Instructor's Resource Guide
Volume 2

for

Understanding Business

Tenth Edition

William G. Nickels
University of Maryland

James M. McHugh
St. Louis Community College at Forest Park

Susan M. McHugh
Applied Learning Systems

Prepared by
Pam McElligott
St. Louis Community College at Meramec

Molly McHugh

The McGraw-Hill Companies

Instructor's Resource Guide, Volume 2 for
UNDERSTANDING BUSINESS
William G. Nickels, James M. McHugh, and Susan M. McHugh

Published by McGraw-Hill/Irwin, an imprint of The McGraw-Hill Companies, Inc., 1221 Avenue of the Americas, New York, NY 10020.

1 2 3 4 5 6 7 8 9 0 QDB/QDB 10 9 8 7 6 5 4 3 2

ISBN: 978-0-07-747439-3
MHID: 0-07-747439-2

www.mhhe.com

Contents

Marketing: Helping Buyers Buy

chapter 13

critical thinking exercises

what's new in this edition

additions to the 10th edition:

- Getting to Know Joseph Jimenez of Novartis
- Name That Company: KFC Canada
- Social Media in Business: Calling All Businesses!
- Spotlight on Small Business: Let's Go to the Movies
- Thinking Green: How Green Is Green?
- Video case

revisions to the 10th edition:

- Text was revised to eliminate redundancy and tighten discussions.
- Statistical data and examples throughout the chapter were updated to reflect current information.

deletions from the 9th edition:

- Getting to Know Cricket Lee, Creator of Fitlogic
- Name That Company: Campbell Soup
- Spotlight on Small Business
- Thinking Green
- Reaching Beyond Our Borders

brief chapter outline and learning goals

chapter 13

Marketing: Helping Buyers Buy

Getting To Know JOSEPH JIMEMEZ of NOVARTIS

learning goal 1

Define *marketing*, and apply the marketing concept to both for-profit and nonprofit organizations.

I. WHAT IS MARKETING?

A. The Evolution of Marketing

1. The Production Era
2. The Selling Era
3. The Marketing Concept Era
4. The Customer Relationship Era

B. Nonprofit Organizations and Marketing

learning goal 2

Describe the four Ps of marketing.

II. THE MARKETING MIX

A. Applying the Marketing Process

B. Designing a Product to Meet Consumer Needs

C. Setting an Appropriate Price

D. Getting the Product to the Right Place

E. Developing an Effective Promotional Strategy

learning goal 3

Summarize the marketing research process.

III. PROVIDING MARKETERS WITH INFORMATION

A. The Marketing Research Process

learning goal 4

Show how marketers use environmental scanning to learn about the changing marketing environment.

IV. THE MARKETING ENVIRONMENT

A. Global Factors

B. Technological Factors

C. Sociocultural Factors

D. Competitive Factors

E. Economic Factors

V. TWO DIFFERENT MARKETS: CONSUMER AND BUSINESS-TO-BUSINESS (B2B)

learning goal 5

Explain how marketers apply the tools of market segmentation, relationship marketing, and the study of consumer behavior.

VI. THE CONSUMER MARKET

A. Segmenting the Consumer Market

B. Reaching Smaller Market Segments

C. Moving toward Relationship Marketing

D. The Consumer Decision-Making Process

learning goal 6

Compare the business-to-business market and the consumer market.

VII. THE BUSINESS-TO-BUSINESS MARKET

VIII. YOUR PROSPECTS IN MARKETING

IX. SUMMARY

lecture outline

Getting to Know JOSEPH JIMENEZ of NOVARTIS

Jimenez put his marketing experience to use when he took the CEO job at one of the world's largest pharmaceutical companies. He restructured the sales force to address consumer needs and increased the company's social responsibilities.

Where's the beef? Many people don't care about the answer to that question anymore. As the trend toward vegetarianism grows, this well-known company in Canada offers a vegan version of its chicken sandwich in 500 of its 750 stores. Name that company.

(Students should read the chapter before guessing the company's name: KFC Canada)

learning goal 1

Define *marketing*, and apply the marketing concept to both for-profit and nonprofit organizations.

I. WHAT IS MARKETING?

A. ***MARKETING*** is the activity, set of institutions, and processes for creating, communicating, delivering, and exchanging offerings that have value for customers, clients, partners, and society at large.

1. Selling and advertising are only part of marketing.
2. Marketing includes the activities buyers and sellers perform to facilitate mutually satisfying exchanges.
3. In the past, marketing focused on helping the seller sell.
    a. Some people still think of marketing as mostly selling, advertising, and distribution from the seller to the buyer.
    b. Today marketing is more about helping the buyer buy.

lecture notes

PPT 13-1
Chapter Title

PPT 13-2
Learning Goals

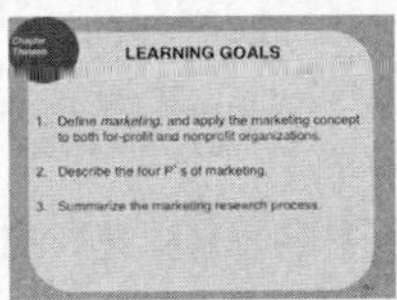

(See complete PowerPoint slide notes on page 13.34.)

PPT 13-3
Learning Goals

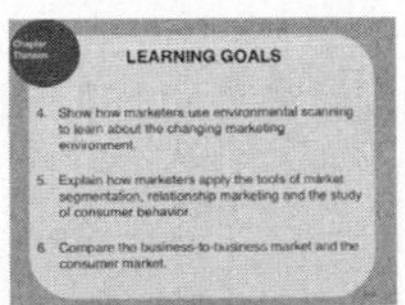

(See complete PowerPoint slide notes on page 13.34.)

PPT 13-4
Joseph Jimenez

(See complete PowerPoint slide notes on page 13.35.)

PPT 13-5
Name That Company

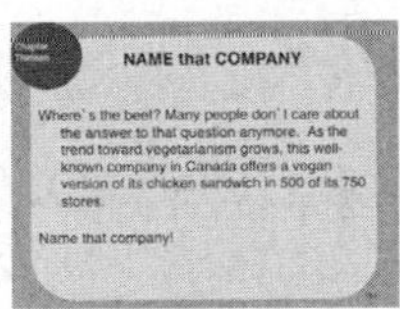

(See complete PowerPoint slide notes on page 13.35.)

PPT 13-6
What's Marketing?

(See complete PowerPoint slide notes on page 13.35.)

bonus case 13-1

CUSTOMER-ORIENTED MARKETING CONCEPTS AT THERMOS

To become a world-class competitor, Thermos completely reinvented the way it conducted its marketing operations. (See the complete case, discussion questions, and suggested answers beginning on page 13.74 of this manual.)

c. *The text uses the example of buying a new or used car, using websites to research before buying.*

4. Helping the buyer buy also helps the seller sell.
5. Traditional retailers who rely solely on traditional advertising and selling are losing out to new ways of marketing.

B. **THE EVOLUTION OF MARKETING**

1. Marketing in the U.S. has passed through four eras.
2. **THE PRODUCTION ERA**
   a. Until the early 1900s, the general philosophy was to "produce as much as you can because there is a limitless market."
   b. The goals of business **CENTERED ON PRODUCTION.**
   c. The greatest marketing need was for more production and improved distribution and storage.
3. **THE SELLING ERA**
   a. By the 1920s, capacity often exceeded market needs.
   b. The business philosophy turned to an **EMPHASIS ON SELLING AND ADVERTISING** to sell existing products.
4. **THE MARKETING CONCEPT ERA**
   a. The **BABY BOOM** after WWII created a tremendous demand for goods and services.

PPT 13-7
Focus of Contemporary Marketing

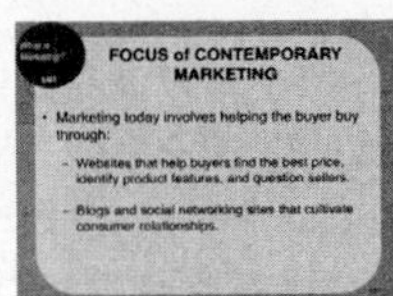

(See complete PowerPoint slide notes on page 13.36.)

SPOTLIGHT ON **small business**
(Text page 354)

PPT 13-8
Let's Go to the Movies

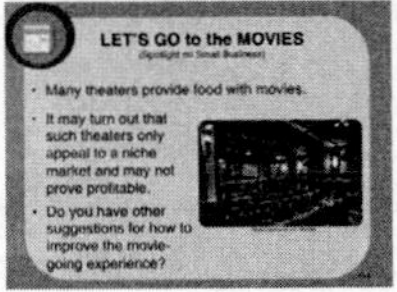

(See complete PowerPoint slide notes on page 13.36.)

PPT 13-9
Four Eras of U.S. Marketing

(See complete PowerPoint slide notes on page 13.36.)

TEXT FIGURE 13.1
Marketing Eras
(Text page 353)

This text figure shows the four eras in the evolution of marketing in the United States

PPT 13-10
The Production and Selling Eras

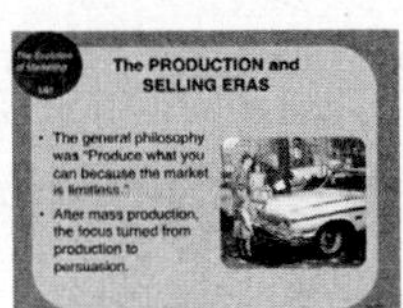

(See complete PowerPoint slide notes on page 13.37.)

PPT 13-11
The Marketing Concept Era

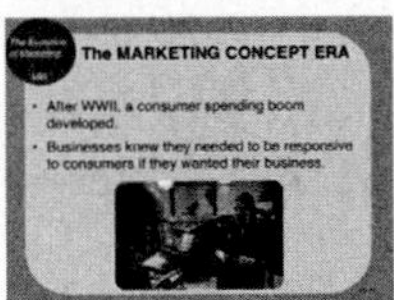

(See complete PowerPoint slide notes on page 13.37.)

   i. Competition for the consumer's dollar was fierce.
   ii. If they wanted to get their business, businesses had to be **RESPONSIVE TO CONSUMERS.**
  b. The **MARKETING CONCEPT** emerged in the 1950s.
  c. The ***MARKETING CONCEPT*** is a three-part business philosophy:
   i. A **CUSTOMER ORIENTATION**: Find out what consumers want and provide it.
   ii. A **SERVICE ORIENTATION:** Make sure everyone in the organization has the same objective: **CUSTOMER SATISFACTION.**
   iii. A **PROFIT ORIENTATION:** Focus on those goods and services that will earn the most profit.
  d. During the 1980s, business began to apply the marketing concept more aggressively.
5. **THE CUSTOMER RELATIONSHIP ERA**
  a. ***CUSTOMER RELATIONSHIP MANAGEMENT(CRM)*** is the process of learning as much as possible about customers and doing everything you can to satisfy them—or even exceed their expectations—with goods and services over time.
  b. The goal is to enhance customer satisfaction and stimulate long-term customer loyalty.

lecture notes

lecture link 13-1

UPDATING THE MARKETING CONCEPT

Twenty-first-century marketers have to readjust their strategies to meet the needs of modern consumers—that means each of the elements of the marketing concept. (See the complete lecture link on page 13.52 in this manual.)

PPT 13-12

Applying the Marketing Concept

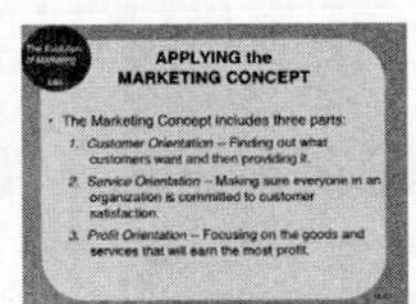

(See complete PowerPoint slide notes on page 13.37.)

lecture link 13-2

PAT CROCE'S TEN COMMANDMENTS

Pat Croce, minority owner of the Philadelphia 76ers NBA team, is a fanatic for customer service. He created the "ten commandments" of customer service. (See the complete lecture link on page 13.53 in this manual.)

PPT 13-13

The Customer Relationship Era

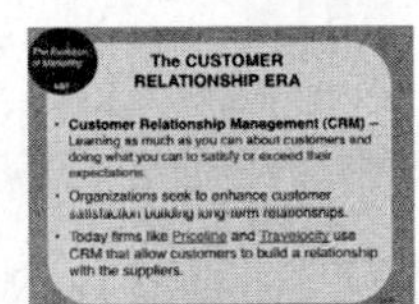

(See complete PowerPoint slide notes on page 13.38.)

PPT 13-14

Service with a Smile

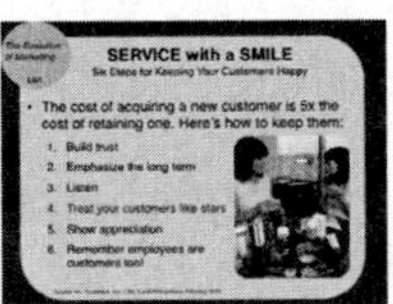

(See complete PowerPoint slide notes on page 13.38.)

lecture link 13-3

SMALL BUSINESSES GOING MOBILE

The newest "want" from customers is the ability to buy whatever they want, whenever they want. mShopper is helping small businesses constantly reach their customers. (See the complete lecture link on page 13.54 in this manual.)

c. Customer relationship building now involves social networks, online communities, and blogs.

6. The newest in CRM efforts is **CUSTOMER-MANAGED RELATIONSHIPS (CMR).**

C. **NONPROFIT ORGANIZATIONS AND MARKETING**

1. Marketing is a crucial part of almost all organizations, profit and nonprofit.
2. Charities, churches, politicians, states, and many other organizations all use marketing.

learning goal 2

Describe the four Ps of marketing.

II. THE MARKETING MIX

A. Pleasing customers has become a priority.

1. The **FOUR FACTORS OF MARKETING** are:
   a. Product
   b. Price
   c. Place
   d. Promotion
2. **CONTROLLABLE PARTS** of the marketing process involve:
   a. Designing a want-satisfying **PRODUCT**
   b. Setting a **PRICE** for the product
   c. Putting the product in a **PLACE** where people will buy it
   d. **PROMOTING** the product

bonus case 13-2
FOOD MARKETING IN THE INNER CITY

This case focuses on how food marketing in the inner city is different from that in suburban neighborhoods. (See the complete case, discussion questions, and suggested answers beginning on page 13.76 of this manual.)

PPT 13-15
Nonprofit Marketing

(See complete PowerPoint slide notes on page 13.38.)

PPT 13-16
Marketing Strategies for Nonprofits

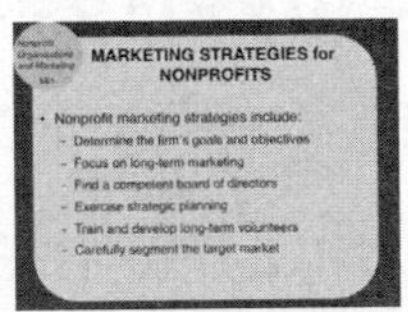

(See complete PowerPoint slide notes on page 13.39.)

thinking green
(Text page 356)

PPT 13-17
How Green Is Green?

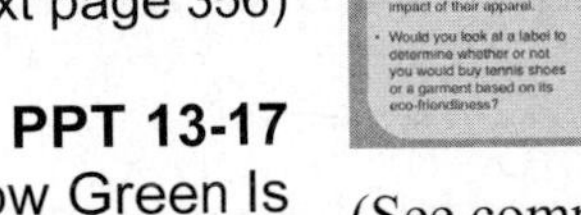

(See complete PowerPoint slide notes on page 13.39.)

PPT 13-18
The Four Ps

TEXT FIGURE 13.2
Marketing Managers and the Marketing Mix
(Text page 357)

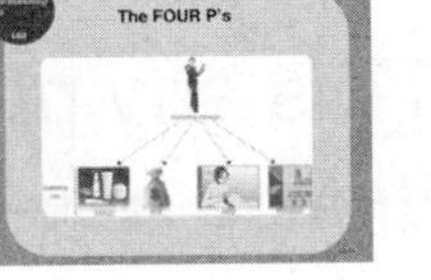

(See complete PowerPoint slide notes on page 13.40.)

bonus case 13-3
LINING UP FOR FREE APPS

The founders of Line Snob created their product while in college. (See the complete case, discussion questions, and suggested answers beginning on page 13.78 of this manual.)

3. These factors are known as the ***MARKETING MIX***, the ingredients that go into a marketing program: product, price, place, and promotion.

B. **APPLYING THE MARKETING PROCESS**

1. To present an overview of the marketing process, *the text takes a hypothetical vegetarian restaurant, Very Vegetarian, through the marketing process.*

2. **The process involves:**

   a. Recognizing a need

   b. Researching the market

   c. Identifying the **TARGET MARKET** (the people you will try to persuade to buy your product)

C. **DESIGNING A PRODUCT TO MEET CONSUMER NEEDS**

1. First, develop a product to fill the identified need (*the text continues the example of the vegetarian restaurant).*

2. A ***PRODUCT*** is any physical good, service, or idea that satisfies a want or need plus anything that would enhance the product in the eye of consumers, such as the brand.

3. The next step is **CONCEPT TESTING,** developing an accurate description of your product and asking people whether or not the concept (the idea of the restaurant) appeals to them.

4. ***TEST MARKETING*** is the process of testing products among potential users.

TEXT FIGURE 13.3
The Marketing Process with the Four Ps
(Text page 358)

This text figure shows the process that leads to the development and sale of a product.

PPT 13-19
Developing a Product

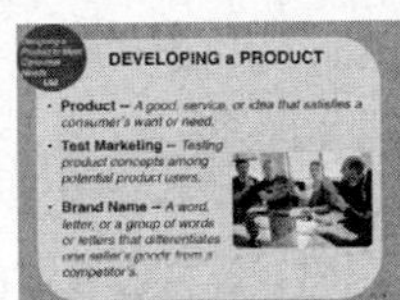

(See complete PowerPoint slide notes on page 13.40.)

critical thinking exercise 13-1
FIND A NEED AND FILL IT

This exercise asks the student to look around himself or herself to identify a need that is unfilled. (See complete exercise on page 13.61 of this manual.)

5. Next, decide which brand names should be offered to attract customers.

6. A ***BRAND NAME*** is a word, letter, or group of words or letters that differentiates one seller's goods and services from those of competitors.

7. These steps create **THE FIRST "P"—PRODUCT.**

D. **SETTING AN APPROPRIATE PRICE** (the second "P")

1. The price depends on a number of factors, such as the price of competing restaurants.

2. You also have to consider the costs of producing, distributing, and promoting the product.

E. **GETTING THE PRODUCT TO THE RIGHT PLACE** (the third "P")

1. Once the product is manufactured, you have to decide how to get it to the consumer.

2. You may want to sell your product through **INTERMEDIARIES (MARKETING MIDDLEMEN),** organizations that specialize in distributing goods from producer to customer.

F. **DEVELOPING AN EFFECTIVE PROMOTIONAL STRATEGY** (the fourth "P")

1. ***PROMOTION*** includes all the techniques sellers use to inform people and motivate them to buy products or services.

2. **RELATIONSHIP BUILDING WITH CUSTOMERS** includes responding to any suggestions they may make to improve the product or the marketing of the product.

3. Listening to customers is the key to marketing.

lecture link 13-4

DISCONTINUING DISCOUNTS

As the economy is starting to recover, companies are struggling to increase the prices of their recession discounts. (See the complete lecture link on page 13.55 of this manual.)

PPT 13-20

Pricing and Placing a Product

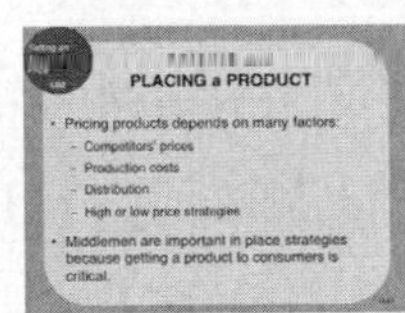

(See complete PowerPoint slide notes on page 13.40.)

lecture link 13-5

MARKETING IS MORE LISTENING THAN PERSUADING

Promotion is part of marketing, but marketing is more about relationship building. (See complete lecture link on page 13.55 of this manual.)

PPT 13-21

Promoting the Product

(See complete PowerPoint slide notes on page 13.41.)

lecture link 13-6

KFC'S IDENTITY CRISIS

Franchise owners are upset with how KFC is now promoting its stores and products. (See the complete lecture link on page 13.56 of this manual.)

PPT 13-22

Perfect Promotion

(See complete PowerPoint slide notes on page 13.41.)

lecture outline

learning goal 3

Summarize the marketing research process.

III. PROVIDING MARKETERS WITH INFORMATION

A. ***MARKETING RESEARCH*** is the analysis of markets to determine opportunities and challenges, and to find the information needed to make good decisions.

1. One goal is to determine exactly what consumers want and need, now and in the future.
2. Businesses need information to compete effectively, and **MARKETING RESEARCH** is the activity that gathers that information.
3. In addition to customers, marketers should pay attention to the views of employees, shareholders, consumer advocates, and other stakeholders.

B. **THE MARKETING RESEARCH PROCESS**

1. ***STEP 1.*** Defining the problem and determining the present situation
2. ***STEP 2.*** Collecting data
   a. Research can be quite expensive, so **SOME TRADE-OFF** must be made between information needed and the cost.
   b. ***SECONDARY DATA*** is information that has already been compiled by others and published in journals and books or made available online.
   c. Despite its name, secondary data should be gathered first as it is the least expensive.
   d. When secondary data don't provide all the necessary information, marketers must do their own research.

PPT 13-23
Tangled Web of Promotion

(See complete PowerPoint slide notes on page 13.41.)

media in business

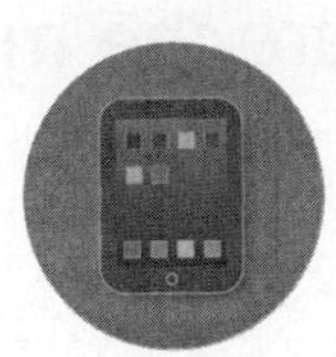

(Text page 360)

PPT 13-24
Calling All Businesses!

(See complete PowerPoint slide notes on page 13.42.)

progress assessment

(Text page 360)

PPT 13-25
Progress Assessment

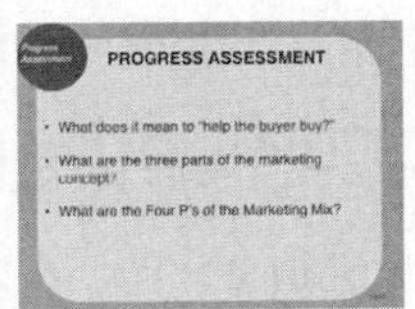

(See complete PowerPoint slide notes on page 13.42.)

PPT 13-26
Searching for Information

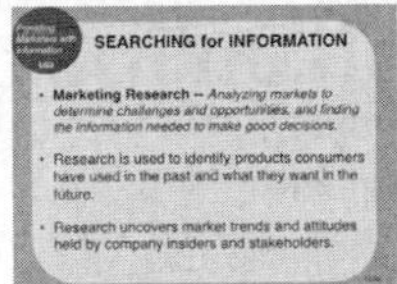

(See complete PowerPoint slide notes on page 13.42.)

PPT 13-27
Four Steps in the Marketing Research Process

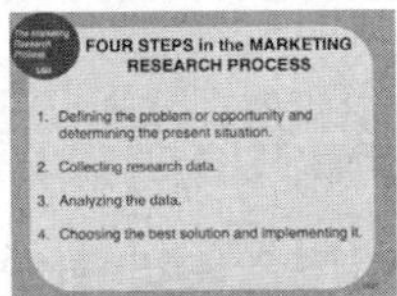

(See complete PowerPoint slide notes on page 13.43.)

PPT 13-28
Defining the Problem or Opportunity

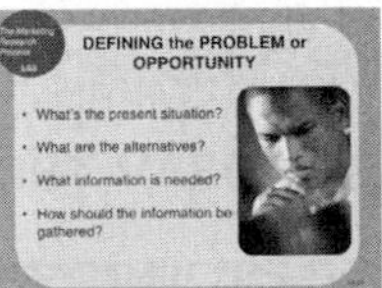

(See complete PowerPoint slide notes on page 13.43.)

e. The result of new studies is ***PRIMARY DATA***, data that you gather yourself (not from secondary sources such as books and magazines).

f. Telephone surveys, online surveys, mail surveys, and personal interviews are the most common methods of gathering survey information.

g. A ***FOCUS GROUP*** is a small group of people who meet under the direction of a discussion leader to communicate their opinions about an organization, its product, or other given issues.

h. Marketers can now gather both secondary and primary data online.

3. ***STEP 3.*** Analyzing the research data

   a. The data collected must be turned into useful information.

   b. Careful, honest interpretation of the data can reveal specific marketing challenges.

4. ***STEP 4.*** Choosing the best solution and implementing it

   a. Researchers determine **ALTERNATIVE STRATEGIES** and make recommendations as to which strategy may be best.

   b. The actions taken should be **FOLLOWED UP** to see if results were as expected.

5. Marketing is an **ONGOING PROCESS**; companies must continually adapt to changes in the market.

PPT 13-29
Collecting Secondary Research Data

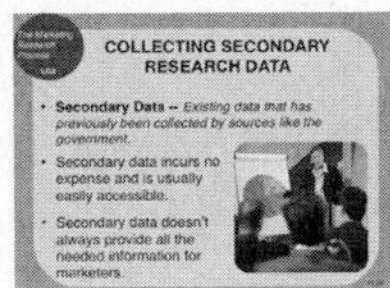

(See complete PowerPoint slide notes on page 13.43.)

TEXT FIGURE 13.4
Selected Sources of Primary and Secondary Information
(Text page 362)

This text figure lists the principal sources of secondary marketing research information.

critical thinking exercise 13-2
GOOD TO THE LAST DROP

This exercise involves an in-class product comparison. Can students identify the taste of their favorite cola in a blind taste test? (See complete exercise on page 13.63 of this manual.)

PPT 13-30
Collecting Primary Research Data

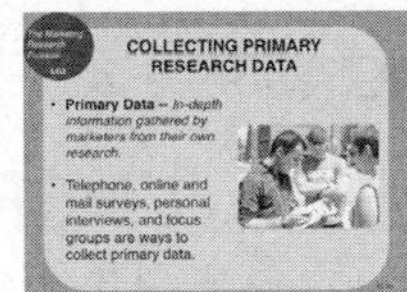

(See complete PowerPoint slide notes on page 13.44.)

PPT 13-31
Focus Groups

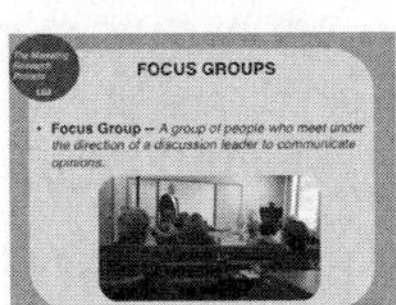

(See complete PowerPoint slide notes on page 13.44.)

PPT 13-32
Analyzing the Data and Implementing the Decision

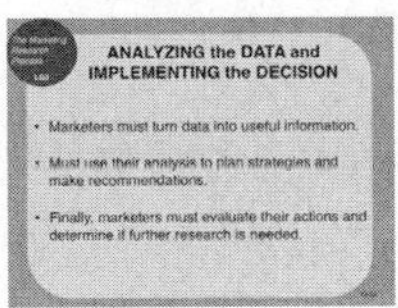

(See complete PowerPoint slide notes on page 13.44.)

PPT 13-33
Key Benefits of Marketing Research

(See complete PowerPoint slide notes on page 13.45.)

lecture outline

learning goal 4

Show how marketers use environmental scanning to learn about the changing marketing environment.

IV. THE MARKETING ENVIRONMENT

A. ***ENVIRONMENTAL SCANNING*** is the process of identifying the factors that can affect marketing success.

B. **GLOBAL FACTORS**

1. The most important global change today is the growth of the Internet.
2. Globalization has also put pressure on companies that deliver products.

C. **TECHNOLOGICAL FACTORS** include the Internet, the growth of consumer databases, flexible manufacturing, and mass customization.

D. **SOCIOCULTURAL FACTORS** include population growth and changing demographics, such as the aging population and the preferences of various ethnic groups.

E. **COMPETITIVE FACTORS**

1. Brick-and-mortar companies must adjust to new competition from the Internet.
2. They have to adapt to competitors, who can deliver products quickly or provide excellent service.

F. **ECONOMIC FACTORS**

1. Marketers must pay close attention to the economic environment in the U.S. and globally.
2. The economic collapse starting in 2008 slowed sales, and became global in scope.

PPT 13-34
Ways to Find Out What Consumers Think

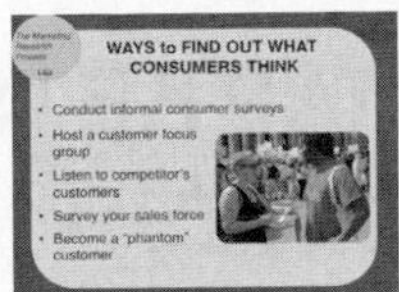

(See complete PowerPoint slide notes on page 13.45.)

PPT 13-35
Scanning the Marketing Environment

(See complete PowerPoint slide notes on page 13.46.)

PPT 13-36
The Marketing Environment

TEXT FIGURE 13.5
The Marketing Environment
(Text page 364)

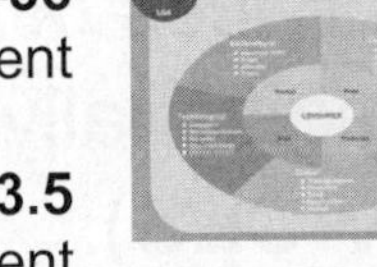

(See complete PowerPoint slide notes on page 13.46.)

lecture link 13-7
THE COLA WARS IN INDIA

Coke dominates Pepsi, but not in India. Coke is now ramping up its promotion in India to try and oust its main competitor. (See the complete lecture link on page 13.57 in this manual.)

bonus case 13-4
MARKETING TO THE BABY BOOM GENERATION

The baby boomer generation, the largest population group, is a profitable market for targeted products and services. (See the complete case, discussion questions, and suggested answers beginning on page 13.80 of this manual.)

PPT 13-37
The ABCs of Marketing

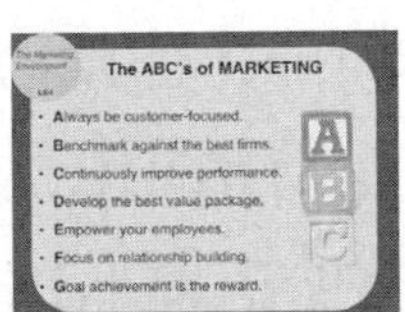

(See complete PowerPoint slide notes on page 13.46.)

V. TWO DIFFERENT MARKETS: CONSUMER AND BUSINESS-TO-BUSINESS (B2B)

A. **THERE ARE TWO MAJOR MARKETS:**

1. The ***CONSUMER MARKET*** is made up of all the individuals or households that want goods and services for personal consumption or use.
2. The ***BUSINESS-TO-BUSINESS (B2B) MARKET*** consists of all the individuals and organizations that want goods and services to use in producing other goods and services or to sell, rent, or supply goods to others (traditionally called **INDUSTRIAL GOODS** and **SERVICES**).

B. The buyer's **REASON FOR BUYING** and the **END USE** of the product determine whether it is considered a consumer product or a B2B product.

learning goal 5

Explain how marketers apply the tools of market segmentation, relationship marketing, and the study of consumer behavior.

VI. THE CONSUMER MARKET

A. Consumer groups differ greatly in age, education level, income, and taste.

1. Marketers must first decide which group to serve and then develop products and services specially tailored to their needs (*as Campbell Soup Company does).*
2. ***MARKET SEGMENTATION*** is the process of dividing the total market into groups whose members have similar characteristics.

PPT 13-38
The Consumer and B2B Market

(See complete PowerPoint slide notes on page 13.46.)

progress assessment
(Text page 366)

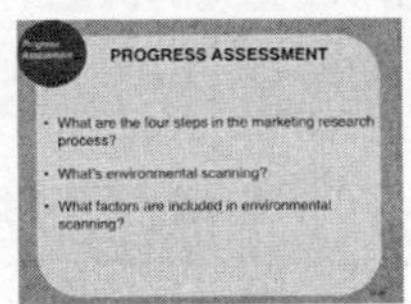

PPT 13-39
Progress Assessment

(See complete PowerPoint slide notes on page 13.47.)

PPT 13-40
Marketing to Consumers

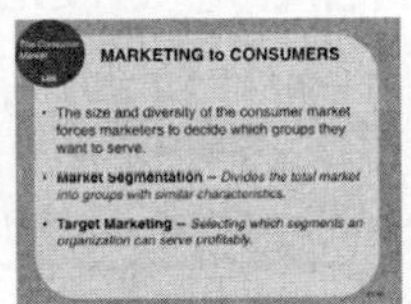

(See complete PowerPoint slide notes on page 13.47.)

critical thinking exercise 13-3
IDENTIFYING THE TARGET MARKET

This exercise asks the student to identify the target market for various products and services. (See complete exercise on page 13.67 of this manual.)

lecture link 13-8
DEWALT IDENTIFIES ITS TARGET MARKET

DeWalt Tools discovered that it was targeting the wrong target market. (See the complete lecture link on page 13.57 in this manual.)

3. ***TARGET MARKETING*** is marketing directly toward those groups (market segments) an organization decides it can serve profitably.

B. **SEGMENTING THE CONSUMER MARKET**

1. ***GEOGRAPHIC SEGMENTATION*** is dividing a market by cities, counties, states, or regions.
2. ***DEMOGRAPHIC SEGMENTATION*** is dividing the market by age, income, and education level.
3. ***PSYCHOGRAPHIC SEGMENTATION*** is dividing the market using the group's values, attitudes, and interests.
4. ***BENEFIT SEGMENTATION*** is dividing the market by determining which benefits of the product to talk about.
5. ***VOLUME, OR USAGE, SEGMENTATION*** is dividing the market by usage (volume of use).
6. The best segmentation strategy is to **USE ALL THE VARIABLES** to come up with a consumer profile that's sizable, reachable, and profitable.

C. **REACHING SMALLER MARKET SEGMENTS**

1. ***NICHE MARKETING*** is the process of finding small but profitable market segments and designing custom-made products for them.
2. *The text uses the example of Fridgedoor.com selling refrigerator magnets.*
3. ***ONE-TO-ONE MARKETING*** means developing a unique mix of goods and services for each individual customer.

PPT 13-41
Segmenting the Consumer Market

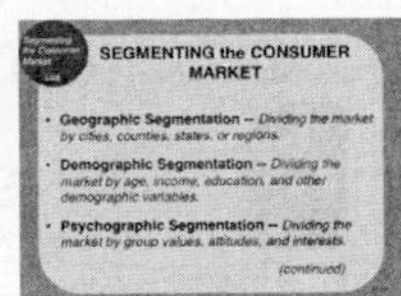

(See complete PowerPoint slide notes on page 13.47.)

TEXT FIGURE 13.6
Market Segmentation
(Text page 367)

This text figure shows some of the methods marketers use to divide the market.

PPT 13-42
Segmenting the Consumer Market

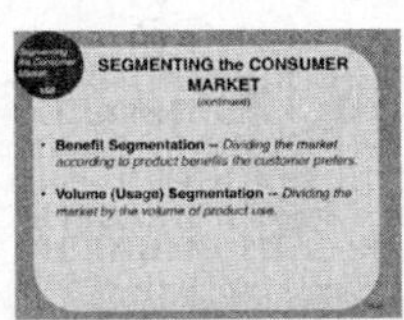

(See complete PowerPoint slide notes on page 13.48.)

PPT 13-43
Marketing to Small Segments

(See complete PowerPoint slide notes on page 13.48.)

4. It is easier to do one-to-one marketing in B2B markets, but is becoming possible in consumer markets as well.

D. **MOVING TOWARD RELATIONSHIP MARKETING**

1. ***MASS MARKETING*** means developing products and promotions to please large groups of people.
   a. The mass marketer tries to sell products to as many people as possible.
   b. That means using mass media, such as TV, radio, and newspapers.
2. ***RELATIONSHIP MARKETING*** is a marketing strategy with the goal of keeping individual customers over time by offering them products that exactly meet their requirements.
   a. **RELATIONSHIP MARKETING** moves away from mass production toward **CUSTOM-MADE GOODS**.
   b. The latest in **TECHNOLOGY** enables sellers to work with buyers to determine their individual wants and needs and to develop goods and services specifically designed for those individuals.

E. **THE CONSUMER DECISION-MAKING PROCESS**

1. Studying consumer behavior centers on studying the **CONSUMER PURCHASE DECISION PROCESS:**
   a. Recognize the problem.
   b. Do the information search.
   c. Evaluate the alternatives.

PPT 13-44
Mass Marketing vs. Relationship Marketing

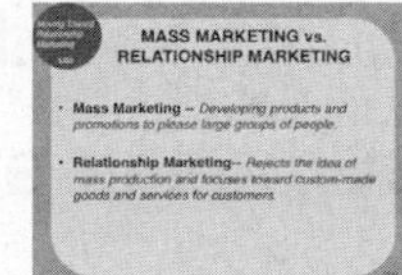

(See complete PowerPoint slide notes on page 13.48.)

PPT 13-45
Keys to Successful Relationship Marketing

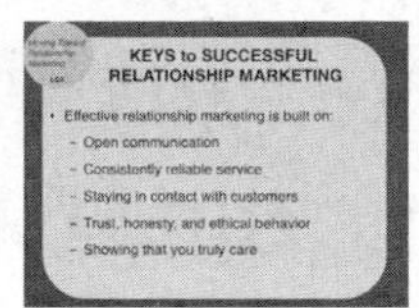

(See complete PowerPoint slide notes on page 13.49.)

lecture link 13-9
RELATIONSHIP MARKETING: GOING BEYOND THE EXPECTED

It is often easier to get present customers to buy more than to get new customers. (See the complete lecture link on page 13.58 in this manual.)

critical thinking exercise 13-4
THE MARKETING OPPORTUNITY

This exercise presents a potentially revolutionary new product and asks the students to consider some key marketing questions. (See complete exercise on page 13.70 of this manual.)

PPT 13-46
Steps in the Consumer Decision-Making Process

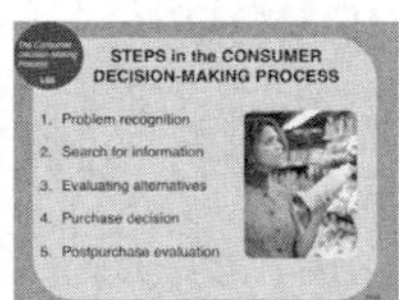

(See complete PowerPoint slide notes on page 13.49.)

lecture link 13-10
FAMILY LIFE CYCLE THEORY UPDATED

Family life cycle characteristics can be used to understand consumers' buying behavior over time.)

   d. Make the purchase decision.
   e. Do a postpurchase evaluation.
2. Consumer behavior researchers also study the various influences that impact **CONSUMER BEHAVIOR**.
   a. **MARKETING MIX VARIABLES** (the four Ps)
   b. **PSYCHOLOGICAL INFLUENCES** such as perception and attitudes
   c. **SITUATIONAL INFLUENCES** such as the type of purchase and physical surroundings
   d. **SOCIOCULTURAL INFLUENCES** such as reference groups and culture
3. Consumer behavior is also influenced by other factors:
   a. **LEARNING** creates changes in an individual's behavior resulting from previous experiences and information.
   b. A **REFERENCE GROUP** is the group that an individual uses as a reference point in formation of his or her beliefs, attitudes, values, or behavior.
   c. **CULTURE** is the set of values, attitudes, and ways of doing things that are transmitted from one generation to another in a given society.
   d. **SUBCULTURE** is the set of values, attitudes, and ways of doing things that results from belonging to a certain group with which one closely identifies.

PPT 13-47
The Consumer Decision-Making Process and Outside Influences

TEXT FIGURE 13.7
The Consumer Decision-Making Process and Outside Influences
(Text page 370)

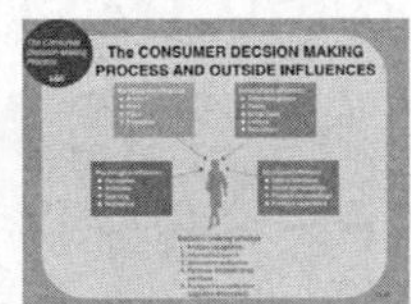

(See complete PowerPoint slide notes on page 13.49.)

PPT 13-48
Key Factors in Consumer Decision Making

(See complete PowerPoint slide notes on page 13.50.)

e. **COGNITIVE DISSONANCE** is the type of psychological conflict that can occur after a purchase—such as doubts about whether they got the best product at the best price.

learning goal 6

Compare the business-to-business market and the consumer market.

VII. THE BUSINESS-TO-BUSINESS MARKET

A. Marketers of goods and services to manufacturers, institutions, commercial operations, and the government are called **B2B MARKETERS.**

B. Several factors make **BUSINESS-TO-BUSINESS MARKETING DIFFERENT**.

1. **NUMBER:** There are relatively few customers compared to the consumer market.
2. **SIZE:** Though few in number, industrial customers are relatively very large.
3. **GEOGRAPHICALLY CONCENTRATED:** B2B markets tend to be concentrated in certain areas of the country.
4. **RATIONAL:** Business buyers are generally more rational in their purchase decisions.
5. **DIRECT:** B2B sales tend to be direct.
6. **PERSONAL SELLING:** There is much more emphasis on personal selling than in the consumer market.

VIII. YOUR PROSPECTS IN MARKETING

There is a wider variety of careers in marketing than in most business areas.

IX. SUMMARY

critical thinking exercise 13-5
CONSUMER OR B2B GOOD?

This exercise asks students to classify various products and services as being a consumer good, a B2B good, or both. (See complete exercise on page 13.72 of this manual.)

PPT 13-49
Business-to-Business Market (B2B)

(See complete PowerPoint slide notes on page 13.50.)

PPT 13-50
B2B Market Differences

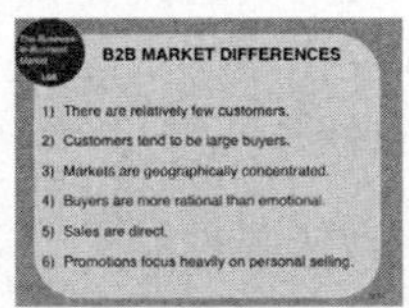

(See complete PowerPoint slide notes on page 13.50.)

TEXT FIGURE 13.8
Comparing Business-to-Business and Consumer Buying Behavior
(Text page 371)

This text figure shows some of the differences between buying behavior in the B2B market and in the consumer market.

progress assessment
(Text page 372)

PPT 13-51
Progress Assessment

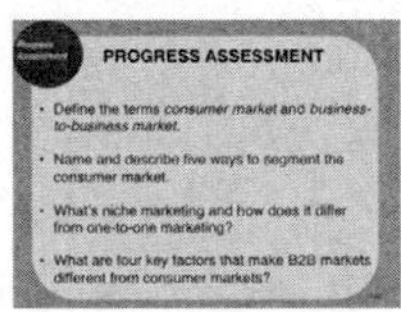

(See complete PowerPoint slide notes on page 13.51.)

PowerPoint slide notes

PPT 13-1
Chapter Title

PPT 13-2
Learning Goals

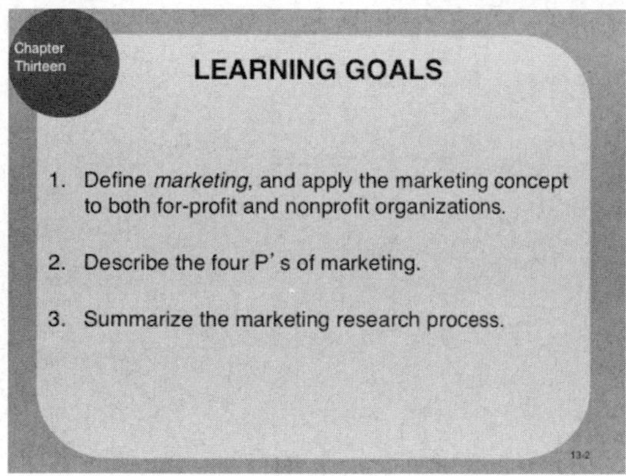

PPT 13-3
Learning Goals

Chapter
Thirteen

LEARNING GOALS

4. Show how marketers use environmental scanning to learn about the changing marketing environment.
5. Explain how marketers apply the tools of market segmentation, relationship marketing and the study of consumer behavior.
6. Compare the business-to-business market and the consumer market.

13-3

PPT 13-4
Joseph Jimenez

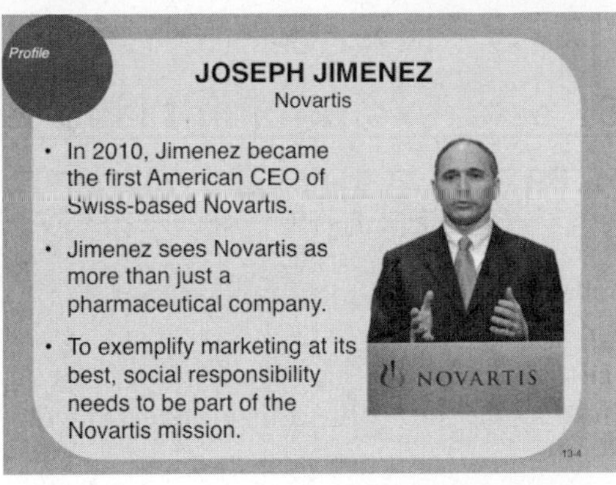

PPT 13-5
Name That Company

Company: KFC Canada

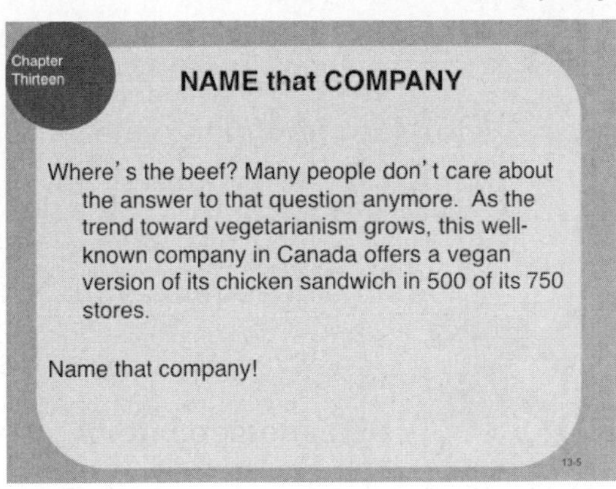

PPT 13-6
What's Marketing?

Simply put, marketing is activities buyers and sellers perform to facilitate mutually beneficial exchanges.

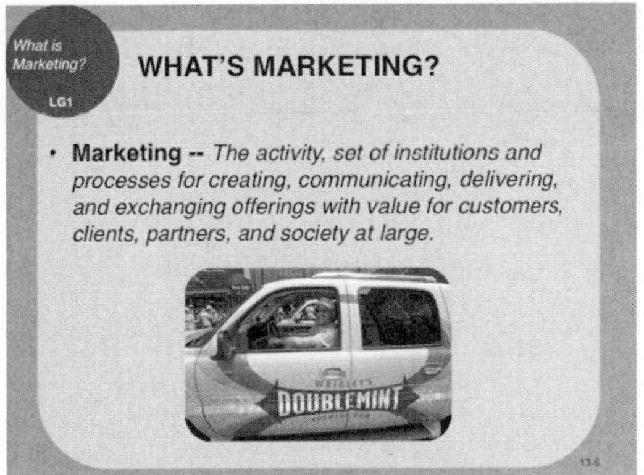

PPT 13-7
Focus of Contemporary Marketing

PPT 13-8
Let's Go to the Movies

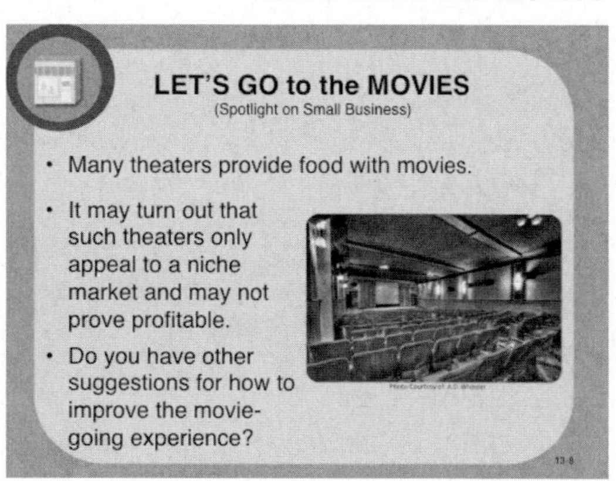

PPT 13-9
Four Eras of U.S. Marketing

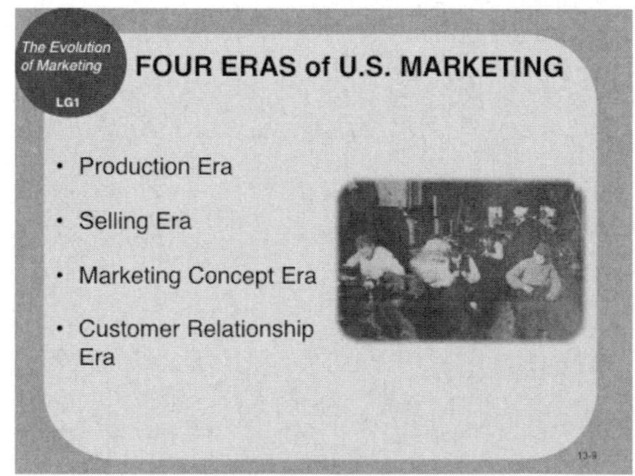

In the United States, marketing has evolved through four eras: (1) production, (2) selling, (3) marketing concept, and (4) customer relationship.

PPT 13-10
The Production and Selling Eras

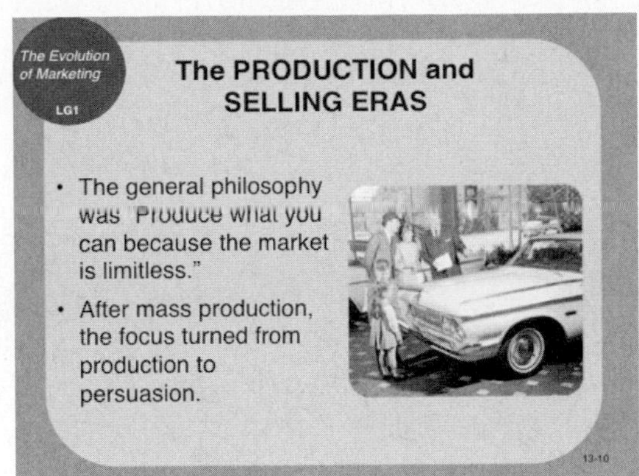

PPT 13-11
The Marketing Concept Era

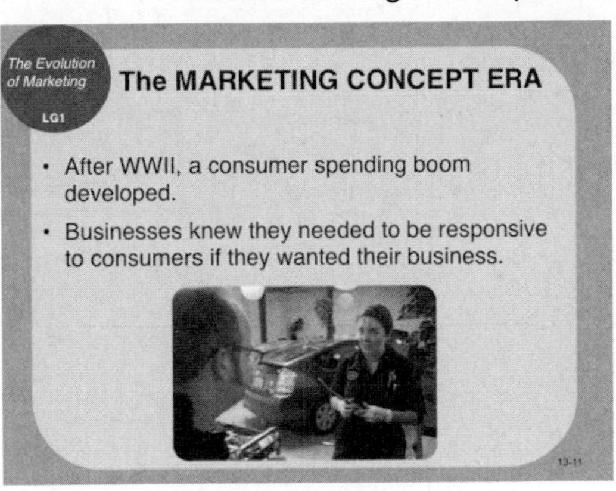

PPT 13-12
Applying the Marketing Concept

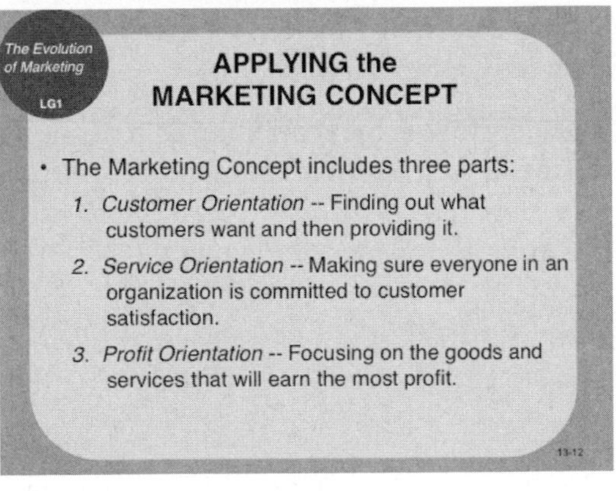

PPT 13-13
The Customer Relationship Era

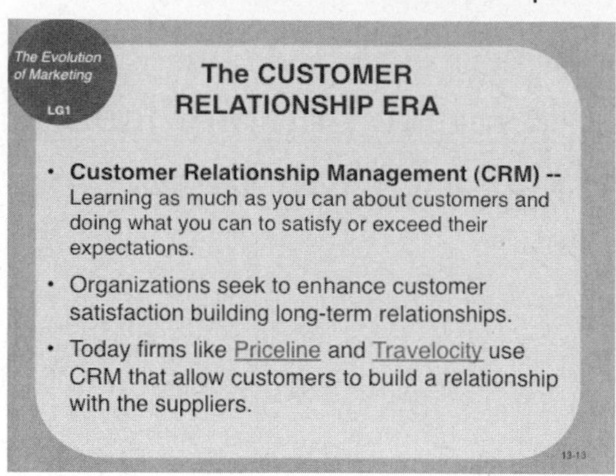

PPT 13-14
Service with a Smile

PPT 13-15
Nonprofit Marketing

1. This slide identifies marketing tactics nonprofits can use to market their organizations.
2. Nonprofits must effectively market their causes in order to reach their target audience.
3. Ask the students, How is the marketing of a nonprofit different from the marketing of a for-profit product? (*Students should be able to identify that there is little difference between the two.)*

PPT 13-16
Marketing Strategies for Nonprofits

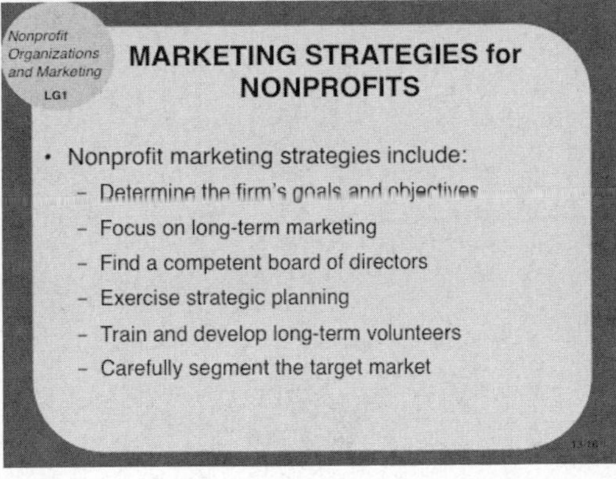

1. This slide identifies many ideas for developing a successful marketing strategy for nonprofit organizations.
2. Regardless of the type or size of the organization, nonprofits will need marketing strategies and techniques to maximize their effectiveness.
3. Marketing tactics nonprofits may consider as a part of an overall marketing program include the following: newspaper inserts, cross promotions, packaging promotions, and corporate newsletters.
4. Public relations will play an important role with recognition and support for building strong community goodwill. Based on the following statistics, nonprofit organizations are very successful:
   - During the past 10 years the number of reporting "public charities" grew by 6.3% annually.
   - The nonprofit sector includes more than 1 million organizations that spend nearly $500 billion each year—more than the GDP of Brazil, Russia, or Australia.
   - Approximately 6% of all organizations in the United States are nonprofits, and 1 in every 15 people works for a nonprofit.

PPT 13-17
How Green Is Green?

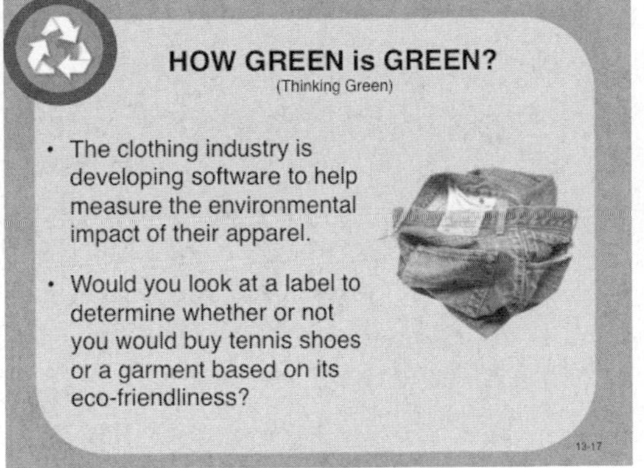

PPT 13-18
The Four Ps

The Four Ps are also known as the marketing mix.

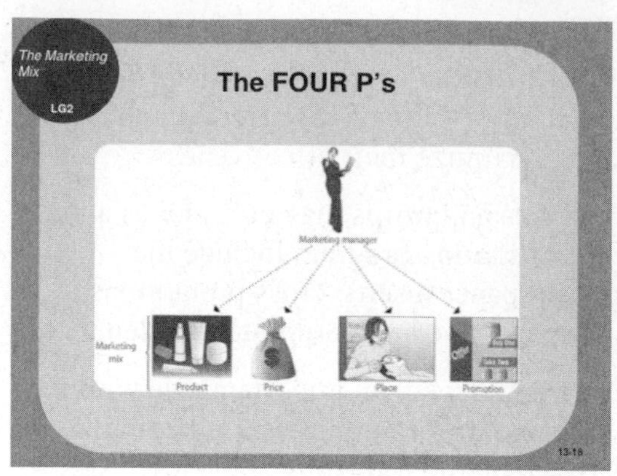

PPT 13-19
Developing a Product

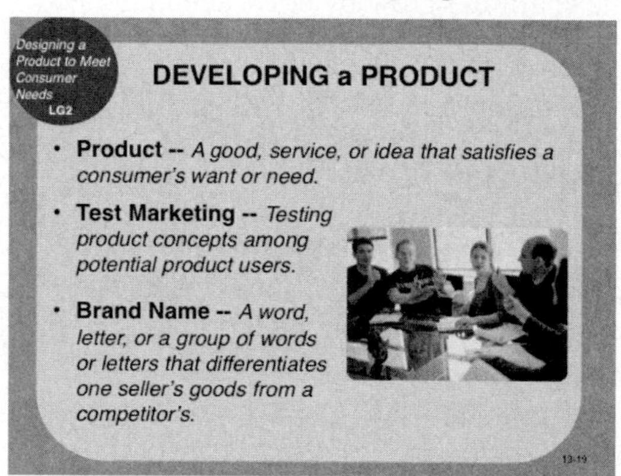

PPT 13-20
Pricing and Placing a Product

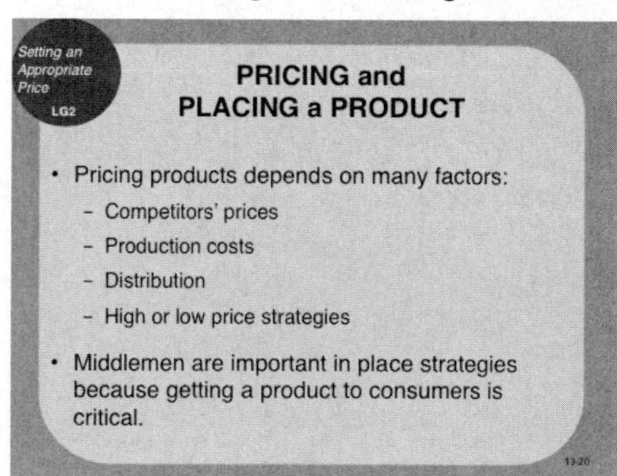

PPT 13-21
Promoting the Product

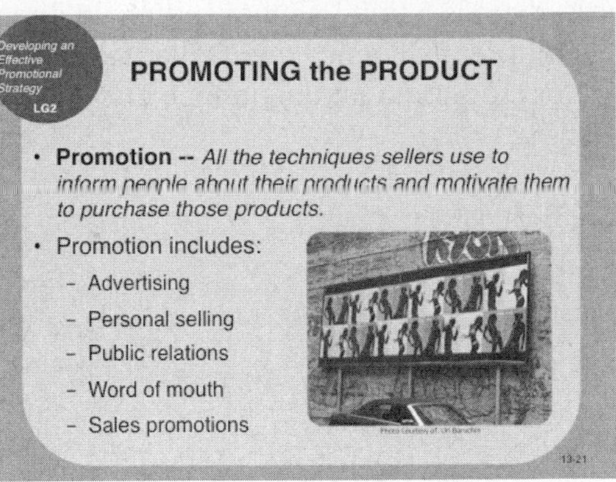

PPT 13-22
Perfect Promotion

1. Companies are working more to create products that are "built to love." These products, like the iPad, create excitement and loyalty from the get-go.
2. Customers, in addition to looking for an amazing product, look for salespeople who they feel are their friends. The key to repeat business is the likability factor.
3. Ask the students, Have you ever gone back to a specific store because of a particular salesperson? If you were in sales, what would you do to increase your likability factor?

PPT 13-23
Tangled Web of Promotion

1. Companies often create websites because they believe they *have* to. However, if it's not done right, it could cause you to lose customers.
2. Not enough emphasis is put on checking the analytics. As noted in this chapter, market research is extremely important. The same goes for Web research.
3. Ask the students, Can you think of other things to add to this list? What are some companies that have good websites? Bad websites?

PPT 13-24
Calling All Businesses!

Some retailers are hoping to use social media to enter the mobile market. Although many companies use social media to create awareness, there is a trend now of setting up direct outlets on social platforms. JCPenney and Delta Airlines have been in talks for months about obtaining a direct presence on Facebook.

PPT 13-25
Progress Assessment

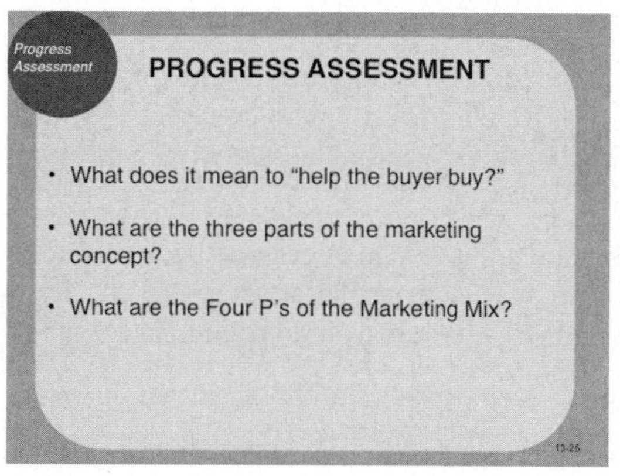

1. In the past, marketing focused entirely on helping the seller sell the product. Today, marketing has changed from selling to instead helping the buyer buy. It is critical that organizations do everything to help buyers make decisions.
2. The three parts of the marketing concept are customer orientation, service orientation, and a profit orientation.
3. The four Ps of the marketing mix are (1) product, (2) price, (3) place, and (4) promotion.

PPT 13-26
Searching for Information

Providing Marketers with Information
LG3
SEARCHING for INFORMATION

- **Marketing Research --** *Analyzing markets to determine challenges and opportunities, and finding the information needed to make good decisions.*
- Research is used to identify products consumers have used in the past and what they want in the future.
- Research uncovers market trends and attitudes held by company insiders and stakeholders.

13-26

To understand customer wants and needs, it is critical to conduct market research. Good market research will identify products consumers have used and want to use in the future, and market trends.

PPT 13-27
Four Steps in the Marketing Research Process

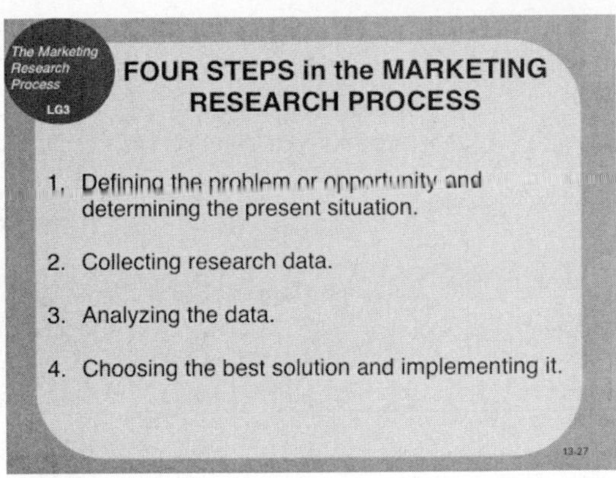

PPT 13-28
Defining the Problem or Opportunity

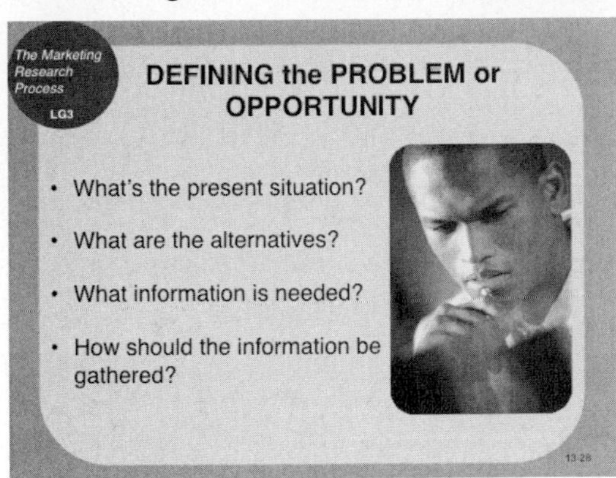

PPT 13-29
Collecting Secondary Research Data

Secondary research is cheaper and often easier to gather than primary research, but may be outdated.

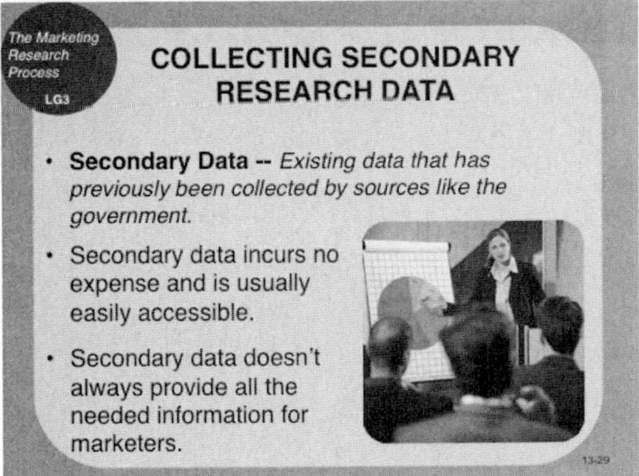

PPT 13-30
Collecting Primary Research Data

Primary data are timely, but can be expensive and time-consuming to gather.

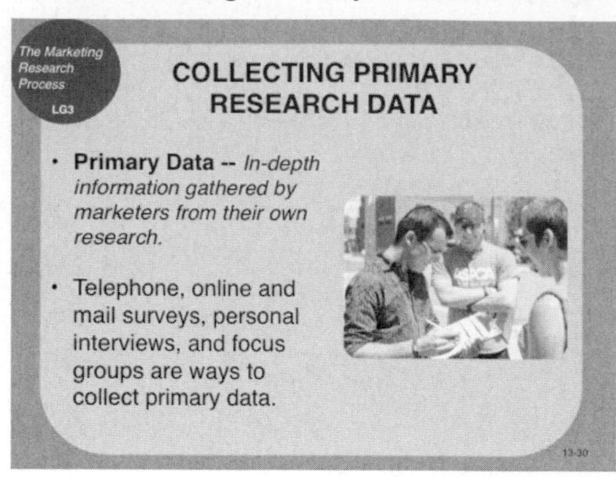

PPT 13-31
Focus Groups

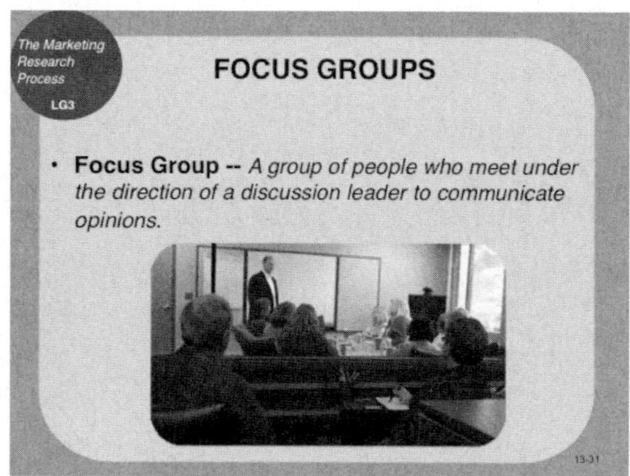

PPT 13-32
Analyzing the Data and Implementing the Decision

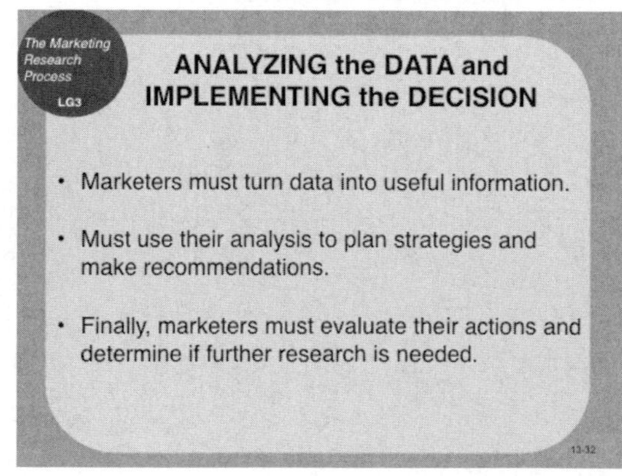

PPT 13-33
Key Benefits of Marketing Research

1. This slide identifies the key benefits of marketing research.
2. As discussed early in the chapter, marketing is about understanding customers' wants and needs. To accomplish this goal marketers must conduct marketing research.
3. Ask the students, How has the Internet changed the way market research is conducted? (*The Internet has made gathering both primary and secondary information easier and quicker. Also, information can now be gathered via blogs and social networks.)*

PPT 13-34
Ways to Find Out What Consumers Think

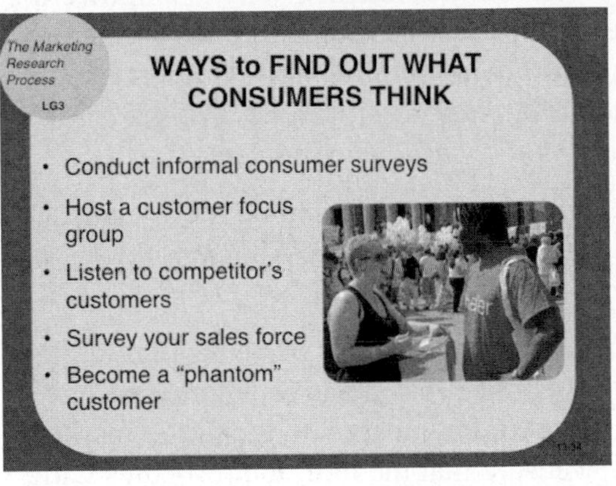

1. The goal of market research is to better understand what consumers are thinking.
2. This slide addresses some of the ways that organizations can discover consumer wants and needs.

PPT 13-35
Scanning the Marketing Environment

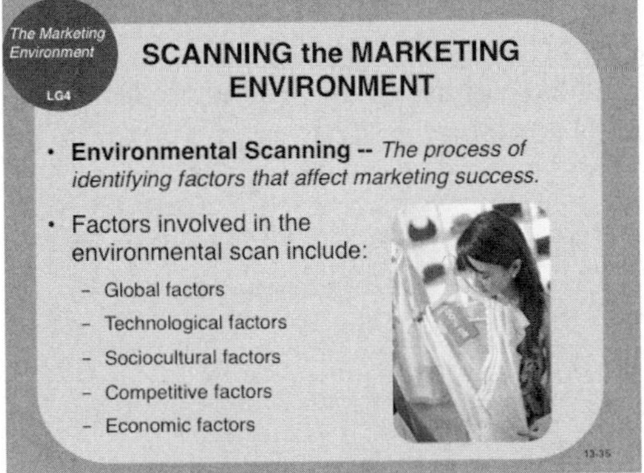

Environmental scanning is the process of identifying factors that affect marketing success. The environment of marketing is changing faster than at any time in history. Companies that don't keep up will fail to survive. Today's marketing environment is influenced by the global marketplace and the explosion of the information age. To be fully prepared, a company must recognize and understand cultural influences; governmental and political influences; demographic and lifestyle trends; local, national, and world economic trends; the strengths of multinational competitors; and the influence of technology on physical distribution.

PPT 13-36
The Marketing Environment

To effectively understand the marketing environment, it is critical that companies continually scan the environment

PPT 13-37
The ABCs of Marketing

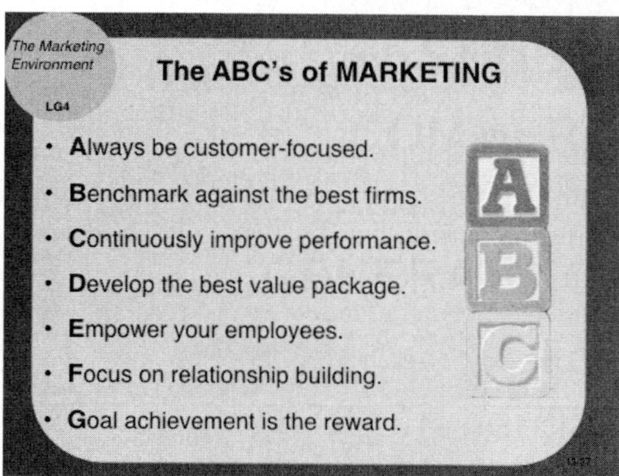

1. This slide identifies keys to marketing success.
2. One point on this slide mentions the empowerment of employees. Ask the students, Why is empowering employees a key to successful marketing? (*Answers will vary, but should focus on how empowerment should lead to greater employee motivation, creating a more customer-focused environment.)*
3. A key to marketing is understanding the organization's strengths and weaknesses and its ultimate customer.
4. Once you have identified your strengths and weaknesses, what you really sell and to whom, and have reviewed your communication to the target market, you need to ensure that the message resonates with the consumer positively. You can do that by engaging in savvy public relations (newsletters, press releases, etc.).

PPT 13-38
The Consumer and B2B Market

The buyer's intended end use of the product determines whether a product is consumer or B2B.

PPT 13-39
Progress Assessment

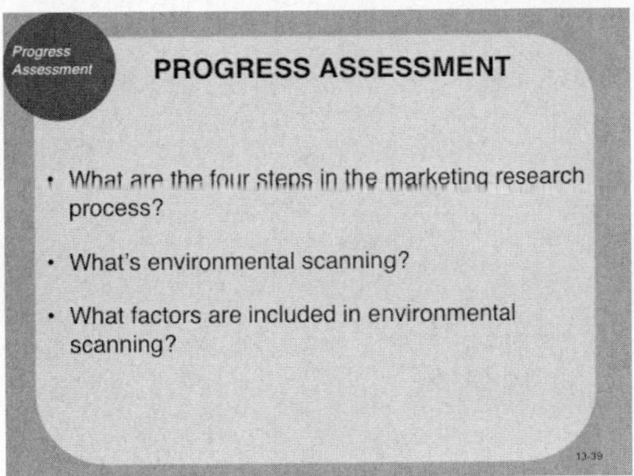

1. The steps in the marketing research process are as follows: (1) Define the problem and determine the present situation, (2) collect the research data, (3) analyze the research data, and (4) choose the best solution and then implement it.
2. Environmental scanning is the process of identifying factors that can affect marketing success. The factors in environmental scanning include global, technological, sociocultural, competitive, and economic influences.

PPT 13-40
Marketing to Consumers

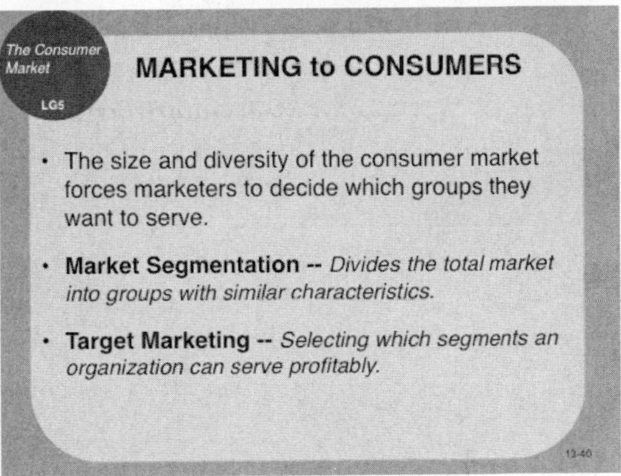

PPT 13-41
Segmenting the Consumer Market

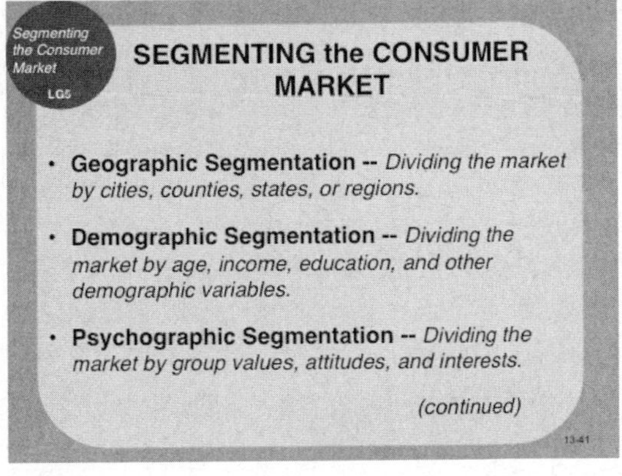

PPT 13-42
Segmenting the Consumer Market

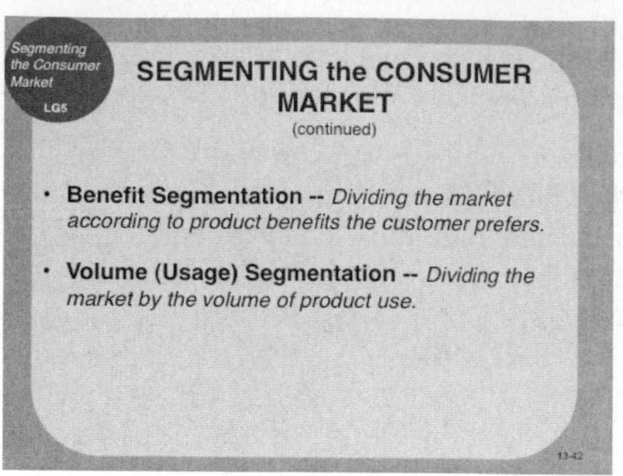

PPT 13-43
Marketing to Small Segments

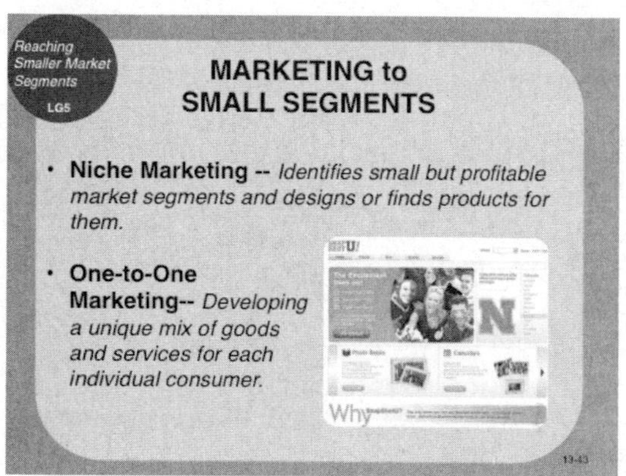

PPT 13-44
Mass Marketing vs. Relationship Marketing

Mass marketing uses little market segmentation. The goal of relationship marketing is to keep customers happy by offering products that meet their exact expectations.

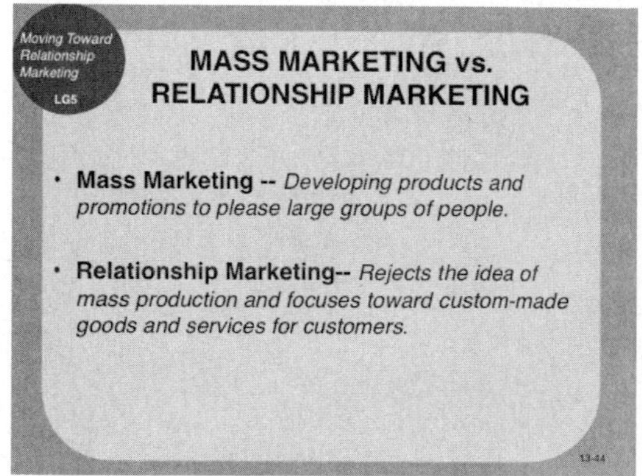

PPT 13-45
Keys to Successful
Relationship Marketing

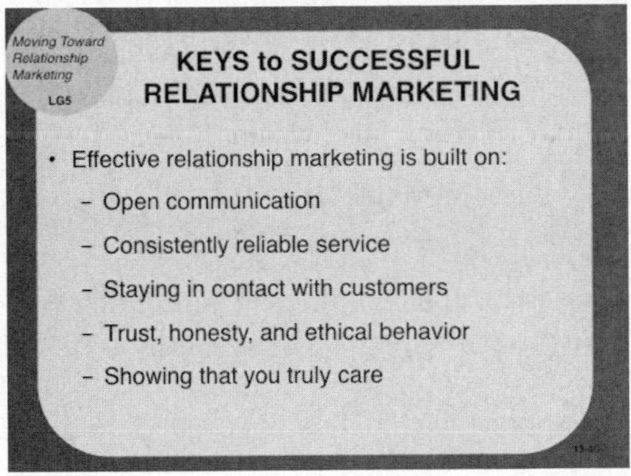

1. Relationship marketing is all about moving away from mass production and toward custom-made goods and services.
2. This slide identifies the keys to successful relationship marketing.
3. The goal of relationship marketing is to retain individual customers over time by offering them new products that meet their expectations.
4. Nike uses relationship marketing by creating custom-made shoes via NikeiD. Explore NikeiD in class at www.nike.com to see relationship marketing in action.

PPT 13-46
Steps in the Consumer Decision-Making Process

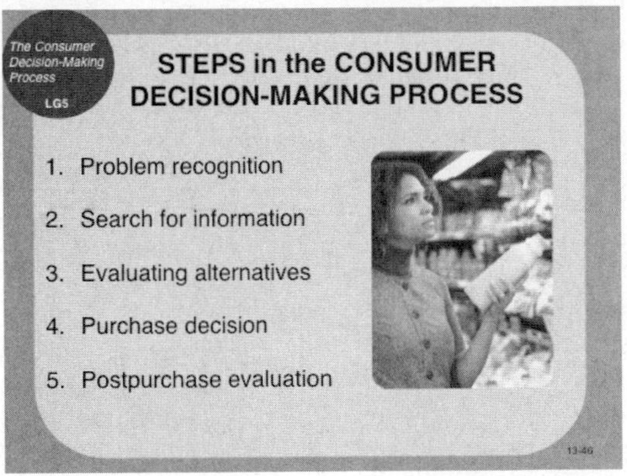

PPT 13-47
The Consumer Decision-Making Process and Outside Influences

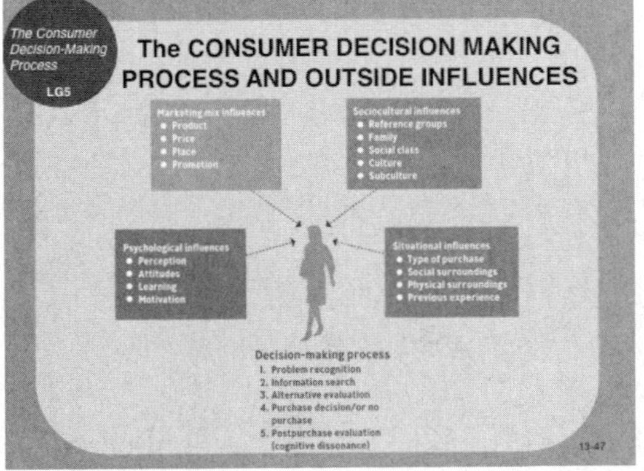

PPT 13-48
Key Factors in Consumer Decision Making

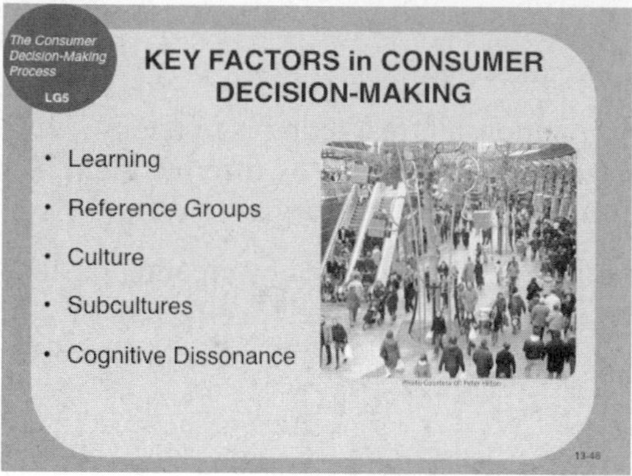

- Learning: Creates changes in consumer behavior through experiences and information
- Reference groups: Reference points in forming beliefs, attitudes, values. or behaviors
- Culture: The set of values, attitudes, and ways of doing things passed from generations
- Subculture: Values, attitudes, and ways of doing things from belonging to a certain group
- Cognitive dissonance: Psychological conflict that may occur after a purchase

PPT 13-49
Business-to-Business Market (B2B)

PPT 13-50
B2B Market Differences

PPT 13-51
Progress Assessment

Progress Assessment

PROGRESS ASSESSMENT

- Define the terms *consumer market* and *business-to-business market.*
- Name and describe five ways to segment the consumer market.
- What's niche marketing and how does it differ from one-to-one marketing?
- What are four key factors that make B2B markets different from consumer markets?

13-51

1. The consumer market consists of all the individuals or households that want goods and services for personal consumption or use and have the resources to buy them. Business-to-business markets consist of all the individuals and organizations that want goods and services to use in producing other goods and services or to sell, rent, or supply goods to others.
2. Geographic segmentation is the process of dividing the market by cities, counties, states, or regions. Demographic segmentation involves dividing the market by age, income, education level, religion, race, and occupation. Psychographic segmentation is the process of dividing the market by values, attitudes, and interests. Benefit segmentation involves determining which benefits to promote. Volume or usage segmentation is the process of determining how your customers purchase and use the product.
3. Niche marketing is identifying small but profitable market segments and designing or finding products for them. One-to-one marketing means developing a unique mix of goods and service for each individual customer.
4. The four key factors that make B2B markets different from consumer markets are as follows : (1) customers in B2B markets are relatively few as compared to households in the consumer market, (2) B2B customers tend to be geographically centered, (3) B2B sales tend to be direct, and (4) in the B2B marketplace sales are based on personal selling.

lecture links

"Consumers are statistics. Customers are people."
Stanley Marcus

"Before you build a better mousetrap, it helps to know if there are any mice out there."
Mortimer B. Zuckerman

"Market research can establish beyond the shadow of a doubt that the egg is a sad and sorry product and that it obviously will not continue to sell. Because after all, eggs won't stand up by themselves, they roll too easily, are too easily broken, require special packaging, look alike, are difficult to open, won't stack on the shelf."
Robert Pliskin

"Your most unhappy customers are your greatest source of learning."
Bill Gates

"It's really hard to design products by focus groups. A lot of times, people don't know what they want until you show it to them."
Steve Jobs

lecture link 13-1

UPDATING THE MARKETING CONCEPT

As we noted earlier in the chapter, the marketing concept was developed in the 1950s to meet the consumer needs of the time. Now that we're in the 21st century, marketers have to readjust their strategies to meet the needs of modern consumers. That means each of the elements of the marketing concept—a consumer orientation, a service orientation, and a profit orientation—all have to be updated. Let's explore each of those changes next.

FROM PROVIDING CUSTOMER SATISFACTION TO EXCEEDING EXPECTATIONS

Marketing's goal in the past was to provide customer satisfaction. Today, the goal of some Six Sigma quality firms is to exceed customer expectations by providing goods and services that exactly meet their requirements. One objective of a company's marketing effort, therefore, is to make sure that the response to customer wants and needs is so fast and courteous that customers are truly surprised and pleased by the experience.

You don't have to look far to see that most organizations haven't yet reached the goal of meeting, much less exceeding, customer expectations. Retail stores, government agencies, and other organizations may still irritate customers as often as they please them. Nonetheless, global competition is forcing organizations to adopt quality concepts, which means, above all, adapting organizations to customers.

Businesses have learned that employees won't provide first-class goods and services to customers unless they receive first-class treatment themselves. Marketers must therefore work with others in the firm, such as human resource personnel, to help make sure that employees are pleased. In some firms, such as IBM, employees are called internal customers to show the need to treat them well—like customers.

BENCHMARKING AND UNITING ORGANIZATIONS

As we explained in Chapter 8, determining whether organizations are providing world-class service and quality is done through competitive benchmarking. That means that companies compare their processes and products with those of the best companies in the world to learn how to improve them. Xerox Corporation, for example, has benchmarked its functions against corporate leaders such as American Express (for billing), Ford (for manufacturing floor layout), Mary Kay Cosmetics (for warehousing and distribution), and Florida Power & Light (for quality processes).

Manufacturers, unfortunately, cannot always exceed customer expectations on their own. They need the cooperation of suppliers to assure customers that they are getting the finest parts. They need close relationships with dealers to make sure that the dealers are providing fast, friendly service. We will discuss the close relationships among marketing intermediaries in Chapter 15.

MAINTAINING A PROFIT ORIENTATION

Marketing managers must make sure that everyone in the organization understands that the purpose behind pleasing customers and uniting organizations is to ensure a profit for the firm. Using that profit, the organization can then satisfy other stakeholders of the firm such as stockholders, environmentalists, and the local community.

It has been estimated that reducing by 5% the number of customers who defect—that is, who switch from buying your products to buying another company's—can increase profit by as much as 85% (though this figure varies by industry). Some of that profit comes from increased purchases and some from referrals. Thus, customer relationship management is becoming an intimate part of any organization seeking to maximize profits.

lecture link 13-2

PAT CROCE'S TEN COMMANDMENTS

Pat Croce, a minority owner and former president of the Philadelphia 76er NBA team, can be described as the fusion of promotion and customer service. He is best known for revitalizing the failing franchise through promotional stunts and "wanton acts of customer and employee pampering." He once rappelled 110 feet from the rafters of the First Union Center. He has climbed to the top of the Walt Whitman bridge to unfurl a 76ers banner. Since he joined the 76ers after the 1995–1996 season, the 76ers have increased attendance by 64%.

Before coming to the 76ers, Croce used his experiences in training athletes to found Sports Physical Therapists. The 1980s fitness boom was in full swing, and Croce was able to attract well-known athletes, including NBA legend Julius Erving. Ten years after he opened his first center, there were 40 stores in 11 states.

Pat Croce's philosophy of customer service developed during his days at SPT. A story from these years illustrates his obsession with customer service. On his way to an executives-only meeting at SPT, Croce stopped in a lavatory to find an overflowing towel bin, toilet paper on the floor, and clothing dangling from half-closed lockers. He gathered his execs and marched them into that lavatory, where, scrub brushes and buckets in tow, he conducted the meeting.

To communicate his philosophy to employees, he developed his "ten commandments." He says he wanted a "cookbook" for his employees to follow using the strength-training principle of KISS: Keep it simple, stupid. His employees knew all 10. He had the commandments posted in every cubicle and every office in the facility. "I wanted to make sure people used first names, that they listened, that 'Do it now' was always at the forefront of their minds." These principles came from his own life experiences. "I put them down in a very instructive way for people to use. People need that; they need ABCs."

CROCE'S TEN COMMANDMENTS WITH HIS COMMENTS

- **Every customer gets a hello and a goodbye.** "It's common courtesy. I love it when someone says hello to me. Goodbye requires a little more caring and passion. If I make all the guards say 'good night' to people as they leave, they're more likely to come back."
- **Establish a friendly, first-name basis.** "I believe a name is the sweetest sound to anyone's ear. And if you say thank you with it, that's all the better."
- **Listen, listen, listen.** "That is really one of the secrets to my success. I learned at an early age that opportunity sometimes knocks very softly, so you truly have to listen."
- **Communicate clearly**. "It's the back half of 'listen, listen, listen.' You have to communicate so that you don't leave any windows of miscommunication open."
- **Be neat, clean, and fit.** "Everyone likes an environment conducive to business. I don't care if it's bubble-gum on a seat or lying on a treatment table and there's rain-soaked stains on a drop ceiling. That kills me. We never had it."
- **Be prompt and professional.** "Tardiness is a lack of discipline. I don't think you should disrespect anyone's time. Carpe diem! But it's hard to seize the day if someone's messing with it."
- **Be positive.** "Life has a way of becoming a self-fulfilling prophecy. So think success. If you go at something as if you can't fail, many times you won't. Do you know how many people said I couldn't get the 76ers?"
- **Extend compliments.** "When you feel better about yourself and the world, you're more apt to give an encouraging word to someone."
- **Have fun.** "Most people don't, so it's a commandment. It's easy to be caught up in the drudgery of work. Try to make it fun. It's contagious."
- **Do it now.** "If you wait till tomorrow to use what you learned today, you're two steps late."[i]

lecture link 13-3

SMALL BUSINESSES GOING MOBILE

In this digital age, setting up shop online is vital for most retail businesses. But having a presence on computers alone isn't enough anymore. As iPhones and Androids have grown in popularity, so has the public's interest in using their phones to shop. Big retailers are already mining the smartphone market for a fortune. Amazon, for instance, earned more than $1 billion from phone purchases in 2009.

Translating a company's current online presence into something suited for a smartphone isn't difficult for large retailers with vast resources. For small businesses, however, migrating to the mobile medium can be tricky. The array of devices available and lack of uniform design standards presents a challenge to Web designers, thus increasing the cost of going mobile. But as Amazon's smartphone sales suggests, making the leap from laptop to touchscreen may become essential for the survival of small retailers.

In September 2010, matters got easier for businesses hoping to break into the mobile world when the Boulder-based company mShopper introduced the Mobile Commerce Platform, or mStore. The service takes the guesswork out of constructing a mobile site by providing design and search engine tools along with an analytics dashboard to track traffic and sales. The actual cash from the transaction, though, goes straight into the retailer's current online shopping cart in order to streamline records and retain customer service processes. mShopper charges a licensing fee on a sliding scale ranging from $99 to $999, depending on Web traffic. Since mShopper doesn't get paid if its clients' stores don't get hits, the company also offers a marketing system that sends out promotional texts and discounts to customers on an mStore's mailing list.[ii]

lecture link 13-4

DISCONTINUING DISCOUNTS

Although the recession technically ended in 2010, its effects are likely to linger for years to come. But for many of the companies that slashed prices during the downturn, sticking with those discounts until the economy fully recovers could be unwise. The longer companies discount a product, the more that item becomes devalued. Once the economy starts improving in earnest, companies will have a harder time explaining why a product that cost $10 for four years is now suddenly $15.

Pricing, like packaging or size, is just another one of a product's attributes. And just as shoes come in a number of styles and colors, prices can be adaptive, too. For instance, Procter & Gamble confronted customers' value-centric mindset during the recession by "versioning" its product line. Its one-ply toilet roll Charmin Basic cost 15 to 25% less than the company's standard product to appeal to customers who wanted to spend less without sacrificing quality. Most importantly, though, P&G didn't have to lower the price of its regular and premium rolls at all. The sales of its Basic line simply made up for the shortfall in other brands.

Sometimes a clever promotion can keep prices competitive without resorting to versioning. In the automotive industry, rampant price cuts didn't help move many cars as consumers felt wary of such a large investment even with a discount. To counter these fears, Hyundai initiated its Assurance program that allowed customers who lost their jobs to stop making payments and return their cars. As the rest of the auto industry saw U.S. sales drop 20%, Hyundai's safety net policy helped increase revenues by 8% without slashing prices any further. Even better, the cost of the promotion was minimal as customers returned fewer than 50 cars total. The central advantage of adaptive pricing, though, is that once the economy rebounds, companies can simply phase out their new brands and promotions. P&G has quietly begun removing Tide Basic from shelves while Hyundai stopped highlighting its Assurance program in its commercials.[iii]

lecture link 13-5

MARKETING IS MORE LISTENING THAN PERSUADING

It is often fun to play what might be called "the psychologist's game" in class. The professor says *sky* and the students say *blue*. *Fish* and *water*. Then the professor says *marketing*. What words come up? Usually students will say words like *selling*, *advertising*, *promotion*, *money, business,* and the like. In other words, they think marketing is basically a business function that sells and advertises things to people for money. A real challenge would be to change that perception 180 degrees. But that's exactly what some professors try to do when introducing marketing to students. Here's how it's done.

Imagine a road leading into town that is divided in the middle by a grassy divider. On that divider is a woman waving her right arm in the direction of downtown. All the cars on that side of the road are going downtown, so it might look like the woman was making them go that way. In fact, many of the drivers believe that the woman is indeed making the cars go that way. They wonder at her powers and wish they had such powers. "Who is she?" they ask. "That's Miss Marketing," is the reply. "She stands there every day and notes that the cars all go in the direction she is indicating."

A man from a nonprofit organization drives by and notices the woman. He immediately thinks that she would be a major asset to his organization. He thinks that it would be a good idea to hire her and have her tell people what to do. He has seen her at work (on the road) and knows she is effective at persuasion. So her hires her and puts her back next to the road. Except this time, she is telling people what nonprofit organizations want people to do. She is saying, "Drive 55! Wear your seat belts! Save a whale!" No one seems to be paying attention. Why? Before, she was telling people what to do and they all seemed to be doing it. Now, she was standing at the same spot, but people were ignoring her. She was waving them in one direction and they were going in the other. Why?

The answer is that people will do what you tell them to do if you tell them to do what they already are doing or want to do. On the other hand, they rarely do what they don't want to do—no matter how effective the promoter is. The secret to marketing, therefore, is to find out what people want and then give it to them. If you do that, you will look very powerful as a promoter because people will buy what you are selling. They will buy what you are selling because you are selling what they want.

So, how do you find out what people want? One way would be to ask them, but you rarely have anyone stop you on the street and ask you what you want. So that's not the way most marketers learn what you want. The easiest way to find out what people want is to observe what they are already buying. For example, it is obvious that many college men drink beer. Most of them also watch sports on TV. Therefore, it would be effective to promote beer to college students during football games. You may have noticed that marketers are already doing that. They are very effective at getting college men to buy what they already want: mountain bikes, cars, beer, soda, snow boards, and the like. They are not so effective at getting most college men to buy things like tofu, broccoli, and sprouts. An effective marketer, therefore, is one who listens (or observes) and responds to what people want. Listening is the opposite of talking (promoting) and responding is the opposite of persuading. Thus effective marketing is about 180 degrees from what most students think it is. It is more about listening than selling and advertising and more about responding than persuading. Furthermore, marketing is not limited to businesses. Ask the students, What nonbusinesses do marketing? With some prompting, they will see that charities, churches, nonprofit hospitals and schools, and causes all do marketing. And they are not businesses. Also, students themselves do marketing when they try to get a job.

How do you successfully market yourself? Do you write a good resume to sell yourself? Or is it better to listen to what companies are looking for and respond accordingly? Sure, promotion is part of marketing, but it works best when you listen first to what people want. People have two ears and only one mouth because listening is more important than talking in relationship building. And marketing is a relationship building function.

lecture link 13-6

KFC'S IDENTITY CRISIS

Recently KFC angered its franchisees with an Oprah-sponsored grilled chicken giveaway. Though the promotion failed, KFC's corporate offices continued to heavily market grilled chicken and its line of sandwiches in order to distract health conscious customers from the "fried" part of Kentucky Fried Chicken. The company's new slogan read "Unthink KFC," which is exactly what many customers did, only not in the way CEO Roger Eaton intended. KFC's second-quarter sales at U.S. stores open at least a year fell 7%, not to mention that a survey showed franchisees ended up throwing away almost 50% of their grilled chicken supplies.

In January 2010 the KFC National Council & Advertising Cooperative, which represents all U.S. franchisees, filed suit against KFC corporate to gain control of its ad strategy. KFC rebuffed the claim, calling it "baseless." A spokesperson for the company defended the "Unthink KFC" strategy by claiming it was "derived from extensive consumer research." But franchisees aren't having it. Another group of KFC storeowners, the Association of Kentucky Fried Chicken Franchisees, recently hired a former McDonald's CFO to help increase local marketing instead of standing by the advertising demands of headquarters.

To franchisees, the idea that calorie counters would flock toward a new brand of grilled KFC chicken only slightly healthier than their original recipe is absurd. In their experience, customers come to Kentucky Fried Chicken for, well, the fried chicken. In fact, franchisees feel that the company's marketing strategy demonized the restaurant's flagship blend of 11 herbs and spices. Granted, KFC has long tried to distance itself from its most famous product, preferring to grace new storefronts with just the company's acronym instead of its full name. But the "Unthink KFC" campaign was the first time the chain's advertising had taken an active stance against its namesake. And it doesn't look like franchisees will back down until they can get back to selling KFC chicken the old-fashioned way.[iv]

lecture link 13-7

THE COLA WARS IN INDIA

When it comes to global branding, nobody beats Coca-Cola. The soft drink is the de facto name for soda in dozens of countries, consistently besting both local and multinational competitors to become the world's most recognized brand. That is, with one notable exception: In India, Pepsi—not Coke—is the catchall word for all cold, fizzy drinks.

Pepsi earned this rare honor simply by arriving in the Indian market before Coke did. Technically, Coke was the first Western soft drink to hit India's shores after it set up a small presence there in the 1970s. But government regulations that would have forced Coke to partner with an Indian firm and reveal its secret recipe sent the company packing in 1977. A decade later, PepsiCo joined up with two Indian companies and began selling its flagship brand by 1990. Coke tried to enter the market three years later upon repeal of the previous regulations, but by then Pepsi had a long head start on becoming the nation's ubiquitous Western cola brand.

Losing the cola race certainly didn't deter Coke's efforts in India, however. Instead of focusing on increasing the popularity of Coca-Cola itself, the company competes by offering other beverages. After all, 90% of Indian beverage brands are tea, milk, or coffee products, leaving less than 5% of the total market to cola drinks. Since it entered the market in 1993, Coke added many Indian drink brands to its roster, including a lemon drink called Limca and an orange one called Gold Spot. As its portfolio of brands increased, so have its revenues. Sales by volume increased by 31% in 2009 along with a 25% increase in sales of Coca-Cola, Diet Coke, and Coke Zero. Pepsi is countering by pushing its nondrink brands like Frito Lay snacks and Quaker Oats. Though not as successful as its namesake product, retail sales of Pepsi's expanded product lineup totaled a healthy $1.5 billion in 2009.[v]

lecture link 13-8

DEWALT IDENTIFIES ITS TARGET MARKET

By the late 1980s the DeWalt brand of power tools was failing. The production of the line was halted, and the brand was shelved. Makita, a Japanese tool company, had taken over the market. It "had eaten our lunch throughout the '80s," says Nola Archibald, CEO of Black & Decker, which owns the DeWalt name. "So we started doing a bunch of research." The findings were surprising. Consumers were lukewarm about DeWalt tools, but professional tool users had a high regard for the brand. "The light went on," says Archibald. Black & Decker launched a line of portable electric power tools under the DeWalt name in 1992, and then an innovative line of cordless tools two years later.

In a short time, the company has become one of Black & Decker's most profitable divisions. With $1 billion in annual sales, it commands a 35% share of the professional-tool market.

How did DeWalt fix itself? The company decided to market DeWalt primarily to professionals—who make up 69% of U.S. tool sales. It followed up by making the tools more rugged and reliable. That was important to people who use tools every day; it also allowed the company to charge a higher price.

Then the company got creative. An army of tool guys in bright-yellow trucks swarmed construction sites around the country to get workers to test and critique DeWalt tools on the spot. They camped out in Home Depot and Lowe's parking lots, inviting passersby to test their tools.

To reach Hispanics—who represent nearly 20% of DeWalt's customers—DeWalt hired Ethnic Marketing Group (EMG), a Los Angeles–based agency. DeWalt and EMG launched a contest to find the most dedicated, respected Spanish-speaking construction worker in the Southeast. The contest has expanded into other cities, from San Diego to Orlando, and Black & Decker has doubled DeWalt Hispanic marketing budget along the way.

What DeWalt doesn't do is just as interesting. It doesn't do TV commercials, and it doesn't sell at Wal-Mart. The strategy is all about controlling distribution and protecting the brand, and keeping its marketing efforts directly focused on the correct target market—the professional user.[vi]

lecture link 13-9

RELATIONSHIP MARKETING: GOING BEYOND THE EXPECTED

If you pay any attention at all to what marketers do, it becomes clear rather quickly that most marketers are more concerned with getting new customers than keeping and nurturing old customers. Most ads on TV are trying to get new people to try new things, like a new kind of soda (pop) or new detergent or new workout equipment. There are very few ads telling present users how to get more use out of products we already own. Selling more to more people is the traditional way of doing marketing. On the other hand, such marketing gets harder over time as fewer and fewer people aren't already using your product. Everyone seems to know what a Coke is—and a Pepsi and a Big Mac. To sell more, a company may have to go overseas. Costs go up, ad effectiveness goes down, and everything seems to get harder. When that happens, it may occur to marketers that it is often easier to get present customers to buy more than to get totally new customers. Thus, McDonald's says, "Would you like fries with that?" People have been encouraged to ask for a Number One (hamburger, Coke, and fries) rather than order each separately. That is relationship marketing. It tries to get present customers to buy more by offering them deals (a Number One costs less than the items would if bought separately).

Once you catch on to the idea, you can see how more companies could benefit by doing more to please present customers rather than trying to attract new customers all the time. Your local clothing store, for example, might keep track of what you buy there. Once it learned of your style and habits, it could call you when something new came in that would probably fit into your wardrobe. The store could also notify you when things you want go on sale. In short, you would establish a relationship with the owners. It might have a customer party occasionally. Note how Harley-Davidson has created a following among people who ride its bikes. They wear Harley clothes, go to Harley meeting places, and hang around with other Harley riders. A store that sells fly fishing gear could do the same. Customers might enjoy wearing the same kind of clothes, fishing together in the best streams, and hanging around talking with other fisherpeople.

Electronic databases make it much easier to do relationship marketing. Supermarkets, for example, give out identification pieces that you can use to get discounts. Once you have shopped at a supermarket for a while, it knows what you buy and how often. It knows if you have a dog and what you eat during the holidays. Using that information, it can send you promotional pieces offering you specials on the things that you want and need: dog food, holiday food, and so on. It might even sponsor a party where everyone with similar tastes might get together. It could hold cooking classes, wine tasting classes, or gourmet dinners where it teaches people clever ways of cooking their foods.

The whole idea of relationship marketing is to exceed customer expectations. When they come in for a checkup for the car, wash it for them free. Offer them special deals on oil changes and engine tune-ups periodically. Keep track of when they last changed their oil and let them know its time to come in again. Offer to give people a free loaner car if their car needs repair. Offer to drive them to work or to the bus if they must leave their car. Surprise them with free coffee and donuts or the like. Enterprise doesn't just loan you a car, it picks you up at your home and takes you to the rental place. Hotels might put flowers in your room and a free box of chocolates.

The whole idea of relationship marketing is so fun that the class might enjoy brainstorming what relationship marketing might look like at various local establishments. What might they do for you at the local gas station that would go way beyond expectations? At the local pizza shop? At the local department store, supermarket, movie theater, and so on?

lecture link 13-10

FAMILY LIFE CYCLE THEORY UPDATED

Age, population patterns, income, and regional differences are all market characteristics that affect the marketing of goods and services. But some marketing experts feel that life cycle characteristics are a stronger determinant of consumers' buying habits than any of the other characteristics. For two decades, business schools have taught family life cycle theory to marketing students.

Life cycle theory assumes that people pass through a series of stages or family situations in their lives. These stages, or cycles, are characterized by different interests, financial situations, and buying habits. Regardless of their age, for instance, newly married couples will probably purchase kitchen appliances, furniture, and life insurance. Young married couples with a small child will purchase toys, shoes, and medical care. Life cycle theory also identifies groups that are the heaviest purchasers of individual products and allows marketers to target their marketing strategy to narrower target markets.

EARLY FAMILY LIFE CYCLE THEORY

The first versions of life cycle theory identified five stages of life:

- Young, single, just starting out
- Childless couple, both working, in their late 20s
- Two-income household with children in school
- Middle-aged working couple with no dependent children
- Elderly retired person

UPDATED LIFE CYCLE THEORY

Purchasing habits fluctuate over time with every generation. Because of increased access to new technology and uncertainty due to world events, the consumer trends of generations have changed. The current version of family life cycle theory uses the following categories.

BIRTH TO 12 YEARS OLD

It is no longer just colorful toys that attract this consumer segment, and it is no longer possible to lump "subteens" together under the same marketing roof. Because of the changing tastes of these subteens toward consumer electronics and fashion goodies, marketing for this age group has now been split into four distinct under-13 segments:

- Newborns to 3-year-olds
- 3- to 5-year-olds
- 5- to 8-year-olds
- 8- to 12-year-olds

In the wake of the September 11, 2001, tragedy, children are leading more protected lives that include more organized activities and closer parental supervision. Stores can market products to children and parents at the same time by selling products that both can enjoy together.

Today, children within this market segment also differ from their predecessors in that they are technically empowered. They have grown up in a world with ready access to multifunctional gaming consoles and Internet connections. Due to this empowerment at such an early age, they could well evolve into the most progressive and/or demanding generation of consumers. Marketing aimed at this consumer segment should focus on these new media preferences. Products and marketing campaigns that are fun are also a priority, as they are still children.

13 TO 17 YEARS OLD

The image of the typical teenager has changed from that of a lazy underachiever to an optimistic, ambitious, self-assured person with a more confident and positive outlook on life. This age group is much more accustomed to being the targets of sales pitches and is sometimes critical of their motives. Because teenagers are accustomed to multitasking, products need to be presented in a way that will catch the attention of the consumer. Community involvement and global awareness have become more important due to the widespread use of the Internet, so products that are "earth and community friendly" may be more appealing.

18 TO 34 YEARS OLD

This market segment, also referred to as the "bling generation," includes those who were raised on TV images of the Vietnam War on one end and those who grew up watching MTV on the other. Another result of this uncertainty is the increased demand for luxury products. Technology and luxury seem to be two things this generation clearly desires. Social responsibility plays an important role in selling products to this age group. Because people in this age group are so diverse, they can be difficult to market to as a whole. Appealing to this generation requires a product with good design; good value, preferably luxury; at least the appearance of some social responsibility; and an advertising campaign that sells *with* the consumers, not *at* them.

35 TO 54 YEARS OLD

This generation, called the "trailing boomers," is characterized by spending a lot but spending carefully. This segment has three primary characteristics: (1) They are quite sophisticated in the use of technology to get information; (2) they have the money to buy things, and they are still in the householder life stage, many raising teens; and (3) they want to spend more—they need to indulge themselves a bit. This market segment wants to get a deal but not sacrifice quality. A good marketing strategy for this group is product segmentation. If a product works well for a specific consumer, price will not be a major issue; but different products will appeal to different consumers. This age group also values fitness and well-being. To reach this group the marketing approach should be based on state of health and ability to get out and do things instead of on age.

55+ YEARS OLD

Today, this generation is looking toward retirement characterized by youthful vigor, prosperity, and personal fulfillment. They define themselves based on their values and attitudes, giving marketers opportunities in the areas of financial, hospitality, and wellness products and services.

In order for businesses to appeal to these consumers, they need to understand what the buying habits are, how they have changed, and what techniques can be used to reach this life stage.

critical thinking exercises

Name: ______________________________

Date: ______________________________

critical thinking exercise 13-1

FIND A NEED AND FILL IT

The text emphasizes that marketing is not a matter of taking a product and selling it, but of finding a need and filling it. Look around you—around your campus, your home, or your job: Do you see a need that is unfilled? If you're having trouble finding a need, try to remember the times you've said, "Somebody ought to do_____," or "Somebody ought to make______." That somebody is going to be you!

Fill the need you have identified by following the steps listed below. Write down what you would do at each step.

STEPS IN THE MARKETING PROCESS

1. Find a need:

2. Design a product or service:

3. Test your concept:

4. Make up a prototype and test market your product or service:

5. Design packaging, think of a name, and set a price:

6. Decide how to distribute the product to consumers:

7. Develop a promotional strategy:

notes on critical thinking exercise 13-1

This is an excellent exercise for getting students to begin looking for market opportunities and hearing other students do the same. If more than one student sees the same opportunity, that may be a good business to pursue. Just thinking their way through the marketing process is a great way to remember the concepts later.

Name: ______________________

Date: ______________________

critical thinking exercise 13-2

GOOD TO THE LAST DROP

"Good to the last drop" was Coca-Cola's slogan long before it was used in Maxwell House Coffee ads. Coke used it way back in 1900. Other Coke slogans included "Thirst knows no season" (1922); "It had to be good to get where it is" (1925); "Around the corner from everywhere" (1927); "Coke Is It," "Life Tastes Good," and "Have a Coke and a Smile"—Coca-Cola spent $700 million in advertising during its first 90 years. Today, that figure is probably in the billions.

Of course, Pepsi has spent its share of advertising dollars. In fact, Pepsi probably created the most famous jingle of all. The company was about to go bankrupt during the Depression. Even though it was selling six-ounce bottles for only five cents, Coke was beating Pepsi in the market. So the company decided to sell twice as much for the same price. Here is the jingle it used to introduce the new size:

"Pepsi-Cola hits the spot.
Twelve full ounces, that's a lot.
Twice as much for a nickel, too.
Pepsi-Cola's the drink for you."

How important are these jingles and slogans? Needless to say, the market responded to the Pepsi jingle, saving Pepsi from bankruptcy. Why do people buy particular colas? Is it because of the taste? Or does the advertising play a larger role in their cola brand preference?

Let's do a little tasty marketing research ourselves. Many of us drink colas, and more than a few of us have our favorite cola. Let's see if your friends can pick out their favorite from three other colas. You may want to do this project as a class or at least in groups—colas don't sell for a nickel anymore and the cost can add up!

When you have finished gathering your data using the following method instructions and recording sheets, answer these questions:

1. How many of your tasters could identify their favorite cola?

2. How many correctly identified the other colas?

3. How did the responses given when the brands were unknown compare with the responses given when the brands were known?

4. What do your results tell you about the power of advertising?

critical thinking exercise 13-2 (continued)

METHOD

1. Cool bottles or cans of four colas to the same temperature. Don't use some colas in bottles and others in cans because the packaging process could affect taste. Be sure to include Coca-Cola to test those Coke loyalists. It's also interesting to include a diet cola and an "off" brand.

2. Ask 10 people to sample the colas. Test each person individually. Don't let the others watch the test to avoid influencing their own decisions.

3. Each person will be tested in two rounds. In the first round, don't tell the person what he or she is tasting. Refer to each cola as A, B, C, or D. Pour a little in each of four cups (be careful not to get them mixed up). After each cup, ask the taster to describe the flavor, carbonation, and aftertaste. Record the responses on the following record sheet by circling the appropriate response. (You will need one sheet for each taster.) Let each taster take a bite of bread between each cola to clean his or her palate.

4. On the second round, tell the taster which brands he or she is drinking. Don't offer them in the same order as the first round to avoid a simple repetition of responses. Record the responses on the record sheet. It may help you compare responses if you use different colors to record each round. (Don't forget the bread!)

5. Rearrange the order of the colas between tasters. You need to do this for two reasons: (1) Overheard comments can influence your other tasters; and (2) many people will choose C if there is any doubt about an answer.

6. Compile your results and answer the questions.

critical thinking exercise 13-2 (continued)

TASTER NUMBER:______ What's your favorite cola?________________________

Do you think you could identify the brand in a taste test? ☐ YES ☐ NO

COLA A:

Flavor:	Good	•	•	Fair	•	•	Bad
Carbonation:	Heavy	•	•	Fair	•	•	Light
Aftertaste:	Strong	•	•	Fair	•	•	Light

What's your overall opinion of the cola? ________________________

What brand is it? ________________ Would buy it? ☐ YES ☐ NO

COLA B:

Flavor:	Good	•	•	Fair	•	•	Bad
Carbonation:	Heavy	•	•	Fair	•	•	Light
Aftertaste:	Strong	•	•	Fair	•	•	Light

What's your overall opinion of the cola? ________________________

What brand is it? ________________ Would buy it? ☐ YES ☐ NO

COLA C:

Flavor:	Good	•	•	Fair	•	•	Bad
Carbonation:	Heavy	•	•	Fair	•	•	Light
Aftertaste:	Strong	•	•	Fair	•	•	Light

What's your overall opinion of the cola? ________________________

What brand is it? ________________ Would buy it? ☐ YES ☐ NO

COLA D:

Flavor:	Good	•	•	Fair	•	•	Bad
Carbonation:	Heavy	•	•	Fair	•	•	Light
Aftertaste:	Strong	•	•	Fair	•	•	Light

What's your overall opinion of the cola? ________________________

What brand is it? ________________ Would buy it? ☐ YES ☐ NO

notes on critical thinking exercise 13-2

If the results of the students' research are similar to the dozens of similar projects conducted in our classrooms, they should indicate that individuals usually cannot identify their favorite colas on blind taste tests. However, when they are told the brands they are tasting, these same individuals will usually select their favorite as the "best" of those offered.

If taste isn't the criterion for cola selection, why are we loyal to certain brands above others? This should lead to an interesting class discussion.

Name: ______________________________

Date: ______________________________

critical thinking exercise 13-3

IDENTIFYING THE TARGET MARKET

For each of the products below, identify the target market. Be specific. For example, the target market for Just For Men hair color could be broadly defined as "men." However, by analyzing the potential users and characteristics, a narrower market segment can be defined—men, over 40, involved in a romantic relationship, with some amount of disposable income, who care about looking younger.

PRODUCT/SERVICE	TARGET MARKET
1. Lipitor prescription drug	
2. Zebco spinning reel (for fishing)	
3. Luvs disposable diaper	
4. Avon cosmetics	
5. Cesar gourmet canned dog food	
6. First-class airline ticket to London	
7. Set of twin-sized bed linens	
8. Sterling silver flatware, one setting	
9. Hummer automobile	
10. Romantic novel from Amazon.com	

notes on critical thinking exercise 13-3

PRODUCT/SERVICE	TARGET MARKET
1. Lipitor prescription drug	Two separate target markets. One is consumers who are aware that they have high cholesterol who seek medical help. However, there is a more important target market: the physicians who prescribe the drug. This is an example of a product for which there are separate decision-makers and buyers.
2. Zebco spinning reel (for fishing)	Broadly, the target market for a fishing reel would be sport fisherpeople. If you have students who regularly fish, they may be able to more specifically identify a market. Zebco reels are entry-level items, bought by first-time fisherpeople or as gifts for children.
3. Luvs disposable diaper	The temptation is to say "babies," but this is incorrect. A baby doesn't decide which product to buy; his or her parent (or caregiver) does. Marketing should target parents of children less than two years old.
4. Avon cosmetics	First, broadly, the target market is women. However, this market can be narrowed to women in the appropriate age range—not toddlers, not nursing home patients. The market could also be narrowed by income. Very low-income consumers would be more likely to shop for lower-priced cosmetics at discount stores. Very high-income buyers can afford the pricey cosmetics sold in high-end boutique stores.
5. Cesar gourmet canned dog food	The target market here is owners of small dogs who have the financial resources to pamper their pets with gourmet pet food. Small cans of food would be impractical for large breeds of dog or working dogs.
6. First-class airline ticket to London	The target market is what used to be referred to as "jet setters," well-off individuals who love to travel and value luxury and comfort. The average tourist could probably not afford the first-class ticket, and only top-level businesspeople would have the expense account to pay for premium travel.
7. Set of twin-sized bed linens	The target market for twin-sized bed linens is harder to narrowly segment. Parents of young children would be one market. First-year college students are another. Perhaps newly single adults who are downsizing are a third market.

8. Sterling silver flatware, one setting	This is easy—friends and family of couples about to marry, or newly marrieds.
9. Hummer automobile	Adults with high disposable income who value status, safety, and "muscle" would be the target market. You could probably eliminate customers who live in densely populated cities such as New York City, sports car enthusiasts, and nondrivers.
10. Romantic novel from Amazon.com	The typical buyer of a romance novel is a woman who enjoys reading. In addition, the buyer (who could be male) would need to own or have access to a computer, have some Internet experience, use a credit card, and feel safe buying online.

Name: ______________________

Date: ______________________

critical thinking exercise 13-4

THE MARKETING OPPORTUNITY

Suppose your roommate just invented an electronic pencil that senses when a word being written is misspelled, beeps, and shows the correct spelling on a small screen on the side of the pencil. He figures the pencil can be manufactured for about $5, since the cost of computer chips has dropped so low.

Your roommate comes to you for advice and money. He will make you a 40% owner if you help manufacture and sell the pencils. He asks you to put up $500 for materials for the first 100 units. He asks that you help make and sell the pencils after classes.

Since your roommate is studying electronic engineering, he knows about as much about marketing as you know about electronics. You agree to study the possibilities. You make a list of questions that need to be answered before you commit your $500.

1. What need does this product fill?

2. What is the potential market for the product?

3. What are the target markets for such a product?

4. What type of consumer good is this product?

5. How will you distribute the product?

6. How could the consumer be convinced to purchase the product?

7. What are the other questions that need to be answered before a decision is made?

notes on critical thinking exercise 13-4

1. *What need does this product fill?*

   This pencil will help those students who are not good spellers to learn how to spell better and to make sure that what they write is spelled correctly.

2. *What is the potential market for the product?*

   The potential market includes everyone who uses a pencil to write words rather than numbers.

3. *What are the target markets for such a product?*

   Especially interested may be students, writers, and editors.

4. *What type of consumer good is this product?*

   It is a shopping good in that it will compete with other pencils and pens of comparable cost.

5. *How will you distribute the product?*

   Eventually you would want as wide a distribution as possible, including drugstore counters, business supply stores, campus bookstores, and so forth. At first, however, it may be best to focus on campus bookstores and business supply stores.

6. *How could the consumer be convinced to purchase the product?*

   Usually the best way to convince someone of the benefit of a new product is to have him or her sample one. Such samples could be placed on the counters of the bookstores and business supply stores. You would have to train the store personnel in how to use the product. You could also recruit student salespeople to do demonstrations and sell the product on campus. Word of mouth and publicity would likely help in creating sales. It is doubtful that much advertising would be needed at first, but if the product is successful, it could be advertised widely.

7. *What are the other questions that need to be answered before a decision is made?*

   Can such a pencil really be made? Do you have a patent or are you getting one? What should the initial price be? Who should make the pencil? Do other people know about this idea? Where can I find the $500 quickly?

Name: ______________________________

Date: ______________________________

critical thinking exercise 13-5

CONSUMER OR B2B GOOD?

For each product below, indicate whether it is a consumer good, a B2B (industrial) good, or both. Explain the reasons for your choices.

ITEM	TYPE OF GOOD	RATIONALE
1. McDonald's Big Mac	☐ Consumer ☐ B2B ☐ Both	
2. Xerox copy paper	☐ Consumer ☐ B2B ☐ Both	
3. 14-pound bag of sugar	☐ Consumer ☐ B2B ☐ Both	
4. John Deere front-end loader	☐ Consumer ☐ B2B ☐ Both	
5. Hewlett-Packard laser printer	☐ Consumer ☐ B2B ☐ Both	
6. Band-Aid strips	☐ Consumer ☐ B2B ☐ Both	
7. Designer wedding dress	☐ Consumer ☐ B2B ☐ Both	
8. 20-pound box of framing nails	☐ Consumer ☐ B2B ☐ Both	
9. Craftsman 48-inch-cut riding lawn-mower	☐ Consumer ☐ B2B ☐ Both	
10. TurboTax tax preparation software	☐ Consumer ☐ B2B ☐ Both	

notes on critical thinking exercise 13-5

ITEM	TYPE OF GOOD	RATIONALE
1. McDonald's Big Mac	☒ Consumer ☐ B2B ☐ Both	A McDonald's Big Mac probably could not be used to create another consumer product.
2. Xerox copy paper	☐ Consumer ☐ B2B ☒ Both	An office could use the copy paper to create reports for another customer (B2B good), but it could also be sold to a customer for home use.
3. 14-pound bag of sugar	☐ Consumer ☐ B2B ☒ Both	A bag of sugar delivered to a restaurant would be a B2B good because it is used to create baked goods for sale. It can also be sold to a customer to be used in his or her morning coffee.
4. John Deere front-end loader	☐ Consumer ☒ B2B ☐ Both	A front-end loader is a specialized piece of equipment used in construction projects. Your average homeowner doesn't need one.
5. Hewlett-Packard laser printer	☐ Consumer ☐ B2B ☒ Both	Again, could be used in an office or in the home of a consumer.
6. Band-Aid strips	☐ Consumer ☐ B2B ☒ Both	In a hospital, Band-Aids would be a B2B good, used to create a consumer service (health care). In a buyer's home, it is a consumer good.
7. Designer wedding dress	☒ Consumer ☐ B2B ☐ Both	The only product a designer wedding dress can create is a marriage.
8. 20-pound box of framing nails	☐ Consumer ☒ B2B ☐ Both	If the question were about a *1-pound* box of framing nails, it could be a consumer good, used in a home renovation project. However, the size of this product seems to indicate that a commercial contractor will use it.
9. Craftsman 48-inch-cut riding lawnmower	☐ Consumer ☐ B2B ☒ Both	The lawnmower could be used by a lawn-care service (B2B) to create a service or by a homeowner in his or her own yard (consumer).
10. TurboTax tax preparation software	☒ Consumer ☐ B2B ☐ Both	A tax preparation service would probably use a professional tax preparation software service. TurboTax is a stripped-down tax preparation program aimed at individual taxpayers.

bonus cases

bonus case 13-1

CUSTOMER-ORIENTED MARKETING CONCEPTS AT THERMOS

Thermos is the company made famous by its Thermos bottles and lunch boxes. Thermos also manufactures cookout grills. Its competitors include Sunbeam and Weber. To become a world-class competitor, Thermos completely reinvented the way it conducted its marketing operations. By reviewing what Thermos did, you can see how new marketing concepts affect organizations.

First, Thermos modified its corporate culture. It had become a bureaucratic firm organized by function: design, engineering, manufacturing, marketing, and so on. That organizational structure was replaced by flexible, cross-functional, self-managed teams. The idea was to focus on a customer group—for example, buyers of outdoor grills—and build a product development team to create a product for that market.

The product development team for grills consisted of six middle managers from various disciplines, including engineering, manufacturing, finance, and marketing. They called themselves the Lifestyle Team because their job was to study grill users to see how they lived and what they were looking for in an outdoor grill. To get a fresh perspective, the company hired Fitch, Inc., an outside consulting firm, to help with design and marketing research. Team leadership was rotated based on needs of the moment. For example, the marketing person took the lead in doing field research, but the R&D person took over when technical developments became the issue.

The team's first step was to analyze the market. Together, team members spent about a month on the road talking with people, videotaping barbecues, conducting focus groups, and learning what people wanted in an outdoor grill. The company found that people wanted a nice-looking grill that didn't pollute the air and was easy to use. It also had to be safe enough for apartment dwellers, which meant it had to be electric.

As the research results came in, engineering began playing with ways to improve electric grills. Manufacturing kept in touch to make sure that any new ideas could be produced economically. Design people were already building models of the new product. R&D people relied heavily on Thermos's core strength—the vacuum technology it had developed to keep hot things hot and cold things cold in Thermos bottles. Drawing on that technology, the engineers developed a domed lid that contained the heat inside the grill.

Once a prototype was developed, the company showed the model to potential customers, who suggested several changes. Employees also took sample grills home and tried to find weaknesses. Using the input from potential customers and employees, the company used continuous improvement to manufacture what became a world-class outdoor grill.

No product can become a success without communicating with the market. The team took the grill on the road, showing it at trade shows and in retail stores. The product was such a success that Thermos is now using self-managed, customer-oriented teams to develop all its product lines.

discussion questions for bonus case 13-1

1. How can Thermos now build a closer relationship with its customers using the Internet?

2. What other products might Thermos develop that would appeal to the same market segment that uses outdoor grills?

3. What do you think the Thermos team would have found if it had asked customers what they thought about having consumers put the grills together rather than buying them assembled? What other questions might Thermos place on its website to learn more about customer wants and needs?

notes on discussion questions for bonus case 13-1

1. *How can Thermos now build a closer relationship with its customers using the Internet?*

   Customers can ask questions and make comments on the Internet so that Thermos can continuously improve its products and add more products to its offering.

2. *What other products might Thermos develop that would appeal to the same market segment that uses outdoor grills?*

   In general, it might be said that more men than women use outdoor grills. Those men may be interested in other outdoor products such as leaf blowers, lawn mowers, trashcans, rakes and other tools, and the like. The class may enjoy brainstorming this question.

3. *What do you think the Thermos team would have found if it had asked customers what they thought about having consumers put the grills together rather than buying them assembled? What other questions might Thermos place on its website to learn more about customer wants and needs?*

   Some people enjoy putting things together, especially if it results in a lower price. Other questions may include questions about customer desire for cooking products, including meats, fish, condiments, and tools for cooking. The class may have creative questions to ask.

bonus case 13-2

FOOD MARKETING IN THE INNER CITY

In many cases, food marketers don't even try to sell products for the health-conscious in low-income neighborhoods. Businesses both big and small thus contribute to the cycle of poor nutrition in the inner city. A spokesperson for Kraft General Foods said, "We aren't a miniature Health and Human Services Department. A company doesn't have a social obligation to instruct consumers on the best way to handle their health."

At the Friendly Pal supermarket in Brooklyn, the Continental Baking delivery person puts up lots of Wonder Bread and two small loaves of whole wheat and another two of light wheat. The salesperson says, "Whole wheat is for the old people, light wheat is for the skinny people, and all this white bread, it's for the fat people." In low-income Bedford Stuyvesant, only 25 of 149 small grocers carry low-fat milk. A store across the street from one of Chicago's low-income housing projects offers only two cartons of low-fat milk and two cartons of skim. The store sells lots of Snickers, Coke, and Frito Lay products, beer, and cigarettes.

In Harlem, Little Debbie's cupcakes sell like hotcakes. One Harlem storeowner tried stocking his store with fresh fruits and vegetables and Del Monte fruit in light syrup. His peaches, grapes, lettuce, and tomatoes were ignored. Now he sells just potatoes and bananas.

Although African Americans suffer more from hypertension, for which doctors prescribe low-salt diets, the Special Request line of low-sodium soups from Campbell is hard to find in the inner city where many African Americans live. Campbell soup says it is easier to fish where the fish are and doesn't try to promote its more nutritious soup to inner-city people.

Many supermarket chains have abandoned inner cities and have left the market to smaller stores that charge between 10 and 20% more for the same food. This isn't a rip-off of consumers as much as a passing on of higher costs. Smaller stores simply can't buy at the same low prices as larger supermarkets can.

discussion questions for bonus case 13-2

1. Major food companies and smaller grocery stores in the inner city are applying the marketing concept as they learned it. They are giving people what they want, as measured by store sales. They are not making much of an effort to encourage people to buy products that are more nutritious. Is this a problem as you see it?

2. Food costs more in the inner city than it does in the more affluent suburbs. Do marketers have any responsibility to change the situation? If not, does the government have any responsibility, or should people be free to buy, sell, and eat whatever they want at whatever cost, with no interference from the outside?

3. Poor health costs all of us in higher medical bills and lower productivity of the workforce. If major food companies will not promote nutrition to poor people, should that function be taken over by nonprofit organizations such as churches, schools, and the government? What would you recommend?

4. Inner-city stores sell lots of snack items, soda, beer, and cigarettes, but little fruit and vegetables. Would you try to do anything different if you were a grocery store owner? What would motivate you to try to sell items that are more nutritious?

notes on discussion questions for bonus case 13-2

1. *Major food companies and smaller grocery stores in the inner city are applying the marketing concept as they learned it. They are giving people what they want, as measured by store sales. They are not making much of an effort to encourage people to buy products that are more nutritious. Is this a problem as you see it?*

   This is an ethical problem and an economic problem of deep significance. Marketers today do not see much of an obligation to guide consumers to purchase what is good for them. Rather, they give consumers what they want. This satisfies consumers and sellers. The only people not satisfied are those who want to change society. They too have a right to market their ideas, but perhaps their efforts should not be mixed into the retailing system as it now exists. Rather, nutrition and other information should be provided in schools, newspapers, and other means. Then consumers will ask for more nutritious food, and retailers will be glad to sell it to them.

2. *Food costs more in the inner city than it does in the more affluent suburbs. Do marketers have any responsibility to change the situation? If not, does the government have any responsibility, or should people be free to buy, sell, and eat whatever they want at whatever cost, with no interference from the outside?*

   "Free markets" means truly "free markets." Food often costs more in the inner city because expenses are higher, including rent, insurance, and storage. Furthermore, many inner-city stores are smaller and don't have the advantage of bulk purchasing that the giants have. The government can do little to change such circumstances except to give businesses tax breaks and other concessions to locate in the city.

3. *Poor health costs all of us in higher medical bills and lower productivity of the workforce. If major food companies will not promote nutrition to poor people, should that function be taken over by nonprofit organizations such as churches, schools, and the government? What would you recommend?*

   Yes, schools, nonprofit organizations, and the government should all try to educate people to eat better, to exercise, and so on. People are eating better today—less meat, more fish, and so on. The educational process is working. Now people need to be taught to exercise more, to buy more nutritious products, and to eat less.

4. *Inner-city stores sell lots of snack items, soda, beer, and cigarettes, but little fruit and vegetables. Would you try to do anything different if you were a grocery store owner? What would motivate you to try to sell items that are more nutritious?*

   It all depends on your goals. If your goal is to make money, then give consumers what they want and stock soft drinks, beer, and so forth. If you also have social goals for your store, you might try to educate consumers to buy more nutritious drinks, such as bottled water or milk, especially for children or pregnant women. Most businesspeople make minimal profits in the inner city to begin with and could lose more by trying to sell what people do not want. On the other hand, they have a captive audience if they can convince people to buy fresh produce and other goods not being sold in the area at the present time.

bonus case 13-3

LINING UP FOR FREE APPS

In this digital age of free information, it can be a chore to convince consumers, especially young ones, to purchase some products. After all, for every Web app or program that isn't already distributed freely, there are about a dozen other ways to obtain it through easy but extralegal means. Nevertheless, information and the ways in which it is transmitted will become no more restrained in five years than they are now. Rather than react with higher prices and stringent policies, entrepreneurs must adapt and find ways to integrate the free flow of information into their moneymaking schemes.

For instance, in 2006 Eric Alder and Julien Chabbott graduated from college with an idea for a smartphone app that would provide regular updates on the wait times of lines around town. The app was to be driven by social media with individual users providing the app with the estimated length of the lines they were standing in. But the pair of young entrepreneurs faced a quandary. Without accurate line times built in, nobody would use the app. And if nobody used the app, there wouldn't be enough reliable data to formulate accurate line times.

In order to get the app off the ground, Alder and Chabbott first distributed Line Snob for free on the iPhone marketplace. Then the pair rewarded users who reported wait times with points that could be redeemed for coupons. And rather than rely solely on word of mouth, Line Snob ingratiated itself with popular venues that uploaded data on their own lines and posted fliers about the app around their queues. Once Chabbott and Alder established their user base, they began making money by charging companies a monthly fee for using the app. Line Snob is especially popular in Las Vegas, where hotels use it to announce which buffet or club lines are the shortest. The app remains free for regular users, and the company hopes to unveil soon a new feature that can predict line waits before they occur.[vii]

discussion questions for bonus case 13-3

1. What key entrepreneurial characteristics seemed to drive Alder and Chabbott?

2. What's the major challenge for Line Snob going forward?

notes on discussion questions for bonus case 13-3

1. *What key entrepreneurial characteristics seemed to drive Alder and Chabbott?*

   As described in Chapter 6, both entrepreneurs seemed to be self-nurturing and action-oriented. They continued to believe in their product even though it faced many ups and downs. They had the burning desire to build their dream into a reality.

2. *What's the major challenge for Line Snob going forward?*

   The flow of information continues to move unrestrained at a fast pace with competition forever on the horizon. Line Snob needs to continuously add new features and services that reach target customers and top competitors.

bonus case 13-4

MARKETING TO THE BABY BOOM GENERATION

The nation's 78 million baby boomers, born between 1946 and 1964, are the wealthiest group of Americans. They have an estimated $1 trillion in annual disposable income and three-quarters of the nation's financial assets, but only 10% of advertising dollars are directed specifically at the 50-plus market. Marketers aim for the "sweet spot," the demographic group between 18 and 49. But as the aging boomers hurdle toward retirement, some marketers are realizing the commercial potential of such a huge, affluent market.

The baby boom generation has transformed every age and stage it has passed through. As children, boomers created a market for disposable diapers and strained peas in jars. As teenagers, they introduced the nation to long hair, rock-and-roll music, tie-dyed clothes, and skateboards. As the generation became parents, they demanded organic baby food, quality health care, and SUVs. Today market researchers are looking at the marketing opportunities for the wealthiest generation steadily moving into retirement. Almost 8 million Americans turned 60 in 2006. By 2010, one in three adults will be 50 or older. This huge demographic group will not go gently into retirement like earlier generations have done.

The conventional wisdom among marketers is that you have to get consumers to commit to your brand early in life and once they commit they will be loyal to your brand forever. However, a study conducted by AARP showed that consumers aged 45 and older switch brands just as readily as younger generations. This has tremendous implications for savvy marketers.

Half of all boomers live in households without kids. Companies like General Mills changed the packaging for its Pillsbury dinner rolls and Green Giant vegetables to resealable freezer bags that allow for several smaller portions instead of family-sized portions.

Boomer retirees will leave their primary career near age 62 to 65, but most will not completely leave the job market. Many will pursue volunteer opportunities, take a low-stress part-time job, or start a completely new business. A study by Merrill Lynch found that 76% of boomers said they will probably hold down a job in retirement, and a majority of that group said they expect to shift back and forth between leisure and work.

Savvy entrepreneurs can capitalize on the unique qualities of this generation. Take Re/Max agent Kathy Sperl-Bell. Sperl-Bell is a Senior Real Estate Specialist (SRES), 1 of more than 14,000 real estate agents nationwide with an SRES designation, up from 5,000 in 2002. Agents go through a two-day training program, which includes analysis of the different generational needs and attitudes of those 55 and older, as well as the types of housing options available for that market. SRES agents specialize in dealing with this growing market segment that have specific needs—taxes, elder care, estate sales, health care availability—and also a large amount of disposable income to meet them.

This generation also has the income and leisure time to become doting grandparents. Disney has targeted this trend with TV commercials showing multiple generations enjoying theme-park attractions.

Retiring boomers don't want to look like retirees. From Botox to cosmetic peels to plastic surgery, the race is on to profit from the generation's desire to be forever young. Every cosmetic company from Avon to L'Oreal is rolling out wrinkle creams and serums to halt sagging skin and wrinkles.

But marketers must tailor their marketing carefully. According to one researcher, "Anything marketing to silver hair is bad marketing. Don't talk to their chronological age; talk to their self-image." That 50-year-old boomer probably still feels like a 30-something.[viii]

discussion questions for bonus case 13-4

1. Based on this upcoming, large spending group, what other types of products/services might be popular and attention getting to this market? Why would these products/services be a good fit to this group?

2. Is there a segment of the baby boomers who are more conservative and not interested in buying products that speak to a younger living lifestyle as portrayed in this case study? If so, how would you define this segment and what potential would there be to sell products and services to them?

3. For those baby boomers who would like to become entrepreneurs, what might be types of businesses that they would be good fits to operate? What would be their motivation to own and operate their own business?

notes on discussion questions for bonus case 13-4

1. *Based on this upcoming, large spending group, what other types of products/services might be popular and attention getting to this market? Why would these products/services be a good fit to this group?*

   Students will have lots of ideas to share about these questions. Some of the obvious areas to consider are travel, auto styles, insurance, health products, and home choices. Marketing to this group will be best done by appealing to their emotional enjoyment of the product and service experience, and there will be many different and creative ways to accomplish these objectives.

2. *Is there a segment of the baby boomers who are more conservative and not interested in buying products that speak to a younger living lifestyle as portrayed in this case study? If so, how would you define this segment and what potential would there be to sell products and services to them?*

   Without question, there will be opportunities to do more traditional marketing to the baby boomer generation and have successful results. Some segments of this generation will not be as well-off and have other basic needs that will need to be addressed. Finding these "other" segments might be less popular and less spenders but will have needs that will need to be met considering their lifestyles that call for more traditional ideologies of the products and services that will meet their needs.

3. *For those baby boomers who would like to become entrepreneurs, what might be types of businesses that they would be good fits to operate? What would be their motivation to own and operate their own business?*

   Business ideas for baby boomers might be a growing, yet-to-be-determined market opportunity. Potential business ideas might range from craft and antique shops to other retail ventures. Baby boomers might be good business owners because of their insight and dedication to the business ideas they choose to operate. Their heritage of hard work and dedication to their job, families, and lives might come out in their business ownership opportunities.

endnotes

---

[i] *Source*: Brian L. Clark, "Pat Croce's Secret," *Fortune Small Business*, November 13, 2001.

[ii] *Source:* Jason Ankeny, "Setting Sale on Smartphones," *Entrepreneur*, December 2010.

[iii] *Source:* Rafi Mohammed, "Ditching the Discounts," *Harvard Business Review*, January–February 2011.

[iv] *Source:* Burt Helm, "KFC Owners Wonder What Happened to the 'F'," *Bloomberg Businessweek*, August 16, 2010.

[v] *Source:* Mehul Srivastava, "For India's Consumers, Pepsi Is the Real Thing," *Bloomberg Businessweek*, September 16, 2010.

[vi] *Source*: Juile Schlosser, "DeWalt, Lesson: Know Your Customer," *Fortune*, October 31, 2005.

[vii] *Source:* Joel Howard, "Your Wait Is Over," *Entrepreneur*, November 2010.

[viii] *Sources*: Kristin Davis, "Oldies but Goodies," *U.S. News & World Report*, March 14, 2005; Farrell Kramer, "Affluent Baby Boomers Don't Expect to Retire Like Their Parents; Three-Quarters of Working Baby Boomers Plan to Remain in Workforce When They Hit Retirement Age," *PR Newswire*, November 17, 2004; Pete Bach, "Aging Baby Boomers Will Have a Wide-Reaching Economic Impact," *The Post-Crescent* [Appleton, Wisconsin], March 6, 2006; Sally Stich, "Special Agents," *Time*, August 2006.

Developing and Pricing Goods and Services

chapter 14

what's new in this edition

additions to the 10th edition:

- Getting to Know Mary Barra of GM
- Name That Company: Virgin Airlines
- Subsection Distributed Product Development added to section Product Development and the Total Product Offer.
- Term **distributed product development** added to Key Terms and Glossary.
- Spotlight on Small Business: Don't Come to Me; I'll Come to You
- Thinking Green: Quality and Sustainability
- Reaching Beyond Our Borders: The Name Game
- Video case

revisions to the 10th edition:

- Text was revised to eliminate redundancy and tighten discussions.
- Statistical data and examples throughout the chapter were updated to reflect current information.
- Key Term **manufacturers' brands** replaces **manufacturers' brand names**

deletions from the 9th edition:

- Getting to Know Ratan Tata from the Tata Group
- Name That Company: Zipper
- Spotlight on Small Business
- Thinking Green
- Reaching Beyond Our Borders

brief chapter outline and learning goals

chapter 14

Developing and Pricing Goods and Services

Getting To Know MARY BARRA from GM

learning goal 1

Describe a total product offer.

I. PRODUCT DEVELOPMENT AND THE TOTAL PRODUCT OFFER

- **A. Distributed Product Development**
- **B. Developing a Total Product Offer**
- **C. Product Lines and the Product Mix**

learning goal 2

Identify the various kinds of consumer and industrial goods.

II. PRODUCT DIFFERENTIATION

- **A. Marketing Different Classes of Consumer Goods and Services**
- **B. Marketing Industrial Goods and Services**

learning goal 3

Summarize the functions of packaging.

III. PACKAGING CHANGES THE PRODUCT

- **A. The Growing Importance of Packaging**

learning goal 4

Contrast *brand, brand name*, and *trademark* and show the value of brand equity.

IV. BRANDING AND BRAND EQUITY

- **A. Brand Categories**
- **B. Generating Brand Equity and Loyalty**
- **C. Creating Brand Associations**
- **D. Brand Management**

learning goal 5

Explain the steps in the new-product development process.

V. THE NEW-PRODUCT DEVELOPMENT PROCESS

A. Generating New-Product Ideas

B. Product Screening

C. Product Analysis

D. Product Development and Testing

E. Commercialization

learning goal 6

Describe the product life cycle.

VI. THE PRODUCT LIFE CYCLE

A. Example of the Product Life Cycle

B. Using the Product Life Cycle

learning goal 7

Identify various pricing objectives and strategies.

VII. COMPETITIVE PRICING

A. Pricing Objectives

B. Cost-Based Pricing

C. Demand-Based Pricing

D. Competition-Based Pricing

E. Break-Even Analysis

F. Other Pricing Strategies

G. How Market Forces Affect Pricing

VIII. NONPRICE COMPETITION

IX. SUMMARY

lecture
outline

Getting to Know MARY BARRA from GM

Barra is General Motors's (GM) highest-ranking woman and the senior vice president of global product development. She focuses on the customer in the area of global design, vehicle and power train engineering, program management, and quality. GM is working to increase its presence in the hybrid market.

It's no secret that the airline industry is extremely competitive and many airlines have cut basic services like free baggage and food. In order to set itself apart from its competitors, this company takes a different path by offering door-to-door limousine service and in-flight massages. Name that company.

(Students should read the chapter before guessing the company's name: Virgin Airlines)

learning goal 1

Describe a total product offer.

I. PRODUCT DEVELOPMENT AND THE TOTAL PRODUCT OFFER

A. This chapter explores two key parts of the marketing mix: **PRODUCT** and **PRICE**.

1. To prevent losing customers, marketers must **DESIGN AND PROMOTE** better products, products that customers perceive as having better **VALUE.**
2. The American Marketing Association defines **MARKETING** as "a set of processes for creating, communicating, and delivering value to customers."
3. ***VALUE*** is good quality at a fair price.
4. When consumers calculate the value of a product, they look at the **BENEFITS** and then subtract the

lecture notes

PPT 14-1
Chapter Title

PPT 14-2
Learning Goals

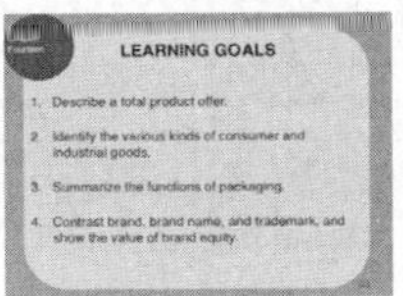

(See complete PowerPoint slide notes on page 14.42)

PPT 14-3
Learning Goals

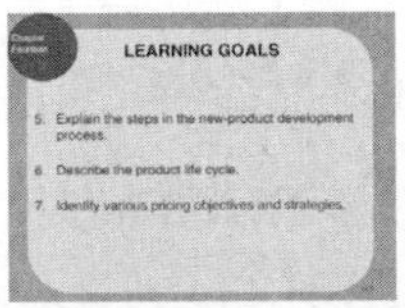

(See complete PowerPoint slide notes on page 14.42.)

PPT 14-4
Mary Barra

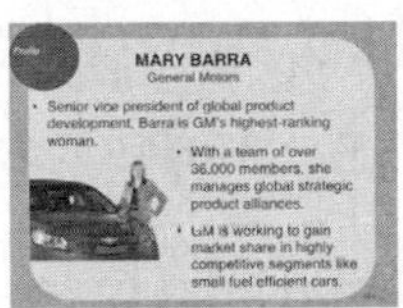

(See complete PowerPoint slide notes on page 14.43.)

PPT 14-5
Name That Company

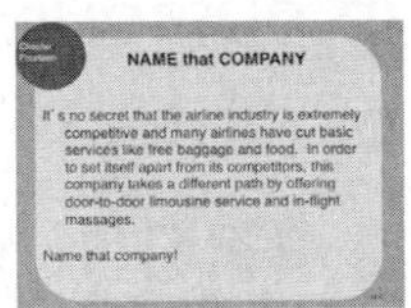

(See complete PowerPoint slide notes on page 14.43.)

lecture link 14-1
THERE IS NO SUCH THING AS A "BETTER" PRODUCT

The best product is the one that best meets your needs. (See the complete lecture link on page 14.61 in this manual.)

PPT 14-6
Developing Value

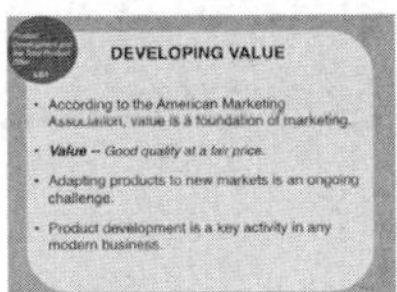

(See complete PowerPoint slide notes on page 14.43.)

COSTS to see if the benefits exceed the costs.

5. To satisfy consumers, marketers must **LISTEN TO** and constantly **ADAPT TO** changing market demands and competitors' pricing.
6. Because customers' needs change over time, they must be **CONSTANTLY MONITORED.**
7. The text uses several examples:
   a. *McDonald's new-product developments in the fast-food market, a fast-changing market.*
   b. *Companies such as 7-Eleven, KFC, Arby's, Burger King, and Wendy's introducing new fast food.*
8. Companies also need to adapt their offerings to local conditions, both here and abroad.
9. Product development is key in any business.

B. **DISTRIBUTED PRODUCT DEVELOPMENT**

1. The increase in outsourcing has resulted in efforts requiring use of multiple organizations.
2. **DISTRIBUTED PRODUCT DEVELOPMENT** is handing off various parts of your innovation process—often to companies in other countries.

C. **DEVELOPING A TOTAL PRODUCT OFFER**

1. A ***TOTAL PRODUCT OFFER*** consists of everything that consumers evaluate when deciding whether or not to buy something (also called the value package).
   a. The basic product may be a physical good or service.
   b. Some people call the basic product the

lecture notes

PPT 14-7
Products Consumers Won't Give Up

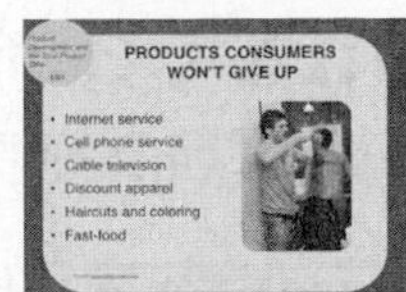

(See complete PowerPoint slide notes on page 14.44.)

PPT 14-8
Products "Expendable" by Spending Cuts

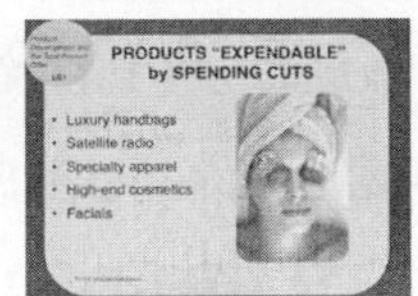

(See complete PowerPoint slide notes on page 14.44.)

bonus case 14-1
PANERA EXPANDS PAY-WHAT-YOU-CAN EXPERIMENT

Panera adapted its pricing plan in a Missouri store to include an honor system where customers can weigh their own cost versus value. (See the complete case, discussion questions, and suggested answers beginning on page 14.78 of this manual.)

lecture link 14-2
THE VENETIAN'S TROUBLES IN MACAO

Popular Las Vegas hotels are building in China but some have missed the mark in what their customers want. Operators need to find out how to fix their problems. (See the complete lecture link on page 14.62 in this manual.)

PPT 14-9
Distributed Product Development

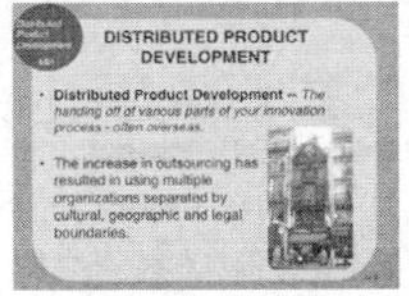

(See complete PowerPoint slide notes on page 14.44.)

bonus case 14-2
THE VALUE OF A PRODUCT OFFER

This case uses the comparison of value between a Ford and a BMW. (See the complete case, discussion questions, and suggested answers beginning on page 14.80 of this manual.)

PPT 14-10
Developing a Total Product

(See complete PowerPoint slide notes on page 14.45.)

PPT 14-11
Product Innovation during the Great Depression

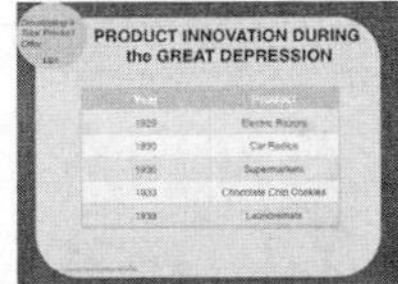

(See complete PowerPoint slide notes on page 14.45.)

"CORE PRODUCT" and the total product offer the **"AUGMENTED PRODUCT."**

c. **TANGIBLE ATTRIBUTES** are the product itself and the packaging.

d. **INTANGIBLE ATTRIBUTES** include image created by advertising, guarantee, and reputation of the producer.

e. Consumers evaluate the total product offer as a collection of impressions.

2. Different customers may want different total product offers, so marketers may develop a variety of offerings.

D. **PRODUCT LINES AND THE PRODUCT MIX**

1. Companies usually sell several different, but complementary, products.

2. The ***PRODUCT LINE*** is a group of products that are physically similar or are intended for a similar market *(example: Coke's varied offerings).*

3. The ***PRODUCT MIX*** is the combination of product lines offered by a manufacturer *(Proctor & Gamble's laundry detergent line).*

4. **SERVICE PROVIDERS** also have product lines and product mixes *(banking products and services offered by a credit union or bank).*

learning goal 2

Identify the various kinds of consumer and industrial goods .

II. PRODUCT DIFFERENTIATION

A. ***PRODUCT DIFFERENTIATION*** is the creation of real or perceived product differences.

lecture notes

PPT 14-12
Anything You Can Do . . .

(See complete PowerPoint slide notes on page 14.45.)

PPT 14-13
Potential Components of a Total Product Offer

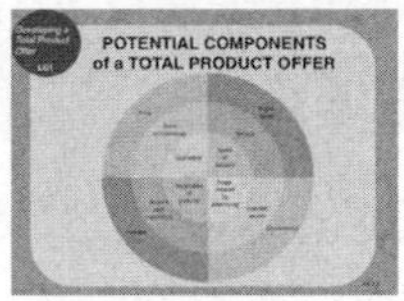

TEXT FIGURE 14.1
Potential Components of a Total Product Offer
(Text page 380)

(See complete PowerPoint slide notes on page 14.46.)

Thinking green
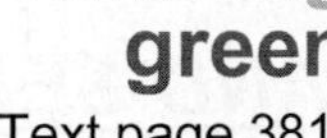
(Text page 381)

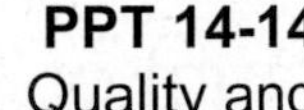

PPT 14-14
Quality and Sustainability

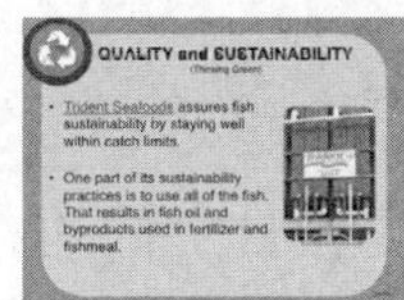

(See complete PowerPoint slide notes on page 14.46.)

PPT 14-15
Understanding Product Lines

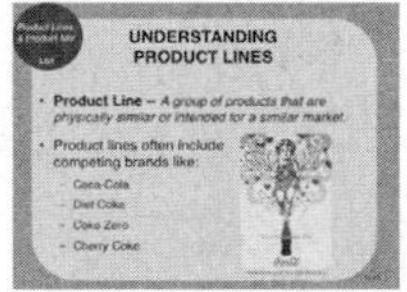

(See complete PowerPoint slide notes on page 14.46.)

PPT 14-16
The Product Mix

(See complete PowerPoint slide notes on page 14.47.)

1. Actual product differences are sometimes quite small, so marketers must create a **UNIQUE, ATTRACTIVE IMAGE** *(example: various brands of bottled water).*
2. Small businesses can often win market share with **CREATIVE PRODUCT DIFFERENTIATION** *(example: Charlie Clark's yearbook photography offers multiple backgrounds and special allowances).*

B. **MARKETING DIFFERENT CLASSES OF CONSUMER GOODS AND SERVICES**

1. ***<u>CONVENIENCE GOODS AND SERVICES</u>*** are products that the consumer wants to purchase frequently and with a minimum of effort.
   a. For these, location, brand awareness, and image are important for marketers.
   b. *Examples*: *candy, milk, snacks, gas, and banking services.*
   c. The Internet provides another level of convenience.
   d. *Best marketing strategy:* make them readily available and create the proper image.
2. ***<u>SHOPPING GOODS AND SERVICES</u>*** are those products that the consumer buys only after comparing value, quality, price, and style from a variety of sellers.
   a. Shopping goods and services are usually sold through shopping centers where consumers can make comparisons.

PPT 14-17
Differentiating Products

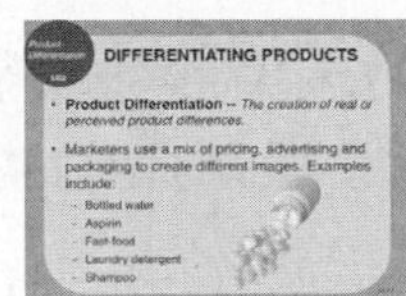

(See complete PowerPoint slide notes on page 14.47.)

PPT 14-18
Classifying Consumer Goods and Services

(See complete PowerPoint slide notes on page 14.47.)

PPT 14-19
Classifying Shopping Goods and Services

(See complete PowerPoint slide notes on page 14.48.)

b. *Examples: clothes, shoes, appliances, and auto repair services.*

c. *Target is an example of a store selling primarily shopping goods.*

d. *Best marketing strategy:* emphasize price differences, quality differences, or some combination.

3. ***SPECIALTY GOODS AND SERVICES*** are consumer products with unique characteristics and brand identity.

   a. Because these products are perceived as having no reasonable substitute, the consumer makes a special effort to buy them.

   b. *Examples: specialty foods, expensive wine, and jewelry.*

   c. These products are often marketed through specialty magazines.

   d. Interactive websites make purchasing specialty goods more convenient.

   e. *Best marketing strategy:* advertising that reaches special market segments.

4. ***UNSOUGHT GOODS AND SERVICES*** are products that consumers are unaware of, haven't necessarily thought of buying, or find that they need to solve an unexpected problem.

   a. *Examples: emergency car-towing services.*

   b. Unsought goods are best sold through personal selling and the Yellow Pages.

lecture notes

bonus case 14-3

THE TOY STORY ISN'T OVER JUST YET

Specialty toys, like Disney-Pixar's Woody and Buzz, are a hot commodity among kids. Though the movie trilogy has finished, the company is finding new ways to keep these characters' toys in the hands of kids. (See the complete case, discussion questions, and suggested answers beginning on page 14.83 of this manual.)

PPT 14-20
Classifying Specialty Goods and Services

(See complete PowerPoint slide notes on page 14.48.)

PPT 14-21
Specialty Goods Aren't Just for Humans

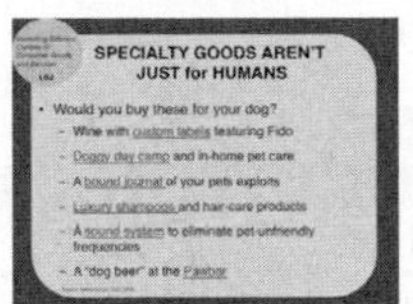

(See complete PowerPoint slide notes on page 14.48.)

PPT 14-22
Classifying Unsought Goods and Services

(See complete PowerPoint slide notes on page 14.49.)

PPT 14-23
Identifying Consumer Goods Classifications

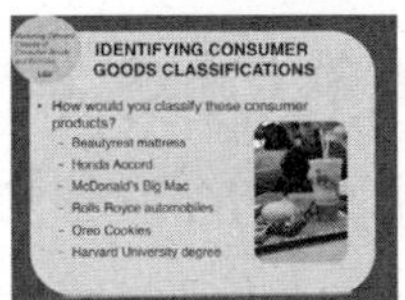

(See complete PowerPoint slide notes on page 14.49.)

5. The marketing task varies depending on the category of product.
6. The **INDIVIDUAL CONSUMER** determines whether or not a good or service falls into a particular class.

C. **MARKETING INDUSTRIAL GOODS AND SERVICES**

1. Many goods could be classified as consumer goods or industrial goods, based on their uses.
2. ***INDUSTRIAL GOODS*** are products used in the production of other products: sometimes called business goods or B2B goods.
3. The buyer's intended use of the product determines whether it is a consumer or an industrial product.
4. Industrial goods are more likely to be sold by salespeople or on the Internet.
5. **CATEGORIES:**
    a. **INSTALLATIONS** consist of major capital equipment such as *new factories and heavy equipment.*
    b. **CAPITAL ITEMS** are products that last a long time and cost a lot of money.
    c. **ACCESSORY EQUIPMENT** consists of capital items that are not quite as long lasting or expensive as installations, such as *computers and photocopy machines.*

PPT 14-24
Odd Product Ideas That Were Successful

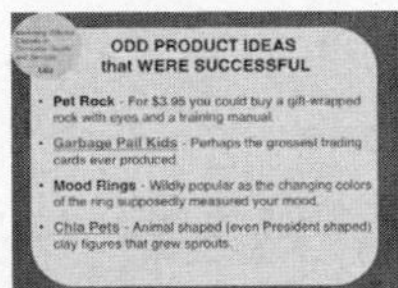

(See complete PowerPoint slide notes on page 14.49.)

PPT 14-25
Classifying Industrial Goods and Services

(See complete PowerPoint slide notes on page 14.50.)

TEXT FIGURE 14.2
Various Categories of Consumer and Industrial Goods and Services
(Text page 385)

This text figure shows some of the categories of both consumer and industrial goods.

progress assessment
(Text page 384)

PPT 14-26
Progress Assessment

(See complete PowerPoint slide notes on page 14.50.)

learning goal 3

Summarize the functions of packaging.

III. PACKAGING CHANGES THE PRODUCT

A. **PACKAGING** plays an important role in customers' evaluation of the value package.

1. It can **CHANGE AND IMPROVE** its basic product *(for example, the packaging of salt).*
2. *Other packaging improvements: squeezable ketchup, square paint cans, aromatic bottle caps.*
3. **PACKAGING MUST DO THE FOLLOWING:**
    a. **ATTRACT THE BUYER'S ATTENTION**
    b. **PROTECT THE GOODS INSIDE**, stand up under handling and storage, be tamperproof, deter theft, and be easy to open
    c. **BE EASY TO OPEN AND USE**
    d. **DESCRIBE THE CONTENTS** and give information about the contents
    e. **EXPLAIN THE BENEFITS** of the goods inside
    f. **PROVIDE INFORMATION** on warranties, warnings, and other consumer matters
    g. Give some **INDICATION OF PRICE, VALUE, AND USES**
4. Packaging can also help make a **PRODUCT MORE ATTRACTIVE TO RETAILERS** *(UPCs on packages help stores control inventory).*
5. Packaging changes the product by changing its **VISIBILITY, USEFULNESS,** or **ATTRACTIVENESS.**

PPT 14-27
Uses of Packaging

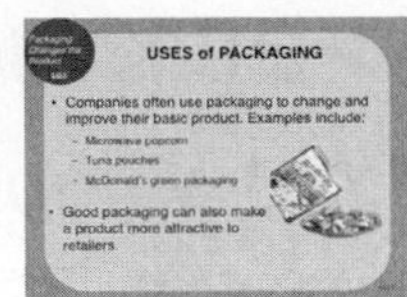

(See complete PowerPoint slide notes on page 14.51.)

lecture link 14-3
A CANVAS ON A KLEENEX BOX

Kleenex has turned the tissue box into a work of art and uses that in promotion. (See the complete lecture link on page 14.63 in this manual.)

PPT 14-28
Some Key Functions of Packaging

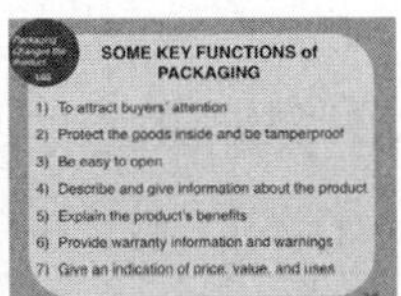

(See complete PowerPoint slide notes on page 14.51.)

lecture link 14-4
THE NEW BARCODES

After years of using a 12-digit UPC barcode, U.S. companies are now using the same 13-digit standard that has long been the worldwide standard. (See the complete lecture link on page 14.63 of this manual.)

lecture link 14-5
THE 100-CALORIE SNACK ATTACK

Food companies such as Kraft are introducing individual 100-calorie packages of popular snacks such as Cheetos and Oreos. (See complete lecture link on page 14.64 of this manual.)

B. **THE GROWING IMPORTANCE OF PACKAGING**

1. The package is more important for promotion now than in the past.
2. The **FAIR PACKAGING AND LABELING ACT** requires that packages contain quantity and value comparison.
3. Packaging can use a strategy called **BUNDLING** that combines goods and/or services for a single price.
4. ***BUNDLING*** is grouping two or more products together and pricing them as a unit.
   a. Marketers must not include so much that the price gets too high.
   b. The best strategy is to work with customers to develop value that meets their needs.

learning goal 4

Contrast brand, brand name, and trademark, and show the value of brand equity.

IV. BRANDING AND BRAND EQUITY

A. A ***BRAND*** is a name, symbol, or design (or combination thereof) that identifies the goods or services of one seller or group of sellers and distinguishes them from the goods and services of competitors.

1. **BRAND NAME** is that part of the brand consisting of a word, letter, or group of words or letters comprising a name that differentiates a seller's goods or services from those of competitors. *Examples: Red Bull, Sony, Del Monte, Levis, Google.*
2. A ***TRADEMARK*** is a brand that has been given exclusive legal protection for both the brand name

PPT 14-29
Bundling

(See complete PowerPoint slide notes on page 14.51.)

critical thinking exercise 14-1
CHOOSING A BRAND NAME

This exercise gives students a chance to create unique brand names for several consumer products. (See complete exercise on page 14.69 of this manual.)

lecture link 14-6
THE MOST VALUABLE BRANDS

Interbrand, a research company, annually ranks the most valuable brands in the world. The top global brands for 2010 are listed. (See the complete lecture link on page 14.64 of this manual.)

PPT 14-30
Understanding Branding

(See complete PowerPoint slide notes on page 14.52.)

and its design (*example: McDonald's golden arches).*

3. Most people **CHOOSE A BRAND-NAME PRODUCT** over a nonbranded one, even when they say there's no difference.
4. A brand name has benefits for both buyers and sellers.
    a. For the **BUYER**, a brand name ensures quality, reduces search time, and adds prestige.
    b. For the **SELLER**, brand names facilitate new-product introductions, help promotional efforts, add to repeat purchases, and differentiate products.

B. **BRAND CATEGORIES**

1. ***MANUFACTURERS' BRANDS*** are the brand names of manufacturers that distribute products nationally.
2. ***DEALER (PRIVATE-LABEL) BRANDS*** are products that do not carry the manufacturer's name, but carry a distributor or retailer's name instead *(examples: Kenmore and Diehard brands sold through Sears).*
3. Many manufacturers fear having their brand name become a **GENERIC NAME,** a name for a product category.
    a. *Names such as nylon, escalator, kerosene, and zipper became so popular that they lost their brand status and became generic.*
    b. Companies today are protecting brand names such as *Xerox and Rollerblade.*

lecture notes

REACHING BEYOND our borders
(Text page 388)

PPT 14-31
The Name Game

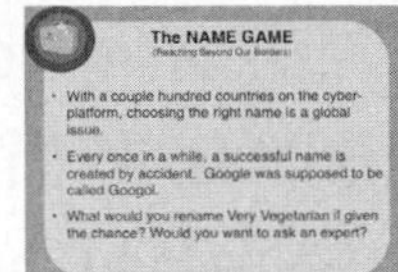

(See complete PowerPoint slide notes on page 14.52.)

PPT 14-32
What's in a Name?

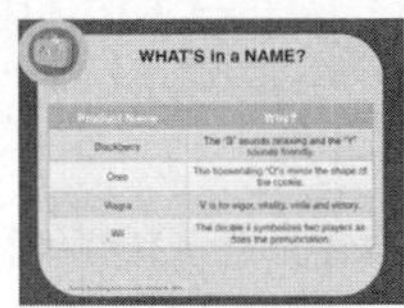

(See complete PowerPoint slide notes on page 14.52.)

lecture link 14-7
BABY PRODUCTS STAY STRONG AS PRICES RISE

Though new parents are often strapped for cash, they still buy brand-name baby products. (See the complete lecture link on page 14.65 in this manual.)

PPT 14-33
Key Brand Categories

(See complete PowerPoint slide notes on page 14.53.)

lecture link 14-8
BRAND MANAGEMENT ICONS

The Michelin man is 75 years old, but he's not the oldest brand mascot. (See the complete lecture link on page 14.66 in this manual.)

PPT 14-34
Key Brand Categories

(See complete PowerPoint slide notes on page 14.53.)

lecture link 14-9
THE MYSTIQUE OF COCA-COLA

The critical element in Coca-Cola's success is the aura of mystery around the product's formula. (See the complete lecture link on page 14.66 in this manual.)

4. ***GENERIC GOODS*** are nonbranded products that usually sell at a sizable discount compared to national or private-label brands.
    a. They have very basic packaging and are backed with little or no advertising.
    b. Because quality has improved, consumers today are buying more generic products.
5. ***KNOCKOFF BRANDS*** are illegal copies of national brand-name goods.

C. **GENERATING BRAND EQUITY AND LOYALTY**

1. ***BRAND EQUITY*** is the value of the brand name and associated symbols.
2. ***BRAND LOYALTY*** is the degree to which customers are satisfied, like the brand, and are committed to further purchases.
3. ***BRAND AWARENESS*** refers to how quickly or easily a given brand name comes to mind when a product category is mentioned.
4. **PERCEIVED QUALITY** is an important part of brand equity.
    a. A product that is perceived as better quality can be priced accordingly.
    b. Factors influencing the perception of quality include price, appearance, and reputation.
    c. Consumers often develop **BRAND PREFERENCE**—they prefer one brand over another.
    d. The product becomes a specialty good when customers reach **BRAND INSISTENCE.**
5. To hold off the challenge from competitors,

PPT 14-35
Establishing Brand Equity and Loyalty

(See complete PowerPoint slide notes on page 14.54.)

PPT 14-36
Most Valuable Brands

(See complete PowerPoint slide notes on page 14.54.)

PPT 14-37
Origins of Automobile Symbols

(See complete PowerPoint slide notes on page 14.54.)

critical thinking exercise 14-2
MOST VALUABLE GLOBAL BRANDS

Interbrand, a research company, annually ranks the most valuable brands in the world. This exercise asks students to research the current year's ranking. (See complete exercise on page 14.71 of this manual.)

PPT 14-38
Building Brand Awareness

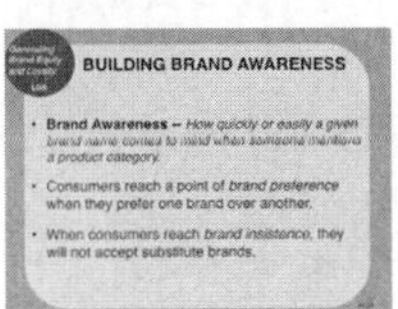

(See complete PowerPoint slide notes on page 14.54.)

brand-name manufacturers have to develop new products faster and promote their names better.

D. **CREATING BRAND ASSOCIATIONS**

1. The name, symbol, and slogan a company uses helps gain brand recognition for that company's products.
2. ***BRAND ASSOCIATION*** is the linking of a brand to other favorable images.
3. Many brands use celebrities or athletes to provide a positive association.
4. The person responsible for building brands is a **BRAND MANAGER** or **PRODUCT MANAGER.**

E. **BRAND MANAGEMENT**

1. A ***BRAND MANAGER*** is a manager who has direct responsibility for one brand or one product line; called a **PRODUCT MANAGER** in some firms.
2. The brand manager is responsible for all the elements of the marketing mix.
3. Brand managers in large consumer-product companies have greater control over new-product development and product promotion.

learning goal 5

Explain the steps in the new-product development process.

V. THE NEW-PRODUCT DEVELOPMENT PROCESS

A. Chances that a **NEW PRODUCT WILL FAIL** are high, as high as 80%.

1. A leading cause of new-product failure is not delivering what is promised.

PPT 14-39
Building Brand Associations

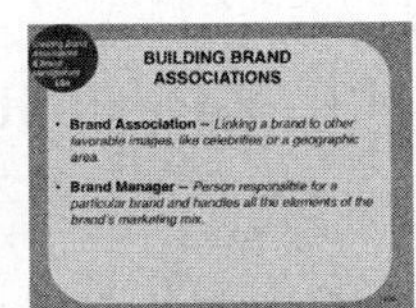

(See complete PowerPoint slide notes on page 14.55.)

progress assessment
(Text page 390)

PPT 14-40
Progress Assessment

PROGRESS ASSESSMENT

- What functions does packaging now perform?
- What's the difference between a brand name and a trademark?
- Explain the difference between a manufacturers' brand, a dealer brand, and a generic brand.
- What are the key elements of brand equity?

(See complete PowerPoint slide notes on page 14.55.)

2. Other **REASONS FOR FAILURE** include getting ready for market too late, poor positioning, not enough differences from competitors, and poor packaging.

B. **THE NEW-PRODUCT DEVELOPMENT PROCESS:**

1. **IDEA GENERATION**, based on consumer wants and needs
2. **PRODUCT SCREENING**
3. **PRODUCT ANALYSIS**
4. **DEVELOPMENT**, including building prototypes
5. **TESTING**
6. **COMMERCIALIZATION** (bringing the product to market)

C. **GENERATING NEW-PRODUCT IDEAS**

1. It now takes about seven ideas to generate one commercial product.
2. The number one **SOURCE OF IDEAS** for industrial products has been employees.
3. Research and development is a major source of new products.
4. Firms should also listen to their **SUPPLIERS** for new-product ideas.

D. **PRODUCT SCREENING**

1. ***PRODUCT SCREENING*** is a process designed to reduce the number of new-product ideas being worked on at any one time.
2. **CRITERIA NEEDED FOR SCREENING** include fit with present products, profit potential, and marketability.

PPT 14-41
The New-Product Development Process

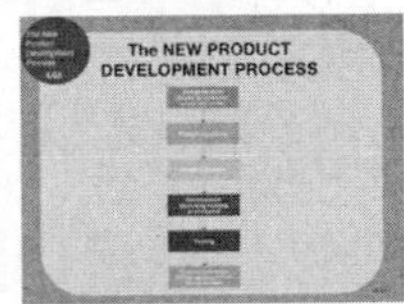

TEXT FIGURE 14.3
The New-Product Development Process
(Text page 391)

(See complete PowerPoint slide notes on page 14.56.)

lecture link 14-10
TOP 10 NEW PRODUCTS IN HISTORY

Research and development executives identify the top 10 new products of all time. (See the complete lecture link on page 14.45 of this manual.)

PPT 14-42
Bringing New Products to the Market

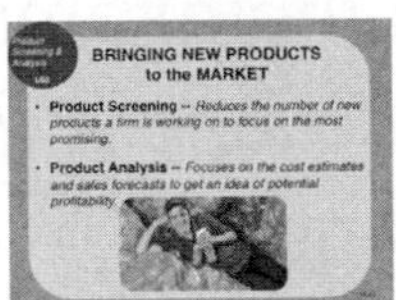

(See complete PowerPoint slide notes on page 14.56.)

E. **PRODUCT ANALYSIS** is done after screening.

1. ***PRODUCT ANALYSIS*** is making cost estimates and sales forecasts to get a feeling for profitability of new-product ideas.
2. Products that don't meet the established criteria are withdrawn from further consideration.

F. **PRODUCT DEVELOPMENT AND TESTING**

1. A **PRODUCT IDEA** can be developed into many different **PRODUCT CONCEPTS**, or alternative product offerings based on the same product idea.
2. The firm may develop a **PROTOTYPE.**
3. ***CONCEPT TESTING*** involves taking a product idea to consumers to test their reactions.

G. **COMMERCIALIZATION**

1. *The text uses the example of the long struggle for the inventor of zippers to gain consumer acceptance of the product.*
2. The marketing effort must include ***COMMERCIALIZATION,*** promoting the product to distributors and retailers to get wide distribution and developing strong advertising and sales campaigns to generate and maintain interest in the product among distributors and consumers.
3. Through promotion on the Internet, new products are getting more rapid exposure to global markets.

PPT 14-43
Bringing New Products to the Market

(See complete PowerPoint slide notes on page 14.56.)

SPOTLIGHT ON
small
business
(Text page 392)

PPT 14-44
Don't Come to Me; I'll Come to You

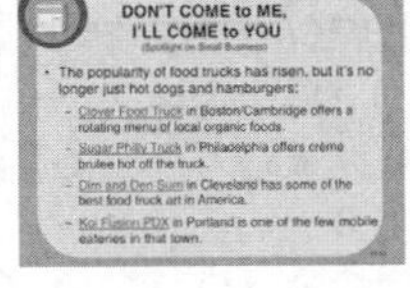

(See complete PowerPoint slide notes on page 14.57.)

learning goal 6

Describe the product life cycle.

VI. THE PRODUCT LIFE CYCLE

A. The ***PRODUCT LIFE CYCLE*** is a *theoretical* model of what happens to sales and profits for a product class over time; the four stages are introduction, growth, maturity, and decline.

1. Not all products follow the life cycle, and some brands may act differently.
2. Knowing what stage in the cycle a product is in helps marketing managers decide when strategic changes are needed.

B. **EXAMPLE OF THE PRODUCT LIFE CYCLE**. *The text uses the example of how instant coffee moved through the product life cycle.*

C. **USING THE PRODUCT LIFE CYCLE**

1. Different stages in the product life cycle call for different strategies.
2. Each stage calls for multiple marketing mix changes.
3. These concepts should be used only as **GUIDE-LINES**.
4. *Example: Every few years Arm and Hammer baking soda promotes new uses for the product to boost sales.*

learning goal 7

Identify the various pricing objectives and strategies.

VII. COMPETITIVE PRICING

A. **PRICE** is a critical ingredient in consumer

PPT 14-45
The Four Stages of a Product Life Cycle

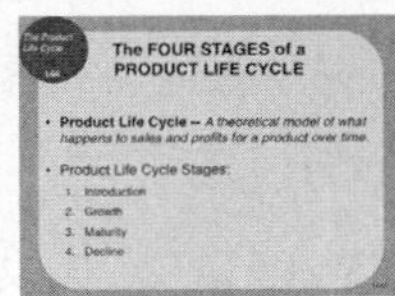

(See complete PowerPoint slide notes on page 14.57.)

PPT 14-46
Sales and Profits during the Product Life Cycle

TEXT FIGURE 14.4
Sales and Profits during the Product Life Cycle
(Text page 393)

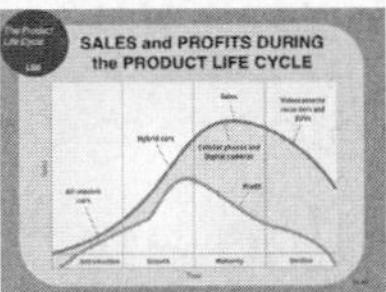

(See complete PowerPoint slide notes on page 14.57.)

lecture link 14-11
EXTENDING THE LIFE CYCLE ON A ROLLER COASTER

Amusement parks have found a way to extend the vacation season—Halloween events complete with haunted houses and scary costumes. (See the complete lecture link on page 14.67 of this manual.)

TEXT FIGURE 14.5
Sample Strategies Followed during the Product Life Cycle
(Text page 394)

This text figure shows that different stages in the product life cycle call for different marketing strategies.

PPT 14-47
Profits beyond the Grave

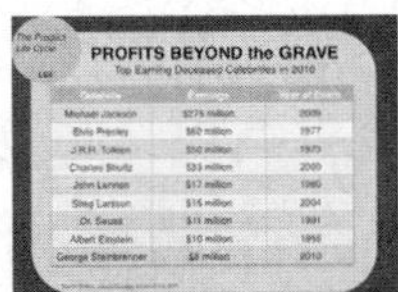

(See complete PowerPoint slide notes on page 14.58.)

lecture link 14-12
EXTENDING SWEETHEARTS

One of the oldest candy companies in the United States is introducing new lines of heart-shaped candies geared to Memorial Day and the movie *Twilight*. (See the complete lecture link on page 14.68 of this manual.)

TEXT FIGURE 14.6
How Sales, Profits, and Competition Vary over the Product Life Cycle
(Text page 395)

This text figure shows in table form what happens to sales volume, profits, and competition during the product life cycle evaluations of the product and a difficult one for marketers to control.

B. **PRICING OBJECTIVES**

1. The firm may have several objectives in mind when setting a pricing strategy.
2. These price objectives must be stated clearly before developing an overall pricing objective.
3. Popular **PRICING STRATEGIES** include:
    a. **ACHIEVING A TARGET RETURN ON INVESTMENT OR PROFIT.** Most first seek to maximize profit.
    b. **BUILDING TRAFFIC**. Low prices on certain products *(loss leaders)* can bring customers into your store.
    c. **ACHIEVING GREATER MARKET SHARE**. Price can be used to capture and hold market share.
    d. **CREATING AN IMAGE**. A high price may present an image of status.
    e. **FURTHERING SOCIAL OBJECTIVES.** A product may be priced low so more people can afford to buy it.
4. A company's **SHORT-TERM PRICING OBJECTIVES** may differ from its **LONG-TERM OBJECTIVES.**
5. Pricing objectives are influenced by other marketing decisions regarding product design, packaging, branding, distribution, and promotion.
6. A product's price and cost to produce aren't always related.

lecture notes

progress assessment
(Text page 390)

PPT 14-48
Progress Assessment

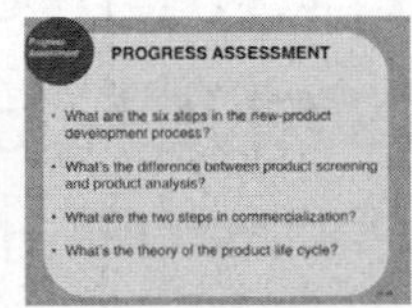

(See complete PowerPoint slide notes on page 14.58.)

PPT 14-49
Pricing Objectives

(See complete PowerPoint slide notes on page 14.59.)

PPT 14-50
Pricing Strategies

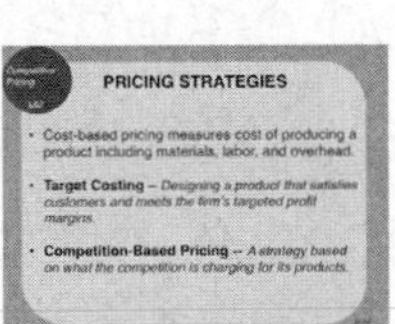

(See complete PowerPoint slide notes on page 14.59.)

C. **COST-BASED PRICING**

1. Producers often use **COST** as a primary basis for setting price.
2. In the long run, **THE MARKET**—not the producer—determines what the price will be.
3. Pricing should take into account product costs, but also expected costs of product updates and marketing.

D. **DEMAND-BASED PRICING**

1. ***TARGET COSTING*** is designing a product so that it satisfies customers and meets the profit margins desired by the firm.
2. Marketers estimate the selling price that people are willing to pay, then subtract the desired profit margin.

E. **COMPETITION-BASED PRICING**

1. ***COMPETITION-BASED PRICING*** is a pricing strategy based on what all the other competitors are doing; the price can be set at, above, or below competitors' prices.
2. ***PRICE LEADERSHIP*** is the procedure by which one or more dominant firms set the pricing practices that all competitors in an industry follow.

F. **BREAK-EVEN ANALYSIS**

1. ***BREAK-EVEN ANALYSIS*** is the process used to determine profitability at various levels of sales.
2. The **BREAK-EVEN POINT (BEP)** is the point where revenues from sales equal all costs.
3. BEP is calculated:

lecture link 14-13
RISING FOOD PRICES

The prices consumers have been used to during the recession are about to rise. Customers had better be ready! (See the complete lecture link on page 14.68 of this manual.)

critical thinking exercise 14-3
SILKY SKIN SOLUTION

This exercise asks students to develop a marketing program for Silky Skin Solution, a technologically advanced wrinkle cream. (See complete exercise on page 14.72 of this manual.)

PPT 14-51
Using Break-Even Analysis

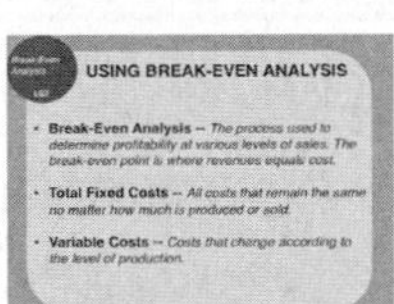

(See complete PowerPoint slide notes on page 14.59.)

$$\frac{\text{Total fixed costs (FC)}}{\text{Price of 1 unit (P)} - \text{Variable costs (VC) of 1 unit}}$$

4. ***TOTAL FIXED COSTS*** are all the expenses that remain the same no matter how many products are made or sold.
5. ***VARIABLE COSTS*** are costs that change according to the level of production.
6. You don't make a profit until you sell more than the break-even sales volume.

G. **OTHER PRICING STRATEGIES**

1. Pricing in the introductory stage is critical.
2. A ***SKIMMING PRICE STRATEGY*** is a strategy in which a new product is priced high to make optimum profit while there is little competition; however, it invites competitors.
3. A ***PENETRATION STRATEGY*** is one in which a product is priced low to attract more customers and discourage competitors; it allows a company to capture market share quickly.
4. **PRICING STRATEGIES USED BY RETAILERS**
   a. ***EVERYDAY LOW PRICING (EDLP)*** is setting prices lower than competitors and then not having any special sales *(example: Home Depot and Wal-Mart).*
   b. The ***HIGH–LOW PRICING STRATEGY*** is setting prices that are higher than EDLP stores, but have many special sales where the prices are lower than competitors.
   c. Consumers can use the Internet to find lower prices, making it harder to use this strategy.

critical thinking exercise 14-4
BREAK-EVEN ANALYSIS

This exercise guides the students through the analysis required to determine a restaurant's break-even point. (See complete exercise on page 14.74 of this manual.)

PPT 14-52
Pricing Alternatives

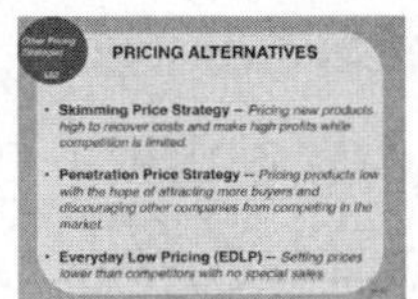

(See complete PowerPoint slide notes on page 14.60.)

PPT 14-53
Pricing Strategies of Retailers

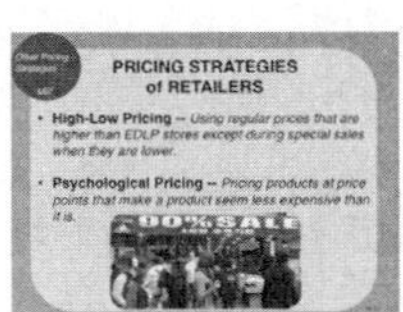

(See complete PowerPoint slide notes on page 14.60.)

d. Some retailers chose the products they carry based on price *(example: stores that sell only products priced at $1).*

e. ***PSYCHOLOGICAL PRICING*** is pricing goods and services at price points that make the product appear less expensive than it is *(example: gasoline priced at $2.99 instead of $3.00).*

H. **HOW MARKET FORCES AFFECT PRICING**

1. Marketers now face a new pricing problem: Customers can compare prices of many goods and services on the **INTERNET.**

2. Internet sellers sometimes use a **"DEMAND COLLECTION SYSTEM,"** in which buyers post the prices they are willing to pay and invite sellers to accept or decline the price.

3. Price competition is going to heat up as consumers have more access to price information from all around the world.

VIII. NONPRICE COMPETITION

A. Marketers often compete on product **ATTRIBUTES OTHER THAN PRICE**.

B. Because price differences are small in products such as candy bars and gas, marketers stress image and benefits.

C. Many smaller organizations promote the services that accompany basic products rather than price in order to compete with bigger firms.

IX. SUMMARY

critical thinking exercise 14-5
COMPARISON SHOPPING ONLINE

This Internet exercise directs students to www.BizRate.com, a website that lets consumers compare both product price and vendor reputation, to comparison shop for a digital camera. (See complete exercise on page 14.77 of this manual.)

progress assessment
(Text page 399)

PPT 14-54
Progress Assessment

(See complete PowerPoint slide notes on page 14.60.)

PowerPoint slide notes

PPT 14-1
Chapter Title

PPT 14-2
Learning Goals

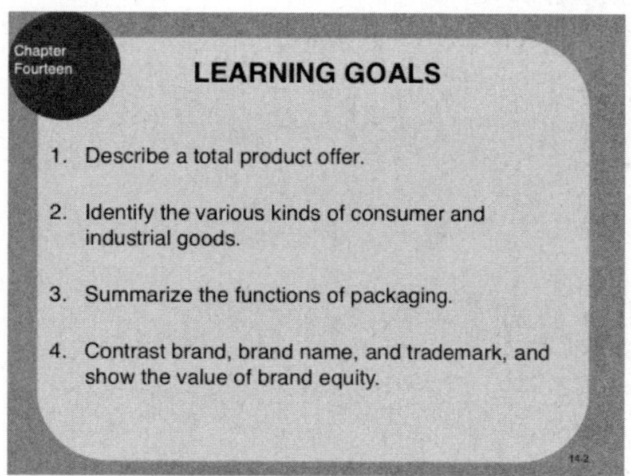

PPT 14-3
Learning Goals

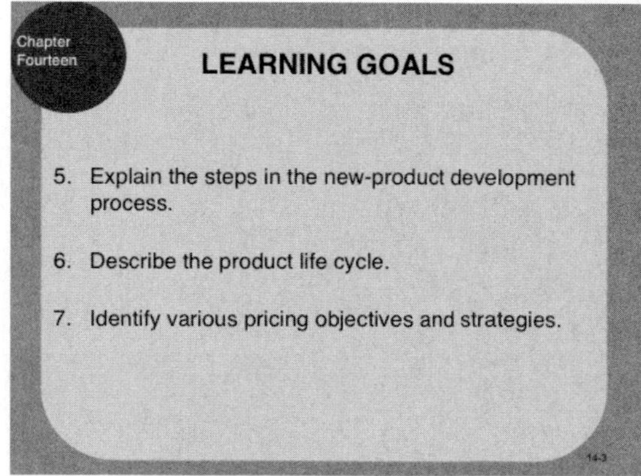

PPT 14-4
Mary Barra

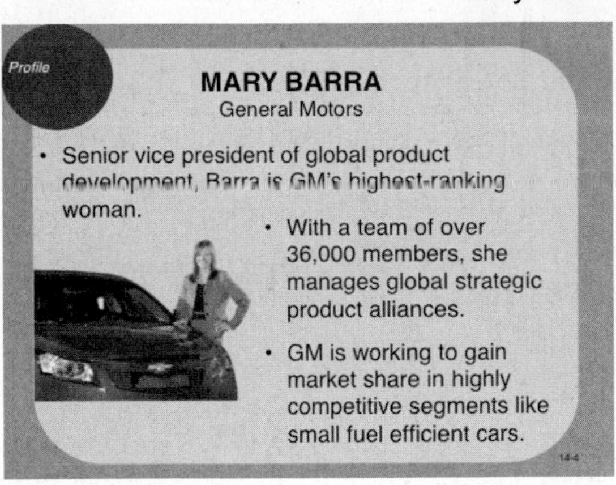

PPT 14-5
Name That Company

Company: Virgin Airlines

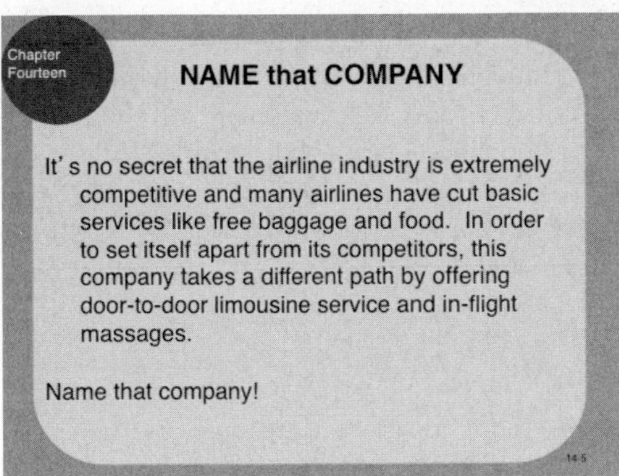

PPT 14-6
Developing Value

PPT 14-7
Products Consumers Won't Give Up

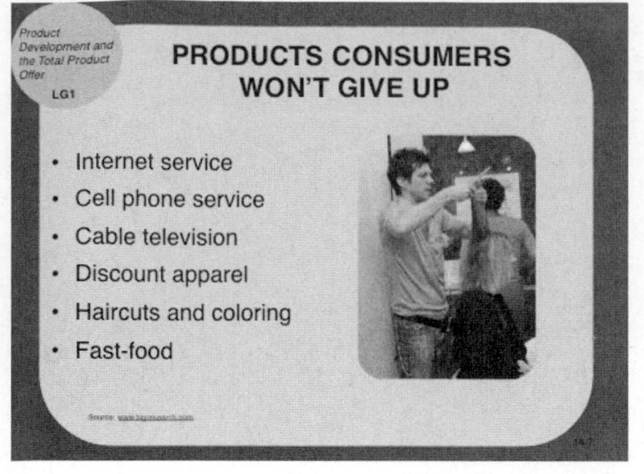

1. This slide profiles some of the goods and services people do not eliminate during a recession.
2. Ask the students, Why are the items listed on the slide considered "untouchables"?
3. To further the discussion ask the students, What items do you consider to be "untouchable" and why?

PPT 14-8
Products "Expendable" by Spending Cuts

1. This slide shows the flipside of the previous slide and lists items that people are most likely to eliminate.
2. Ask the students to get into groups and discuss: Why are these items "expendable," but the items on the previous slide are "untouchable"?

PPT 14-9
Distributed Product Development

PPT 14-10
Developing a Total Product

The total product offering includes tangible as well as intangible benefits.

PPT 14-11
Product Innovation during the Great Depression

1. The late 1920s and 1930s are associated with the Great Depression, but the period was also one of great product innovation.
2. The items on the slide were invented during the Great Depression.
3. Have students look at the items and ask, Why do you think these items were developed during a time when most Americans had very little discretionary income?
4. Have students work with a partner or small group to come up with specific reasons they think these products developed.

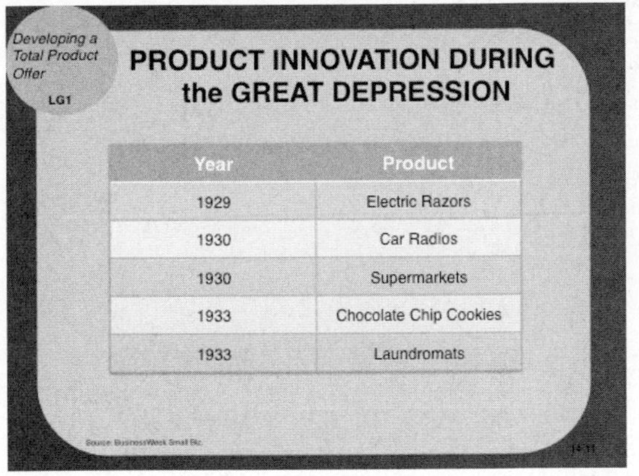

PPT 14-12
Anything You Can Do . . .

1. This slide shows that companies that innovated and create new products don't always remain the market leaders.
2. Point out that while Apple didn't introduce cell phones, video recorders, or game players, it has become the market leader by listening to consumers and improving these products to meet consumers' wants and needs.

PPT 14-13
Potential Components of a Total Product Offer

A product can be divided into the physical and the total product. Marketing managers must take the physical and add value to create the total product offer.

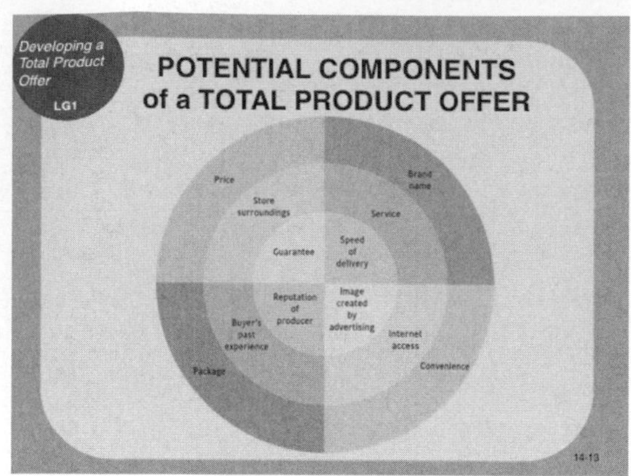

PPT 14-14
Quality and Sustainability

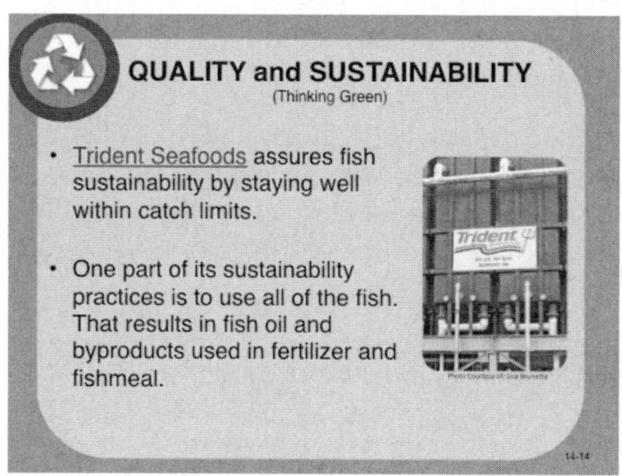

PPT 14-15
Understanding Product Lines

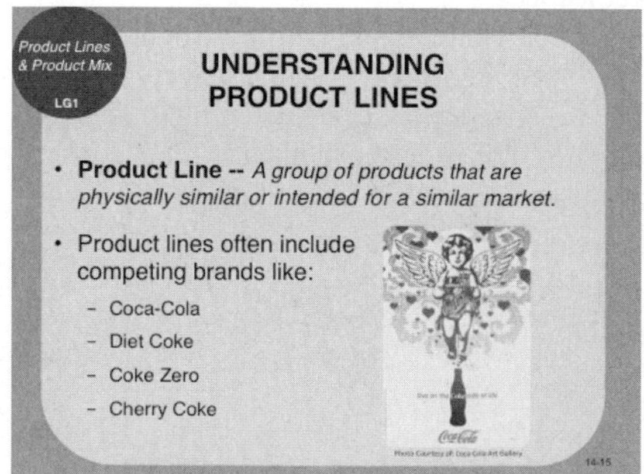

PPT 14-16
The Product Mix

To give students a visual of the products offered by Procter & Gamble, use its website at www.pg.com and click on the products tab.

PPT 14-17
Differentiating Products

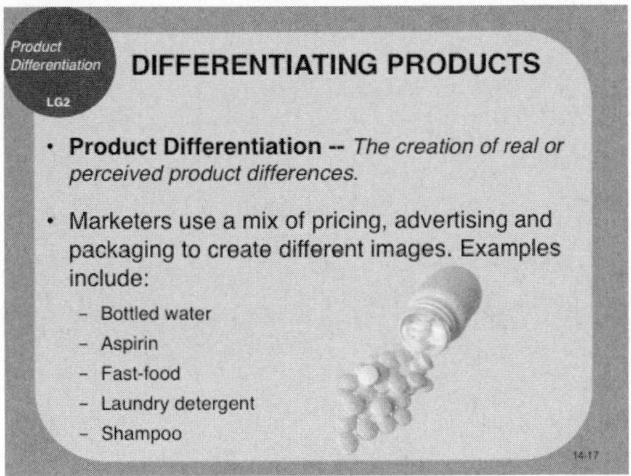

PPT 14-18
Classifying Consumer Goods and Services

Location, brand awareness, and image are important in marketing these goods and services.

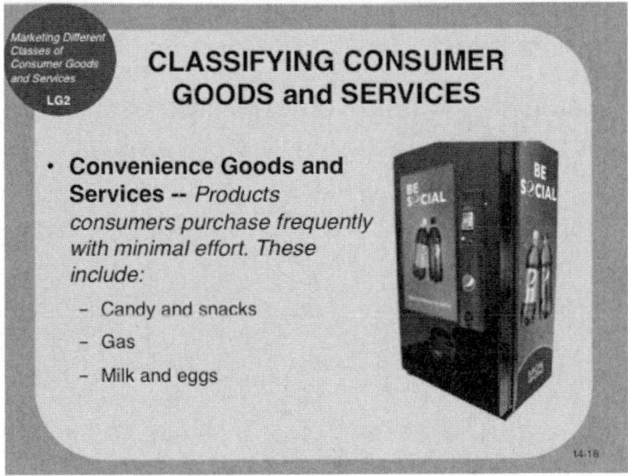

PPT 14-19
Classifying Shopping Goods and Services

Brand name, price, and quality differences are important in marketing these goods and services.

PPT 14-20
Classifying Specialty Goods and Services

PPT 14-21
Specialty Goods Aren't Just for Humans

1. People are doting on their pets more than ever. These links show just a few things you could buy for your best friend.
2. Ask the students, Would you ever purchase any of these for your pet? Do you have a pet product idea?

PPT 14-22
Classifying Unsought Goods and Services

Unsought goods and services often rely on personal selling or specialty advertising—like the Yellow Pages.

PPT 14-23
Identifying Consumer Goods Classifications

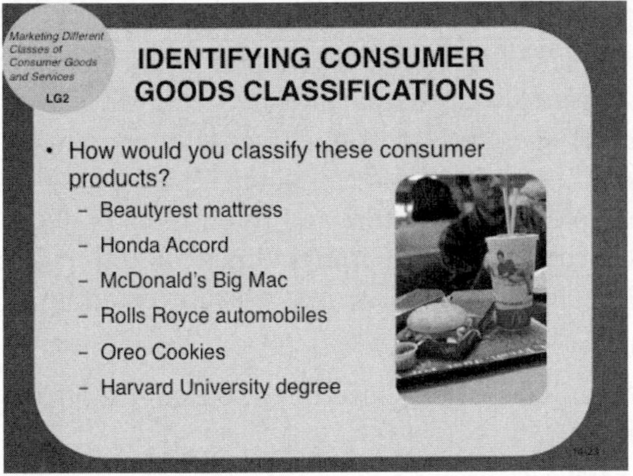

- Beautyrest mattress—shopping good
- Honda Accord—shopping good
- McDonald's Big Mac—convenience good
- Rolls-Royce automobiles—specialty good
- Oreo Cookies—convenience good
- Harvard University degree—specialty good

PPT 14-24
Odd Product Ideas That Were Successful

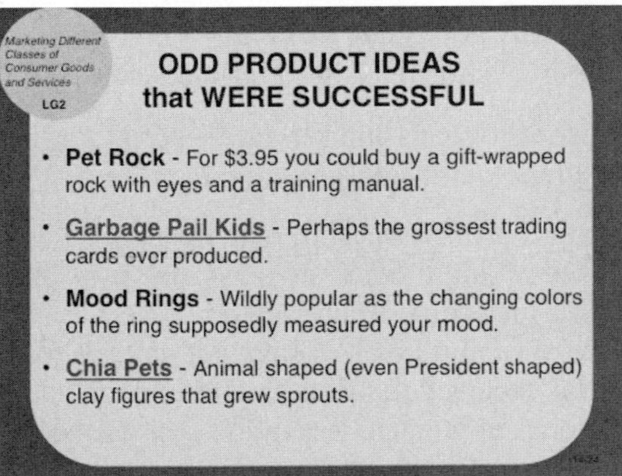

1. Not all successful products necessarily make sense. Take, for example, the products mentioned on this slide.
2. To start a discussion on odd product offerings ask the students, What are some other examples of odd products that were successful or unsuccessful?
3. For more examples of odd products that were not successful go to www.businessadministration.org/blog/15-ridiculous-products-that-actually-sell.

PPT 14-25
Classifying Industrial Goods and Services

PPT 14-26
Progress Assessment

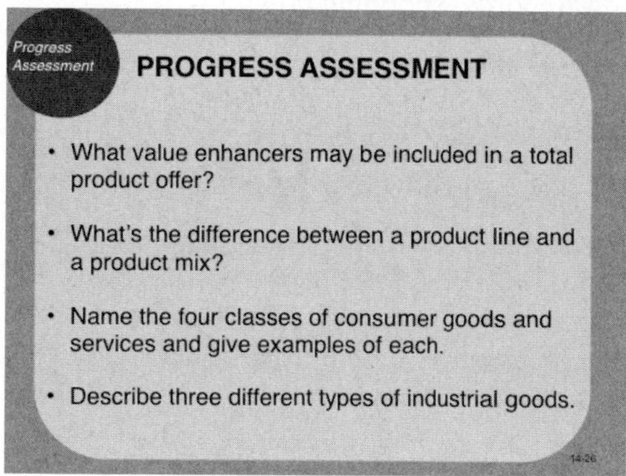

1. Some value enhancers that may be included in the total product offering include brand name, warranty, service, store surroundings, and speed of delivery.
2. *Product line* refers to the group of products that are physically similar or intended for a similar market. These products may face similar competition. For example, you can purchase a Diet Coke, Diet Coke with Splenda, and so on. The product mix is the total of the product lines offered by a particular company. The text uses the example of Procter & Gamble.
3. The four classes of consumer goods and services include:
    - Convenience goods and services—candy, gum and milk
    - Shopping goods and services—clothes, shoe, and appliances
    - Specialty goods and services—fur coats, imported chocolates, and business consultants
    - Unsought goods and services—burial service, insurance, and emergency drain cleaning
4. Installation goods consist of major capital equipment. Capital items are expensive products that last a long time. Accessory equipment consists of capital items that are not quite as long-lasting or expensive as installations and include computers, copy machines, and various tools.

PPT 14-27
Uses of Packaging

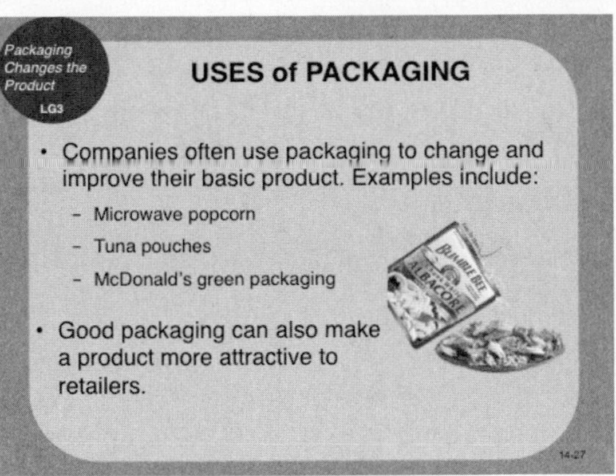

PPT 14-28
Some Key Functions of Packaging

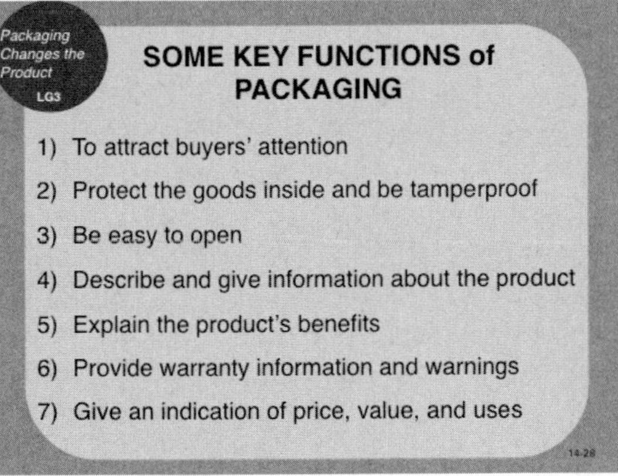

PPT 14-29
Bundling

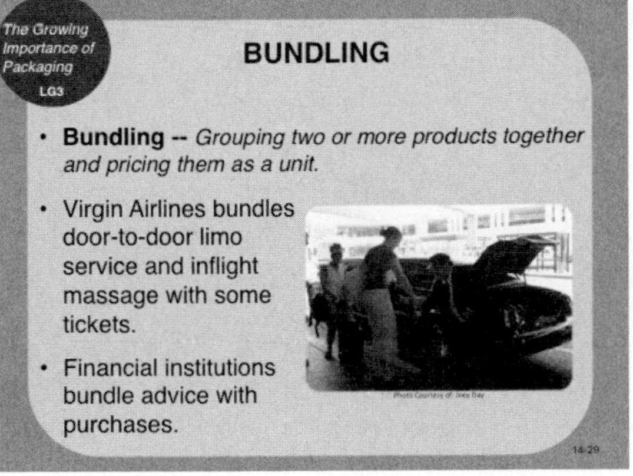

PPT 14-30
Understanding Branding

Recognized trademarks include the Nike Swoosh, the Pillsbury Doughboy, and Apple's Apple.

PPT 14-31
The Name Game

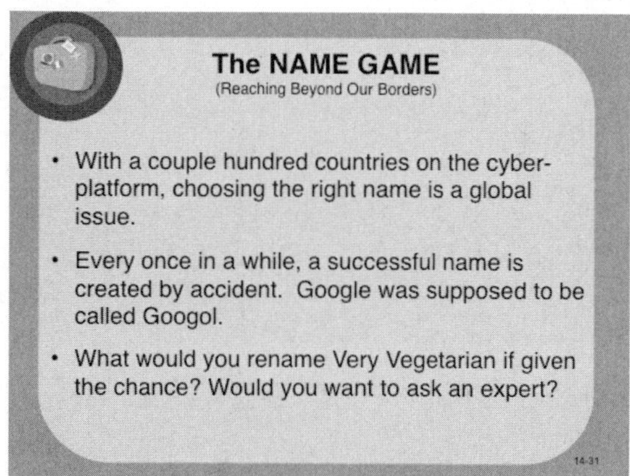

PPT 14-32
What's in a Name?

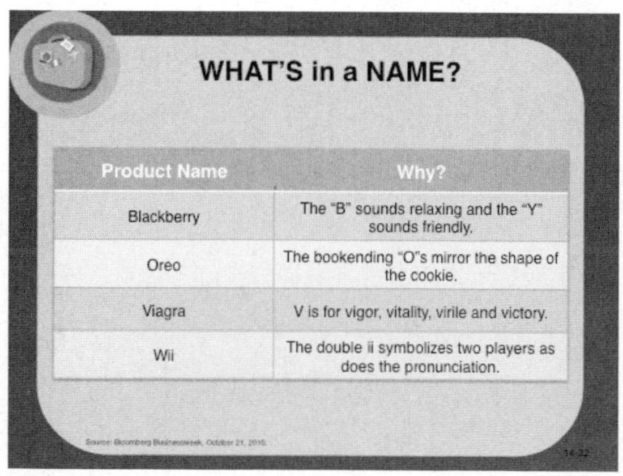

Product Name	Why?
Blackberry	The "B" sounds relaxing and the "Y" sounds friendly.
Oreo	The bookending "O"s mirror the shape of the cookie.
Viagra	V is for vigor, vitality, virile and victory.
Wii	The double ii symbolizes two players as does the pronunciation.

1. Product names are not decided on lightly.
2. Many companies seek professional advice regarding corporate identity.

PPT 14-33
Key Brand Categories

Manufacturers' brand examples include Ford, Microsoft, and Xerox. A dealer brand example is Kenmore, from Sears.

PPT 14-34
Key Brand Categories

PPT 14-35
Establishing Brand Equity and Loyalty

Generating Brand Equity and Loyalty
LG4

ESTABLISHING BRAND EQUITY and LOYALTY

- **Brand Equity –** *The value of the brand name and associated symbols.*
- **Brand Loyalty --** *The degree to which consumers are satisfied and are committed to further purchases.*

Coca-Cola Ziploc

14-35

Coca-Cola and Ziploc have strong brand equity.

PPT 14-36
Most Valuable Brands

Generating Brand Equity and Loyalty LG4

MOST VALUABLE BRANDS

Brand	Value
Apple	$57.4 billion
Microsoft	$56.6 billion
Coca-Cola	$55.4 billion
IBM	$43 billion
Google	$39.7 billion
McDonald's	$35.9 billion
GE	$33.7 billion
Marlboro	$29.1 billion
Intel	$28.6 billion
Nokia	$27.4 billion

Source: Forbes, August 30, 2010.

1. This slide lists the 10 most valuable brands according to *Forbes*.
2. As you can see, six of the most valuable brands are tech companies.

PPT 14-37
Origins of Automobile Symbols

1. This slide presents the origins of car symbols.
2. Ask the students, How important is the name and symbol of a product? What aspects should be considered in the naming process? (Most students should suggest that the name of your product is very important, because it represents your company, tells the customers what the product is, and should mean something.)
3. Given that there are so many models of cars in so many different countries, naming cars becomes a very complex process. Should only one name be used in all countries or different names for the same model in different countries?

PPT 14-38
Building Brand Awareness

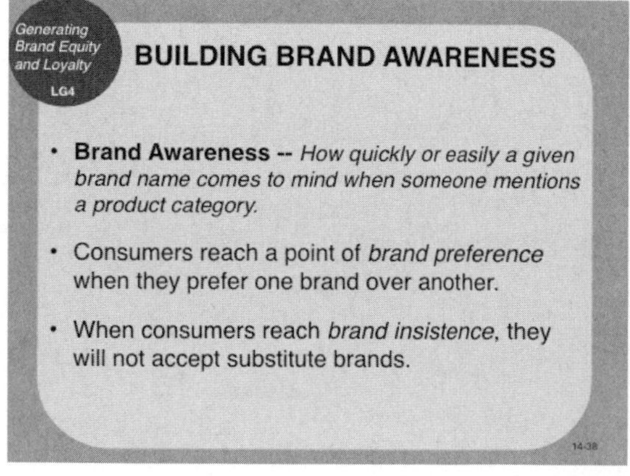

PPT 14-39
Building Brand Associations

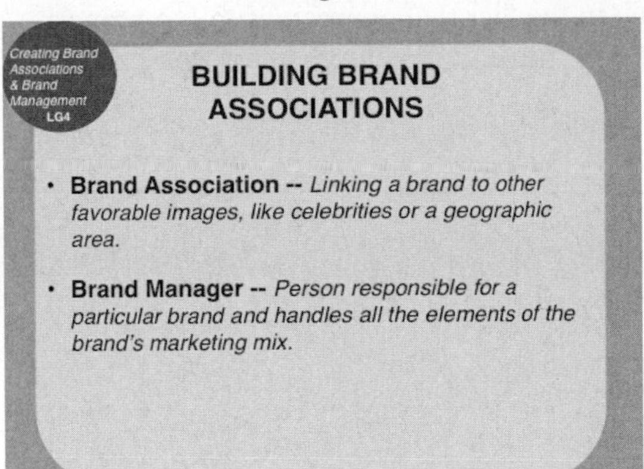

PPT 14-40
Progress Assessment

Progress Assessment

PROGRESS ASSESSMENT

- What functions does packaging now perform?
- What's the difference between a brand name and a trademark?
- Explain the difference between a manufacturers' brand, a dealer brand, and a generic brand.
- What are the key elements of brand equity?

14-40

1. The functions packaging performs include (1) attract the buyer's attention; (2) protect the goods inside; (3) be easy to open; (4) describe and give information; (5) explain the benefits of the good inside; (6) provide information on warranties, warnings and other consumer matters; and (7) give some indication of price, value, and uses.
2. Brand names consist of a word, letter, or group of words or letters that set it apart from other goods and services. A trademark is a brand that has exclusive legal protection for both its brand name and design.
3. A manufacturers' brand represents manufacturers that distribute their products nationally such as Xerox or Dell. A dealer brand is often referred to as a private label and will not carry the manufacturer's name, but rather carries the name of the distributor instead. For example, Kenmore is a dealer brand sold via Sears. A generic brand is the name of an entire product category.
4. Brand equity is the value of the brand name and associated symbols. The elements of brand equity include brand loyalty, brand awareness, and brand association.

PPT 14-41
The New-Product Development Process

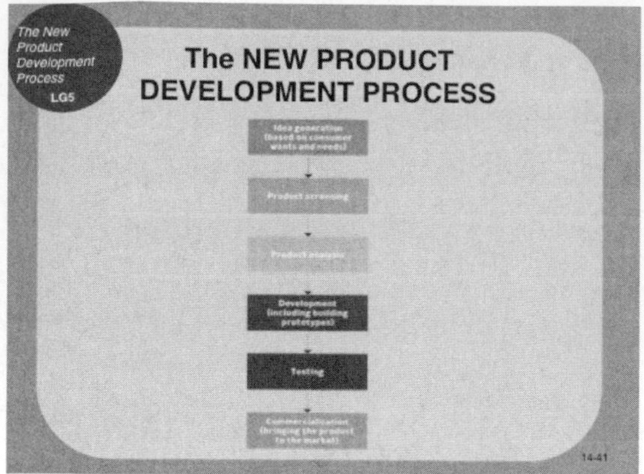

Green Ketchup and New Coke are two of the many thousands of products that failed. New-product failure is common due to the fact that companies fail to properly manage the new-product development process.

PPT 14-42
Bringing New Products to the Market

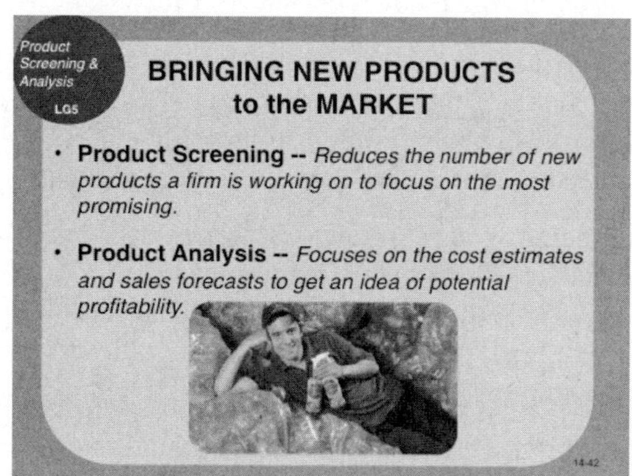

PPT 14-43
Bringing New Products to the Market

PPT 14-44
Don't Come to Me; I'll Come to You

PPT 14-45
The Four Stages of a Product Life Cycle

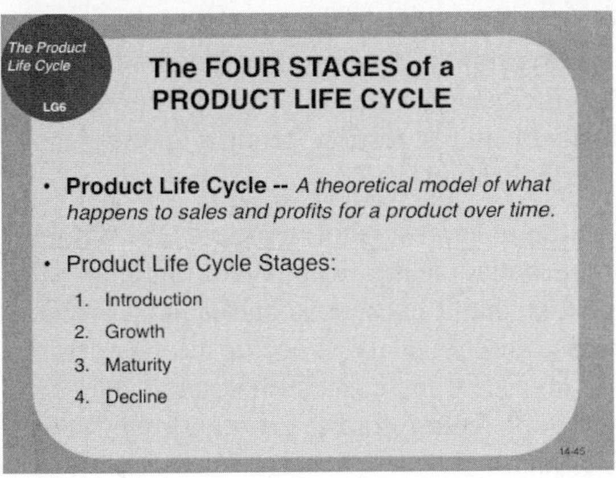

PPT 14-46
Sales and Profits during the
Product Life Cycle

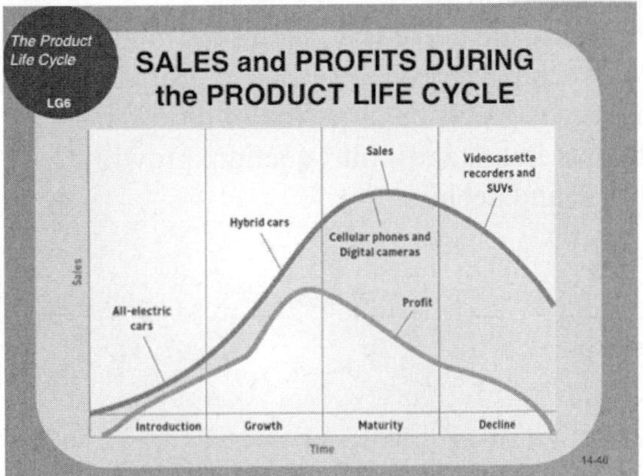

PPT 14-47
Profits beyond the Grave

The Product Life Cycle
LG6

PROFITS BEYOND the GRAVE
Top Earning Deceased Celebrities in 2010

Celebrity	Earnings	Year of Death
Michael Jackson	$275 million	2009
Elvis Presley	$60 million	1977
J.R.R. Tolkien	$50 million	1973
Charles Shultz	$33 million	2000
John Lennon	$17 million	1980
Stieg Larsson	$15 million	2004
Dr. Seuss	$11 million	1991
Albert Einstein	$10 million	1955
George Steinbrenner	$8 million	2010

Source: Forbes, www.forbes.com, accessed July 2011.

14-47

1. This slide explores the top earnings of deceased celebrities.
2. Ask the students, Albert Einstein is associated with all things "brainy." His earnings weren't generated by sales of any products he invented, so how did his estate bring in $10 million in 2010? *(Einstein's name appears on such things as Baby Einstein products, Chrysler's Ram brand truck ads, and a collection of A.J. Morgan "geek chic" glasses. A new brain video game for Nintendo DS retails for about $50. Go to www.forbes.com/2010/10/22/top-earning-dead-celebrities-business-entertainment-dead-celebs-10_land.html to read more about each of the deceased celebrities on the slide.)*
3. Ask the students, What do you think the future earnings of Michael Jackson will be?

PPT 14-48
Progress Assessment

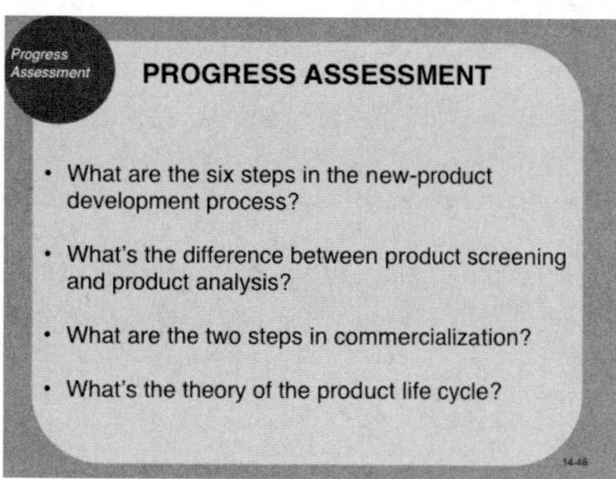

1. The six steps in the new-product development process include idea generation, development, product screenings, testing, product analysis, and commercialization.
2. During the product screening process the number of new-product ideas a firm is working on is reduced, so that it may focus on the most promising ideas. Product analysis occurs after screening and involves making cost estimates and sales forecasts to get a feeling for the profitability of new-product ideas.
3. The two steps in commercialization involve promoting the product to distributors and retailers, and developing strong advertising and sales campaigns.
4. The product life cycle is a theoretical model that explains what happens to sales and profit for a product over a particular period of time. This model has four stages: introduction, growth, maturity, and decline.

PPT 14-49
Pricing Objectives

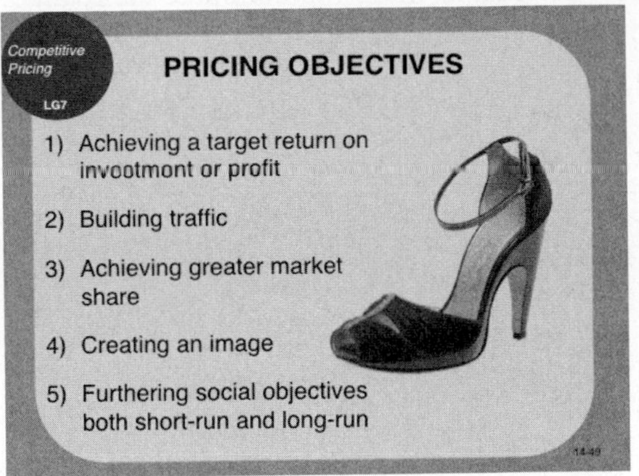

One strategy many students have experienced but might not fully understand is the loss leader strategy. This strategy is often used around the Thanksgiving holiday when grocery stores offer to sell customers turkeys for much less than their actual cost in an effort to attract consumers into the store. This leads to more traffic and sales of more products.

PPT 14-50
Pricing Strategies

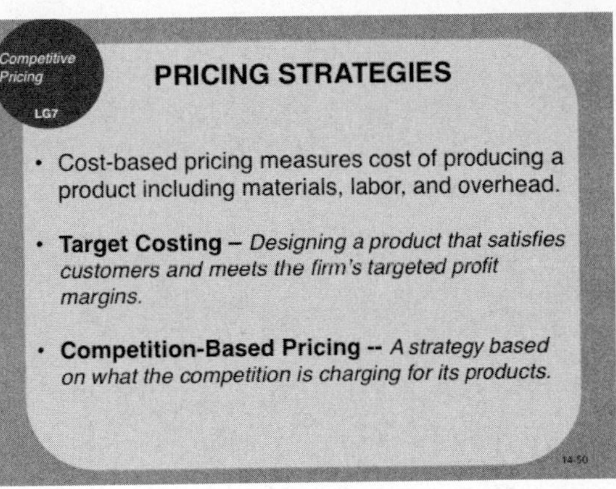

PPT 14-51
Using Break-Even Analysis

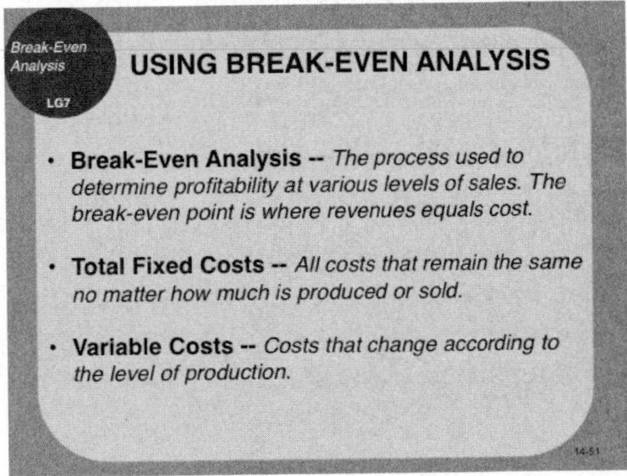

PPT 14-52
Pricing Alternatives

Other Pricing Strategies
LG7

PRICING ALTERNATIVES

- **Skimming Price Strategy** -- *Pricing new products high to recover costs and make high profits while competition is limited.*
- **Penetration Price Strategy** -- *Pricing products low with the hope of attracting more buyers and discouraging other companies from competing in the market.*
- **Everyday Low Pricing (EDLP)** -- *Setting prices lower than competitors with no special sales.*

14-52

When Apple introduced the iPhone, it used a skimming price strategy. Wal-Mart has effectively used everyday low pricing, or EDLP, to dominate the retail sector.

PPT 14-53
Pricing Strategies of Retailers

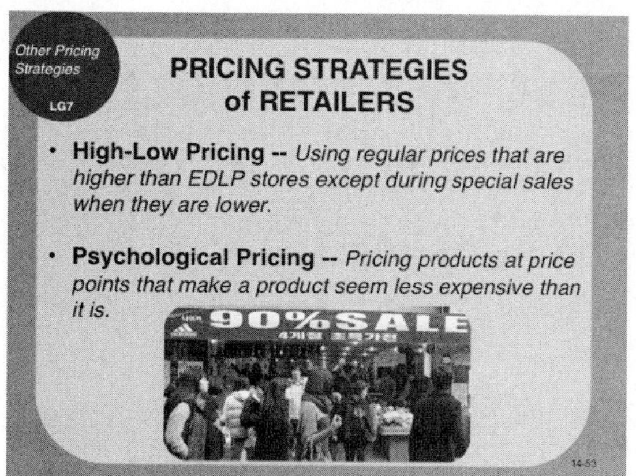

PPT 14-54
Progress Assessment

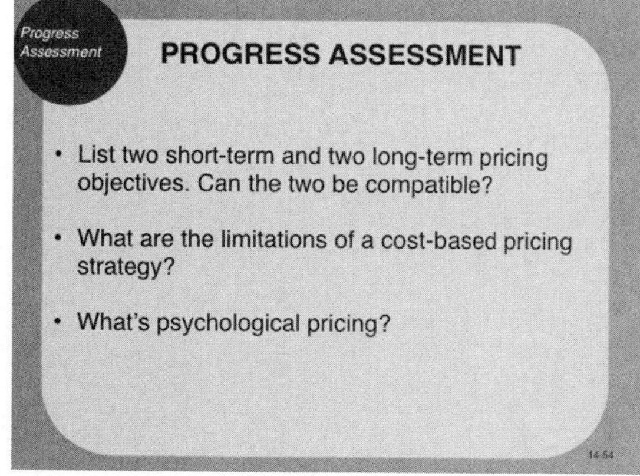

1. Short-term pricing objectives include loss leaders and are designed to build traffic as well as achieving greater market share. Long-term pricing objectives include achieving a target return on investment and creating a certain image. It is important that marketing managers set pricing objectives in context of other marketing decisions, since the pricing objectives may differ greatly.
2. The limit of a cost-based pricing system is that in the long run it is not the producer that establishes price but rather the marketplace. To effectively establish price, the producer must take into account competitor prices, marketing objectives, actual cost, and the expected cost of product updates.
3. Psychological pricing involves setting the price of goods or services at price points that make the product appear less expensive. For example, a TV may be priced at $999, since it sounds less expensive than $1,000.

lecture links

"People want economy and they will pay any price to get it."
Lee Iacocca

"It's impossible to make things foolproof because fools are so ingenious."
Murphy's Law #8

"The aim of marketing is to know and understand the customer so well the product or service fits him and sells itself."
Peter F. Drucker

"Good design can't fix broken business models."
Jeffrey Veen

lecture link 14-1

THERE IS NO SUCH THING AS A "BETTER" PRODUCT

It may seem outrageous at first to see think that "There is no such thing as a 'better' product," but hear me out. Often it is best to understand a concept by looking at some examples. So, here goes. Which school offers the better product: Harvard, Berkeley, or this school? To answer that question, one has to ask, "What do you mean by 'better product'?" If you mean, "Which product is perceived as better by the most people," that's one thing. If you mean, "Which is the most affordable?" that's something else.

Doesn't it make sense that the best product is the one that best meets your needs? If that is true, then there is no such thing as a better product for everyone. Some students may prefer Harvard, others Berkeley, and others this school. Each may have his or her own reasons. But, the bottom line is that there is no such thing as a better school for students. The school that best meets an individual student's needs is the best school for him or her. Those needs include the need for accessibility (Is the school close?), affordability, completability (Can I graduate?), and more.

One mistake people make is to think that *better* means *better quality*. That often happens in engineering schools, but it can happen anywhere. If you cannot afford a Cadillac and Cadillac improves the quality of the car, is the car now a better car for you? Of course not. You couldn't afford one without increased quality. It is not likely you could afford one that cost more because of increased quality. Do you always buy the best-quality goods? Why not? Because they are not the best product for you. Are you getting the idea that the notion of a good product includes a lot more than just quality? It may include a good price, a good style, a good location, and more—much more. What's important to you may not be important to me. What's a better product for you, therefore, may not be a better product for me.

So, how does one determine what a better product is? One way is to see what people actually buy. To them, that was the better product—for them. This is a very hard notion to comprehend, but a very important one for marketers to understand. There is no one standard for *better*. Not quality, not price, not any one thing. *You* may think something is better because it has a better reputation or it is stronger or faster or whatever, but that doesn't make it better from a marketing perspective. A better product, from a marketing perspective is the one that people will buy. When designing a product, therefore, it is important to ask people what they want. When you give people what they want, you then create a better product, even if it is inferior in quality.

For example, a BMW is not a better product than a Ford just because it costs more or has more prestige. In fact, a Ford may be a better product for a lot more people because it is more affordable. Can you see that a product you can't afford is not better, at least not for you? But it's clear that there are many products that are *perceived* as better. For example, a BMW is usually perceived as better than a Ford. On the other hand, I may not like the way BMW cars look or the price or the snob appeal. My perception may be that Ford is better because it is American-made, more stylish, and so on. No one's perception is wrong; it is just their perception.

In the marketplace, perceptions are critical. One way to make a product better, then, is to change perceptions. If I tell you that my product is "new and improved" and you believe me, I've now made my product better. Of course, if you don't believe me, the product is not better. Similarly, if I improve a product's quality dramatically, and you don't know I've done that, then the product is not really better yet. In marketing, therefore, perception is often more important than reality.

One way to make a product better in marketing is to improve your advertising or to improve your marketing communications in general. By creating a better impression of your product, you make it more attractive to consumers; that is, you make it better in their minds. If there is some benefit to your product that people don't know about and you tell them about it in your ad, you then make your product better even though you've made no changes in the physical good itself. On the other hand, if a competitor convinces people that your product is not better, then it's not better, even though by most objective measures it may be. To make a product better, it is a good idea to find out what people want and make sure your product has what they want. But your product won't truly be better to them until they hear about it; that is, until they change their perception. Think about it. What are some more examples?

lecture link 14-2

THE VENETIAN'S TROUBLES IN MACAO

The business world is no stranger to gamblers. Entrepreneurs take risks every day pursuing various ventures that could either make them a bundle or send them home with an empty wallet. For Sheldon Adelson, chair of the casino corporation Las Vegas Sands, opening a branch of his hit hotel and casino The Venetian in Asia seemed like a sure thing. The Vegas Venetian had been a massive success, accommodating scores of gamblers and tourists alike with world-class restaurants, shows, and a massive casino. After the tiny Chinese protectorate of Macao loosened its gaming laws in 2002, Adelson assumed the region was the perfect place for an Asian branch of the Venetian brand.

As it turned out, Adelson was right about the casino, but wrong about the brand. While the Venetian Macao, operated by Adelson's Sands China, has kept afloat thanks to legions of steady gamblers, the rest of the casino's attractions remain lifeless. Revenues for nongambling services at the Venetian Macao accounted for 14% of Sands China's overall sales, just half of what they are in Vegas. In the third quarter alone, room revenues dropped 11.9% while retail sales plummeted 23.8%. As a result, stock in Sands China has slipped significantly from its $2.5 billion initial public offering.

Adelson and other Western developers went into Macao hoping to turn it into an Asian Vegas, complete with ornately appointed hotels and big-name attractions like Cirque de Soleil. What Adelson and company failed to take into account was that Macao's clientele of Chinese gamblers don't tend to take their families with them on casino trips. Their customers focus on the tables and slot machines, not the theaters and restaurants. While the Vegas contingent has watched their stock plunge, other Hong Kong–based IPOs have soared. Adelson may be in too deep to solve his problems, though. Sands China has no choice but to proceed on the $2.4 billion hotels and a casino already under construction in Macao, in addition to completing a $5.4 billion casino in Singapore.[i]

lecture link 14-3

A CANVAS ON A KLEENEX BOX

Though the cardboard box that encases a stack of tissues adds little to the functionality of the product itself, Kleenex has turned the once unassuming tissue box into a work of art and, more importantly, into one of its central selling tools. Sales of Kleenex dropped 5% since 2007 as consumers turn to cheaper generic brands. In an effort to bring sales back up, Kleenex's parent Kimberly-Clark set its sights on a more style conscious market by offering over 100 different Kleenex box designs.

For decades following its 1924 founding, solid colors and a small array of floral designs were the only design choices available to Kleenex customers. Nowadays Kleenex designers work constantly in their own three-story building where each design is meticulously produced and reviewed. Kleenex plans new box designs two years in advance and constantly mines its customers for data to ensure that every box is tailored flawlessly for the market. Kimberly-Clark's research includes finding out which color boxes sell best on the East Coast compared to the West Coast, how age groups compare on box loyalty, and what percentage of households hide Kleenex boxes in cozies.

Kleenex has a few ground rules that every box design must follow: The box must appeal to women, fit home décor trends, and look "trustworthy." The color blue is a dependable mainstay. But even with so much research, it's difficult to predict that boxes will sell best. One unshakeable tradition, however, is Kleenex's feathery Flame Stitch design, which has been its best selling box for 25 years. Still can't find the box you love? Now you can design your own box at www.MyKleenexTissue.com. Of course, this luxury comes at a price you might sniff at.[ii]

lecture link 14-4

THE NEW BARCODES

The Universal Product Code (UPC) found on all consumer products has undergone a makeover in the U.S. market. While the rest of the world has long used a 13-digit barcode, U.S. companies resisted changing from their 12-digit system. In 2004, the Uniform Code Council, the nonprofit industry group that oversees barcode standards in North America, adopted the global standard in 2004, and gave retail stores just months to update their systems to accept the new codes. For retailers, the changeover did not affect cash-register scanning. These machines could already read the longer codes. Retailer conversion problems involved the back-end software systems that retailers use for inventory control and automated reordering.

The new codes have four groups of numbers, each encoded with a specific type of information. In a code such as 12 34567 89012 8, the individual digit groups reveal the following:

- The first group (**12**) is the country code. Numbers 00 through 13 indicate companies based in the United States or Canada. Codes 54 and 76 would signify Belgium and Switzerland, respectively.
- The five-digit group that follows (**34567**) is the company code, identifying each manufacturer in the world.
- The second group of five digits (**89012**) is the article code, assigned to individual products by manufacturers and registered in centralized databases through regional authorities like the Uniform Code Council.
- The final digit (**8**) is a check digit. The 12 previous digits are run through a mathematical algorithm that produces a single digit. This number is used to verify that a barcode is scanned correctly.

Contrary to popular opinion, the UPC code does not include the product's price. When the barcode is scanned, the digits in the UPC code are fed into the retailer's central computer where the code is matched with current price listing.[iii]

lecture link 14-5

THE 100-CALORIE SNACK ATTACK

For years, mothers have carefully portioned out handfuls of crackers or cookies and packed them in sandwich bags for their children. America's fast-food companies finally noticed the trend and began designing products for this market. Store shelves are now crowded with boxes of 100-calorie snack packs—Cheetos, graham crackers, Lorna Doones, even M&Ms.

Kraft kicked off the trend in 2004 with wafer-like versions of popular Nabisco treats, such as Oreos and Chips Ahoy cookies. In the first year, these products took in more than $100 million in revenue. That's a remarkable achievement that fewer than 1% of new packaged-good products have achieved. Since then, a growing number of food companies have scrambled to copy Kraft's success, from Coke's mini-cans to Hershey's 100-calorie candy bars.

Some products are reformulated for the small package, such as Cheetos Asteroids. Other products are simply existing products packaged in smaller portions.

Customers could emulate those mothers and bag their own snacks, but increasingly they are letting companies such as Kraft and Nabisco do it for them, even thought they pay significantly more per serving for the product. Also driving the trend is America's ongoing weight-loss quest. Customers appear to be willing to pay a little more to bolster their self-control.[iv]

lecture link 14-6

THE MOST VALUABLE BRANDS

Interbrand, a research consulting firm, annually calculates the world's most valuable global brands. For 2010, Coca-Cola was the top brand, for the ninth year in a row.[v]

2010 Rank	2009 Rank	Brand	Country of Origin	Sector	2010 Brand Value ($m)	Change in Value
1	1	Coca-Cola	United States	Beverages	70,452	2
2	2	IBM	United States	Business Services	64,727	7
3	3	Microsoft	United States	Computer Software	60,895	7

4	7	Google	United States	Internet Services	43,557	36
5	4	GE	United States	Diversified	42,808	-10
6	6	McDonald's	United States	Restaurants	33,578	4
7	9	Intel	United States	Electronics	32,015	4
8	5	Nokia	Finland	Electronics	29,495	-15
9	10	Disney	United States	Media	28,731	1
10	11	Hewlett-Packard	United States	Electronics	26,867	12
11	8	Toyota	Japan	Automotive	26,192	-16
12	12	Mercedes-Benz	Germany	Automotive	25,179	6
13	13	Gillette	United States	Personal Care	23,298	2
14	14	Cisco	United States	Business Services	23,219	5
15	15	BMW	Germany	Automotive	22,322	3
16	16	Louis Vuitton	France	Luxury	21,860	4
17	20	Apple	United States	Electronics	21,143	37
18	17	Marlboro	United States	Tobacco	19,961	5
19	19	Samsung	South Korea	Electronics	19,491	11
20	18	Honda	Japan	Automotive	18,506	4

lecture link 14-7

BABY PRODUCTS STAY STRONG AS PRICES RISE

Thanks to rising commodities costs, the product discounts that people enjoyed during the recession are on the decline. With prices on brand-name items spiking across the board, consumers once again are flocking to generic equivalents to lessen the impact on their wallets. But at least one retail sector is enjoying stable sales at the premium level. Sales of name-brand baby items from diapers to clothing are staying steady as parents cut corners on their own personal products, but pay the higher prices for kids' merchandise.

Market analysts found that shoppers are less likely to buy cheaper brands of baby products than many other items. A recent study found that just 10% of consumers switched to a cheaper diaper brand because "it's not worth paying more in this category." Conversely, nearly a third surveyed said they had switched brands of liquid soap and bottled water. With that info in hand, Kimberly-Clark and Procter & Gamble, makers of Huggies and Pampers, respectively, are increasing prices of diapers and wipes by as much as 7%. Similarly, though sales in men's, women's and teen fashion have been anemic for years, retailers have been able to hold the line for the most part when it comes to children's clothing.

Part of the reason why prices are rising now is because companies can't find any more places to cut corners. Trimming overhead became a top priority for many businesses during the recession, especially for retailers. Now that they're out of ideas about how to cut costs any leaner, companies say they have no choice but to raise prices. Nevertheless, many businesses could face consumer backlash as they switch to private labels and generic products. Necessities like toilet paper and diapers are in a different league, however, since it's harder to reduce consumption of those items. With a larger market share at their command, brands like Huggies, Pampers, and even Charmin have more power to increase prices than others. Still, Kimberly-Clark at least remains wary about driving prices too high. The company plans to reduce sticker shock by reducing the volume of the packages rather than raising the price immediately.[vi]

lecture link 14-8

BRAND MANAGEMENT ICONS

Most Americans recognize the Michelin man—the symbol of what is now the world's leading tire company. Today he is pictured as a friendly younger cousin to the cuddly Pillsbury Doughboy, but he was far from cuddly in his earliest incarnations.

The Michelin man made his first appearance in an 1898 ad. He was pictured as a frightening, mummy-like gladiator. Back then he was also known as the "road drunkard." To this day his official name is Bibendum, Latin for "drinking to be done." In the first posters featuring him, he was depicted hoisting a champagne goblet filled with nails and broken glass. The message was "Michelin tires drink up obstacles."

Some people wonder why, if he is to represent tires, his rings are white, not black. Simple answer: Tires weren't black until 1912, when makers first began adding carbon black as a preservative. Until then they were a light gray-white.

Through the years, his image has been softened. Like Mickey Mouse, Bibendum's head has grown larger relative to his body, his eyes bigger relative to his head, and his limbs pudgier. In 1929 he ditched his signature cigar during an outbreak of tuberculosis.

The Michelin man is not the oldest corporate mascot. The Quaker Oats Pilgrim goes back to 1877, and Aunt Jemima to at least 1893. Other brand icons with long heritages: the Morton Salt Umbrella Girl (1911), Mr. Peanut (1916), Betty Crocker (1921), the Jolly Green Giant (1925), and Reddy Kilowatt (1926).vii

lecture link 14-9

THE MYSTIQUE OF COCA-COLA

One of the masters in product differentiation is Coca-Cola. The brand is worth $65 billion worldwide. A critical element in this success is the aura of mystery around the product's formula.

The 120-year-old formula for Coca-Cola is stored in a vault in the bowels of a SunTrust Bank in Atlanta. That is one certainty. Everything else surrounding it—the need for a vote by Coke's board of directors to open the vault, for example—may be urban legend.

Myth or not, at least three people recently risked jail time to breech the company's air of mystery. The three, including a former administrative assistant at Coke's Atlanta headquarters, pleaded guilty in a plot to sell Coca-Cola trade secrets to Pepsi for $1.5 million. The plot fizzled when Pepsi alerted Coca-Cola, which then contacted the FBI.

The incident sparked fresh questions about whether the formula is an actual trade secret or mystical marketing.

History suggests it's a mixture of both. In 1886 John Pemberton, a pharmacist, started Coca-Cola with a recipe he created in his lab. Pemberton sold the concoction a few years later to Asa Candle, a businessman, who helped transform the soft drink into a success. This in turn made competitors and consumers curious about what exactly went into the drink. Some swore that the main ingredient was cocaine, a claim that the company denies. By 1919, when the Candlers sold Coca-Cola to a group of investors, the secrecy surrounding the formula had become a marketing tool. The new owners made the formula a pop culture legend when they placed the recipe in the Atlanta vault.

Experts say it is not impossible to decipher the formula and effectively clone Coca-Cola—but not 100%. Besides, copying it is pointless, say others, because it's not the secret, it's the branding that has made Coke such a success.[viii]

lecture link 14-10

TOP 10 NEW PRODUCTS IN HISTORY

Three hundred and fifty research and development executives were polled by *New Product Development* newsletter on the top 10 new products of all time. Their choices, in order, were:

1. The wheel
2. The bow and arrow
3. Telegraph
4. Electric light
5. Plow
6. Steam engine
7. Vaccine
8. Telephone
9. Paper
10. Flush toilet

lecture link 14-11

EXTENDING THE LIFE CYCLE ON A ROLLER COASTER

America's love affair with the roller coaster has lasted over a century. In the final decades of the past century, newer and scarier coasters were constructed to satisfy increasing sophisticated riders. Theme-park owners scrambled trying to find creative ways to keep customers coming through the turnstiles.

Now many parks are finding a new lure—the haunted amusement park. Each October, Knott's Berry Farms sponsors a month-long Halloween celebration. A cast of 1,000 actors dressed in monster costumes take over the amusement park, growling at unsuspecting bystanders. According to one actor, "People scream, they flinch, they run, they faint because they get so scared." The customers love it.

The haunted amusement park phenomenon, which started in the 1970s, has become a surefire way for parks to keep riders happy and to extend peak travel season beyond the summer months.

Knott's Berry Farm is not the only amusement park to use the scary approach. Disney World's Magic Kingdom devoted a record 15 nights to Halloween in the 2005 Halloween season. All Six Flags parks in the United States celebrate Halloween with haunted houses. Magic Mountain in Valencia, California, includes a roller coaster that rides backward.

A few of the parks prevent kids from entering during the haunted days. Most parks stress that the events are rated PG-13 and try to discourage parents from bringing children. But a few parks actually cater to children and their families. Mickey's Not-So-Scary Halloween Party at Disney World offers a parade, fireworks, story telling, and pictures with characters in Halloween costumes.[ix]

lecture link 14-12

EXTENDING SWEETHEARTS

Every Valentine's Day millions of them appear on desks, tables, and lunch counters—the heart-shaped candies inscribed with messages like "I Love You" and "Kiss Me." The Sweethearts candies are manufactured and sold by the New England Confectionery Company (NECCO). Necco is one of the country's oldest candy companies, founded in 1847. When it began production, there were only 29 states. When it began making its signature Sweetheart Conversation Hearts in 1866, the Civil War had just ended.

Today Necco is planning an expansion in its product line. It recently unveiled a new line of Sweethearts connected to *Twilight*, the young-adult vampire-romance book series. They were released to coincide with the DVD launch of the movie by the same name and include sayings such as "Bite me" and "Bedazzle." Around Memorial Day, Necco also introduced "Red, White and You" series aimed at veterans returning from Iraq with messages like "Proud" and "Love the USA."

The changes began in 2003 when the company moved out of a 1926 red brick factory next to a water tower with painted images of Necco Wafers. The new 820,000-square-foot factory in Revere, Massachusetts, is 60% bigger and will better accommodate planned expansion.

Necco, the nation's oldest multiline candy business, needs to expand its brand now in the United States so that it can expand globally later. CEO Richard Krause is aiming for 30% growth within two years for Necco. Says Krause, "There are some iconic brands here that are just marvelous. We thought it was an excellent opportunity to take this company to the next level."[x]

lecture link 14-13

RISING FOOD PRICES

Throughout the recession, value reigned supreme in the retail sector. Customers continue to cut/download coupons at the highest rate in years as stores entice them with sales and price reductions. But the deals in grocery stores are about to fade as worldwide increases in food prices lead to higher prices to consumers. In recent months prices of supermarket staples like milk, beef, coffee, and sugar have risen sharply, leading retailers and producers to warn that consumers too will have to shoulder the burden of soaring costs.

In the overall economy, inflation has been growing slowly. The consumer price index for all items except food and energy rose just 0.8% over the last year, the lowest 12-month increase since 1961. Food prices, on the other hand, have been going through the roof due to increase demand for meat in China and India, leading to higher prices for grain as well as chicken and steak. As a result, the food index rose by 1.4% last year. The Department of Agriculture predicts that food prices could inflate by as much as 3% next year.

Food producers Kraft, Sara Lee, and General Mills have reported that prices on certain products will increase soon. In response, grocery chains like Kroger and Safeway say they'll also be forced to increase product prices to cover their growing supplier costs. As for restaurants, they have a tighter rope to walk since many money-conscious diners can choose to cook at home rather than endure the higher cost of going out. At the casual-dining chain BJ's restaurants, the company will raise its prices by 2.5% in 2011, but only after each location's table settings and décor are revamped. The idea is that customers should enjoy a finer dining experience if they must pay steeper prices for the same dishes. Meanwhile, Domino's is attempting to covertly increase prices by offering to upgrade its $5.99 two-topping medium pie into a "premium pizza" with more toppings for $2.00 more.[xi]

critical thinking exercises

Name: ______________________________

Date: ______________________________

critical thinking exercise 14-1

CHOOSING A BRAND NAME

Suggest an appropriate brand name for each of the following consumer products:

1. A cable TV network targeted at new parents with features on babies and toddlers

2. A chocolate-flavored vitamin drink

3. A sporty car targeted at middle-aged women

4. A glow-in-the-dark light switch

5. A breakthrough prescription drug to treat childhood diabetes

6. A restaurant serving Japanese and Chinese food

7. An easy-to-use handheld e-mail device targeted at technology-phobic senior citizens

8. An inexpensive line of cosmetics featuring vibrant colors

9. A magazine targeted on single career women

10. A high-end all-natural cat food

11. An exclusive line of children's sports shoes

critical thinking exercise 14-1 (continued)

12. A banana-flavored breakfast cereal

13. A mobile dental clinic

14. A digital camera/GPS (global positioning satellite) combination preloaded with maps of North America

Name: ____________________

Date: ____________________

critical thinking exercise 14-2

MOST VALUABLE GLOBAL BRANDS

As stated earlier, Interbrand, a research consulting firm, annually calculates the world's most valuable global brands. For 2010, Coca-Cola was the top brand, for the ninth year in a row.

Go to the Interbrand website (www.interbrand.com)[xii] and search for the current year's ranking. (Sometimes the Web address for a location changes. You might need to search to find the exact location mentioned.) Complete the table below.[xiii]

RANK	BRAND	VALUE ($ MILLIONS)	COUNTRY OF ORIGIN	SECTOR
1				
2				
3				
4				
5				
6				
7				
8				
9				
10				

Name: ____________________

Date: ____________________

critical thinking exercise 14-3

SILKY SKIN SOLUTION

Your company has just made the scientific breakthrough of the century. It has invented a wrinkle cream that really works. One application results in smooth, wrinkle-free skin without costly and painful plastic surgery. There are other products that claim they eliminate wrinkles, but they only conceal them for an hour or two. Your cream works so well it needs to be used only once a month to keep skin silky. The cream is relatively inexpensive to produce with a total production cost of 20 cents per ounce. The cream could, therefore, be priced at either a competitive level or below it. The firm is not sure which policy is the best to follow.

When your Silky Skin Solution is promoted, your firm wants to have as many tubes as possible on the retailers' shelves. Thus, the firm plans to offer its wholesalers a much larger discount than is normal.

If the product is handled correctly, the return on investment should be between 40 and 70% after taxes. It would be the most profitable product in your firm.

Assume that you are the product manager for Silky Skin Solution. Don't forget to justify your answers.

1. What pricing policy will you follow?

2. What marketing approach will you use?

3. How will you treat your wholesalers?

notes on critical thinking exercise 14-3

1. *What pricing policy will you follow?*

   To recover the research and development costs, the price of the product should be set fairly high. The product would be protected from competition by the patent for a few years. You could lower the price when competition became stiff.

2. *What marketing approach will you use?*

   You could probably use testimonials from users and from doctors in your advertising. You could try to get the widest distribution possible in all drugstores and supermarkets. Sampling would be a good way to prove to consumers that the product worked. Word of mouth would then make the product very successful in the market with little need for more promotion.

3. *How will you treat your wholesalers?*

   You should treat wholesalers well because they are your tool for getting wide distribution. You could give them incentives and bonuses to get the product out quickly.

Name: ____________________

Date: ____________________

critical thinking exercise 14-4

BREAK-EVEN ANALYSIS

You just inherited a million dollars from your grandfather. You always had a talent for cooking and have long dreamed of opening an expensive gourmet restaurant. You are happy living near your college's campus and would like to open a four-star restaurant across the street from school.

Of course, the restaurant would have certain fixed costs; for example, management salaries, utilities, interest, license fees, and property taxes. The only variable costs would be the food, beverages, and preparation costs. The fixed costs are estimated at $440,000 per year while the average variable cost per meal is estimated at $15. These meals would be sold for an average of $27 each.

1. Perform a break-even analysis of your proposed business.

2. How many units will you have to sell each year to break even?

3. How many units will you have to sell each evening (use a 365-day year) to break even?

4. Considering your community, does it seem likely that there is a large enough market for gourmet food for the restaurant to operate at or beyond the break-even point?

5. How much profit will the restaurant earn on sales of 40,000 meals?

notes on critical thinking exercise 14-4

1. *Perform a break-even analysis of your proposed business.*

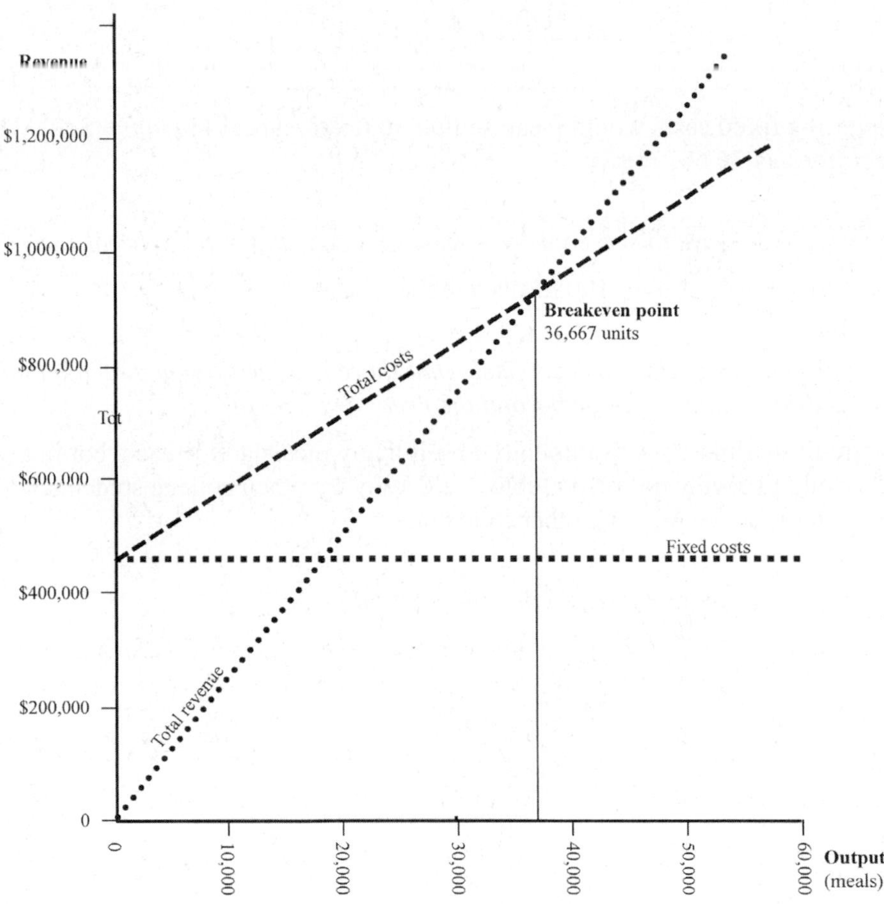

The restaurant will need to sell 36,667 meals to break even.

2. *How many units will you have to sell each year to break even?*

The break-even point can be calculated using a formula or using a break-even chart. The break-even chart shows the point at which the total cost curve intersects with total revenue.

	0	10,000	20,000	30,000	40,000	50,000
Total Revenue ($27)	$0	$270,000	$540,000	$810,000	$1,080,000	$1,350,000
Fixed Costs	$440,000	$440,000	$440,000	$440,000	$440,000	$440,000
Variable Costs ($15)	$0	$150,000	$300,000	$450,000	$600,000	$750,000
Total Costs	$440,000	$590,000	$740,000	$890,000	$1,040,000	$1,190,000
Profit (Loss)	($440,000)	($320,000)	($200,000)	($80,000)	$40,000	$160,000

Using the formula, you can plug in the data and calculate the break-even volume: total fixed costs of $440,000, variable costs of $15, and a sale price of $27. Subtracting $15 from $27 shows that you would make $12 per sale.

$$\frac{\text{Total fixed costs (FC)}}{\text{Price of 1 unit} - \text{Variable costs of 1 unit}}$$

$$\frac{\$440{,}000}{\$27 - \$15}$$

To cover the fixed costs would mean selling 36,667 meals ($440,000 ÷ $12). The break-even point, therefore, is 36,667 meals.

3. *How many units will you have to sell each evening (use a 365-day year) to break even?*

   You would have to sell a little over 100 meals a night.

4. *Considering your community, does it seem likely that there is a large enough market for gourmet food for the restaurant to operate at or beyond the break-even point?*

   It would be difficult in almost any community to sell many meals at $27 each, but in a college community, it would probably not be possible at all. Why try when college students would respond much better to a deli or some other food outlet?

5. *How much profit will the restaurant earn on sales of 40,000 meals?*

   You would make about $40,000 selling 40,000 meals a year. That is a very small profit for a restaurant.

Name: ______________________________

Date: ______________________________

critical thinking exercise 14-5

COMPARISON SHOPPING ONLINE

It is possible to compare prices for products at many Internet sites. But how do you know that the lowest-price product will be delivered on time and as expected? One way is to go to a website that compares both prices and retailer reputation.

One such site is www.BizRate.com. BizRate collects feedback from customers immediately after they buy. Customers rate which stores are good, why they are good, and how their service varies.

Go to the BizRate.com website at www.BizRate.com.[xiv] Search for price information for digital cameras. (Sometimes the Web address for a location changes. You might need to search to find the exact location mentioned.)

1. Which features of the product are important in comparing the cameras?

2. How important would the brand name be in your product selection?

3. Choose one camera model and compare prices for various vendors. Is there a relationship between price and customer satisfaction?

4. In which classification of product would you put digital cameras?

5. Would you use a website such as BizRate.com to buy a digital camera? A DVD player? DVDs?

bonus cases

bonus case 14-1

PANERA EXPANDS PAY-WHAT-YOU-CAN EXPERIMENT

When it comes to corporate philanthropy, many companies don't go much further than cutting a check. While it is certainly generous to give money to a good cause, donating to charities and food banks simply wasn't enough for Ronald Shaich, chair of the bakery-café chain Panera Bread. He wanted to lend assistance to those in need in a way that was integrated within the day-to-day operations of one of his stores.

In the end he decided to use one of his locations in Clayton, Missouri, for a radical experiment: let the customers decide how much they want to pay for food. The idea is that those who have money to spend would pay full price, or even more if they so chose, while cash-strapped customers would pay whatever they could afford. The net revenue that is left over after the company covers its overhead costs would be given to charity. In essence, Shaich's nonprofit plan is a large-scale version of a community kitchen, where people who need a discount or even free food can get it if they need it. The only difference is that Panera is a successful restaurant operation with more than 1,400 locations across the country, not exactly your normal nonprofit.

Shaich says the honor system experiment started out shaky, with one teenager walking out with $40 worth of food after putting just few dollars on his credit card. But after one month in operation, most of the customers abide by the goals of the program. About 60 to 70% of customers pay full price, while 15% leave a little more and a further 15% either pay less or nothing at all. Within its first month the non-profit Panera grossed $100,000, but Shaich won't reveal the margin between total costs and revenue. Still, the company must be happy enough with the results since it plans to open two more nonprofit locations within the next few months. Like the affluent but accessible Clayton location, the next two nonprofit Paneras will be located in upscale neighborhoods that can be easily reached by poorer customers, but still retain a wealthier core population that can pay full price.[xv]

discussion questions for bonus case 14-1

1. What seems to be the strength of Panera's nonprofit locations plan?

2. Do you suspect competitors will follow Panera's lead?

notes on discussion questions for bonus case 14-1

1. *What seems to be the strength of Panera's nonprofit locations plan?*

   Most would have to agree that the concept is certainly unique. Also, it lifts the burden of those who cannot afford to pay full price for a Panera meal to paying what they can manage. Other customers have total control over what they wish to contribute to the charity Panera's profits will support

2. *Do you suspect competitors will follow Panera's lead?*

   It's too early to tell yet. Panera experimented with only one store, and while the results were positive, it's not yet certain whether the concept will work for the company in the long run. However, if the results pan out for Panera, look for copycat programs from competitors to surface.

bonus case 14-2

THE VALUE OF A PRODUCT OFFER

The heart of a successful marketing program is a product offer that people want and need. But what do we mean when we say "product offer"? Is a service part of a product offer? Yes. Is an idea part of a product offer? Sure, people try to market (and sell) ideas. A product offer, then, is not necessarily something tangible nor is it always visible. Let's see if we can clarify what the term *product offer* means to a marketer.

First of all, notice that the same physical good (for example, a car) is worth different amounts to different people. How can that be? Clearly, a product offer's value is not determined by the good (e.g., car) itself but by the perceptions of the consumer; otherwise all physical goods would have the same value to different consumers. So the consumer determines a product offer's value.

Also, notice that product offers have value that goes beyond tangible features. For example, a car may have status value. A painting may have additional value simply because it is rare. A product offer's value, therefore, is determined by the consumers' tastes and desire to be different as well as the physical characteristics.

From a marketing standpoint, therefore, a product offer includes an intangible sense of value that the consumer perceives when evaluating the product offer. In simpler terms, a product offer is what the consumer thinks it is. If a consumer thinks a product offer is valuable, it is valuable to him or her. And if a consumer thinks a product offer has no value, it has no value until the consumer is convinced it does. The consumer, not the producer, determines a product offer's value.

There is no such thing as a "better" product offer in marketing. There are only product offers that consumers think are better. Many marketers make the mistake of making a better-quality product with the hope that consumers will buy the better quality. But a product has no quality until consumers perceive it. Since consumers can't see quality, they are not moved to buy by better quality unless it can be shown. Ford, Chrysler, and other American automobile producers are saying that "Quality is Job 1" and other such slogans, but until consumers perceive that quality, it does not exist (from a marketing perspective). Many consumers still believe that the Japanese make better-quality cars, whether or not that is true in reality.

To make a product offer better, make consumers think it is better. It does no good to improve a product unless consumers can be convinced that the improvement is there. This sounds confusing, but it becomes clear when we look at an example:

Which is a better product, a BMW Z4 Roadster or a Ford Focus? Be careful and think before you answer. (Take a poll of the class by having them raise their hands. Almost everyone will say that BMW is a better product.) If BMW is a better product, why do more people buy Ford Focuses? Someone must think that Ford Focuses are better products. (No," your students will say. "They know that BMW is better; they simply cannot afford one.")

Another point, then, is that cost is obviously an important part of what a consumer looks at when evaluating a product. We could say that a consumer looks at benefits of a product and then subtracts cost to get value. When evaluating a BMW versus a Focus, therefore, a consumer's evaluation process might look like this:

BENEFITS OF A BMW		**BENEFITS OF A FOCUS**	
Comfort		Price	
Status		Mileage	
Quality			
Durability			
Reliability			
Value of a BMW	$35,000	Value of a Focus	$18,000
Cost of a BMW	–$50,000	Cost of a Focus	–$16,000
Net value	**–$15,000**	Net value	**$2,000**

In this case, the Focus would be the better product because it had more value to the consumer. That is why more consumers buy Focuses than BMWs. "But wait a minute," you say. "A BMW is still a better car." Yes, but the car is not the product. The product is the car as seen through the eyes of the consumer who is evaluating not just the car and its quality, but price as well.

The answer to the question "Which is the better product, a BMW or a Ford Focus?" is that *it all depends*. To some people, a BMW is a better product because they put more value on comfort, status, and so forth. To others, the Ford Focus is a better product because they put more value on price and mileage. Neither is a better product inherently, although we largely would agree that the BMW is a better car.

discussion questions for bonus case 14-2

1. What is the product of a community college? (Be careful; the product is not what the school offers, but what the school offers as seen through the eyes of students.)

2. Which is the better product, what you get at a community college, or what you get at Harvard?

3. How can you make a product better?

4. Is a better-quality product perceived as a better product by consumers?

notes on discussion questions for bonus case 14-2

1. *What is the product of a community college? (Be careful; the product is not what the school offers, but what the school offers as seen through the eyes of students.)*

   The product is what students, faculty, parents, and community people think it is. It is convenience, quality teaching, or whatever people think it is. It is not just what the school hopes it is in the mind of consumers.

2. *Which is the better product, what you get at a community college, or what you get at Harvard?*

   "It all depends." Community colleges have many benefits and lower cost. Harvard has many different benefits and a much higher cost. The value of both institutions depends on the needs and wants of the student. Neither has an inherently better product, even though Harvard is known as a better school. One has to ask, "Better for what?" It certainly is not better for a student who cannot compete with other Harvard students or who does not have the money. That is why so many older students are going to community college; they see more value there.

3. *How can you make a product better?*

   By making people think it's better. If consumers think that a product is better, it is better from a marketing perspective. A school can appear better by promoting its quality students and faculty, by telling the public more about its offerings, and by generally providing more information that makes people see more value.

4. *Is a better-quality product perceived as a better product by consumers?*

   Not usually, because it usually comes with a higher cost as well. Most people seem to prefer moderate quality at moderate prices. This is true in cars, clothes, and most other goods and services. Consumers often know which goods have better quality, but that is not usually their number one concern. The best product to consumers is one that has enough quality at a good price; that is, the product with the most value.

bonus case 14-3

THE TOY STORY ISN'T OVER JUST YET

More than a decade ago, Disney's computer animation arm Pixar introduced the world to Woody and Buzz Lightyear, the stars of its Toy Story franchise. After three movies and billions of dollars in box office sales, the probability of a reunion of the animated pair in another feature-length film appears highly unlikely. Pixar operates independently of the rest of the Disney creative machine and is famously devoted to the artistic integrity of its inventions.

Still, the Toy Story properties, especially Woody and Buzz, remain a hot commodity for Disney after the release of *Toy Story 3*. The company estimates toys and other products from the last film will generate $7.3 billion in retail sales, making it the fourth most profitable merchandise franchise of 2010. With sales exceeding even Mattel's Barbie line, Disney isn't ready to keep its golden cowboy and space ranger off the big screen for good just yet.

In lieu of another feature film, Disney plans to keep the Toy Story brand fresh in consumers' minds through a series of short films produced by Pixar's satellite studio in Vancouver, British Columbia. The first Toy Story "toon" can be seen at the beginning of *Cars 2*, the company's second-largest blockbuster franchise. Preceding showings of its films with a short is well-worn territory for Pixar. Along with wholly original creations, the company has also produced a slew of quick cartoons featuring characters from *Cars* and *Monster's Inc*. In the case of the former, new videos and short clips have been prevalent online and on Disney's television networks since 2007. Disney officials credit the consistent appearance of *Cars* characters in new adventures as a key contributor to the franchise's 11% rise in merchandise sales for 2010. Toy Story is an even more lucrative enterprise, leading many to speculate that the 2011 summer short film will not be the last time the public sees Woody and Buzz in action.[xvi]

discussion questions for bonus case 14-3

1. With no new Toy Story feature movies planned, can Woody and Buzz remain hot?

2. What's the marketing advantage of animated characters like Woody and Buzz?

notes on discussion questions for bonus case 14-3

1. *With no new Toy Story feature movies planned, can Woody and Buzz remain hot?*

   There's no doubt that they can. Disney classic movies and characters are always being made available to new audiences of children who watch them for the first time. Look for Woody and Buzz to be on toy shelves for many years to come.

2. *What's the marketing advantage of animated characters like Woody and Buzz?*

   Unlike the rest of us, Woody and Buzz never get old. Consider that Mickey Mouse was created in 1928. By our calculations that puts him at 83 years old. Although Disney often updates the appearance or wardrobe of a character, the essence of that character doesn't change.

endnotes

[i] *Source.* Frederik Balfour, "Shelly Adelson's Misstep in Macao," *Bloomberg Businessweek*, December 14, 2009.

[ii] *Source:* Anne Kadet, "The Sniffler's Choice," *SmartMoney*, April 2009.

[iii] *Source.* Kevin Kelleher, "Barcodes Get One Better," *Business 2.0*, October 2004.

[iv] *Source:* Jennifer Barrett, "The 100-Calorie Snack Attack," *Newsweek*, August 14, 2006.

[v] *Source: Interbrand,* www.interbrand.com, accessed August 17, 2011.

[vi] *Source:* Ellen Byron and Paul Ziobro, "Whoa Baby, Prices Are Jumping for Diapers, Other Family Basics," *The Wall Street Journal*, April 26, 2011.

[vii] *Source:* Roger Parloff, "Michelin Man: The Inside Story," *Fortune*, September 19, 2005.

[viii] *Source:* Jessica Ramirez, "Coca-Cola's Holy Grail," *Newsweek*, November 6, 2006.

[ix] *Source:* Ramin Setoodeh, "Mummy, Let's Ride Again," *Newsweek*, October 17 2005.

[x] *Source:* Russell Contreras, "A Change of Heart," *The (Baton Rouge) Advocate*/Associated Press, February 8, 2009.

[xi] *Source:* Julie Jargon and Ilan Brat, "Food Sellers Grit Teeth, Raise Prices," *The Wall Street Journal*, November 4, 2010.

[xii] The Internet is a dynamic, changing information source. Web links noted in this manual were checked at the time of publication, but content may change over time. Please review the website before recommending it to your students.

[xiii] *Sources*: Interbrand, www.interbrand.com, accessed August 17, 2011; "Cult Brands," *BusinessWeek*, August 9, 2004; "The 100 Top Brands, 2005," *BusinessWeek,* August 30, 2005; Lesley Kump, Kurt Badenhausen, and Maya Roney, "Brand Values," *Forbes*, January 2, 2005.

[xiv] The Internet is a dynamic, changing information source. Web links noted in this manual were checked at the time of publication, but content may change over time. Please review the website before recommending it to your students.

[xv] *Source:* Christopher Leonard, "Panera to Open More Pay-What-You-Wish Restaurants," Associated Press, June 27, 2010.

[xvi] *Source:* Ronald Grover, "Disney's Toy Branding Strategy," *Bloomberg Businessweek*, June 2, 2011.

Distributing Products

chapter 15

critical thinking exercises 15.66

bonus cases 15.73

what's new in this edition

additions to the 10th edition:

- Getting to Know Tony Hsieh, CEO of Zappos
- Name That Company: Kia
- Spotlight on Small Business: Pop! Goes the Retail Store
- Reaching Beyond Our Borders: The Global Supply Chain for Services
- Thinking Green: Distribution and Sustainability
- Video case

revisions to the 10th edition:

- Text was revised to eliminate redundancy and tighten discussions.
- Statistical data and examples throughout the chapter were updated to reflect current information.

deletions from the 9th edition:

- Getting to Know Mark Stern of Doggypads.com
- Name That Company: Wal-Mart
- Spotlight on Small Business
- Reaching Beyond Our Borders
- Thinking Green

brief chapter outline and learning goals

chapter 15

Distributing Products

Getting To Know TONY HSIEH of ZAPPOS

learning goal 1

Explain the concept of marketing channels and their value.

I. THE EMERGENCE OF MARKETING INTERMEDIARIES

A. Why Marketing Needs Intermediaries

B. How Intermediaries Create Exchange Efficiency

C. The Value versus the Cost of Intermediaries

learning goal 2

Demonstrate how intermediaries perform the six marketing utilities.

II. THE UTILITIES CREATED BY INTERMEDIARIES

A. Form Utility

B. Time Utility

C. Place Utility

D. Possession Utility

E. Information Utility

F. Service Utility

learning goal 3

Identify the types of wholesale intermediaries in the distribution system.

III. WHOLESALE INTERMEDIARIES

A. Merchant Wholesalers

B. Agent and Brokers

learning goal 4

Compare the distribution strategies retailers use.

IV. RETAIL INTERMEDIARIES

A. Retail Distribution Strategy

learning goal 5

Explain the various kinds of nonstore retailing.

V. NONSTORE RETAILING

A. Electronic Retailing

B. Telemarketing

C. Vending Machines, Kiosks, and Carts

D. Direct Selling

E. Multilevel Marketing

F. Direct Marketing

learning goal 6

Explain the various ways to build cooperation in channel systems.

VI. BUILDING COOPERATION IN CHANNEL SYSTEMS

A. Corporate Distribution Systems

B. Contractual Distribution Systems

C. Administered Distribution Systems

D. Supply Chains

learning goal 7

Describe logistics and outline how intermediaries manage the transportation and storage of goods.

VII. LOGISTICS: GETTING GOODS TO CONSUMERS EFFICIENTLY

A. Trains Are Great for Large Shipments.

B. Trucks Are Good for Small Shipments to Remote Locations.

C. Water Transportation Is Inexpensive but Slow.

D. Pipelines Are Fast and Efficient.

E. Air Transportation Is Really Fast but Expensive.

F. Intermodal Shipping

G. The Storage Function

H. Tracking Goods

VIII. WHAT ALL THIS MEANS TO YOU

IX. SUMMARY

lecture outline

Getting to Know TONY HSIEH of ZAPPOS

E-tailers sometimes fall short of brick-and-mortal rivals in customer service. That's not the case for Zappos. Hsieh wanted to make sure his site was different; he wanted to wow customers with service. Call-center staffers have freedom to do whatever they can to remedy a situation. His commitment to quality and service has grown Zappos into an online powerhouse.

Although this automobile manufacturer builds its cars in South Korea, the 30,000 components come from all over the world. For example, the airbags come from a Swedish company that makes them in Utah. Its supply chain is truly interfirm and international. Name that company.

(Students should read the chapter before guessing the company's name: Kia)

learning goal 1

Explain the concept of marketing channels and their value.

I. THE EMERGENCE OF MARKETING INTERMEDIARIES

A. THE IMPORTANCE OF DISTRIBUTION

1. There are hundreds of thousands of marketing intermediaries that help move goods through the distribution network from producers to customers.

2. ***MARKETING INTERMEDIARIES*** are organizations that assist in moving goods and services from producer to business (B2B) and business to consumer (B2C).

   a. These are organizations in the middle of the series of organizations that distribute goods from producers to consumers.

   b. A ***CHANNEL OF DISTRIBUTION*** is the whole series of marketing intermediaries, such as

lecture notes

PPT 15-1
Chapter Title

PPT 15-2
Learning Goals

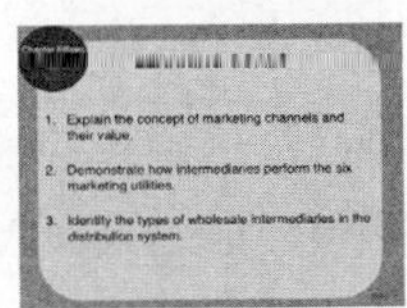

(See complete PowerPoint slide notes on page 15.40)

PPT 15-3
Learning Goals

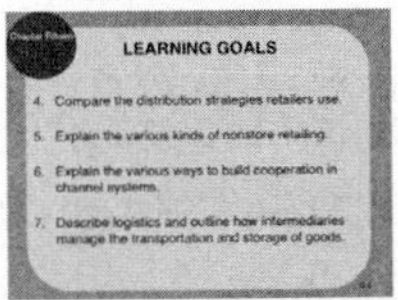

(See complete PowerPoint slide notes on page 15.40.)

PPT 15-4
Tony Hsieh

(See complete PowerPoint slide notes on page 15.41.)

PPT 15-5
Name That Company

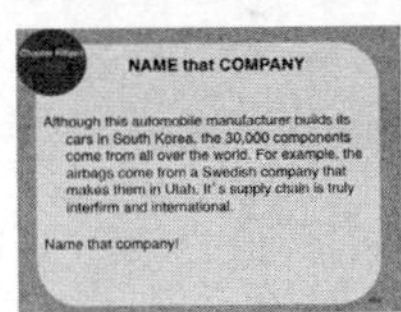

(See complete PowerPoint slide notes on page 15.41.)

lecture link 15-1
WHY THERE ARE NO INDIAN WAL-MARTS

There are millions of small shop owners in India who are fighting to keep the big retail chains out of the country. (See the complete lecture link on page 15.58 in this manual.)

PPT 15-6
What Are Marketing Intermediaries?

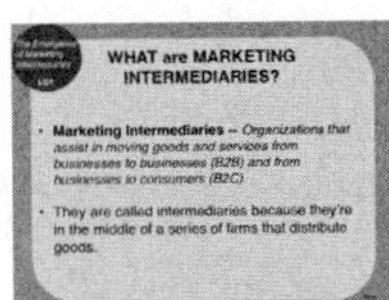

(See complete PowerPoint slide notes on page 15.41.)

PPT 15-7
What Are Marketing Intermediaries?

(See complete PowerPoint slide notes on page 15.42.)

agents, brokers, wholesalers, and retailers, that join together to transport and store goods in their path (or channel) from producers to consumers

c. ***AGENTS/BROKERS*** are marketing intermediaries that bring buyers and sellers together and assist in negotiating an exchange, but do not take title to the goods.

d. A ***WHOLESALER*** is a marketing intermediary that sells to other organizations.

e. A ***RETAILER*** is an organization that sells to ultimate consumers.

3. **CHANNELS OF DISTRIBUTION** enhance communication flows and the flow of money and title to goods.

B. **WHY MARKETING NEEDS INTERMEDIARIES**

1. Not all manufacturers need marketing intermediaries to sell their goods to consumer and business markets.

2. Intermediaries perform certain marketing functions **FASTER AND CHEAPER** than most manufacturers; these functions include transporting, storing, selling, advertising, and relationship building.

3. Agents and brokers facilitate the exchange process.

C. **HOW INTERMEDIARIES CREATE EXCHANGE EFFICIENCY**

1. Intermediaries **CREATE EXCHANGE EFFICIENCY** by decreasing the number of

thinking green
(Text page 407)

PPT 15-8
Distribution and Sustainability

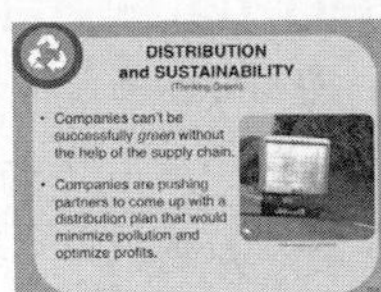

(See complete PowerPoint slide notes on page 15.42.)

PPT 15-9
Types of Marketing Intermediaries?

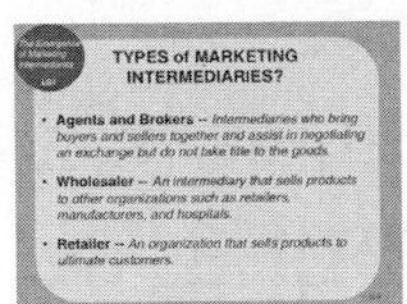

(See complete PowerPoint slide notes on page 15.42.)

critical thinking exercise 15-1
TOP 100 RETAILERS

This exercise asks students to use the Internet to research the top 100 U.S. retailers. (See complete exercise on page 15.66 of this manual.)

PPT 15-10
Selected Channels of Distribution

TEXT FIGURE 15.1
Selected Channels of Distribution for Consumer and Industrial Goods and Services
(Text page 408)

(See complete PowerPoint slide notes on page 15.43.)

PPT 15-11
Why Marketing Needs Intermediaries

(See complete PowerPoint slide notes on page 15.43.)

PPT 15-12
How Intermediaries Create Exchange Efficiency

TEXT FIGURE 15.2
How Intermediaries Create Exchange Efficiency
(Text page 409)

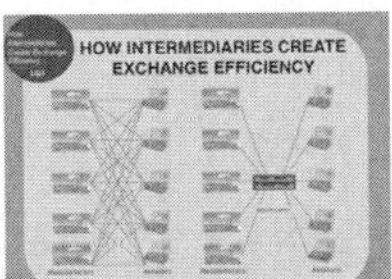

(See complete PowerPoint slide notes on page 15.43.)

contacts needed to establish marketing exchanges.

2. Intermediaries **ADD VALUE** that greatly exceeds their cost.

D. **THE VALUE VERSUS THE COST OF INTERMEDIARIES**

1. Some people think that if we could **GET RID OF INTERMEDIARIES**, we could greatly reduce the cost of the things we buy.
2. *The text uses the example of a breakfast cereal to illustrate how marketing intermediaries facilitate the movement of goods.*
3. Values discussed include:
   a. The value of not driving to Michigan to buy a box of cereal
   b. The value of saving time
   c. The effort saved by not having to drive to a wholesaler on the outskirts of town
4. The text emphasizes **THREE BASIC FACTS ABOUT INTERMEDIARIES:**
   a. Intermediaries can be eliminated, but their **ACTIVITIES** cannot.
   b. Intermediary organizations have survived because they perform marketing functions **FASTER AND CHEAPER** than others do.
   c. Although intermediaries add costs to products, these costs are usually offset by values they create.

bonus case 15-1

UNITED STATIONERS: OFFICE-SUPPLY INTERMEDIARY

This case focuses on Randall Larrimore of United Stationers. Larrimore modified the company's distribution strategy to compete with office-supply giants such as Office Depot and Staples. (See the complete case, discussion questions, and suggested answers beginning on page 15.73 of this manual.)

PPT 15-13
Three Key Facts about Marketing Intermediaries

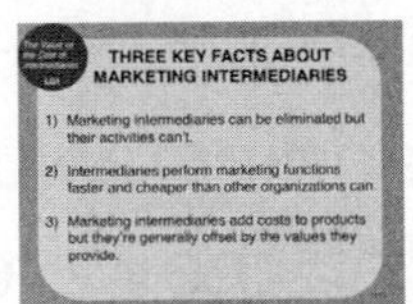

(See complete PowerPoint slide notes on page 15.44.)

PPT 15-14
Distribution's Effect on Your Food Dollar

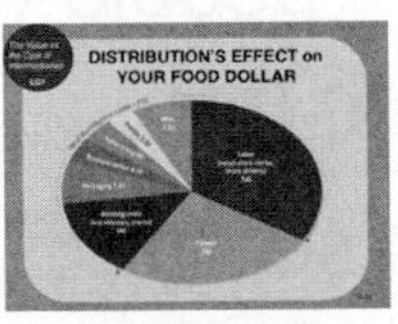

TEXT FIGURE 15.3
Distribution's Effect on Your Food Dollar
(Text page 410)

(See complete PowerPoint slide notes on page 15.44.)

lecture outline

learning goal 2

Demonstrate how intermediaries perform the six marketing utilities.

II. THE UTILITIES CREATED BY INTERMEDIARIES

A. ***UTILITY***, in economics, is the want-satisfying ability, or value, that organizations add to goods or services; the products are made more useful or accessible to consumers than they were before.

B. **FORM UTILITY** is taking raw materials and changing their form so that they become useful products.

   1. This type of utility has traditionally been performed by producers.

   2. By customizing products, retailers sometimes perform form utility also.

C. ***TIME UTILITY*** is adding value to products by making them available when they are needed.

D. ***PLACE UTILITY*** is adding value to products by having them where people want them.

E. **POSSESSION UTILITY**

   1. Intermediaries add ***POSSESSION UTILITY***—doing whatever is necessary to transfer ownership from one party to another, including providing credit, delivery, installation, guarantees, and follow-up service.

   2. Possession utility also allows customers to use goods through **RENTING**.

F. ***INFORMATION UTILITY*** is adding value to products by opening two-way flows of information between marketing participants.

critical thinking
exercise 15-2
FORMS OF UTILITY

This exercise presents a series of businesses and asks the students to describe how they create each type of utility. (See the complete exercise on page 15.68 of this manual.)

PPT 15-15
Intermediaries Create Utility

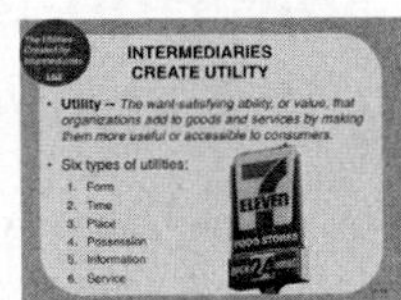

(See complete PowerPoint slide notes on page 15.44.)

lecture link 15-2
WHATEVER HAPPENED TO DOOR-TO-DOOR DELIVERY?

Many new developments have been made the door-to-door salesperson obsolete. (See the complete lecture link on page 15.59 in this manual.)

PPT 15-16
How Marketers Use Utility

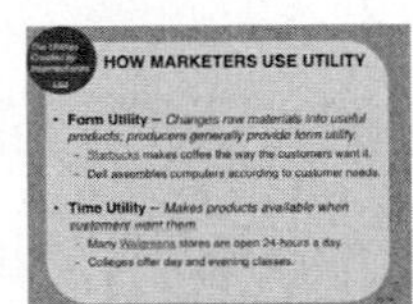

(See complete PowerPoint slide notes on page 15.45.)

PPT 15-17
How Marketers Use Utility

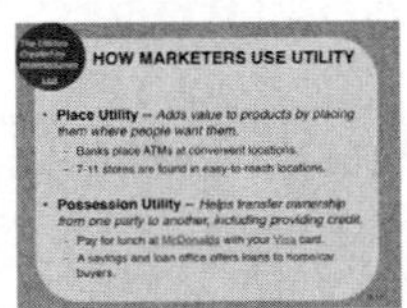

(See complete PowerPoint slide notes on page 15.45.)

PPT 15-18
How Marketers Use Utility

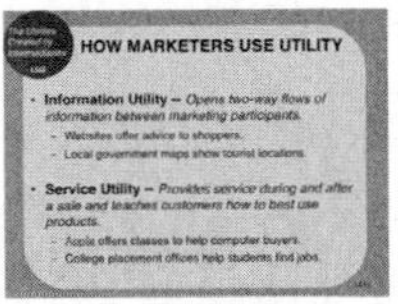

(See complete PowerPoint slide notes on page 15.45.)

G. **SERVICE UTILITY**

1. Intermediaries create ***SERVICE UTILITY***; adding value by providing fast, friendly service during and after the sale and teaching customers how to best use products over time.
2. For retailers, service utility is becoming **THE MOST IMPORTANT UTILITY**.

learning goal 3

Identify the types of wholesale intermediaries in the distribution system.

III. WHOLESALE INTERMEDIARIES

A. **DIFFERENCES BETWEEN WHOLESALERS AND RETAILERS**

1. Some producers will sell only to wholesalers.
2. Others sell some of their merchandise to other intermediaries, but also sell to ultimate consumers.
3. A **RETAIL SALE** is the sale of goods and services to consumers for their own use.
4. A **WHOLESALE SALE** is a sale to businesses and institutions for use in the business or to wholesalers or retailers for reuse.

B. ***MERCHANT WHOLESALERS*** are independently owned firms that take title to (own) the goods that they handle.

1. **FULL-SERVICE WHOLESALERS** perform all of the distribution functions.
2. **LIMITED-FUNCTION WHOLESALERS** perform only selected functions, but try to do them especially well.

lecture notes

progress assessment
(Text page 412)

PPT 15-19
Progress Assessment

PROGRESS ASSESSMENT

- What's a channel of distribution and what intermediaries participate in it?
- Why do we need intermediaries? Illustrate how intermediaries create exchange efficiency.
- How would you defend intermediaries to someone who said getting rid of them would save consumers millions of dollars?
- Give examples of the utilities intermediaries create and how they provide them.

(See complete PowerPoint slide notes on page 15.46.)

PPT 15-20
Wholesale Intermediaries

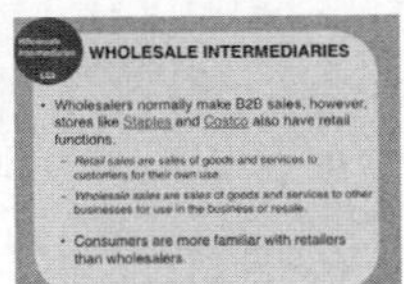

(See complete PowerPoint slide notes on page 15.47.)

lecture link 15-3
WHOLESALE CLUBS THRIVE IN THE RECESSION

Wholesale clubs are drawing in penny pinchers during our economic downturn. (See the complete lecture link on page 15.59 in this manual.)

lecture link 15-4
WHAT INTERMEDIARIES TO USE WHEN GOING INTERNATIONAL

What intermediaries are needed to reach the international customer? (See the complete lecture link on page 15.60 of this manual.)

critical thinking exercise 15-3
DISTRIBUTION CHANNELS

This exercise asks students to identify the channels of distribution of manufacturers in their areas. (See the complete exercise on page 15.69 of this manual.)

PPT 15-21
Types of Wholesale Intermediaries

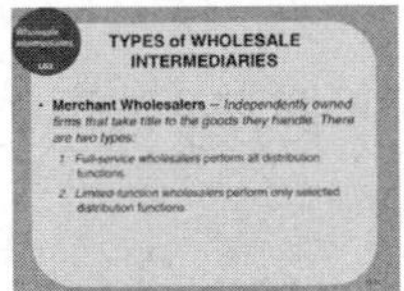

(See complete PowerPoint slide notes on page 15.47.)

TEXT FIGURE 15.4
A Full-Service Wholesaler
(Text page 414)

This text figure shows the functions performed by a full-service wholesaler.

3. ***RACK JOBBERS*** are wholesalers that furnish racks or shelves full of merchandise to retailers, display products, and sell on consignment.
4. ***CASH-AND-CARRY WHOLESALERS*** are wholesalers that serve mostly smaller retailers with a limited assortment of products.
5. ***DROP SHIPPERS*** are wholesalers that solicit orders from retailers and other wholesalers and have the merchandise shipped directly from a producer to a buyer.

C. **AGENTS AND BROKERS**

1. Agents and brokers bring buyers and sellers together and help **NEGOTIATE AN EXCHANGE,** but they never own the products.
   a. They do not usually carry inventory.
   b. Agents and brokers earn commissions or fees based on a percentage of the sales revenues.
   c. **AGENTS** maintain long-term relationships with the people they represent.
   d. **BROKERS** are usually hired on a temporary basis.
2. Agents who represent producers are known as **MANUFACTURER'S AGENTS** or **SALES AGENTS.**
   a. **MANUFACTURER'S AGENTS** may represent several manufacturers in a specific territory.
   b. **SALES AGENTS** represent a single producer in a larger territory.

lecture notes

PPT 15-22
Types of Limited-Function Wholesalers

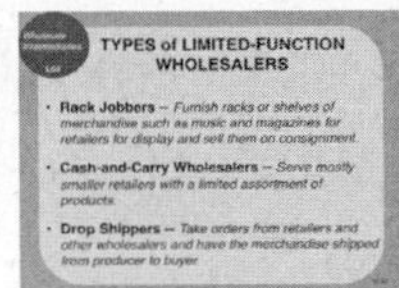

(See complete PowerPoint slide notes on page 15.47.)

PPT 15-23
Roles of Agents and Brokers

(See complete PowerPoint slide notes on page 15.48.)

lecture link 15-5
THE MARKETING FIRM STOCKING AMERICA'S GROCERIES

Jacksonville-based Acosta is responsible for getting big retailers to stock their clients' products. (See complete lecture link on page 15.60 of this manual.)

PPT 15-24
Retailing in the U.S.

(See complete PowerPoint slide notes on page 15.48.)

SPOTLIGHT ON small business
(Text page 416)

PPT 15-25
Pop! Goes the Retail Store

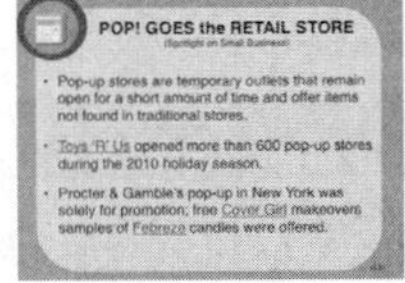

(See complete PowerPoint slide notes on page 15.48.)

3. Brokers have no continuous relationship with the buyer or the seller.

learning goal 4

Compare the distribution strategies retailers use.

IV. RETAIL INTERMEDIARIES

A. A **RETAILER** is an intermediary that sells to consumers.

1. The U.S. has about 2.3 million retail stores, not including websites.
2. About 11 million people work for retail organizations.

B. **RETAIL DISTRIBUTION STRATEGY**

1. Different products call for different retail distribution strategies.
2. ***INTENSIVE DISTRIBUTION*** puts products into as many retail outlets as possible; includes vending machines (used for convenience goods *such as candy and cigarettes*).
3. ***SELECTIVE DISTRIBUTION*** sends products to only a preferred group of retailers in an area (used for shopping goods *such as appliances or furniture*).
4. ***EXCLUSIVE DISTRIBUTION*** is distribution that sends products to only one retail outlet in a given geographic area (used for specialty goods *such as luxury automobiles*).

PPT 15-26
Fastest-Growing Retail Categories

(See complete PowerPoint slide notes on page 15.49.)

PPT 15-27
How to Prevent Coupon Fraud

(See complete PowerPoint slide notes on page 15.49.)

PPT 15-28
How to Prevent Return Policy Fraud

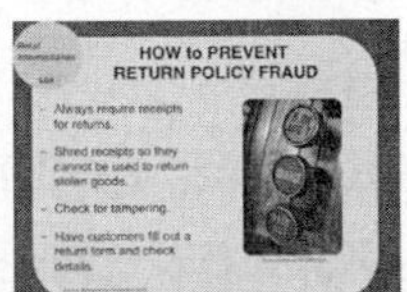

(See complete PowerPoint slide notes on page 15.49.)

lecture link 15-6
HOW RETAILERS COMPETE

Retailers compete for the consumer's dollar in five major ways. (See the complete lecture link on page 15.61 of this manual.)

PPT 15-29
Types of Retail Stores

TEXT FIGURE 15.5
Types of Retail Stores
(Text page 415)

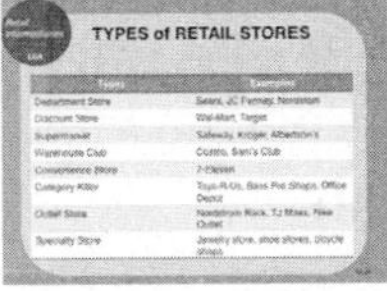

(See complete PowerPoint slide notes on page 15.50.)

PPT 15-30
Retail Distribution Strategies

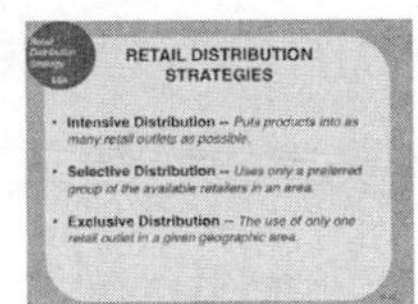

(See complete PowerPoint slide notes on page 15.50.)

critical thinking exercise 15-4
RETAIL DISTRIBUTION STRATEGY

This exercise asks students to give examples of each category of distribution strategy. (See complete exercise on page 15.70 of this manual.)

PPT 15-31
Pick a Strategy . . .

(See complete PowerPoint slide notes on page 15.50.)

<u>learning goal 5</u>

Explain the various kinds of nonstore retailing.

V. NONSTORE RETAILING

A. Nonstore retailing includes Internet retailing, telemarketing, vending machines, direct selling, and so on.

B. **ELECTRONIC RETAILING**

1. ***ELECTRONIC RETAILING*** is selling goods and services to ultimate consumers (e.g., you and me) over the Internet.
2. Attracting customers is only half the battle; the other half is delivering the goods, providing service, and keeping your customers.
3. Internet retailers have had difficulties with **SERVICE AFTER THE SALE**, such as handling complaints and returns.
   a. Most Internet retailers provide e-mail confirmation.
   b. Some websites have live chat functions.
4. Old brick-and-mortar stores are going online; these are sometimes called **"BRICK-AND-CLICK" STORES.**
5. To be successful in the future, companies will need both a real store and an online presence.
6. Both traditional retailers and new Internet retailers need to develop new distribution strategies to satisfy Internet-savvy shoppers *(example: Sears learned to use a new kind of distribution).*

C. **TELEMARKETING**

1. ***TELEMARKETING*** is the sale of goods and services by telephone.

progress assessment
(Text page 417)

PPT 15-32
Progress Assessment

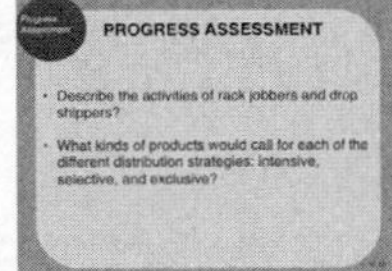

(See complete PowerPoint slide notes on page 15.51.)

PPT 15-33
Forms of Nonstore Retailing

(See complete PowerPoint slide notes on page 15.51.)

PPT 15-34
What Online Sites Need

(See complete PowerPoint slide notes on page 15.51.)

critical thinking exercise 15-6
INTERNET AUCTIONS: BYPASSING THE RETAILER

This Internet exercise directs students to the Internet auction site eBay to explore how such sites are changing the channel of distribution for consumer goods. (See complete exercise on page 15.72 of this manual.)

bonus case 15-2
STARTING AN ONLINE BUSINESS

Joseph Cohen started an online business at age 14. (See the complete case, discussion questions, and suggested answers beginning on page 15.75 of this manual.)

2. Many companies use telemarketing to supplement in-store selling.

D. **VENDING MACHINES, KIOSKS, AND CARTS**

1. The benefit of vending machines is their **CONVENIENT LOCATION.**
2. **CARTS** and **KIOSKS** have lower costs than stores, so they can offer lower prices.
3. Kiosks also serve as gateways to the Internet.

E. **DIRECT SELLING**

1. ***DIRECT SELLING*** is selling to consumers in their homes or where they work.
2. Many companies are sponsoring parties at workplaces and on weekends and evenings to accommodate working women.

F. **MULTILEVEL MARKETING**

1. Multilevel marketing salespeople work as independent contractors.
   a. They **EARN COMMISSIONS** on their own sales and create commissions for the "upliners" who recruited them.
   b. MLM salespeople also **RECEIVE COMMISSIONS** from "downliners" whom they recruit to sell.
2. The main attraction of multilevel marketing is the **LOW COST OF ENTRY.**
3. Because of some unethical MLM schemes, potential salespeople should carefully check out the organization.

lecture link 15-7
PARTY ON

The days of the old-fashioned Tupperware party are over, but some companies are using the direct-to-home distribution method for more unusual products. (See the complete lecture link on page 15.63 in this manual.)

PPT 15-35
Forms of Nonstore Retailing

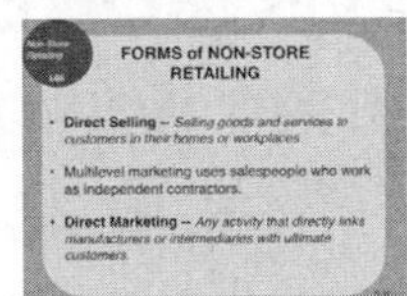

(See complete PowerPoint slide notes on page 15.52.)

bonus case 15-3
MULTILEVEL MARKETING

Multilevel marketing often gets a bad rap. But when multilevel marketing companies succeed, their growth can be astonishing. (See the complete case, discussion questions, and suggested answers beginning on page 15.77 of this manual.)

G. **DIRECT MARKETING**

1. One of the fastest-growing aspects of retailing is **DIRECT MARKETING.**
   a. ***DIRECT MARKETING*** is any activity that directly links manufacturers or intermediaries with the ultimate consumer.
   b. Direct retail marketing includes direct mail, catalog sales, telemarketing, and online marketing.
2. *Examples are L.L. Bean, Lands' End, Dell Computers, and Coldwater Creek.*
3. Direct marketing is **MORE CONVENIENT FOR CONSUMERS** than going to stores.
4. Sellers can provide information on websites to create **INTERACTIVE EXCHANGES.**
5. In order for consumers to receive the maximum benefit from marketing intermediaries, **THE ORGANIZATIONS MUST WORK TOGETHER.**

learning goal 6

Explain the various ways to build cooperation in channel systems.

VI. BUILDING COOPERATION IN CHANNEL SYSTEMS

A. Traditional retailers can stay competitive by making the whole system more efficient and cost competitive.

1. Manufacturers, wholesalers, and retailers must work closely together to form a unified system.
2. One way is to link the firms together in a formal relationship.

critical thinking exercise 15-5

CAREERS IN DISTRIBUTION

This Internet exercise asks students to research a career in distribution. (See complete exercise on page 15.71 of this manual.)

PPT 15-36

The Four Systems of Channel Relationships

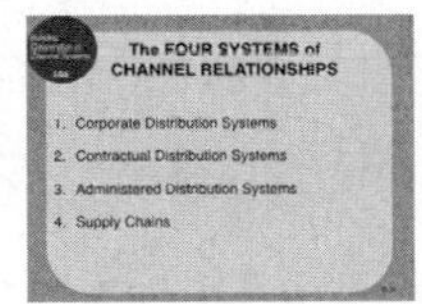

(See complete PowerPoint slide notes on page 15.52.)

B. A ***CORPORATE DISTRIBUTION SYSTEM*** is a distribution system in which all the organizations in the channel of distribution are owned by one firm *(example: Sherwin-Williams).*

C. ***CONTRACTUAL DISTRIBUTION SYSTEM*** is a distribution system in which members are bound to cooperate through contractual agreements.

   1. In **FRANCHISING SYSTEMS** *(such as McDonald's, KFC, Baskin-Robbins, and AAMCO),* the franchisee agrees to all of the rules, regulations, and procedures of the franchisor.
   2. In **WHOLESALER-SPONSORED CHAINS** *(Ace Hardware and IGA food stores)*, each store agrees to use the same name, participate in chain promotions, and cooperate even though each store is independently owned.
   3. A **RETAIL COOPERATE** *(Associated Grocers)* resembles a wholesaler-sponsored chain except the retailers initiate it.

D. **ADMINISTERED DISTRIBUTION SYSTEM**

   1. Producers can manage all the marketing functions themselves if they can't get retailers to cooperate.
   2. An ***ADMINISTERED DISTRIBUTION SYSTEM*** is distribution system in which producers manage all the marketing functions at the retail level.
   3. Retailers cooperate with producer-managed systems because they get so much free help.

E. **SUPPLY CHAINS**

   1. The ***SUPPLY CHAIN*** (or ***VALUE CHAIN***) is the

PPT 15-37
Corporate Distribution Systems

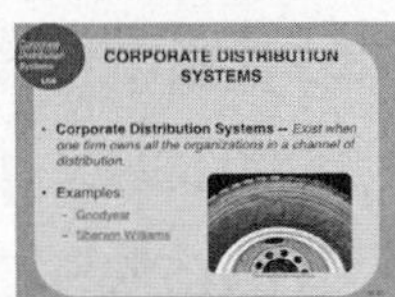

(See complete PowerPoint slide notes on page 15.52.)

PPT 15-38
Contractual Distribution Systems

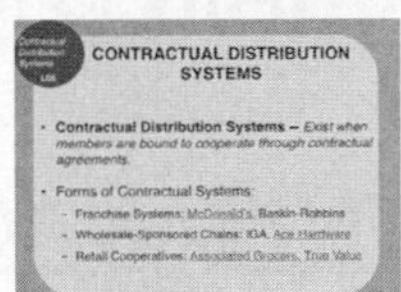

(See complete PowerPoint slide notes on page 15.53.)

PPT 15-39
Administered Distribution Systems

(See complete PowerPoint slide notes on page 15.53.)

PPT 15-40
Supply Chains

(See complete PowerPoint slide notes on page 15.53.)

sequence of linked activities that must be performed by various organizations to move goods from the sources or raw materials to ultimate consumers.

2. The **SUPPLY CHAIN** is longer than the channel of distribution.
3. ***SUPPLY-CHAIN MANAGEMENT*** is the process of managing the movement of raw materials, parts, work in progress, finished goods, and related information through all the organizations involved in the supply chain; managing the return of such goods, if necessary; and recycling material when appropriate.
4. *The text uses the example of the Kia Sorento model and its complex supply chain.*
5. Computers make it possible to coordinate the movement of goods and information to create products with the least amount of materials, inventory, and time.
6. Such systems are sometimes called **VALUE CHAINS** because they are so effective and efficient.
7. Firms often outsource the whole supply-chain management process because it is so complex.
8. *The text uses the example of how Cardinal Health became more successful after reorganizing its supply chain.*

lecture link 15-8
WHEN THE SUPPLY CHAIN BREAKS

The unexpected closure of a key player in the supply chain can create chaos in the market. (See the complete lecture link on page 15.63 in this manual.)

PPT 15-41
The Supply Chain

TEXT FIGURE 15.6
The Supply Chain
(Text page 421)

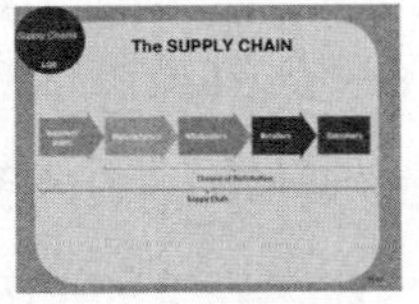

(See complete PowerPoint slide notes on page 15.54.)

REACHING BEYOND our borders
(Text page 422)

PPT 15-42
The Global Supply Chain for Services

The GLOBAL SUPPLY CHAIN for SERVICES
- Much movie animation takes place in the Philippines while companies in China provide research and development services.
- The competition among foreign suppliers is intense, including the need to find workers with strong language skills.
- One country that could be a leader in supplying supply-chain services is the U.S.

(See complete PowerPoint slide notes on page 15.54.)

lecture outline

learning goal 7

Describe logistics and outline how intermediaries manage the transportation and storage of goods.

VII. LOGISTICS: GETTING GOODS TO CONSUMERS EFFICIENTLY

A. Shipping costs have risen dramatically.

1. Shipping from city to city or state to state must to be fast but cost-effective.
2. Many companies turn to Web-based trade compliance systems to manage customs problems.
3. Distributing goods globally is more complicated than distributing domestically.

B. ***LOGISTICS*** is the marketing activity that involves planning, implementing, and controlling the physical flow of materials, final goods, and related information from points of origin to points of consumption to meet customer requirements at a profit.

1. ***INBOUND LOGISTICS*** is the area of logistics that involves bringing raw materials, packaging, other goods and services, and information from suppliers to producers.
2. ***MATERIALS HANDLING*** is the movement of goods within a warehouse, from warehouses to the factory floor, and from the factory floor to various workstations.
3. **FACTORY PROCESSES** change raw materials and parts into goods.
4. ***OUTBOUND LOGISTICS*** is the area of logistics that involves managing the flow of finished products and information to business buyers and

PPT 15-43
Using Logistics

(See complete PowerPoint slide notes on page 15.54.)

PPT 15-44
Logistics Applications

(See complete PowerPoint slide notes on page 15.55.)

PPT 15-45
Logistics Applications

(See complete PowerPoint slide notes on page 15.55.)

ultimate consumers (people like you and me).

5. ***REVERSE LOGISTICS*** is the area of logistics that involves bringing goods back to the manufacturer because of defects or for recycling materials.

C. Logistics is as much about the movement of **INFORMATION** as it is about the movement of **GOODS**.

1. **THIRD-PARTY LOGISTICS** is the use of outside firms to help move goods from here to there.
2. *Text example: Texas Instruments International warehouses are handled by a third-party logistics service.*

D. **SELLERS HAVE MANY DELIVERY OPTIONS.**

1. Sellers can deliver the goods themselves, use a shipping specialist, or outsource the distribution function to specialists.
2. Choosing the most efficient method of distribution system requires evaluating on basic service criteria.

E. **TRAINS ARE GREAT FOR LARGE SHIPMENTS.**

1. The largest percentage of goods (by volume) is shipped by **RAIL.**
2. Railroad shipment is best for bulky items, *such as coal or wheat.*
3. In **PIGGYBACK SHIPPING**, a truck trailer is loaded onto a railroad flatcar, taken to a destination, offloaded, and driven to customers' plants.
4. Railroad shipment is a relatively energy-efficient way to move goods.

lecture notes

PPT 15-46
Comparing Transportation Modes

TEXT FIGURE 15.7
Comparing Transportation Modes
(Text page 424)

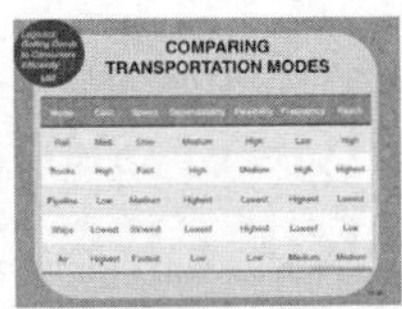

(See complete PowerPoint slide notes on page 15.55.)

lecture link 15-9

THE HIGH-TECH FUTURE OF FREIGHT

Railroads continue to play a vital role in the shipping industry, but changes need to be made to enjoy the benefits of our digital age. (See the complete lecture link on page 15.64 in this manual.)

PPT 15-47
Logistics Specialists

(See complete PowerPoint slide notes on page 15.56.)

5. Smaller manufacturers that don't ship enough products to fill a railcar or truck can use a freight forwarder.
6. A ***FREIGHT FORWARDER*** is an organization that puts many small shipments together to create a single large shipment that can be transported cost-effectively to the final destination.

F. **TRUCKS ARE GOOD FOR SMALL SHIPMENTS TO REMOTE LOCATIONS.**

1. The second-largest surface transportation mode is **MOTOR VEHICLES.**
2. Trucks reach more locations than trains.
3. A company can own its own trucks or hire a trucking specialist.
4. **PIGGYBACKING** methods now involve 20-foot-high railroad cars, called **DOUBLE-STACKS.**
5. The cost of trucking rises when fuel prices rise.
6. The newest measure of transportation from farm to consumer is the **CARBON COST,** and the fewer the miles food travels the better for the environment.

G. **WATER TRANSPORTATION IS INEXPENSIVE BUT SLOW.**

1. Water transportation isn't appropriate for goods that need to be delivered quickly, but it is often the least expensive method.
2. River transport, shipping on the Great Lakes, and shipping along coasts are options.

PPT 15-48
Types of Intermodal Shipping

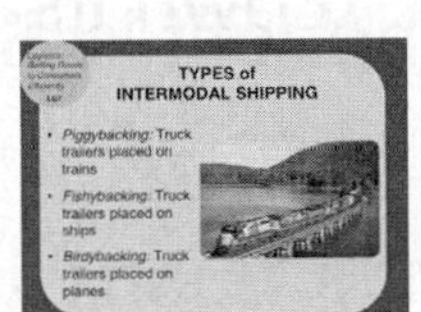

(See complete PowerPoint slide notes on page 15.56.)

3. When truck trailers are placed on ships, the process is called **FISHYBACK**.
4. When these trailers are placed in airplanes, the process is called **BIRDYBACK**.

H. **PIPELINES ARE FAST AND EFFICIENT.**

1. Pipelines are used primarily for transporting water, petroleum, and petroleum products.
2. Other products, such as coal in water, can be sent by pipelines.

I. **AIR TRANSPORT IS FAST BUT EXPENSIVE.**

1. Only a small part of shipping is done by **AIR**, but it is a critical factor in many industries.
2. The primary benefit is **SPEED** *(examples: FedEx and UPS).*
3. The air freight industry is starting to focus on global distribution *(example: KLM Royal Dutch Airlines).*

J. **INTERMODAL SHIPPING**

1. ***INTERMODAL SHIPPING*** is the use of multiple modes of transportation to complete a single long-distance movement of freight.
2. Services specializing in intermodal shipping are called **INTERMODAL MARKETING COMPANIES.**
3. Railroads are merging with each other and other transportation companies to offer intermodal distribution.

K. **THE STORAGE FUNCTION**

1. Marketers must have goods available in various

PPT 15-49
Get Your Product There

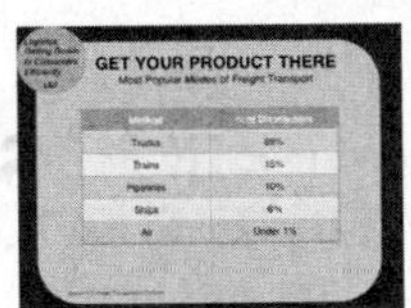

(See complete PowerPoint slide notes on page 15.56.)

parts of the country ready to be shipped locally when ordered.

2. A significant part of the total cost of logistics is for storage.
3. There are two major kinds of warehouses:
   a. A **STORAGE WAREHOUSE** holds products for a relatively long time. *(Example: seasonal products.)*
   b. **DISTRIBUTION WAREHOUSES** are facilities that gather and redistribute products. *(Examples: FedEx or UPS.)*

L. **TRACKING GOODS**

1. Managing the flow of goods means being able to keep track of where goods are at any given time.
2. **UNIVERSAL PRODUCT CODES (UPCs)** keep track of inventory.
3. **RADIO FREQUENCY IDENTIFICATION (RFID) TAGS** allow merchandise to be tracked through the distribution channel.
4. *For example, UPS uses a mix of Bluetooth's short-range radio capabilities and wireless receivers to track merchandise.*

VIII. WHAT ALL THIS MEANS TO YOU

A. The success of a firm depends on its ability to take orders, process them, and get the goods to customers.

B. There are many new jobs available in the area of supply-chain management.

IX. SUMMARY

PPT 15-50
Storage Warehouses

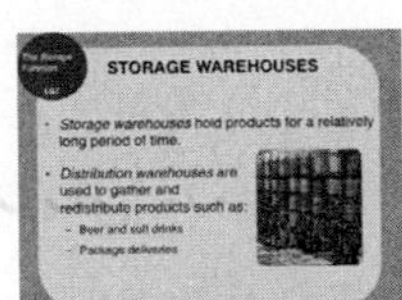

(See complete PowerPoint slide notes on page 15.57.)

progress
assessment
(Text page 428)

PPT 15-51
Progress Assessment

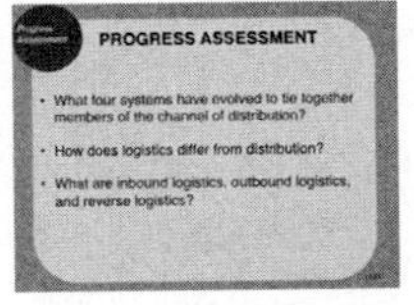

(See complete PowerPoint slide notes on page 15.57.)

PowerPoint slide notes

PPT 15-1
Chapter Title

PPT 15-2
Learning Goals

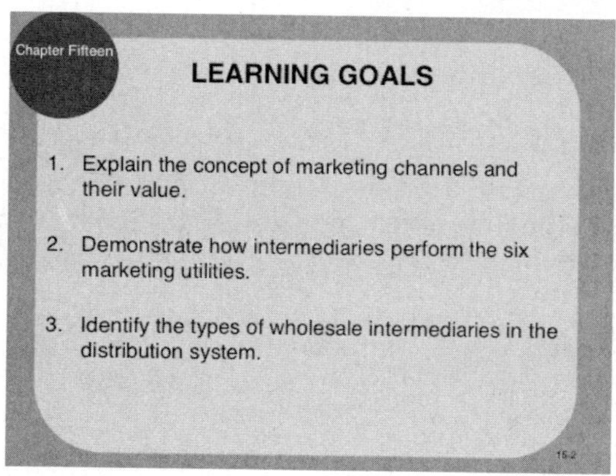

PPT 15-3
Learning Goals

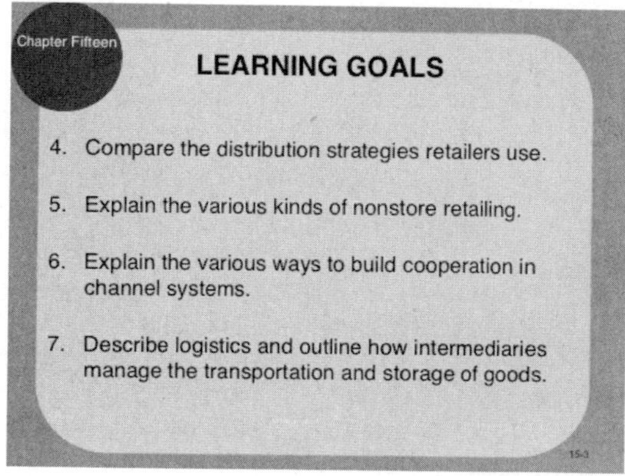

PPT 15-4
Tony Hsieh

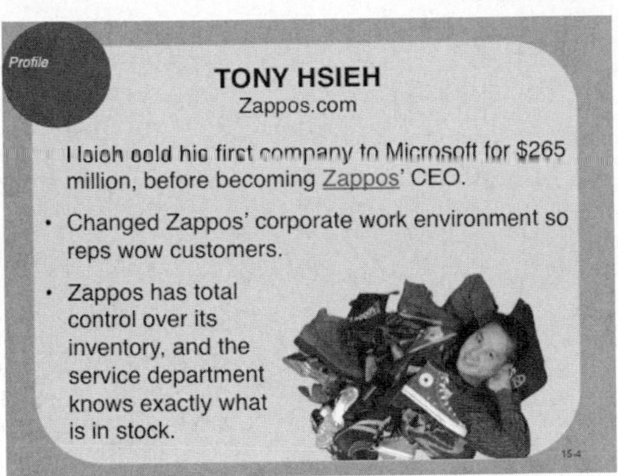

PPT 15-5
Name That Company

Company: Kia

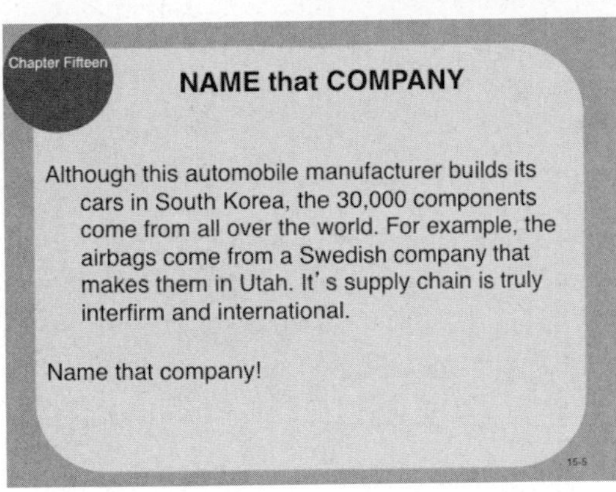

PPT 15-6
What Are Marketing Intermediaries?

1. Ask the students, How many of you think marketing intermediaries are an unnecessary cost? (*Often a majority of students will respond emphatically with a yes.*)
2. Use this as a basis to begin this chapter and an opportunity to explain the benefits these intermediaries play.

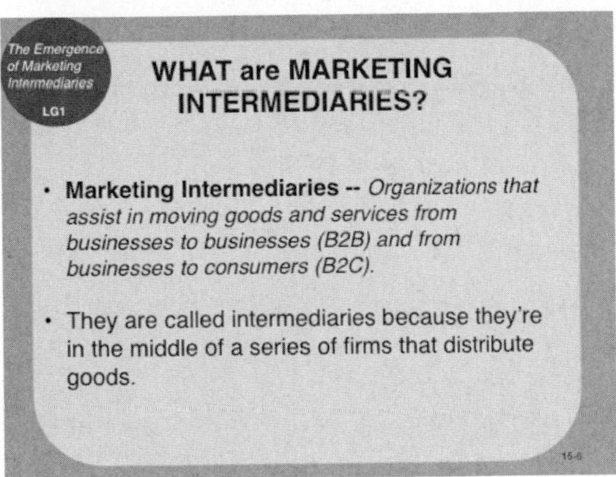

PPT 15-7
What Are Marketing Intermediaries?

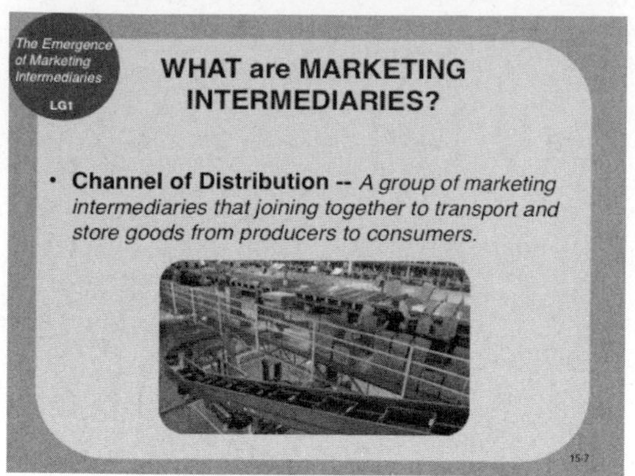

PPT 15-8
Distribution and Sustainability

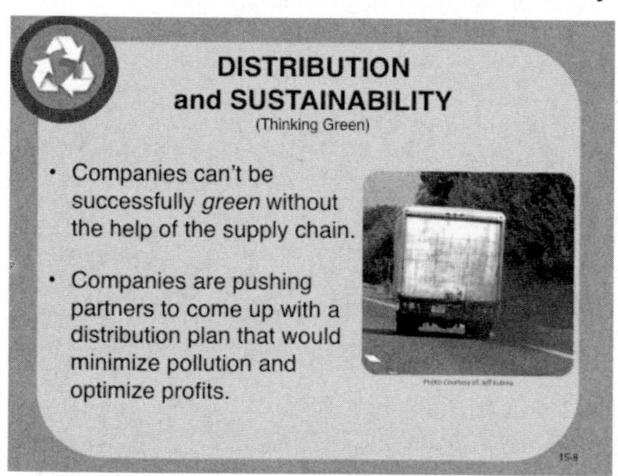

PPT 15-9
Types of Marketing Intermediaries?

There are different types of marketing intermediaries, each with a different role.

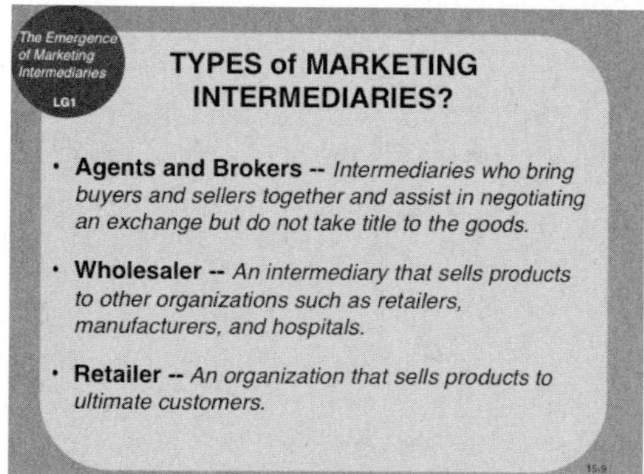

PPT 15-10
Selected Channels of Distribution

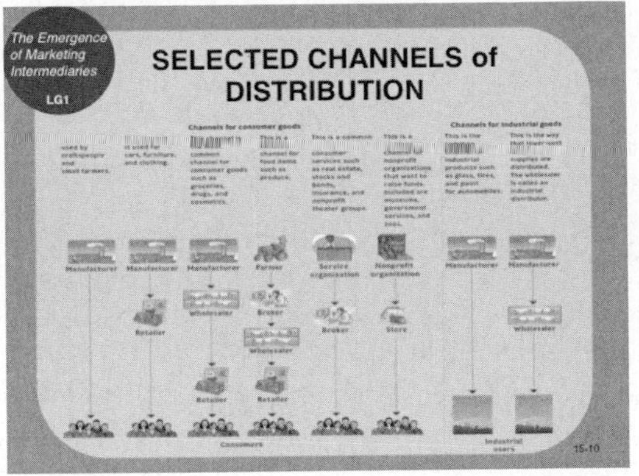

1. Different types of products will get to market via different channels of distribution.
2. Often small producers will bypass wholesalers and retailers, taking their products directly to the marketplace.

PPT 15-11
Why Marketing Needs Intermediaries

PPT 15-12
How Intermediaries Create Exchange Efficiency

How Intermediaries Create Exchange Efficiency
LG1
HOW INTERMEDIARIES CREATE EXCHANGE EFFICIENCY
Manufacturers
Retailers
Wholesaler
Manufacturers
Retailers
15-12

Intermediaries do add cost, as many assume, but they also create an efficient exchange of product. Many students are surprised how intermediaries create value for the consumer.

PPT 15-13
Three Key Facts about Marketing Intermediaries

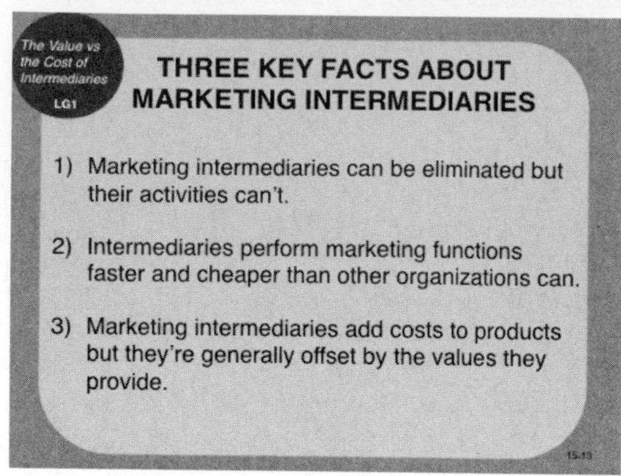

PPT 15-14
Distribution's Effect on Your Food Dollar

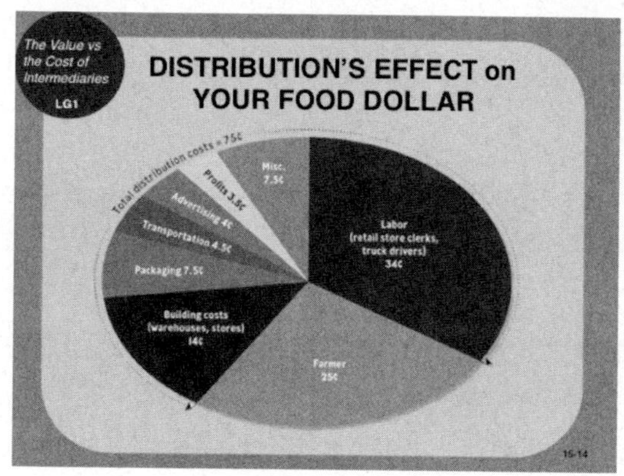

PPT 15-15
Intermediaries Create Utility

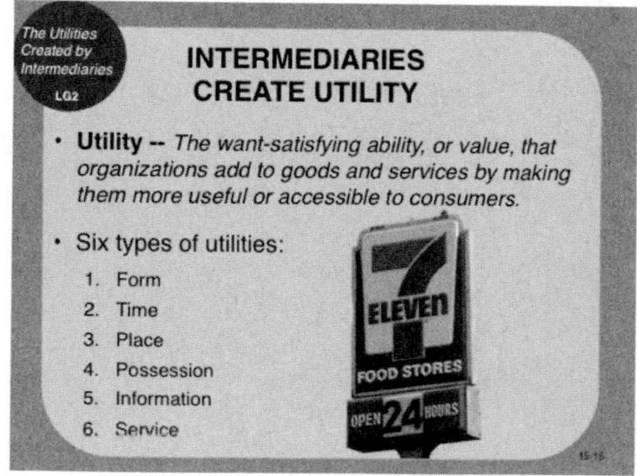

PPT 15-16
How Marketers Use Utility

PPT 15-17
How Marketers Use Utility

PPT 15-18
How Marketers Use Utility

PPT 15-19
Progress Assessment

1. A channel of distribution consists of agents, brokers, wholesalers, and retailers that join together to transport and store goods in their path or channel.
2. Marketing intermediaries perform tasks such as transporting, storing, selling, advertising, and relationship building. They are able to perform these tasks faster and more cheaply than most manufacturers, creating a cost savings.
3. The reason that marketing intermediaries have not been eliminated is they add value that greatly exceeds their cost.
4. There are six types of utility provided by intermediaries:
   - Form utility occurs when raw materials are changed into useful products. For example, retail butchers cut pork chops from a larger piece of meat.
   - Time utility is added to products by making them available to consumers when they want them. Convenience stores like 7-Eleven and QuikTrip provide time utility since they are open 24 hours a day.
   - Place utility occurs when products are placed where people want them. Again 7-Eleven and QuikTrip provide place utility, since they are in easy to reach locations.
   - Possession utility is added by doing whatever is necessary to transfer ownership from one party to another. Activities associated with possession utility include delivery, installation, guarantees, and follow-up service.
   - Information utility is created by opening two-way flows of information between marketing participants. Newspapers, websites, and salespeople all provide information utility.
   - Service utility is added by providing fast, friendly service before and after the sale. This is a critical area for most retailers, since without service utility they would lose business to the Internet or to catalogs.

PPT 15-20
Wholesale Intermediaries

WHOLESALE INTERMEDIARIES

- Wholesalers normally make B2B sales, however, stores like Staples and Costco also have retail functions.
  - *Retail sales* are sales of goods and services to customers for their own use.
  - *Wholesale sales* are sales of goods and services to other businesses for use in the business or resale.
- Consumers are more familiar with retailers than wholesalers.

15-20

PPT 15-21
Types of Wholesale Intermediaries

TYPES of WHOLESALE INTERMEDIARIES

- **Merchant Wholesalers --** *Independently owned firms that take title to the goods they handle. There are two types:*
  1. *Full-service wholesalers* perform all distribution functions.
  2. *Limited-function wholesalers* perform only selected distribution functions.

15-21

PPT 15-22
Types of Limited-Function Wholesalers

TYPES of LIMITED-FUNCTION WHOLESALERS

- **Rack Jobbers --** *Furnish racks or shelves of merchandise such as music and magazines for retailers for display and sell them on consignment.*
- **Cash-and-Carry Wholesalers --** *Serve mostly smaller retailers with a limited assortment of products.*
- **Drop Shippers --** *Take orders from retailers and other wholesalers and have the merchandise shipped from producer to buyer.*

15-22

PPT 15-23
Roles of Agents and Brokers

Agents and brokers do not take title or possession of the product but simply represent the interest of their clients.

PPT 15-24
Retailing in the U.S.

PPT 15-25
Pop! Goes the Retail Store

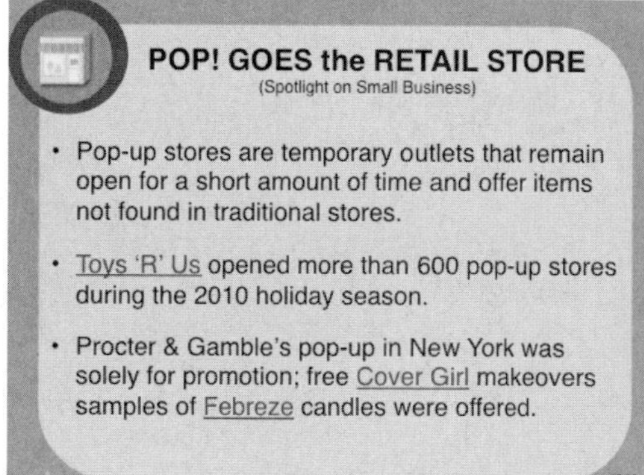

The aim of these types of pop-ups is to create lasting relationships with customers, rather than just distribute the products.

PPT 15-26
Fastest-Growing Retail Categories

1. This slide presents the fastest-growing retail categories.
2. Have students brainstorm reasons why they believe these categories are growing at a fast rate.
3. Ask the students, What value do consumers see in these particular categories?

PPT 15-27
How to Prevent Coupon Fraud

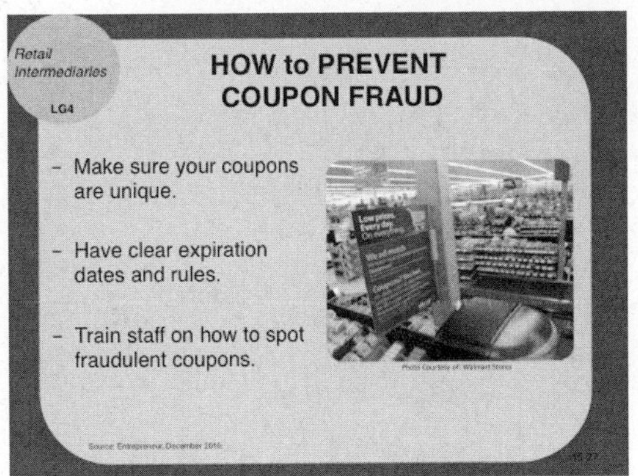

1. Retail fraud cost the industry approximately $10 billion a year.
2. In our current economic state, coupon fraud is becoming more and more prevalent.
3. This slide shows how businesses can protect themselves.
4. Ask the students, Is it illegal to counterfeit coupons? Is it ethical?

PPT 15-28
How to Prevent Return Policy Fraud

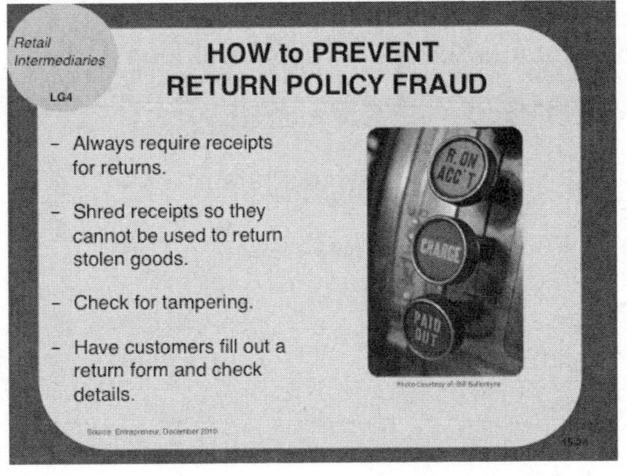

1. Retail fraud cost the industry approximately $10 billion a year.
2. In our current economic state, more and more customers are returning products after personal use.
3. This slide shows how businesses can protect themselves.
4. Ask the students, Should retailers have stricter return policies? What would you do if you owned a shop and customers were returning used goods?

PPT 15-29
Types of Retail Stores

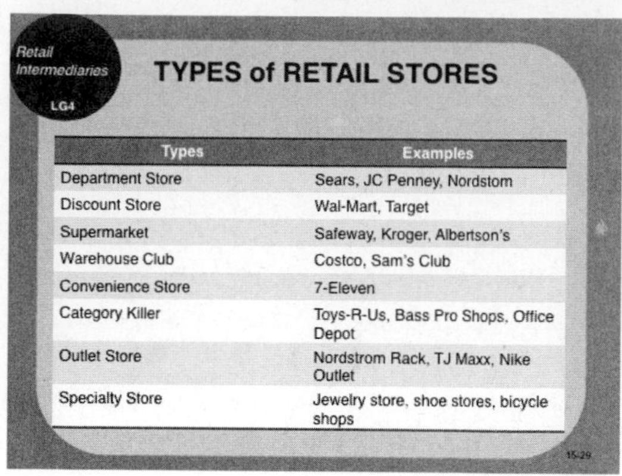

PPT 15-30
Retail Distribution Strategies

The retail strategy employed often depends on the product one is selling.

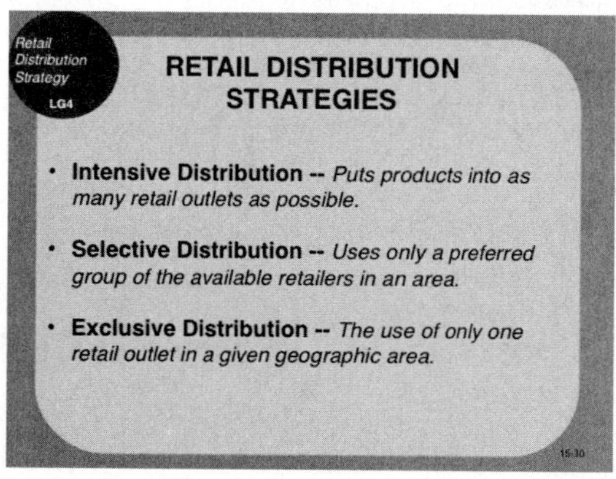

PPT 15-31
Pick a Strategy . . .

- Ralph Lauren Polo shirts—selective strategy
- Diet Pepsi—intensive strategy
- Rolls-Royce automobiles—exclusive strategy
- Calloway golf clubs—selective strategy
- Snickers candy bars—intensive strategy
- Steinway pianos—exclusive strategy

PPT 15-32
Progress Assessment

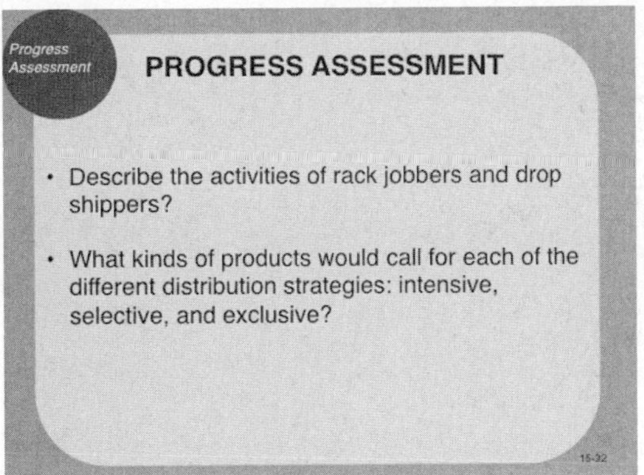

1. Rack jobbers furnish racks full of merchandise like toys and health and beauty aids to retailers. They display the items and sell them on consignment, keeping title to the goods until they are sold. Drop shippers solicit orders and have the merchandise shipped directly from producer to the buyer. They own the merchandise but do not handle it, stock it, or deliver it
2. Intensive distribution includes convenience items such as gum, magazines, candy, and cigarettes. Selective distribution includes items such as appliances, furniture, and clothing. Exclusive distribution includes specialty products such as fly-fishing gear or equipment for snow skiing.

PPT 15-33
Forms of Non-Store Retailing

In many countries vending machines, kiosks, and carts are more popular than in the United States. The Japanese Vending Machine Manufacturers Association estimates there is one vending machine for every 23 people, selling everything from soft drinks to umbrellas.

PPT 15-34
What Online Stores Need

1. Online retailing is relatively new and is evolving to be more customer-friendly.
2. This slide gives students an idea of the important features on e-commerce websites.
3. The lack of these features often causes people to shy away from making purchases online.
4. Ask the students, Do you have hesitations about shopping online? Why or why not?

PPT 15-35
Forms of Non-Store Retailing

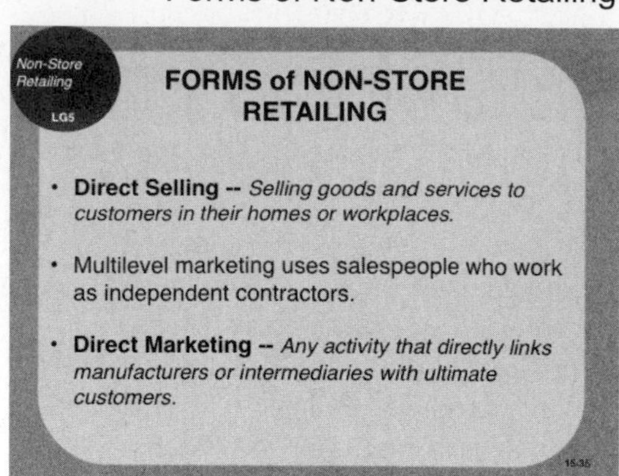

PPT 15-36
The Four Systems of Channel Relationships

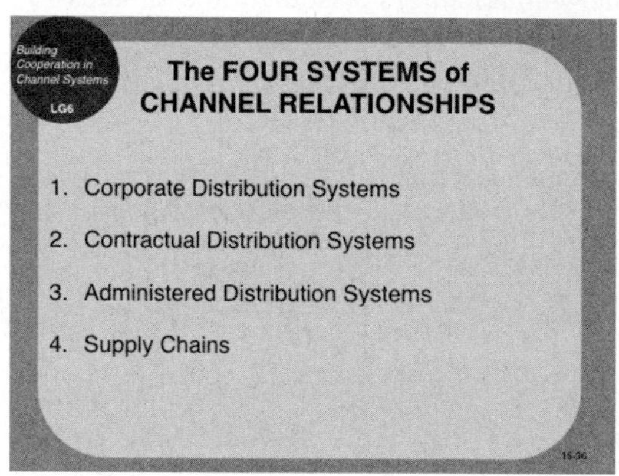

PPT 15-37
Corporate Distribution Systems

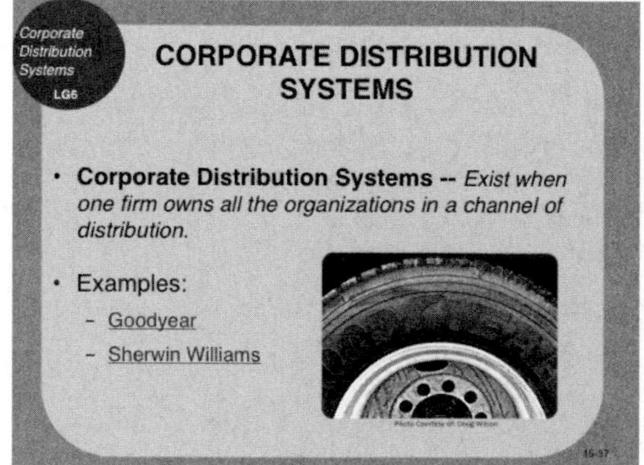

PPT 15-38
Contractual Distribution Systems

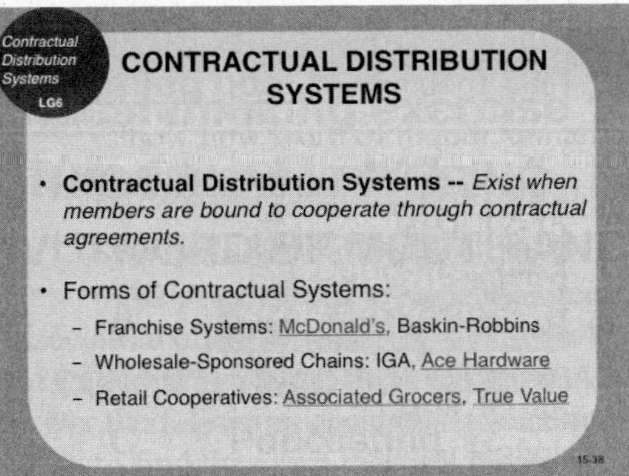

PPT 15-39
Administered Distribution Systems

PPT 15-40
Supply Chains

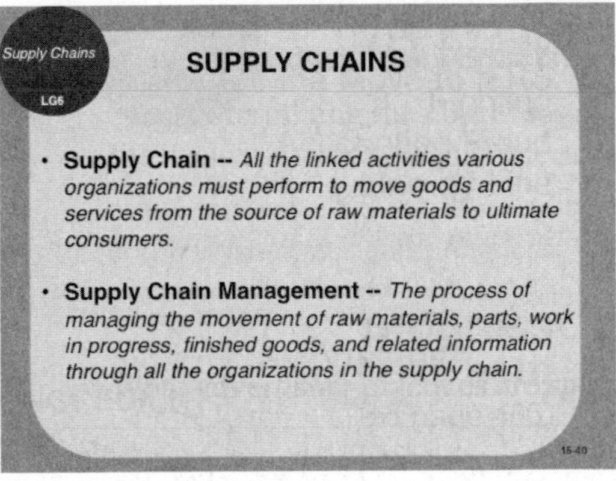

PPT 15-41
The Supply Chain

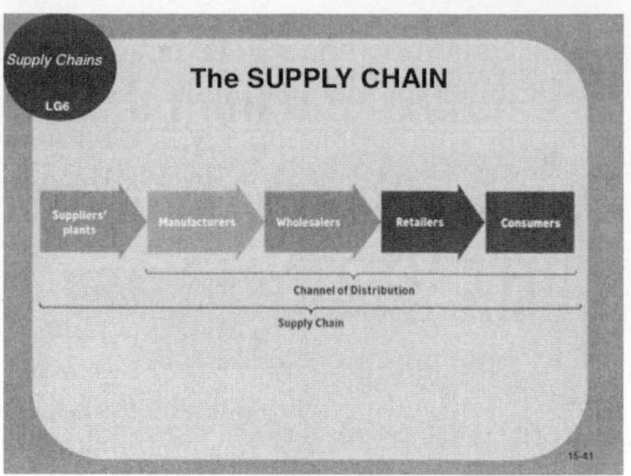

Supply-chain management is a key to effective distribution in the 21st century. This slide illustrates to students how supply chains are structured and implemented in the market.

PPT 15-42
The Global Supply Chain for Services

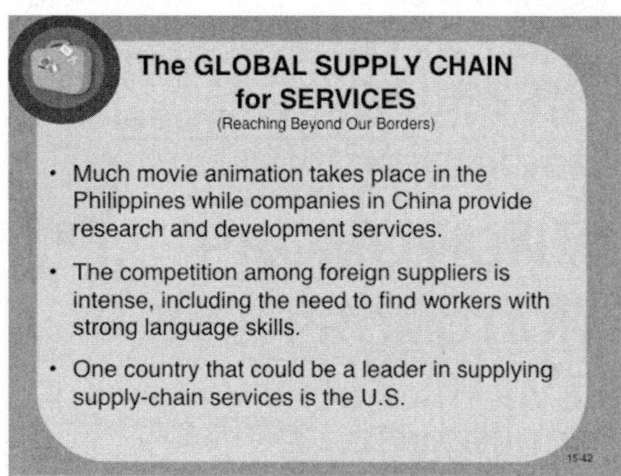

PPT 15-43
Using Logistics

PPT 15-44
Logistics Applications

PPT 15-45
Logistics Applications

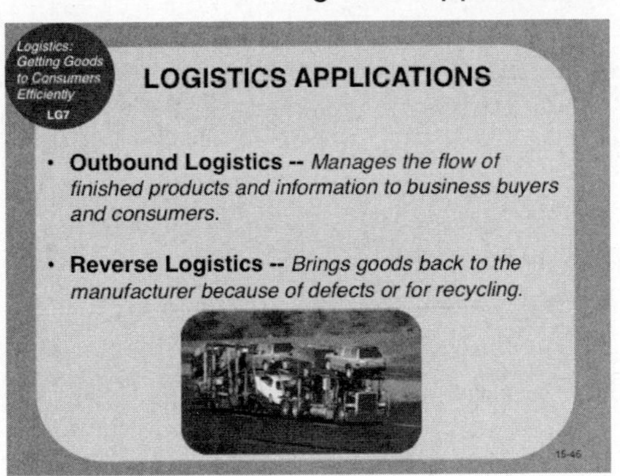

PPT 15-46
Comparing Transportation Modes

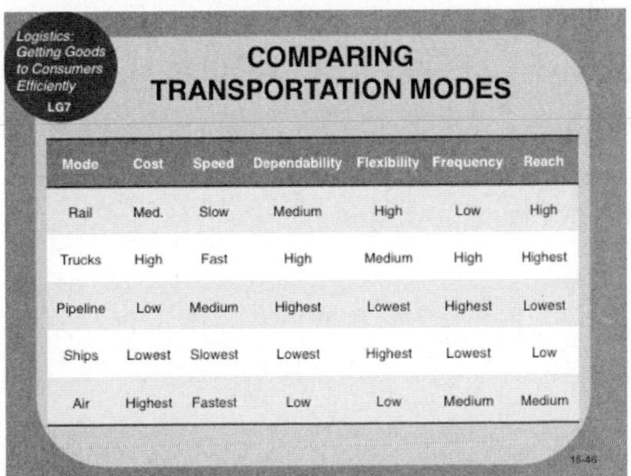

Mode	Cost	Speed	Dependability	Flexibility	Frequency	Reach
Rail	Med.	Slow	Medium	High	Low	High
Trucks	High	Fast	High	Medium	High	Highest
Pipeline	Low	Medium	Highest	Lowest	Highest	Lowest
Ships	Lowest	Slowest	Lowest	Highest	Lowest	Low
Air	Highest	Fastest	Low	Low	Medium	Medium

PPT 15-47
Logistics Specialists

PPT 15-48
Types of Intermodal Shipping

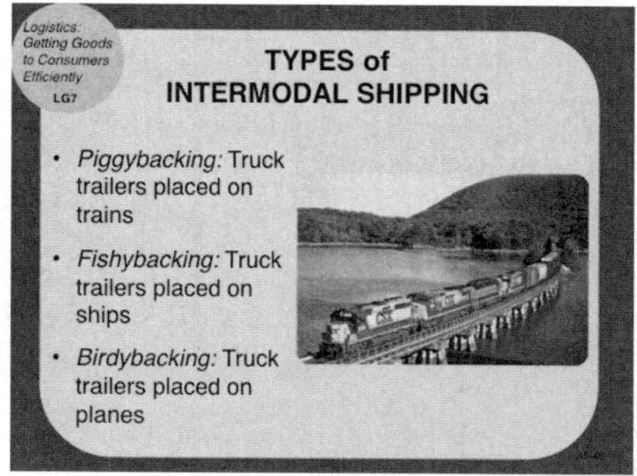

A truck driver from North Carolina, Malcolm McLean, invented container shipping in 1956.

PPT 15-49
Get Your Product There

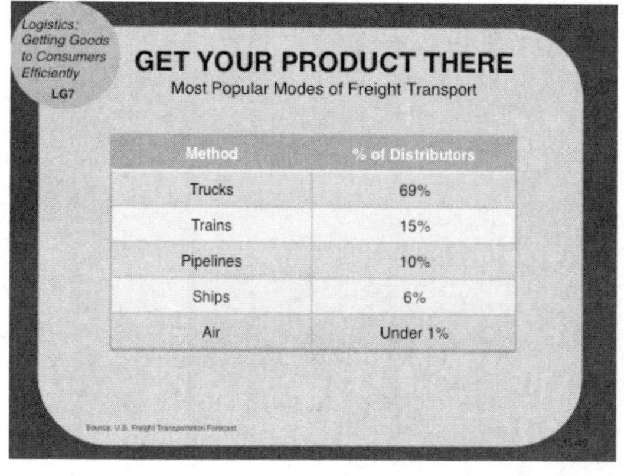

Method	% of Distributors
Trucks	69%
Trains	15%
Pipelines	10%
Ships	6%
Air	Under 1%

1. Not only must a manufacturer produce a product, it then must figure out the best way to ship the product.
2. This slide gives students insight into the most popular methods of freight transportation.
3. To make sure students understand this slide, discuss with the class the advantages and disadvantages of each method of transportation.

PPT 15-50
Storage Warehouses

Seasonal items, like snow shovels and lawnmowers, are often held in storage warehouses.

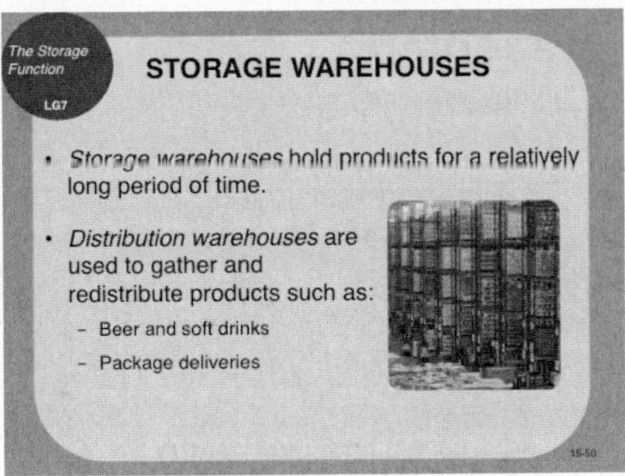

PPT 15-51
Progress Assessment

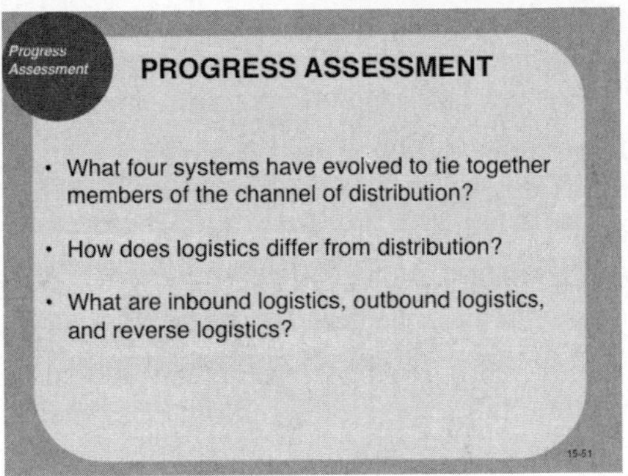

1. The four systems that have emerged to tie firms together are corporate systems, contractual systems, administered systems, and supply chains.
2. Logistics differs from distribution in many ways. Logistics is the planning, implementing, and controlling of the physical flow of materials, final goods, and related information from points of origin to points of consumption to meet customer requirements at a profit. Distribution is much less complex than logistics and simply involves moving the product from the manufacturer to the end consumer.
3. Inbound logistics is the process of bringing raw materials, packaging, other goods and services, and information from suppliers to producers. Outbound logistics manages the flow of finished products and information to business buyers and them to consumers. Reverse logistics brings goods back to the manufacturer because of defects or for recycling.

lecture links

"The solving of the problem lies in finding the solvers."
Van Herpen's Law

"The question for us is are you creating value? The Internet is a great place for companies of all kinds that are creating genuine value for customers and it is a terrible place for companies that are not."
Jeff Bezos

"If you don't need it and don't want it, there's always plenty of it."
Murphy's Law of Supply

lecture link 15-1

WHY THERE ARE NO INDIAN WAL-MARTS

If you needed to buy a bag of rice or a CD player in Delhi, India, you wouldn't be able to go to the local Wal-Mart to buy it. You probably would wind up at the Big Bazaar store, where electronic equipment is displayed alongside women's panties, tennis balls next to handbags. The feeling at Big Bazaar, and at most Indian stores, is like a typical bazaar. Colorful, chaotic, and a little cluttered. Most shopkeepers know that this is the way Delhi residents like it.

The Big Bazaar, 1 of 90 owned by Pantaloon, India's largest retail group, draws up to 8,000 customers a day with its wide array of merchandise and air conditioning. India's growing middle class fuels this commercial boom. The middle class now makes up a third of the country's 1.1 billion population.

Big retailers like Wal-Mart and Tesco have long eyed this huge this market, but you won't find a single store in the country. Those big retailers can't enter the Indian market, thanks to restrictions on foreign investment. Even the promise of lower prices and more efficient supply chains haven't been enough to overcome the political power of India's 12 million shopkeepers. These small entrepreneurs account for 97% of the country's $258 billion in annual retail sales. Large Indian companies are also urging the government to slow down reforms that would open the market to foreign competition. Opponents of foreign investment estimate that 8 million people would lose their jobs if Wal-Mart or similar stores took just 20% of the retail trade.

India's Commerce Minister Kamal Nath is considering an incremental plan that would create new jobs, while not replacing or displacing employment in small neighborhood shops. Nath's plan would initially limit companies like Wal-Mart to India's six biggest cities and allow them to open only one store a year in each city. These stores would have to be at least 100,000 square feet, so they couldn't be located in inner-city neighborhoods. The plan has not gotten much traction due to delays by the business lobby and factions in India's government.

Retail sales are increasing in India by an average of 10% a year, and spending on luxury goods is rising nearly twice as fast. With two-thirds of India's population under 35, consumer demand is clearly growing. However, India's two political parties say they have no intention of relaxing their position and do not expect government reforms in the foreseeable future.i

lecture link 15-2

WHATEVER HAPPENED TO DOOR-TO-DOOR DELIVERY?

Not too long ago in America, there were vendors who delivered goods door-to-door. One person brought milk and left it on the porch. Another person brought ice for the "ice box." They are now called refrigerators and have their own icemakers. Still other people brought bread or coffee. Now, most of those people are out of business. But is the idea a bad one? Maybe we can learn from the "good old days."

Many new developments have made the old door-to-door delivery person obsolete. A major change has been the emergence of neighborhood 7-Eleven stores and other "convenience" stores that have made it possible to quickly obtain milk and bread and eggs and other items: candy, soft drinks, and ice cream. But another trend has emerged that has greatly increased the potential for door-to-door delivery. The percentage of people over 65 has skyrocketed in the last few years and will continue to grow very rapidly. Many of these people live in high-rise communities and have limited means for getting around. Many have difficulty walking and some can't drive.

Imagine, if you will, a mobile 7-Eleven store. It would come to each community at the same time every day with staples such as milk, bread, eggs, soft drinks, butter, cheese, and the like. Over time, the vendor would listen to customers and learn of special needs, like medicine from the local pharmacy. Soon the mobile 7-Eleven would be like a custom-made retailer to the people served. You could call or e-mail the night before and place your order for special items not normally carried on the truck.

It would be more expensive to buy such goods because there are added costs, but the convenience may far exceed the additional costs. And the vendor could make a *lot* of money. Do you see how such marketing intermediaries emerge?

lecture link 15-3

WHOLESALE CLUBS THRIVE IN THE RECESSION

If there's a silver lining to the recession, it's that consumers have become more cost-conscious regarding the items they need and buy. But while this may be a lesson well learned for most people, it's been a nightmare for retail companies. Even stores that offer essential items like food have taken a beating. Thanks to increased price competition as well as the harsh economy, chains like Kroger and Wal-Mart have seen their once lucrative food sales plummet. Wal-Mart, for instance, saw sales at stores that have been open for more than a year drop 1.6% overall last year.

Wal-Mart might not have much cause for worry, though, as sales at its wholesale counterpart Sam's Club rose 0.7% last year. In fact, as supermarkets watch their profits tumble, wholesale clubs report record profits. Costco, the largest wholesale company in the nation, reported a mammoth 25% rise in profit in the second quarter. Revenue also climbed for BJ's Wholesale Club, which reported a 5% rise in profits for the fourth quarter. Both companies also saw club memberships increase, adding more revenue through annual member fees.

Wholesale clubs enjoy several advantages that supermarkets can't compete with. First of all, the clubs' high volume and low-cost model draws many penny-pinching consumers away from pricier grocery stores. Clubs also eliminate or greatly reduce advertising since the promise of cheap bulk goods is enough to appeal to most consumers. Rising gas prices were also a boon to wholesale clubs, as many own banks of gas pumps on store premises. Still, while groceries and gasoline sales may be up, sales of discretionary items remain low and are expected to stay meager as long as the recession persists.

lecture link 15-4

WHAT INTERMEDIARIES TO USE WHEN GOING INTERNATIONAL

It's one thing to decide to sell a product internationally; it's something else again to try to implement such a program. How are you going to reach the consumer? You could, of course, send sales representatives to contact people directly, but that would be costly and risky. How can you get your product into foreign markets at a minimum cost and still have wide distribution?

USE BROKERS. As explained in the chapter text, a broker is an intermediary who keeps no inventory and takes no risk. A broker can find distributors for you. Brokers sell for you and make a commission on the sale. This is the least expensive way to enter foreign markets, but you still assume the risks of transportation.

USE IMPORTERS AND EXPORTERS. Importers and exporters take all the risks of business and sell your products to international markets. Their commission is much higher than that of brokers, but they do much more for you. They may find you distributors or do the selling to ultimate consumers themselves.

CALL ON DISTRIBUTORS DIRECTLY. You can bypass exporters and brokers and call on distributors yourself. In that case, you actually become your own exporter and deliver directly to distributors, but again you assume the risks of transportation.

SELL DIRECT. The most costly and risky way to sell internationally is to set up your own distribution system of wholesalers and retailers. On the other hand, this maximizes potential profits in the long run. Many firms start out selling through importers and exporters and end up setting up their own distribution system as sales increase.

USE THIRD-PARTY LOGISTICS (3PL) PROVIDERS. This new kind of company will distribute goods worldwide for you. The U.S. market leader is Ryder Integrated Logistics. Ryder designs, implements, and manages the whole system for delivering goods in the United States and overseas.

lecture link 15-5

THE MARKETING FIRM STOCKING AMERICA'S GROCERIES

Given the immense size of many supermarkets, the complicated process that brings food to store shelves may be lost on many consumers. After all, retailers have a nearly limitless choice of items and brands they could stock. While a few customer staples might be natural selections, a good deal of thought and consideration goes into filling the rest of a store's shelf space. That's where food-marketing companies like the Jacksonville-based Acosta come in. It's Acosta's job to convince big retailers like Kroger and Wal-Mart to carry its clients' products.

Acosta employs 13,000 people to patrol more than 130,000 stores in the United States and Canada in order to secure prominent shelf space for clients like Kellogg, Procter & Gamble, and Nestlé. As the so-called brand behind the brands, Acosta earned more than $1 billion in commissions last year. Even as food prices climb and companies scale back on expenses, insiders expect Acosta's revenue to rise regardless. Part of the reason behind the company's success is its entrenchment in many prominent food companies. One expert in marketing strategy claimed, "Acosta has a seat in the boardroom when it comes to a brand's overall business strategy."

Of course, Acosta's services expand beyond securing Cap'n Crunch a spot on the shelf befitting his naval rank. It also spearheads manufacturer-funded promotions and sales scheduled for busy shopping times. Perhaps most importantly, though, Acosta helps steer its clients through any crises that may occur. For instance, in 2009 flooding and manufacturing mishaps led to the temporary closing of two out of the four plants that produce Eggo waffles. As a result, shortages forced the Kellogg-owned brand to watch its share of the frozen breakfast market fall by one-third to 19% by early 2010. Once the plants came back online, Acosta collaborated with Kellogg to plot the waffle's comeback. They settled on a back-to-school promotion that knocked $2 off Eggo's most popular flavors. After that, Acosta parlayed with retailers to sell them on the idea as well as ensure ample shelf space. By the beginning of 2011 Eggo's market share rose back to 30%.[ii]

lecture link 15-6

HOW RETAILERS COMPETE

There are five major ways in which retailers compete for the consumer's dollar: price, service, location, selection, and entertainment. Since consumers are constantly comparing retailers on price, service, and variety, it is important for retailers to use benchmarking to compare themselves against the best in the field to make sure that their practices and procedures are the most advanced. The following sections describe the five means of competition.

PRICE COMPETITION

Discount stores such as Wal-Mart, Target, Kmart, and T.J.Maxx/Marshalls—not to mention all the various Internet discount sites—succeed by offering low prices. It's hard to compete with these price discounters over time, especially when they offer good service as well.

Service organizations also compete on price. Note, for example, Southwest Airlines' success with its low-price strategy. The same is true of H&R Block in income tax preparation services, Hyatt Legal Plans for legal services, and Motel 6 or Red Roof Inns for motel-room rentals.

Price competition is getting fiercer as Internet firms like mySimon.com help consumers find the best prices on a wide range of items. Look up BotSpot (www.botspot.com) for other companies that do price searches. As you learned earlier, prices are easy to match, so most retailers have to turn to other strategies—like service—to win and keep customers.

SERVICE COMPETITION

A second competitive strategy for retailers is service. Retail service involves putting the customer first. This requires all frontline people to be courteous and accommodating to customers. Retail service also means follow-up service such as on-time delivery, guarantees, and fast installation. Consumers are frequently willing to pay a little more for goods and services if the retailer offers outstanding service.

The benchmark companies in this regard include Macy's, Lord & Taylor, and Nordstrom. These retailers show that if you hire good people, train them well, and pay them fairly, you will be able to provide world-class service. Service organizations that have successfully competed using service include Scandinavian Airlines, Tokyo's Imperial Hotel, and Florida Power & Light. Sheraton hotels are offering your money back or a free night if you aren't happy with their services. Small service providers, such as The Hair Cuttery, Sam's Auto Repair, and Beautiful Nails, also compete by offering superior service.

LOCATION COMPETITION

Many services, especially convenience services like banks and dry cleaners, compete effectively by having good locations. That's why you find automated teller machines in convenient places such as supermarkets and train stations. Many fast-food stores, such as Burger King and Pizza Hut, now have locations on college campuses so that students can reach them quickly. Some dry cleaners pick up and deliver laundry at your home or business.

Often, nothing is more convenient than shopping online: You don't have to go outside at all and fight crowds or traffic. But online retailers have to learn to deliver goods faster and more reliably and handle returns better, or they will lose the advantage of convenience. Also, many consumers are nervous about giving their credit card numbers to online retailers for fear of having them stolen. Each of these problems will be solved someday, but meanwhile competition between brick-and-mortar retailers and online retailers will intensify.

SELECTION COMPETITION

A fourth competitive strategy for retailers is selection. Selection is the offering of a wide variety of items in the same product category. Category killer stores offer wide selection at competitive prices. They are called category killers because they are so competitive that they usually overpower smaller competitors that don't offer comparable selection or price and drive them out of business. Tower Records carries over 75,000 titles. Borders Books carries some 150,000 different titles. Sport Mart carries over 100,000 sporting goods items. PetSmart and other pet food superstores have some 10,000 items each.

Despite their initial success, many category killer stores are in turn being killed by discount department stores like Wal-Mart. Wal-Mart has become a huge challenge to Toys "R" Us. Consumers are finding it more convenient to shop for multiple items at stores like Costco rather than go out of their way to find stores selling only sports equipment or only pet supplies. Thus, location may be more important than selection for consumer items.

Internet stores can offer products from dozens of suppliers and offer almost unlimited selection (e.g., Amazon.com). Small retailers sometimes compete by offering wide selection within one or a few categories of items. Thus, you have successful small stores that sell nothing but coffee beans or party products. Small retailers also compete by offering personalized service. Restoration Hardware, with stores in the Bay Area of California and around the country, is one store that has survived the competition with Home Depot and the other giant lumber and hardware stores. Restoration was able to succeed by offering consumers products that couldn't be found in the other stores.

Service organizations that compete successfully on selection include Blockbuster (wide selection of rental videos and DVDs), most community colleges (wide selection of courses), and Schwab Mutual Funds (hundreds of funds).

ENTERTAINMENT COMPETITION

The Internet may be a convenient place to shop, but it can't possibly be as much fun as a brick-and-mortar store designed to provide entertainment as well as a place to buy things. When you approach a Jordan's furniture store in New England, for example, you notice that the design team has recreated French Quarter facades like those in New Orleans. As you walk in, you see a Louis Armstrong look-alike playing in a room that resembles Bourbon Street (in New Orleans). There is even a replica of a riverboat that features live music every weekend. You can eat a free fresh-baked cookie and, if it's raining, you can get an umbrella.

One mall calls it "shoppertainment." In any case, it's making it more fun to shop at stores and malls. At Bass Pro Shops, you are treated to giant aquariums, waterfalls, trout ponds, rifle ranges, and classes in everything from ice fishing to conservation. In San Francisco, Sony's Metreon is a Sony Entertainment Center with a restaurant, an IMAX theater, and lots of exciting video games to play. You get to see and experience all the latest high-tech equipment and have fun at the same time. Vans, Inc., a sporting goods retailer, opened a 60,000-square-foot skate park and off-road bicycle track at Ontario Mills Mall.

lecture link 15-7

PARTY ON

The days of the neighborhood Tupperware parties are over, but other types of home selling are making a rebound. Twenty years ago, most home-party purchasers were friends of the hostess and could be counted on for sales anyway. The new generation product parties are lively gatherings guided by a consultant who doesn't necessarily know the partygoers.

Pampered Chef embraced the home shopping party. The company, which offers kitchen-supply parties, was so successful that Warren Buffet purchased it in 2002. The same year, Crayola introduced its Big Yellow Box program, bringing kids and parents together to make crafts. Tommy Tools attracts women customers with woman-friendly products such as lightweight toolboxes and scaled-down hacksaws.

Lane Nemeth's house parties feature special seat belts, chewable rubber toys, and venison-jerky treats. Her products are targeted at the parents of a new breed of child: pets. Petlane, her pet-products company, reached $1 million sales in 2005, up from $300,000 the year before. Her sales team of 225 "pet advisors" in 12 states and expanding every year.

She is banking on American's increasing obsession with their pets, which is fueling the 6% annual growth in the $34 billion pet-care industry. "Pets are the new kids," she says, noting that young couples see pets as a parenting test run. Her sales people teach pet care to their customers. Nemeth's obsession is teaching pet owners how pets communicate.

Nemeth is no stranger to success in direct sales. Inspired in 1978 to find stimulating toys for her daughter, she started Discovery Toys. The educational-toy company grew from a $5,000 garage-based enterprise into an international direct sales company with $100 million in revenues by 1997, when she sold it to Avon.[iii]

lecture link 15-8

WHEN THE SUPPLY CHAIN BREAKS

The supply chain is only as strong as its weakest link. The unexpected closure of Clark Foam in December 2005 clearly illustrates this. Clark, a Laguna Niguel, California, company, mass-produced foam blocks used to create customized surfboards. Gordon Clark pioneered the technology in 1961. The foam blanks, which cost between $50 and $90, are bought by custom surfboard makers. The boards are first smoothed and shaved with sandpaper and shavers. Painters then add color and design before the board is covered in fiberglass.

Clark enjoyed a virtual monopoly on the blocks (called "blanks"). It supplied unshaped blanks for about 90% of all custom-made boards purchased worldwide. Before the Clark closure, custom-made boards sold for between $300 and $800. Suddenly manufacturers were scrambling to purchase the last supplies of the polyurethane blanks. The price for a classic longboard rose from $100 to $1,000 shortly after Clark closed.

Clark Foam closed because California's Orange County Fire Authority had repeatedly reported Clark Foam to other government agencies, including the EPA. The government agency cited the company for its continued use of the toxic chemical toluene diisocyanate, which can cause severe and chronic lung problems.

Clark finally shut down the facility of his own volition, rather than face the legal fallout. The media attention on Clark's closure focused light on this and other environmental problems associated with the production of surfboards, such as the use of polyester-based resins, which are harmful to the worker and emit noxious fumes. Most of the industry, long silent on the fact that manufacturing a surfboard is a dirty process, was poised for change.

In the weeks following Clark's closure, board builders scrambled to find the remaining Clark blanks. They were even available on eBay. Bidding for blanks went as high as $50,000. Scraps of Clark Foam were even being sold as pieces of history, starting at $1.

Before the closure, Clark had churned out about 1,000 blanks a day. Gradually smaller producers like JustFoam in San Clemente began to ramp up production. JustFoam was able to increase daily production from 24 to 350.

But Clark's closure may turn out to be the best thing to happen to the sport. Surfers have been forced to find a new ride. A handful of small companies had already been working, some for up to 20 years, on cleaner surfboard-making technologies that would cost the same as the dirtier ones. But they couldn't find a hole in Clark's monopoly to successfully introduce a product. Among the contenders was Homeblown U.S., an independently owned six-employee foam producer that had developed a foam production system that was similar to Clark's but was safer to workers because it didn't emit volatile fumes.

Homeblown started in Britain in the late 1980s and held a 50% share of the market for blanks there. But Clark had such a dominant position in the market that it wasn't practical for Homeblown to open in the United States until the Clark factory closed.

Today, Homeblown has gained a toehold in the U.S. market—though it still produces only 75 to 100 foam blanks a day, compared to Clark's 1,000 a day production. It is ramping up its efforts to bring more sustainable surfboards into the market. The end of Clark's monopoly in surfboard blanks has paved the way for cleaner ways of making surfboards, with independent businesses taking the lead.

Companies like California's Firewire Surfboards and France's Salomon have caught the attention of high-ranking pro surfers by bringing innovative materials and construction methods to surfboards, something that already worked for skis, snowboards, and the wings of Boeing jetliners. The buzzwords are *flex memory,* the way a board snaps back into its original shape in a turn or maneuver, something that conventional polyurethane boards simply could not do. The new materials have a memory of the original curve, and they return to that curve very quickly.

The new composites are crafted from foams of varying densities as well as fiberglass, resins, carbon fibers, and wood in various configurations, some devised with sophisticated computer modeling. These materials have allowed designers to tinker with the board's outline, giving more or less curve, and fins, the design element critical for responsiveness and control.

Salomon, a brand famous for its skis and snowboards, introduced an "S-Core" design that creates a shock-absorber-like effect using foam stringers in a hollow carbon core, covered by a foam shell—an airplane wing on the water. High-ranking surfers love the new boards—they can be custom shaped, are 20% lighter, and last up to 10 times as long as foam boards.[iv]

lecture link 15-9

THE HIGH-TECH FUTURE OF FREIGHT

The freight railroad system is one of the country's earliest network businesses. And unlike so many other older national networks, such as the U.S. Post Office, that have had trouble adapting to the modern age, railroads continue to play a vital role in the shipping industry. In spite of its longevity the freight railroad system needs to initiate changes that will allow it to enjoy the benefits that this digital age can provide. In light of recent deadly train crashes, regulators and industry officials have been pushing railway companies to integrate technology more deeply into America's railways.

The biggest change arriving on the freight train scene is a new traffic system called positive train control (PTC). Onboard computers and GPS gear allow trains to be tracked by a central station and even stopped if an engineer misses a signal. Following a pair of major train crashes in 2008, the federal government mandated that PTC be implemented by 2015 on all major train lines that carry passengers or corrosive chemicals. Industry insiders estimate the system will cost $13 billion to install and maintain over the next 20 years.

Indeed, the soaring costs associated with upgrading have kept railway companies reluctant to change their entrenched ways on a wide scale. For example, a new type of electronically controlled brakes improves vastly on the air-based brakes used on locomotives for ages. Though the electronic system enhances handling and shortens braking distance, the cost and technical complication involved with installation will prevent widespread adoption at least for the near future. Other upgrades are too young to judge what kind of impact they'll eventually have on the industry. One process uses cameras to take a 360-degree picture of every car on a train in order to indentify mechanical problems early on. This so-called CAT scan for freight cars is currently being tested at the Transportation Technology Center in Colorado.[v]

critical thinking exercises

Name: ______________________

Date: ______________________

critical thinking exercise 15-1

TOP 100 RETAILERS

The National Retail Foundation's (NRF) website (www.nrf.com)[vi] contains numerous resources for retailers and people interested in a retailing career. The site also provides links to other sites related to retailing. (Sometimes the Web address for a location changes. You might need to search to find the exact location mentioned.)

NRF publishes an online magazine, *Stores*, that contains stories about successful retail stores, unique promotions, and retail statistics. It also publishes a listing of the year's top 100 retailers. Go to the *Stores* website (www.stores.org), navigate to the list of recent articles, and find the current listings for the Top 100 Retailers. Use the information presented there to fill in the information below.

1. Which retailer has the highest revenue for the current year? ______________________

   a. Where is the headquarters?

   b. Give the current year's **revenue** figure.

   c. Is this an increase or decrease from the previous year? By what percentage?

   d. Give the current year's **earnings**.

   e. How many stores does the company have?

critical thinking exercise 15-1 (continued)

2. Choose two other retail companies that you are familiar with and answer the same questions.

COMPANY 1: ____

a. Where is the headquarters?

b. Give the current year's **revenue** figure.

c. Is this an increase or decrease from the previous year? By what percentage?

d. Give the current year's **earnings**.

e. How many stores does the company have?

f. Why did you choose this company?

COMPANY 2: ____

a. Where is the headquarters?

b. Give the current year's **revenue** figure.

c. Is this an increase or decrease from the previous year? By what percentage?

d. Give the current year's **earnings**.

e. How many stores does the company have?

f. Why did you choose this company?

Name: ______________________________

Date: ______________________________

critical thinking exercise 15-2

FORMS OF UTILITY

The text discusses five types of utility created by marketing. For **one** of the companies below, describe how it creates each type of utility with its goods or services.

a. Albertsons Grocery

b. Barnes & Noble bookstore

c. Buzy B's Hair and Nail Styles

d. Disney World

e. H&R Block tax preparation service

f. DirecTV satellite service

g. *Time* magazine

Name: ______________________

Date: ______________________

critical thinking exercise 15-3
DISTRIBUTION CHANNELS

Let's find out about the kinds of distribution channels that manufacturers in your area use. Call or visit five manufacturers in your area and ask them the following questions. Record your answers on the chart below.

1. What is your main product?
2. How do you distribute your product to consumers? Do you use a direct channel (straight from you to consumers) or an indirect channel (through intermediaries)?
3. If you use wholesalers, what kind?

MANUFACTURER	MAIN PRODUCT	DISTRIBUTION CHANNEL DIRECT OR INDIRECT	WHOLESALERS

Name: ______________________________

Date: ______________________________

critical thinking exercise 15-4

RETAIL DISTRIBUTION STRATEGY

The text discusses three categories of retail distribution—intensive distribution, selective distribution, and exclusive distribution. For each of the categories, summarize the distribution strategy and give three examples of each that are *not* included in the text discussion.

INTENSIVE DISTRIBUTION

Summarize the strategy:

Example 1: ______________________________

Example 2: ______________________________

Example 3: ______________________________

SELECTIVE DISTRIBUTION

Summarize the strategy:

Example 1: ______________________________

Example 2: ______________________________

Example 3: ______________________________

EXCLUSIVE DISTRIBUTION

Summarize the strategy:

Example 1: ______________________________

Example 2: ______________________________

Example 3: ______________________________

Name: ___________________________

Date: ___________________________

critical thinking exercise 15-5

CAREERS IN DISTRIBUTION

What would a career in distribution involve? What are the educational requirements? The future job prospects?

The U.S. Bureau of Labor Statistics publishes the *Occupational Outlook Handbook*, a comprehensive analysis for thousands of careers. The handbook is available online at the Bureau's website (www.bls.gov/oco).[vii] (Sometimes the Web address for a location changes. You might need to search to find the exact location mentioned.)

Choose a career in one of the distribution-related fields, such as retail sales representative, wholesale sales representative, or manufacturing sales representative. Summarize below the information given in the *Handbook*.

1. Describe the nature of the work for this career.

2. What are the working conditions?

3. What training and qualifications are needed?

4. How many jobs are available in this career area?

5. What is the job outlook for the next decade?

6. What are the median annual earnings for this career?

Name: ____________________

Date: ____________________

critical thinking exercise 15-6

INTERNET AUCTIONS: BYPASSING THE RETAILER

The traditional method for consumers to purchase goods is through a retail outlet. Even electronic retailing involves an intermediary, the online retail store. But small sellers are now finding a new chain of distribution—direct to consumers through online auction sites such as eBay and Amazon.com. Go to the website for eBay (www.eBay.com).[viii] Search the site for fax machines offered for sale. (Sometimes the Web address for a location changes. You might need to search to find the exact location mentioned.)

1. Open two listings for fax machines: the least expensive offered and the most expensive. Choose items that have approximately 24 hours before expiration. Write down the description and current price bid. Why do you think sellers of the lower-priced item are asking such a low price?

2. Check the eBay site after 8 to 24 hours. How have the bids changed?

3. What type of payment is accepted for each of these items? How do these payment types differ from payment options at brick-and-mortar stores? Why?

4. What type of business would be able to use an online auction site effectively to sell its products?

5. eBay also offers an option for businesses to establish nonauction "eBay stores" to sell products through the website. What would be the advantages to a small business of establishing such a store rather than a brick-and-mortar store? Would there be any disadvantages? Explain.

bonus cases

bonus case 15-1

UNITED STATIONERS: OFFICE-SUPPLY INTERMEDIARY

The Internet has created rapid change in the sale and distribution of most goods. Perhaps nowhere is such change more apparent than in the office-supply market. By the early 1990s, half of the smaller stationers in the United States had gone out of business—about 6,000 stores. Staples, Office Depot, and other large retailers, many of them with online services, rapidly replaced them. So, what happened to companies like United Stationers that supplied those small stationers with the products they sold?

When Randall Larrimore became the company's chief executive in 1994, United Stationers wasn't doing too well. Larrimore was determined to reverse the company's fortunes. He modernized United Stationers by using the latest supply-chain concepts.

Come with us to Ketchum, Idaho, to visit a stationer called Business as Usual. It's a small store; only 1,500 square feet. Despite its size, its prices are competitive with those of not only the office superstores in nearby Twin Falls but also online sellers. The reason Business as Usual remains competitive is that United Stationers can readily provide it with some 35,000 items from more than 500 manufacturers at prices lower than those it could get by ordering directly from the manufacturers. United Stationers can purchase the products from the manufacturers more cheaply than small stores because it orders in such large volumes. It can then pass on part of the savings to its customers.

If Business as Usual places an order to United Stationers by 4 p.m., the store gets the supplies by the next day. Even better, Business as Usual can have United Stationers send the supplies directly to its customers. By providing a large inventory and speedy delivery low prices, United Stationers has made it possible for small companies to survive. It was Randall Larrimore who helped make all this possible.

Staples and Office Depot also use the services of United Stationers. These superstores order in such large volumes that they buy most of their products directly from manufacturers. However, there are many products that are not very popular but that superstores must carry in order to become one-stop shopping centers for office supplies. Since ordering these products directly from the manufacturer is not efficient, the superstores turn to United Stationers. United Stationers also supplies many of the office products that get sold online by Dell Computer and 125 other companies.

In the United States, there are hundreds of thousands of suppliers like United Stationers, providing similar services to retailers of products ranging from automobile suppliers to zoo shop souvenirs.

The whole system for distributing goods has changed over the last decade or so. The advent of online retailers has altered the way customers buy and the way manufacturers sell. The Internet has also changed the way goods are distributed.[ix]

discussion questions for bonus case 15-1

1. What does this case teach you about the need for constant change in marketing?

2. Does this case indicate that intermediaries are becoming less or more important to marketers?

3. What do you see as the future of online marketing in general and B2B online marketing in particular?

notes on discussion questions for bonus case 15-1

1. *What does this case teach you about the need for constant change in marketing?*

   If United Stationers had not changed the way it functioned, it would be out of business, just like the thousands of small stationery stores it serviced. Business is constantly changing, and the Internet is only making such changes come more rapidly. There are many disruptions caused in the channel of distribution, but just as many opportunities are created.

2. *Does this case indicate that intermediaries are becoming less or more important to marketers?*

   Intermediaries will always be needed as long as they can provide a service faster or cheaper or better than a company could do it by itself. There will always be a need for FedEx and UPS and other intermediaries. There will always be a need for retailers, but their character may change dramatically. Retailing has always been in a state of flux, and will continue to be. Intermediaries are not any less or more important; they are equally important. They just have different tasks to perform.

3. *What do you see as the future of online marketing in general and B2B online marketing in particular?*

   Online marketing can only continue to grow. Just watch the growth of eBay, for example. The same will be true for B2B sales. The failures of the past are no indication of the future. Growth simply came too fast, and there was not enough planning. People learn from mistakes, however, and the future of online marketing looks bright indeed.

bonus case 15-2

STARTING AN ONLINE BUSINESS

When Joseph Cohen's parents left for a weeklong trip out of town, the 14-year-old Brooklyn didn't plan a big parents-free party. He called a cab, collected the money he had saved up working for his dad, and drove into Manhattan. He returned with $3,000 worth of Christmas decorations, toys, and lights. Joseph put the goods online, adopting the name of his family's hardware store, Polsteins.

For about $1,000 a month, Joseph opened a Yahoo store account to handle online payments. He also signed onto some Web ad services to generate traffic. Every time someone keyed "Christmas lights" into a Web search engine, Joseph paid 10¢ to 50¢ for a link to Polsteins.com. By the time his parents returned, he had doubled his money and bought more goods to sell.

Soon after selling out the Christmas items, he put a $50 battery-operated Pinocchio doll on his site; 1,000 orders came in. Another early success was a $10 animated kung fu hamster that 2,000 people ordered. Within three years, Joseph's operation was selling $1.9 million worth of goods annually.

Despite his entrepreneurial ability, Joseph is still a teenager and still has to attend school. He runs his online enterprise out of his office/warehouse after school. He does admit to taking "sick days" from school when business is heavy.

He has made some mistakes, however. The summer he turned 15, Joseph took his eye off the business, doing what kids do during the summer. He went to travel camp, visiting a different North American city each week. At the time, Polsteins was selling a 50-foot rolled flat hose for $20. While he was away for six weeks, thousands of orders poured in and were automatically put on back order.

When he returned from camp, Joseph rushed out the $30,000 worth of back orders, only to discover that the hoses were defective. Once they were returned, he had to repay customers, while applying for refunds from the manufacturer. And because no one had been minding the online store in his absence, the hoses had been left on the site all summer, running up $43,000 in ad charges, built up every time someone clicked on "garden hose." He stopped the ads, negotiated discounts on shipping, and spent the next three months paying off his debts and rebuilding his store.

A surprise best seller: mason jars for canning. These jars had become hard to find, and Joseph was able to sell thousands to people canning summer fruits and vegetables. Polsteins.com is now the largest customer for Ball and Kerr jars.

Recently Polsteins.com established a partnership with its giant former rival Amazon.com. The company also changed its name to HomeandBeyond.com and announced the introduction of a home shopping catalog filled with household tips and recipes to be called @Home. Cohen, who is now company CEO, said, "Changing our name from Polsteins.com to HomeandBeyond.com allows us to better brand our site as one dedicated to home shopping."[x]

discussion questions for bonus case 15-2

1. If you were to start an online business, what kind of products would you be interested in selling? What would you anticipate to be your biggest problem?

2. What do you see as the advantages of starting an online store versus a brick-and-mortar store?

3. What are the advantages and disadvantages of starting an online business while you are still in school?

notes on discussion questions for bonus case 15-2

1. *If you were to start an online business, what kind of products would you be interested in selling? What would you anticipate to be your biggest problem?*

   Students may enjoy hearing the ideas of other students about what could be sold online. In fact, almost anything can be sold online, including houses, cars, and more. Often the biggest problem is learning the best way to ship products. Ensuring payment is another.

2. *What do you see as the advantages of starting an online store versus a brick-and-mortar store?*

   Advantages include the ease of start-up, including start-up fees. It is easier to sell a wide variety of things online; there is almost no limit. Hours of operation are 24/7, but you don't have to work all of that time. In short, there is the potential for more free time. When lots of people want to buy at the same time, you don't experience long lines, but can answer orders one at a time. Students may come up with more and more creative answers.

3. *What are the advantages and disadvantages of starting an online business while you are still in school?*

   Students may enjoy brainstorming this answer. They should consider things like lower grades in school because of less study time, less free time for whatever, more responsibility and stress, less desire for advanced degrees, and more.

bonus case 15-3

MULTILEVEL MARKETING

Multilevel marketing often doesn't get the respect it deserves in marketing literature. When multilevel marketing companies succeed, their growth is often unbelievable. At least six multilevel marketing companies have reached the $500 million level in sales.

Multilevel marketing companies work like this: The founders begin by recruiting a few good people to go out and find managers to sell their products and to recruit other supervisors. These supervisors then recruit additional salespeople. That is, 20 people recruit 6 people each. That means 120 salespeople. Those people then recruit 6 people each, and you have 720 salespeople. If in turn those people all recruit 6 people, you then have almost 5,000 salespeople. All supervisors earn commissions on what they sell as well as on what everyone under them sells. When you get thousands of salespeople selling for you, commissions can be quite large. One company promotes the fact that 1% from 100 salespeople is as good as 100% from one successful salesperson. Companies often add new products or expand to other countries to keep a continuous growth pattern.

Distribution under multilevel marketing is relatively easy. Often the salespeople will carry inventory in their own homes and deliver products as ordered. Many companies also offer direct shipping to customers using UPS or other delivery firms.

Marketers cannot ignore the success of this sales and distribution strategy. Nu Skin (a seller of health and beauty products) alone will soon have $1 billion in sales. Looking for more growth, the company started a new division, Interior Design Nutrition, to make and sell vitamins and weight-control products. Amway, perhaps one of the most well-known multilevel marketers, has chosen the international route for growth; recently, its sales of home and personal care products increased by over $1 billion in one year.

discussion questions for bonus case 15-3

1. Amway and others have been successful in Japan. To what other countries could you lead such companies so that you could become a top earner?

2. What will happen as multilevel marketing distributors begin selling and recruiting others using the latest in technology such as the Internet?

3. Why do you suppose multilevel marketing hasn't received the same acceptance as other retail innovations such as catalog sales? What could the companies do to improve their image?

4. If multilevel marketing works so well for beauty and health care products, why not use the same concept to sell other products?

notes on discussion questions for bonus case 15-3

1. *Amway and others have been successful in Japan. To what other countries could you lead such companies so that you could become a top earner?*

   Many developing countries would have the consumer purchasing power for network marketing to be successful. Central and Southern American countries come to mind, as do the eastern European countries formerly a part of the Soviet Union.

2. *What will happen as multilevel marketing distributors begin selling and recruiting others using the latest in technology such as the Internet?*

   It will be interesting to see what answers your students come up with. So much of network marketing is dependent on personal sales that impersonal Internet selling does not seem feasible. Many network marketers use telemarketing rather than in-home visits. There may be other possibilities.

3. *Why do you suppose multilevel marketing hasn't received the same acceptance as other retail innovations such as catalog sales? What could the companies do to improve their image?*

   Unfortunately, many multilevel marketing schemes have been little more than fraud. The term *pyramid sales* still evokes the image of unscrupulous marketers and risky investments. In order to make multilevel marketing more acceptable, salespeople will need to convince customers of the value of their product. One easy way to start would be to offer a money-back guarantee in writing.

4. *If multilevel marketing works so well for beauty and health care products, why not use the same concept to sell other products?*

   Any product with a high profit margin is a possible candidate for multilevel marketing. There are some products that people would rather buy in the store (for example, feminine hygiene products) and don't want to face a human. Others have a high time utility, and the distribution lag would be a problem. Americans, however, are very creative in their approach to competition, so anything is possible.

endnotes

[i] *Source:* "John Elliott, "Why There Are No Indian Wal-Marts," *Fortune*, May 25, 2006.

[ii] *Source:* Matthew Boyle, "How Acosta Stocks Your Grocer's Shelf," *Bloomberg Businessweek*, March 24, 2011.

[iii] *Sources*: Coco Masters, Let's Pawty!" *Time Inside Business*, May 2005; Alyssa Danigells, "Party One," *Fast Company*, May 2006.

[iv] *Sources*: Associated Press, *The Clarion-Ledger*, December 10, 2005; Robert Whitfield, "Clark Foam Surfboard Blanks on eBay," *The Orange County Register,* December 15, 2005; Nancy Luna, "Former Clark Foam Employees Say They've Formed a New Foam-Making Factory," *The Orange County Register*, March 4, 2005; Nancy Luna, "Buyers Flood Clark Foam Auction," *The Orange County Register,* March 9, 2006; Coco Masters, "Surfing's New Wave," *Time*, July 17, 2006.

[v] *Source:* Daniel Machalaba, "The Little Engine Really Could," *The Wall Street Journal*, May 23, 2011.

[vi] The Internet is a dynamic, changing information source. Web links noted of this manual were checked at the time of publication, but content may change over time. Please review the website before recommending it to your students.

[vii] The Internet is a dynamic, changing information source. Web links noted of this manual were checked at the time of publication, but content may change over time. Please review the website before recommending it to your students.

[viii] The Internet is a dynamic, changing information source. Web links noted of this manual were checked at the time of publication, but content may change over time. Please review the website before recommending it to your students.

[ix] *Sources*: Ashlea Eblin, "Paper Tiger," *Forbes*, February 21, 2000, pp. 71–74; "ebuyxpress.com, Leading B2B MRO Procurement Web Site, Cuts Cost of Goods 20% by Eliminating Distribution Layer and Aggregating Millions in Buying Power," *Business Wire*, May 2, 2000; Marshall L. Fisher, Ananth Raman, and Anna Sheen McClelland, "Rocket Science Retailing Is Almost Here: Are You Ready?" *Harvard Business Review*, July–August 2000, pp. 115–124.

[x] *Sources*: Phyllis Berman, "The Merchant of Bay Ridge," *Forbes*, December 27, 2004; "Polsteins.com to Operate Under New Name: HomeandBeyond.com," PRWeb, October 17, 2005; "Polsteins.com Announces Partnership with Amazon.com, www.polsteins.com, October 17, 2005; www.homeandbeyond.com/.

Using Effective Promotions

chapter 16

what's new in this edition

additions to the 10th edition:

- Getting to Know Andrew Mason, CEO of Groupon
- Name That Company: Dr Pepper
- Subsection Using Social Media to Monitor Ad Effectiveness added to section Advertising: Information, Persuading, and Reminding
- Social Media in Business: Social Media Complements Other Promotions
- Spotlight on Small Business: Fresh-Baked Promotion
- Reaching Beyond Our Borders: Promotion in Rural India
- Making Ethical Decisions: Electronic Ethics
- Video case

revisions to the 10th edition:

- Text was revised to eliminate redundancy and tighten discussions.
- Statistical data and examples throughout the chapter were updated to reflect current information.

deletions from the 9th edition:

- Getting to Know Laurel Richie, Chief Marketing Officer of the Girl Scouts
- Name That Company: Garden.com
- Thinking Green
- Reaching Beyond Our Borders

brief chapter outline and learning goals

chapter 16

Using Effective Promotions

Getting To Know ANDREW MASON of GROUPON

learning goal 1

Identify the new and traditional tools that make up the promotion mix.

I. PROMOTION AND THE PROMOTION MIX

learning goal 2

Contrast the advantages and disadvantages of various advertising media, including the Internet and social media.

II. ADVERTISING: INFORMING, PERSUADING, AND REMINDING

- **A. Television Advertising**
- **B. Product Placement**
- **C. Infomercials**
- **D. Online Advertising**
- **E. Using Social Media to Monitor Ad Effectiveness**
- **F. Global Advertising**

learning goal 3

Illustrate the steps of the B2B and B2C selling processes.

III. PERSONAL SELLING: PROVIDING PERSONAL ATTENTION

- **A. Steps in the Selling Process**
- **B. The Business-to-Consumer (B2C) Sales Process**

learning goal 4

Describe the role of the public relations department, and show how publicity fits in that role.

IV. PUBLIC RELATIONS: BUILDING RELATIONSHIPS

- **A. Publicity: The Talking Arm of PR**

learning goal 5

Assess the effectiveness of various forms of sales promotion, including sampling

V. SALES PROMOTION: GIVING BUYERS INCENTIVES

learning goal 6

Show how word of mouth, e-mail marketing, viral marketing, blogging, podcasting, and mobile marketing work.

VI. WORD OF MOUTH AND OTHER PROMOTIONAL TOOLS

A. Viral Marketing

B. Blogging

C. Podcasting

D. E-Mail Promotions

E. Mobile Media

VII. MANAGING THE PROMOTION MIX: PUTTING IT ALL TOGETHER

A. Promotional Strategies

VIII. SUMMARY

lecture outline

Getting to Know ANDREW MASON of GROUPON

Mason's Groupon combines social networking with discounting. The site has grown faster than any Web company in history and Mason has even turned down offers of $6 billion for his company. Mason's simplicity in running his site is what is credited for its success. There are many competitors out there, which has led to Groupon expanding into mobile marketing.

This beverage company has 8.5 million Facebook friends. It posts two daily messages and then monitors how many times each message is reviewed, how many times it's shared, and what the fan response to the messages are. It also uses Facebook to test potential ads be-fore airing them on traditional media, like TV. Name that company

(Students should read the chapter before guessing the company's name: Dr Pepper)

learning goal 1

Identify the new and traditional tools that make up the promotion mix.

I. PROMOTION AND THE PROMOTION MIX

A. **PROMOTION** consists of all the techniques sellers use to motivate people to buy their products or services.

1. These tools include advertising, personal selling, public relations, and sales promotion.
2. The combination of promotional tools an organization uses is called its ***PROMOTION MIX.***

B. ***INTEGRATED MARKETING COMMUNICATION (IMC)*** is a technique that combines all the promotional tools into one comprehensive and unified promotional strategy.

lecture notes

PPT 16-1
Chapter Title

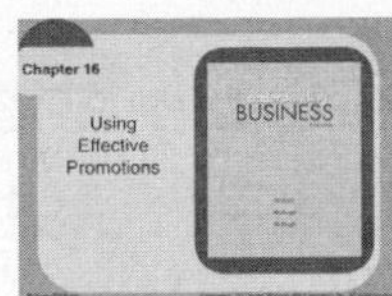

PPT 16-2
Learning Goals

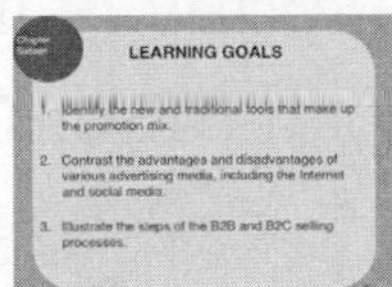

(See complete PowerPoint slide notes on page 16.42.)

PPT 16-3
Learning Goals

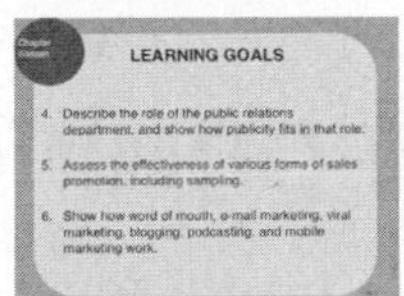

(See complete PowerPoint slide notes on page 16.42.)

PPT 16-4
Andrew Mason

(See complete PowerPoint slide notes on page 16.43.)

bonus case 16-1
GROUPON'S TIGHT WALK TOWARD A RICH FUTURE

Andrew Mason made headlines when he turned down a $6 billion buyout. (See the complete case, discussion questions, and suggested answers beginning on page 16.73 of this manual.)

PPT 16-5
Name That Company

(See complete PowerPoint slide notes on page 16.43.)

lecture link 16-1
MURPHY'S LAWS OF MARKETING

The study of marketing doesn't always have to be serious and academic. For a good shot of irreverence, try *Murphy's Laws* by Arthur Bloch. (See the complete lecture link on page 16.59 in this manual.)

PPT 16-6
Promotion in an Organization

TEXT FIGURE 16.1
The Traditional Promotion Mix
(Text page 436)

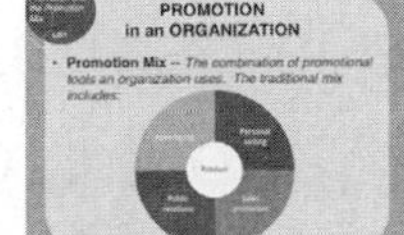

(See complete PowerPoint slide notes on page 16.43.)

PPT 16-7
Integrated Marketing Communication (IMC)

(See complete PowerPoint slide notes on page 16.44.)

1. All promotional tools and company resources are used to build better relationships with customers.
2. The emphasis today is integrating traditional media with social media.

learning goal 2

Contrast the advantages and disadvantages of various advertising media, including the Internet and social media.

II. ADVERTISING: INFORMING, PERSUADING, AND REMINDING

A. ***ADVERTISING*** is paid, nonpersonal communication through various media by organizations and individuals who are in some way identified in the advertising message.

1. **PROPAGANDA** is nonpersonal communication that does not have an identified sponsor.
2. Total ad volume exceeds $241 billion yearly.
   a. **DIRECT MAIL** is the number one advertising medium in terms of total dollars spent.
   b. **TELEVISION** is number two.
   c. **NEWSPAPERS** are falling because of mobile media.
3. The public **BENEFITS FROM ADVERTISING**:
   a. Advertising is informative–it provides information about products, prices, features, and so on.

SPOTLIGHT ON
small
business
(Text page 437)

PPT 16-8
Fresh-Baked
Promotion

(See complete PowerPoint slide notes on page 16.44.)

PPT 16-9
Steps in a Promotional Campaign

TEXT FIGURE 16.2
Steps in a Promotional Campaign
(Text page 437)

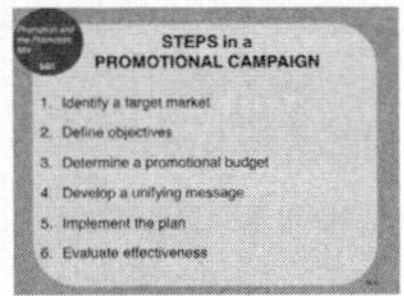

(See complete PowerPoint slide notes on page 16.44.)

PPT 16-10
Classic Campaigns

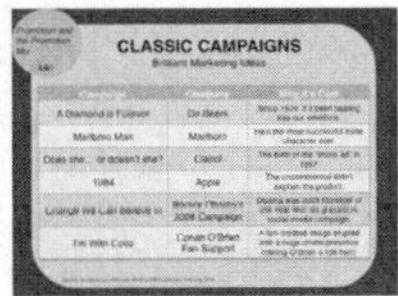

(See complete PowerPoint slide notes on page 16.45.)

PPT 16-11
Advertising in the Firm

(See complete PowerPoint slide notes on page 16.45.)

PPT 16-12
Impact of Advertising

(See complete PowerPoint slide notes on page 16.45.)

PPT 16-13
Social Advertising

(See complete PowerPoint slide notes on page 16.46.)

PPT 16-14
Major Categories of Advertising

TEXT FIGURE 16.3
Major Categories of Advertising
(Text page 438)

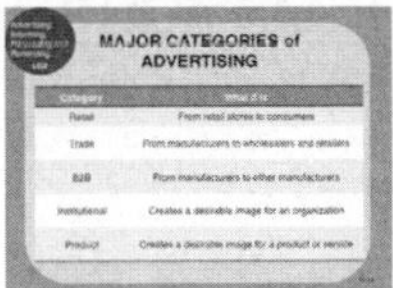

(See complete PowerPoint slide notes on page 16.46.)

  b. Advertising provides us with free TV and radio programs, because advertisers cover most of the production costs.
  c. Advertising costs cover the major costs of producing newspapers and magazines.
4. Newspapers, radio, and the Yellow Pages are especially attractive to **LOCAL ADVERTISERS.**
5. Marketers must choose which media and which programs will best reach the audience they desire.
  a. **RADIO ADVERTISING** is less expensive than TV advertising and often reaches people when they have few distractions.
6. Mobile marketing can include text messages, reminders, and recipes.
7. Appealing to consumers through green marketing has also been successful.

B. **TELEVISION ADVERTISING**
1. TV has many advantages to national advertisers, but it is expensive.
2. However, few other media can **REACH AS MANY PEOPLE** with such impact.
3. TV advertising is still a dominant medium despite growth in alternative media advertising.
4. New services, such as video on demand and DVRs, make it difficult for TV advertisers to reach consumers.

PPT 16-15
Major Categories of Advertising

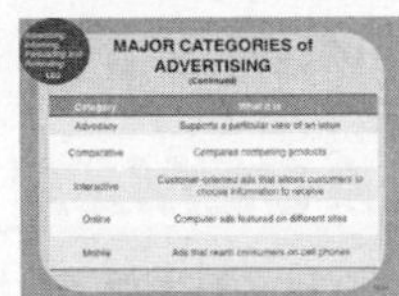

(See complete PowerPoint slide notes on page 16.46.)

PPT 16-16
Advertising Expenditures by Media in $ Millions

TEXT FIGURE 16.4
Advertising Expenditure by Media (in millions of dollars)
(Text page 439)

(See complete PowerPoint slide notes on page 16.47.)

PPT 16-17
Dear Mr. Postman . . .

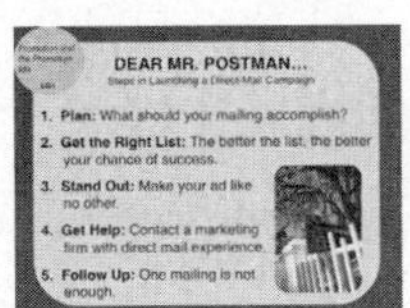

(See complete PowerPoint slide notes on page 16.47.)

TEXT FIGURE 16.5
Advantages and Disadvantages of Various Advertising Media
(Text page 440)

This text figure presents the advantages and disadvantages of various advertising media to the advertiser.

PPT 16-18
Match Game

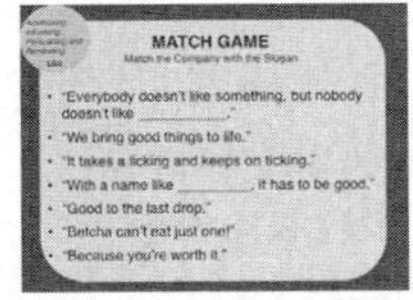

(See complete PowerPoint slide notes on page 16.47.)

lecture link 16-2
EFFECTIVE ADVERTISING: CELEBRITY VOICE-OVERS

Celebrity voice-overs are effective in reaching consumers, but are most effective when consumers can't quite identify the celebrity. (See the complete lecture link on page 16.60 in this manual.)

PPT 16-19
It's a Dog's Life

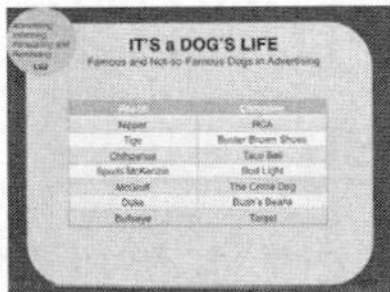

(See complete PowerPoint slide notes on page 16.48.)

PPT 16-20
Popular Advertising Media

(See complete PowerPoint slide notes on page 16.48.)

C. **PRODUCT PLACEMENT**

1. ***PRODUCT PLACEMENT*** is putting products into TV shows and movies where they will be seen.
2. Another type of placement puts virtual products into video games.

D. **INFOMERCIALS**

1. An ***INFOMERCIAL*** is a full-length TV program devoted exclusively to promoting goods and services.
2. They are so successful because they show the product in great detail.
3. A half-hour infomercial is the equivalent of sending your best salespeople into a person's home.
4. Some products, such as real estate programs and work-out tapes, are hard to sell without showing testimonials.

E. **ONLINE ADVERTISING**

1. Some advertisers are putting their ads online.
   a. Marketers can reach customers as they are researching their product through advertising on popular online sites.
   b. If users click through an ad to the website, the company gets to interact with the customer.
   c. The goal is to **GET CUSTOMERS AND POTENTIAL CUSTOMERS TO A WEBSITE** where they can learn more about the company and its products.

lecture link 16-3
PRODUCT PLACEMENT IN POP

Product placement is not just for television anymore. Products are now mentioned and shown within pop songs and their videos. (See the complete lecture link on page 16.60 in this manual.)

PPT 16-21
Let's Go to the Movies

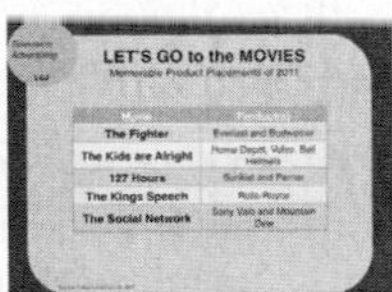

(See complete PowerPoint slide notes on page 16.48.)

PPT 16-22
Infomercials and Online Advertising

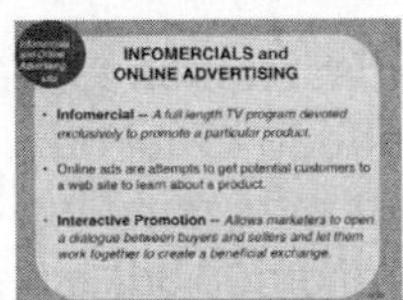

(See complete PowerPoint slide notes on page 16.49.)

PPT 16-23
Infomercial Hall of Fame

(See complete PowerPoint slide notes on page 16.49.)

critical thinking exercise 16-1
ADVERTISING ON GOOGLE

A popular method of Internet advertising is buying an ad on a Web search engine such as Google. This Internet exercise lets students explore exactly what this involves. (See complete exercise on page 16.65 of this manual.)

critical thinking exercise 16-2
ADVERTISING APPEALS

This exercise explores the different advertising appeals that marketers use in television advertising. (See complete exercise on page 16.66 of this manual.)

critical thinking exercise 16-3
IDENTIFYING PRODUCT PLACEMENT

This exercise asks students to watch prime-time television to identify product placements in television shows. (See complete exercise on page 16.68 of this manual.)

PPT 16-24
Online Experience

(See complete PowerPoint slide notes on page 16.49.)

2. **E-MAIL MARKETING** has become a huge component of online advertising.
3. However, advertisers have to be careful not to overuse it because customers can rebel.
4. ***INTERACTIVE PROMOTION*** is a promotion process that allows marketers to go beyond a monologue, where sellers tried to persuade buyers to buy things, to a dialogue in which buyers and sellers can work together to create mutually beneficial exchange relationships.
5. **TECHNOLOGY** has improved the speed and potential of Internet dialogues.
   a. Many companies provide online videos, chat rooms, and other services in a virtual store where customer can ask questions, examine goods, and buy products.
   b. The Internet is fundamentally changing the way marketers work with customers.
   c. The current trend in Internet marketing is to **BUILD RELATIONSHIPS** with customers over time.
   d. *Text example: Vita-Mix and K-Tec used interactive promotion to sell food blenders.*
6. Advertisers can track how many people click through the commercial and what websites they read and watch.

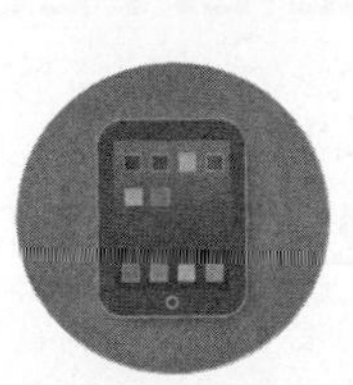

social media in business
(Text page 443)

PPT 16-25
Social Media Complements Other Promotion

(See complete PowerPoint slide notes on page 16.50.)

PPT 16-26
Social Scammers

(See complete PowerPoint slide notes on page 16.50)

lecture link 16-4
RANKING TV OUTSIDE THE NIELSEN SPECTRUM

Our favorite shows can now be seen on our favorite devices and Optimedia is there to redo the current rating system. (See the complete lecture link on page 16.61 of this manual.)

PPT 16-27
Monitoring Ad Effectiveness

(See complete PowerPoint slide notes on page 16.50.)

PPT 16-28
Socially Superior

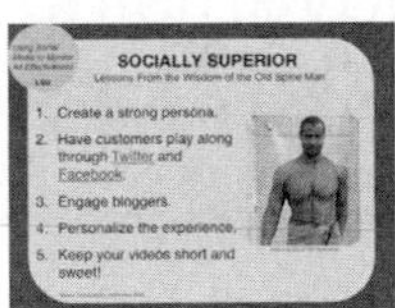

(See complete PowerPoint slide notes on page 16.51.)

MAKING ethical decisions
(Text page 445)

PPT 16-29
Electronic Ethics

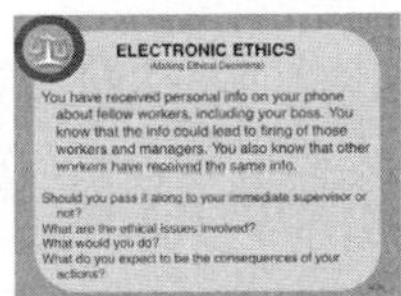

(See complete PowerPoint slide notes on page 16.51.)

F. **USING SOCIAL MEDIA TO MONITOR AD EFFECTIVENESS**

1. Social media have made it possible for companies to **test ads** before airing them.
2. *The text uses the example of Dr. Pepper's Facebook page.*
3. Social media also allow **top managers** into the customer–company dialogue.

G. **GLOBAL ADVERTISING**

1. **GLOBAL ADVERTISING** refers to developing a product and promotional strategy that can be implemented worldwide.
2. Because of differences in culture, language, and buying habits, promotional efforts designed specifically for individual countries may work best.
3. Getting the words right in international advertising is critical, but tricky.
4. International advertising calls for researching **THE WANTS AND NEEDS OF PEOPLE** in each country.
5. Even in the U.S., selected groups are large enough and different enough to call for specially designed promotions.
6. Advertising today is evolving from **GLOBALISM** (one ad for everyone in the world) to **REGIONALISM** (specific ads for each country or for specific groups within a country).

lecture link 16-5
AS SEEN ON SOCIAL MEDIA

Guthy-Renker, an infomercial powerhouse, is turning to social media to advertise products for younger audiences. (See complete lecture link on page 16.61 of this manual.)

PPT 16-30
Global Advertising

(See complete PowerPoint slide notes on page 16.51.)

critical thinking exercise 16-4
ETHICS IN ADVERTISING

The American Association of Advertising Agencies is the professional organization representing the major advertising agencies. Its website provides guidelines for ethical behavior in advertising. (See complete exercise on page 16.69 of this manual.)

critical thinking exercise 16-5
DESIGNING A WEBSITE

A well-designed website is a powerful promotional tool. This exercise asks students to design a basic website—developing an overall message, developing interesting visual features, and building a basic page hierarchy. (See complete exercise on page 16.70 of this manual.)

REACHING BEYOND our borders
(Text page 446)

PPT 16-31
Promotion in Rural India

(See complete PowerPoint slide notes on page 16.52.)

lecture outline

learning goal 3

Illustrate the steps of the B2B and B2C selling processes.

III. PERSONAL SELLING: PROVIDING PERSONAL ATTENTION

A. ***PERSONAL SELLING*** is the face-to-face presentation and promotion of products and services.

1. It also involves searching out prospects and providing follow-up service after the sale.
2. Effective selling today is more than persuading others to buy; it is helping them **SATISFY THEIR WANTS AND NEEDS.**
3. Salespeople now use **TECHNOLOGY,** such as the Internet, laptops, and iPads, to help customers and to complete the sale.
4. The benefit of personal selling is having a person help you complete a transaction.
5. Companies that retain salespeople must train them to be effective, efficient, and helpful.
6. The average cost of a single sales call to a potential B2B buyer is about $400.

B. **STEPS IN THE SELLING PROCESS**

1. **CUSTOMER RELATIONSHIP MANAGEMENT (CRM) SOFTWARE** is becoming critically important to establishing long-term relationships with customers.
   a. *The text uses the example of a software salesperson.*
   b. The selling process for B2B and for consumer products is similar.

PPT 16-32
Personal Selling

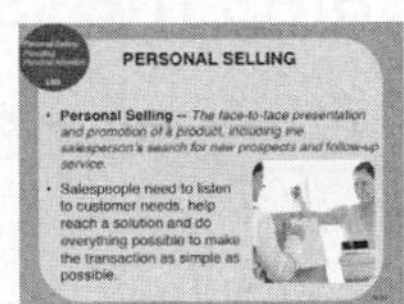

(See complete PowerPoint slide notes on page 16.52.)

PPT 16-33
Steps in the Selling Process

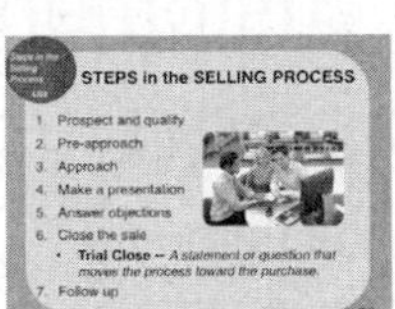

(See complete PowerPoint slide notes on page 16.52.)

c. In both, it is critical for the salesperson to know the product well and know how the product compares to those of competitors.

2. ***STEP 1.* PROSPECT AND QUALIFY**
   a. ***PROSPECTING*** involves researching potential buyers and choosing those most likely to buy.
   b. In the selling process, ***QUALIFYING*** is making sure that people have the need for a product, the authority to buy, and the willingness to listen to a sales message.
   c. A ***PROSPECT*** is a person with the means to buy a product, the authority to buy, and the willingness to listen to a sales message.
   d. The best prospects are people recommended by existing customers.
3. ***STEP 2.* PREAPPROACH**
   a. Before making a sales call, sales representatives must do further **RESEARCH** to learn as much as possible about customers and their wants and needs.
   b. All this information should be in a **DATABASE**.
   c. Gathering information before the sale takes place is critical.
4. ***STEP 3.* APPROACH**
   a. You don't have a second chance to make a **FIRST IMPRESSION**.
   b. The approach should give an impression of friendly professionalism to create rapport, to build credibility, and to start a relationship.

PPT 16-34
Prospecting and Qualifying in Selling

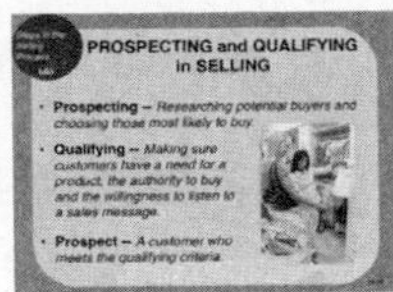

(See complete PowerPoint slide notes on page 16.53.)

PPT 16-35
Buy This!

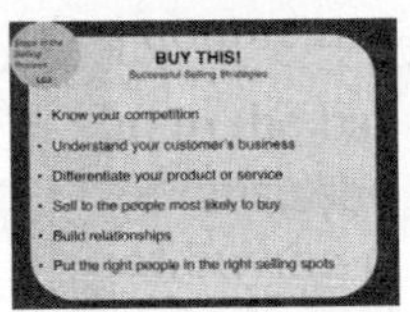

(See complete PowerPoint slide notes on page 16.53.)

PPT 16-36
Whoops!

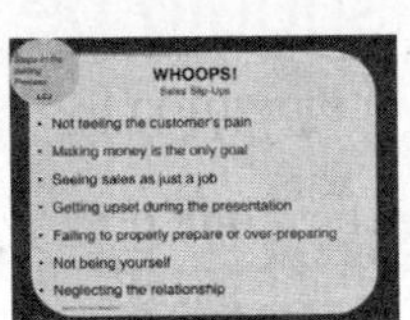

(See complete PowerPoint slide notes on page 16.53.)

5. ***STEP 4.* MAKE PRESENTATION**
   a. The idea is to match the benefits of your value package to the client's needs.
   b. Software tools help the salesperson tailor the presentation.
   c. This is a good time to use **TESTIMONIALS**.
6. ***STEP 5.* ANSWER OBJECTIONS**
   a. A salesperson should anticipate potential objections and determine proper responses.
   b. Questions should be viewed as opportunities for creating better relationships.
7. ***STEP 6.* CLOSE SALE**
   a. The ***TRIAL CLOSE*** is a step in the selling process that consists of a question or statement that moves the selling process toward the actual close.
   b. The final step is to **ASK FOR THE ORDER**.
   c. Salespeople must close many times before a long-term relationship is established.
8. ***STEP 7.* FOLLOW UP**
   a. The selling process isn't over until the order is approved and the customer is happy.
   b. Selling goes beyond simply sales—it includes **ESTABLISHING RELATIONSHIPS**, not just selling goods and services.
   c. **FOLLOW-UP** includes handling customer complaints, making sure that the customer's questions are answered, and supplying what the customer wants.

lecture notes

d. Often, customer **SERVICE** is as important to the sale as the product itself.

9. The **SELLING PROCESS VARIES** somewhat among different goods and services, but the general idea is the same.
   a. The goal is to help the buyer buy and make sure the buyer is satisfied after the sale.
   b. **SALES FORCE AUTOMATION (SFA)** includes software programs that help salespeople design products, close deals, tap into intranets, and more.

C. **THE BUSINESS-TO-CONSUMER (B2C) SALES PROCESS**

1. B2C selling differs from B2B selling.
   a. In **B2C SALES**, the salesperson does not have to do as much prospecting or qualifying.
   b. Retail salespeople don't usually have to go through a preapproach step.
2. The first formal step in the B2C process is the **APPROACH**.
3. Don't say "May I help you"; instead say "What can I help you with?"
4. After the initial approach, a salesperson then **MAKES A PRESENTATION** to show customers how the company's products meet their needs.
5. Next, the salesperson should answer customers' questions to help them choose the products that are right for them.

PPT 16-37
Steps in the B2C Selling Process

TEXT FIGURE 16.6
Steps in the Business-to-Consumer (B2C) Selling Process
(Text page 449)

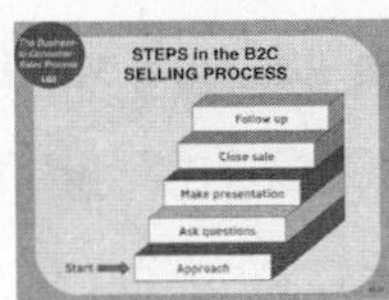

(See complete PowerPoint slide notes on page 16.54.)

bonus case 16-2

THE NEW BREED OF SALESPERSON

This case discusses how one salesperson used new technologies to change the approach to personal selling. (See the complete case, discussion questions, and suggested answers beginning on page 16.75 of this manual.)

progress assessment

(Text page 450)

PPT 16-38
Progress Assessment

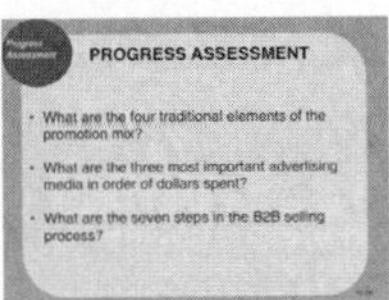

(See complete PowerPoint slide notes on page 16.54.)

6. In B2C selling, it is important to make a **TRIAL CLOSE**, walking a fine line between being helpful and being pushy.
7. **AFTER-SALE FOLLOW-UP** is an important but often neglected step in B2C sales.

learning goal 4

Describe the role of the public relations department, and tell how publicity fits in that role.

IV. PUBLIC RELATIONS: BUILDING RELATIONSHIPS

A. PUBLIC RELATIONS

1. ***PUBLIC RELATIONS (PR)*** is the management function that evaluates public attitudes, changes policies and procedures in response to the public's requests, and executes a program of action and information to earn public understanding and acceptance.
2. **A GOOD PUBLIC RELATIONS PROGRAM HAS THREE STEPS:**
   a. **LISTEN TO THE PUBLIC**: start with good marketing research.
   b. **CHANGE POLICIES AND PROCEDURES**: listen, in different forums, to what customers want.
   c. **INFORM PEOPLE** that you're being responsive to their needs.
3. The public relations department has responsibility for **MAINTAINING CLOSE RELATIONSHIPS** with the media, community leaders, government officials, and other stakeholders.

PPT 16-39
Using Public Relations in Promotion

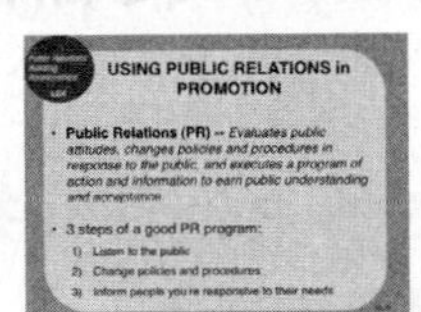

(See complete PowerPoint slide notes on page 16.54.)

B. **PUBLICITY: THE TALKING ARM OF PR**

1. ***PUBLICITY*** is any information about an individual, product, or an organization that is distributed to the public through the media, and that's not paid for or controlled by the sponsor.
   a. **PRESS RELEASES** must be carefully written so the media will publish them.
   b. Publicity works only if the media find the material interesting or newsworthy.
2. **ADVANTAGES OF PUBLICITY:**
   a. Publicity is **FREE**.
   b. Publicity may reach people who wouldn't read an ad.
   c. The greatest advantage of publicity may be its **BELIEVABILITY**.
3. **DISADVANTAGES OF PUBLICITY** include:
   a. Marketers have no control over how, when, or if the media will use the story.
   b. Media do not have to publish it.
   c. The story can be altered so it's not positive.
   d. There is good publicity and there is bad publicity.
   e. Stories are not likely to be repeated; advertising can be repeated as often as needed.
4. To see that publicity is handled well by the media, the marketer should establish a **FRIENDLY RELATIONSHIP WITH THE MEDIA** and cooperate with them.

PPT 16-40
Publicity

(See complete PowerPoint slide notes on page 16.55.)

PPT 16-41
Disadvantages of Publicity

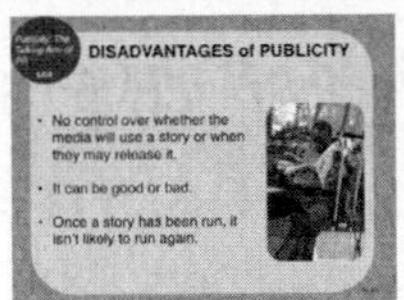

(See complete PowerPoint slide notes on page 16.55.)

bonus case 16-3
BP'S CRUDE REPUTATION

Following the 2010 oil spill in the Gulf, BP had a lot of repairs to make and one of the biggest was to its reputation (See the complete case, discussion questions, and suggested answers beginning on page 16.77 of this manual.)

lecture outline

<u>learning goal 5</u>

Assess the effectiveness of various forms of sales promotion, including sampling.

V. SALES PROMOTION: GIVING BUYERS INCENTIVES

A. SALES PROMOTION

1. ***SALES PROMOTION*** is the promotional tool that stimulates consumer purchasing and dealer interest by means of short-term activities.
   a. *Sales promotion techniques include displays, trade shows and exhibitions, event sponsorships, and contests.*
   b. *Examples of consumer sales promotions include free samples, cents-off coupons, and prizes.*
   c. Sales promotion programs are designed to **SUPPLEMENT** personal selling, advertising, and public relations by creating enthusiasm for the overall promotional program.
   d. There has been a big increase in sales promotions in the 21st century.
2. **INTERNAL SALES PROMOTIONS** (within the company) generate employee enthusiasm about a product, including:
   a. Sales training
   b. Development of sales aids *such as flip charts, portable audiovisual displays, and videos*
   c. Participation in trade shows
3. **EXTERNAL SALES PROMOTION** (outside the company, including distributors and dealers)

PPT 16-42
Sales Promotions

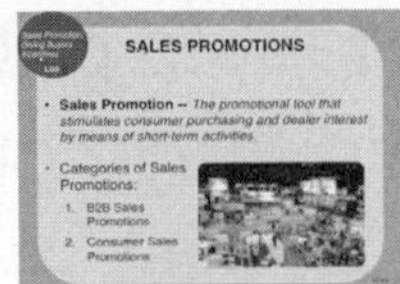

(See complete PowerPoint slide notes on page 16.55.)

TEXT FIGURE 16.7
Business-to-Business Sales Promotion Techniques
(Text page 451)

This text figure lists some B2B sales promotion techniques.

PPT 16-43
Some Key Consumer Promotions

(See complete PowerPoint slide notes on page 16.56.)

lecture link 16-6
AMERICANS RETURN TO CLIPPING COUPONS

Coupon use in the U.S. declined steadily since 1992. But once our economic downturn started in 2008, coupon use has been climbing yet again. (See the complete lecture link on page 16.62 of this manual.)

PPT 16-44
Clip These

(See complete PowerPoint slide notes on page 16.56.)

TEXT FIGURE 16.8
Consumer Sales Promotion Techniques
(Text page 452)

This text figure lists some consumer sales promotion techniques.

  a. It is important to get distributors and dealers involved so they, too, are enthusiastic.
  b. **TRADE SHOWS** are important because buyers are able to see products from many different sellers.
  c. **VIRTUAL TRADE SHOWS**—trade shows on the Internet—enable buyers to see many products without leaving the office.
4. The next step is to **PROMOTE TO FINAL CONSUMERS.**
  a. Techniques include *samples, coupons, cents-off deals, displays, contests, rebates, and so on.*
  b. Sales promotion is an ongoing effort to maintain enthusiasm.

B. ***SAMPLING*** is a promotional tool in which a company lets consumers have a small sample of a product for no charge.
  1. Using sampling in **GROCERY STORES** is a quick, effective way of demonstrating a product's superiority at the time consumers are making a purchase decision.
  2. Companies use sampling in conjunction with other techniques such as **EVENT MARKETING.**
  3. *The text uses the example of Pepsi's introduction of SoBe.*

progress assessment
(Text page 453)

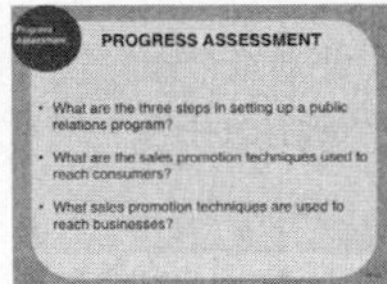

PPT 16-45
Progress Assessment

(See complete PowerPoint slide notes on page 16.56.)

PPT 16-46
Using Word-of-Mouth Promotion

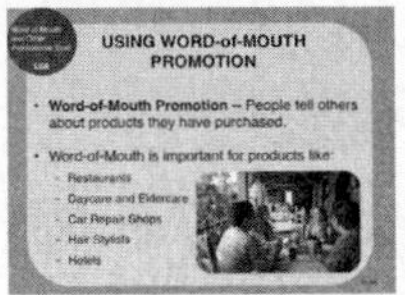

(See complete PowerPoint slide notes on page 16.57.)

lecture link 16-7
WRAP YOUR SUV

Some companies will pay hundreds of dollars to put their ads on cars of everyday citizens. (See the complete lecture link on page 16.62 in this manual.)

PPT 16-47
Emerging Promotional Tools

(See complete PowerPoint slide notes on page 16.57.)

lecture outline

learning goal 6

Show how word of mouth, e-mail marketing, viral marketing, blogging, podcasting, and mobile marketing work.

VI. WORD OF MOUTH AND OTHER PROMOTIONAL TOOLS

A. **WORD OF MOUTH** is one of the most effective promotional tools.

1. ***WORD-OF-MOUTH PROMOTION*** is a promotional tool that involves people telling other people about products they have purchased.
2. Anything that encourages people to talk favorably about an organization is effective word of mouth.
3. Clever commercials and samples can generate word of mouth.

B. **VIRAL MARKETING**

1. Some companies have begun creating word of mouth by paying people to go online and hyping the product in chat rooms.
2. These people get free tickets, T-shirts, and other merchandise that the industry calls **SWAG**.
3. ***VIRAL MARKETING*** is the term now used to describe everything from paying people to say positive things on the Internet to setting up multilevel selling schemes whereby consumers get commissions for directing friends to specific websites.
4. An effective strategy for spreading word of mouth is to send **TESTIMONIALS** to current customers.
   a. These are effective in confirming customers' belief that they chose the right company and are effective in promotion to new customers.

bonus case 16-4
GUERILLA MARKETING

Dietrich Mateschitz is the man who introduced Red Bull to the U.S. market. The secret to Red Bull's success is something called guerrilla marketing. (See the complete case, discussion questions, and suggested answers beginning on page 16.79 of this manual.)

b. But negative word of mouth can hurt a firm.

c. Upset customers are now publishing their complaints on the Internet.

C. **BLOGGING**

1. A ***BLOG*** is an online diary (Web log) that looks like a Web page but is easier to create and update by posting text, photos, or links to other sites.

2. There are millions of blogs on the Internet.

D. **PODCASTING**

1. ***PODCASTING*** is a means of distributing audio and video programs via the Internet that lets users subscribe to a number of files, also known as feeds, and then hear or view the material at the time they choose.

2. Podcasting gives broadcast radio or television programs a new distribution method.

3. Many companies have also found success in creating video for YouTube.

E. **E-MAIL PROMOTIONS**

1. Many companies use e-mail to announce new products and provide product updates.

2. While e-mails may lose their power over time, they are still gaining in popularity.

3. One key to success is to keep the message brief for mobile users.

F. **MOBILE MEDIA**

1. Marketers use the cell phone to send texts to promote sweepstakes, send news and alerts, and give company information.

PPT 16-48
Blogs, Podcasts, and E-Mails

(See complete PowerPoint slide notes on page 16.57.)

lecture link 16-8
CONAN'S TWITTER TRIUMPH

After losing the *Tonight Show,* Conan O'Brien's future looked grim. How did he reinvent himself? Through Twitter. (See the complete lecture link on page 16.63 in this manual.)

lecture link 16-9
BLOGS FOR SMALL BUSINESSES

Small companies are discovering that using blogs can help them create a brand identity. (See the complete lecture link on page 16.64 in this manual.)

PPT 16-49
Mobile Media

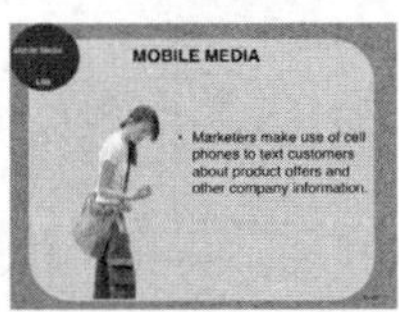

(See complete PowerPoint slide notes on page 16.58.)

2. **TRADITIONAL PROMOTIONAL** methods are slowly but surely being replaced by new technology.

VII. MANAGING THE PROMOTION MIX: PUTTING IT ALL TOGETHER

A. Each target group calls for a separate promotion mix.

1. Large, homogeneous groups of consumers are most efficiently reached through **ADVERTISING**.
2. Large organizations are best reached through **PERSONAL SELLING**.
3. **SALES PROMOTION** motivates people to buy now rather than later.
4. **PUBLICITY** adds support to the other efforts and can create a good impression.
5. **WORD OF MOUTH** is often the most powerful promotional tool; often including blogs and podcasting.

B. **PROMOTION STRATEGIES**

1. In a ***PUSH STRATEGY,*** the producer uses advertising, personal selling, sales promotion, and all other promotional tools to convince wholesalers and retailer to stock and sell merchandise.
2. In a ***PULL STRATEGY,*** heavy advertising and sales promotion efforts are directed toward consumers so they will request the products from retailers.
3. A company can use **BOTH** push and pull strategies at the same time.

bonus case 16-5

WIEDEN + KENNEDY: EXPERIMENTAL PROMOTIONS

Wieden + Kennedy is known as one of the most creative advertising agencies in the United States. One of its ads even used a streaker (See the complete case, discussion questions, and suggested answers beginning on page 16.81 of this manual.)

PPT 16-50

Push, Pull, and Pick Promotional Strategies

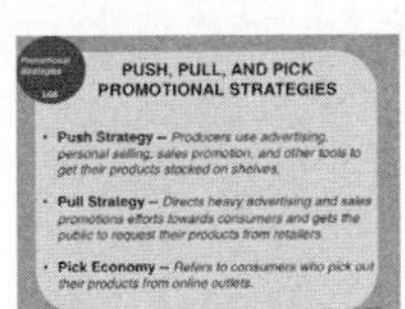

(See complete PowerPoint slide notes on page 16.58.)

4. The latest in pull and push strategies are being conducted on the **INTERNET**.
5. It is important to make promotion part of a **TOTAL SYSTEMS APPROACH** to marketing.
    a. Thus, promotion would be an integral part of supply-chain efforts.
    b. The idea would be to develop a **total product offer** to appeal to everyone: manufacturers, distributors, retailers, and consumers.
6. Today push and pull strategies seem to be losing some effectiveness.
    a. Customers are increasingly using the Internet to shop for products.
    b. The term ***PICK ECONOMY*** refers to those consumers who pick out their products from online outlets or who do online comparison shopping.

VIII. SUMMARY

lecture notes

progress assessment
(Text page 456)

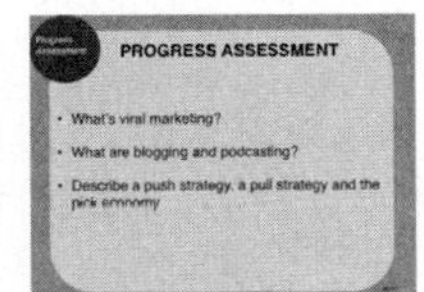

PPT 16-51
Progress Assessment

(See complete PowerPoint slide notes on page 16.58.)

PowerPoint slide notes

PPT 16-1
Chapter Title

PPT 16-2
Learning Goals

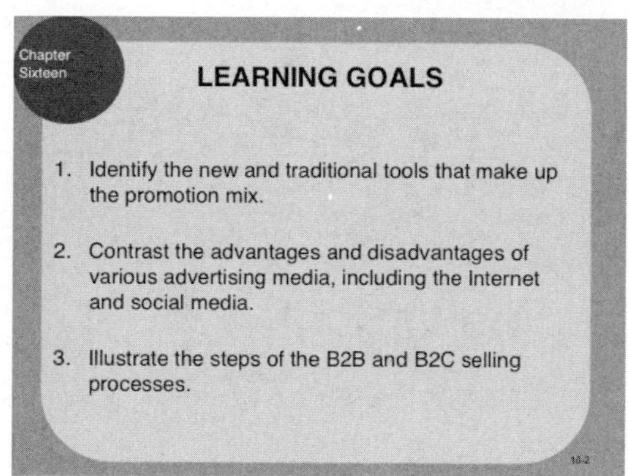

PPT 16-3
Learning Goals

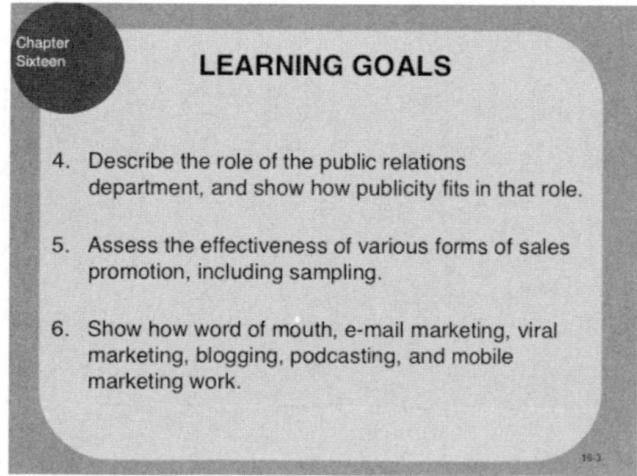

PPT 16-4
Andrew Mason

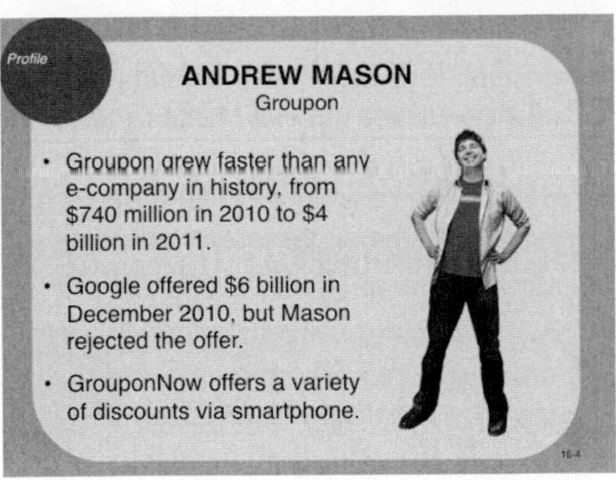

PPT 16-5
Name That Company

Company: Dr. Pepper

PPT 16-6
Promotion in an Organization

PPT 16-7
Integrated Marketing Communication (IMC)

Emphasis today is on integrating traditional media with social media.

PPT 16-8
Fresh-Baked Promotion

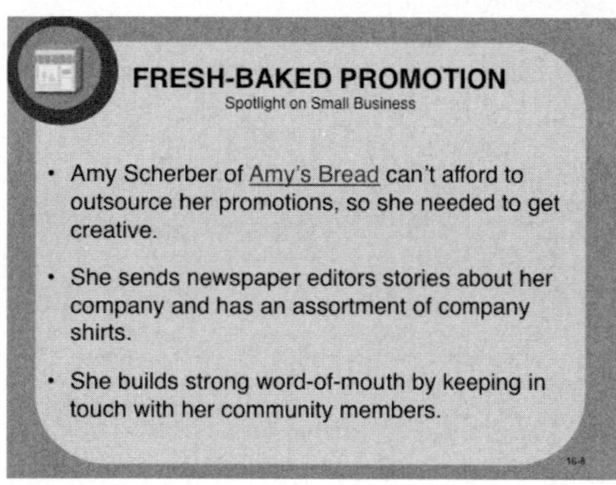

PPT 16-9
Steps in a Promotional Campaign

PPT 16-10
Classic Campaigns

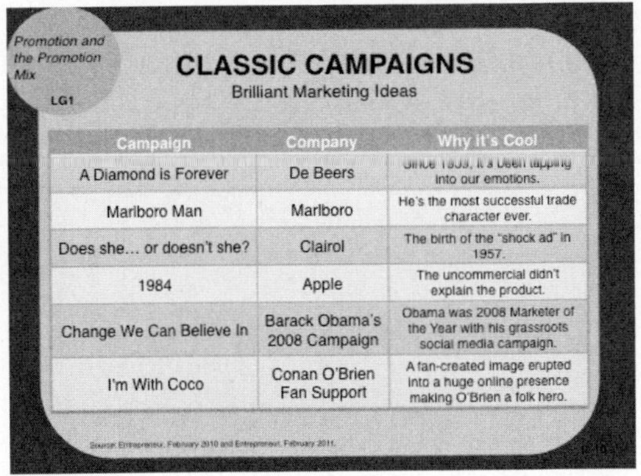

Campaign	Company	Why It's Cool
A Diamond is Forever	De Beers	[illegible] into our emotions.
Marlboro Man	Marlboro	He's the most successful trade character ever.
Does she... or doesn't she?	Clairol	The birth of the "shock ad" in 1957.
1984	Apple	The uncommercial didn't explain the product.
Change We Can Believe In	Barack Obama's 2008 Campaign	Obama was 2008 Marketer of the Year with his grassroots social media campaign.
I'm With Coco	Conan O'Brien Fan Support	A fan-created image erupted into a huge online presence making O'Brien a folk hero.

1. This slide shows the evolution of marketing campaigns from pulling on heartstrings to shocking viewers to engaging customers.
2. Ask the students, Do you expect social media to continue to play a big part in marketing? How are campaigns like Dove's "Real Beauty" and Burger King's "Subservient Chicken" gaining a new customer base?

PPT 16-11
Advertising in the Firm

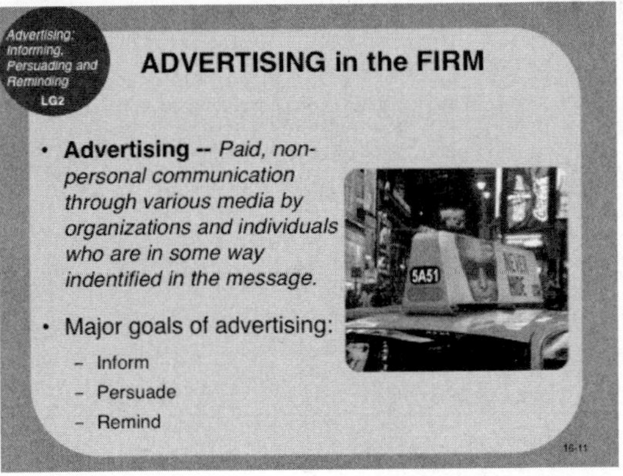

Advertising is different from public relations, since advertising is paid and public relations is free.

PPT 16-12
Impact of Advertising

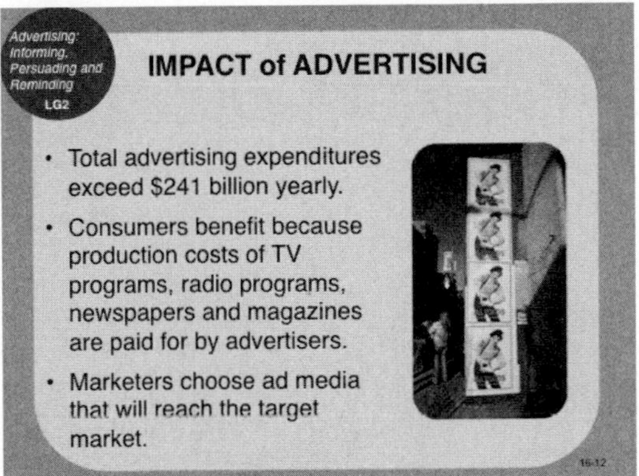

PPT 16-13
Social Advertising

PPT 16-14
Major Categories of Advertising

If time permits, ask students to bring magazines and newspapers with examples of the previously mentioned advertising categories.

Advertising: Informing, Persuading and Reminding
LG2

MAJOR CATEGORIES of ADVERTISING

Category	What it is
Retail	From retail stores to consumers
Trade	From manufacturers to wholesalers and retailers
B2B	From manufacturers to other manufacturers
Institutional	Creates a desirable image for an organization
Product	Creates a desirable image for a product or service

16-14

PPT 16-15
Major Categories of Advertising

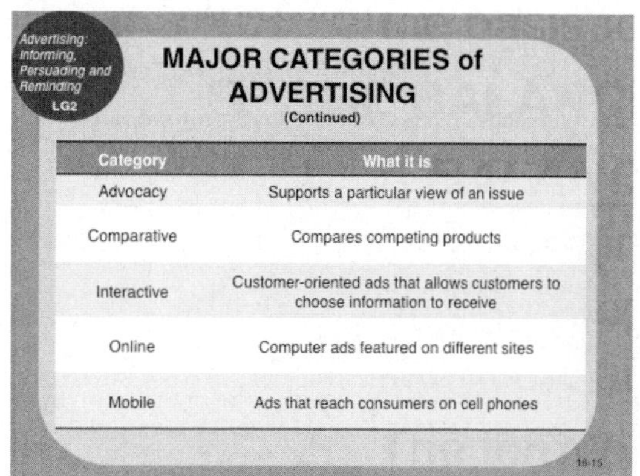

Category	What it is
Advocacy	Supports a particular view of an issue
Comparative	Compares competing products
Interactive	Customer-oriented ads that allows customers to choose information to receive
Online	Computer ads featured on different sites
Mobile	Ads that reach consumers on cell phones

PPT 16-16
Advertising Expenditure by Media in $ Millions

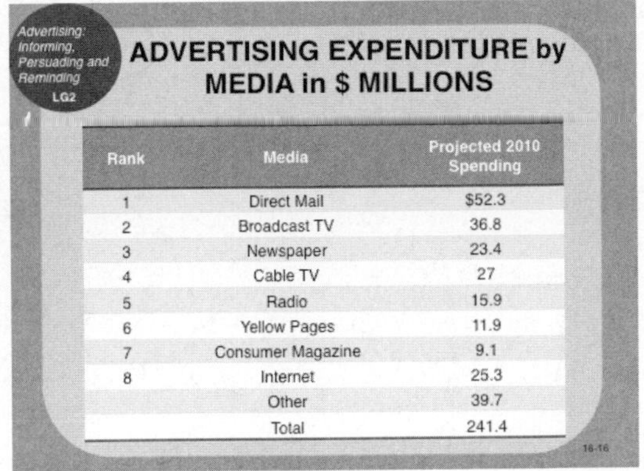

Rank	Media	Projected 2010 Spending
1	Direct Mail	$52.3
2	Broadcast TV	36.8
3	Newspaper	23.4
4	Cable TV	27
5	Radio	15.9
6	Yellow Pages	11.9
7	Consumer Magazine	9.1
8	Internet	25.3
	Other	39.7
	Total	241.4

Before showing this slide, ask students to guess the top five forms of direct advertising.

PPT 16-17
Dear Mr. Postman . . .

Promotion and the Promotion Mix
LG1

DEAR MR. POSTMAN...
Steps in Launching a Direct-Mail Campaign

1. **Plan:** What should your mailing accomplish?
2. **Get the Right List:** The better the list, the better your chance of success.
3. **Stand Out:** Make your ad like no other.
4. **Get Help:** Contact a marketing firm with direct mail experience.
5. **Follow Up:** One mailing is not enough.

1. This slide highlights the steps in launching a direct-mail campaign
2. Direct mail is the number one form of advertising, accounting for 21.6% of all ad dollars spent.
3. Ask the students, Why is direct mail so popular as a form of advertising? *(Answers may vary, but students should understand that the cost of direct mail and the ability to target specific demographic groups make direct mail a popular choice.)*
4. Once students have discussed the benefits of direct mail, ask them about the drawbacks of this form of advertising. *(The main drawback* to *this form of advertising is that people will look at each mailer as just more junk and throw it in the trashcan.)*

PPT 16-18
Match Game

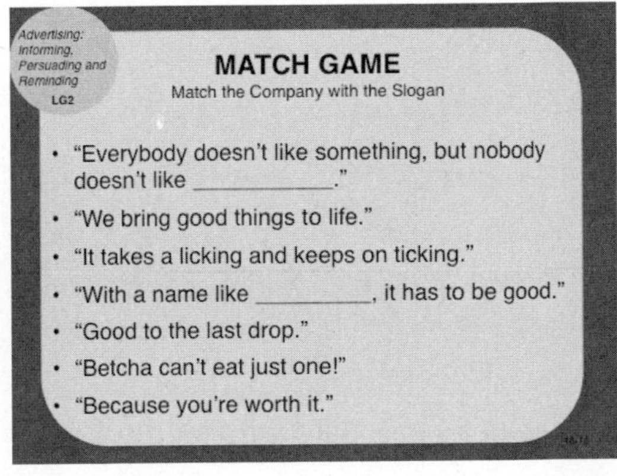

1. This slide represents a few of the most recognized taglines in the United States. It will be interesting to see how many students recognize the taglines.
2. Ask the students, Do you know what products these taglines represent? Taglines are very important to a company's advertising message. Companies want people to respond to their message, therefore these taglines must tell individuals how the product benefits them:

   Sara Lee, GE, Timex , Smucker's, Maxwell House, Lay's, L'Oréal

PPT 16-19
It's a Dog's Life

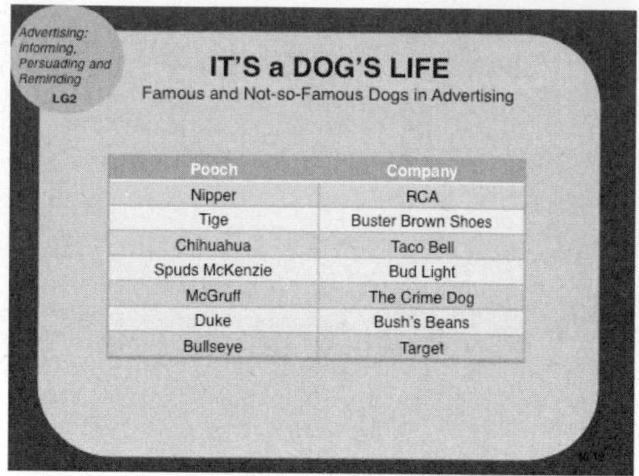

1. Dogs have been used in advertising for years.
2. This slide highlights some of the famous and not-so-famous dogs used in advertising.
3. Ask the students, Why are dogs so popular in advertising?

PPT 16-20
Popular Advertising Media

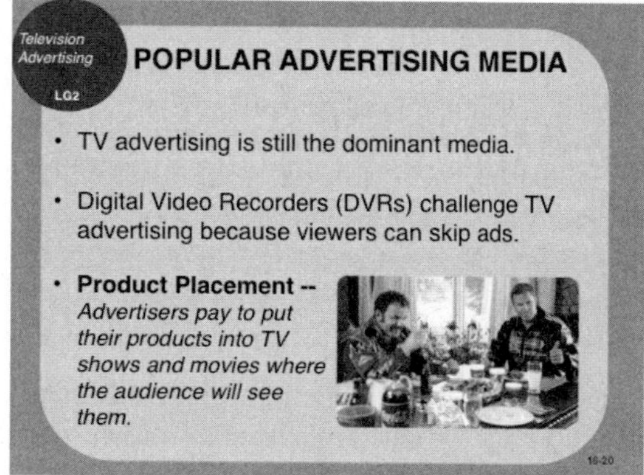

PPT 16-21
Let's Go to the Movies

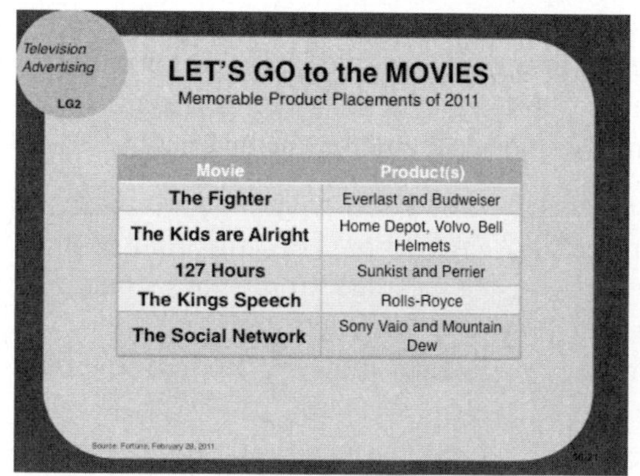

1. This slide shows examples of memorable product placement in 2011 Oscar-nominated films.
2. Ask the students, Do you find product placements distracting? Do you not notice them at all? Do you think product placements help you choose products?

PPT 16-22
Infomercials and Online Advertising

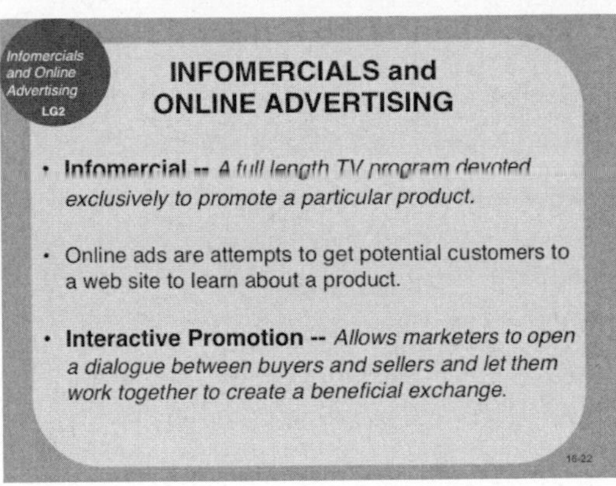

Infomercials are expected to rise to over $170 billion in 2014

PPT 16-23
Infomercial Hall of Fame

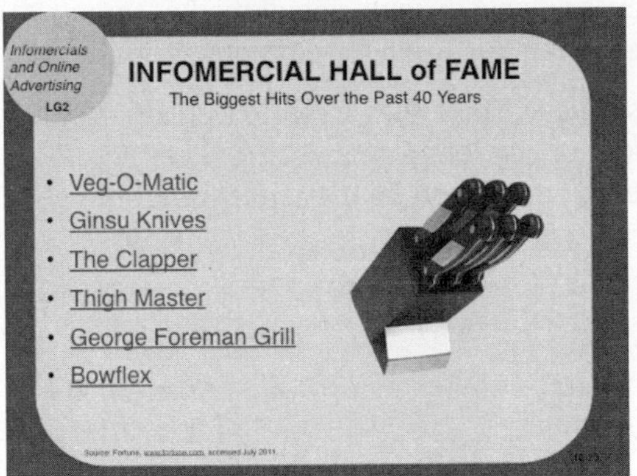

1. This slide presents the biggest infomercial hits over the past 40 years.
2. Ask the students, Why are infomercials on the air? *(Simple; they work. It is estimated that infomercials make up 25% of all television commercials and that 66% of adults have watched them.)*
3. The following link is from YouTube and features the top 10 worst infomercials of all time. Students love to watch this video and laugh at some of the products featured (www.youtube.com/watch?v=duaiVk_aRgQ).

PPT 16-24
Online Experience

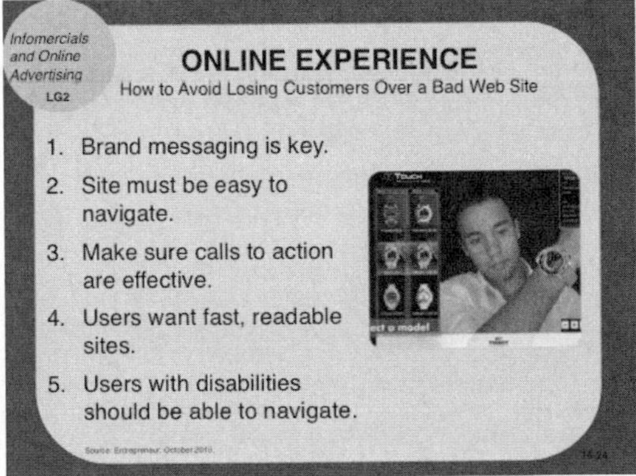

1. Failing to deliver an online experience to customers may result in losing them.
2. This slide shows ways to avoid a bad customer experience.
3. Ask the students, What are examples of company or product websites you like? Navigate through sites mentioned and ask other students to chime in on why they think it's a good customer experience.

PPT 16-25
Social Media Complements
Other Promotion

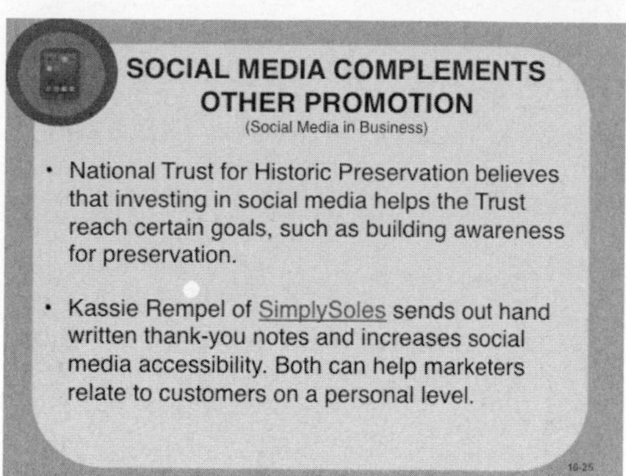

PPT 16-26
Social Scammers

1. Although businesses want you to spread the word about their products through social media, some groups are using this trend to scam others.
2. Ask the students, Have they experienced strange requests or application problems? How else could you protect yourself and your friends from online scammers?

PPT 16-27
Monitoring Ad Effectiveness

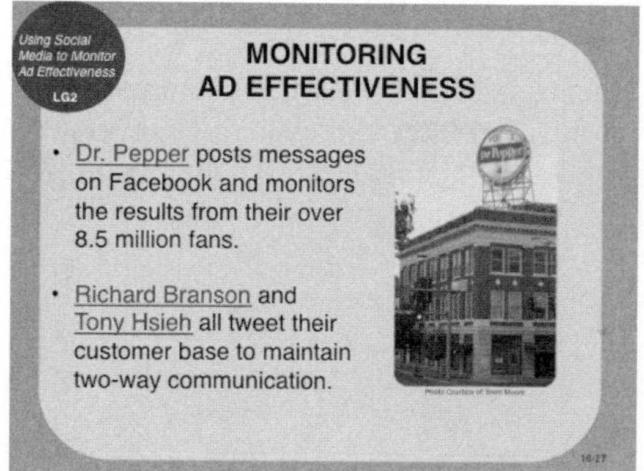

PPT 16-28
Socially Superior

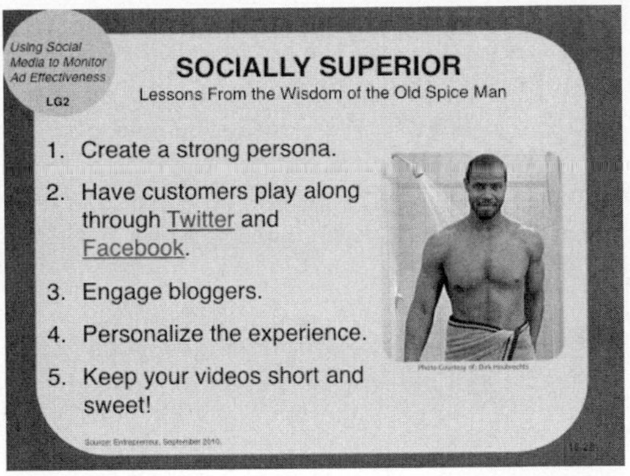

1. This slide shows five essentials to a successful online campaign.
2. Ask the students, Have you seen the YouTube videos featuring Isaiah Mustafa and Old Spice products? Did you forward these videos to friends or have videos forwarded to you? Here is a link to one of the commercials: www.youtube.com/watch?v=owGykVbfgUE.
3. Companies are incorporating social media into their promotional plans and are creating Web-exclusive content to engage customers.

PPT 16-29
Electronic Ethics

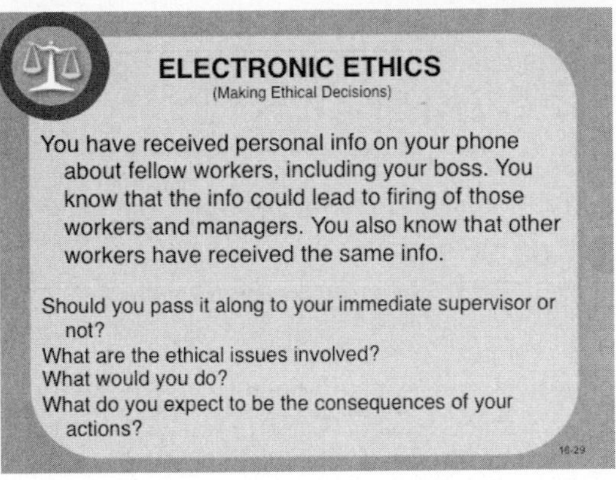

PPT 16-30
Global Advertising

Culturally sensitive advertising is key to successful international marketing.

PPT 16-31
Promotion in Rural India

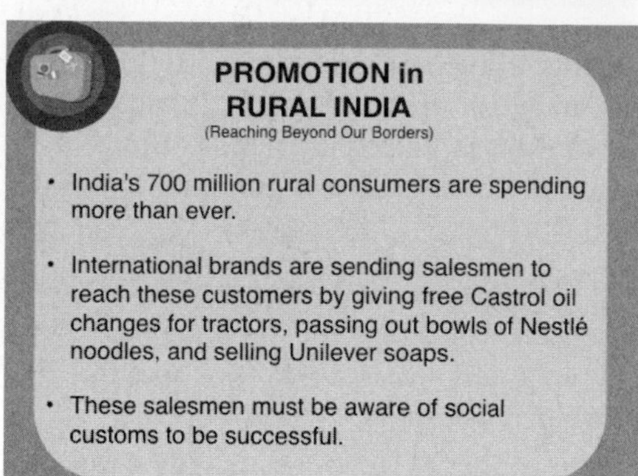

PPT 16-32
Personal Selling

Selling is about more than trying to convince someone to buy a product; it is about listening to the needs of the customer.

Personal Selling: Providing Personal Attention
LG3

PERSONAL SELLING

- **Personal Selling** -- *The face-to-face presentation and promotion of a product, including the salesperson's search for new prospects and follow-up service.*
- Salespeople need to listen to customer needs, help reach a solution and do everything possible to make the transaction as simple as possible.

16-32

PPT 16-33
Steps in the Selling Process

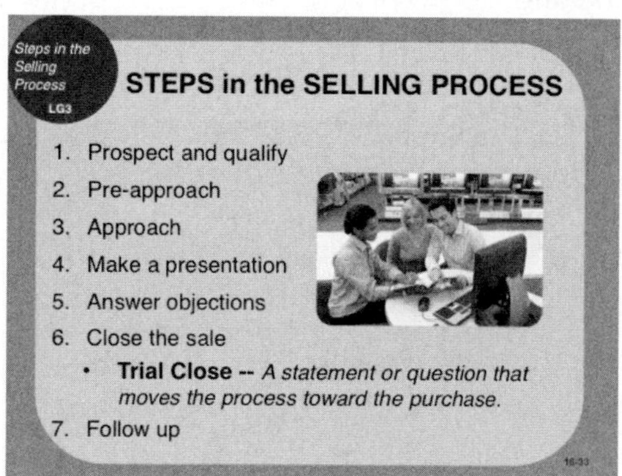

PPT 16-34
Prospecting and Qualifying in Selling

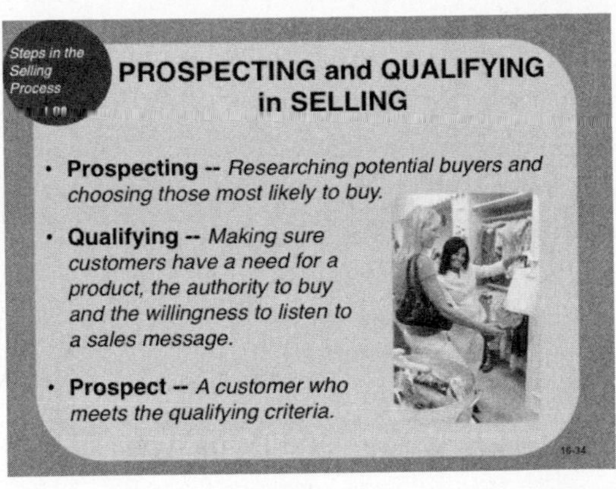

A key to B2B selling is qualifying customers, so that time is not wasted on customers who do not have a need.

PPT 16-35
Buy This!

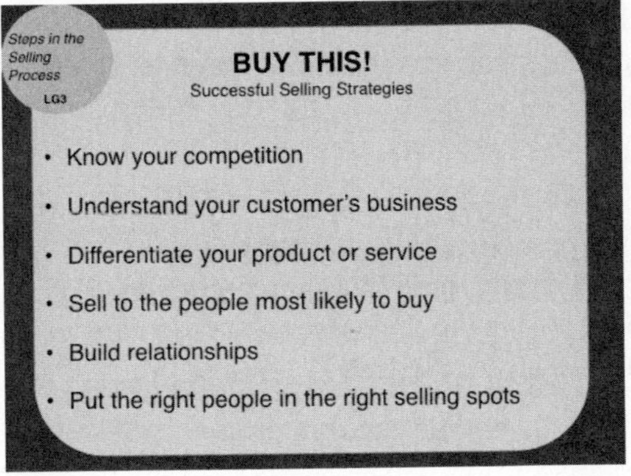

1. There are several strategies for selling that have been proven to work. Some of those are listed on this slide.
2. Ask students to get into small groups or turn to a neighbor and discuss why they think these strategies work.
3. Have students think about which of these strategies they think are the most successful (rank order) and support their answers. Ask the students, Was it easy to rank order these? Do you think some are more effective than others? Why?

PPT 16-36
Whoops!

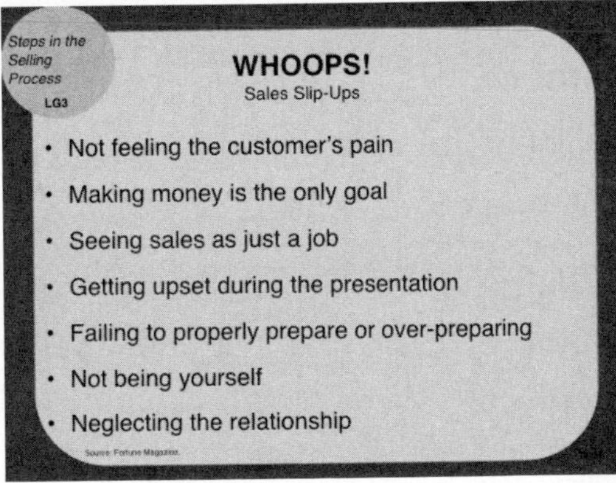

There are several mistakes people make when trying to make the sale. Those are listed on this slide.

1. Ask the students, Have you ever decided not to purchase something because of a sales person? What made you not want to buy from that particular person?

PPT 16-37
Steps in the B2C Selling Process

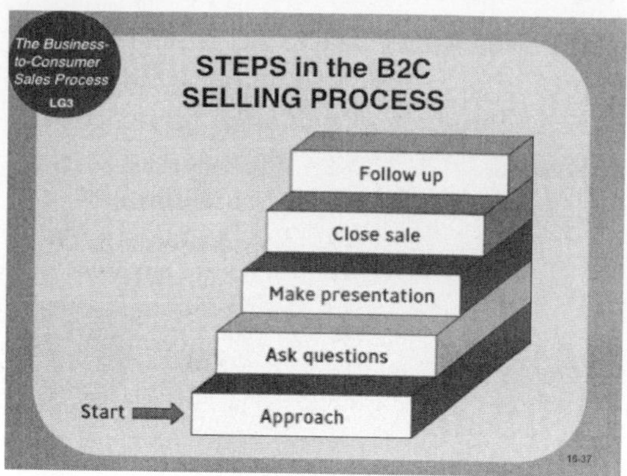

PPT 16-38
Progress Assessment

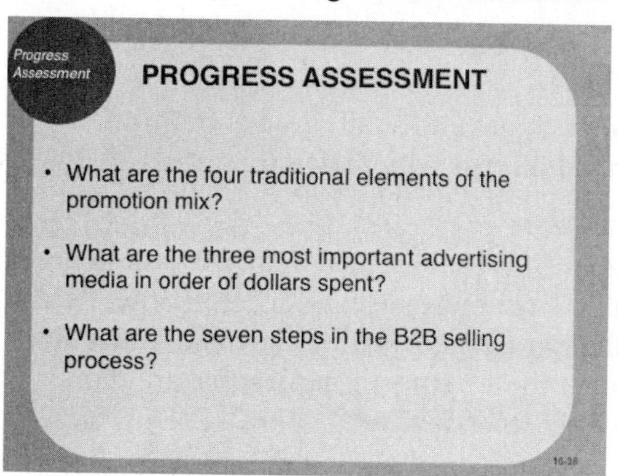

1. The four traditional elements of the promotion mix include advertising, personal selling, public relations, and sales promotion.
2. The the three most important advertising media in order of dollar spent are direct mail, broadcast television, and cable TV networks. (Internet advertising is climbing quickly and may move to the upper ranks soon.)
3. The seven steps in the B2B selling process are (1) prospect and qualify, (2) preapproach, (3) approach, (4) make the presentation, (5) answer objections, (6) close sale, and (7) follow up.

PPT 16-39
Using Public Relations in Promotion

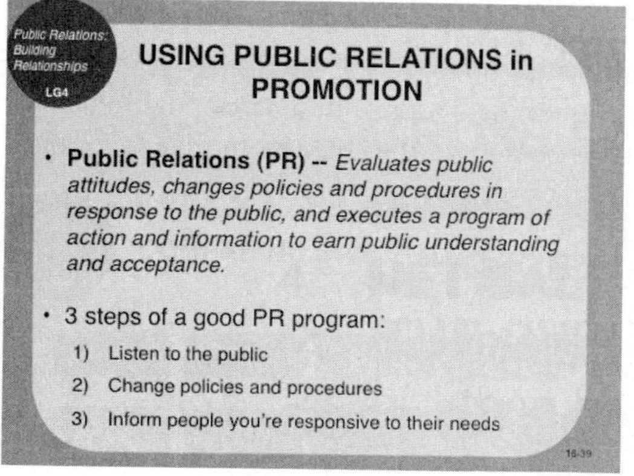

PPT 16-40
Publicity

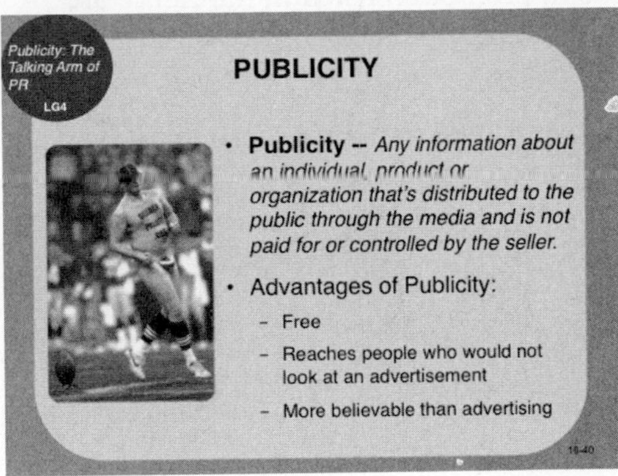

PPT 16-41
Disadvantages of Publicity

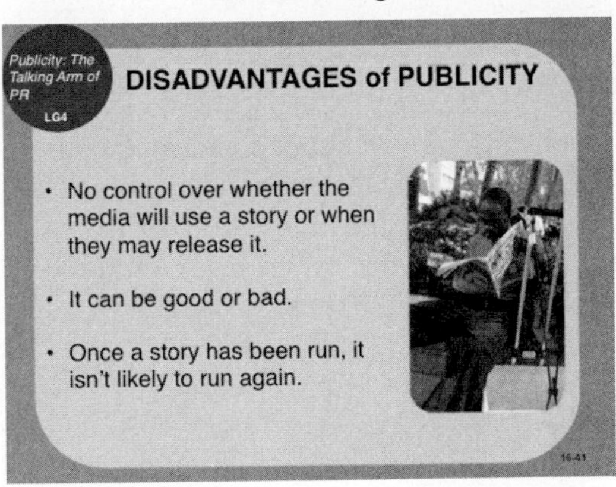

PPT 16-42
Sales Promotions

PPT 16-43
Some Key Consumer Promotions

1. Information in this slide is based on Figure 16.8.
2. Other forms of promotion listed in the figure are cents-off promotions, premiums, bonuses, catalogs, special events, and lotteries.
3. Promotion needs to tie into the overall marketing strategy of the product being sold.

PPT 16-44
Clip These

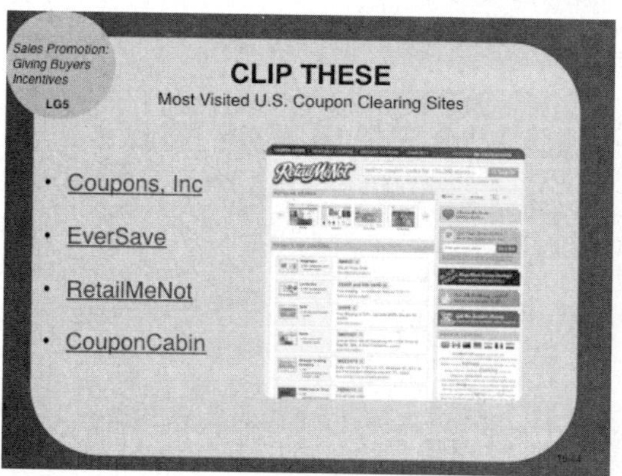

1. Coupons are no longer found only in the Sunday newspaper; now we have websites dedicated to coupon clipping.
2. First coupon was distributed in 1894 for Coca-Cola.
3. Ask the students, Have you clipped and used coupons? Where did you find the coupons that you used? Was clipping the coupon the motivation for trying the product? What was your experience? Would you have tried the product without the coupons?
4. Ask the students, Would using coupons be a push or pull strategy? *(Pull strategy)*

PPT 16-45
Progress Assessment

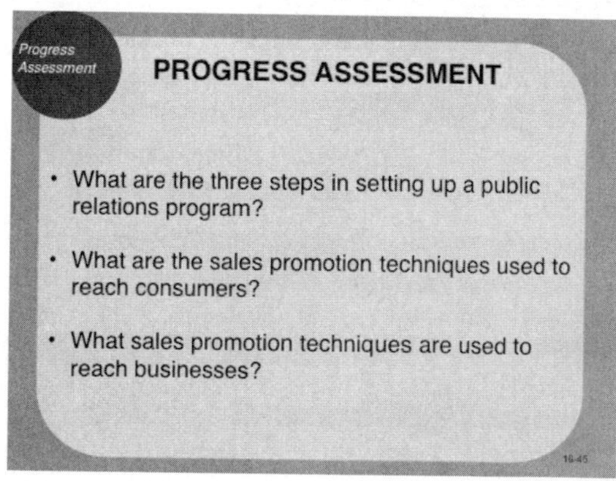

1. The three steps in a public relations program include (1) listen to the public, (2) develop policies and procedures in the public interest, and (3) tell people you're being responsive to their needs.
2. External sales promotions to consumers rely on samples, coupons, cents-off deals, displays, store demonstrators, premiums, and other incentives.
3. Internal sales promotion activities include sales training, sales aids, audiovisual displays, and trade shows.

PPT 16-46
Using Word-of-Mouth Promotion

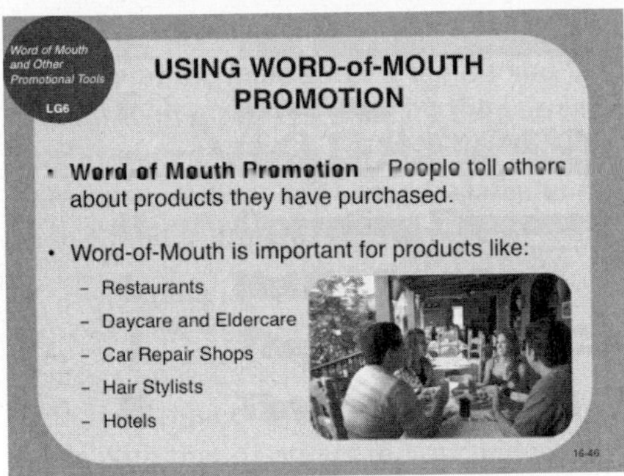

PPT 16-47
Emerging Promotional Tools

PPT 16-48
Blogs, Podcasts, and E-Mails

Tweeting, blogging, and podcasting are rapidly changing how products are promoted.

PPT 16-49
Mobile Media

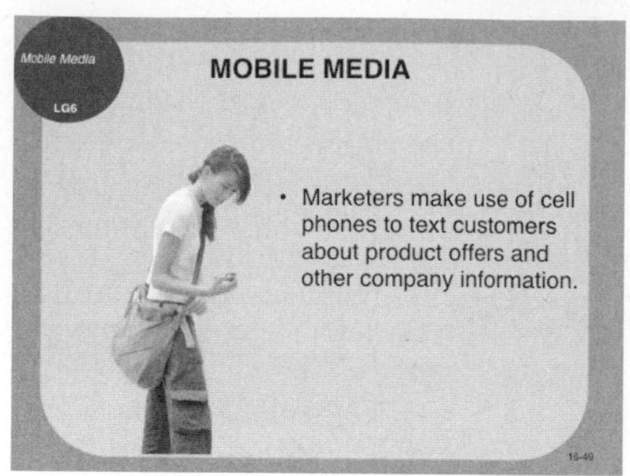

PPT 16-50
Push, Pull, and Pick Promotional Strategies

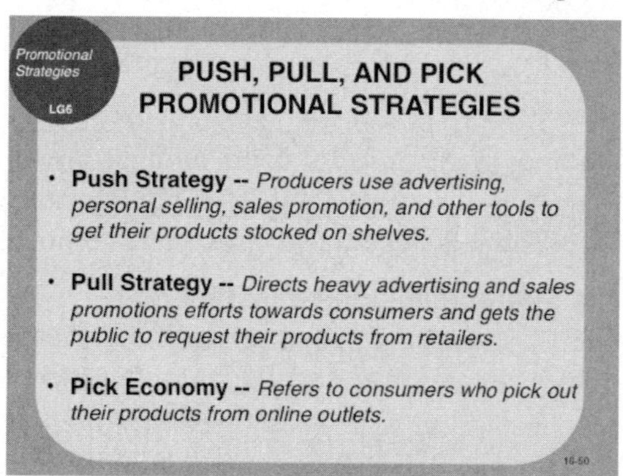

PPT 16-51
Progress Assessment

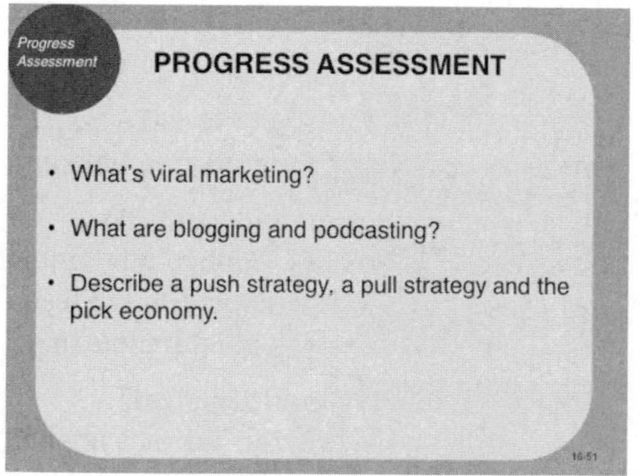

1. *Viral marketing* is a broad term that describes everything from paying customers to say positive things about a product or service on the Internet, to setting up multilevel selling schemes whereby consumers get commissions for directing friends to specific websites.
2. A blog (Web log) is an online diary that allows the user to create and update by posting text, photos, or links to other sites. Podcasting is a means of distributing audio and video programs via the Internet.
3. In a push strategy, the producer uses advertising, personal selling, sales promotion, and all other promotional tools to convince wholesalers and retailers to stock and sell merchandise. A pull strategy directs all advertising and sales promotion toward the consumer. The pick economy refers to those consumers who pick their products out from online outlets.

lecture links

"The first rule of business is never sell something you love. Otherwise, you may as well be selling your children"
Hugh Macleod

"If everything seems to be going well, you have obviously overlooked something."
Steven White

"Doing business without advertising is like winking at a girl in the dark. You know what you are doing, but nobody else does."
Stuart Henderson

lecture link 16-1

MURPHY'S LAWS OF MARKETING

The study of marketing doesn't always have to be serious and academic. When you need some irreverence, a good source is Arthur Bloch's book, *Murphy's Laws*, first published in 1978. To celebrate the 25th anniversary of its publication, Arthur Block reissued it as *Murphy's Law: The 25th Anniversary Edition*. Following are a few of Murphy's laws of marketing.

ROBBIN'S RULES OF MARKETING

1. Your share of the market is lower than you think.
2. The combined market position goals of all competitors always totals at least 150%.
3. The existence of a market does not ensure the existence of a customer.
4. Beware of alleged needs that have no real market.
5. Low price and long shipment will win over high price and short shipment.
6. If the customer buys lunch, you've lost the order.

THINGS THAT CAN BE COUNTED ON IN A CRISIS

MARKETING says yes.

FINANCE says no.

LEGAL has to review it.

PERSONNEL is concerned.

PLANNING is frantic.

ENGINEERING is above it all.

MANUFACTURING wants more floor space.

TOP MANAGEMENT wants someone responsible.

LEWIS'S LAW

People will buy anything that's one to a customer.

BROOK'S LAW OF RETAILING

Security isn't.

Management can't.

Sales promotions don't.

Consumer assistance doesn't.

Workers won't.

lecture link 16-2

EFFECTIVE ADVERTISING: CELEBRITY VOICE-OVERS

Good news for the actors who moonlight doing voice-overs for television commercials. According to the *Journal of Consumer Research*, celebrity voice-overs are effective in reaching consumers. But voice-overs are most effective when people recognize the voice—but can't quite put a name to it. Researchers studied reactions to TV commercials with actors Robert Downey Jr., John Krasinski, Sarah Silverman, and Jon Hamm doing voice-overs for Nissan, Carnival Cruise Lines, Vitamin Water, and Mercedes-Benz. The commercial watchers' prior attitudes toward the celebrity influenced how much they liked or disliked the brand, but the celebrity endorsements created stronger feelings for the brand when viewers weren't sure to whom the familiar voice belonged.

According to researcher Mark Forehand, who ran the study, "When they [viewers] recognize the celebrity, it seems potentially manipulative, and they wind up overcompensating. But when they don't recognize the celebrity, they generalize over to the brand."[i]

lecture link 16-3

PRODUCT PLACEMENT IN POP

The last decade has been tough for the recording industry, and not just because of online piracy. Although Apple's iTunes store brought in some much-needed business, the 99 cents per song model has all but killed sales of the traditional album format. With most of the money generated by just a few singles, the new challenge for recording artists and producers is make as much money as possible from one song.

In such a setting, product placement can be a powerful tool, both for marketers and producers. Industry executives first noted the practice's power in 2002 when Busta Rhymes' song "Pass the Courvoisier" sent sales of the cognac skyrocketing. Nevertheless, direct product placement in pop music is still relatively new territory. To bridge the gap between companies and artists, agents like Adam Kluger act as intermediaries. Kluger has experience in both the entertainment and retail sectors.

Kluger has a client list ranging from products and services like a soft drink called Drank to the dating site Zoosk as well as relationships with big-name performers like Flo Rida and Lady Gaga. In 2009, Zoosk paid "in the mid-to high six figures" to appear in the lyrics and video for a song called "Zoosk Girl," performed by Kluger's up-and-coming client JRandall and superstar T-Pain. The fee more than covered the song's production costs, leading to a wider margin of profit for the tune. Fees with Kluger's agency and others range from $40,000 and $250,000 per video placement while a lyrical name check can run as much as $500,000. Kluger's agency generated $5 million in revenue last year and expects to grow even bigger as record companies rely on placements to make up for profits lost from album sales.[ii]

lecture link 16-4

RANKING TV OUTSIDE THE NIELSEN SPECTRUM

For years, television programming didn't reach much further than viewers' living rooms. People could watch their preferred shows only at the appointed time scheduled by the networks. Discussion of the previous night's shows took place in person at places like the company water cooler or in the school cafeteria. But with the current media landscape forever transformed by the Internet, viewers have a seemingly endless avenue at their disposal to both watch and discuss the latest shows on their own time.

Due to this technological shift, many advertisers and networks are growing less confident in the Nielsen rating system's role as the sole measure of a show's audience. According to research agencies like Optimedia US, buzz on social media sites and the blogosphere contributes to a more accurate picture of a show's impact. For instance, Nielsen's standings rank NBC's *The Office* at 105th place for an average week. According to Optimedia's Content Power Ratings (CPR) system, however, online discussion and dissemination of clips across the Web kicks the show up to 6th place. Similarly, though Comedy Central's *South Park* wallows at 211th place on the Nielsen charts, the show rests comfortably at 4th on the CPR index.

New measurements by companies like Optimedia could have a sizable effect on the advertising industry in years to come. Given that many networks are raising prices for commercial time this coming season, companies are expected to become pickier about the shows they choose to push their products on. Optimedia's new ranking system may provide the fresh perspective that advertisers need. What's more, Optimedia's research teams can also track how advertising during a certain program affects sales as well as consumers' perception of the product. Nevertheless, the system is too young to command any change in pricing models for ads at the present time.[iii]

lecture link 16-5

AS SEEN ON SOCIAL MEDIA

Turn the TV on any station after midnight and you're bound to find an infomercial for a Guthy-Renker product. Since 1988 the company has made a mint by promoting everything from the Malibu Pilates Chair to Tony Robbins's landmark audiobook *Personal Power*. Currently, Guthy-Renker's shining star is Proactiv, an acne cream endorsed by celebrities like Justin Beiber and Katy Perry. Of the $1 billion Guthy-Renker earned through cosmetic sales last year, $800 million of it came from Proactiv.

While Proactiv remains a major cash cow for the company, G-R's traditional method of infomercial inundation may not always be the most effective promotional vehicle for its consumers. After all, today's self-conscious teenagers aren't exactly the types who would suffer through a 30-minute spiel on skin care. They live their lives through texts and tweets, harboring little patience for advertisements longer than an average commercial break. To compensate, G-R has dipped its toe into the social media pool. So far Proactiv has amassed more than 56,000 Facebook fans and 25,000 Twitter followers. Its celebrity spots have done well, too, with several million views on YouTube.

Still, G-R is a company modeled on old media. The $10 to $15 million it pays stars to promote Proactiv isn't even included in the company's gargantuan $200 million media budget, most of which is spent on airtime. Also, up until recently G-R controlled more than 10,000 1-800 numbers with each one allotted to a particular region. That way the company is able to tell exactly where and when they are selling their goods. Now as G-R spends $11 million on billboard, magazine, and television ads there's no telling what markets they are tapping into. With social media, however, G-R can use the access to the origins and interests of its fans to deliver customized, meaningful advertisements. Only time will tell if G-R is too entrenched in the infomercial format to completely break through to this increasingly connected generation.[iv]

lecture link 16-6

AMERICANS RETURN TO CLIPPING COUPONS

Way back in 1992, coupon use in the United States peaked as Americans redeemed over 7.9 billion coupons for discounted items. In the following years, however, coupon use declined steadily, reaching an ultimate low of 2.6 billion coupons redeemed in 2006. Overall coupon redemption continued to languish at that number until late 2008 when, as we all know too well, the economy took its sharp turn south. From then on, coupon use has increased exponentially quarter after quarter, rising by over 20% in 2009 to hit 3.2 billion coupons redeemed.

Even as the economy has begun to recover, coupon use is still on the rise. What was once considered an unfashionable and all too thrifty way of saving money has once again become an easy, everyday way for consumers to save cash at the counter. Besides the usual coupon sheets that come bundled in most local papers, many Americans have turned to the Web in search of savings. Coupons.com, for instance, allows consumers to print coupons for various household items off its website. In 2008 users printed $313 million worth of coupons from the site. By June 2009 the site had already surpassed that mark, and by year's end consumers had printed off nearly $1 billion in savings.

Companies are benefiting from increased coupon usage as well. After anemic sales during the 2008 holiday season, businesses found themselves marking down products by 60 or 70% just to get them off the shelves. In December 2010, though, companies anticipated another sparse holiday by reducing inventories at the end of the year. With limited inventory and no apparent markdowns available, the burden of finding deals went to the consumers, who inevitably turned to coupons. This way companies were able to maintain decent profit margins by keeping their supplies low while the consumer hunted for savings in their coupon books, not the clearance rack.[v]

lecture link 16-7

WRAP YOUR SUV

Some companies pay millions to have their logos on Dale Earnhardt Jr.'s racecar, but others prefer to pay $500 to put their ads on cars of everyday citizens such as Brian Katz of Manhattan. Katz is one of tens of thousands of motorists who have signed up to have their cars and trucks wrapped in advertisements in exchange for a monthly stipend.

These offers are becoming so popular that car owners have been willing to limit where they shop and abide by a code of conduct while they are behind the wheel. People whose cars were wrapped with ads for two Coca-Cola products—Planet Java and Vault—were cautioned against sipping Pepsi products behind the wheel or parking at restaurant chains like KFC or Pizza Hut that serve Pepsi exclusively.

Vehicle wrapping started in 1993 when PepsiCo bought the rights to paint six Seattle city buses with its logo. Pepsi planned to put the buses in a paint shop for six weeks, but Louis Hoffman, general manager for a Seattle printing company called SuperGraphics, persuaded Pepsi to have the buses wrapped instead. Wrapping, using a vinyl material made by 3M, could be applied in less than two days. 3M uses an adhesive similar to the one on its Post-it notes that makes the "wrap" possible. Far from hurting the paint job, the wrap preserves it.

Brian Katz has had his car wrapped for several companies, including Jamba Juice and Verizon Wireless. Katz says the experience has been great, although he often has to roll down his window to answer strangers' questions about Verizon's calling plans.

Katz was matched with his advertisers by FreeCar Media, a Los Angeles ad agency that has a database of more than a million car owners who say they will wrap their cars for a fee, says Drew Livingston, president of the company. According to Livingston, companies like Procter & Gamble believe the wrap advertising is a low-cost, effective way to reach the demographic they desire. For example, the target market for a new version of Tide detergent could be defined as "stay-at-home moms with two-plus children who live in selected markets." Livingston's company would then find drivers in that demographic. "We feel that when you can wrap a mom's car and get it to her P.T.A. meeting or Curves gym, you are getting the acceptance from her social circle."

Another FreeCar participant, Jerome Harris, was in his junior year at Temple University when he had his Nissan Altima wrapped for a promotion for Trolls dolls. He earned $500 a month while his car was wrapped. In addition, he was required to hand out Trolls pens to fellow students during finals week.

The vehicle ad technique seems to pay off. Brian Morris, owner of We Fix Ugly Pools, a pool repair company in Phoenix, wrapped more than 30 vehicles in his fleet in ads for his company. He says he has earned more than $1 million in revenue over a year from people seeing one of his trucks in a driveway or in traffic. Morris advises his drivers to find the slowest lane in rush-hour traffic and "sit in it." He pays for the time and the gas. "The people behind you can't help but sit and stare."vi

lecture link 16-8

CONAN'S TWITTER TRIUMPH

In the winter of 2010, the future looked dim for late-night TV personality Conan O'Brien. Having taken over hosting duties on NBC's *Tonight Show* just seven months earlier, Conan left the show in a furor after a scheduling dispute would have pushed his timeslot forward a half-hour. Although his exit reaped him a cool $32.5 million, a contract stipulation that prohibited him from appearing on television for months left him depressed. After 17 years as a fixture of late-night television, Conan's ban from the airwaves could have destroyed his career completely.

Luckily, Conan had the good fortune to get fired just as Twitter was growing from a niche online tool to a widespread communication service among young people. As his battle with NBC raged, a devoted fan stayed up all night crafting a triumphant picture of Conan placed in front of an American flag emblazoned with the message "I'm with Coco." A Facebook fan page quickly appeared and used the image as the standard bearer of its cause, attracting hundreds of thousands of fans in a short time. After seeing the success of this grassroots social media movement, Conan launched his own Twitter account shortly after he left the *Tonight Show* for good. The feed gathered hundreds of fans overnight, which soon turned into thousands, then hundreds of thousands. Today, Conan's Twitter boasts more than 2.7 million followers and counting.

Conan's social media presence ensured that viewers would not forget him during the months they had to wait before his new talk show on TBS premiered. During this downtime Conan and his producers realized the potential of his massive online following. Conan's live act, "The Legally Prohibited from Being Funny on Television Tour," was advertised solely through Twitter, with most shows selling out hours after tickets went on sale. Once his TBS show began, Conan used his newfound creative control to remain in charge of all his online content. Every video clip posted to the show's website is owned by his own Team Coco production company. And as Conan's ratings have skyrocketed among the coveted 18- to 49-year-olds, his online presence ensures that people can access his content on their own time, not according to the will of the TV execs that took Conan off in the first place. With his enormous reach and open access, insiders speculate that Conan's online branding could revolutionize the medium of television.[vii]

lecture link 16-9

BLOGS FOR SMALL BUSINESSES

Many businesspeople believe that blogs are for large national brands. Blogs have enabled corporate executives like Jonathan Schwartz, president of Sun Microsystems, to talk directly to customers and employees.

However, many small companies are discovering that using blogs can help them create a brand identity. Blogs have also helped Paul Chaney gain national recognition for his Tupelo, Mississippi, based Radiant Marketing Group. Chaney is a professional blogger and uses the tool to gain recognition in cyberspace. Because blogs are text-based, updated frequently, and heavily linked to other blogs and websites, search engines like Google find them easily.

Type "radiant marketing" into Google and, although other companies with nearly the same name exist, 9 of 10 links on the first page point to Chaney. "Blogs are great business marketing tools," Chaney says. "It gets your message out there, establishes you as an industry leader, and puts a personal face on your business that encourages customer loyalty."

Unlike a website, blogs are easy to set up, a plus for small businesses. They are also written in a more informal, shoot-from-the hip style that conveys the writer's personality. Posts are short and updated daily or weekly. Because the blog is dynamic, viewers return more often.[viii]

critical thinking exercises

Name: ____________________________

Date: ____________________________

critical thinking exercise 16-1

ADVERTISING ON GOOGLE

One of the most popular types of online advertising involves buying an ad-link on search engines like Google, Yahoo, or Bing.[ix] Advertisers can narrowly target potential customers by buying an ad that will be placed next to the search results for a specific term. For instance, if you used Yahoo search engine and typed in "spaghetti," you would get 13 million results, ranging from spaghetti recipes, to encyclopedia references, to a link for the "Church of the Flying Spaghetti Monster." In the right column are "sponsored results"—ads for spaghetti cookbooks, pasta making equipment, and several distributors of spaghetti sauce.

Each search engine's advertising system is unique, but you can get a basic understanding of the process by investigating Google's system called "AdWords." Go to the AdWords website (https://adwords.google.com) and then answer the following questions. If the link does not work, you can start at www.google.com and click on "advertising programs" to get to the AdWords site.

1. Explain how the price of an ad on Google is calculated.

2. When purchasing search term advertising, a critical decision is identifying as many possible key terms to describe your product as possible. Suppose you were an online organic food store and you wanted to advertise your vegetarian spaghetti sauce on Google. What specific keywords would you want to include? (*Hint:* Use the "keyword tool.") List the best prospects.

3. Assume your daily advertising budget is $50. What would be the best combination of key terms and cost per click to reach your target audience?

Name: ____________________

Date: ____________________

critical thinking exercise 16-2

ADVERTISING APPEALS

Advertising is not a collection of homogeneous commercials. Each company and even different brands within the company use different advertising appeals. Humor works best for some commercials; honesty for others.

Watch television for several days and identify commercials that use the following appeals. Then decide what TV commercial shown in the last year you remember best, and which commercial irritated you the most.

1. Identify television commercials that use the following appeals:

   a. Honesty:

   b. Fear:

   c. Emotion:

   d. Sex:

   e. Humor:

   f. Irritation:

   g. Cost-comparison:

2. What TV commercial in the last year do you remember best? Why do you remember it?

3. What is the most obnoxious or irritating or disgusting TV advertisement you have seen recently? Why do you remember it?

notes on critical thinking exercise 16-2

1. *Identify television commercials that use the following appeals: honesty, fear, emotion, sex, humor, irritation, and cost-comparison.*

   Honesty. Ads featuring children are perceived by the public as more honest than those featuring adults. Children project an innocent, honest image. To an extent, celebrity testimonials try to use honesty as an appeal, but may not work.

   Fear. Fear is a powerful advertising hook. Life insurance companies have used it for decades to sell their product. Products as varied as smoke detectors, mouthwash, deodorant, and insect sprays use fear to develop sales.

   Emotion. One of the pioneers in using emotional appeals to sell products is Hallmark Cards. For years, wives have been shown presenting the perfect card to doting husbands and grandmothers crying over a cherished Christmas card.

   Sex. The old Madison Avenue adage "sex sells" still is true. Marketers of perfume use little else. Automobiles are shown driven by seductive women or well-dressed, elegant men. Cosmetics makers and perfume companies toot the advantages to one's social life of their brand of eye shadow or cologne.

   Humor. Used judicially, humor can be very effective. Each year the new Bud Lite advertisement, unveiled during the Super Bowl, is anticipated almost as much as the game itself.

   Irritation. These are the commercials we as consumers generally hate. They irritate us with repetition or stupidity, but we remember them. One pain relief product advertises "Head-On, applied directly to the forehead. Head-On, applied directly to the forehead, . . ." ad infinitum. The commercial is irritating, but gets the message across. Charmin bathroom tissue scored big several decades ago with its "Mr. Whipple" commercials a decade ago. One survey showed that more elementary school kids could identify Mr. Whipple than could identify the president of the United States.

   Cost-comparison. Cost comparison commercials appeal to the logical and rational side of us. Internet service providers frequently use cost comparisons to differentiate their services.

2. *What TV commercial in the last year do you remember best? Why do you remember it?*

   This will change with the whims of Madison Avenue.

3. *What is the most obnoxious or irritating or disgusting TV advertisement you have seen recently? Why do you remember it?*

   This, also, will vary. There are some truly disgusting advertisements on the air at any given time. Feminine hygiene products, adult diapers, and local furniture companies and automobile dealers usually top the list. Late-night ads for dial-a

Name: ____________________

Date: ____________________

critical thinking exercise 16-3

IDENTIFYING PRODUCT PLACEMENT

Your assignment is to watch prime-time television. Not a bad assignment, right? Watch at least two hours of prime-time programming. Try to include one drama, one comedy, and one reality program. Watch closely and try to identify brand-name products that are featured. Record the name of the program and the television channel. Then analyze the effect of the product placement and whether the placement is positive or negative.

	Program Name	Network	Products Featured	Is Placement Effect Positive or Negative? Why?
Drama				
Comedy				
Reality				

Name: ______________________________

Date: ______________________________

critical thinking exercise 16-4

ETHICS IN ADVERTISING

The professional organization representing the major advertising agencies is the American Association of Advertising Agencies (AAAA). The AAAA website explains the organization's mission and standards of practice. Go to the AAAA site (www.aaaa.org) and use the information you find there to answer the following questions. (Sometimes the Web address for a location changes. You might need to search to find the exact location mentioned.)

1. Give a brief summary of the organization's history, purpose, and membership.

2. What is the mission of the AAAA?

3. Find the AAAA's Standards of Practice. What does this document say about the basic beliefs or codes of conduct for advertisers?

4. What advertising practices are specifically excluded on ethical grounds?

Name: ______________________________

Date: ______________________________

critical thinking exercise 16-5

DESIGNING A WEBSITE

A well-designed website is one of the most important promotional tools for a company. The site should be designed to present a consistent message in a way that appeals to visitors. The information below is a guide to designing a simple website. The Microsoft Office site has a wealth of information on creating websites. Go to http://office.microsoft.com/en-us/assistance/HA010429391033.aspx. If the link is broken, you can go to the Office website (http://office.microsoft.com) and follow the links below.

Assistance > FrontPage > Creating web pages > Piecing together the Web page puzzle.

EXERCISE

You are the director of promotion for a new restaurant. Design a simple Web page to promote the restaurant. Choose one of the restaurant suggestions below or develop your own. Think through the message you wish to convey to consumers. Consider the structure of your site—what subpages would be appropriate (for example "menus," "about us," etc.) Then use the blank template on the next page to unveil the website for your company.

a. Shell-Fish Shuck: baked, broiled, and blackened seafood cuisine

b. Very Vegetarian: a vegetarian restaurant

c. The Cajun Platter: specializing in South Louisiana cuisine

d. Blues Bistro: southern cooking with great music

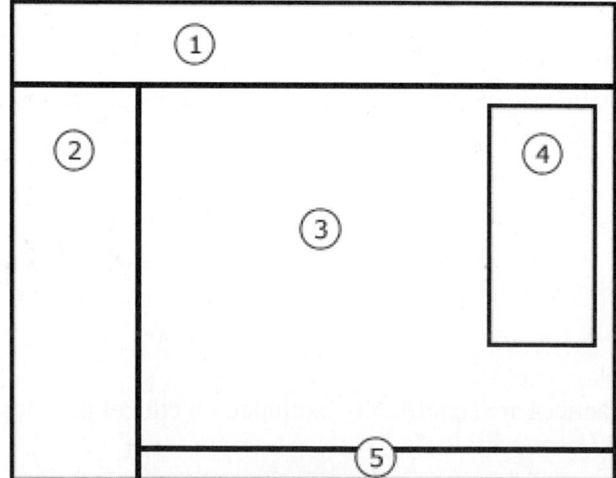

1. **Site identifier**—lets visitors know where they are; may include logo, name, or other graphics.
2. **Navigation bar**—shows visitors the structure of your website; helps them find content

3. **Main content**—the page title, headings, text, and images are what your visitors actually come to see.
4. **Secondary content**—may include advertising, announcements, news, and links.
5. **Identification bar**—copyright, last updated, contact information, security/privacy links, and name of Web developer.

critical thinking exercise 16-5 (continued)

bonus cases

bonus case 16-1

GROUPON'S TIGHT WALK TOWARD A RICH FUTURE

The tech industry moves at a lightning pace capable of generating scores of catastrophic flops and meteoric successes without ever looking back to take stock. The social media discount site Groupon seems to be destined to join the latter category since its launch just two years ago. A revenue-gushing juggernaut, the already astronomical $500 million Groupon rakes in annually is only expected to grow in the coming years. Naturally, Silicon Valley's biggest stars have been salivating over the company for ages (in tech industry time, of course), culminating in December 2010 with a whopping $6 billion buyout offer from Google. In an even bolder statement of the site's anticipated success, Groupon CEO Andrew Mason turned down Google.

Only time will tell if he made the right decision. One thing is certain, though: Groupon is not assured the throne of Internet discount dominance. The company faces several high-profile start-ups such as Tippr and the Amazon-backed LivingSocial as well as established review sites like Yelp. Also, a new study shows that employees disgruntled about the influx in deal seekers can actually harm the business more than the promotion helps. Restaurant servers and workers in niche industries not accustomed to coupon clippers can come to resent the new customers' disinclination to tip or their perceived sense of entitlement. As a result, the employee has no motivation to provide a positive experience, thus lessening the chance that Groupon will create repeat customers.

For now, the biggest asset at Groupon's disposal is its powerful brand name. Still, the sanctity of the Groupon name is far from secure. In fact, the company may have done irreparable harm to its brand with a series of poorly received Super Bowl ads in 2011. Conceived as a parody of public service announcements, each of the commercials featured a celebrity speaking seriously about an important social cause before abruptly changing the subject to extol about the deals one can find at Groupon. The joke didn't sit well with viewers, many of whom found the ads offensive and told Groupon as much in a flood of social media backlash. After five days Mason pulled the ads and apologized on his blog. While there's no telling how this PR snafu affected Groupon just yet, the incident serves as a lesson for the young company about how delicate even the mightiest brand name can be.[x]

discussion questions for bonus case 16-1

1. Will Groupon's Super Bowl ad disaster cause permanent damage to the brand?

2. What's the major challenge for Groupon going forward?

notes on discussion questions for bonus case 16-1

1. *Will Groupon's Super Bowl ad disaster cause permanent damage to the brand?*

   Without a doubt, Groupon took a hit to its image with the firm's poorly conceived Super Bowl ads. However, we suspect the damage will have a short-term effect and Groupon loyalists will come back to the fold. The quick apology and action by the Groupon CEO helped the firm regain its favorable footing.

2. *What's the major challenge for Groupon going forward?*

   As noted, competition is breathing down the firm's neck and a budding negative perception in the restaurant/service sector could cause some companies to rethink their Groupon participation. CEO Mason needs to address both problems.

bonus case 16-2

THE NEW BREED OF SALESPERSON

Tina Damron's job as a sales representative for Coordinated Resources has changed dramatically since she started working for the San Jose, California, office furniture business. Just a couple of years ago, Damron had very little to do with computers or high technology in general. She was a traditional salesperson; that is, one who relied more on personality and service than on high-tech tools. For example, she would write orders using three sheets of carbon paper; if she made a mistake, she would have to recopy the whole thing.

Today, Coordinated Resources's high-tech tools help make Damron a better salesperson. Using her laptop computer, she can make dramatic three-dimensional presentations of desks, chairs, and cubicles. She can also chat with other salespeople on the computer, obtain up-to-date information on furniture (e.g., the latest models and prices), and send orders. On one call, she knew that the customer was looking at a competitor's products, so she went on the Internet and found information about those products. She learned, for example, that you couldn't plug anything into the walls of the competitors' cubicles. That became a major selling point for Coordinated Resources's product.

Damron also has access to a website called UpShot.com, which tracks new customer leads. When salespeople find leads, they put all the information into UpShot where all the other salespeople can access it. The salesperson who previously had Damron's job left all kinds of information in UpShot. For example, he wrote that one customer didn't like to joke around. Damron was able to use that information on all her calls to that account. Before UpShot, Damron made all of her notes in a folder, but folders can get lost and are not always easy to share with others. Now all the information is available online, easily accessible to any colleagues who may need it.

Damron's customers place orders online and, as a result, receive faster delivery compared to those who place orders in person. Whereas an order used to take five weeks to be delivered, it can now be delivered within five days. What pleases Damron most about working online is that she can do more of her work at home. She's a single mother, and flexibility is important to her.

Damron is just one of thousands of salespeople whose jobs are changing because of the Internet. Buyers can now learn about product benefits online, so the salesperson's role is changing to one of an in-house consultant, helping customers solve problems. Although many questions can be handled online, there is still nothing like the personal attention and help a trained salesperson can provide.

Changes in technology have had a dramatic effect on all areas of promotion, not just selling. Advertising, for example, is changing because there are so many channels for a consumer to watch that advertising on, any one of them simply is not effective as it was when there were just a few. Furthermore, advertising on the Internet is very different from traditional advertising. Consumers can now get coupons over the Internet, and companies are completely rethinking the whole promotional process. [xi]

discussion questions for bonus case 16-2

1. What have you learned from this case about the changing role of the salesperson? What was the biggest influence on this change?

2. What changes might new technologies like TiVo have on TV advertising?

3. Has the role of the salesperson changed dramatically or is it just different now that the salesperson has so many technological tools to help?

notes on discussion questions for bonus case 16-2

1. *What have you learned from this case about the changing role of the salesperson? What was the biggest influence on this change?*

   Sales has changed in that sales force automation (SFA) has made the job easier and more complex both at the same time. A salesperson now has much more information at his or her command, but more expertise is expected from him or her as a result. The Internet and SFA will continue to have a major influence on the role of the salesperson. He or she is now more of a consultant. The information provided in the past in now ready in a cheaper, faster, 24/7 way on the Internet.

2. *What changes might new technologies like TiVo have on TV advertising?*

   TiVo makes it possible to record your favorite TV shows and watch them later without the commercials. Those advertisers who relied on TV exposure for sales are worried. What if people stopped watching commercials on TV? How would advertisers reach large audiences without TV advertising? The answer is to use radio, billboards, and other media. But none of them has the power of TV. Students may enjoy looking at the consequences and possible alternatives.

3. *Has the role of the salesperson changed dramatically or is it just different now that the salesperson has so many technological tools to help?*

   The role of the salesperson has not changed that dramatically. It's just that he or she has so much more information available now. Sharing that information with potential customers in an efficient way is critical. The salesperson must be able to present information faster, easier, and more effectively than could be done online or by a kiosk.

bonus case 16-3

BP'S CRUDE REPUTATION

We've passed the anniversary of the catastrophic oil spill at BP's Deepwater Horizon drilling rig. Although the story disappeared from the front page, the effects of the spill are still glaringly apparent to the residents of the Gulf shore. Oil slicks continue to sheen the water's surface in certain areas. Even worse, the 1.9 million gallons of toxic dispersants used by BP to counteract the spill led to a wave of sickness and even deaths of Gulf residents.

Nevertheless, BP's reputation at the corporate level remains strong. The company recently placed in the top three on the Lundquist Employer Branding list, which studies what a company offers, its recruitment process, and the accessibility of its website. But for a modern company in the age of social media and constant connectivity, industry accolades are not enough. Companies need to demonstrate a legitimate interest in the consequences of their actions rather than obsessing solely over how their failures will affect the brand. If a business chooses the latter option, as BP did, consumers have countless avenues at their disposal to express their outrage. And even after the mainstream media have moved on to the next scandal, Internet denizens will make sure that the company's unflattering online image remains intact.

For instance, a month after the spill a young comedy writer began the Twitter account BPGlobalPR. Sarcastic tweets like "Can't we just start calling it the oil ocean and move on please?" quickly garnered him a massive following. Although the oil spill has been absent from many mainstream news outlets for months, BPGloberPR remains active with more than 175,000 followers. Along with acerbic humor, the feed also posts links to articles about the spill that many would likely not have read were it not for the accessibility of Twitter. In the past, once a PR disaster stopped making headlines public perception against the company would cool down in turn. Now, however, as BP becomes ever more reluctant to address the spill, there is still plenty of information available to help the public neither forgive nor forget anytime soon.[xii]

discussion questions for bonus case 16-3

1. How are the social media changing the process of public relations?

2. Moving forward, what's the best course for BP to follow?

notes on discussion questions for bonus case 16-3

1. *How are the social media changing the process of public relations?*

   In the past, after a story ran its course in the main media (i.e., newspapers, television), the public tended to forget an issue or put it on the backburner. With the continuous presence of connectivity through new media, issues will not just fade into oblivion but will be kept alive.

2. *Moving forward, what's the best course for BP to follow?*

   BP may be best served by providing extended attention to the damage the oil spill caused and the lingering problems associated with it. With brand image becoming ever more important in today's global market, a short-term fix may not be not the best option.

bonus case 16-4

GUERILLA MARKETING

Many a student sits with a can of Red Bull next to him or her when preparing for a big exam. Red Bull, Monster, and Full Throttle are all energy drinks with giant doses of caffeine in them.

Dietrich Mateschitz is the man who introduced Red Bull to the U.S. market. Mateschitz graduated from the Vienna University of Economics and Business Administration. His major was world trade, and for a while he worked on the marketing of Procter & Gamble's Blendax toothpaste. He also did some marketing for Unilever and Jacobs Coffee. In 1987, he founded Red Bull with two Thai partners. Now he is a billionaire.

Mateschitz is an example of a billionaire who did not invent a wonderful new product. Instead, he made his money through creative marketing. Mateschitz bought a Thai company that already had an energy drink called Krating Daeng (red water buffalo). He changed the ingredients and the name (a little) and added carbonation. Red Bull is not known for tasting great. Furthermore, the name isn't very appealing and the price is high. So what made it so popular? For one thing, Red Bull has a lot of wake-up power, including 80 milligrams of caffeine. It also has mysterious ingredients such as taurine and glucuronolactone.

But the secret to Red Bull's success is something called guerrilla marketing. Guerrilla (not gorilla) marketing means studying the market for your product very carefully and then going after that market using nontraditional promotional means such as sponsoring sports events and creating word of mouth with sometimes outrageous promotions. Event marketing began with the sponsorship of mountain biking, paragliding, snowboarding, and hang-gliding competitions.

Mateschitz also sponsors Red Bull's Flutag (flying day) contest, in which competitors fly homemade contraptions over water. All together, Red Bull supports about 500 world-class extreme sports athletes. It also sponsors parties on various university campuses.

In addition to sponsoring extreme sports, Mateschitz sponsors the World Stunt Awards. He bought the Formula I Team Jaguar Racing from Ford and renamed it Red Bull Racing. In other words, the brand Red Bull has become closely associated with those who live large and are not afraid to take chances, including drinking something that has a lot of kick.

The success of Red Bull led to the introduction of more than 100 competitors, including Monster, whose slogan is "Unleash the Beast." There are lots of energy drinks available today, but Red Bull still stands out in the crowd because of its unusual promotions. This chapter is about effective promotional techniques. You will explore traditional promotional tools such as advertising, selling, and public relations. But you will also delve into some nontraditional promotional tools.[xiii]

discussion questions for bonus case 16-4

1. In this case of Red Bull, is it a success because of the producer discovering a real market need or is it strictly an example of all marketing hype and very little product substance? Could it be a combination of both factors?
2. If you were to define the marketing demographics of the target customer for Red Bull, what would they be? How has their success created more products that are similar in the marketplace?
3. How have the entire marketing efforts of the Red Bull product been different than some of the traditional marketing efforts or other drink products? Describe what is meant by "guerrilla marketing"?
4. How much do you see the success of Red Bull to market timing or marketing perseverance? Explain.

notes on discussion questions for bonus case 16-4

1. *In this case of Red Bull, is it a success because of the producer discovering a real market need or is it strictly an example of all marketing hype and very little product substance? Could it be a combination of both factors?*

   Red Bull is successful both because of the product image and target market demographics. The fact that it has more caffeine than other products makes it somewhat unique, but it is only a more caffeinated version of sodas like Mountain Dew that have already proved successful. As a result, the success of Red bull is probably a combination of a newly designed product and savvy marketing campaigns.

2. *If you were to define the marketing demographics of the target customer for Red Bull, what would they be? How has their success created more products that are similar in the marketplace?*

   Red Bull should market to a young crowd looking to identify with a contemporary and cool product. The punch of the caffeine is the hook.

3. *How have the entire marketing efforts of the Red Bull product been different then some of the traditional marketing efforts or other drink products? Describe what is meant by "guerrilla marketing"?*

   Because of the age group (primarily college students and other similar young adults), the company should probably put more emphasis on event marketing and other nontraditional marketing tools like podcasting and blogging. This age group tends to have more free time and is easily encouraged to participate in product promotional events designed for their age group. Guerrilla marketing is best defined by more local, event-planned marketing campaigns as opposed to more traditional print, magazine, and billboard media advertising mediums.

4. *How much do you see the success of Red Bull to market timing or marketing perseverance? Explain.*

   It appears Red Bull is successful because its young audience was ready to move on from soda and other caffeinated drinks. Market timing and successful marketing have both contributed to the product's success.

bonus case 16-5

WIEDEN + KENNEDY: EXPERIMENTAL PROMOTIONS

You may not know the name Dan Wieden, but you are likely to have seen his work. He is the person who created the "Just Do It" slogan for Nike. His company, Wieden + Kennedy, is known as one of the most creative advertising agencies in the United States.

One of the most controversial Nike ads from W+K featured a streaker running around a stadium during a soccer game. The filming was so realistic that many people thought that they were witnessing an actual event. In fact, the people in the stands were extras who were hired for the shoot. The commercial took five days to create in near freezing weather. It's no wonder the man in the commercial ran so fast! With the tagline "MoreGo," the commercial promoted Nike's ShoxNZ.

W+K was started in Portland, Oregon, in 1982 with Nike as its sole client. By the 1990s, Nike ads featuring Michael Jordan, Spike Lee, and Tiger Woods were being hailed as industry leaders. Wieden was credited with bringing in a new, postmodern school of advertising that blended influences from the popular culture, the art scene, independent film, and rock and rap music. For example, rapper Snoop Dogg was featured in a disco Nike ad. W+K now has many other clients, including ESPN and Miller Brewing.

As an independent ad agency, W+K is freer to experiment and take risks than traditional agencies are. Part of that risk-taking is to move the agency into entertainment as well as advertising. For example, W+K is putting together a Broadway musical about basketball that is set to a hip-hop beat. Its Tokyo office is launching a record label. You might also see documentary films, a weekly TV series, and MTV music videos coming out of the agency. W+K's first piece of self-funded entertainment was a book about dogs in Portland. It hit the bestseller lists overseas. You can see the appeal of the book by looking at the cover. It says, "Cat Spelled Backward Doesn't Spell God," an obvious dig at cat owners.

Why is an advertising agency getting involved in so many other ventures? Part of the answer is that the ad business was battered by the recession in early 2000, hurt tremendously by the fall of dot-coms, and threatened by new technology. In the early 2000s, companies wishing to promote their products began looking for ways of promotion more creative than the typical 30-second TV commercial. Companies feared, for one thing, that many consumers, armed with TiVo and other digital recorders, would simply skip watching commercials on TV by programming their recorders to avoid them.

Pop-up ads on the Internet have proved too annoying to be a powerful promotional tool. Nonetheless, many companies are using websites packed with product information, entertainment, and branding messages. Promoters tend toward using a variety of promotional companies rather than one huge agency that promises to do it all for them. That means that companies are hiring public relations firms, Internet specialists, media buying specialists, and international specialists to provide them with variety and expertise. That includes, of course, hiring an agency like W+K to come up with creative ads that people don't soon forget.[xiv]

discussion questions for bonus case 16-5

1. What are your favorite commercials or magazine ads? What makes them special to you?

2. What celebrities' endorsements have attracted you to buy a product? Which have turned you away from such a purchase?

3. If you were to obtain a job in advertising, what would you enjoy doing the most: creative, writing ad material, creating art, selling advertising to businesses, analyzing markets, shooting commercials, buying media, or what?

notes on discussion questions for bonus case 16-5

1. *What are your favorite commercials or magazine ads? What makes them special to you?*

   This is a great discussion starter. You may be amazed at the different reasons for enjoying commercials. What medium is mentioned the most? Is that a surprise? What kinds of products are featured?

2. *What celebrities' endorsements have attracted you to buy a product? Which have turned you away from such a purchase?*

   This question opens up the whole area of celebrity endorsements and their value to advertisers. Do students respond as favorably to celebrities such as Tiger Woods as you would expect from their wide use? Which celebrities are most attractive to students? Why?

3. *If you were to obtain a job in advertising, what would you enjoy doing the most: creative, writing ad material, creating art, selling advertising to businesses, analyzing markets, shooting commercials, buying media, or what?*

   A great chance to talk about the variety of jobs in advertising, including (surprisingly) accounting.

endnotes

---

[i] *Sources*: Barbara Kiviat, "Voice Lessons," *Time Inside Business,* June 2005; "Guess the Celebrity Voice-Over," *Entertainment Weekly,* August 5, 2011.

[ii] *Source:* Burt Helm, "He Puts the Soda in Pop Songs," *Bloomberg Businessweek*, December 2, 2010.

[iii] *Source:* Emily Steele, "New Tools for Picking TV Hits," *The Wall Street Journal*, May 23, 2011.

[iv] *Source:* Lacey Rose, "Shill Shocked," *Forbes*, November 22, 2010.

[v] *Source:* Sandra M. Jones, "Coupon Use: Consumers Hunt Savings Online, Increasing Usage for First Time since 1992," *Chicago Tribune*, December 10, 2009.

[vi] *Source:* Andrew Adam Newman, "Your Ad Here, on My S.U.V.? And You'll Pay?" *The New York Times*, August 27, 2007.

[vii] *Source:* Douglas Alden Warshaw, "Conan 2.0," *Fortune*, February 10, 2011.

[viii] *Source*: Emily Lecoz, "'Blogs' Changing Way Companies, People Create Their Brand Identity," *Northeast Mississippi Daily Journal*, January 31, 2005.

[ix] The Internet is a dynamic, changing information source. Web links noted in this manual were checked at the time of publication, but content may change over time. Please review the website before recommending it to your students.

[x] *Sources:* Brad Stone and Douglas MacMillan, "Groupon's $6 Billion Snub," *Bloomberg Businessweek*, December 8, 2010; Utpal M. Dholakia, "Why Employees Can Wreck Promotional Offers," *Harvard Business Review*, January–February 2011; Nathan Olivarez-Giles, "Groupon Pulls Controversial Super Bowl Ads," *Los Angeles Times*, February 11, 2011.

[xi] *Sources*: Andrea Peterson, "Making the Sale," *The Wall Street Journal*, November 15, 1999, p. R16; Philip B. Clark and Sean Callahan, "Sales Staffs: Adapt or Die," *BtoB*, April 10, 2000, pp. B1, B8, B55; Rekha Balu, "Life of a (Digital) Salesman," *Fast Company,* May 2000, pp. 377–378.

[xii] *Sources:* Anya Kamenetz, "Not So Slick," *Fast Company*, October 2010; Dahr Jamil, "Gulf Spill Sickness Wrecking Lives," *Aljazeera English*, March 9, 2011; Eric Silvers, "BP Ranked High for Employer Branding Despite Spill," *The Telegraph*, March 17, 2011.

[xiii] *Sources:* Kerry A. Dolan, "The Soda with Buzz," *Forbes*, March 28, 2005; Christopher Palmeri, "Hansen Natural," *BusinessWeek* , June 6, 2005; Wikipedia (online encyclopedia); Gwendolyn Bounds, "Move Over, Coke," *The Wall Street Journal* , January 30, 2006, pp. R1 and R3; Andrew Murr, "Monster vs. Red Bull," *Newsweek*, March 28, 2006.

[xiv] *Sources*: Warren Berger, "Just Do It. Again," *Business 2.0*, September 2002, pp. 77–84; Gerry Khermouch, "The 5 Rules of the Ad Game," *BusinessWeek*, January 20, 2003, pp. 12–13.

Understanding Accounting and Financial Information

chapter 17

critical thinking exercises

bonus cases

what's new in this edition

additions to the 10th edition:

- Getting to Know Siggi Hilmarsson of Siggi's Yogurt
- Name That Company: QuickBooks and Peachtree
- Legal Briefcase: Fighting Accounting Fraud Line-by-Line
- Making Ethical Decisions: Barking Up the Wrong Financial Statement
- Reaching Beyond Our Borders: Accountants of the World United
- Video case

revisions to the 10th edition:

- Text was revised to eliminate redundancy and tighten discussions.
- Statistical data and examples throughout the chapter were updated to reflect current information.

deletions from the 9th edition:

- Getting to Know Sean Perich of Bakery Barn
- Name That Company: Arthur Andersen
- Legal Briefcase
- Making Ethical Decisions
- Reaching Beyond Our Borders

brief chapter outline and learning goals

chapter 17

Understanding Accounting and Financial Information

Getting To Know SIGGI HILMARSSON of SIGGI'S YOGURT

learning goal 1

Demonstrate the role that accounting and financial information play for a business and for its stakeholders.

I. THE ROLE OF ACCOUNTING INFORMATION

A. What Is Accounting?

learning goal 2

Identify the different disciplines within the accounting profession.

II. ACCOUNTING DISCIPLINES

A. Managerial Accounting

B. Financial Accounting

C. Auditing

D. Tax Accounting

E. Governmental and Not-for-Profit Accounting

learning goal 3

List the steps in the accounting cycle, distinguish between accounting and bookkeeping, and explain how computers are used in accounting.

III. THE ACCOUNTING CYCLE

A. Accounting Technology

learning goal 4

Explain how the major financial statements differ.

IV. UNDERSTANDING KEY FINANCIAL STATEMENTS

A. The Fundamental Accounting Equation

B. The Balance Sheet

C. Classifying Assets

D. Liabilities and Owners' Equity Accounts

E. The Income Statement

F. Revenue

G. Cost of Goods Sold

H. Operating Expenses

I. Net Profit or Loss

J. The Statement of Cash Flows

K. The Need for Cash Flow Analysis

learning goal 5

Demonstrate the application of ratio analysis in reporting financial in-formation.

V. ANALYZING FINANCIAL PERFORMANCE USING RATIOS

A. Liquidity Ratios

B. Leverage (Debt) Ratios

C. Profitability (Performance) Ratios

D. Activity Ratios

VI. SUMMARY

lecture outline

Getting to Know SIGGI HILMARSSON of SIGGI'S YOGURT

He took a job with Deloitte after leaving Iceland for college at Columbia. Adjusting to American life proved to be difficult for Siggi and he missed some of his favorite foods, like skyr. After perfecting his recipe, financing came from one of his professors from Columbia and he found an underused dairy plant to make his goods. Siggi has faced cost issues, but as an accountant he knows what to look out for.

Until the development of accounting software simplified the accounting process, account-ants had to enter all financial information by hand. Today accounting software makes it possible for businesses to have financial information available whenever they need it. Name those two products.

(Students should read the chapter before guessing the company's name: QuickBooks and Peachtree)

learning goal 1

Demonstrate the role that accounting and financial information play for a business and for its stakeholders.

I. THE ROLE OF ACCOUNTING INFORMATION

A. Financial information is the **HEARTBEAT OF COMPETITIVE BUSINESS MANAGEMENT.**

1. You have to know something about accounting if you want to understand business.
2. You need to **LEARN BASIC ACCOUNTING TERMS** and understand basics of how accounts are kept.
3. To run a business effectively you need to be able to read, understand, and analyze accounting reports and financial statements.
4. Accounting reports and financial statements are as revealing of the **HEALTH OF A BUSINESS** as pulse rate and blood pressure reports are in revealing the health of a person.

lecture notes

PPT 17-1
Chapter Title

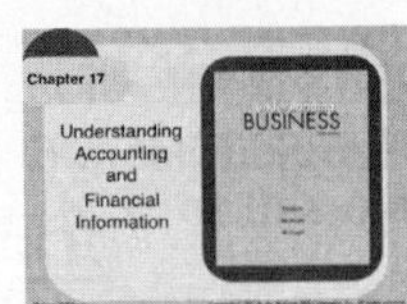

PPT 17-2
Learning Goals

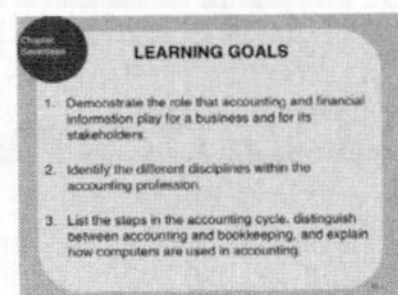

(See complete PowerPoint slide notes on page 17.50.)

PPT 17-3
Learning Goals

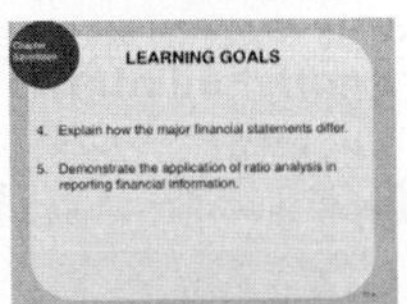

(See complete PowerPoint slide notes on page 17.50.)

PPT 17-4
Siggi Hilmarsson

(See complete PowerPoint slide notes on page 17.51.)

PPT 17-5
Name That Company

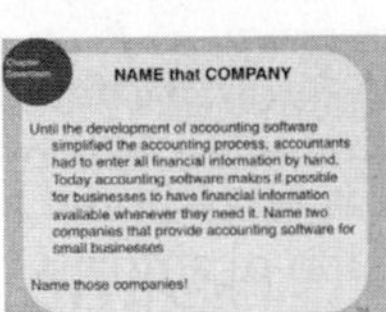

(See complete PowerPoint slide notes on page 17.51.)

lecture link 17-1
INNOVATING WITH OPEN BOOKS AND SHARED PROFITS

A little investment can go a long way to improving efficiency and profit margins. This is sometimes forgotten during recessions. (See the complete lecture link on page 17.69 in this manual.)

B. **WHAT IS ACCOUNTING?**

1. ***ACCOUNTING*** is the recording, classifying, summarizing, and interpreting of financial events and transactions to provide management and other interested parties with the information they need to make good decisions.

   a. **FINANCIAL TRANSACTIONS** include

      i. Buying and selling goods and services

      ii. Acquiring insurance

      iii. Paying employees

      iv. Using supplies

   b. An **ACCOUNTING SYSTEM** is the method used to record and summarize accounting data into reports.

2. **PURPOSES OF ACCOUNTING:**

   a. To give managers basic financial information so they may make better decisions.

   b. To report financial information to **PEOPLE OUTSIDE THE FIRM** such as owners, creditors, suppliers, employees, investors, and the government.

learning goal 2

Identify the different disciplines within the accounting profession.

II. ACCOUNTING DISCIPLINES

A. Accounting has been called the **LANGUAGE OF BUSINESS.**

1. Accounting is also the language used to report financial information about nonprofit organizations.

PPT 17-6
What's Accounting?

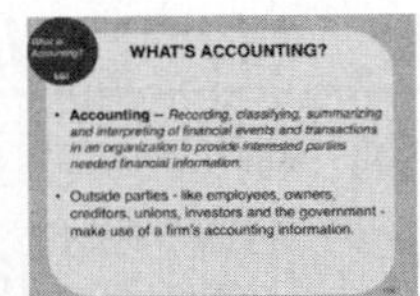

(See complete PowerPoint slide notes on page 17.51.)

TEXT FIGURE 17.1
The Accounting System
(Text page 465)

PPT 17-7
The Accounting System

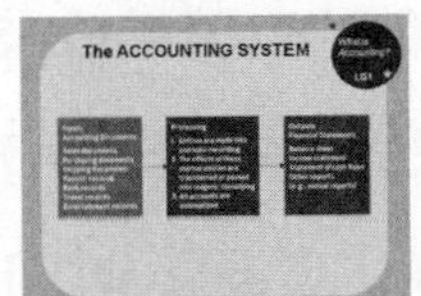

(See complete PowerPoint slide notes on page 17.52.)

TEXT FIGURE 17.2
Users of Accounting Information and the Required Reports
(Text page 465)

This text figure shows the various users of accounting information and the types of reports used to report to them.

PPT 17-8
Accountants' Responsibilities

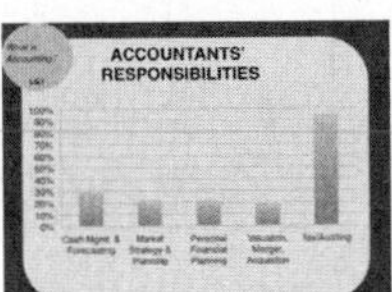

(See complete PowerPoint slide notes on page 17.52.)

2. Five key areas of the accounting profession are:
    a. Managerial accounting
    b. Financial accounting
    c. Auditing
    d. Tax accounting
    e. Governmental and not-for-profit accounting

B. **MANAGERIAL ACCOUNTING**

1. ***MANAGERIAL ACCOUNTING*** is accounting used to provide information and analyses to managers within the organization to assist them in decision making.
2. Managerial accounting is concerned with:
    a. **MEASURING AND REPORTING COSTS** of production, marketing, and other functions
    b. **PREPARING BUDGETS** (planning)
    c. Checking whether or not units are **STAYING WITHIN THEIR BUDGETS** (controlling)
    d. **DESIGNING STRATEGIES TO MINIMIZE TAXES**
3. A ***CERTIFIED MANAGEMENT ACCOUNTANT (CMA)*** is a professional accountant who has met certain educational and experience requirements, passed a qualifying exam in the field, and been certified by the Institute of Certified Management Accountants.

C. **FINANCIAL ACCOUNTING**

1. ***FINANCIAL ACCOUNTING*** is accounting information and analyses prepared for people outside

PPT 17-9
Managerial Accounting

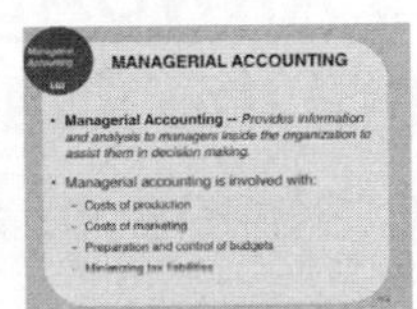

(See complete PowerPoint slide notes on page 17.53.)

lecture link 17-2
MANAGERIAL ACCOUNTING AND THE BUDGET PROCESS

In addition to the balance sheet, income statement, and cash flow statement, managers need other forms of financial information, especially information for budgeting and cost accounting. (See the complete lecture link on page 17.70 in this manual.)

PPT 17-10
Users of Accounting Information

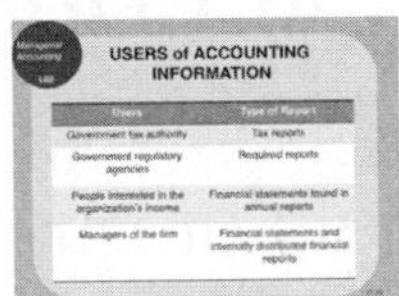

(See complete PowerPoint slide notes on page 17.53.)

the organization (owners and prospective owners, creditors and lenders, employee unions, customers, suppliers, governmental units, and the general public).

a. These **EXTERNAL USERS** are interested in the organization's profits and other financial information.

b. Much of this information is contained in the company's ***ANNUAL REPORT***, a yearly statement of the financial condition, progress, and expectations of an organization.

2. It is critical for firms to keep accurate financial information.

   a. A ***PRIVATE ACCOUNTANT*** is an accountant who works for a single firm, government agency, or nonprofit organization.

   b. A ***PUBLIC ACCOUNTANT*** is an accountant who provides his or her accounting services to individuals or businesses on a fee basis.

   c. **PUBLIC ACCOUNTANTS** help firms by:

      i. Designing an accounting system for a firm

      ii. Helping select the correct computer and software to run the system

      iii. Analyzing the financial strength of an organization

3. A ***CERTIFIED PUBLIC ACCOUNTANT (CPA)*** is an accountant who has passed a series of examinations established by the American Institute of Certified Public Accountants (AICPA).

PPT 17-11
Financial Accounting

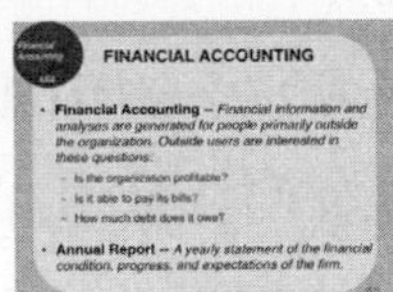

(See complete PowerPoint slide notes on page 17.54.)

critical thinking exercise 17-1
ANNUAL REPORTS ONLINE

This exercise asks the students to explore the annual report of a specific company by visiting the company's website. (See complete exercise on page 17.78 of this manual.)

PPT 17-12
How to Read an Annual Report

(See complete PowerPoint slide notes on page 17.54.)

PPT 17-13
Public versus Private Accountants

(See complete PowerPoint slide notes on page 17.55.)

4. Professional accounting assures users of financial information that financial reports of organizations are accurate.
   a. The independent financial accounting standards board (FASB) defines what are **GENERALLY ACCEPTED ACCOUNTING PRINCIPLES (GAAP)** that accountants must follow.
   b. If financial reports are prepared "in accordance with GAAP," users know the information is reported professionally.
5. In the early 2000s, several **SCANDALS** rocked the accounting industry.
   a. After scandals involving companies including WorldCom, Enron, and Tyco, the public has lost faith in corporate integrity.
   b. Arthur Andersen was convicted of obstruction of justice for its actions in the Enron case.
6. Scrutiny of the accounting industry is becoming more intense.
7. In response, Congress passed the **SARBANES-OXLEY ACT** that created:
   a. New government reporting standards for publicly traded companies
   b. The Public Company Accounting Oversight Board (PCAOB), charged with overseeing professional accountants
8. The recent financial crisis led to the **DODD-FRANK WALL STREET REFORM AND CONSUMER PROTECTION ACT**.

lecture link 17-3
COMING SOON—THE WIDE WORLD OF ACCOUNTING

Accounting standards may be going global in a big way. (See the complete lecture link on page 17.71 in this manual.)

PPT 17-14
Ways to Improve Accounting Practices

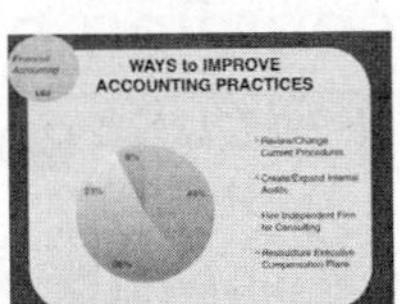

(See complete PowerPoint slide notes on page 17.55.)

TEXT FIGURE 17.3
Key Provisions of the Sarbanes-Oxley Act
(Text page 467)

The passage of the Sarbanes-Oxley Act was a landmark antifraud law, long overdue. However, one section of the law has caused problems for companies.

a. Dodd-Frank increased financial regulation.

b. CPAs must complete 150 hours of training and an exam, take about 40 hours of continuing education, qualify for recertification, and pass an ethics exam.

D. **AUDITING**

1. ***AUDITING*** is the job of reviewing and evaluating the records used to prepare the company's financial statements.

   a. Private accountants within the organization often perform **INTERNAL AUDITS** to ensure proper accounting procedures and reporting are carried on within the organization.

   b. Public accountants also conduct **INDEPENDENT AUDITS** of accounting records.

2. An ***INDEPENDENT AUDIT*** is an evaluation and unbiased opinion about the accuracy of company's financial statements.

3. To restore accounting's reputation, new rules for auditing and consulting have been instated.

4. A ***CERTIFIED INTERNAL AUDITOR (CIA)*** is an accountant who has a bachelor's degree and two years of experience in internal auditing, and who has passed an exam administered by the Institute of Internal Auditors.

E. **TAX ACCOUNTING**

1. All levels of government require **SUBMISSION OF TAX RETURNS,** filed at specific times and in a precise format.

lecture link 17-4

NEW REGULATIONS HIT WALL STREET

President Obama signed the Dodd-Frank Act into law. This new legislation should have dramatic effects on the future of American commerce. (See the complete lecture link on page 17.72 of this manual.)

PPT 17-15
The Dodd-Frank Act

(See complete PowerPoint slide notes on page 17.56.)

lecture link 17-5

THE POWER OF THE INTERNAL AUDITOR

The largest bankruptcy in U.S. history started with an internal auditor following an unexplained piece of financial information. (See complete lecture link on page 17.73 of this manual.)

PPT 17-16
Auditing Checks Accuracy

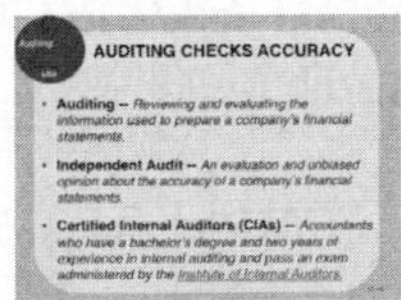

(See complete PowerPoint slide notes on page 17.57.)

legal briefcase
(Text page 468)

PPT 17-17
Fighting Accounting Fraud Line-by-Line

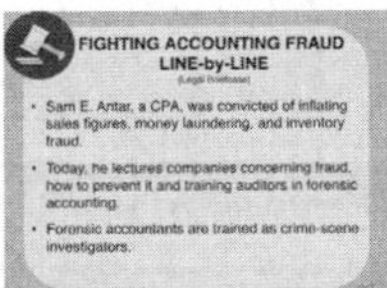

(See complete PowerPoint slide notes on page 17.57.)

2. A ***TAX ACCOUNTANT*** is an accountant trained in tax law and responsible for preparing tax returns and developing tax strategies.
3. As the burden of taxes grows, the role of the tax accountant becomes more important.

F. **GOVERNMENT AND NOT-FOR-PROFIT ACCOUNTING**

1. ***GOVERNMENT AND NOT-FOR-PROFIT ACCOUNTING*** is the accounting system for organizations whose purpose is not generating a profit but serving ratepayers, taxpayers, and others according to a duly approved budget.
2. Users of government accounting information, such as citizens and special interest groups, want to ensure that government is **MAKING THE PROPER USE OF TAXPAYERS' MONEY**.
3. Governmental standards are set by the Governmental Accounting Standards Board (GASB).
4. **NOT-FOR-PROFIT ORGANIZATIONS** have a growing need for trained accountants since contributors want to see exactly how and where the funds are being spent.

learning goal 3

List the steps in the accounting cycle, distinguish between accounting and bookkeeping, and explain how computers are used in accounting.

III. THE ACCOUNTING CYCLE

A. The ***ACCOUNTING CYCLE*** is a six-step procedure that results in the preparation and analysis of the major financial statements.

lecture link 17-6
WHERE THE JOBS WILL BE

During the recent recession, millions of jobs disappeared. However, one sector that may have a bright future is accounting. (See the complete lecture link on page 17.73 of this manual.)

PPT 17-18
Specialized Accountants

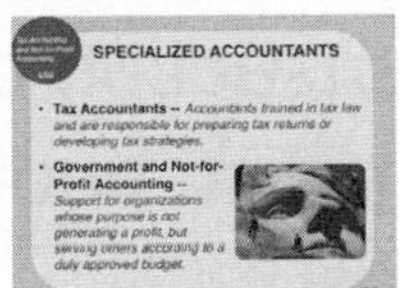

(See complete PowerPoint slide notes on page 17.57.)

progress assessment
(Text page 469)

PPT 17-19
Progress Assessment

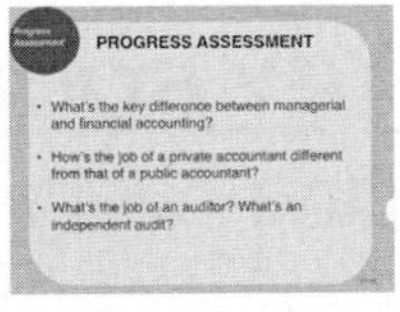

(See complete PowerPoint slide notes on page 17.58.)

lecture outline

1. ***BOOKKEEPING*** is the recording of business transactions.
   a. Accounting goes far beyond the mere recording of data to classify, summarize, interpret, and report data to managers.
   b. They suggest strategies for improving the financial condition of the company.
2. **WHAT BOOKKEEPERS DO**
   a. The first task of bookkeepers is to divide all the paperwork into **MEANINGFUL CATEGORIES.**
   b. Then they **RECORD THE DATA** from the original transaction documents (sales slips, etc.) into record books called **JOURNALS**.
   c. A ***JOURNAL*** is the record book or computer program where accounting data are first entered.
3. ***DOUBLE-ENTRY BOOKKEEPING*** is the concept of writing every business transaction in two places.
   a. In **DOUBLE-ENTRY BOOKKEEPING**, two entries in the journal are required for each company transaction.
   b. Bookkeepers can check one list against the other to make sure they add up to the same amount.
4. A ***LEDGER*** is a specialized accounting book or computer program in which information from accounting journals is accumulated into specific categories and posted so that managers can find

TEXT FIGURE 17.4
Steps in the Accounting Cycle
(Text page 470)

PPT 17-20
The Accounting Cycle

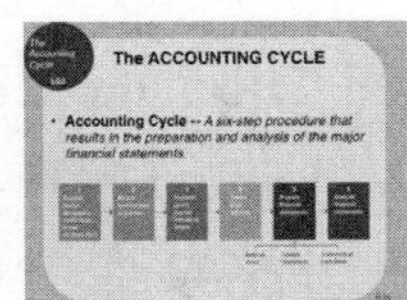

(See complete PowerPoint slide notes on page 17.58.)

PPT 17-21
Bookkeeper's Role

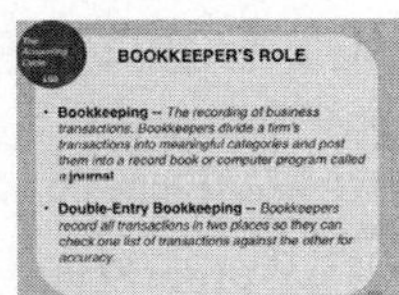

(See complete PowerPoint slide notes on page 17.59.)

PPT 17-22
Bookkeeper's Tools

(See complete PowerPoint slide notes on page 17.59.)

all the information about one account in the same place.

5. The six-step accounting cycle includes:
   a. ***Step 1.*** **ANALYZING** and **CATEGORIZING** documents
   b. ***Step 2.*** Putting the information into **JOURNALS**
   c. ***Step 3.*** Posting that information into **LEDGERS**
   d. ***Step 4.*** Preparing a ***TRIAL BALANCE*** (a summary of all the data in the account ledgers to show whether the figures are correct and balanced).
   e. ***Step 5.*** **PREPARING** an income statement, balance sheet, and statement of cash flows
   f. ***Step 6.*** **ANALYZING** the financial statements and determining the financial health of the company

B. **ACCOUNTING TECHNOLOGY**
   1. Computers have **SIMPLIFIED THE TASKS** involved in accounting so users get reports when and how they want them.
      a. Computers rapidly handle large amounts of financial information, so accountants are free to do more important tasks such as **FINANCIAL ANALYSIS.**
      b. Many **SMALL-BUSINESS ACCOUNTING PACKAGES** *(such as QuickBooks and Peachtree)* address the specific accounting needs of a small business.

PPT 17-23
Technology and Accounting

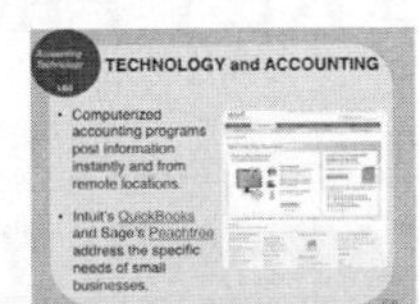

(See complete PowerPoint slide notes on page 17.59.)

c. Small-business owners should hire or consult with an accountant before they get started in business.

2. Computers do not make financial decisions by themselves.

   a. They are a **TOOL** for businesspeople to use.

   b. Computers help make accounting work **LESS MONOTONOUS.**

3. The work of an accountant requires training and very specific competencies.

learning goal 4

Explain how the major financial statements differ.

IV. UNDERSTANDING KEY FINANCIAL STATEMENTS

A. A ***FINANCIAL STATEMENT*** is the summary of all transactions that have occurred over a particular period.

1. These indicate a firm's financial health and stability.

2. **THE KEY FINANCIAL STATEMENTS** are:

   a. The **BALANCE SHEET**, which reports the firm's financial condition on a specific date.

   b. The **INCOME STATEMENT**, which summarizes revenues, cost of goods, and expenses for a specific period and highlights the total profit or loss the firm experienced during that period.

   c. The **STATEMENT OF CASH FLOWS,** which provides a summary of money coming into and going out of the firm.

Progress
assessment
(Text page 471)

PPT 17-24
Progress Assessment

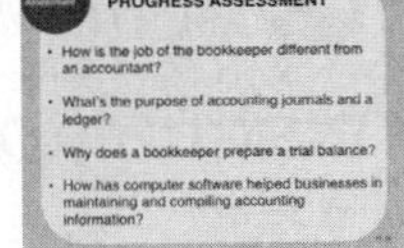

(See complete PowerPoint slide notes on page 17.60.)

PPT 17-25
Financial Statements

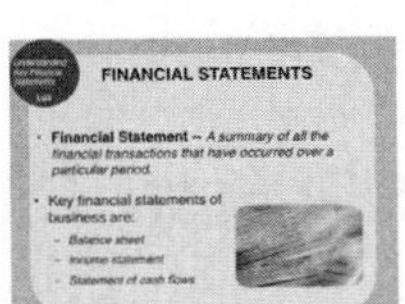

(See complete PowerPoint slide notes on page 17.60.)

3. The **DIFFERENCES** among the financial statements:
    a. The **BALANCE SHEET** details what the company owns and owes on a certain day.
    b. The **INCOME STATEMENT** shows the revenue a firm earned selling its products compared to its selling costs over a specific period of time.
    c. The **STATEMENT OF CASH FLOWS** shows the difference between cash coming in and cash going out of a business.

B. **THE FUNDAMENTAL ACCOUNTING EQUATION**
1. Your assets are equal to **WHAT YOU OWE** plus **WHAT YOU OWN.**
    a. This equation must always be balanced.
    b. Each business transaction is a recording of two transactions.
2. The ***FUNDAMENTAL ACCOUNTING EQUATION*** is **Assets = Liabilities + Owners' equity**; this is the basis for the balance sheet.

C. **THE BALANCE SHEET**
1. A ***BALANCE SHEET*** is the financial statement that reports a firm's financial condition at a specific time and is composed of three major accounts: assets, liabilities, and owners' equity.
2. The term *balance sheet* implies that the report shows a **BALANCE BETWEEN TWO FIGURES**—a firm's assets and its liabilities and owners' equity.

PPT 17-26
The Fundamental Accounting Equation

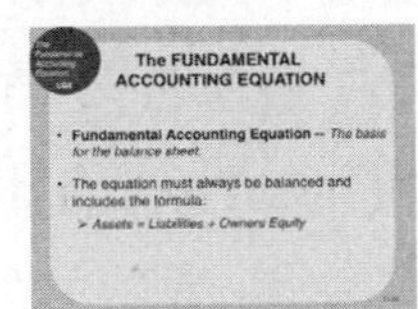

(See complete PowerPoint slide notes on page 17.60.)

PPT 17-27
The Balance Sheet

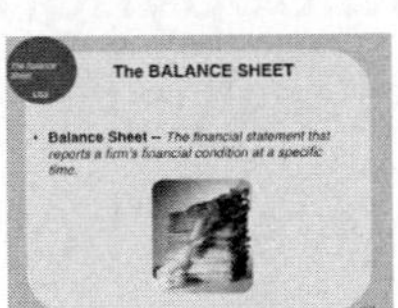

(See complete PowerPoint slide notes on page 17.61.)

3. It is important to follow **GENERALLY ACCEPTED ACCOUNTING PRINCIPLES (GAAP).**

D. **CLASSIFYING ASSETS**

1. ***ASSETS*** are economic resources (things of value) owned by the company.
   a. *Examples: equipment, buildings, land, patents, copyrights, and goodwill.*
   b. Assets include productive, **TANGIBLE** items that help generate income, as well as **INTANGIBLES** of value.
   c. **GOODWILL** represents the value attached to factors such as a firm's reputation, location, and superior products.
   d. Intangibles—such as brand names, trade-marks, and copyrights—can be among the firm's most valuable assets.
2. ***LIQUIDITY*** refers to how fast an asset can be converted into cash.
   a. Speedier conversion means higher liquidity.
   b. An **ACCOUNT RECEIVABLE** is the amount of money owed to the firm that it expects to receive within one year—it is considered a **LIQUID ASSET.**
   c. **LAND** is considered a **FIXED** or **LONG-TERM ASSET**, because it takes time, effort, and paperwork to sell.

TEXT FIGURE 17.5
Sample Very Vegetarian Balance Sheet
(Text page 473)

This text figure presents a sample balance sheet for Very Vegetarian, showing the major accounts.

PPT 17-28
Assets

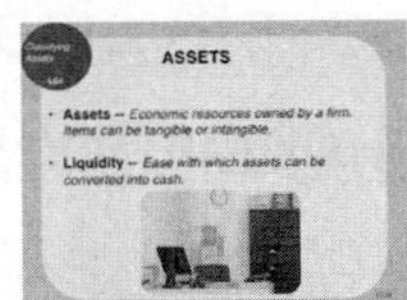

(See complete PowerPoint slide notes on page 17.61.)

lecture link 17-7
FINDING A FRIENDLY FACTOR

Factoring companies such as Receivables Exchange let businesses exchange accounts receivables for badly needed cash. (See the complete lecture link on page 17.74 in this manual.)

PPT 17-29
Classifying Assets

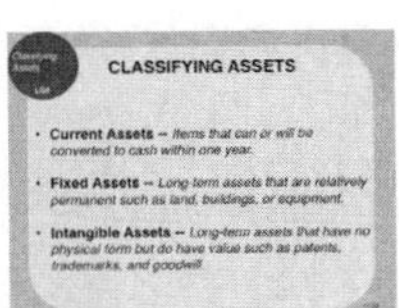

(See complete PowerPoint slide notes on page 17.61.)

3. **ASSETS ARE CHARACTERIZED BASED ON LIQUIDITY.**
   a. ***CURRENT ASSETS*** are items that can or will be converted to cash within one year *(examples: cash, accounts receivable, and inventory).*
   b. ***FIXED ASSETS*** are assets that are relatively permanent, *such as land, buildings, and equipment*.
   c. ***INTANGIBLE ASSETS*** are long-term assets *(e.g., patents, trademarks, copyrights)* that have no real physical form but do have value.

E. **LIABILITIES AND OWNERS' EQUITY ACCOUNTS**
   1. ***LIABILITIES*** are what the business owes to others (**DEBTS**).
      a. **CURRENT LIABILITIES** are debts due in one year or less.
      b. **LONG-TERM LIABILITIES** are debts not due for one year or longer.
      c. Common liabilities:
         i. ***ACCOUNTS PAYABLE*** are current liabilities or bills the company owes to others for merchandise or services purchased on credit but not yet paid for.
         ii. ***NOTES PAYABLE*** are short-term or long-term liabilities that a business promises to repay by a certain date.
         iii. ***BONDS PAYABLE*** are long-term liabilities that represent money lent to the firm that must be paid back.

PPT 17-30
Classifying Liabilities

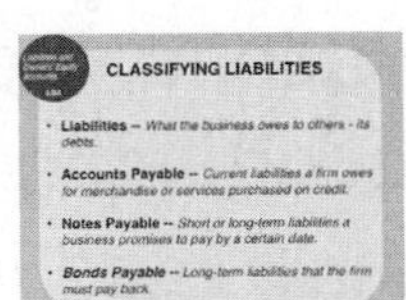

(See complete PowerPoint slide notes on page 17.62.)

2. **EQUITY** is the value of things you **OWN** (assets) minus the amount of money you **OWE** others (liabilities).
   a. The value of what stockholders own in a firm (minus liabilities) is called **STOCKHOLDERS'** (or **SHAREHOLDERS') EQUITY**.
   b. ***OWNERS' EQUITY*** is the amount of the business that belongs to the owners minus any liabilities owned by the business.
   c. The formula for **OWNERS' EQUITY:**

      Owners' equity = Assets ▤ Liabilities

   d. Businesses that are not incorporated identify this as a **CAPITAL ACCOUNT**.
   e. For corporations, the **OWNERS' EQUITY** account records the owners' claims to funds they have invested in the firm plus retained earnings.
   f. ***RETAINED EARNINGS*** are the accumulated earnings from a firm's profitable operations that were reinvested in the business and not paid out to stockholders in dividends.

F. **THE INCOME STATEMENT**
   1. The ***INCOME STATEMENT*** is the financial statement that shows a firm's profit after costs, expenses, and taxes; it summarizes all of the resources that have come into the firm (revenue), all the resources that have left the firm, and the resulting net income.
   2. ***NET INCOME OR NET LOSS*** is revenue left over after all costs and expenses, including taxes, are paid.

lecture notes

PPT 17-31
Owners' Equity Accounts

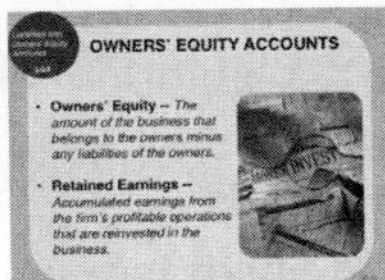

(See complete PowerPoint slide notes on page 17.62.)

TEXT FIGURE 17.6
You, Incorporated
(Text page 475)

This text figure helps students develop a personal balance sheet.

progress assessment
(Text page 475)

PPT 17-32
Progress Assessment

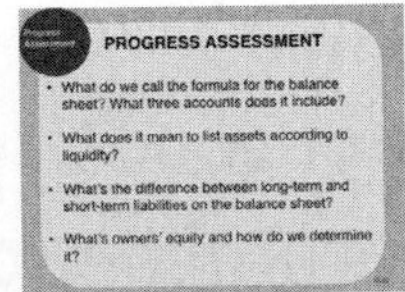

(See complete PowerPoint slide notes on page 17.62.)

PPT 17-33
The Income Statement

(See complete PowerPoint slide notes on page 17.63.)

lecture link 17-8
WHEN IS A SALE A SALE?

Small-business owners need to understand the distinction between cash-based and accrual-based accounting. (See the complete lecture link on page 17.75 in this manual.)

3. The income statement reports the results of operations over a particular period of time.
4. This statement includes valuable financial information for stockholders, lenders, investors, and employees.
5. The income statement is arranged according to **GENERALLY ACCEPTED ACCOUNTING PRINCIPLES (GAAP):**

   Revenue
   – Cost of goods sold
   = Gross profit (gross margin)
   – Operating expenses
   = Net income before taxes
   – Taxes
   = Net income or loss

G. **REVENUE** is the value of what is received for goods sold, services rendered, and other financial sources.

1. There is a difference between revenue and sales.
2. Most revenue comes from **SALES**, but other sources of revenue include rents earned, interest earned, and so forth.
3. **GROSS SALES** are the total of all sales the firm completed.
4. **NET SALES** are gross sales minus returns, discounts, and allowances.

H. **COST OF GOODS SOLD**

1. ***COST OF GOODS SOLD** (or **COST OF GOODS MANUFACTURED**)* is a measure of the cost of merchandise sold or cost of raw materials and supplies used for producing items for resale.

TEXT FIGURE 17.7
Sample Very Vegetarian Income Statement
(Text page 477)

This text figure shows the calculations involved in creating Very Vegetarian's income statement.

PPT 17-34
The Income Statement

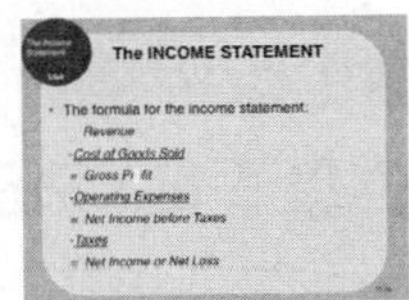

(See complete PowerPoint slide notes on page 17.63.)

PPT 17-35
Accounts of the Income Statement

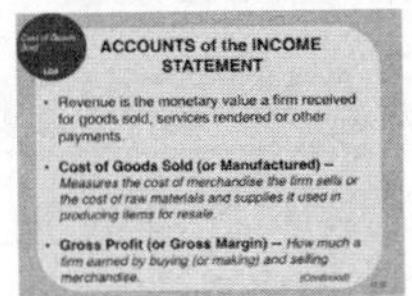

(See complete PowerPoint slide notes on page 17.64.)

   a. The cost of goods sold includes the purchase price plus any costs associated with obtaining and storing the goods.
   b. Valuing a firm's **INVENTORY** is complicated—it doesn't matter when an item was placed in inventory; what matters is how an accountant records the cost of the item when it was sold.
2. ***GROSS PROFIT (GROSS MARGIN)*** is how much a firm earned by buying (or making) and selling merchandise.
3. A service firm may have no cost of goods sold—gross profit would equal net revenue.
4. The gross profit doesn't tell you everything—you must **SUBTRACT EXPENSES** to determine net profit or loss.

I. **OPERATING EXPENSES**

1. ***OPERATING EXPENSES*** are costs involved in operating a business, such as rent, utilities, and salaries.
2. ***DEPRECIATION*** is the systemic write-off of the cost of a tangible asset over its estimated useful life.
   a. Assets such as equipment and machinery are considered depreciable subject to accounting rules.
   b. Companies are permitted to recapture the cost of assets using **DEPRECIATION** as a business operation expense.
3. **OPERATING EXPENSES** can be classified into two categories:

PPT 17-36
Accounts of the Income Statement

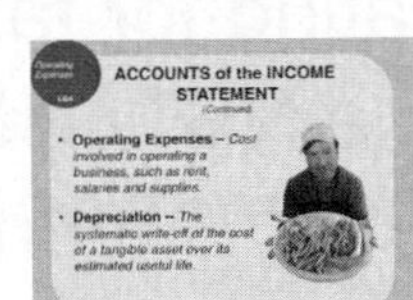

(See complete PowerPoint slide notes on page 17.64.)

critical thinking exercise 17-2
THE PIZZA STAND

A student organization plans to operate a pizza stand during homecoming weekend. This exercise asks students to prepare a budget and calculate expected profit. (See complete exercise on page 17.80 of this manual.)

   a. **SELLING EXPENSES** are expenses related to the marketing and distribution of the firm's goods or services.
   b. **GENERAL EXPENSES** are administrative expenses of the firm, such as depreciation and rent.

J. **NET PROFIT OR LOSS**

1. After all expenses are deducted, the firm's **NET INCOME BEFORE TAXES** is determined.
   a. Net income can also be referred to as **NET EARNINGS** or **NET PROFIT.**
   b. After allocating for taxes, you get to the bottom line, the **NET INCOME** (or perhaps **NET LOSS**) the firm incurred from revenue minus sales returns, costs, expenses, and taxes.
2. Businesses need to keep track of how much money they earn, spend, how much cash they have on hand, and so on.
3. Users of financial information are very interested in the **FLOW OF CASH** into and the flow of cash out of a business.

K. **THE STATEMENT OF CASH FLOWS**

1. The ***STATEMENT OF CASH FLOWS*** is the financial statement that reports cash receipts and disbursement related to the firm's three major activities: operations, investment, and financing.
   a. **OPERATIONS**: Cash transactions associated with running the business
   b. **INVESTMENTS**: Cash used in or provided by the firm's investment activities

SPOTLIGHT ON
small business
(Text page 478)

PPT 17-37
What's Coming and Going at the College Bookstore

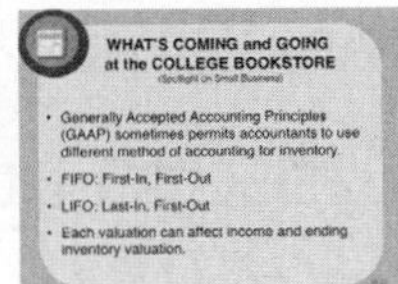

(See complete PowerPoint slide notes on page 17.64.)

critical thinking exercise 17-3
PREPARING FINANCIAL STATEMENTS

This exercise directs students to use a given list of accounts to create a balance sheet and income statement. (See complete exercise on page 17.84 of this manual.)

PPT 17-38
The Statement of Cash Flows

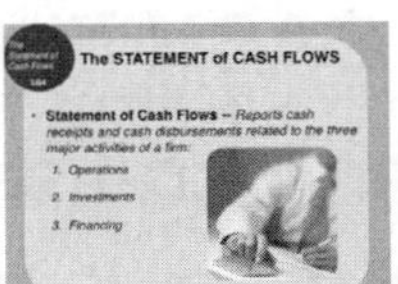

(See complete PowerPoint slide notes on page 17.64.)

   c. **FINANCING**: Cash raised from the issuance of new debt or equity capital or cash used to pay business expenses, past debts, or company dividends

2. Accountants analyze all of the **CASH CHANGES** that have occurred from operating, investing, and financing to determine the firm's net cash position.
3. Cash flow analysis answers questions such as:
   a. How much cash came into the business from current operations?
   b. Was cash used to buy stocks, bonds, or other investments?
   c. Were investments sold that brought in cash?
   d. How much money came in from issuing stock?
4. Managing cash flow can mean the success or failure of a business.

L. **THE NEED FOR CASH FLOW ANALYSIS**

1. A business can increase sales and increase profit and still suffer cash flow problems.
2. ***CASH FLOW*** is the difference between cash coming in and cash going out of a business.
3. Poor cash flow is a major problem for business and is particularly difficult for small business.
   a. In order to meet the demands of customers, a business buys more and more goods on credit.

lecture link 17-9

USING THE STATEMENT OF CASH FLOWS

Companies do not go out of business because they report net losses—they fail because they run out of cash. (See the complete lecture link on page 17.75 in this manual.)

PPT 17-39

Understanding Cash Flow

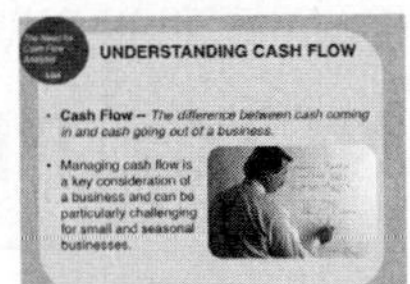

(See complete PowerPoint slide notes on page 17.65.)

TEXT FIGURE 17.8

Sample Very Vegetarian Statement of Cash Flows

(Text page 480)

This text figure shows a statement of cash flows, again using the example of Very Vegetarian.

bonus case 17-1

THE BEST-LAID PLANS OFTEN GO AWRY

This case discusses how offering credit to customers affected the finances of a pottery import firm. (See the complete case, discussion questions, and suggested answers beginning on page 17.95 of this manual.)

b. It is selling its goods and services, but isn't getting paid in time to turn around and pay its own bills.

c. When the firm's credit limit is reached, the bank may refuse further loans.

d. Too often, the company goes into **BANKRUPTCY** because there is no cash available when it is most needed.

4. Accountants can advise the firm whether it needs cash and, if so, how much.

learning goal 5

Demonstrate the application of ratio analysis in reporting financial information.

V. ANALYZING FINANCIAL PERFORMANCE USING RATIOS

A. Accountants use accurate financial information to prepare a financial analysis.

1. ***RATIO ANALYSIS*** is the assessment of a firm's financial condition using calculations and interpretations of financial ratios developed from the firm's financial statements.

2. **FINANCIAL RATIOS** are helpful in analyzing the actual performance of the company compared to its financial objectives.

3. They also provide key insights into the firm's performance compared to other firms in the industry.

B. **LIQUIDITY RATIOS** measure the company's ability to turn assets into cash to pay its short-term debts.

1. Short-term debts are expected to be repaid within one year.

MAKING **ethical decisions**
(Text page 481)

PPT 17-10
Barking Up the Wrong Financial Statement

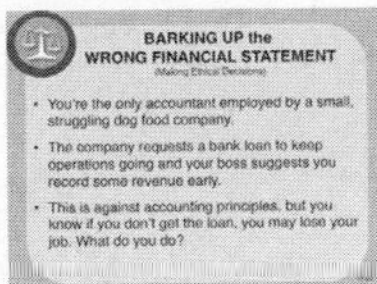

(See complete PowerPoint slide notes on page 17.65.)

progress assessment
(Text page 481)

PPT 17-41
Progress Assessment

PROGRESS ASSESSMENT
• What are the key steps in preparing an income statement?
• What's the difference between revenue and income on the income statement?
• Why is the statement of cash flows important in evaluating a firm's operations?

(See complete PowerPoint slide notes on page 17.65.)

lecture link 17-10
STAYING ALIVE IN TOUGH ECONOMIC TIMES

Having enough cash on hand is especially critical for entrepreneurs during tough economic times. (See the complete lecture link on page 17.53 of this manual.)

PPT 17-42
Using Financial Ratios

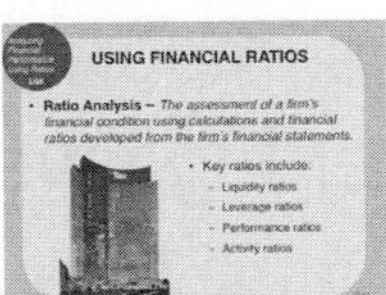

(See complete PowerPoint slide notes on page 17.66.)

2. The **CURRENT RATIO** is the ratio of a firm's current assets to its current liabilities.
   a. Current ratio = $\frac{\text{Current assets}}{\text{Current liabilities}}$
   b. Usually, a company with a current ratio of 2 or better is considered a safe credit risk.
   c. The ratio should be compared to that of competing firms within the industry and to the company's current ratio in the previous year.
3. The **ACID-TEST RATIO** (or **QUICK RATIO**) measures the cash, marketable securities, and receivables of the firm, to its current liabilities.
   a. **Acid-test ratio =**

      $$\frac{\text{Cash + Accounts receivable + Marketable securities}}{\text{Current liabilities}}$$

   b. This ratio is important to firms that have difficulty converting inventory into quick cash.

C. **LEVERAGE (DEBT) RATIOS** measure the degree to which a firm relies on borrowed funds in its operations.

1. The **DEBT TO OWNERS' EQUITY RATIO** measures the degree to which the company is financed by borrowed funds that must be repaid.
   a. **Debt to owners' equity ratio =**

      $$\frac{\text{Total liabilities}}{\text{Owners' equity}}$$

   b. A ratio above 1 (above 100%) shows that a firm has more debt than equity.
2. It is important to **COMPARE RATIOS** to those of other firms in the same industry and to the company's ratios in previous years.

critical thinking exercise 17-4

CALCULATING FINANCIAL RATIOS (ADVANCED)

This exercise directs students to use the financial reports of a company to calculate key financial ratios. (See complete exercise on page 17.87 of this manual.)

PPT 17-43
Commonly Used Liquidity Ratios

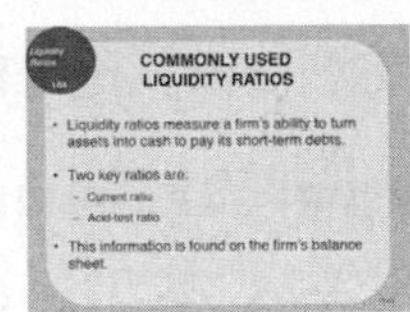

(See complete PowerPoint slide notes on page 17.66.)

critical thinking exercise 17-5

COMPARING INDUSTRY RATIOS (BASIC)

An investor is considering investing in a regional hotel chain. This exercise lets students compare the financial results for four possible investments. (See complete exercise on page 17.92 of this manual.)

PPT 17-44
Leverage Ratios

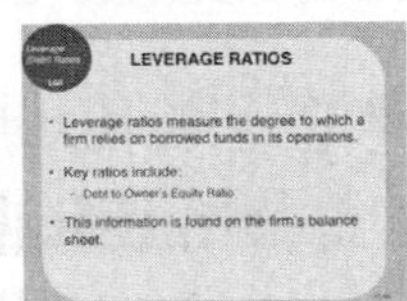

(See complete PowerPoint slide notes on page 17.67.)

D. **PROFITABILITY (PERFORMANCE) RATIOS** measure how effectively a firm is using its various resources to achieve profits.

1. **EARNINGS PER SHARE (EPS)** is an important ratio because earnings help stimulate growth.
   a. The Financial Accounting Standards Board requires companies to report their quarterly earning per share two ways: basic and diluted.
   b. **BASIC EARNINGS PER SHARE (BASIC EPS)** measures the amount of profit earned by a company for each share of common stock it has outstanding.
   c. **Basic earnings per share =**

$$\frac{\textbf{Net income after taxes}}{\textbf{Number of shares common stock outstanding}}$$

   d. **DILUTED EARNINGS PER SHARE (DILUTED EPS)** measures the amount of profit earned by a company for each share of outstanding common stock, but also takes into consideration stock options, warrants, preferred stock, and convertible debt securities that can be converted into common stock.

3. **RETURN ON SALES** is calculated by comparing a company's net income with its total sales.

$$\textbf{Return on sales} = \frac{\textbf{Net income}}{\textbf{Net sales}}$$

4. **RETURN ON EQUITY** (ROE) measures how much was earned for each dollar invested by owners.

PPT 17-45
Profitability Ratios

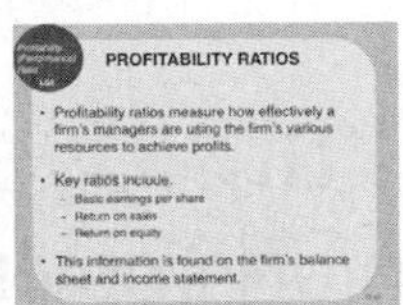

(See complete PowerPoint slide notes on page 17.67.)

a. The higher the **RISK** involved in an industry, the higher the **RETURN** investors expect on their investment.

b. It is calculated by comparing a company's net income with its total owner's equity.

c. **Return on equity =** $\frac{\textbf{Net income after taxes}}{\textbf{Total owners' equity}}$

5. These and other profitability ratios are vital measurements of company growth and management performance.

E. **ACTIVITY RATIOS** measure the effectiveness of the firm's management in using the assets that are available.

1. **INVENTORY TURNOVER RATIO** measures the speed of inventory moving through the firm and its conversion into sales.

a. The more efficiently a firm manages its inventory, the higher the return.

b. **Inventory turnover ratio =**

$$\frac{\textbf{Cost of goods sold}}{\textbf{Average inventory}}$$

c. A lower than average inventory turnover ratio often indicates obsolete merchandise on hand or poor buying practices.

d. Proper inventory control and expected inventory turnover should be monitored.

F. Finance professionals use several other specific ratios to learn more about a firm's financial condition.

VI. SUMMARY

TEXT FIGURE 17.9
Accounts in the Balance Sheet and Income Statement
(Text page 485)

This figure shows the major accounts included on the income statement and the balance sheet.

lecture link 17-11
USING YOUR COMPUTER IN SMALL-BUSINESS ACCOUNTING

The computer can be a priceless tool for a small-business owner. (See the complete lecture link on page 17.77 of this manual.)

PPT 17-46
Activity Ratios

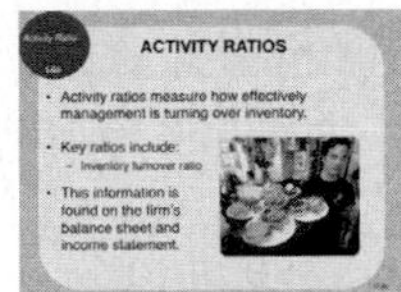

(See complete PowerPoint slide notes on page 17.67.)

bonus case 17-2
MANAGING BY THE NUMBERS

This case discusses how financially knowledgeable workers helped improve one company's finances. (See the complete case, discussion questions, and suggested answers beginning on page 17.97 of this manual.)

REACHING BEYOND our borders
(Text page 486

PPT 17-47
Accountants of the World United

(See complete PowerPoint slide notes on page 17.68.)

PPT 17-48
Timeline for the Move to IFRS

(See complete PowerPoint slide notes on page 17.68.)

progress assessment
(Text page 486)

PPT 17-49
Progress Assessment

(See complete PowerPoint slide notes on page 17.68.)

PowerPoint slide notes

PPT 17-1
Chapter Title

PPT 17-2
Learning Goals

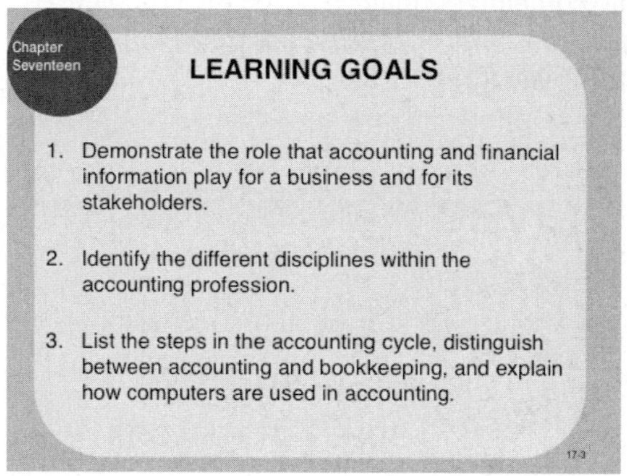

PPT 17-3
Learning Goals

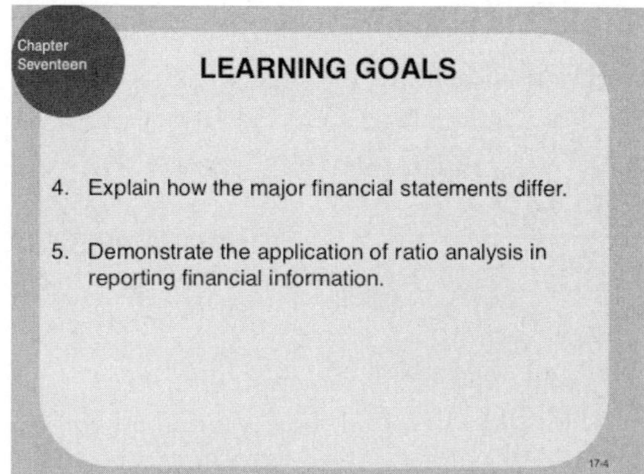

PPT 17-4
Siggi Hilmarsson

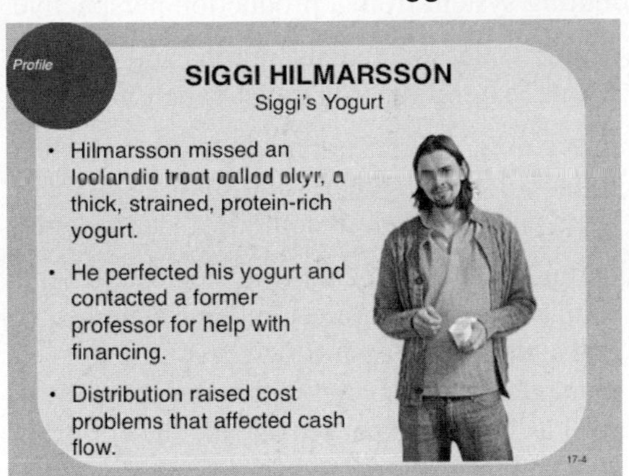

PPT 17-5
Name That Company

Companies: Intuit's QuickBooks and Sage's Peachtree

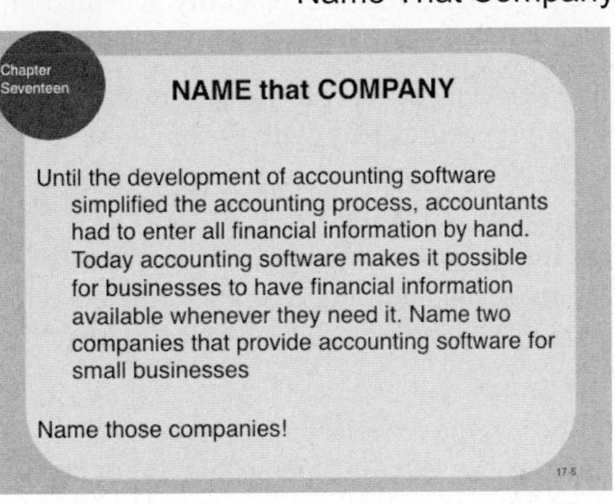

PPT 17-6
What's Accounting?

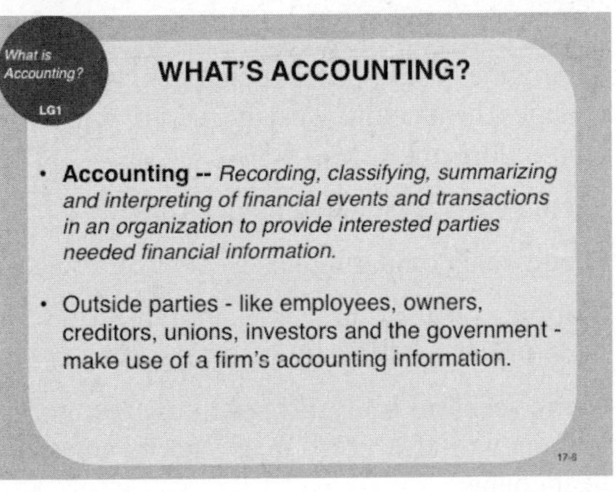

PPT 17-7
The Accounting System

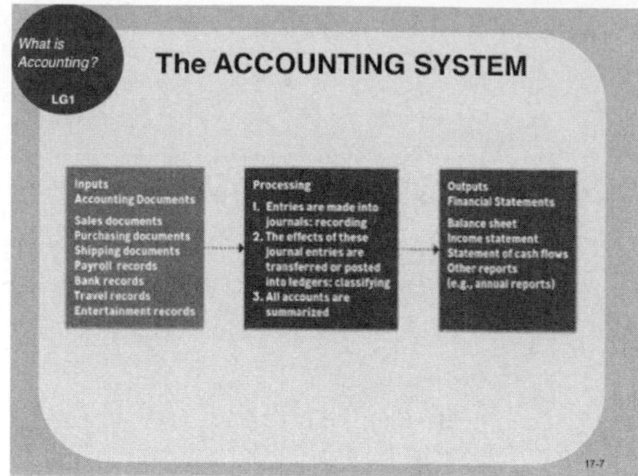

1. For students who are not taking an accounting class this slide can help them understand an accounting system from a production perspective:
   - Inputs: Sales documents, purchasing documents, payroll records travel expenses, etc.
   - Processing: Entries are made to journals; then transferred into ledgers; and finally summarized and reviewed to compile a trial balance.
   - Outputs: Development of financial statements such as the balance sheet, income statement, and statement of cash flows, prepared for management personnel within the company as well as interested parties outside the company.
2. It is very important for students to understand the importance of integrity when calculating numbers. Generally accepted accounting principles (GAAP) outline procedures that are generally accepted in the accounting field.
3. Ask the students, What role did questionable accounting procedures play with Enron, Fannie Mae, and WorldCom?

PPT 17-8
Accountants' Responsibilities

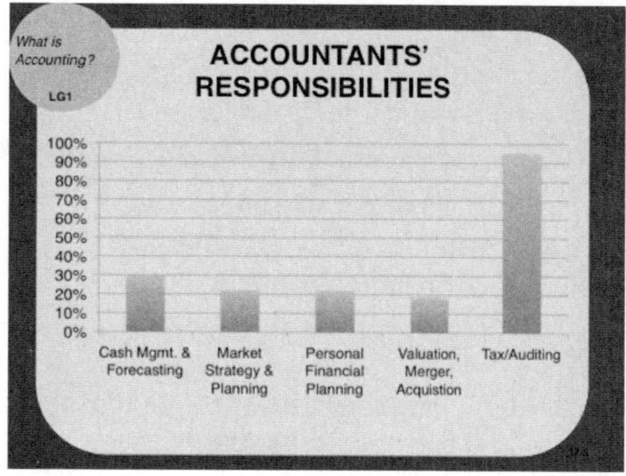

1. One of the biggest uses of accountants by business is taxes and auditing. Explain to the class that the theme of "integrity of numbers" is critical for business.
2. In addition to the reasons listed on the slide, accountants can offer businesses the following value-added services:
   - Getting complete visibility of processes
   - Seeing the true cost of a process or part of a process
   - Seeing the cost of process changes, volume changes, headcount, wastage, scrap, rejects, nonconformance, downtime
   - Seeing costs by job and by department
   - Seeing and comparing costs of outsourcing
   - Mapping business processes, organization-wide or job specific
   - Using scenario analysis to see how reengineering will affect resources such as costs and headcounts

PPT 17-9
Managerial Accounting

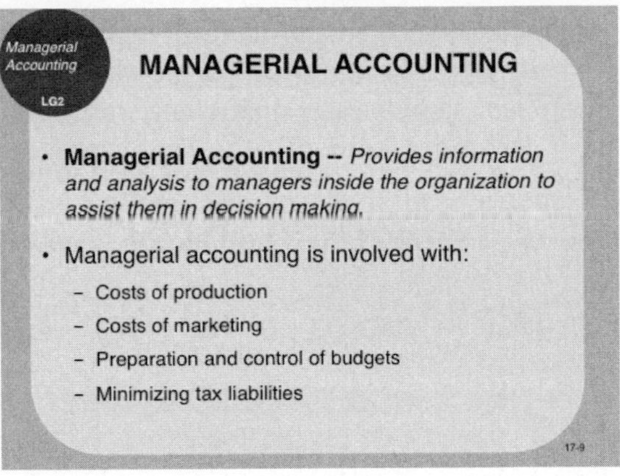

PPT 17-10
Users of Accounting Information

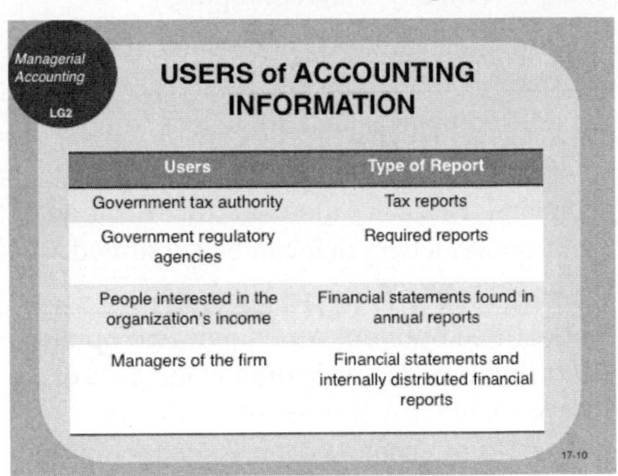

1. This slide (based on Figure 17.2) gives the students an overview of the importance of accounting information when managing a business. Accounting procedures are the foundation for controlling mechanisms that businesses put in place to measure performance and plan for the future. Accounting influences decisions for managers in the following ways:
   - Understanding cost behavior and perform cost–volume profit analysis
   - Using cost allocation in planning and control
   - Using job-order-costing and process-costing to track the flow of costs to products
   - Using relevant information to make marketing and production decisions
   - Using capital budgeting techniques to make long-term capital investment decisions
2. Accounting information can improve a company's ability to compete by:
   - Using competitor information and sales analysis to bring new concepts to the financial planning process
   - Learning to spot financial trends to predict strategic business decisions
   - Learning how to integrate technology into decision making
3. Explain to students the most important point of using this information to influence decision making is to make sure you have the RIGHT information, at the RIGHT time, and in the RIGHT format.

PPT 17-11
Financial Accounting

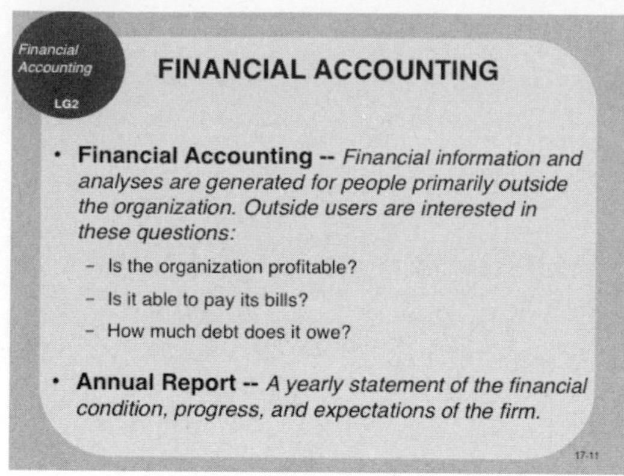

PPT 17-12
How to Read an Annual Report

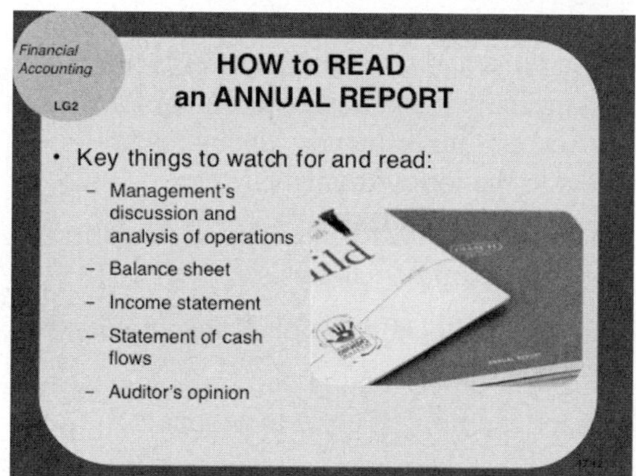

1. This slide presents the key areas to read when analyzing a company's annual report.
2. It is important that students understand that the annual report is more than a balance sheet but contains different areas that are just as important.
3. The auditor's opinion is a critical area for students to understand. Basically there are four different types of opinion letters that can be submitted. They are:
   A. Unqualified opinion: An unqualified opinion letter involves a certification made by the independent CPA firm that the company's financial statements were prepared in conformity with GAAP, and fairly represented the firm's financial condition on the statement date.
   B. Qualified opinion: A qualified auditor's opinion letter is one in which the CPA has included one or more specific qualifications to its assurance that the customer's financial statements follow GAAP. This means that one or more irregularities were found, and that the customer could not or would not correct these irregularities.
   C. Adverse opinion: This is the most serious of all the opinion letters that can accompany a customer's financial statements. When a CPA firm discovers information during the course of its audit that demonstrates material noncompliance with GAAP accounting rules, the CPA may choose to submit an adverse opinion letter to accompany the financial statements of the company under review.

(continued)

PPT 17-12
How to Read an Annual Report (continued)

D. Disclaimer of opinion: Due to scope limitations, a CPA may be unwilling to express any opinion about the accuracy of a customer's financial statements. A disclaimer of opinion letter means the CPA does not assume responsibility for the accuracy of the company's financial statements. (Source: www.encyclopediaofcredit.com.)

PPT 17-13
Public versus Private Accountants

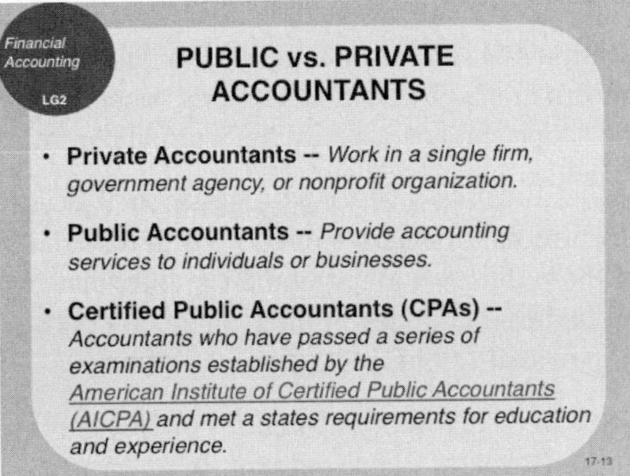

This slide helps highlight the difference in public and private accounting. This may be a good time to discuss what accounting or finance careers will do for students:

- Develop them into a well-rounded business executives
- Help them learn how to analyze and forecast financial goals through utilization of historical data, competitor information and financial data/information
- Make an impression at a multibillion-dollar corporation
- See the company increase its financial vitality by being a part of the financial planning and reporting process

(*Source:* www.Retailology.com.)

PPT 17-14
Ways to Improve Accounting Practices

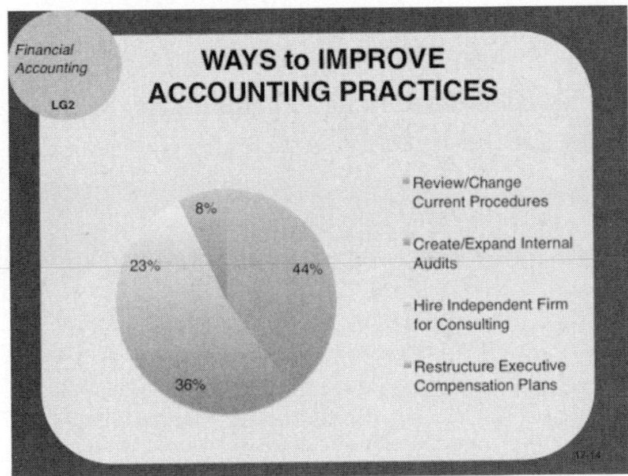

1. This slide charts how to improve accounting practices.
2. If the events of the last 10 years have taught us anything, it is that accurate financial data is critical for creditors, investors, and managers to make informed decisions.
3. The federal government has reacted with the passage of Sarbanes-Oxley. This law, which went into effect in 2002, has five major components:
   - Section 302: Periodic statutory financial reports are to include certifications that the signing officers have reviewed the report; the report does not contain any material untrue statements or material omission or be considered misleading; the financial statements and related information fairly present the financial condition and the results in all material respects; the signing officers are responsible for internal controls and have evaluated these internal controls within the previous 90 days and have reported on their findings; a list is

(continued)

PPT 17-14
Ways to Improve Accounting Practices
(continued)

provided of all deficiencies in the internal controls and information on any fraud that involves employees who are involved with internal activities; and any significant changes in internal controls or related factors that could have a negative impact on the internal controls are reported.

- Section 401: Financial statements published by issuers are required to be accurate and presented in a manner that does not contain incorrect statements.
- Section 404: Issuers are required to publish information in their annual reports concerning the scope and adequacy of the internal control structure and procedures for financial reporting.
- Section 409: Issuers are required to disclose to the public, on an urgent basis, information on material changes in their financial condition or operations.
- Section 802: Imposes penalties or fines and/or up to 20 years' imprisonment for altering, destroying, mutilating, concealing, or falsifying records, documents, or tangible objects with the intent to obstruct, impede, or influence a legal investigation.

(*Source:* www.soxlaw.com.)

PPT 17-15
Dodd-Frank Act

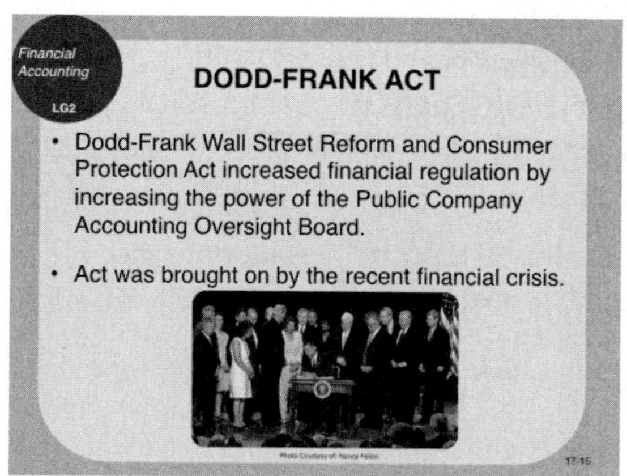

PPT 17-16
Auditing Checks Accuracy

AUDITING CHECKS ACCURACY

- **Auditing** -- *Reviewing and evaluating the information used to prepare a company's financial statements.*
- **Independent Audit** -- *An evaluation and unbiased opinion about the accuracy of a company's financial statements.*
- **Certified Internal Auditors (CIAs)** -- *Accountants who have a bachelor's degree and two years of experience in internal auditing and pass an exam administered by the Institute of Internal Auditors.*

17-16

PPT 17-17
Fighting Accounting Fraud Line-by-Line

FIGHTING ACCOUNTING FRAUD LINE-by-LINE
(Legal Briefcase)

- Sam E. Antar, a CPA, was convicted of inflating sales figures, money laundering, and inventory fraud.
- Today, he lectures companies concerning fraud, how to prevent it and training auditors in forensic accounting.
- Forensic accountants are trained as crime-scene investigators.

17-17

PPT 17-18
Specialized Accountants

SPECIALIZED ACCOUNTANTS

- **Tax Accountants** -- *Accountants trained in tax law and are responsible for preparing tax returns or developing tax strategies.*
- **Government and Not-for-Profit Accounting** -- *Support for organizations whose purpose is not generating a profit, but serving others according to a duly approved budget.*

17-18

PPT 17-19
Progress Assessment

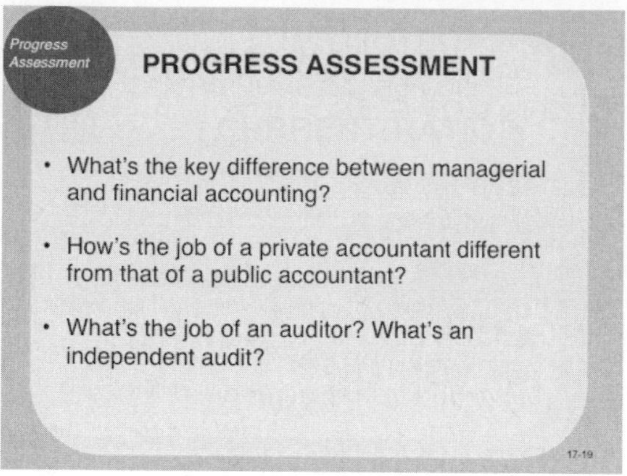

1. Managerial accounting provides information and analysis to the managers inside the organization and helps them make better-informed decisions. Managerial accounting is concerned with measuring and reporting cost of production, marketing, and other functions; preparing budgets; making sure business units stay within their budgets; and designing strategies to minimize taxes. Financial accounting differs from managerial accounting in that financial accounting generates information for people primarily outside the organization.
2. The private accountant works for a single firm, government agency, or nonprofit organization while public accountants work for accounting firms that provide accounting services for a fee. Public accountants provide services to individuals or businesses that include designing an accounting system, selecting software to run the accounting system, and analyzing an organization's financial performance.
3. Auditors are responsible for examining the financial health of the organization as well as looking into the operational effectiveness and efficiencies of the organization. An independent audit is an audit conducted by public accountants who provide an evaluation and unbiased opinion about the accuracy of a company's financial statements.

PPT 17-20
The Accounting Cycle

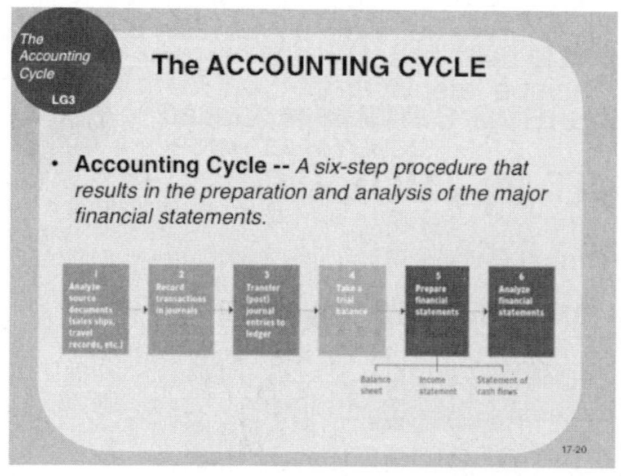

With this slide (based on Figure 17.4) students are provided with the step-by-step progression of the accounting cycle. Place particular emphasis on the accounting cycle to give the student an overview of reporting requirements. To start a discussion with students ask the following questions before showing the next few slides:

- Can you explain the differences between accounting and bookkeeping?
- What's the difference between an accounting journal and a ledger?
- Why does a bookkeeper prepare a trial balance?

PPT 17-21
Bookkeeper's Role

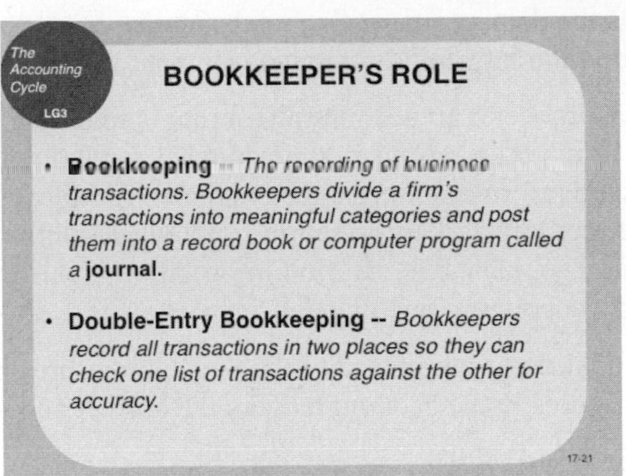

PPT 17-22
Bookkeeper's Tools

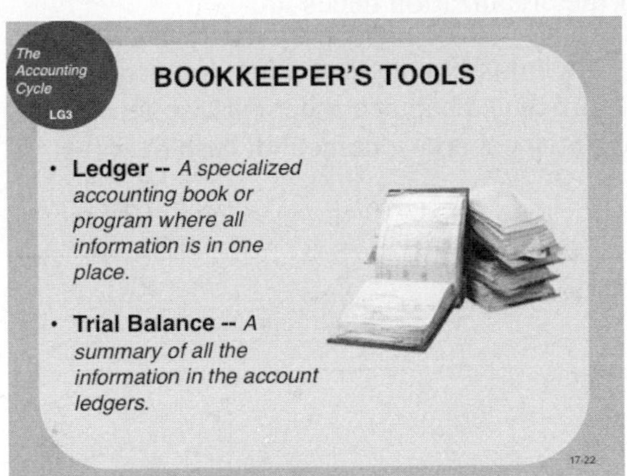

With this slide (based on Figure 17.4) students are provided with the step-by-step progression of the accounting cycle. Place particular emphasis on the accounting cycle to give the student an overview of reporting requirements. To start a discussion with students ask the following questions before showing the next few slides:

- Can you explain the differences between accounting and bookkeeping?
- What's the difference between an accounting journal and a ledger?
- Why does a bookkeeper prepare a trial balance?

PPT 17-23
Technology and Accounting

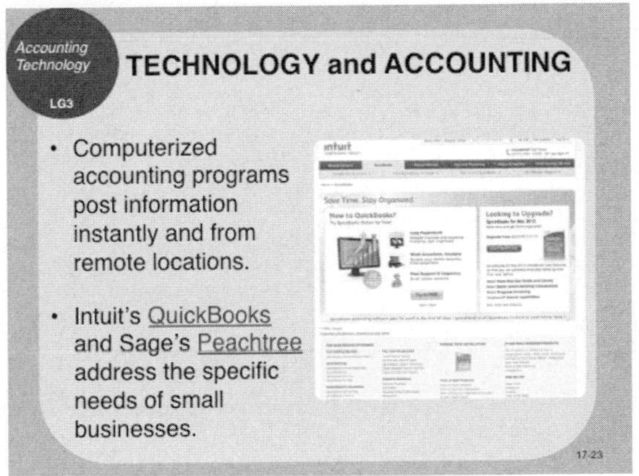

PPT 17-24
Progress Assessment

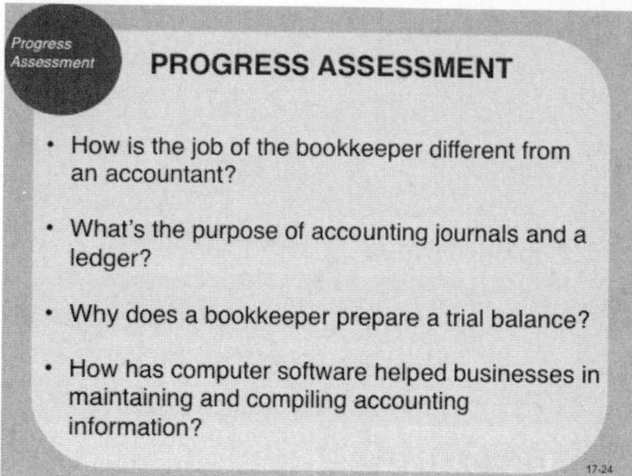

1. A bookkeeper classifies and summarizes the firm's financial data, while an accountant interprets the data, prepares financial statements, and reports the information to management.
2. The purpose of an accounting journal is to divide the firm's transactions into meaningful categories to keep information organized and manageable. A ledger transfers information from an accounting journal so managers can find information about a single account in one place.
3. A bookkeeper prepares a trial balance to ensure the figures in the account ledgers are correct and balanced.
4. Computer software post information from journals instantaneously even from remote locations so financial information is readily available whenever the organization needs it.

PPT 17-25
Financial Statements

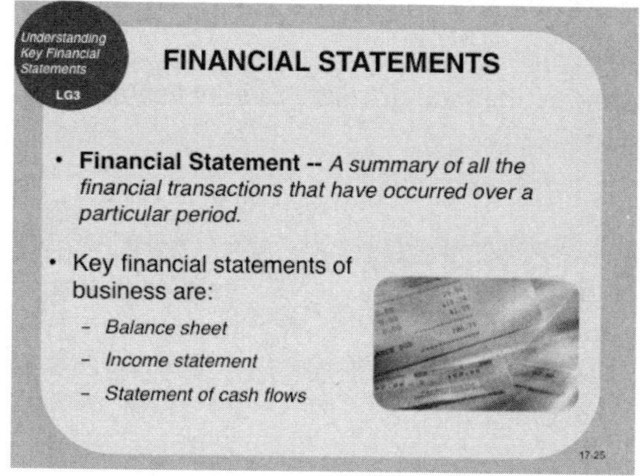

Students often do not understand that financial statements are more than a balance sheet but also incorporate the income statement and statement of cash flows

PPT 17-26
The Fundamental Accounting Equation

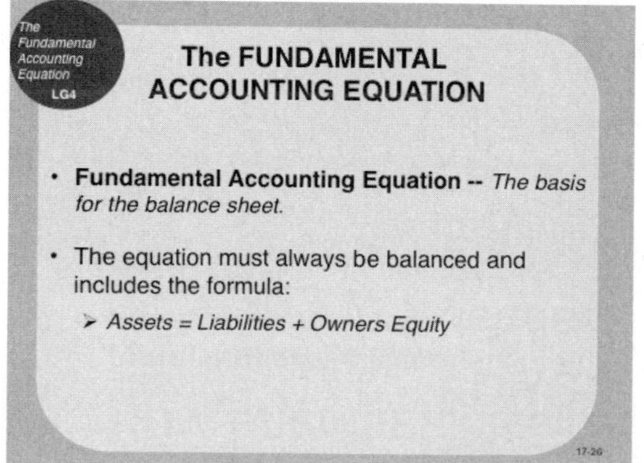

.

PPT 17-27
The Balance Sheet

See Figure 17.5 in the text for a sample balance sheet for Very Vegetarian.

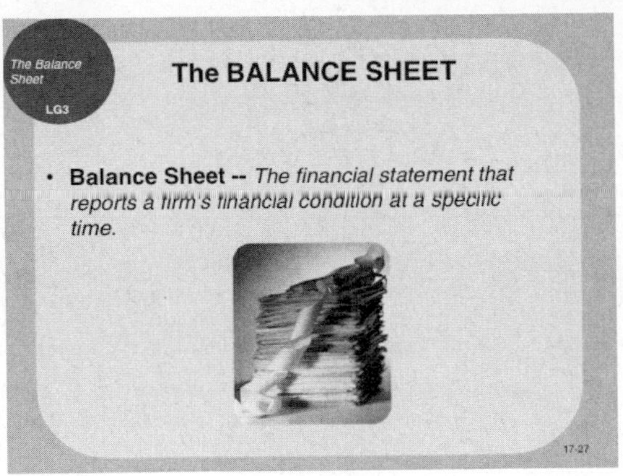

PPT 17-28
Assets

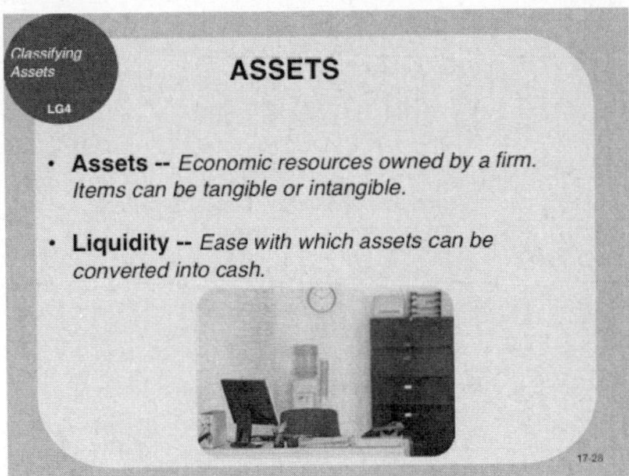

PPT 17-29
Classifying Assets

Assets are divided into three categories according to how fast they can be converted into cash.

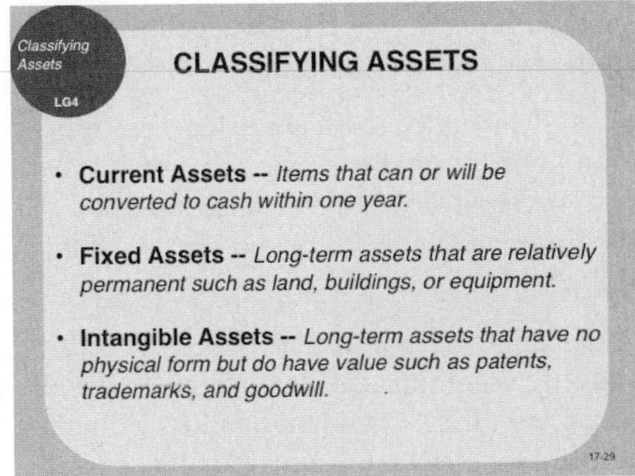

PPT 17-30
Classifying Liabilities

CLASSIFYING LIABILITIES

- **Liabilities** -- *What the business owes to others - its debts.*
- **Accounts Payable** -- *Current liabilities a firm owes for merchandise or services purchased on credit.*
- **Notes Payable** -- *Short or long-term liabilities a business promises to pay by a certain date.*
- ***Bonds Payable*** -- *Long-term liabilities that the firm must pay back.*

17-30

PPT 17-31
Owners' Equity Accounts

OWNERS' EQUITY ACCOUNTS

- **Owners' Equity** -- *The amount of the business that belongs to the owners minus any liabilities of the owners.*
- **Retained Earnings** -- *Accumulated earnings from the firm's profitable operations that are reinvested in the business.*

17-31

PPT 17-32
Progress Assessment

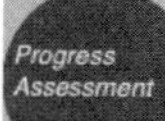

PROGRESS ASSESSMENT

- What do we call the formula for the balance sheet? What three accounts does it include?
- What does it mean to list assets according to liquidity?
- What's the difference between long-term and short-term liabilities on the balance sheet?
- What's owners' equity and how do we determine it?

17-32

1. The formula for the balance sheet is referred to as the fundamental accounting equation. This equation includes the following three accounts: assets, liabilities, and owners' equity.
2. Assets on the balance sheet are listed according to how quickly they can be converted to cash. Therefore, as you move down the balance sheet it becomes more difficult to convert the assets into "liquid" cash.
3. Liabilities are what the business owes to others. The liability account is divided into current and long-term liabilities. Common liability accounts include accounts payable, notes payable, and bonds payable.
4. Owners' equity is the amount of the business that belongs to the owners, minus any liabilities the business owes. The formula for owners' equity is assets minus liabilities.

PPT 17-33
The Income Statement

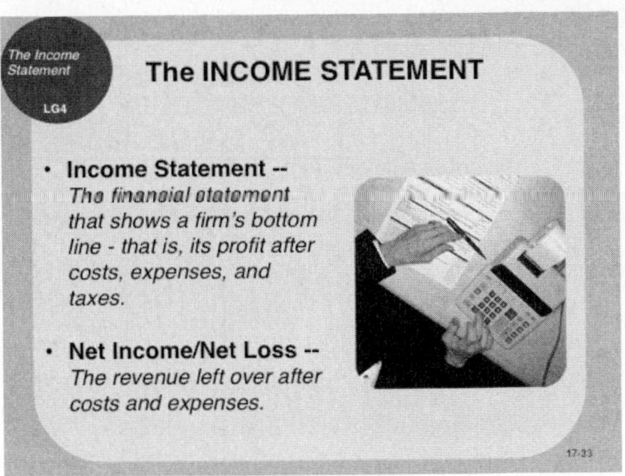

PPT 17-34
The Income Statement

See Figure 17.7 in the text for a sample income statement for Very Vegetarian.

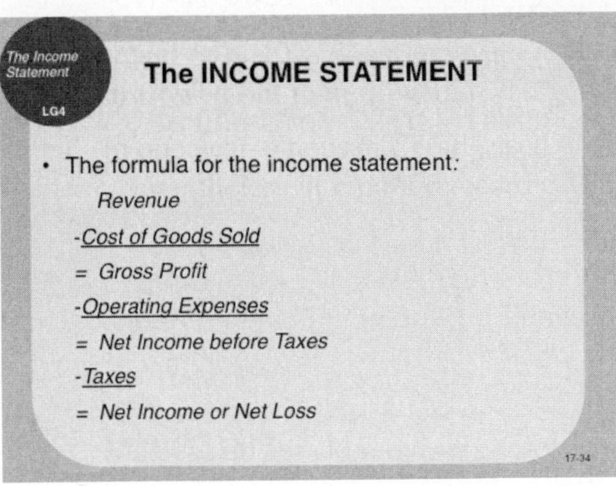

PPT 17-35
Accounts of the Income Statement

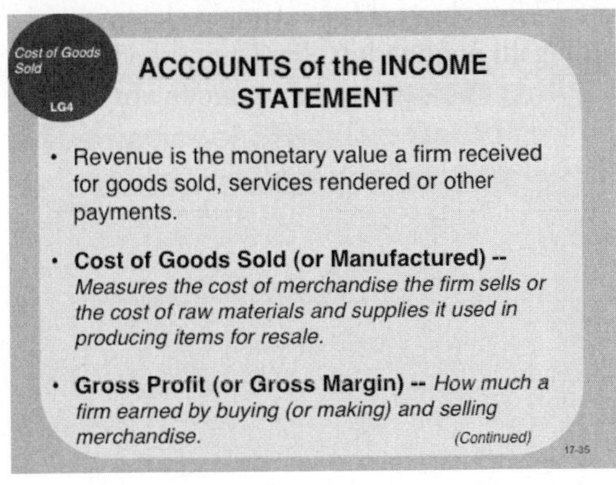

PPT 17-36
Accounts of the Income Statement

While depreciation is an expense, it is a noncash expense for the company.

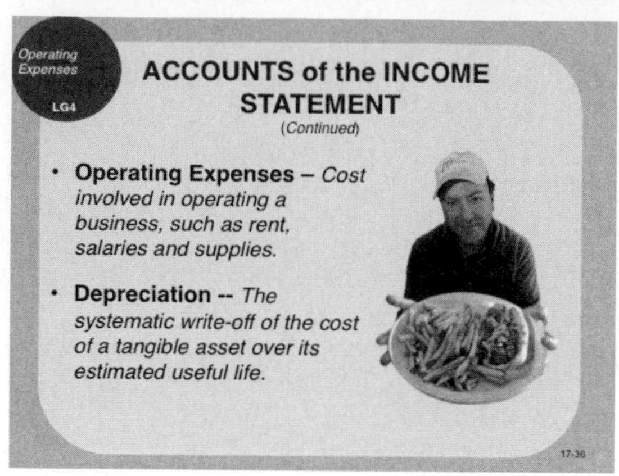

PPT 17-37
What's Coming and Going at the College Bookstore

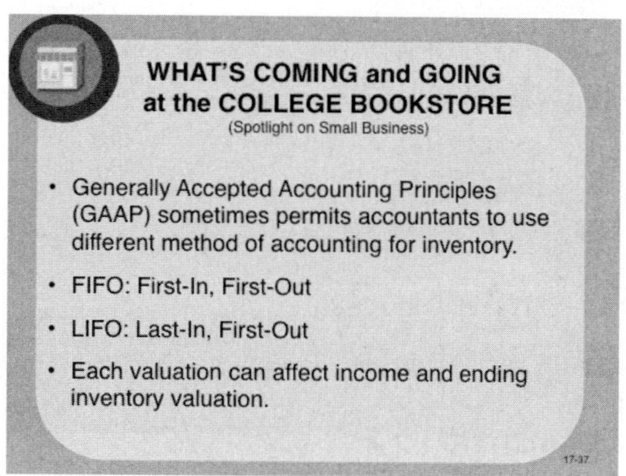

PPT 17-38
The Statement of Cash Flows

See Figure 17.8 in the text for a sample statement of cash flows for Very Vegetarian.

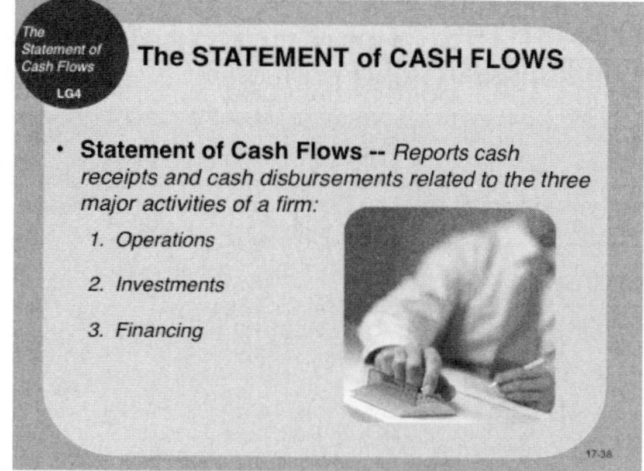

PPT 17-39
Understanding Cash Flow

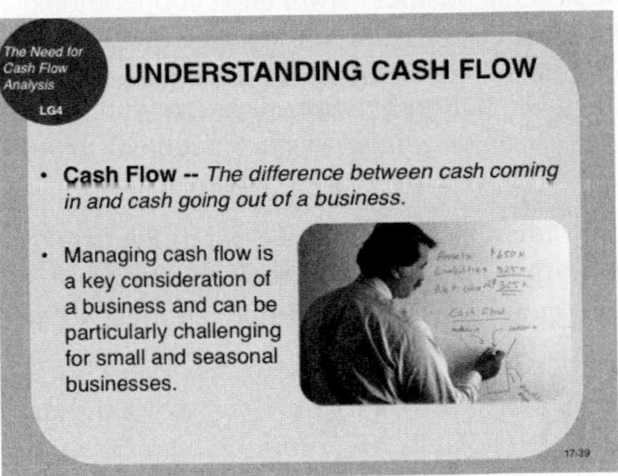

PPT 17-40
Barking Up the Wrong Financial Statement

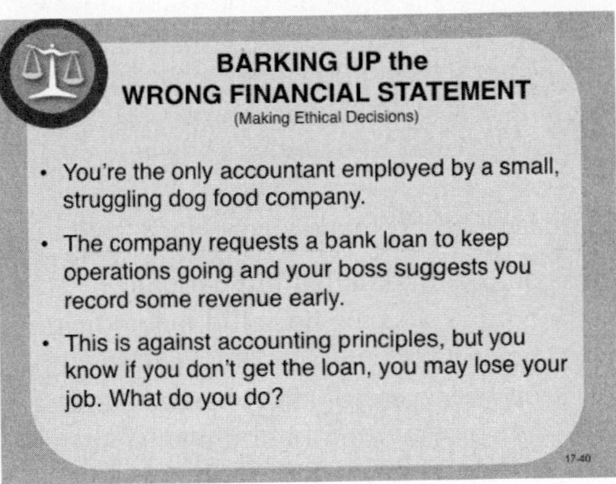

PPT 17-41
Progress Assessment

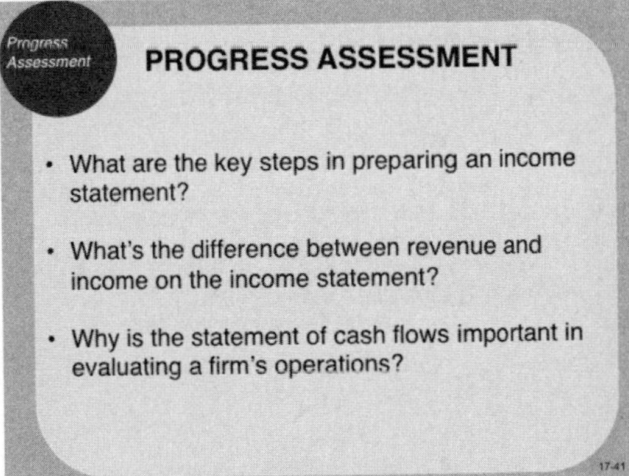

1. The key steps in preparing an income statement are:

   Revenue
   – Cost of goods sold
   = Gross profit (gross margin)
   – Operating expenses
   = Net income before taxes
   – Taxes
   = Net income or loss

2. Revenue is the monetary value of what a firm receives for goods sold, services rendered, and other payments such as rent. Income refers to the bottom line which is the net income (or perhaps net loss) the firm incurs from revenue minus sales returns, costs, expenses, and taxes over a period of time.

(continued)

PPT 17-41
Progress Assessment
(continued)

3. The statement of cash flows is important because it answers such questions as, How much cash came into the business from current operations? Did the firm use cash to buy stocks, bonds, or other investments? Did it sell some investments that brought in cash?

PPT 17-42
Using Financial Ratios

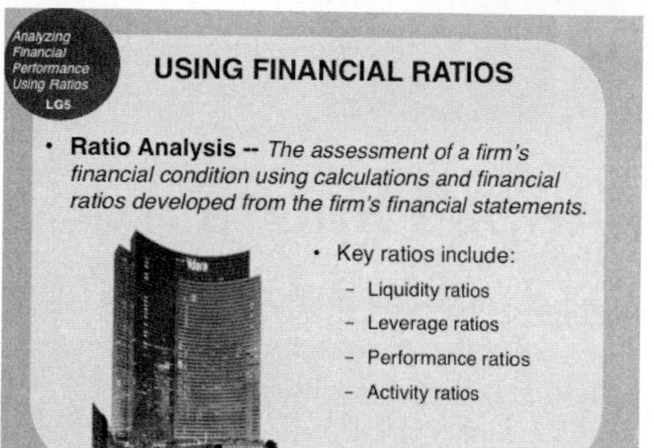

Ratio analysis provides an assessment of the firm's financial condition. It can be extremely useful when results of a ratio analysis are compared to industry peers.

PPT 17-43
Commonly Used Liquidity Ratios

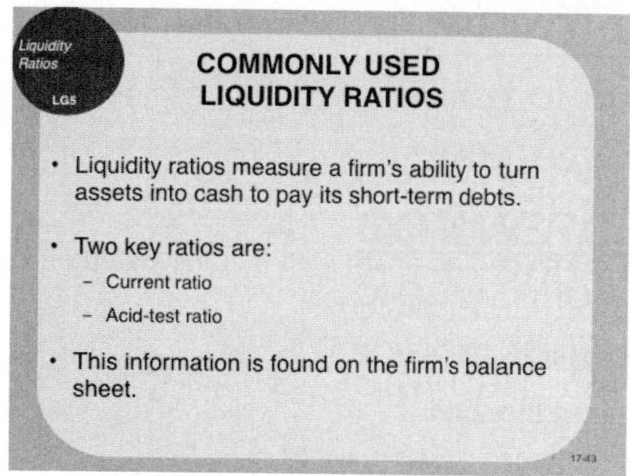

The acid-test ratio is sometimes referred to as the quick ratio.

PPT 17-44
Leverage Ratios

Leverage (Debt) Ratios
LG5

LEVERAGE RATIOS

- Leverage ratios measure the degree to which a firm relies on borrowed funds in its operations.
- Key ratios include:
  - Debt to Owner's Equity Ratio
- This information is found on the firm's balance sheet.

17-44

PPT 17-45
Profitability Ratios

Profitability (Performance) Ratio
LG5

PROFITABILITY RATIOS

- Profitability ratios measure how effectively a firm's managers are using the firm's various resources to achieve profits.
- Key ratios include:
  - Basic earnings per share
  - Return on sales
  - Return on equity
- This information is found on the firm's balance sheet and income statement.

17-45

PPT 17-46
Activity Ratios

ACTIVITY RATIOS

- Activity ratios measure how effectively management is turning over inventory.
- Key ratios include:
  - Inventory turnover ratio
- This information is found on the firm's balance sheet and income statement.

17-46

PPT 17-47
Accountants of the World United

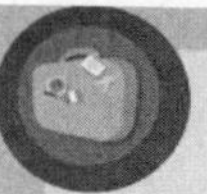

ACCOUNTANTS of the WORLD UNITED
(Reaching Beyond Our Borders)

- Multinational companies must adapt their accounting reporting to the rules of multiple countries.
- Many countries have adopted International Financial Reporting Standards (IFRS) and are pushing to make them standard.
- The U.S. Securities & Exchange Commission believes there should be such a standard.

17-47

PPT 17-48
Timeline for the Move to IFRS

TIMELINE for the MOVE to IFRS

- **2008:** SEC offered proposed timeline
- **2009:** 110 large companies have the option of using IFRS
- **2011:** SEC assesses progress of IFRS
- **2013:** Final decision on the move to IFRS
- **2014:** Large public companies will be required to report in IFRS (pending SEC decision)
- **2016:** All companies will be required to report in IFRS (pending SEC decision)

Source: IFRS.org, accessed July 2011.

17-48

1. This slide profiles the timeline for the move to International Financial Reporting Standards
2. International Financial Reporting Standards (IFRS) are a set of accounting standards developed by the International Accounting Standards Board (IASB) that is becoming the global standard for the preparation of public company financial statements.
3. Ask the students, What are some of the benefits of international accounting standards?
4. If time permits, have students explore the IFRS website (www.ifrs.com) and review some of the accounting case studies that the site presents.

PPT 17-49
Progress Assessment

PROGRESS ASSESSMENT

- What's the primary purpose of performing ratio analysis using the firm's financial statements?
- What are the four main categories of financial ratios?

17-49

1. Ratio analysis is the assessment of a firm's financial condition, using calculations and financial ratios. Financial ratios are especially useful in comparing the company's performance to its financial objectives and to the performance of others in the industry.
2. The four main categories of financial ratios are liquidity, leverage, profitability, and activity.

lecture links

"In the business world, the rearview mirror is always clearer than the windshield."
Warren Buffett

"There is no job so simple that it can't be done wrong."
Perrussel's Law

"It comes from saying no to 1,000 things to make sure we don't get on the wrong track or try to do too much."
Steve Jobs

lecture link 17-1

INNOVATING WITH OPEN BOOKS AND SHARED PROFITS

During a recessionary economy, cutting costs becomes the primary focus of most companies. Anything that detracts from a business's bottom line is excised and nothing that could burden the books is added. But with all their penny-pinching, many managers fail to heed one of the simplest maxims in business: You have to spend money to make money. In most cases, a little investment in a company's employees through open accounting and profit sharing can go a long way toward improving efficiency and, ultimately, profit margins.

By opening the books to employees and cutting them in on profits, staffers become more motivated to do a good job since they can see how their salary is tied to their performance. But most importantly, open-book management spurs innovation in every level of the company. For instance, at the small packaging business Great Little Box, employees equally split 15% of the company's pretax earnings. Thanks to the staff's level playing field, a maintenance worker suggested to upper management that they trim a quarter-inch of cardboard off some boxes. The employee's recommendation resulted in thousands of dollars in savings each month for Great Little Box. Also, each employee acts as a sort of mini-manager by keeping tabs on their colleagues' productivity, since any amount of slacking could result in less money for everybody.

A recent study by the Institute for Health and Social Policy at McGill University found comprehensive employee empowerment to be a common thread in successful companies both big and small. In fact, a survey by *Inc.* magazine revealed that 40% of the 500 fastest-growing companies in the United States use open-book management. Nevertheless, only 1% of American companies grant employees access to accounting records. And those few that employ profit sharing usually reserve it only for managers. In the end, most companies feel they can't afford to include their staff in their already slim profit margins. But as the recession wears on, businesses could find that short-term cost-cutting measures could come back to bite them in the long term.[i]

lecture link 17-2

MANAGERIAL ACCOUNTING AND THE BUDGET PROCESS

In addition to the balance sheet, income statement, and cash flow statement, managers need other forms of financial information—especially for the budgeting process. They also need this information to help make decisions such as when to replace a machine, whether to hire extra people, how much wages can be raised, and if advertising should be increased or decreased. Detailed reports are needed on such things as departmental costs, special projects, cash flow, financial analyses, taxes, and labor costs. These reports, which are a part of managerial accounting, do not have to be standardized but can be tailored to the firm's individual needs.

BUDGETING AND BUDGETARY CONTROL

Two of the primary functions of management are planning and control. When these two functions are combined with the accounting techniques we have studied, they provide one of management's most useful tools: the budgeting process. This process, in turn, involves both budgeting and budgetary control.

Budgeting is simply stating in dollars-and-cents terms what the firm wants to accomplish in a given period of time. Most individuals have some informal plan at the beginning of the month as to how they are going to spend their money. They know, in general, what their expected income is and what expenses they must use that money for.

Businesses must use more formal plans, but they follow the same procedure an individual does—determine how much revenue will come into the firm, divide that revenue among the expenses, and determine the expected profit or loss from operations. In essence, the firm is preparing a "planned" income statement when it sets up a budget.

The starting point in budgeting is estimating expected revenue, which is the total amount of goods or services that company expects to sell. For management to get an accurate figure, the firm's sales department must give a realistic estimate of probable sales. This figure will be a blend of past sales figures, expected business conditions, and company objectives. For example, if 1,200,000 units are to be sold, and the expected price per unit is $7, the total revenue should be $8,400,000.

Next, expected expenses are calculated by the departments in the firm that will be involved. The production department should submit a plan showing how much it will cost to produce those items, including such costs as raw materials, wages, electricity, and maintenance. The marketing department should develop a plan for sales activities such as advertising, personal selling, and sales promotion. Then administrative, depreciation, and other costs must be computed.

After all the firm's departments have submitted their estimates, management can calculate the projected net income by subtracting total expected expenses from expected revenues.

At this point, management adds its plans and projections to the raw figures and begins "fine-tuning" the budget. The departmental budgets may be sent back for further work and the first few steps repeated until a comprehensive budget acceptable to all is created. Each department then develops a departmental budget based on the figures in the comprehensive budget.

The budgeting process does not end here. The only thing you have at this point is a plan, stated in monetary terms, of what you expect to do during the next year. Unless budgetary control is added, the budget becomes useless. Budgetary control involves comparing actual performance against planned performance and taking corrective action if differences are found.

For instance, the production department budget may call for spending $490,000 each month to produce one month's output of 100,000 units. If, at the end of the month, the chief accountant finds that $505,000 has been spent, he or she knows that actual expenses are exceeding planned expenses by $15,000 and can notify the production manager to take corrective action.

With this information, the manager can investigate the problem. Are raw materials being wasted? Was there an increase in the cost of these materials? On the basis of the results of this investigation, a change may be made in production methods or a new supplier may be found. If it is found that the original budget was not realistic, the budget itself may be changed to show realistic goals. In this way, management makes adjustments in order to meet the goals it has set. Budgets and budgetary control are excellent planning and control tools.

DETERMINING COSTS AND SETTING PRICES

The income statement shows an item called "cost of sales" or "cost of goods sold," which includes various costs—material, labor, and overhead. Analyses that are more detailed can be made to relate these costs to each product, and costs can be compared with the income from the sales of that product. This shows what the present cost–profit situation is at a given level of sales. Another study is usually made to find out what the situation would be if sales increased or decreased.

Each company has its own approach to cost accounting. Some emphasize quality, others price. Cost analysis provides a basis for determining which approach to follow. All involve a trade-off of value against cost.

DECIDING ON CAPITAL INVESTMENTS

Managers must make daily and long-term capital investment decisions. Daily decisions may be made on whether to use machine A or machine B for a given operation. Should a salesperson visit customer X on this trip or the next? Should Jones's order be produced today to ensure on-time delivery, or can it wait?

Capital investment decisions are concerned with changes in fixed assets that affect longer periods of time. Should a manual operation be replaced with a machine? Should a piece of equipment be replaced, rebuilt, or discarded? Many of these decisions involve large sums of money and have long-term effects on the company. Special consideration must therefore be given to such decisions, including such factors as interest charges and the unavailability of money for other purposes, called opportunity cost.

These and other capital investment studies consume much time and involve many people. They also involve the use of detailed accounting records to obtain costs for their analysis.

lecture link 17-3

COMING SOON—THE WIDE WORLD OF ACCOUNTING

It would be nearly impossible to make it through a day in the United States using only products that were "Made in America" or owned by American companies. Globalization is a fact of life we have come to accept in the 21st century. Nevertheless, there is one last vestige of Made in America that has persisted. The U.S. accounting system is still based on generally accepted accounting principles (GAAP) under the oversight of the Financial Accounting Standards Board (FASB). However, this lone ranger of U.S. financial leadership may soon give way to the unstoppable surge of globalization much like other industries before it.

The move from GAAP to International Financial Reporting Standards (IFRS) seems to be an inevitable conclusion. Accountants no longer talk about *if* GAAP and IFRS will converge but *when* the transformation will take place. The U.S. Securities and Exchange Commission has even devised a roadmap for the incorporation of IFRS with a whisper date of 2013 for implementation. Many accountants, however, believe that certain changes in the international standards need to be met first and U.S. companies won't make the switch to IFRS until 2016.

At one time, many felt GAAP would become the gold standard worldwide as many European and Asian companies rolled out accounting numbers in the preferred U.S. style as well as their own. However, support for GAAP seemed to collapse globally as it became more and more bloated (25,000 pages versus 2,500 for the IFRS) and heavily rules-riddled. Even Robert H. Herz, chair of FASB, admitted GAAP was better suited to a different era, one that was not global. One concern that does bother many accountants about IFRS is its relative youth. The International Accounting Standards Board (IASB), the body that regulates IFRS, has been in existence only since 2001. Still Europe adopted IFRS early, and nations such as Japan, China, India, Brazil, and Canada have announced their intention to move toward IFRS adoption as well.

The change to IFRS is far from a done deal. Many questions persist about the implementation and what it would mean for American companies and investors. Jeffrey Mahoney, general counsel of the Council of Institutional Investors, says IASB needs to answer six questions before U.S. companies switch to IFRS:

- Do international standards produce the same quality of reporting as GAAP?
- Will the application and enforcement of international standards in the United States be as rigorous as they are in the case of GAAP?
- Does IASB have an adequate and stable source of funding that's not dependent on private donors?
- Does IASB have a competent, full-time, capable staff?
- Does IASB pay the most attention to the views of customers of financial reports—in other words, investors?
- Does IASB have a structure, process, and adequate governmental support to keep its standards work from "being overridden by the political process"?

Others have questions about the membership of the board, whether it should be based on expertise, geography, or some other measure. Needless to say, the banking and financial crisis of 2008–2009 did little to help the transition to global accounting standards and will most likely stall its implementation. Still, accountants ranging from academia, the Big Four, not-for-profits, and so on agree that global change is in the air.[ii]

lecture link 17-4

NEW REGULATIONS HIT WALL STREET

More than two years after the near collapse of America's financial system, President Obama signed the Dodd-Frank Financial Reform and Consumer Protection Act into law in 2010. Although the bill took awhile to run through the congressional wringer, the provisions included in it will have a dramatic effect on the future of American commerce. First of all, the new legislation gives the government power to seize and shutter large financial institutions on the verge of collapse in an effort to prevent further bailouts. It also subjects derivatives, the complicated financial deals that fueled the crisis, to strict governmental oversight.

Perhaps most important to the general public, though, is the law's formation of an independent consumer protection agency housed within the Federal Reserve. The new agency protects borrowers against a host of financial abuses ranging from payday loans to mortgages and credit cards. As Harvard law professor and consumer protection pioneer Elizabeth Warren said: "For the first time, there will be a financial regulator in Washington watching out for families instead of banks." Still, the agency is not without its critics. Some consumer advocates worry about the agency's location within the Federal Reserve, an institution that has done little to protect consumers in the past. Also, a number of entities are exempt from regulation by the agency. For example, car dealers, originators of nearly 80% of auto loans, are not liable to the agency's jurisdiction.

In its most controversial move, the reform act does nothing to restructure the government-owned Fannie Mae and Freddie Mac. In fact, it leaves all of the nation's biggest financial institutions almost completely intact. Loopholes litter the nearly 2,000-page measure as well, potentially setting the stage for future economic meltdowns. For all its faults, though, the reform act represents the most sweeping change in financial regulation since the Great Depression. It may not be a miracle cure, but at least it resolves some of the most pressing issues facing our economy today while setting the stage for a stronger financial future.[iii]

lecture link 17-5

THE POWER OF THE INTERNAL AUDITOR

The largest bankruptcy in U.S. history was the 2002 collapse of telecom giant WorldCom. The company's downfall was caused by a fraudulent $11 billion accounting scheme. The unlikely heroine at the center of this story is an internal auditor who wouldn't stop asking questions.

Cynthia Cooper admits that she was "literally scared to death" during the process of uncovering WorldCom's fraudulent activities. In the course of a routine internal audit into the obscure area of line cost expenses, Cooper uncovered something that didn't look right. Other executives told her she was wasting her time and the department's resources by pursuing the audit. But she never allowed herself to be intimidated. It was the urging to move onto something else that encouraged her to keep looking. Her department eventually discovered $3.8 billion in fraudulent accounting involving line fees—fees WorldCom paid to other telephone companies for the right to use their lines.

Cooper said there was a spider web of entries used to disguise the fraud. After her auditing staff traced them backward and forward, they still couldn't understand what was happening. When she confronted former controller David Myers about the entries, he was honest and said there was no support to back up the accounting.

According to Cooper, the internal audit department never considered backing down once it began the investigation. "We were at a crossroads," Cooper said of the internal auditing team. "The decision to come forward was easy, but doing the right thing doesn't come without a cost." The role of whistleblower isn't one she relishes.

The WorldCom debacle eventually sent several executives to prison. Bernie Ebbers, former chief executive officer and cofounder, was sentenced to 25 years after being found guilty of fraud and conspiracy for his role in the accounting scheme. This is the harshest sentence ever given in a white-collar criminal case. Scott Sullivan, the former chief financial officer who testified against Ebbers, received five years. Cooper has trouble reconciling those sentences.

Cooper now runs Cynthia Cooper Consulting Company and spends a great deal of time speaking on the events surrounding the WorldCom scandal. "Small decisions matter. Make sure your moral compass is pointed a true North. Never allow yourself to be intimidated."[iv]

lecture link 17-6

WHERE THE JOBS WILL BE

Although America's unemployment problems are far from solved, the market has stop hemorrhaging jobs at least for the moment. Still, it's difficult to overestimate the amount of work lost during the recession. Approximately 8.75 million jobs disappeared, more than the previous four recessions combined. Filling such a huge gap will be difficult, but there are some areas of U.S. business where the job market is finally expanding.

One sector that offers a bright future to workers is accounting. Since the American economy is based on finance now more than ever, keeping track of all that money has become an essential service.

The Bureau of Labor Statistics expects accounting jobs to grow by 22% between 2008 and 2018. Information technology jobs present an even better avenue of opportunity with an estimated growth of 30% through the same time period. These jobs aren't necessarily exclusive to computer science majors, either. Employees can enter the IT world through a help desk at a tech firm and move on to analysis or management.

Nevertheless, these are just two growing industries in a complex economy. To offset the losses made during the recession would require the addition of 135,000 jobs per month. Even when the jobs do come back that doesn't mean everything will return to normal. Many of the new jobs people took since the recession don't match the pay, the benefits or the hours of the jobs they held before the downturn. For instance, while the Bureau of Labor Statistics estimates that the number of food preparation and serving jobs will increase by nearly 400,000 through 2018, the average wage will be only $16,430 including tips. At the top level, however, employees will see fewer jobs but at more pay. Over the next decade financial examiner positions will expand by just 11,000, but will net a median income of $70,930. In order to truly reinvigorate the economy, newly created jobs must pay a salary comparable to pre-recession levels on both ends of the employment spectrum, not just the high end.[v]

lecture link 17-7

FINDING A FRIENDLY FACTOR

The recession of 2009 has dried up credit markets to the point that the term *cash squeeze* has become a part of many companies' everyday lives. Take Data Drive Thru, for example. The demand for its high-speed data-transfer technology was growing, but the company's cash cupboard was bare. CFO Brad Oldham knew that the frozen credit market would make finding a bank loan for the company almost impossible. His other option was selling receivables to a traditional factor that might very well harm the company's cash flow position. What is a growing company to do?

Help may be on the way through the Receivables Exchange, an online bidding platform that does for many companies what eBay does for consumer's used merchandise. Unlike eBay, however, buyers don't take possession of the products they buy. Instead they bid an interest rate they will accept to lend against the company's receivables. For example, receivables a company may hold from a top-notch company like Wal-Mart will procure a good rate. The Receivables Exchange offers companies greater control, faster remittances for receivables, access to global buyers, and lower transactions costs than traditional factors.

CFO Oldham found his first experience with the exchange very rewarding. His firm found a buyer willing to extend $100,000 for Data Drive Thru receivables with terms the company found very fair. The next morning the company had cash in hand.

The Receivables Exchange provides an example of the good elements of financial innovation—linking buyers and sellers who would not have come together otherwise. It's likely small and medium-sized businesses that hold receivables from reputable companies will find the exchange a true friend. In fact, firms like Quorum Technical Services, a provider of IT staff to global firms, uses the exchange on a regular basis. Says CEO Jack Karamanoukian, "we tally invoices on Friday and post them on the exchange on Monday." Let the bidding begin.[vi, vii]

lecture link 17-8

WHEN IS A SALE A SALE?

For entrepreneurs, there is no shortage of advice about what types of specialized assistance is needed to get their business up-and-running and on the road to long-term survival. Legions of small business consultants recommend marketing and finance experts, lawyers, management gurus, tax specialists, and technology buffs, just to name a few. Unfortunately, most entrepreneurs lack the financial resources to hire such an elite team and settle on one expert they consider critical—an outside accountant.

To be sure, an outside accountant can be an important resource to a business. Still, while outside accountants may be well intentioned and very good at their craft, they often deal with so many clients that they may not have the time needed to oversee a small company's finances. Therefore, like it or not, entrepreneurs need to set aside their fear of the financial unknown and understand the numbers of their business. One concept that's especially important is the distinction between cash-based and accrual-based accounting.

With cash-based accounting, sales and expenses are recorded only when money changes hands. In other words, a sale is not recognized until you get paid for it, and an expense is not recognized until you pay for it. Generally, businesses that provide services like auto mechanics, dentists, and landscaping use cash-based accounting.

In using accrual-based accounting, sales and expenses are recorded when you do the work involved in creating and delivering a product or service a customer has agreed to purchase. Manufacturers and companies with inventory generally use accrual accounting.

Individuals and most small businesses use cash-based accounting in the preparation of their income taxes. Unfortunately, tax laws limit the ability of small businesses to deduct money that is never paid to them under the cash-based method. For example, if a service provider such as a dentist does not get paid, he or she is out the time and everything else involved in the treatment. The provider cannot deduct this bad debt on his or her taxes. On the other hand, a manufacturer who ships goods to a customer can record the sale when it occurs. The manufacturer can also claim a tax deduction if the customer never pays the bill.

Understanding accounting information could be the difference between a successful firm that builds a bright future and one that closes its doors due to poor financial management.[viii]

lecture link 17-9

USING THE STATEMENT OF CASH FLOWS

Rather than studying the income statement, many investors are choosing to look beyond that list of a company's revenues and expenses to the cash flow statement. And because cash flow is key to financing many takeovers and leveraged buyouts, understanding and profiting from acquisitions often means understanding figures such as "operating cash flow" and "free cash flow."

Companies do not go out of business because they report net losses. They fade away because they run out of cash. Monitoring your ability to generate cash flow is critical to success. To maximize long-term value, a company must continually evaluate its consistent capacity for generating cash. Commercial lenders realize that it is cash flow, not net income, which will repay their loans.

The true definition of *cash flow* is unclear. It is one of the most overused and least agreed upon terms in corporate finance. Cash flows can be divided into three primary categories:

- Cash flows from operating activities
- Cash flows from investing activities
- Cash flows from financing activities

Investors have been coming in more contact with cash flow statements recently. Since November 1987, public companies have been required to include cash flow statements when presenting full financial statements. Cash flow is simply how much money a company spends, and where it has gone; and how much is received, and from whom. The cash flow statement is a hard-nosed and pragmatic financial statement.

Cash flow is often a better measure of company health than earnings, analysts say, because earnings can be puffed up or hidden through accounting changes or other manipulations that don't reflect the true state of a company's business. When times are tough, companies can fool around with tax rates and make timing adjustments. Due to such manipulations, many analysts rate the usefulness of cash flow statements far above earnings statements.

In today's competitive environment, it is vital for the owner/operator to monitor current and future cash flow requirements. Careful tracking of cash flow is especially important for industries facing seasonal fluctuations, such as the retail industry. These companies must prepare projections of cash inflows and outflows, preferably on a monthly basis, but certainly no less than on a quarterly basis. A forecast of the company's monthly balance sheet is also important to show its financial position and available assets, such as accounts receivable and inventory, which can be used as collateral for working capital loans.

Based on these projections, periods of negative cash flow will be highlighted and anticipated. To lessen the effect of periods of negative cash flow, many factors should be considered, including the company's business cycle and its ability to fund the negative cash flow period.

In anticipation of these down times, it's necessary to pay particular attention to cash-producing assets, such as accounts receivable, and cash flow–draining liabilities, such as accounts payable. Steps to speed up time for collections of receivables might include reducing the time between the sale and mailing the invoice to the customer or changing sales terms to cash on delivery. It may also be worthwhile to meet with the company's banker to review the cash flow requirements of the company and obtain a seasonal line of credit to cover the negative cash flow periods.

Cash flow can be used in different ways for different types of companies:

- For developing companies, cash flow and free cash flow are usually negative because the company is burdened with low sales and one-time expenses necessary to build the business. Matching the cash being lost in a cash flow statement to the assets on hand to pay bills can predict how long the company can survive.
- Minding cash flow is especially crucial in energy and real estate companies, whose bottom line often is obscured by heavy depreciation and depletion allowances.
- Companies that recently have made takeovers often have depressed earnings because they must write off massive amounts of goodwill carried on their balance sheet. The goodwill comes from paying a premium over a company's book value to buy the company.

Monitoring cash flows is crucial to a company's success. As owners and financial statement users become more familiar with the concept and use of cash flow ratios, their decision-making process will improve greatly and become more focused on the cash flow impact of their decisions.

lecture link 17-10

STAYING ALIVE IN TOUGH ECONOMIC TIMES

Going broke is an idea that any business hates to think about. However, if you are going to go broke in the United States, it helps to be a large, established company. For example, after the September 11, 2001, terrorist attacks, the government stepped in and saved major air carriers like American and United. More recently quasi-government agencies like Fannie Mae and Freddie Mac received money from the government to stay afloat despite poor practices in the mortgage business. Banks that risked capital on risky investments like derivatives and credit swaps were also beneficiaries of the federal government's largesse. Even automakers whose managers misjudged the market were propped up by government dollars. Which leads us to the question, "What if small-business owners run out of cash?"

The simple answer is, it's goodbye to the business. That's why having enough cash on hand (liquidity) is especially critical for entrepreneurs during economic tough times. Unfortunately, this is no simple task. Liquidity for small companies can change almost immediately due to some unexpected event such as a major customer going out of business or perhaps an unexpected natural catastrophe like a flood. Experts agree that keeping enough liquid assets (like cash and cash equivalents like bonds) to fund the next six months is a good rule of thumb. If you keep a reserve of liquid assets, you have time to work on a remedy if a crisis hits rather than having to close your doors.

Accountants and financial managers also advise small businesses to be particularly aware of three ratios to make sure the business is liquid enough to survive: current ratio, quick ratio, and the debt-to-equity ratio.

- **Current ratio:** current assets divided by current liabilities. Most bankers like the ratio to be at least 2:1.
- **Quick ratio:** cash and receivables divided by current liabilities. This ratio addresses the scary question of whether or not a company can meet its obligations if sales suddenly fall or dry up. A ratio greater than 1:1 is often acceptable.
- **Debt-to-equity ratio:** total liabilities divided by shareholders equity. The higher this ratio is the less likely bankers can deal with you. A ratio below 3:1 is often considered safe for small businesses.

The key to remember as a small business is that you are not AIG or General Motors. No one is there to catch you if you fall.

lecture link 17-11

USING YOUR COMPUTER IN SMALL-BUSINESS ACCOUNTING

Small-business owners are always touted as the backbone of American capitalism. A small business can be categorized in several different ways and can employ as few as one and as many as a few hundred. The beauty of a small-business owner is that he (or she) is "the man." We have all heard the phrase, "I'm going to stick it to the man." Well, if you become a small-business owner, you ARE the man.

Now being "the man" can be a double-edged sword. You get to make the decisions, but you also have to make the decisions. Calling the shots can be tougher than you might think. However, if you line yourself up with a good CPA, you've got someone who's got your back. Yet, you don't want to have to totally depend on your accountant for all of your immediate reporting needs that might arise.

The computer becomes a priceless tool for the small-business owner. By loading accounting software like QuickBooks and becoming experienced in a spreadsheet tool like Excel, the owner can become "report-savvy" and keep tabs on current numbers. By doing this, he or she can keep an up-to-date account of sales versus cost of goods sold figures and know immediately what some key gross numbers are. This will help him or her make any needed "on-the-fly" changes in a certain problem area, should there be one.

As in anything, a person cannot be too knowledgeable. With technology changing as rapidly as it does, it's become vital for small-business owners to keep tabs on the hot topics that can help them better their business. More times than not, a small business is not going to be in the financial shape to have an R&D department to keep track of these things.[ix]

critical thinking exercises

Name: ______________________

Date: ______________________

critical thinking exercise 17-1

ANNUAL REPORTS ONLINE

Locating corporate annual reports is easier than it has ever been. AnnualReports.com hosts a website (www.reportgallery.com)[x] containing annual reports for hundreds of corporations. The site is comprehensive and easy to use.

Go to the website (www.reportgallery.com) and choose one company to research. Use the information given in this report to answer the following questions. (Sometimes the Web address for a location changes. You might need to search to find the exact location mentioned.)

COMPANY NAME ______________________ **FINANCIAL YEAR** ______________________

1. Locate the report of the independent auditors.
   a. Who are the auditors?

   b. Are there any auditor reservations—anything that the auditors flag with the term "except"? Give details.

2. Locate the report of management. Since the passage of the Sarbanes-Oxley Act in 2002, corporate management has to certify these financial results. Who signed the management report?

3. Which intangible assets are listed on the balance sheet?

4. How much income tax did the company pay?

critical thinking exercise 17-1 (continued)

5. Using the financial ratios discussed in this chapter, answer the following:

   a. What is the current ratio?

   b. What is the debt-to-equity ratio?

6. What is the basic earnings per share? Diluted earnings per share.

Name: ______________________

Date: ______________________

critical thinking exercise 17-2

THE PIZZA STAND

A student organization has been given permission to operate a pizza stand during the upcoming homecoming weekend. The stand will be located just outside the football stadium, making it accessible during the ball game. The location is also convenient for visitors as they tour the campus at other times during the weekend. An estimated 2,500 visitors will be on campus, in addition to the campus population of 1,500.

Each pizza requires:

1/2 lb. pizza flour

2 oz. pizza sauce

1/8 lb. pepperoni

1/2 lb. cheese

Pizza flour costs $8.00 per 10-lb. bag; pizza sauce, $4.80 per 64-oz. jar; pepperoni, $18.00 per 5-lb. package; and cheese, $15.00 per 5-lb. package. Club members will cook the pizzas and staff the stand on a volunteer basis. The university requires each vendor to pay a $25.00 permit fee and a $50.00 refundable deposit on the building. Your club plans to donate the profits from the pizza sales to a local children's hospital.

1. How many pizzas can you anticipate selling?

2. What price should you charge per pizza?

3. How much of each raw material do you need to buy?

4. What will be your probable profit?

5. Develop a financial plan for your weekend enterprise.

notes on critical thinking exercise 17-2

I have used this exercise several times in my classes. Below are two of the potential solutions, one conservative and one very optimistic.

ALTERNATIVE 1

1. *How many pizzas can you anticipate selling?*

   On homecoming weekend, there will be about 4,000 people on campus. The first step in developing a budget is to estimate what percentage of attendees will purchase your pizzas. This can be complicated. Factors such as the weather, time of day, and presence of other food vendors need to be considered. Obviously, you also need to consider the demand for pizzas at several price points. Perhaps the simplest method is to use a percentage, say 10%. Potential sales: 400 pizzas.

2. *What price should you charge per pizza?*

   You could consider several pricing strategies. Chapter 14 covered several possibilities: demand-based pricing, competition-based pricing, cost-based pricing, and break-even analysis. What is the price people are willing to pay? What price is our competition charging? What is the break-even point? To simplify transactions on the day of the sale, you may want to set the price at a whole dollar amount and not have to bother with coin change.

   The analysis below uses cost-based pricing. The fixed costs are quite low—the only one given is the $25.00 permit. Next, calculate the cost of raw materials per pizza, the variable cost.

INGREDIENT	AMOUNT PER PIZZA	OUNCES	COST OF INGREDIENT	COST PER OUNCE	COST PER PIZZA
Pizza flour	1/2 lb.	8 oz.	$8.00 per 10 lb.	$0.05	$0.40
Pizza sauce	2 oz.	2 oz.	$4.80 per 64 oz.	$0.075	$0.15
Pepperoni	1/8 lb.	2 oz.	$18.00 per 5 lb.	$0.225	$0.45
Cheese	1/2 lb.	8 oz.	$15.00 per 5 lb.	$0.1875	$1.50
Total					**$2.50**

   After determining the cost of raw materials, a price can be set that covers these costs and provides the desired profit. Possible prices: $5.00, $7.00, or $9.00.

3. *How much of each raw material do you need to buy?*

INGREDIENT	AMOUNT PER PIZZA	OUNCES	POTENTIAL SALES UNITS	TOTAL OUNCES NEEDED	TOTAL POUNDS
Pizza flour	1/2 lb.	8 oz.	400	3,200 oz.	200 lb.
Pizza sauce	2 oz.	2 oz.	400	800 oz.	
Pepperoni	1/8 lb.	2 oz.	400	800 oz.	50 lb.
Cheese	1/2 lb.	8 oz.	400	3,200 oz.	200 lb.

SUPPLIES NEEDED

Pizza flour	20 10-lb. bags	20 x $8.00	$160.00
Pizza sauce	12 1/2 64-oz. jars	13 x $4.80	$62.40
Pepperoni	10 5-lb. packages	10 x $18.00	$180.00
Cheese	40 5-lb. packages	40 x $15.00	$600.00
Total cost			**$1,002.40**

4. *What will be your probable profit?*

Your profit will depend on the price you charge. Using $7.00:

Price	$7.00
Revenue	$2,800.00 (400 x $7.00)
Variable costs	$1,002.40
Fixed costs	$25.00
Total costs	$1,027.40
Profit	**$1,772.60**

5. *Develop a financial plan for your weekend enterprise.*

PROJECT COSTS

Buy permit			$25.00
Purchase raw materials			
Pizza flour	20 10-lb. bags	20 x $8.00	$160.00
Pizza sauce	12 1/2 64-oz. jars	13 x $4.80	$62.40
Pepperoni	10 5-lb. packages	10 x $18.00	$180.00
Cheese	40 5-lb. packages	40 x $15.00	$600.00
Total cost			**$1,027.40**

(The $50.00 deposit is a wash, $50.00 cost, $50.00 refund. Therefore, it was not used in these calculations.)

PROJECT REVENUE

Assuming sales of 400 pizzas (10% of attendees) and using $7.00 sale price:

400 x $7.00 = **$2,800.00**

PROJECT NET PROFIT

Revenue	$2,800.00
Cost of goods	$1,002.40
Fixed costs	$25.00
Net profit	**$1,772.60**

ALTERNATIVE 2

1. *How many pizzas can you anticipate selling?*

Assume that you will sell pizzas to 75% of the people at homecoming (3,000 pizzas). People will be hungry, and they will want to support the club.

2. *What price should you charge per pizza?*

Charge $10.00 per pizza.

3. *How much of each raw material do you need to buy?*

INGREDIENT	AMOUNT PER PIZZA	OUNCES	POTENTIAL SALES UNITS	TOTAL OUNCES NEEDED	TOTAL POUNDS
Pizza flour	1/2 lb.	8 oz.	3,000	24,000 oz.	1,500 lb.
Pizza sauce	2 oz.	2 oz.	3,000	6,000 oz.	
Pepperoni	1/8 lb.	2 oz.	3,000	6,000 oz.	375 lb.
Cheese	1/2 lb.	8 oz.	3,000	24,000 oz.	1,500 lb.

SUPPLIES NEEDED

Pizza flour	150 10-lb. bags	150 x $8.00	$1,200.00
Pizza sauce	93.75 64-oz. jars	94 x $4.80	$ 451.20
Pepperoni	75 5-lb. packages	75 x $18.00	$1,350.00
Cheese	300 5-lb. packages	300 x $15.00	$4,500.00
Total cost			**$7,501.20**

4. *What will be your probable profit?*

Price is $10.00

Revenue	$30,000.00 (3,000 x $10.00)
Variable costs	$7,501.20
Fixed costs	$25.00
Total costs	$7526.20
Profit	**$22,473.80**

5. *Develop a financial plan for your weekend enterprise.*

Purchase enough raw materials to make 3,000 pizzas and market aggressively. If sales don't meet expectations by the end of the third quarter, lower the price by half. Even at a $5.00 sales price, you will cover the $2.50 variable cost and make $2.50 profit per pizza.

Name: ______________________________

Date: ______________________________

critical thinking exercise 17-3

PREPARING FINANCIAL STATEMENTS

As the accountant for Wheatley International, it is your job to prepare the company's income statement and balance sheet. Use the accounts listed below to construct the statements. Assume that the tax rate is 25%.

List of Accounts for
WHEATLEY INTERNATIONAL

Accounts Receivable	$ 120,600
Land	1,500,000
Notes Receivable	61,200
Insurance Expenses	54,000
Accounts Payable	45,000
Interest Expenses	24,600
Common Stock	1,896,000
Depreciation	400,000
Net Sales	1,053,000
Ending Inventory	126,600
Notes Payable (Long-Term)	210,000
Beginning Inventory	154,800
Retained Earnings	1,459,800
Advertising Expense	90,000
Cash	72,000
Salaries	180,000
Short-Term Notes Payable	15,600
Merchandise Purchased (for Inventory)	316,800
Buildings	1,050,000
Rent	13,800
Utilities	8,400
Equipment & Vehicles	1,066,000
Goodwill	90,000
Bonds Payable	60,000

notes on critical thinking exercise 17-3

The formula for the balance sheet is assets equal liabilities plus stockholders' equity. To prepare a balance sheet, add the assets and liabilities. The difference between the two is stockholders' equity. For the income statement, you subtract cost of goods sold from net sales (revenue). Then you subtract expenses to get gross income. From that, you subtract the income tax of 25% to get net income.

(*Note:* The format of these statements may be slightly different from the format taught in students' accounting courses. The exact format is less important than understanding the overall concepts.)

WHEATLEY INTERNATIONAL
INCOME STATEMENT
FY 201X

REVENUES		
Net Sales		$1,053,000
COST OF GOODS SOLD		
Beginning Inventory	$154,800	
Merchandise Purchased	+ 316,800	
Cost of Goods Available for Sale	471,600	
Less: Ending Inventory	–126,600	
Cost of Goods Sold		$345,000
GROSS PROFIT (GROSS MARGIN)		$708,000
OPERATING EXPENSES		
Selling Expenses		
Salaries	$180,000	
Advertising	90,000	
Total Selling Expenses		$270,000
General Expenses		
Insurance	$54,000	
Interest Expense	24,600	
Rent	13,800	
Utilities	8,400	
Total General Expenses		$100,800
Total Operating Expenses		$370,800
NET PROFIT (INCOME) BEFORE TAXES		$337,200
Less: Income Tax Expenses (25%)		$ 84,300
NET INCOME (PROFIT) AFTER TAXES		**$252,900**

WHEATLEY INTERNATIONAL
BALANCE SHEET
December 31, 201X

ASSETS		
Current Assets		
Cash	$ 72,000	
Accounts Receivable	120,600	
Notes Receivable	61,200	
Inventory	126,600	
Total Current Assets		$380,400
Fixed Assets		
Land	$1,500,000	
Buildings	1,050,000	
Equipment & Vehicles	1,066,000	
Depreciation	– 400,000	
Total Fixed Assets		$3,216,000
Other Assets		
Goodwill	$90,000	
Total Other Assets		$90,000
TOTAL ASSETS		**$3,686,400**
LIABILITIES AND STOCKHOLDERS' EQUITY		
Current Liabilities		
Accounts Payable	$45,000	
Short-Term Notes Payable	15,600	
Total Current Liabilities		$60,600
Long-Term Liabilities		
Notes Payable (Long-Term)	$210,000	
Bonds	60,000	
Total Long-Term Liabilities		$270,000
Total Liabilities		$330,600
Owner's Equity		
Common Stock	$1,896,000	
Retained Earnings	1,459,800	
Total Owners' Equity		$3,355,800
TOTAL LIABILITIES AND STOCKHOLDERS' EQUITY		**$3,686,400**

Name: ______________________________

Date: ______________________________

critical thinking exercise 17-4

CALCULATING FINANCIAL RATIOS (ADVANCED)

You are considering investing in Acme Incorporated. The company has provided you with the balance sheet and income statement for the previous year. The current price of one share of stock is $46.25. Earning per share last year was $1.86.

1. Calculate the requested financial ratios:

   a. Current ratio

   b. Debt-to-equity ratio

   c. Return on sales (use net income AFTER taxes)

   d. Return on equity (use net income AFTER taxes)

   e. Earnings per share (use net income AFTER taxes)

2. Would you invest in Acme Incorporated? Why or why not?

ACME INCORPORATED
STATEMENT OF INCOME
FY 201X

REVENUES		
Net Sales	$4,090,970	
Other Income	+104,227	
Total Revenue		$4,195,197
COST OF GOODS SOLD		$2,673,129
GROSS PROFIT (GROSS MARGIN)		$1,522,068
OPERATING EXPENSES		
Total Selling Expenses		$333,300
Total General Expenses		+ 306,036
Total Operating Expenses		$639,336
NET INCOME BEFORE TAXES		$882,732
Income Tax Paid (25%)		$220,683
NET INCOME AFTER TAXES		**$662,049**

ACME INCORPORATED
BALANCE SHEET
December 31, 201X

ASSETS		
Current Assets		
Cash	$280,928	
Marketable Securities	514,800	
Accounts Receivable	108,694	
Notes Receivable	855,771	
Inventories	218,156	
Prepaid Expenses and Other Current Assets	88,237	
Total Current Assets		$2,066,586
Fixed Assets		
Land	$510,000	
Plant and Buildings	304,096	
Equipment	218,500	
Total Fixed Assets		$1,744,701
Other Assets		
Goodwill, Net	$49,930	
Total Other Assets		$49,930
TOTAL ASSETS		**$3,861,217**
LIABILITIES AND STOCKHOLDERS' EQUITY		
Current Liabilities		
Accounts Payable	$226,977	
Accrued Expenses and Other Current Liabilities	380,496	
Current Portion of Finance Debt	382,579	
Total Current Liabilities		$990,052
Long-Term Liabilities		
Notes Payable	$228,772	
Bonds	380,000	
Other Long-Term Liabilities		$29,478
Total Long-Term Liabilities		638,250
Total Liabilities		$1,628,303
Owner's Equity		
Common Stock (342,196 Shares Outstanding)	$ 389,538	
Retained Earnings	1,843,377	
Total Owners' Equity		$2,232,915
TOTAL LIABILITIES AND STOCKHOLDERS' EQUITY		**$3,861,217**

notes on critical thinking exercise 17-4

1. *Calculate the requested financial ratios.*

   a. *Current ratio.* The current ratio is the ratio of the firm's current assets to its current liabilities, calculated as follows:

   CURRENT RATIO =

   $$\frac{\text{Current assets}}{\text{Current liabilities}} \quad \text{or} \quad \frac{\$2,066,586}{\$\ 990,520}$$

   2.086:1

   b. *Debt-to-equity ratio.* The debt-to-equity ratio measures the degree to which the company is financed by borrowed funds that must be repaid. It is calculated as follows:

   DEBT-TO-EQUITY RATIO =

   $$\frac{\text{Total liabilities}}{\text{Owners' equity}} \quad \text{or} \quad \frac{\$1,628,300}{\$2,232,815}$$

   0.729 or 72.9%

   c. *Return on sales.* Return on sales is calculated by comparing a company's net income with its total sales, calculated as follows:

   RETURN ON SALES =

   $$\frac{\text{Net income}}{\text{Net sales}} \quad \text{or} \quad \frac{\$\ 662,049}{\$4,090,970}$$

   16.18%

   d. *Return on equity.* Return on equity measures how much was earned for each dollar invested by owners. It is calculated by comparing a company's net income with its total owner's equity:

   RETURN ON EQUITY =

   $$\frac{\text{Net income}}{\text{Owners' equity}} \quad \text{or} \quad \frac{\$\ 662,049}{\$2,232,915}$$

   29.65%

   e. *Earnings per share.* Earnings per share measures the amount of profit earned by a company for each share of common stock it has outstanding:

   EARNINGS PER SHARE =

   $$\frac{\text{Net income}}{\text{Number of shares outstanding}} \quad \text{or} \quad \frac{\$662,049}{342,196}$$

   $1.935 per share

2. *Would you invest in Acme Incorporated? Why or why not?*

   a. The **current ratio** of 2.086 means that $2.086 in current assets is available for every $1.00 of current liabilities. The firms should be able to meet short-term debt payments easily.

b. The **debt-to-equity ratio** of 72.9% means that the firm has more equity than debt, which usually means a relatively safe investment.

c. A 16.18% **return on sales ratio** would have to be compared to other firms in the industry, but seems very healthy.

d. The **return on equity** of 19.73% would also need to be judged relative to other firms, but seems solid.

e. **Earnings per share** is the amount the company has earned in profit for every share of stock outstanding. It is meaningful when compared to the previous year's EPS. The earnings per share has risen from $1.86 to $1.935.

Overall, the company seems to be profitable, with a healthy debt-to-equity ratio.

Name: ____________________

Date: ____________________

critical thinking exercise 17-5

COMPARING INDUSTRY RATIOS (BASIC)

You are interested in investing in a regional hotel company and have investigated the financial statements of four potential investments. Use the information in the table below to answer the questions at the bottom of the page.

	HOTEL N	HOTEL J	HOTEL C	HOTEL W
INFORMATION FROM THE INCOME STATEMENT				
Total revenue	$10,099,000	$3,816,000	$428,806	$1,277,550
Total expenses	9,503,000	3,618,000	354,461	1,822,748
INFORMATION FROM THE BALANCE SHEET				
Current assets	1,946,000	1,020,000	68,629	526,549
Total assets	8,668,000	8,183,000	262,388	3,783,127
Current liabilities	2,356,000	895,000	101,091	693,809
Total liabilities	4,587,000	5,944,000	456,441	3,089,318
Total number of common stock outstanding	225,800	389,000	32,312	168,238

(Use the table on the following page for your answers.)

1. What is the net profit (or net loss) for each company?

2. Calculate the return on sales for each company.

3. Calculate the total stockholders' equity for each company.

4. What is the current ratio for each company?

5. Calculate the return on equity ratio for each company.

6. What is the debt-to-equity ratio for each company?

7. Calculate the basic earnings per share for each company.

	HOTEL N	HOTEL J	HOTEL C	HOTEL W
1. Net income (net profit or net loss)				
2. Return on sales				
3. Current ratio				
4. Stockholders' equity				
5. Return on equity				
6. Debt-to-equity ratio				
7. Earnings per share (basic)				

8. Which company would you rather invest in? Why?

notes on critical thinking exercise 17-5

The requested financial information and ratios are given below.

	HOTEL N	HOTEL J	HOTEL C	HOTEL W
1. Net income (net profit or net loss)	$ 596,000	$ 198,000	$ 74,345	($545,198)
2. Return on sales	5.9%	5.2%	17.3%	(42.7%)
3. Current ratio	0.83	1.13	0.68	0.76
4. Stockholders' equity	4,081,000	2,239,000	(194,053)	693,809
5. Return on equity	14.6%	8.8%	Not meaningful	(78.5%)
6. Debt-to-equity ratio	112%	265%	Not meaningful	445%
7. Earnings per share (basic)	$2.64	$0.51	$2.30	($3.24)

HOTEL N Return on sales is in the midrange for the industry. The current ratio, while less than the ideal 2.0, is in line with two of the other three companies. Return on equity is healthy and at the top of the industry, showing that the company has made good use of the funds invested by the investors. The debt-to-equity is much higher than the ideal ratio of 100%. However, when compared to the other companies in the industry, a 112% debt-to-equity ratio looks good. Earnings per share are also at the top range in the industry.

HOTEL J. Return on sales is in the midrange. Current ratio is at the top of the industry, showing a better than average liquidity. Return on equity is not exceptional, but in the midrange for the industry. The debt-to-equity ratio, however, is alarming. With a debt-to-equity ratio of 265%, the company is heavily leveraged. Creditors provide almost three times as much capital as stockholders do. This would be a relatively risky investment.

HOTEL C If you look only at earnings, return on sales, and earnings per share, Hotel C looks like a winner. The 17.3% return on sales is the highest in the industry. Earnings per share is also at the high end. But investors in this company have a significant problem. The company has not only burned through all of the invested capital, but the stockholders' equity is actually in the red. Not a good sign at all. Calculating the return on equity and debt-to-equity ratios is therefore meaningless. Return on a negative is irrelevant. This company is on the edge of bankruptcy, if it has not already filed.

HOTEL W Hotel W has the opposite problem from Hotel C. Stockholders' equity is still in the positive, but the company is hemorrhaging money. The company's return on sales shows that the company is spending almost 43% more than it takes in as revenue—$1.00 in sales costs the company $1.43.

Hotels C and W are horrible investment candidates. That leaves Hotels N and J. Hotel J is heavily leveraged and would be more risky. Hotel N is a steady, safe performer. Knowing that there is a direct relationship between risk and return, the investment decision would depend on the investors' tolerance for risk.

bonus cases

bonus case 17-1

THE BEST-LAID PLANS OFTEN GO AWRY

How you report revenues on the income statement makes a big difference in how profitable a company looks. The problem is that stockholders are often fooled into investing in a firm that is not nearly as profitable as they think. A good example is that of Thousand Trails of Seattle. It sold campground memberships for owners of recreation vehicles. It used the usual expensive promotions to get potential buyers to come to the campgrounds. Once a potential customer was at the site, there was much pressure to buy now, and the campgrounds were quite attractive. Once a customer got home and reconsidered the investment, though, some backed out of the commitment, and that is where Thousand Trails got into difficulty.

The company recorded the full price of a membership (about $7,500) as revenue, even though members paid only 40% down on average. Marketing expenses were running higher than payments, so more cash flowed out than flowed in. To get cash, Thousand Trails sold its receivables.

In one year, Thousand Trails used $52 million more cash than it produced, a definite cash flow problem. Nevertheless, it reported record earnings of $19.1 million, and the stock price went up to over $29.

Two years later, the stock had fallen to less than $5, reflecting a 90% drop in earnings reported (from $19 million to less than $2 million). What happened was that a lot of campground members dropped out before paying in full. So Thousand Trails had to write off $11 million in paper revenues. Marketing expenses were two times greater than down payments. Debt reached a horrendous 244% of stockholders' equity.

Meanwhile, stockholders were left wondering what happened to the company that was growing so fast and making such good profits (at least on the income statement).

discussion questions for bonus case 17-1

1. Thousand Trails did nothing illegal in its reporting of revenues and profits. What does that tell you about the need to carefully read and analyze income statements before you invest?

2. Can you see how cash flow problems can grow to unbelievable proportions in just a short time, even when profits look good?

notes on discussion questions for bonus case 17-1

1. *Thousand Trails did nothing illegal in its reporting of revenues and profits. What does that tell you about the need to carefully read and analyze income statements before you invest?*

   The fact is that income statements and balance sheets are very hard to analyze. Auditors go over them to check for legality, but that doesn't prevent deception of stockholders. One way to invest and not worry about doing your own analysis is to buy mutual funds and leave the digging to professionals.

2. *Can you see how cash flow problems can grow to unbelievable proportions in just a short time, even when profits look good?*

   Yes, cash flow problems plague businesses, especially the ones that grow rapidly. The problem is that the fast-growing firms are also the most attractive as investments. A firm cannot keep borrowing and growing without careful cash flow analysis or it is bound to get caught with too little cash and too many bills to pay. If the bank refuses the business any more loans, the result, more often than not, is bankruptcy.

bonus case 17-2

MANAGING BY THE NUMBERS

Katherine Potter knew a good thing when she saw it. At least, it seemed so at first. She was traveling in Italy when she spotted pottery shops that made beautiful products ranging from ashtrays to lamps. Some of the pottery was stunning in design.

Katherine began importing the products to the United States, and sales took off. Customers immediately realized the quality of the items and were willing to pay top price. Katherine decided to keep prices moderate to expand rapidly, and she did. Sales in the second three months were double those of the first few months. Sales in the second year were double those of the first year.

Every few months, Katherine had to run to the bank to borrow more money. She didn't really discuss her financial situation with her banker because she had no problems getting larger loans. You see, she always paid promptly. To save on the cost of buying goods, Katherine always took trade discounts. That is, she paid all bills within 10 days to save the 2% offered by her suppliers for paying so quickly.

Most customers bought Katherine's products on credit. They would buy a couple of lamps and a pot, and Katherine would allow them to pay over time. Some were very slow in paying her, taking six months or more.

After three years, Katherine noticed a small drop in her business. The local economy was not doing well, and many people were being laid off from their jobs. Nonetheless, Katherine's business stayed level. One day, the bank called Katherine and told her she was late in her payments. She told them she had been so busy that she didn't notice the bills. The problem was that Katherine had no cash available to pay the bank. She frantically called several customers for payment, but they were not able to pay her, either. Katherine was in a classic cash flow bind.

Katherine immediately raised her prices and refused to make sales on credit. She started delaying payment on her bills and paid the extra costs. Then she went to the bank and went over her financial condition with the banker. The banker noted her accounts receivable and assets. He then prepared a cash budget and loaned Katherine more money. Her import business grew much more slowly thereafter, but her financial condition improved greatly. Katherine had nearly gone bankrupt, but she recovered at the last minute.

discussion questions for bonus case 17-2

1. How is it possible to have high sales and high profits and run out of cash?

2. Why did Katherine do better when she raised her prices and refused to sell on credit?

3. What was the nature of Katherine's problem? Was she correct to go to the banker for help, even though she owed the bank money? How could she have prevented some of the problems she eventually found herself faced with?

notes on discussion questions for bonus case 17-2

1. *How is it possible to have high sales and high profits and run out of cash?*

   That is the classic description of a poor cash flow. A firm sells lots of merchandise on credit and buys more, paying promptly. Credit sales are great, and the firm buys more merchandise on credit. One day the creditors ask for money, and the firm cannot collect its accounts receivable fast enough; it is cash poor. It could go bankrupt if it can't borrow money someplace to cover until accounts receivable are collected.

2. *Why did Katherine do better when she raised her prices and refused to sell on credit?*

   Higher prices increase cash flow when the terms are cash and slow the need to borrow funds to buy on credit. Too rapid growth often leads to cash flow problems because the growth is all financed and there is not enough cash available to back it up.

3. *What was the nature of Katherine's problem? Was she correct to go to the banker for help, even though she owed the bank money? How could she have prevented some of the problems she eventually found herself faced with?*

   Katherine had a classic cash flow problem, and, yes, a bank is an excellent place to turn for help. The bank can provide funds, help in designing a cash budget, and provide further guidance to avoid cash flow problems in the future. What got Katherine in trouble in the first place was being too free to grant credit to customers and not being more insistent about collecting overdue accounts. To slow business, she could have raised prices and given credit only to her best customers.

endnotes

---

[i] *Source: Jody Heymann, "Bootstrapping Profits by Opening the Books," Bloomberg Businessweek, September 23, 2010.*

[ii] Lecture Link created by Michael McHugh.

[iii] *Sources:* Brady Dennis, "Congress Passes Financial Reform Bill," *The Washington Post*, July 16, 2010; Paul Davidson, Paul Wiseman, and John Waggoner, "Will New Financial Regulations Prevent Future Meltdowns?" *USA Today*, June 25, 2010.

[iv] *Source:* Scott Waller, "Whistleblower Tells Her Story," *The Clarion-Ledger*, April 29, 2006.

[v] *Sources:* Bill Saporito, "Where the Jobs Are: The Right Spots in the Recovery," *Time*, January 14, 2011; Joshua Zumbrun and Shobhana Chandra, "A U.S. Recovery Built on Low-Paying Jobs," *Bloomberg Businessweek*, February 24, 2011; Ali Velshi, "Today's 'It' Jobs: Accounting and IT," *Money*, January–February 2011.

[vi] Lecture Link created by Michael McHugh.

[vii] *Source:* S. J. Mintz, "Ex-Factors," *CFO Magazine*, April 2009.

[viii] *Sources*: Norm Brodsky, "Our Irrational Fear of Numbers," *Inc. Magazine*, January–February 2009; Joyce M. Rosenberg, "Non-Payers Can Hurt Small Businesses at Tax Time," *AP Online*, February 4, 2009.

[ix] Lecture Link created by Rusty Adcock.

[x] The Internet is a dynamic, changing information source. Web links noted of this manual were checked at the time of publication, but content may change over time. Please review the website before recommending it to your students.

Financial Management

chapter 18

what's new in this edition

additions to the 10th edition:

- Getting to Know Carol Tomé of Home Depot
- Name That Company: General Motors
- Discussion of Credit Card Responsibility Accountability and Disclosure Act added to subsection Credit Cards
- Legal Briefcase: Financial Order of Financial Martial Law?
- Making Ethical Decisions: Good Finance or Bad Medicine?
- Video case

revisions to the 10th edition:

- Text was revised to eliminate redundancy and tighten discussions.
- Statistical data and examples throughout the chapter were updated to reflect current information.
- Subsection title Lessons from the Financial Crisis replaces Financial Management in Trying Times and includes updated discussion of recent financial conditions.
- Reaching Beyond Our Borders: Exploring the Financial Universe.

deletions from the 9th edition:

- Getting to Know Tonya Atonnucci, Commissioner of the Women's Professional Soccer League
- Name That Company: Chrysler
- Making Ethical Decisions
- Spotlight on Small Business
- Legal Briefcase
- Reaching Beyond Our Borders

brief chapter outline and learning goals

chapter 18

Financial Management

Getting To Know CAROL TOMÉ, CFO of HOME DEPOT

learning goal 1

Explain the role and responsibilities of financial managers.

I. THE ROLE OF FINANCE AND FINANCIAL MANAGERS

A. The Value of Understanding Finance

B. What Is Financial Management?

learning goal 2

Outline the financial planning process, and explain the three key budgets in the financial plan.

II. FINANCIAL PLANNING

A. Forecasting Financial Needs

B. Working with the Budget Process

C. Establishing Financial Controls

learning goal 3

Explain why firms need operating funds.

III. THE NEED FOR OPERATING FUNDS

A. Managing Day-by-Day Needs of the Business

B. Controlling Credit Operations

C. Acquiring Needed Inventory

D. Making Capital Expenditures

E. Alternative Sources of Funds

learning goal 4

Identify and describe different sources of short-term financing.

IV. OBTAINING SHORT-TERM FINANCING

A. Trade Credit

B. Family and Friends

C. Commercial Banks

D. Different Forms of Short-Term Loans

E. Factoring Accounts Receivable

F. Commercial Paper

G. Credit Cards

learning goal 5

Identify and describe different sources of long-term financing.

V. OBTAINING LONG-TERM FINANCING

A. Debt Financing

B. Equity Financing

C. Comparing Debt and Equity Financing

D. Lessons from the Financial Crisis

VI. SUMMARY

lecture outline

Getting to Know CAROL TOMÉ, CFO of HOME DEPOT

Tomé started at Home Depot in 1995 and moved up to CFO in 2001. At that time, the country was in a building frenzy and Home Depot was opening new stores left and right. Once building slowed later in the decade, Tomé's financial focus turned from opening new stores to implementing new technology.

At one time this company was the largest automobile maker in the world. Due to severe financial problems in 2009, the company came very close to extinction. A $7 billion government-backed loan and an additional $43 billion government investment in the company helped it survive. It is now attempting a comeback as a much smaller company. Name that company.

(Students should read the chapter before guessing the company's name: GM.)

learning goal 1

Explain the role and responsibilities of financial managers.

I. THE ROLE OF FINANCE AND FINANCE MANAGERS

A. WHAT IS FINANCIAL MANAGEMENT?

1. Finance activities include:
   a. Preparing budgets
   b. Doing cash flow analysis
   c. Planning for the expenditure of funds on assets such as plant, equipment, and machinery
2. ***FINANCE*** is the function in a business that acquires funds for the firm and manages those funds within the firm.
   a. ***FINANCIAL MANAGEMENT*** is the job of managing a firm's resources so it can meet its goals and objectives.

PPT 18-1
Chapter Title

PPT 18-2
Learning Goals

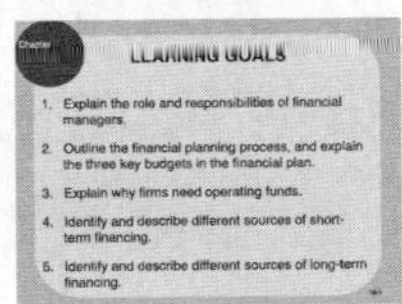

(See complete PowerPoint slide notes on page 18.46.)

PPT 18-3
Carol Tomé

(See complete PowerPoint slide notes on page 18.46.)

PPT 18-4
Name That Company

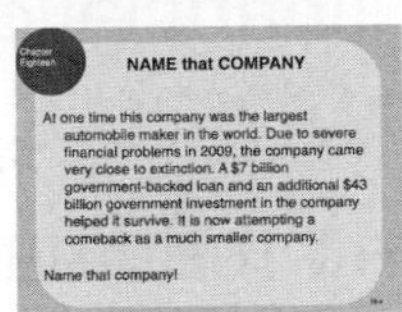

(See complete PowerPoint slide notes on page 18.47.)

lecture link 18-1
LEARNVEST TEACHES THE FINANCIAL BASICS

Financial management skills are essential to sustain personal success. Alexa von Tobel developed a website to help others understand finance. (See the complete lecture link on page 18.63 in this manual.)

PPT 18-5
What's Finance?

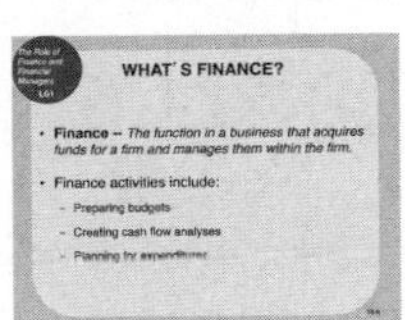

(See complete PowerPoint slide notes on page 18.47.)

PPT 18-6
Financial Management

(See complete PowerPoint slide notes on page 18.47.)

b. The role of an **ACCOUNTANT** is like that of a skilled technician who takes measure of a company's health and writes a report.

c. ***FINANCIAL MANAGERS*** are managers who examine financial data prepared by accountants and recommend strategies for improving the financial performance of the firm.

3. A manager can't make sound financial decisions without understanding accounting information.
   a. Most organizations designate a manager in charge of financial operations, generally the **CHIEF FINANCIAL OFFICER (CFO).**
   b. In large and medium-sized companies, the CFO is responsible for both accounting and finance functions.
   c. Financial management could also be assigned to the company **TREASURER** or **VICE PRESIDENT OF FINANCE.**
   d. A **COMPTROLLER** is the chief accounting officer.
4. Two key responsibilities of the financial manager are:
   a. To obtain funds
   b. To control the use of those funds
5. The need for careful financial management remains an **ONGOING CHALLENGE** in a business throughout its life.
6. *The text gives the example of GM's buyout in 2009.*

PPT 18-7
Financial Managers

(See complete PowerPoint slide notes on page 18.48.)

PPT 18-8
Who's Who in Finance

(See complete PowerPoint slide notes on page 18.48.)

TEXT FIGURE 18.1
What Financial Managers Do
(Text page 495)

PPT 18-9
What Financial Managers Do

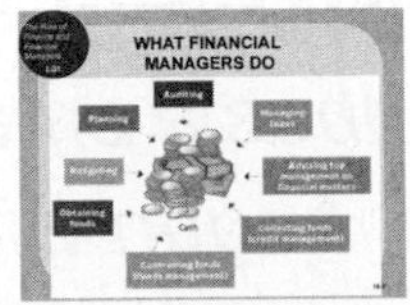

(See complete PowerPoint slide notes on page 18.48.)

lecture link 18-2
THE EXPANDING ROLE OF THE CFO

Today's CFO is a combination strategist, venture capitalist, and chief communicator. (See the complete lecture link on page 18.63 in this manual.)

lecture link 18-3
IVY LEAGUE ENDOWMENT DIFFICULTIES

The Ivy League's investment guru managed to bring in millions through investments. However, after the recession hit, much of that money is needed to pay off debts. (See the complete lecture link on page 18.64 in this manual.)

PPT 18-10
What Worries Financial Managers

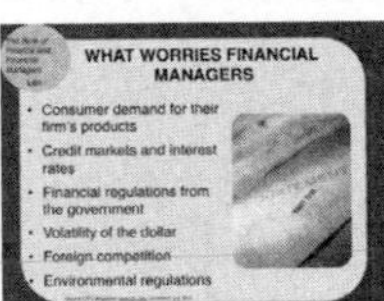

(See complete PowerPoint slide notes on page 18.49.)

B. **THE VALUE OF UNDERSTANDING FINANCE**

1. The most common ways for firms to **FAIL FINANCIALLY** are:
   a. **UNDERCAPITALIZATION**, or not enough funds to start with
   b. Poor **CASH FLOW**, or cash in minus cash out
   c. **INADEQUATE EXPENSE CONTROL**
2. *The text describes a small organization called Parsley Patch, begun with a $5,000 investment.*
   a. The company initially sold its product through gourmet stores.
   b. When the owners expanded into the health-food market, sales soared.
   c. However, neither woman understood cash flow procedures nor how to control expenses, and profits did not materialize.
   d. They eventually hired a CPA and an experienced financial manager, and soon they earned a comfortable margin on operations.
3. This company's experience illustrates the importance of **UNDERSTANDING FINANCE BEFORE** starting a business.
4. Financial understanding is also important to any one who wants to start a business or make an investment.

C. **WHAT IS FINANCIAL MANAGEMENT?**

1. Financial managers are responsible for:

lecture notes

PPT 18-11
Why Do Firms Fail Financially?

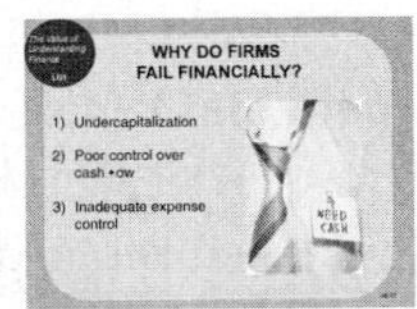

(See complete PowerPoint slide notes on page 18.49.)

PPT 18-12
Top Financial Concerns of Company CFOs—Macro

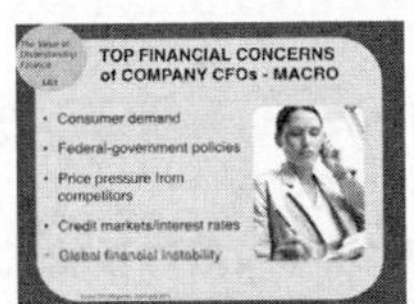

(See complete PowerPoint slide notes on page 18.50.)

PPT 18-13
Top Financial Concerns of Company CFOs—Micro

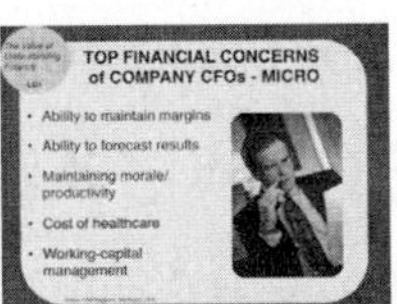

(See complete PowerPoint slide notes on page 18.50.)

a. Buying merchandise on credit (**ACCOUNTS PAYABLE**)

b. Collecting payment from customers (**ACCOUNTS RECEIVABLE**)

c. Making sure the company doesn't lose too much money on **BAD DEBTS**

2. These functions are especially critical to small and medium-sized companies.

3. Financial managers must keep up with opportunities and prepare for change.

4. Financial managers also handle **TAX MANAGEMENT**.

   a. As tax laws change, finance specialists must carefully analyze the **TAX IMPLICATIONS** of various decisions.

   b. Businesses of all sizes constantly manage taxes.

5. It is the **INTERNAL AUDITOR**, usually a member of the firm's finance department, who checks on the journal, ledgers, and financial statements to make sure that all transactions are properly treated.

   a. Without such audits, accounting statements would be less reliable.

   b. It is important that internal auditors be **OBJECTIVE** and **CRITICAL** of any improprieties.

lecture notes

learning goal 2

Outline the financial planning process, and explain the three key budgets in the financial plan.

II. FINANCIAL PLANNING

A. Financial planning is a key responsibility of the financial manager.

1. It involves analyzing short-term and long-term **MONEY FLOWS** to and from the firm.
2. The overall objectives of financial planning are to **OPTIMIZE PROFITS** and make the **BEST USE OF MONEY.**
3. **STEPS IN FINANCIAL PLANNING**:
   a. **FORECASTING** both long-term and short-term financial needs
   b. **DEVELOPING BUDGETS** to meet those needs
   c. **ESTABLISHING FINANCIAL CONTROL** to see how well the company is following the financial plans

B. **FORECASTING FINANCIAL NEEDS**

1. A ***SHORT-TERM FORECAST*** is a forecast that predicts revenues, costs, and expenses for a period of one year or less.
2. A ***CASH FLOW FORECAST*** is a forecast that predicts cash inflows and outflows in future periods, usually months or quarters.
   a. The inflows and outflows of cash are based on expected sales revenues and on various costs and expenses.

PPT 18-14
Financial Planning

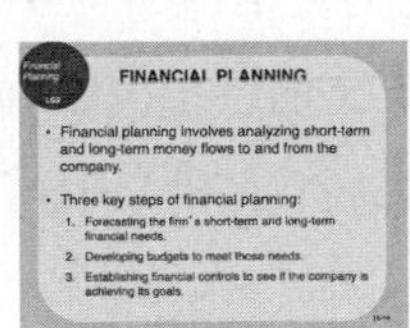

(See complete PowerPoint slide notes on page 18.50.)

PPT 18-15
Financial Forecasting

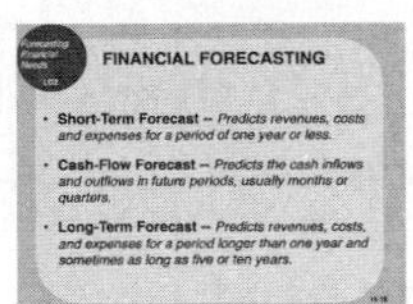

(See complete PowerPoint slide notes on page 18.51.)

   b. A firm often uses its past financial statements as a basis for projecting expected sales and various costs and expenses.

3. A ***LONG-TERM FORECAST*** is a forecast that predicts revenues, costs, and expenses for a period longer than 1 year, sometimes extending 5 or 10 years into the future.
   a. This forecast is crucial to the company's long-term strategic plan.
   b. The long-term financial forecast gives managers an overview of the income or profit potential with different strategic plans.

C. **WORKING WITH THE BUDGET PROCESS**

1. A ***BUDGET*** is a financial plan that sets forth management's expectations, and, on the basis of those expectations, allocates the use of specific resources throughout the firm.
   a. The **KEY FINANCIAL STATEMENTS** form the basis for the budgeting process.
   b. A budget becomes the primary **GUIDE** for the financial operations and financial needs.
2. There are **SEVERAL BUDGETS** in a company:
   a. The ***CAPITAL BUDGET*** is a budget that highlights a firm's spending plans for major asset purchases that often require large sums of money.

critical thinking exercise 18-1
BUDGETARY CONTROL

This exercise asks the students to analyze a company's monthly budgetary report to determine which expenses are over- or underbudget. (See complete exercise on page 18.70 of this manual.)

PPT 18-16
Budgeting

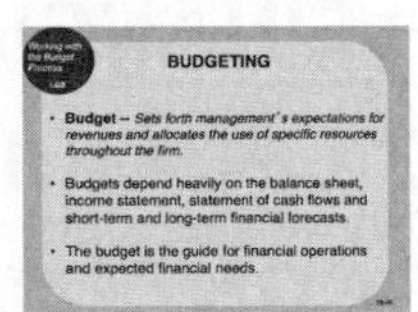

(See complete PowerPoint slide notes on page 18.51.)

PPT 18-17
Types of Budgets

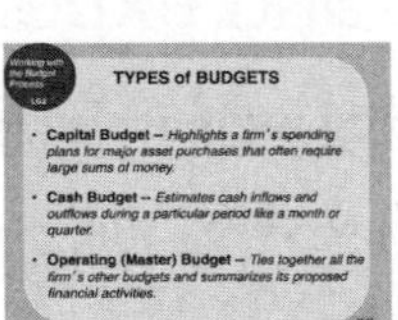

(See complete PowerPoint slide notes on page 18.51.)

b. The ***CASH BUDGET*** estimates cash inflows and outflows during a particular period like a month or a quarter.

c. The ***OPERATING BUDGET (MASTER BUDGET)*** is the budget that ties together all of a firm's other budgets and summarizes its proposed financial activities.

3. Financial planning often determines:
   a. What long-term investments are made
   b. When specific funds will be needed
   c. How the funds will be generated

4. The final step in financial planning is to **ESTABLISH FINANCIAL CONTROLS.**

D. **ESTABLISHING FINANCIAL CONTROLS**

1. ***FINANCIAL CONTROL*** is a process in which a firm periodically compares its actual revenues, costs, and expenses with its budget.
2. Most companies hold monthly financial reviews to ensure financial control.
3. Control procedures help managers identify variances to the financial plan and make corrections if necessary.
4. Financial adjustments to the plan may be needed.
5. *Example: the rapid spike and rapid fall in oil prices in 2011.*

TEXT FIGURE 18.2
Financial Planning
(Text page 497)

PPT 18-18
Financial Planning

(See complete PowerPoint slide notes on page 18.52.)

TEXT FIGURE 18.3
A Sample Cash Budget for Very Vegetarian
(Text page 499)

This text figure presents a sample cash budget for Very Vegetarian, showing the cash inflows and outflows.

TEXT FIGURE 18.4
You Incorporated Monthly Budget
(Text page 500)

Just as with corporations, individuals can compile a monthly budget of income and expenses.

PPT 18-19
Establishing Financial Control

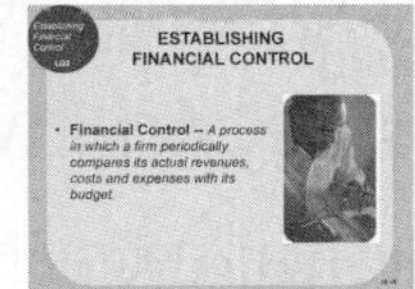

(See complete PowerPoint slide notes on page 18.52.)

PPT 18-20
Factors Used in Assessing Financial Control

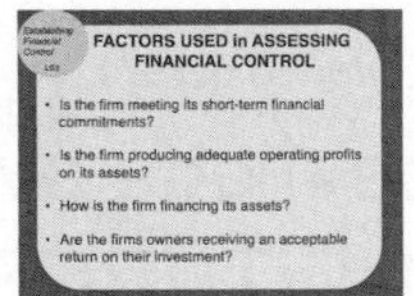

(See complete PowerPoint slide notes on page 18.52.)

progress assessment
(Text page 499)

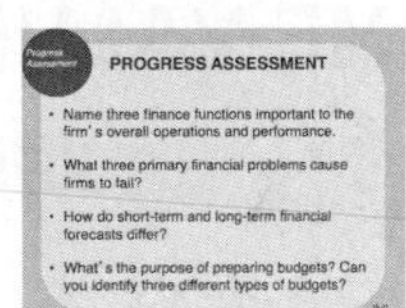

PPT 18-21
Progress Assessment

(See complete PowerPoint slide notes on page 18.53.)

learning goal 3

Explain why firms need operating funds.

III. THE NEED FOR OPERATING FUNDS

A. Businesses continually need operating funds.

1. Financial requirements of a business change as businesses grow or venture into new markets.
2. All organizations need funds for **CERTAIN OPERATIONAL NEEDS:**
    a. Managing day-by-day needs of the business
    b. Controlling credit operations
    c. Acquiring needed inventory
    d. Making capital expenditures

B. **MANAGING DAY-BY-DAY NEEDS OF THE BUSINESS**

1. Funds must be made available to meet **DAILY CASH EXPENDITURES** without endangering the firm's financial health.
2. Money has **TIME VALUE**—$200 today is more valuable than $200 a year from today.
3. Financial managers try to keep cash expenditures to a minimum and invest in interest-bearing accounts.
4. Efficient cash management is particularly important to small firms.

C. **CONTROLLING CREDIT OPERATIONS**

1. Making credit available helps keep current customers happy and attracts new ones.

lecture notes

PPT 18-22
Key Needs for Operational Funds in a Firm

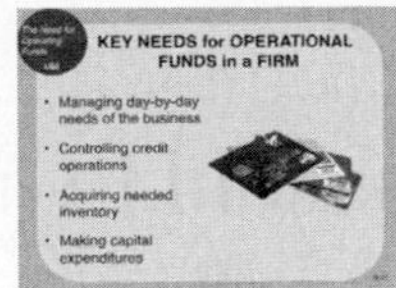

(See complete PowerPoint slide notes on page 18.53.)

legal briefcase

(Text page 501)

PPT 18-23
Financial Order or Financial Martial Law?

(See complete PowerPoint slide notes on page 18.53.)

PPT 18-24
How Small Businesses Can Improve Cash Flow

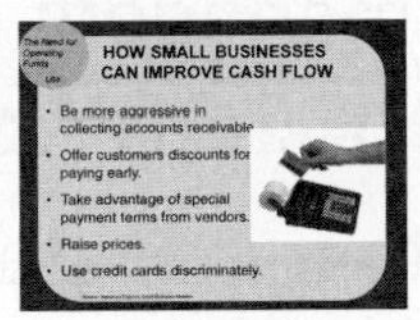

(See complete PowerPoint slide notes on page 18.54.)

MAKING ethical decisions

(Text page 503)

PPT 18-25
Good Finance or Bad Medicine?

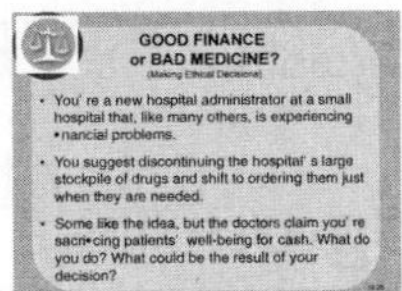

(See complete PowerPoint slide notes on page 18.54.)

2. During 2008, credit was especially critical since banks were hesitant to make loans.
3. If a firm offers credit, as much as 25% of a company's assets can be tied up in **ACCOUNTS RECEIVABLE**.
4. Some of the firm's available funds are needed to pay for the goods or services already sold.
   a. Providing cash or quantity discounts are possible collection procedures.
   b. Financial managers need to scrutinize the **CREDIT HISTORY** of all credit customers.
5. It is possible to minimize the cost of accounts receivable by **ACCEPTING BANK CREDIT CARDS** such as MasterCard or Visa.

D. **ACQUIRING NEEDED INVENTORY**
1. Providing the inventory that customers expect, the business ties up a significant amount of funds.
2. A sound inventory policy helps managers use firm's available funds to maximizing profitability.
3. **JUST-IN-TIME INVENTORY** may help reduce the funds companies must tie up in inventory.

E. **MAKING CAPITAL EXPENDITURES**
1. ***CAPITAL EXPENDITURES*** are major investments in either tangible long-term assets such as land, buildings, and equipment or intangible assets such as patents, trademarks, and copyrights.

critical thinking exercise 18-2
EXTENDING CREDIT

This exercise explores the advantages and disadvantages of accepting credit cards. (See complete exercise on page 18.73 of this manual.)

2. Purchasing major assets uses a huge portion of the organization's funds.
    a. The firm should weigh all possible options before committing major resources.
    b. Financial managers must evaluate the appropriateness of capital expenditures.
3. *Text example: Should an increase in demand be dealt with by building a new plant, purchasing an existing one, or renting space.*
4. The financial manager has to decide how to finance operations.

F. **ALTERNATIVE SOURCES OF FUNDS**
1. Two questions that need answers:
    a. How much money is needed?
    b. What is the appropriate source?
2. **METHODS OF RAISING MONEY**
    a. ***DEBT FINANCING*** refers to funds raised through various forms of borrowing that must be repaid; these funds can be short-term or long-term.
    b. ***EQUITY FINANCING*** is money raised from within the firm, from operations or through the sale of ownership in the firm (stock).
3. **SHORT-TERM VERSUS LONG-TERM FUNDS**
    a. ***SHORT-TERM FINANCING*** are funds needed for a year or less.
    b. ***LONG-TERM FINANCING*** are funds needed for more than a year (usually 2 to 10 years.)

lecture notes

PPT 18-26
Using Alternative Sources of Funds

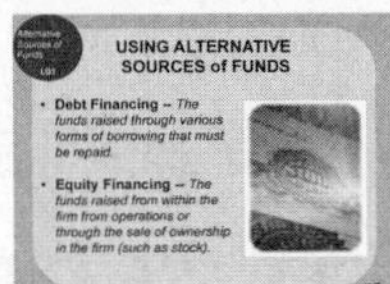

(See complete PowerPoint slide notes on page 18.54.)

PPT 18-27
Short- and Long-Term Financing

(See complete PowerPoint slide notes on page 18.55.)

TEXT FIGURE 18.5
Why Firms Need Funds
(Text page 504)

PPT 18-28
Why Firms Need Financing

(See complete PowerPoint slide notes on page 18.55.)

progress assessment
(Text page 504)

PROGRESS ASSESSMENT
• Money has time value. What does this mean?
• Why is accounts receivable a financial concern of the firm?
• What's the primary reason an organization spends a good deal of its available funds on inventory and capital expenditures?
• What's the difference between debt and equity financing?

PPT 18-29
Progress Assessment

(See complete PowerPoint slide notes on page 18.55.)

learning goal 4

Identify and describe several sources of short-term financing.

IV. OBTAINING SHORT-TERM FINANCING

A. Everyday operation of the firm requires management of short-term financial needs.

1. Firms need to borrow short-term funds to **FINANCE INVENTORY** or **MEET BILLS.**
2. Short-term financing can be either secured or unsecured.

B. **TRADE CREDIT**

1. Trade credit, the most widely used source of short-term funding, is the **LEAST EXPENSIVE** and **MOST CONVENIENT** form of short-term financing.
2. ***TRADE CREDIT*** is the practice of buying goods and services now and paying for them later.
3. The invoice term **2/10, NET 30** means that:
   a. The buyer can take a 2% discount for paying within 10 days
   b. The total bill is due (net) in 30 days if the discount is not taken.
4. Taking the discount is, in effect, saving 36%.
5. If the business has a poor credit rating or history of slow payment, the supplier may insist on a promissory note.
6. A ***PROMISSORY NOTE*** is a written contract with a promise to pay a supplier a specific sum of money at a definite time.

PPT 18-30
Types of Short-Term Financing

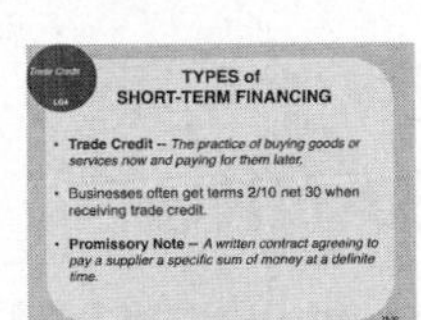

(See complete PowerPoint slide notes on page 18.56.)

C. **FAMILY AND FRIENDS**

1. This source may be convenient, but it can also create problems.
2. It is better not to borrow from friends and relatives.
3. Fewer entrepreneurs today rely on family and friends for funding.
4. If an entrepreneur does borrow from family or friends, it is best to:
   a. Agree on specific loan terms
   b. Put the agreement in writing
   c. Arrange for repayment in the same way you would a bank loan

D. **COMMERCIAL BANKS**

1. Banks are highly **SENSITIVE TO RISK** and hesitate to make small business loans.
2. A promising venture may be able to get a bank loan.
3. The person in charge of finance should keep in **CLOSE TOUCH WITH THE BANK** and visit the banker periodically.

E. **DIFFERENT FORMS OF SHORT-TERM LOANS**

1. A ***SECURED LOAN*** is a loan backed by collateral, something valuable such as property.
   a. The item of value is called **COLLATERAL.**
   b. Accounts receivable are often used as collateral for a loan—known as **PLEDGING.**

PPT 18-31
Types of Short-Term Financing

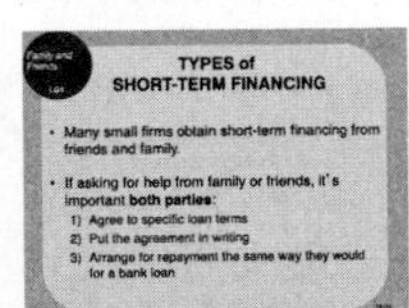

(See complete PowerPoint slide notes on page 18.56.)

PPT 18-32
Difficulty of Obtaining Short-Term Financing

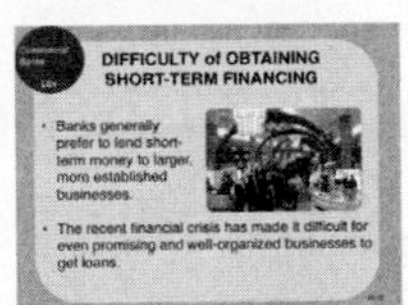

(See complete PowerPoint slide notes on page 18.56.)

SPOTLIGHT ON
small business
(Text page 507)

PPT 18-33
Exploring the Financing Universe

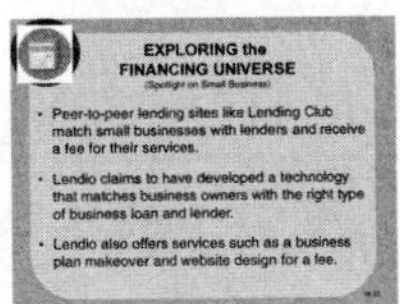

(See complete PowerPoint slide notes on page 18.57.)

2. An ***UNSECURED LOAN*** is a loan that doesn't require any collateral.
   a. These are the most difficult to get.
   b. Only highly regarded customers are approved.
3. ***LINE OF CREDIT*** is a given amount of unsecured short-term funds a bank will lend to a business, provided the funds are readily available.
   a. A line of credit is **NOT GUARANTEED** to a business.
   b. It can, however, speed the borrowing process.
   c. As businesses become more financially secure, the amount of credit may be increased.
   d. ***REVOLVING CREDIT AGREEMENT*** is a line of credit that is guaranteed but usually comes with a fee.
4. ***COMMERCIAL FINANCE COMPANIES*** are organizations that make short-term loans to borrowers that offer tangible assets as collateral.
   a. These **non-deposit-type organizations** (nonbanks) are willing to accept higher degrees of risk than commercial banks.
   b. Interest rates charged are usually higher than banks because they take greater risks.

F. **FACTORING ACCOUNTS RECEIVABLE**

1. ***FACTORING***, the process of selling accounts receivable for cash, is relatively expensive.
   a. A **FACTOR** is a market intermediary that

PPT 18-34
Different Forms of Short-Term Loans

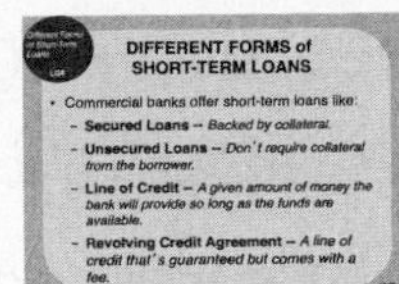

(See complete PowerPoint slide notes on page 18.57.)

critical thinking exercise 18-3

FINDING THE COST OF BANK LOANS

This Internet exercise asks students to go online and research the actual cost of a bank loan. (See complete exercise on page 18.75 of this manual.)

lecture link 18-4

THE NUMBERS SPEAK WHEN DEALING WITH YOUR BANKER

Through ratio analysis the firm's financial statement can tell a banker a lot about the company's financial health. (See the complete lecture link on page 18.65 of this manual.)

PPT 18-35
Factoring

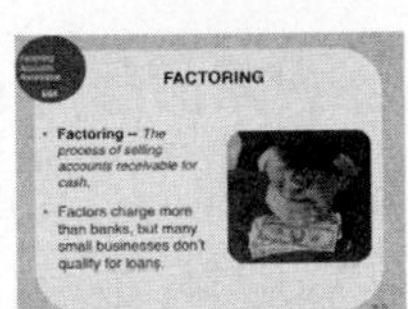

(See complete PowerPoint slide notes on page 18.58.)

agrees to buy the accounts receivable from the firm at a discount for cash.

b. The factor then collects and keeps the money that was owed the firm.

2. Despite the high cost, factoring is very popular among small businesses, especially in the clothing and furniture businesses.
3. Factoring charges are much lower if the company assumes the risk of those accounts who are slow to pay or don't pay at all.
4. Factoring is not a loan—it is the sale of an asset.

G. **COMMERCIAL PAPER**

1. ***COMMERCIAL PAPER*** consists of unsecured promissory notes in amounts of $100,000 and up that mature (come due) in 270 days or less.
2. Only financially stable firms are able to sell commercial paper.
3. Companies can get short-term funds quickly and at a lower interest rate than bank loans.
4. During the recent credit crisis the Federal Reserve stepped in to purchase commercial paper to ease credit.

H. **CREDIT CARDS**

1. About half of all small businesses finance their start-up with credit cards.
2. Credit cards provide a readily available line of credit, but they are extremely risky and costly.
3. Because of their risk and cost, credit cards should be used only as a last resort.

PPT 18-36
Commercial Paper

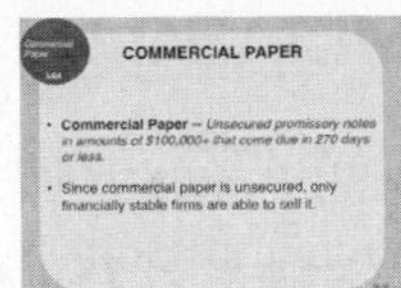

(See complete PowerPoint slide notes on page 18.58.)

PPT 18-37
Credit Cards

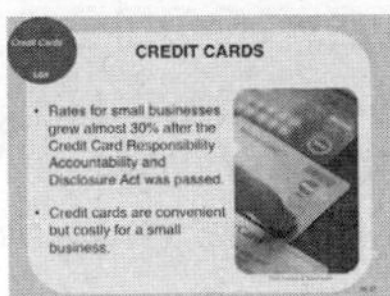

(See complete PowerPoint slide notes on page 18.58.)

PPT 18-38
Ways to Raise Start-Up Capital

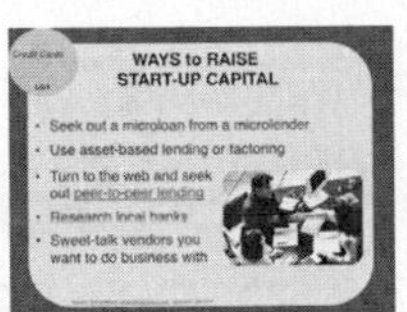

(See complete PowerPoint slide notes on page 18.58.)

Progress assessment
(Text page 509)

PPT 18-39
Progress Assessment

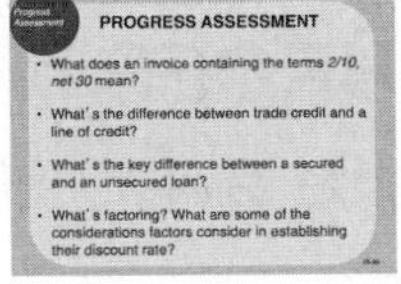

(See complete PowerPoint slide notes on page 18.59.)

learning goal 5

Identify and describe several sources of long-term financing.

V. OBTAINING LONG-TERM FINANCING

A. The **FINANCIAL PLAN** specifies the amount of funding that will be needed over various time periods and the most appropriate sources of those funds.

1. In setting long-term financing objectives, the firm generally asks **THREE MAJOR QUESTIONS**:
   a. What are the organization's long-term **GOALS AND OBJECTIVES?**
   b. What **FUNDS** are needed to achieve these goals and objectives?
   c. What **SOURCES** of long-term funding (capital) are available, and which best fit our needs?
2. **LONG-TERM CAPITAL** is used to buy fixed assets such as plant and equipment and to finance any expansions of the organization.
3. These financing decisions involve high-level management.
4. Long-term financing comes from two sources: **DEBT FINANCING** or **EQUITY FINANCING.**

B. **DEBT FINANCING**

1. **DEBT FINANCING** involves borrowing money, which creates a legal obligation to repay the amount borrowed.

lecture link 18-5
MAKING PAYMENTS OVERSEAS

Some entrepreneurs have found creative ways of paying and being paid overseas. (See complete lecture link on page 18.67 of this manual.)

PPT 18-40
Setting Long-Term Financing Objectives

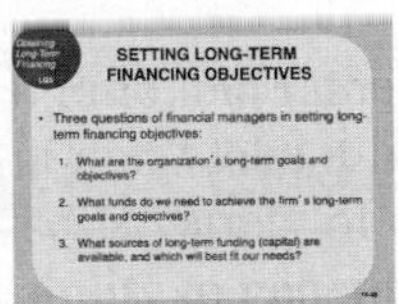

(See complete PowerPoint slide notes on page 18.59.)

PPT 18-41
The Five Cs of Credit

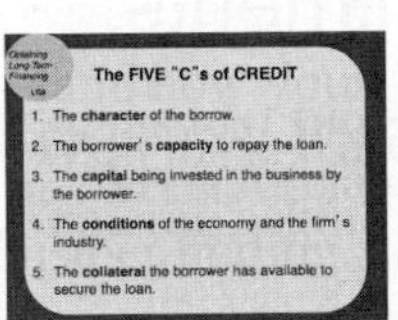

(See complete PowerPoint slide notes on page 18.59.)

PPT 18-42
Using Long-Term Debt Financing

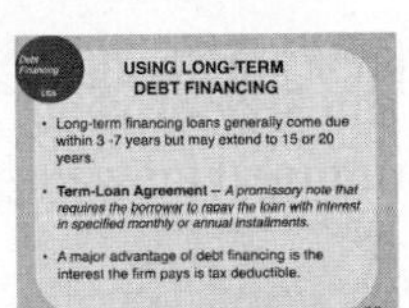

(See complete PowerPoint slide notes on page 18.60.)

2. **DEBT FINANCING BY BORROWING MONEY FROM LENDING INSTITUTIONS.**
   a. Long-term loans are usually repaid within 3 to 7 years, but may extend to 15 or 20 years.
      i. A ***TERM-LOAN AGREEMENT*** is a promissory note that requires the borrower to repay the loan in specified installments.
      ii. A major advantage is that interest paid on a long-term debt is **TAX DEDUCTIBLE**.
   b. **LONG-TERM LOANS** are often more expensive than short-term loans because larger amounts of capital are borrowed and the repayment date is less secure.
      i. Most long-term loans require some form of **COLLATERAL**.
      ii. The greater the risk a lender takes, the higher the rate of interest.
   c. The cost of financing involves the ***RISK/ RETURN TRADE-OFF***, the principle that the greater the risk a lender takes in making a loan, the higher the interest rate required.
   d. Lenders will also often require certain **RESTRICTIONS** on a firm's operations.
3. **DEBT FINANCING BY ISSUING BONDS**
   a. If an organization can't get long-term financing from a lending institution, it may issue bonds.

bonus case 18-1

THE REBUILDING DECISION

A small veterinary clinic is hit by a tornado, ripping off the roof. The partners must make a decision on how to recover. (See the complete case, discussion questions, and suggested answers beginning on page 18.80 of this manual.)

PPT 18-43

Using Debt Financing by Issuing Bonds

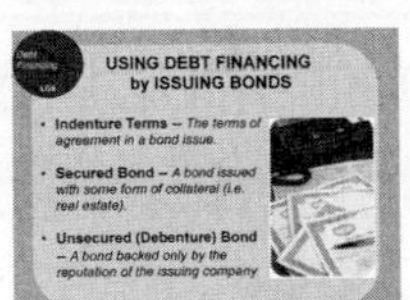

(See complete PowerPoint slide notes on page 18.60.)

i. A **BOND** is a company IOU, a binding contract through which an organization agrees to specific terms with investors in return for investors lending money to the company.

ii. ***INDENTURE TERMS*** are the terms of agreement in a bond issue.

b. Investors in bonds measure the **RISK** involved in purchasing a bond with the **RE-TURN** (interest) the bond promises to pay.

c. A ***SECURED BOND*** is a bond issued with some form of collateral such as real estate, equipment, or other pledged assets.

d. An ***UNSECURED BOND*** is a bond backed only by the reputation of the issuer; also called a debenture bond.

C. **EQUITY FINANCING**

1. **EQUITY FINANCING** comes from the firm's owners.

   a. It involves selling **OWNERSHIP** in the firm in the form of stock, or using retained earnings the firm has reinvested in the business.

   b. A business can also seek equity financing from venture capital.

2. **EQUITY FINANCING BY SELLING STOCK**

   a. One way to obtain needed funds is to sell **OWNERSHIP SHARES (STOCK)** in the firm to the public.

   b. Purchasers of stock become **OWNERS**.

PPT 18-44
Securing Equity Financing

(See complete PowerPoint slide notes on page 18.60.)

critical thinking exercise 18-4
FINANCING OPTIONS

A company needs $1,000 to expand its product line. Which financing option should it use? (See complete exercise on page 18.77 of this manual.)

c. The first time a company offers to sell its stock to the general public is called an **INITIAL PUBLIC OFFERING (IPO).**

d. Companies can issue stock for public purchase only if they meet requirements set by the Securities and Exchange Commission (SEC).

3. **EQUITY FINANCING FROM RETAINED EARNINGS**

   a. The profits the company keeps and reinvests in the firm are called **RETAINED EARNINGS.**

   b. They are a **MAJOR SOURCE OF LONG-TERM FUNDS.**

   c. Retained earnings are the most popular type of financing because:

      i. The company saves interest payments, dividends, and underwriting fees.

      ii. There is no new ownership created.

   d. Many organizations can't use this type of financing because they don't have enough retained earnings.

4. **EQUITY FINANCING FROM VENTURE CAPITAL**

   a. The hardest time for a business to raise money is when it is just starting or in the earliest stages of expansion.

   b. ***VENTURE CAPITAL (VC)*** is money that is invested in new or emerging companies that

PPT 18-45
Want to Attract a Venture Capitalist?

(See complete PowerPoint slide notes on page 18.61.)

are perceived as having great profit potential.

c. The venture capital industry began as an alternative investment vehicle for wealthy families.

   i. Venture capital investment increased during the 1990s, especially in high-tech centers.

   ii. In the early 2000s problems in the economy and in the technology industry resulting in a decrease in VC financing.

   iii. As the economy began to grow again in 2011, venture capital returned to the market.

D. **COMPARING DEBT AND EQUITY FINANCING**

1. ***LEVERAGE*** is raising needed funds through borrowing to increase a firm's rate of return.
2. While debt increases the risk of the firm, it also enhances the firm's profitability.
3. ***COST OF CAPITAL*** is the rate of return a company must earn in order to meet the demands of its lenders and expectations of its equity holders.
4. If the firm earns more than the interest payments on the funds borrowed, stockholders earn a **HIGHER RATE OF RETURN** than if equity financing were used.
5. It is up to each firm to determine exactly what a **PROPER BALANCE** between debt and equity financing is.

lecture link 18-6

THE MYTHS OF VENTURE CAPITAL

Misconceptions about the venture capital industry are based on myths that have developed among firms looking for VC financing. (See the complete lecture link on page 18.68 of this manual.)

TEXT FIGURE 18.6
Differences between Debt and Equity Financing
(Text page 513)

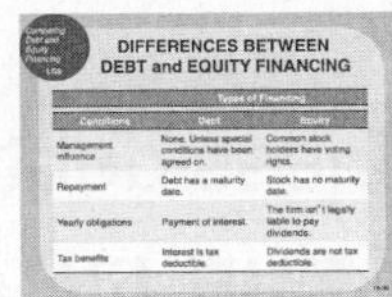

PPT 18-46
Differences between Debt and Equity Financing

(See complete PowerPoint slide notes on page 18.61.)

PPT 18-47
Using Leverage for Funding Needs

(See complete PowerPoint slide notes on page 18.61.)

critical thinking exercise 18-5

OBTAINING FINANCING

This exercise presents three business scenarios and asks the students to suggest financing options. (See complete exercise on page 18.78 of this manual.)

   a. **LEVERAGE RATIOS** are a way to compare leverage relative to other firms in the industry.
   b. The average debt of a large industrial corporation ranges between 33 and 40% of its total assets.
   c. Small-business debt varies considerably.

E. **LESSONS FROM THE FINANCIAL CRISIS**

   1. The collapse of financial markets in 2008 focused attention on the failure of financial management.
   2. Credit tightened as financial institutions instituted more restrictions.
   3. Financial managers will have to earn back the public's trust.

VI. SUMMARY

TEXT FIGURE 18.7
Using Leverage (Debt) versus Equity Financing
(Text page 514)

This text figure shows two options (100% equity and 90% debt/10% equity) for raising the $500,000 that Very Vegetarian needs.

PPT 18-48
Lessons of the Financial Crisis

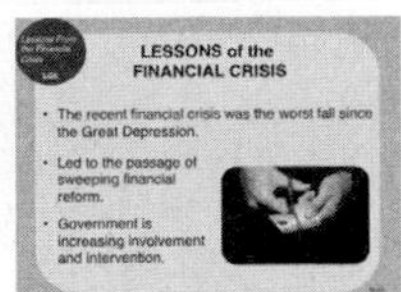

(See complete PowerPoint slide notes on page 18.62.)

lecture link 18-7
AMERICA'S DANGEROUS LACK OF FINANCIAL FACTS

Some believe the recent financial chaos could have been avoided if more companies were transparent with their financial facts (See the complete lecture link on page 18.68 in this manual.)

lecture link 18-8
REAL ESTATE WOES FOR REGIONAL BANKS

Before the recession, local banks lacked the clout to diversify their investments like the big banks. Instead they turned to commercial real estate, and that led to big problems (See the complete lecture link on page 18.69 in this manual.)

progress assessment
(Text page 514)

PPT 18-49
Progress Assessment

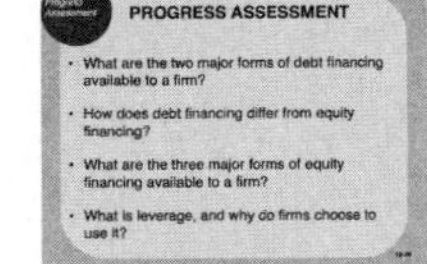

(See complete PowerPoint slide notes on page 18.62.)

PowerPoint slide notes

PPT 18-1
Chapter Title

PPT 18-2
Learning Goals

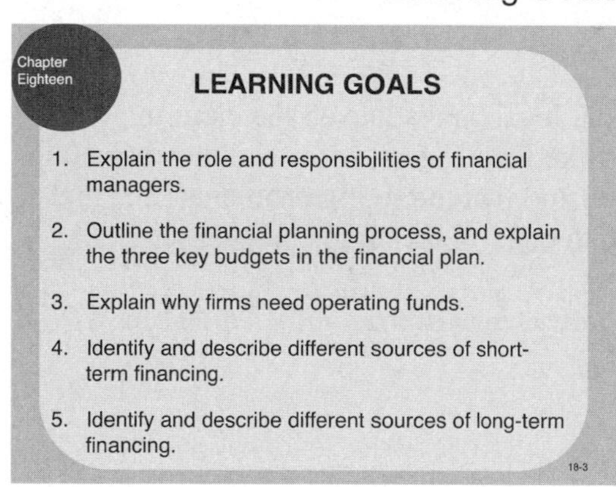

PPT 18-3
Carol Tomé

PPT 18-4
Name That Company

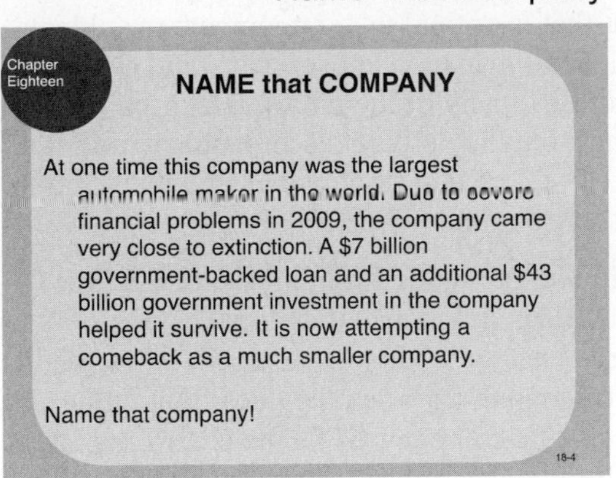

Company: General Motors (GM)

PPT 18-5
What's Finance?

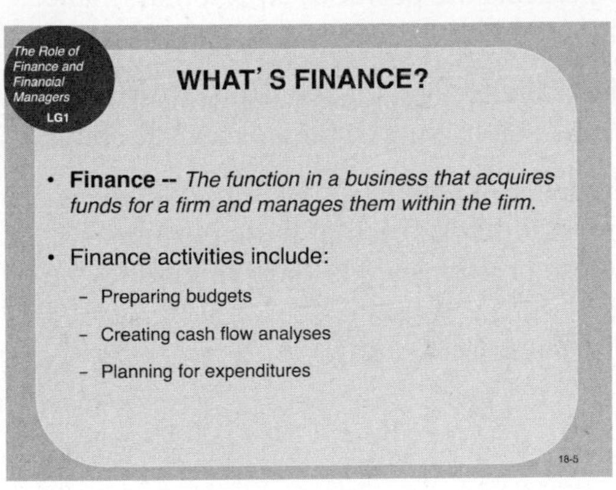

The finance function is responsible for managing a scarce resource—capital.

PPT 18-6
Financial Management

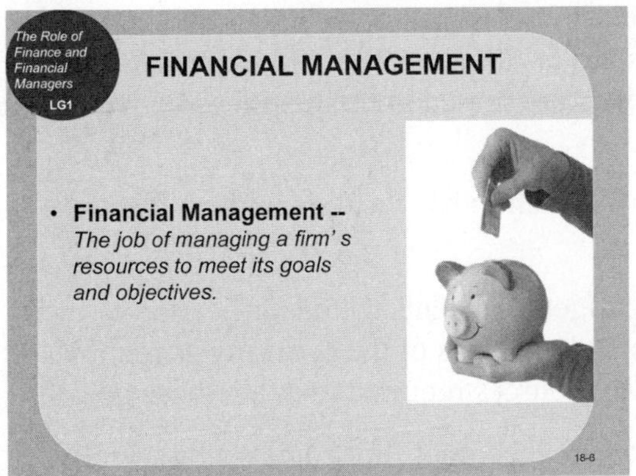

PPT 18-7
Financial Managers

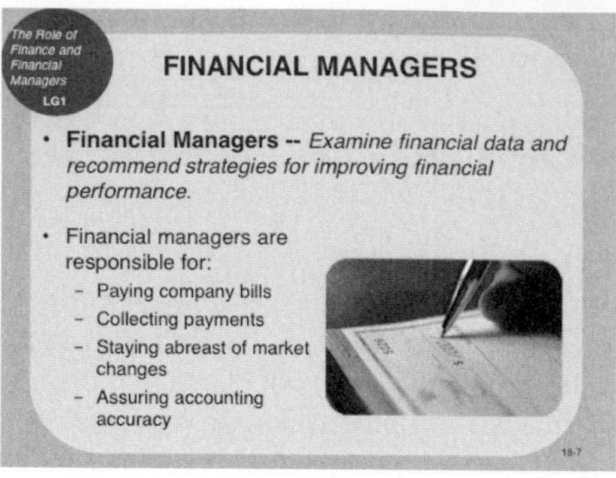

1. This slide provides insight into the role of financial management.
2. One point that is critical to communicate to students is that financial managers must understand accounting (and in fact many of them have backgrounds in accounting), but they are not accountants within the company. They are decision makers and managers in the truest sense of the word.
3. You might want to work through each of the functions of the financial manager and make certain students see exactly what's involved in such a job. Students often perk up when they hear that quite often next to the company CEO, the chief financial officer (CFO) is the highest-paid person within.

PPT 18-8
Who's Who in Finance

1. This slide presents the positions a person in finance might hold.
2. Help students understand that there are a variety of positions a person in finance might strive to obtain.
3. Ask the students, What are some of the functions/responsibilities of each of these positions? How are these positions alike? How might they be different?

PPT 18-9
What Financial Managers Do

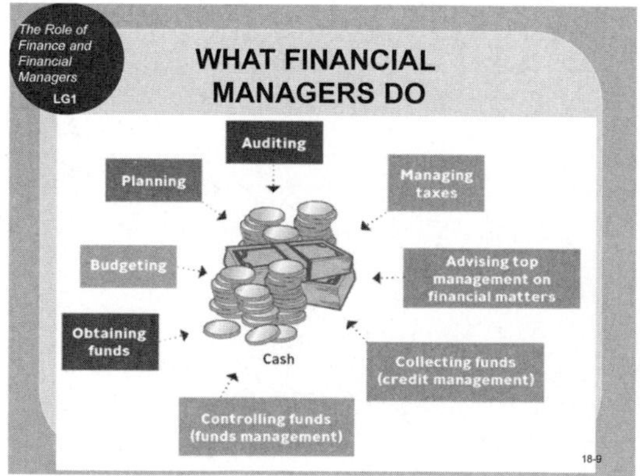

1. This slide (based on Figure 18.1) gives the students a broad overview of what responsibilities financial managers have within a corporation. The CFO's responsibilities are rooted in the functions of "control" and "treasury."
2. The control function has its basis in the budgeting process:
   - The budget represents the quantification of the goals and missions of the company as manifested by the resources required to attain those goals.
   - The budget becomes the scorecard by which the company as a whole is measured.
3. The other area of responsibility for CFOs is the treasury function.

(continued)

PPT 18-9
What Financial Managers Do (continued)

- Procurement of financial resources available to the company
- Ongoing communication with financial sources, investors, and debt holders who must be kept apprised of the firm's financial performance
- Allocation of resources within the context of the company budget

PPT 18-10
What Worries Financial Managers

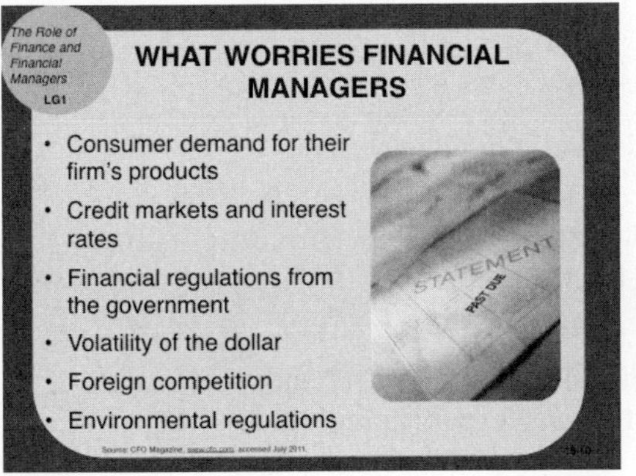

1. This slide highlights the things that worry financial managers.
2. Financial managers are required to wear many hats in the organization. While specific responsibilities of a CFO will vary between large and small companies, and public and closely held companies, the principles of control and treasury responsibilities transgress all boundaries.
3. The number of issues that financial managers face is one reason why they are so well compensated.

PPT 18-11
Why Do Firms Fail Financially?

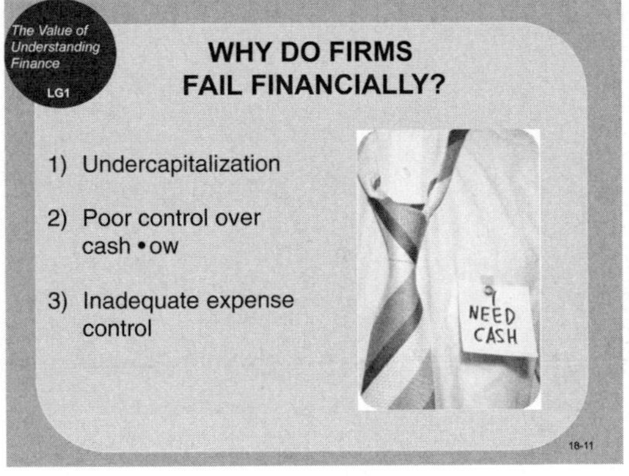

PPT 18-12
Top Financial Concerns of Company CFOs—Macro

1. This slide highlights the top concerns of company CFOs in the macroeconomy (the nation's economy).
2. The chief financial officers of companies must concern themselves with a multitude of issues.

PPT 18-13
Top Financial Concerns of Company CFOs—Micro

1. This slide highlights the top concerns of company CFOs in the microeconomy (within their own businesses).
2. The chief financial officers of companies must concern themselves with a multitude of issues.

PPT 18-14
Financial Planning

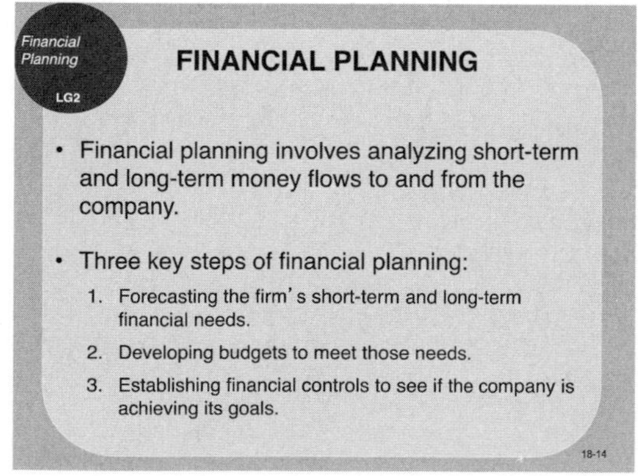

PPT 18-15
Financial Forecasting

FINANCIAL FORECASTING

- **Short-Term Forecast** -- *Predicts revenues, costs and expenses for a period of one year or less.*
- **Cash-Flow Forecast** -- *Predicts the cash inflows and outflows in future periods, usually months or quarters.*
- **Long-Term Forecast** -- *Predicts revenues, costs, and expenses for a period longer than one year and sometimes as long as five or ten years.*

18-15

PPT 18-16
Budgeting

BUDGETING

- **Budget** -- *Sets forth management's expectations for revenues and allocates the use of specific resources throughout the firm.*
- Budgets depend heavily on the balance sheet, income statement, statement of cash flows and short-term and long-term financial forecasts.
- The budget is the guide for financial operations and expected financial needs.

18-16

1. Budgeting is critical for the organization to control expenses and to understand revenue expectations.
2. Think of a budget as a guidepost or a reference point for the organization's managers.

PPT 18-17
Types of Budgets

TYPES of BUDGETS

- **Capital Budget** -- *Highlights a firm's spending plans for major asset purchases that often require large sums of money.*
- **Cash Budget** -- *Estimates cash inflows and outflows during a particular period like a month or quarter.*
- **Operating (Master) Budget** -- *Ties together all the firm's other budgets and summarizes its proposed financial activities.*

18-17

PPT 18-18
Financial Planning

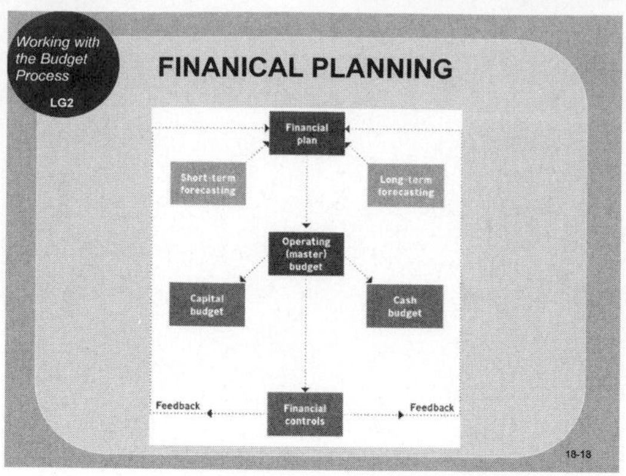

1. This slide is based on Figure 18.2.
2. The capital and cash budgets are part of the operating (master) budget.

PPT 18-19
Establishing Financial Control

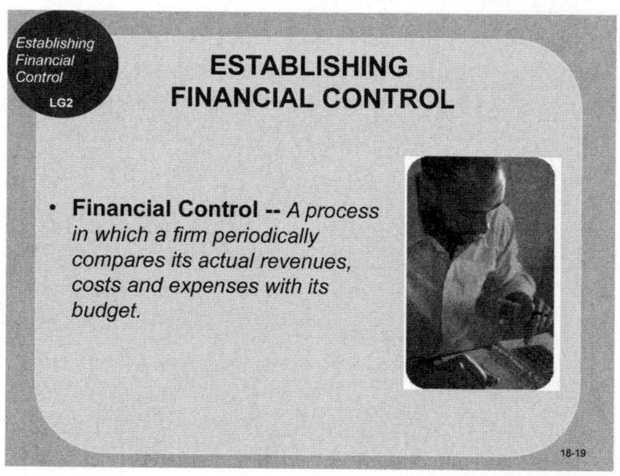

Financial controls also help reveal which specific accounts, departments, and people are varying from the financial plan.

PPT 18-20
Factors Used in Assessing Financial Control

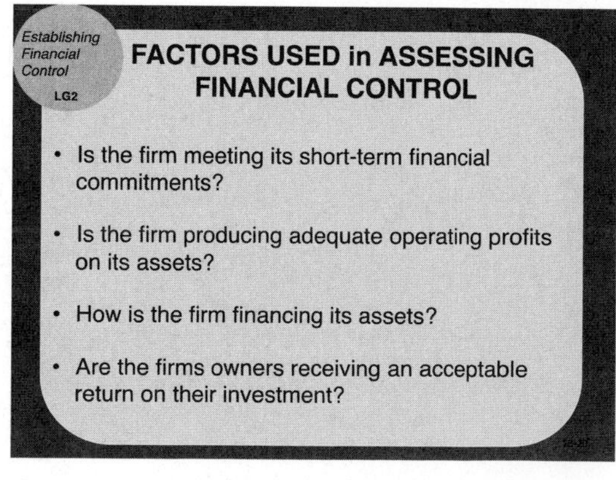

1. This slide highlights the factors used in assessing financial control.
2. Financial control is used in conjunction with the firm's budget to ensure the organization is meeting its commitments and goals.
3. Ask the students, Why is it important for the CFO to maintain financial control?

PPT 18-21
Progress Assessment

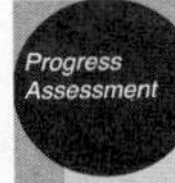

PROGRESS ASSESSMENT

- Name three finance functions important to the firm' s overall operations and performance.
- What three primary financial problems cause firms to fail?
- How do short-term and long-term financial forecasts differ?
- What' s the purpose of preparing budgets? Can you identify three different types of budgets?

18-21

1. The three finance functions are financial planning, budgeting, and the establishment of financial control.
2. The three primary financial problems causing firms to fail are undercapitalization, poor control of cash flow, and inadequate expense control.
3. Short-term forecasts attempt to project revenue, costs, and expenses for a period of one year or less, while long-term forecasts are for a period greater than one year.
4. A budget sets forth management's expectations for revenues and becomes the organization's primary guide for the financial operations as well as expected financial needs. The three types of budgets are capital, cash, and operating.

PPT 18-22
Key Needs for Operational Funds in a Firm

KEY NEEDS for OPERATIONAL FUNDS in a FIRM

- Managing day-by-day needs of the business
- Controlling credit operations
- Acquiring needed inventory
- Making capital expenditures

18-22

PPT 18-23
Financial Order or Financial Martial Law?

FINANCIAL ORDER or FINANCIAL MARTIAL LAW?
(Legal Briefcase)

- In Michigan, half of the state' s communities are in •nancial distress.
- Local Government and School District Fiscal Accountability Act allows cities, towns, and school districts to be taken over by state-appointed emergency •nancial managers (EFMs) selected by the Governor.
- Indiana is considering similar legislation. New York and other states' boards have been given similar power.

18-23

PPT 18-24
How Small Businesses Can Improve Cash Flow

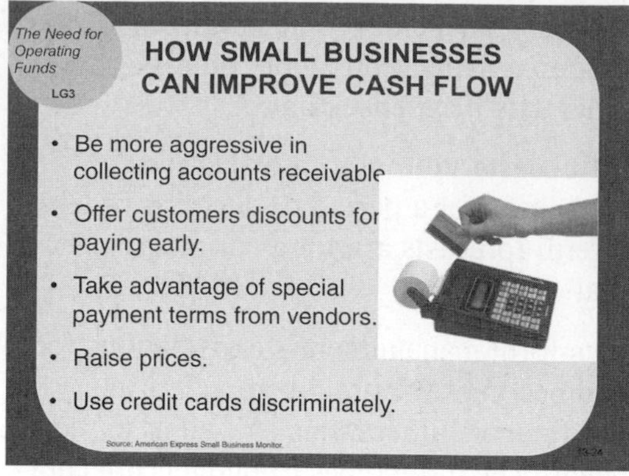

1. The slide lists methods small businesses use to improve cash flow.
2. Lack of cash flow can impact a business of any size and may lead to the business shutting its doors.
3. It is critical that students understand cash is king for a business of any size.

PPT 18-25
Good Finance or Bad Medicine?

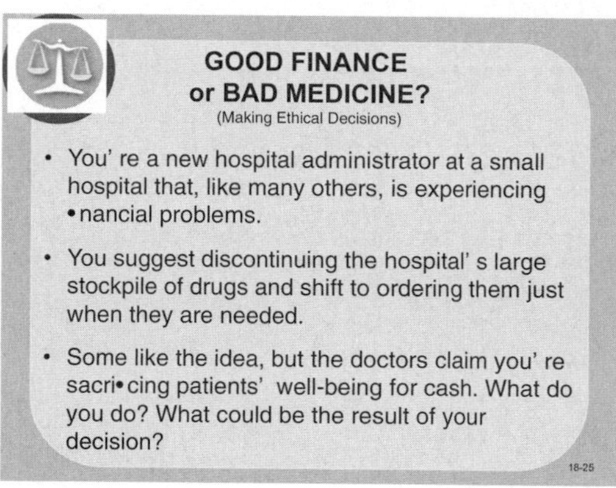

PPT 18-26
Using Alternative Sources of Funds

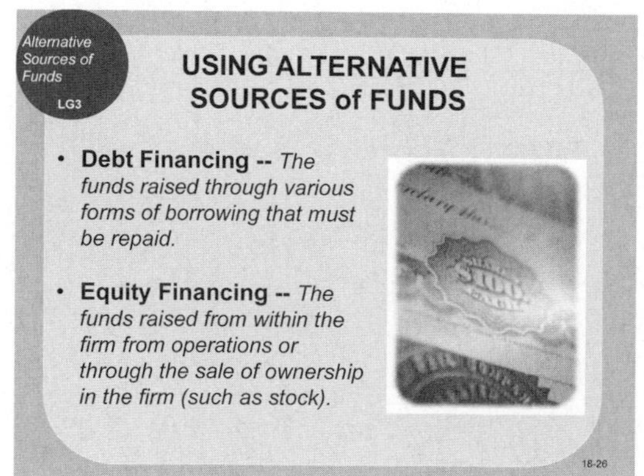

PPT 18-27
Short and Long-Term Financing

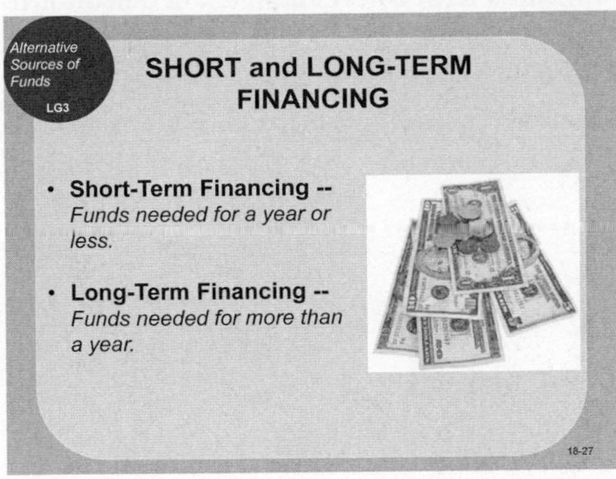

PPT 18-28
Why Firms Need Financing

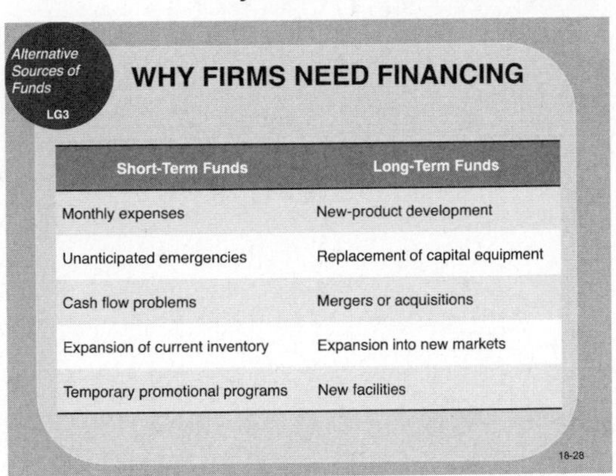

Short-Term Funds	Long-Term Funds
Monthly expenses	New-product development
Unanticipated emergencies	Replacement of capital equipment
Cash flow problems	Mergers or acquisitions
Expansion of current inventory	Expansion into new markets
Temporary promotional programs	New facilities

PPT 18-29
Progress Assessment

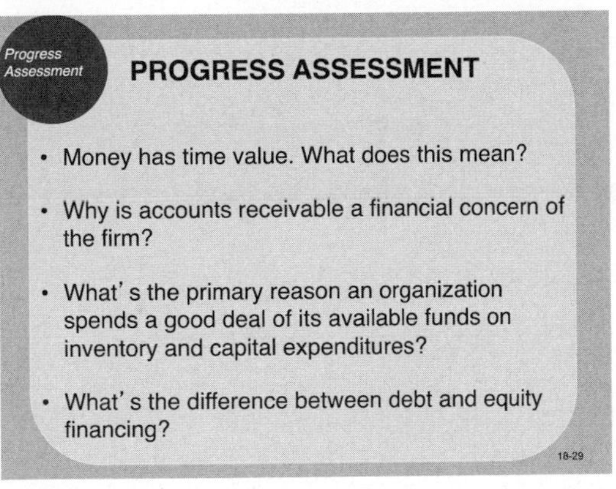

1. Time value of money means money can grow over time through interest earned.
2. Providing credit to customers is often necessary to keep current customers happy and to attract new customers. The problem with selling on credit is that as much as 25% of the firm's assets could be tied up in accounts receivable. This forces the business to use it own funds to pay for goods or services sold to customers who bought on credit.
3. To attract customers a firm must purchase inventory as well as invest in tangible long-term assets such as land, buildings, and equipment, or intangible assets such as patents, trademarks, and copyrights.
4. The primary difference between debt and equity financing is that debt must be repaid at maturity, while there is no obligation to repay equity financing. Interest must be paid on debt while the company is under no obligation to issue dividends on equity financing. The interest paid is tax deductible while dividends are not. Finally, debt holders do not have the right to vote on company matters as equity holders do.

PPT 18-30
Types of Short-Term Financing

Trade Credit

LG4

TYPES of SHORT-TERM FINANCING

- **Trade Credit** -- *The practice of buying goods or services now and paying for them later.*
- Businesses often get terms 2/10 net 30 when receiving trade credit.
- **Promissory Note** -- *A written contract agreeing to pay a supplier a specific sum of money at a definite time.*

18-30

Trade credit is the most common form of financing. The terms 2/10 net 30 mean a firm can receive a 2% discount if the bill is paid within 10 days. If it chooses not to take the discount, the net amount is due in 30 days.

PPT 18-31
Types of Short-Term Financing

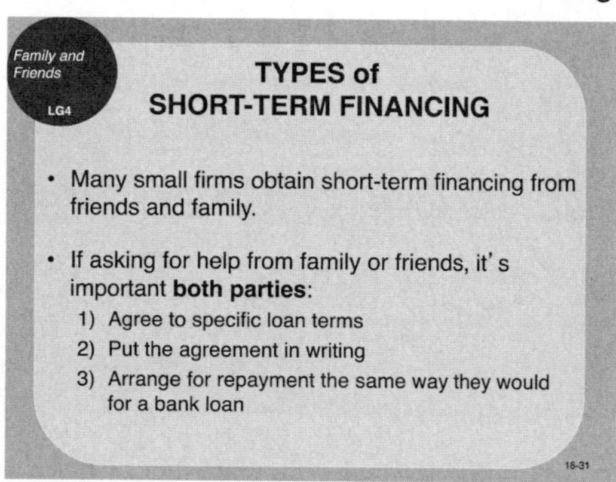

PPT 18-32
Difficulty of Obtaining Short-Term Financing

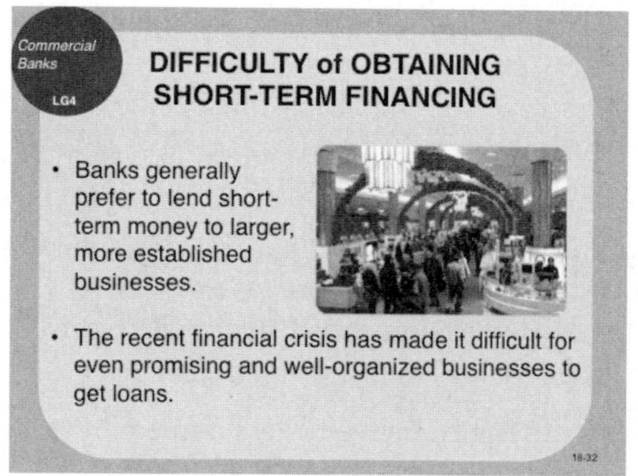

PPT 18-33
Exploring the Financing Universe

EXPLORING the FINANCING UNIVERSE
(Spotlight on Small Business)

- Peer-to-peer lending sites like Lending Club match small businesses with lenders and receive a fee for their services.
- Lendio claims to have developed a technology that matches business owners with the right type of business loan and lender.
- Lendio also offers services such as a business plan makeover and website design for a fee.

18-33

1. Securing capital is the lifeblood to a small business.
2. Students can learn more about Lendio at the website: www.lendio.com.

PPT 18-34
Different Forms of Short-Term Loans

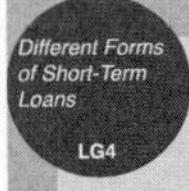

DIFFERENT FORMS of SHORT-TERM LOANS

- Commercial banks offer short-term loans like:
  - **Secured Loans** -- *Backed by collateral.*
  - **Unsecured Loans** -- *Don't require collateral from the borrower.*
  - **Line of Credit** -- *A given amount of money the bank will provide so long as the funds are available.*
  - **Revolving Credit Agreement** -- *A line of credit that's guaranteed but comes with a fee.*

18-34

PPT 18-35
Factoring

FACTORING

- **Factoring** -- *The process of selling accounts receivable for cash.*
- Factors charge more than banks, but many small businesses don't qualify for loans.

18-35

PPT 18-36
Commercial Paper

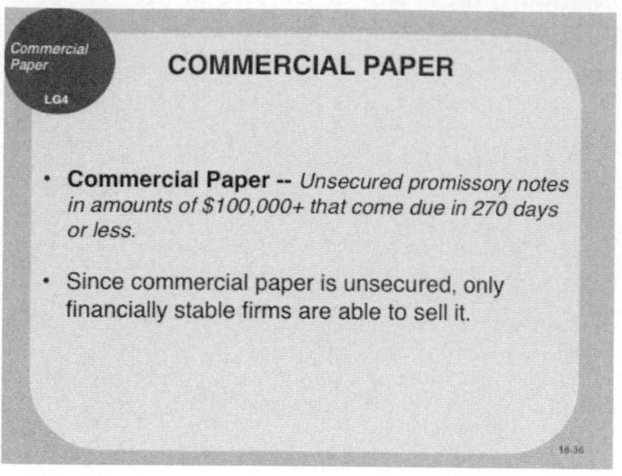

1. The commercial paper market is an important source of funding for financially stable companies.
2. During the financial crisis that started in 2008, this important market completely shut down, forcing the Federal Reserve to step in and assist many companies with their short-term financing by purchasing their commercial paper.

PPT 18-37
Credit Cards

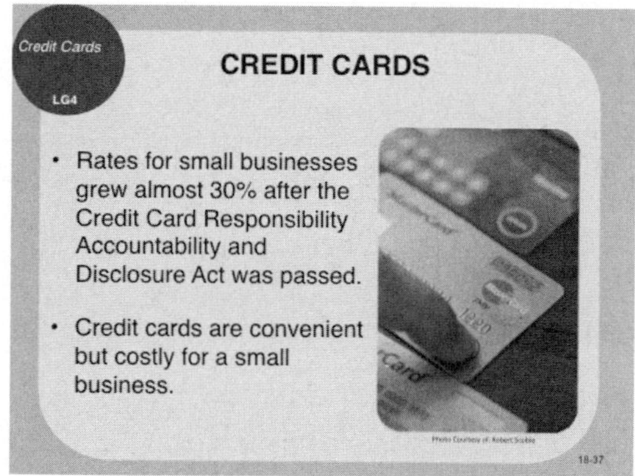

PPT 18-38
Ways to Raise Start-Up Capital

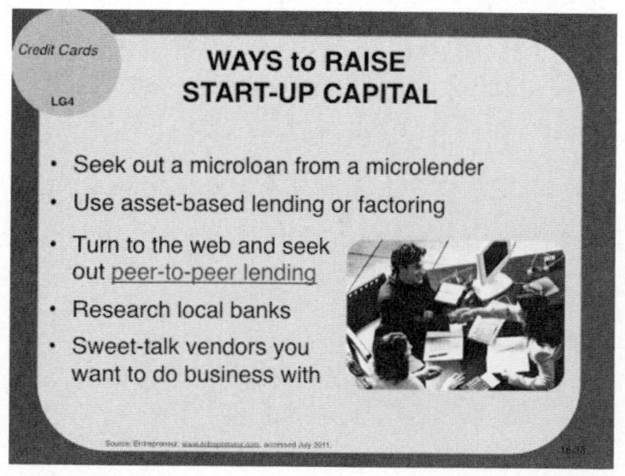

1. This slide profiles some of the unique methods businesses can use to raise capital.
2. Trade credit and factoring are two of the oldest methods of raising capital. To start a discussion with students, ask what are the advantages and disadvantages of using each of these methods.
3. Peer-to-peer lending involves individuals loaning money to other individuals or businesses, thus bypassing traditional lending outlets.
4. For more information on this new method use loan statistics from www.lendingclub.com.

PPT 18-39
Progress Assessment

1. The terms 2/10 net 30 mean a firm can receive a 2% discount if the bill is paid within 10 days. If it chooses not to take the discount, the net amount is due in 30 days.
2. Trade credit is buying goods and services now and paying for them later, while a line of credit is a given amount of unsecured short-term funds a bank will lend a business, provided the funds are readily available.
3. A secured loan requires collateral, whereas an unsecured loan does not.
4. Factoring is the process of sell accounts receivable for cash. Things to consider in establishing the discount rate are age of the accounts receivable, the nature of the business, and the condition of the economy.

PPT 18-40
Setting Long-Term Financing Objectives

PPT 18-41
The Five Cs of Credit

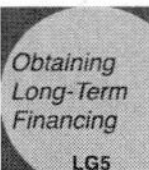

1. This slide highlights the five Cs of credit that lenders use to make decisions.
2. It is essential that lenders make good decisions when deciding whether or not to loan capital to potential borrowers.
3. Go through each of the Cs and have students evaluate how important each one is. Are they equally important for the lenders to consider? Why or why not?
4. Ask the students, Can you think of any other things the lenders should consider before loaning money? (*Note*: These do not have to be words that start with C.)

PPT 18-42
Using Long-Term Debt Financing

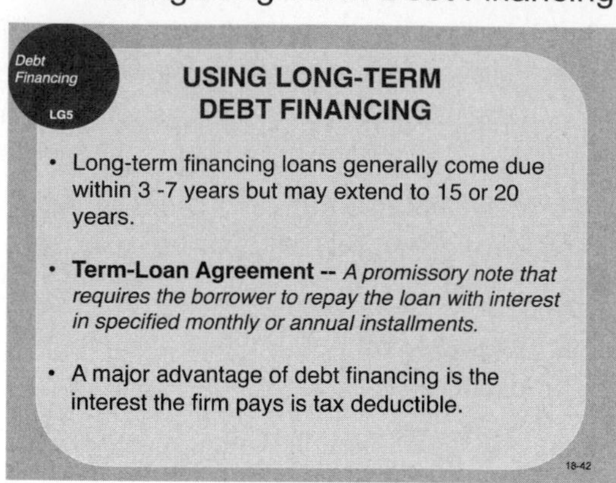

Lenders may also require certain restrictions to force the firm to act responsibly.

PPT 18-43
Using Debt Financing by Issuing Bonds

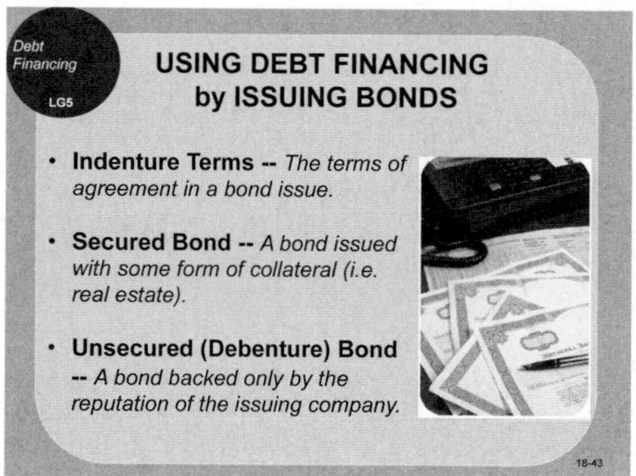

1. It is critical that students understand bonds are a form of debt issued by companies.
2. The terms *debt, bond,* and *loan* are all four-letter words that basically mean the same thing.
3. Students should walk away from this discussion knowing that the government and private industry compete insofar as the sale of bonds to the investing public. The issue of investor security can easily be addressed here, as well as the differences in interest rates paid on specific bonds depending on the issuer. Students should understand that U.S. government bonds are considered the safest investment in the bond market. There is a high probability that students will be familiar with U.S. government savings bonds, and may in fact have received such a bond as a gift. They clearly need to understand the difference between such bonds and issues involving investments in corporate bonds.

PPT 18-44
Securing Equity Financing

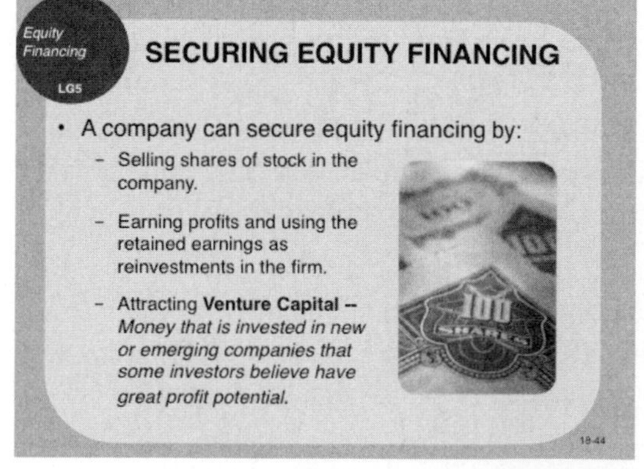

1. This slide shows how venture capitalists assess the many pitches they receive all year.
2. Venture capitalists want to ensure that not only will they get their money back, but that they will also earn more than their investment.
3. Why is a question like "Will it be worth our money and effort?" important to venture capitalists? (VCs want to make sure there is a large return on their investment so they can make money and continue investing in other companies.)

PPT 18-45
Want to Attract a Venture Capitalist?

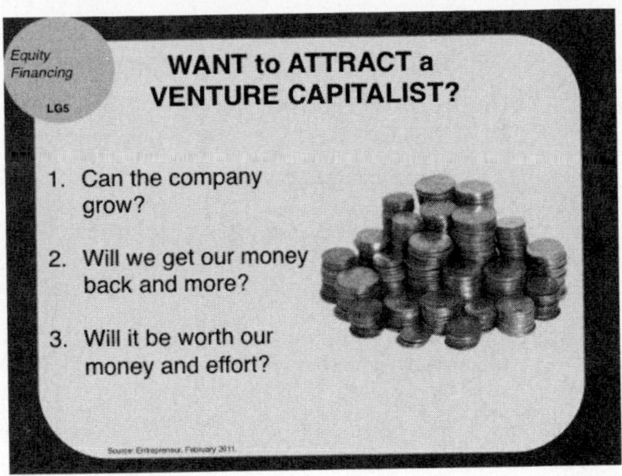

PPT 18-46
Differences between Debt and Equity Financing

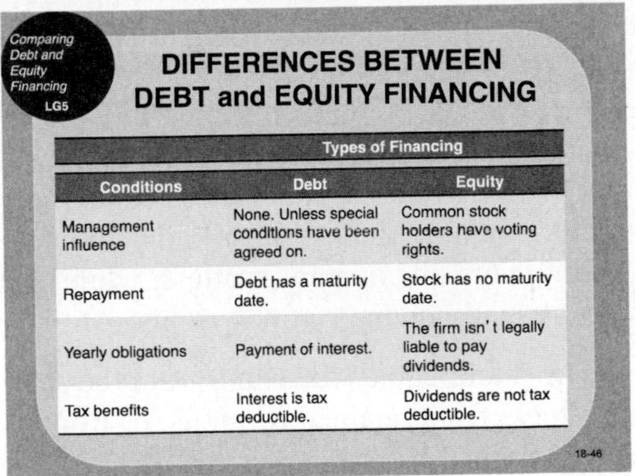

	Types of Financing	
Conditions	Debt	Equity
Management influence	None. Unless special conditions have been agreed on.	Common stock holders have voting rights.
Repayment	Debt has a maturity date.	Stock has no maturity date.
Yearly obligations	Payment of interest.	The firm isn't legally liable to pay dividends.
Tax benefits	Interest is tax deductible.	Dividends are not tax deductible.

1. This slide is based on Figure 18.6.
2. Financial managers must evaluate the benefits of issuing debt or equity and then weigh those benefits with the drawbacks.

PPT 18-47
Using Leverage for Funding Needs

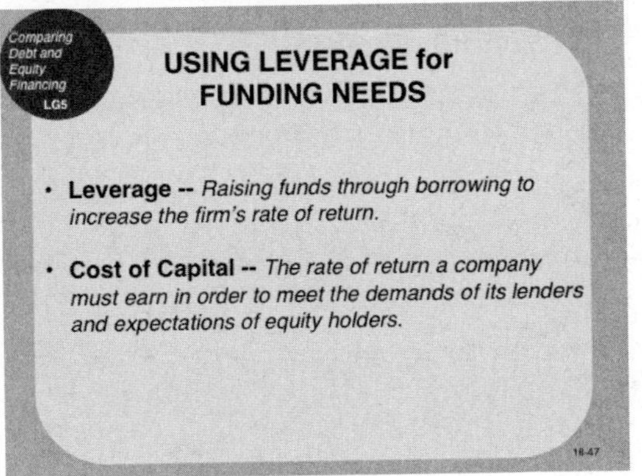

PPT 18-48
Lessons of the Financial Crisis

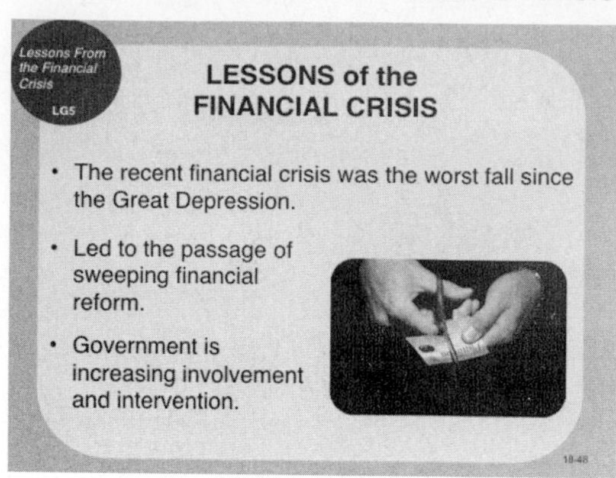

PPT 18-49
Progress Assessment

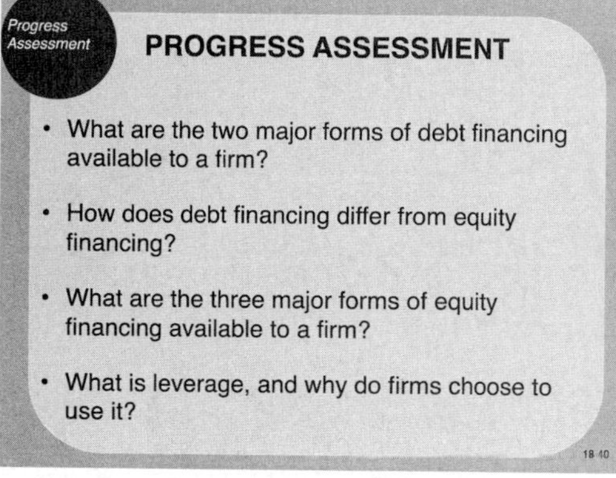

1. A company could issue and sell bonds or it could borrow from financial institutions and individuals.
2. The primary difference between debt financing and equity financing is that debt must be repaid at maturity while there is no obligation to repay equity financing. Interest must be paid on debt, while the company is under no obligation to issue dividends on equity financing. The interest paid is tax deductible, while dividends are not. Finally, debt holders do not have the right to vote on company matters, while equity holders usually do have voting rights.
3. A business can obtain equity financing from the sale of company stock, from retained earnings, or from venture capital firms.
4. Leverage is borrowing funds to invest in expansion, major asset purchases, or research and development. Firms use leverage in an effort to increase the firm's profit.

lecture links

"True genius resides in the capacity for evaluation of uncertain, hazardous, and conflicting information."
Winston Churchill

"Careful planning is no substitute for dumb luck."
Dunn's Law

"Money is made by discounting the obvious and betting on the unexpected."
George Soros

lecture link 18-1

LEARNVEST TEACHES THE FINANCIAL BASICS

Although women's average salary still falls short of men's in the United States, in some major U.S. cities young women are significantly outearning males. For 20-something women in Dallas, the pay gap stretches to as much as 20%. As it is for any ambitious person, responsible personal finance management is a must in order to sustain that success. However, some women reached the highest levels of business only to realize they didn't know enough about what to do with their money.

Such was the case for Alexa von Tobel. A Harvard graduate, von Tobel landed a job with Morgan Stanley shortly after finishing college. As she spent the day managing huge sums of cash and pulling in a healthy salary, von Tobel became unnerved at how little she knew about tending to her own financial needs. After all, how could she broker million-dollar deals every day, but lack the knowledge to plan for her own retirement or pay down her debt? Drawing on a wealth of resources and her valuable education, von Tobel eventually solved her financial quandary. However, her struggle made her think about all the other women out there who were just as intelligent and career-minded, but were nonetheless clueless about personal finance.

Recognizing a niche, von Tobel left her big bank job to found LearnVest.com, a website aimed at making financial literacy relevant and exciting for young women. In her mind female business gurus like Suze Orman and their $25 advice tomes didn't resonate with today's professional females. LearnVest provides information on everything from mortgages to investing, all filtered through a female-oriented design meant to echo the stylish pages of *Vogue* combined with a point-tracking program akin to Weight Watchers. The site personalizes each user's experience. The website first asks visitors about their financial goals. If they want to be better savers, the site provides the fundamentals as well as a series of checklists so the users can track their progress. After less than a year in operation, LearnVest is attracting a dedicated following. With 350,000 hits a month, the site has also amassed $5.5 million in venture capital to expand the brand to the nation's growing number of career-minded women.[i]

lecture link 18-2

THE EXPANDING ROLE OF THE CFO

The role of chief financial officer (CFO) is changing, expanding to that of strategist, venture capitalist, and chief communicator. Bean counters need not apply. Today businesses need someone to fill a much broader role than just supervising transactions and keeping tabs on employee expense reports. He or she needs to be a strategist, communicator, dealmaker, and financier as well as an expert in information technology and risk management. CFOs increasingly step outside the accounting role and focus on bigger issues, and they are gaining more power and respect.

At many firms, the CFO is helping build new businesses from within, by acting as the company venture capitalist. Increasingly, CFOs head up incubators and venture capital arms within their own companies. Dell Computer's former CFO Thomas Meredith recently became the managing director of Dell Ventures, which has invested around $700 million in almost 90 companies.

Now that the Internet is reshaping how companies create value, investors are demanding more and better information. As financial markets become more global, this skill becomes more important.

Today you can get a computer program to do a lot of the more mundane accounting tasks. That frees up the CFO to become more involved in strategic planning and information. Enterprise Software Products already has programs that allow many accounting and financial-modeling tasks to be performed in a fraction of the time it took just a few years ago. The sophistication of these programs will only increase. One expert calls the new technology "CFO-in-a-box."

At Oracle Corporation, a leading innovator in enterprise software itself, expense reports are filed on the company's intranet, eliminating paperwork and labor costs. It allows reimbursements to be paid directly into bank accounts a week faster than was possible back when it used old-fashioned forms.

Another traditional CFO task that is being revolutionized is the reporting of a company's financials and periodic closing of the books. Ultimately, financial information will be available in real-time fashion, making it possible to close the books almost instantaneously. Cisco Systems CFO Larry Carter and CEO John T. Chambers are credited with developing the "virtual close." Cisco is the first company to generate hourly updates on revenues, product margins, discounts, and bookings. It takes Cisco just one day to close its books, while it takes most companies five days and some companies as many as fourteen.ii

lecture link 18-3

IVY LEAGUE ENDOWMENT DIFFICULTIES

From countless investment magazines to television personalities like *Mad Money*'s Jim Cramer, Americans have plenty of places to turn for financial advice. But just because financial "experts" are respected enough to be given a voice in journals or on television shows, they aren't infallible. The business world is a volatile and ever-changing entity that defies the expectations of even the industry's brightest minds. So when it comes to investing, seeking expert advice is a must, but potential investors also have to be careful not to follow their financial advisors blindly.

For instance, from the mid-1980s up until the eve of the financial crisis, Yale's endowment manager David Swensen was the Ivy League's investment guru. Over the course of more than two decades, Swensen poured billions into real estate, private equity, hedge funds, and other nontraditional assets. Swensen's clever investing yielded substantial returns, expanding Yale's endowment at an average annual rate of 16.3% in the decade preceding the credit crunch. Dozens of other wealthy universities copied Swensen's investment strategy, especially Ivy rival Harvard, which boasted a $36.6 billion endowment at the end of fiscal 2008.

But the other shoe dropped with a resounding thud in October 2008. The stock market meltdown left investment-centric colleges with billions tied up in various failing ventures but with little cash on hand to actually run their schools. As a result, 15 wealthy colleges, Harvard and Yale among them, borrowed $7.2 billion between 2008 and 2009. Harvard now spends $87.5 million a year on interest payments to debtors alone. As a result of Harvard's 27.3% endowment nosedive, university officials cut costs at the student level. School administrators nixed hot breakfasts from student dining halls, reduced shuttle bus service, and offered buyouts to professors in an effort to close budget gaps.[iii]

lecture link 18-4

THE NUMBERS SPEAK WHEN DEALING WITH YOUR BANKER

With a few quick calculations, a banker can tell a lot about your company's financial health. If you're in the market for a bank loan, you'd better pay close attention to what your financial statements are telling prospective lenders. Do you have enough cash to repay the loan if sales start to drop? Are you overleveraged? The answers are all there in black and red. By evaluating some key financial ratios from your balance sheet and income statement, a banker can take your company's financial pulse and determine whether it qualifies for the loan request.

Financial ratios, which we studied in Chapter 17, allow bankers to weigh one part of your company's balance sheet against another, such as debt against equity or assets against liabilities. The resulting figures might show that you're carrying too much debt to take on another loan or that your cash flow isn't sufficient to meet the payment terms. The ratios also allow bankers to compare your company's financial status with that of others in your industry.

Of course, plain numbers never tell the whole story. As much as the loan review process seems like an exact science to nonbankers, it isn't. So even if your numbers aren't perfect, other factors will play a role in the overall decision to grant credit. In bank terms, loan requests are measured by the three Cs of credit: namely, the **character** of the borrower, the **collateral** the company brings to the table, and its **capacity** to repay the loan.

Every banker uses both objective criteria and subjective judgment to evaluate these factors. At the beginning of the loan review process, he or she is likely to ask these seven questions:

1. Does the loan meet the bank's market focus and lending policies?
2. What size loan and repayment term are being requested?
3. What is the proposed use of the funds?
4. What is the company's capacity to repay the funds?
5. What is the default risk of this loan?
6. How can the risks be controlled?
7. What loan terms, if any, should we offer?

With those questions in mind, a banker will turn to the numbers on your financial statements, which can sometimes reveal as much about a company's past and future as can its CEO. Here are some of the financial ratios your banker may evaluate:

LEVERAGE RATIO

This ratio tells bankers how much debt your company is carrying in relation to its capital. In other words, the ratio measures how many dollars you have in the company versus how many your creditors have. Assets, liabilities, and owners' equity all are evaluated to determine whether your company can survive bumps in the road and still repay the loan.

Obviously, if your company has more debt than its capital can meet—for example, a debt-to-equity ratio of more than 2:1—your chances of receiving a loan may decrease greatly. Or, at the very least, the bank may try to minimize the risk of making such a loan by asking for other guarantors or requiring the participation of a third party, such as a municipal or state government agency.

CURRENT RATIO

This figure tells bankers whether your company has enough liquid assets to repay a short-term loan, which generally must be repaid in one year. The ratio is calculated by dividing current assets (cash, accounts receivable, and inventory) by current liabilities (debts and obligations due within one year). The standard for the current ratio often is set at 2:1. The higher your ratio, the greater your chances of receiving a short-term loan.

QUICK RATIO

Like the current ratio, a quick ratio gives bankers a look at your company's ability to pay short-term debt. The difference is that the quick ratio doesn't include inventory in its tally of current assets. This helps bankers determine how much of the company could be converted into cash immediately. The quick ratio is especially relevant for service companies, such as law firms and personnel agencies, which don't carry tangible inventory such as raw materials, lumber, or sheet metal.

Again, a quick ratio of more than 1:1 boosts your chances of getting a loan. But remember, other factors may come into play as well. Consider the Smith Jones Law Firm, which recently requested a loan to upgrade its computer equipment and thereby increase efficiency. The law firm's quick ratio is a positive 1:5. Yet, when the banker looks at its assets more closely, he finds that the firm has only two major clients.

This issue, called "business concentration," frequently arises with start-ups and other relatively young companies. It can present a great risk for the bank, even if a company's financial ratios are favorable. Could the law firm, for example, repay the loan if one of its clients sought legal counsel elsewhere or started dragging out its payments? Quite possibly, the firm may be able to overcome this obstacle by providing evidence that its business is growing, perhaps in the form of new contracts.

CASH FLOW ANALYSIS

By analyzing your company's cash flow, a banker can see how it uses money and how much, if any, it needs to borrow. The cash flow analysis includes a number of pieces, each of which helps paint an overall picture of your ability to service new debt. Some of the key factors reviewed:

- **Funds from operations.** This includes your company's net income and noncash charges, such as depreciation and amortization.
- **Net operating capital.** This is the amount your company spends or takes in to operate the business during a given period. It can include increases—or decreases—in receivables, inventories, accounts payable, accrued expenses, and the like.
- **Net cash throw-off.** This is the combined sum of your funds from operations and net operating capital. The surplus or deficit shows how much cash the company has available for its current needs.
- **Other financing required.** If your company's net cash throw-off shows a deficit, you may need other financing such as a short- or long-term loan or an equity investment. This factor helps determine how much—and what type—of capital is needed.

Most important, the cash flow analysis shows bankers whether you have enough funds to support a loan. Suppose, for example, that ABC Clothing Store requests a $100,000 loan to finance new clothing display equipment. The banker walks through the numbers and sees that ABC has a surplus net cash throw-off. The problem: After accounting for financing from other lenders and investors, ABC shows a net cash change, or remaining cash, of only $38,000.

Though ABC's initial cash flow ratios look promising, its current debt demands could affect its ability to repay a loan and still have sufficient cash for operations. Although the banker could try to make the loan work by changing the amount or the terms, the truth is that it may not be in ABC's best interest to take on the debt. Too much debt can limit a company's future business options and hamper its ability to develop the type of positive financial history that banks look for.

SENSITIVITY RATIO

This is not a formal financial ratio, but rather the banker's subjective, gut-level judgment of whether a loan should be made. But don't take it lightly: In some cases, it's the most important factor at play because it encompasses a variety of vital issues, including the credibility of the management team, the business's ability to generate accurate numbers, and the risks inherent to the industry.

The sensitivity ratio becomes especially important when a banker is on the fence about your loan. In the end, he or she wants to see more than ratios and financial statements; the banker also wants to know that you understand how your business makes money, how it will grow, and how you'll manage future hurdles. With the sensitivity analysis, a banker might decide to control its risk by securing the loan with collateral, asking for guarantors, or seeking the participation of a third party such as the SBA.

In some cases, of course, there may not be an immediate solution. But if you're turned down for a loan, don't give up. Good bankers want to develop long-term relationships, and they may be able to help you pursue other financing solutions, such as nonbank lenders or equity investors. Or, the banker may direct you to an accountant or business consultant who can help you focus the business and package a loan request that will be more successful.

Finally, as tedious as it may be, the loan review process itself can help prepare a company for some ups and downs by forcing it to look more closely at its strategies and better plan for the future. As a result, your company may take its first steps toward financial health and open the doors to loans down the road.

lecture link 18-5

MAKING PAYMENTS OVERSEAS

Businesses going global face many difficulties, including cultural differences, currency fluctuations, and tariffs and quotas. Many small businesses also have difficulties making payments for products bought from foreign suppliers. Asian manufacturers typically require either payment in advance or a letter of credit from a bank. Neither option is great for the businesses' cash flow.

Some entrepreneurs have found creative ways of ensuring a steady source of products. When Fred Crosetto's company, Ammex Corp., began importing latex gloves from manufacturers in Malaysia in 1988, he approached potential suppliers to let him pay on open-account terms within 60 to 90 days of his order. Only a few said yes. Crosetto developed these relationships over the years. He has done business on an open-account basis ever since and is now working with seven manufacturers in four countries. He estimates that bypassing letters of credit saves him about $40,000 to $50,000 a year in fees. The practice also keeps his credit line open for other needs.

Crosetto's payment arrangements are relatively rare. He has succeeded through a carefully orchestrated process. To build credibility, Crosetto usually offers to pay first time suppliers half of the balance up front. But even more important to his success is the ongoing communication with these business partners. He visits suppliers two or three times a year to keep them up to date on his business projections.

The approach doesn't work with every business he approaches. According to Crosetto, family-owned businesses make the best prospects, because they are run by people who can make decisions.[iv]

lecture link 18-6

THE MYTHS OF VENTURE CAPITAL

Mention venture capitalists to aspiring entrepreneurs and expect a wide variety of opinions. While one entrepreneur might describe them as angels, another might believe vampire is more appropriate. Venture capitalists believe they have neither wings nor fangs, but agree that most entrepreneurs misunderstand them. According to venture capitalists, misperceptions about the industry are based on *myths* that have developed among capital-seeking entrepreneurs. According to VC firms, the top six *myths* of the industry are the following:

1. **Venture capitalists want to take control of a company.** While most venture capital firms want a fair share of a company in return for the capital invested, they don't consider taking control unless a firm's management fails.
2. **Venture capitalists load their deals with unfair terms.** Though some terms may sound unfair to an entrepreneur, the purpose is to keep the entrepreneur focused. If an entrepreneur remembers that he or she has responsibilities to the VC firm, the entrepreneur will keep his or her mind on growing the business.
3. **Venture capitalists have unrealistic performance expectations.** High expectations, yes; unrealistic, no. VC firms like to remind entrepreneurs that its limited partners are taking on high risk in the firm and therefore expect high rewards.
4. **Venture capitalists won't invest in small deals.** Smaller deals can always get financed if you look in the right places and have a solid business plan.
5. **Venture capitalists are too quick to pull the plug.** It's in the best interest of the VC firm to keep the company afloat. Only in situations that look lost or desperate will it pull the plug.
6. **Venture capitalists are impossible to talk to.** Somewhat true. Venture capitalists would much prefer entrepreneurs send them a business plan they can absorb. They will make the necessary phone calls or set up a meeting.

Even though perceptions of venture capitalists differ, it's obvious they are a growing source of seed funding for aspiring businesses. In 1999, for example, over $20 billion of VC funds were invested in new business ventures. Work on the business plan and know something about the VC firm, and funding might just come your way.[v]

lecture link 18-7

AMERICA'S DANGEROUS LACK OF FINANCIAL FACTS

When the credit crunch came to a head in 2008, not even the financial world's leading experts could make sense out of all the confusion. A jumble of credit default swaps (CDSs), derivatives, and faulty mortgages cluttered the marketplace in multitrillion-dollar heaps. Banks didn't know what they owned, who owed them money, or how much they had lost.

According to the renowned economist Hernando de Soto, all this chaos could possibly have been avoided if investors and regulators had access to genuine financial facts. For almost a century businesses were required to keep all titles, balance sheets, and statements of accounts in a publically accessible "memory system." This way people knew exactly what assets a company held and just how well they were performing. However, over the last two decades deregulation eroded many of these outlets for financial facts, relying almost exclusively on the companies themselves to release the relevant data.

This unaccountability led to a series of massive miscommunications during the 2008 crash. For instance, a number of banks have not been able to foreclose on some defaulted mortgages because they do not possess the proof of ownership. Before the real estate bubble popped banks failed to record the names of the mortgage owners, favoring instead to pool a bunch of mortgages together and trade them as securities. About 60% of the country's residential mortgages are listed as owned by a company called MERS, a shell company used to streamline trading of the mortgages. Now banks that have collected billions in taxpayer money to recover their assets aren't even sure of which assets they actually own.

The economy also suffered thanks to a practice called off-balance-sheet accounting. In the 1990s governments around the world allowed ailing companies to recorded their debts off public balance sheets and on to less accessible ones called special purpose entities. These SPEs allowed companies to game the system by keeping their losses off the public record, thus making them seem healthier to investors. The Dodd-Frank financial reform bill does not address unaccountable mortgage holdings, SPEs, or a number of other maladies limiting our knowledge of the economic system. According to de Soto, without all the necessary facts the world is poised for another wide-scale financial failure.[vi]

lecture link 18-8

REAL ESTATE WOES FOR REGIONAL BANKS

Some of the nation's largest banks have begun to pay back their federal bailout money, leading some to believe that the financial world has already experienced the worst of the recession. While this may be true for the big banks on Wall Street, it's a different story for small regional banks across the nation. Before the recession, regional banks lacked the clout or capital to diversify into stocks and bonds like their multinational colleagues. As a result, regional banks turned to local commercial real estate to expand their portfolios. But as commercial properties across the country continue to fall victim to defaults, regional banks have found themselves mired in a fiscal pickle that could keep them on government support for a while.

In a study of the nation's 35 largest regional banking institutions, lending for commercial property like office parks and shopping malls made up for more than a third of all loans issued. Vacancies and falling real estate prices have ravaged the values of these properties, ensuring that many banks will stay in the red indefinitely. For example, Synovus, a Georgia-based financial services firm, has two-thirds of its loans in commercial property and construction. The company has reported five consecutive quarterly losses. Along with Synovus, eight other banks with more than a third of their holdings in commercial real estate are projected to post steady losses.

Regional banks will also have a tougher time shedding the yoke of governmental control than their Wall Street brethren. Since the big banks have far larger revenue streams and can amass capital quicker, they've had an easier time obtaining federal permission to repay bailout funds. With cash flow stagnant and losses piling up, most regional banks will retain a government presence for years to come. That being the case, regional banks will not be able to declare dividends or make stock repurchases without government approval. These limitations could make regional banks seem less attractive to consumer borrowers than national banks, effectively hamstringing their chances for regrowth. Meanwhile, commercial real estate will keep getting more toxic.[vii]

critical thinking exercises

Name: ____________________

Date: ____________________

critical thinking exercise 18-1

BUDGETARY CONTROL

The Weinstein Manufacturing Company prepared a budget for its production department as follows. At the end of the first month, the production manager compared actual results with budgeted amounts and found that some were over and some were under. An expenditure is considered exceptional if it varies by more than 10% from the budgeted amount.

WEINSTEN MANUFACTURING COMPANY
MONTHLY BUDGETARY CONTROL WORKSHEET

EXPENSE CATEGORY	BUDGETED AMOUNT	ACTUAL EXPENDITURE	DIFFERENCE FROM BUDGET
Labor	$162,500	$195,000	________
Raw materials	172,500	151,500	________
Utilities	6,500	6,300	________
Maintenance	9,750	8,950	________
Other variable expenses	16,750	18,000	________
Fixed overhead expenses	25,000	25,000	________
Total Expenses	**$393,000**	**$404,750**	________

critical thinking exercise 18-1 (continued)

1. Which of the budget items should be investigated?

2. What could be causing the difference?

3. What are some suggestions for improvement?

notes on critical thinking exercise 18-1

WEINSTEN MANUFACTURING COMPANY
MONTHLY BUDGETARY CONTROL WORKSHEET

EXPENSE CATEGORY	BUDGETED AMOUNT	ACTUAL EXPENDITURE	DIFFERENCE FROM BUDGET	
Labor	$162,500	$195,000	+$32,500	**+20.0%**
Raw materials	172,500	151,500	–21,000	**–12.2**
Utilities	6,500	6,300	–200	–3.1
Maintenance	9,750	8,950	–800	–8.2
Other variable expenses	16,750	18,000	+1,250	+7.5
Fixed overhead expenses	25,000	25,000	0	0.0
Total Expenses	**$393,000**	**$404,750**	**+$11,750**	**+3.0%**

1. *Which of the budget items should be investigated?*

   If management looked only at the bottom line, this budget report would appear very positive. The total expenditures are overbudget by only 3%. However, closer inspection of the individual budget items shows that the actual labor cost is exceeding budgeted amount by 20%, a significant overage. This item needs to be investigated—what is causing labor costs to increase so much?

   The second item that needs to be investigated is the expenditure for raw materials. Spending here is 12% below budget. Students may argue that this is good news—why question it? However, the reasons for the decrease need to be identified. Has the cost of raw materials declined? If so, the budget needs to be modified. Are workers using a more efficient production method that uses fewer raw materials? If so, the company needs to make certain that everyone in the organization is using the improved method.

2. *What could be causing the difference?*

   The increased labor costs may be due to an increase in the number of workers or an increase in the amount paid each worker. In other words, has the workforce increased or have individual worker earnings increased? The production department may be relying more on expensive overtime, increasing costs. Or the company may have added additional workers to meet seasonal increases in demand. A critical financial element is missing here—what is the total revenue earned for this period? This budget overage would be less significant if sales revenue is also increasing.

3. *What are some suggestions for improvement?*

   How can workers be used more efficiently? Are there ways to increase productivity? Is automation an option? If the increase is seasonal, how can the company even out the fluctuations? Perhaps the budget report should be prepared more frequently—weekly instead of monthly.

Name: ______________________

Date: ______________________

critical thinking exercise 18-2

EXTENDING CREDIT

You are a partner in Creative Crafts, a small shop in your town's historic district. The district attracts many tourists from nearby states as well as regular customers from town. During your first year, your monthly sales average was about $25,000.

You and your partners invested all your personal savings in the shop. Business has been better than you forecasted, but you believe that sales and profits could have been even better. You sell on a cash-only basis. Your motto has been, "In God we trust; all others pay cash." You are wondering about continuing this policy since one in four people who comes into the store leaves without buying when told you don't accept credit cards.

You and your partners are trying to decide how to go about offering credit to your customers, if you should at all. None of you has experience in dealing with credit, but you each have your own ideas on the matter.

1. Why would you not sell on credit in the first place?

2. Why do you think the lack of credit caused some shoppers not to buy from you?

3. What alternatives for offering credit can you and your partners suggest? Which alternative do you recommend? Justify your answer.

notes on critical thinking exercise 18-2

1. *Why would you not sell on credit in the first place?*

   Selling on credit cuts into profit because you have to pay the credit company a fee. Also, there is also the risk of credit card fraud, which could really cut into profits.

2. *Why do you think the lack of credit caused some shoppers not to buy from you?*

   Buyers are used to buying things on credit. It is the American way. Some people don't carry enough cash on them to make purchases over a small amount. Some of those who walked away may come back when they have the cash. Credit cards are a very convenient way to buy things.

3. *What alternatives for offering credit can you and your partners suggest? Which alternative do you recommend? Justify your answer.*

   You can accept any of the many credit cards available. It is probably best to accept several of the leading cards. Those who carry credit cards will likely have one of the leading ones. You may not want to accept all cards because the paperwork is too burdensome.

Name: ____________________

Date: ____________________

critical thinking exercise 18-3

FINDING THE COST OF BANK LOANS

The Bankrate.com website is devoted to tracking interest rates for bank loans and investment vehicles such as CDs. Currently, the site does not specifically give rates and monthly payments for business loans. The questions below refer to either mortgage rates or personal loan rates as a representative sample of other types of loans. Go to www.bankrate.com[viii] and answer the following questions:

1. Follow the website links to the "interest rate roundup." For each of the following types of loans, record the average interest rate.

   a. Mortgage loan (30-year fixed)

   b. Auto loans

   c. Credit cards

2. Use the "compare rates" tab to compare interest rates in your local area. The site does not specifically give rates for business loans. Use "personal loans" to see similar interest rates. List three bank quotes by lender, rate, rate, and fees and conditions:

   a.

   b.

   c.

3. Follow the website links to find the subpage giving the prime rate.

   a. What is the prime rate this week?

   b. What was the prime rate a month ago?

   c. What was the prime rate a year ago?

critical thinking exercise 18-3 (continued)

4. Use the rate calculator to calculate the monthly payment for 30- and 25-year loans. Again, business loans are not specifically listed. Use the "mortgage payment calculator" to view sample loan payments.

    a. If your company wanted to get a 30-year loan for $165,000 at 7% interest, what would the monthly payments be?

    b. For a $165,000 loan at 7% interest over 15 years?

    c. For a 15-year loan for $165,000 at 10% interest?

    d. For a 15-year loan for $500,000 at 7% interest?

    e. For a 30-year loan for $500,000 at 7% interest?

    f. For a 30-year loan for $500,000 at 10% interest?

5. If your company was considering taking out a $165,000 bank loan:

    a. Would you advise that it borrow the money this week or wait two months? Why?

    b. Would you advise using a 15-year loan or a 30-year loan? Why?

Name: ______________________________

Date: ______________________________

critical thinking exercise 18-4

FINANCING OPTIONS

You've owned a tool and die company for the last five years. Even during the recession, you have been earning a net profit of 30% on your investment and have been able to pay yourself a reasonable salary. You are feeling so confident that you are considering expanding. You believe that your profit potential can improve greatly if you could expand your product line with newer high-tech equipment. You estimate that you will need $1 million for the expansion.

1. What are your financing alternatives?

2. Would you consider selling bonds if you had to pay 12% interest? Why or why not?

3. What are the major advantages of issuing bonds?

4. A venture capital firm has agreed to invest the money you need. In return, the firm will own 75% of the business. You will be replaced as board chair and CEO, though you'll retain the title of company founder and president. The VC firm will hire a new CEO. Would you be willing to take the money but lose control of your business? Why or why not?

Name: ______________________

Date: ______________________

critical thinking exercise 18-5
OBTAINING FINANCING

Many factors influence how businesses are funded. Think about the factors involved in each of the situations below. Solve the problems by applying the concepts in the text. Where can your firm find financing?

1. Your company needs a new copy machine quickly. The high-volume, multifeatured model you want costs $3,000, but your small business doesn't have that much cash on hand right now and doesn't want to borrow at this time.

2. Your firm has a large payment that needs to be made by next week. The company doesn't have the cash available at this time. You already have large outstanding loans, so you don't want to go to the bank. Your stockholders don't want you to sell more stock because it would dilute their control. You can't sell bonds by next week. Your inventory is small but your accounts receivable are large. Your firm sells everything on a 30-day open account, and most of your customers pay on time.

3. You own a dry cleaning store near an apartment complex. The store attracts a growing number of young patrons who find it convenient to drop off their garments on the way back and forth to work. In fact, business is doing so well, your tiny store is starting to feel cramped. Your next-door neighbor, a donut shop, has just offered to sell you his business and real estate for $100,000. You believe that the location and expansion potential are great, but you don't have the cash at the moment.

notes on critical thinking exercise 18-5

1. *Your company needs a new copy machine quickly. The high-volume, multifeatured model you want costs $3,000, but your small business doesn't have that much cash on hand right now and doesn't want to borrow at this time.*

   You would finance the machine through the seller and pay for it over time. You and I face this same situation often. We want to buy something, but don't have the cash. Instead, we finance the deal through the seller. We most often do this for cars.

2. *Your firm has a large payment that needs to be made by next week. The company doesn't have the cash available at this time. You already have large outstanding loans, so you don't want to go to the bank. Your stockholders don't want you to sell more stock because it would dilute their control. You can't sell bonds by next week. Your inventory is small but your accounts receivable are large. Your firm sells everything on a 30-day open account, and most of your customers pay on time.*

   You could sell the appropriate amount of accounts receivable to a factor. You would receive cash immediately, but would lose some of the potential revenue from collecting the accounts yourself. Factors give you only a percentage of the revenues they collect. It varies by the risk involved.

3. *You own a dry cleaning store near an apartment complex. The store attracts a growing number of young patrons who find it convenient to drop off their garments on the way back and forth to work. In fact, business is doing so well, your tiny store is starting to feel cramped. Your next-door neighbor, a donut shop, has just offered to sell you his business and real estate for $100,000. You believe that the location and expansion potential are great, but you don't have the cash at the moment.*

   This is the time to go to the bank and arrange a loan. Your business has had a steady income, and your credit is likely to be good. You can show how the loan will be repaid out of the increased income from the expansion.

bonus case

bonus case 18-1

THE REBUILDING DECISION

After Rob and Janet Colton finished veterinary school in the early 1990, they spent several years working for other veterinary clinics. By 1997, they felt it was time for them to start their own practice. They considered several towns in the south-central United States, visiting local chambers of commerce and studying each town's demographics. They finally settled in Wardston, a small city in Arkansas. Wardston is a regional center for the surrounding counties, located at the intersection of a two major cross-state highways. The industry rule of thumb is that it takes a population of 1,500 pet owners to support one veterinarian. Wardston appeared to be an underserved area, and no other veterinarian in the area was treating large animals. A big factor in their decision also was the fact that Janet's parents and three brothers lived in Wardston. "If we failed, at least we knew we could get a good homemade meal," said Rob.

They bought an abandoned veterinary clinic with a three-quarter-acre plot of land on the major thoroughfare. The clinic, a sturdy 2,000-square-foot cinderblock structure, had been constructed in 1950 and needed major renovations. Rob and Janet were still paying off $45,000 in student loans and had no savings to draw on. However, Janet's parents agreed to deed them a house and tract of land to get started. Now a property owner, Rob was able to borrow $165,000 from a local bank. Rob's family took out a home equity loan to help them complete the renovations. When the clinic opened in May of 1998, the small concrete building had been transformed into the Wardston Animal Hospital, a 4,000-square-foot veterinary clinic, complete with treatment room, surgery, kennels, and offices.

As they had anticipated, the area badly needed another vet clinic, and business began to boom. They were able to pay off the loan from Rob's parents and make improvements to the clinic's parking area. By 2000, the Wardston Animal Hospital had grown large enough to need another vet, and Dr. Wayne Harper joined the practice. He soon became an equal partner with Rob and Janet.

The clinic building, while adequate for a small practice, was still half a century old with an inconvenient traffic flow. The building was designed around a single center hallway going from north to south. Clients going to exam rooms, animals being weighed, vets heading to treatment rooms, staff going to the break room all had to go down same central hallway. The partners always knew that they eventually wanted to build a new "ideal" clinic. Janet kept a notebook full of ideas and possible floor plans that they dubbed their "five-year plan."

Then in April 2005 a line of severe thunderstorms passed through the city. It was a Wednesday afternoon, the clinic's early closure day, and the staff—with the exception of the office manager—had left the building. At 3:00 p.m., a tornado dropped out of the squall line and plowed through the northern part of the city, tearing the roof off the Wardston clinic and wrapping it around several nearby pine trees. For three hours, a steady downpour flooded the damaged building, leaving six inches of water on the treatment room floor. Worse still, the rainwater soaked into the insulation in the walls, the sheetrock on the walls, and the ceiling tiles. Volunteers, staff, even other veterinarians flocked to the clinic to help ferry the boarded animals to temporary homes and clean up the shredded interior. None of the animals were hurt, and no one was injured, although the clinic office manager was in shock for a few days.

Within two weeks, the partners were back in business, operating out of a doublewide trailer set up on the north side of the parking lot. They hired a cleanup service to start the long process of recovery. The cleaning crew soon realized the extent of the damage and told the partners that the cleanup would be very costly. They also warned that the soggy walls and ceiling would probably have mildew problems in the future no matter how thoroughly the building was cleaned.

Rob, Janet, and Wayne had to make a decision about how to proceed. As Rob saw it, there were four options to consider:

PLAN A: Restore the building to its existing condition before the tornado. The $150,000 insurance settlement would just cover the renovation costs. This option would be the least costly, but they would still have the same 55-year-old building with the same bad traffic flow.

PLAN B: Gut the old building and create the "ideal" building within the old shell, total cost approximately $400,000.

PLAN C: Level the old building and rebuild on the site. This option was almost immediately eliminated for several reasons. First, the cost just to demolish the building would be $50,000. Also, the clinic staff was using undamaged parts of the old building for kennel space and storage. The doublewide trailer alone would be inadequate to support the practice if the old building were immediately demolished.

PLAN D: Build the clinic of their dreams on land the partners owned adjacent to the clinic. The clinic would take almost a year to complete at a cost of $650,000.

discussion questions for bonus case 18-1

1. Are there other options that have not been considered? Explain.
2. How should the renovations or rebuilding be financed—debt or equity financing? Why?
3. What would you advise the veterinary partners to do? Why?
4. If the Wardston area suffered a major economic blow, what risks would the partnership face?

notes on discussion questions for bonus case 18-1

1. *Are there other options that have not been considered? Explain.*

   Students can develop other options. The veterinary partners did not consider moving to another location, for example.

2. *How should the renovations or rebuilding be financed—debt or equity financing? Why?*

   Debt financing involves borrowing money, creating a legal obligation. If the revenue created does not meet expectations, the clinic would still have to repay the loan. The advantage of debt financing is that the interest paid is tax deductible.

   Equity financing comes from the firm's owners. None of the veterinary partners had sufficient personal funds needed to finance the rebuilding effort themselves. Using equity financing would involve creating ownership. This would reduce each partner's ownership share.

3. *What would you advise the veterinary partners to do? Why?*

   This case is based on an actual incident. The partners decided to go with plan D, financing the new clinic entirely with a bank loan. According to an industry study, building a new veterinary facility causes an average revenue bump of 20%. Rob believed that the growing practice and influx of Katrina pet owners would enable him to pay off the loan without problems.

   Right after the tornado, Rob put an inexpensive roof on the old building to protect it from further damage. He decided to donate the old clinic to the local animal rescue league, which badly needed the kennels and the office space. Generous and ethical behavior—and a nice tax deduction.

4. *If the Wardston area suffered a major economic blow, what risks would the partnership face?*

   Borrowing funds to build the new clinic creates a legal obligation to repay the loan. If a major economic blow occurred, the partners would run the risk that revenues generated will not cover the monthly loan payment.

   This case is another one of those realistic situations. The two vets are good friends of mine. For months, I listened to Bob (Rob in this scenario) go through the all the angst and indecision. At some point, I pulled out a pencil and started taking notes. Finally, I sat him down just to fill in a few details for the case. Instead, he spent two hours giving me all the details, some very private, about financing the clinic. It was an incredible opportunity to create a decision-based case.

   The outcome: The partners moved into the new clinic in 2006.

endnotes

---

[i] *Source:* Dan Macsai, "A Source of Their Own," *Fast Company*, October 2010.

[ii] *Sources*: Marcia Vickers, "Up from Bean Counter," *BusinessWeek,* August 28, 2000, pp 118–120; Joseph Goedert, "The CFO's Role in IT Negotiations," *Health Data Management,* June 1, 2006.

[iii] *Source:* Michael McDonald, "Paying the Price for Following Yale," *Bloomberg Businessweek*, September 30, 2010.

[iv] *Sources*: Emily Barker, "Global Trade, Zero Angst," *Inc. Magazine*, July 2001; Nadine Heintz, "Breaking Away: Set Your Employees Free—with Paid Sabbaticals," *Inc. Magazine*, October 2004; Michael Tobin, "Debunking the Five Myths of Global Expansion," *Financial Executive*, March 1, 2006

[v] *Sources*: Paul DeCeglie, "The Truth about Venture Capital," *Business Start-Ups*, February 2000, pp. 40–47; Randall E. Stross, "Venture Capitalists Aren't Villians," *The Wall Street Journal*, July 25, 2000, pp. A22; "Ignore All the Myths, Says Hotbed," *Investment Adviser,* November 29, 2004; "WCA Breakfast Examines Myths about Raising Capital," *Westchester County Business Journal,* April 24, 2006.

[vi] *Source:* Hernando de Soto, "The Destruction of Economic Facts," *Bloomberg Businessweek*, April 28, 2011.

[vii] *Source:* Elizabeth Hester and Linda Shen, "A Long Shadow over Small Banks," *Bloomberg Businessweek,* December 21, 2009.

[viii] The Internet is a dynamic, changing information source. Web links noted of this manual were checked at the time of publication, but content may change over time. Please review the website before recommending it to your students.

Using Securities Markets for Financing and Investing Opportunities

chapter **19**

critical thinking exercises

what's new in this edition

additions to the 10th edition:

- Getting to Know Maria Bartiromo of CNBC
- Name That Company: Berkshire Hathaway
- Spotlight on Small Business: A Place for Small Companies to Call Home
- Making Ethical Decisions: Money Going Up in Smoke
- Reaching Beyond Our Borders: The Sun Never Sets on Stock Opportunities
- Legal Briefcase: Cleaning Up the Street
- Video case

revisions to the 10th edition:

- Text was revised to eliminate redundancy and tighten discussions.
- Statistical data and examples throughout the chapter were updated to reflect current information.
- Figure bond ratings revised to include Fitch Ratings as well as Moody's Investors Service and Standard & Poor's

deletions from the 9th edition:

- Getting to Know Warren Buffett, CEO of Berkshire Hathaway
- Name That Company: Standard & Poor's/Moody's
- Making Ethical Decisions
- Reaching Beyond Our Borders
- Thinking Green
- Legal Briefcase

brief chapter outline and learning goals

chapter 19

Using Securities Markets for Financing and Investing Opportunities

Getting To Know MARIA BARTIROMO of CNBC

learning goal 1

Describe the role of securities markets and of investment bankers.

I. THE FUNCTION OF SECURITIES MARKETS

A. **The Role of Investment Bankers**

learning goal 2

Identify the stock exchanges where securities are traded.

II. STOCK EXCHANGES

A. **Securities Regulations and the Securities and Exchange Commission**

B. **Foreign Stock Exchanges**

learning goal 3

Compare the advantages and disadvantages of equity financing by issuing stock, and detail the differences between common and preferred stock.

III. HOW BUSINESSES RAISE CAPITAL BY SELLING STOCK

A. **Advantages and Disadvantages of Issuing Stock**

B. **Issuing Shares of Common Stock**

C. **Issuing Shares of Preferred Stock**

learning goal 4

Compare the advantages and disadvantages of obtaining debt financing by issuing bonds, and identify the classes and features of bonds.

IV. HOW BUSINESSES RAISE CAPITAL BY ISSUING BONDS

A. **Learning the Language of Bonds**

B. Advantages and Disadvantages of Issuing Bonds

C. Different Classes of Bonds

D. Special Bond Features

learning goal 5

Explain how to invest in securities markets and set investment objectives such as long-term growth, income, cash, and protection from inflation.

V. HOW INVESTORS BUY SECURITIES

A. Investing through Online Brokers

B. Choosing the Right Investment Strategy

C. Reducing Risk by Diversifying Investments

learning goal 6

Analyze the opportunities stocks offer as investments.

VI. INVESTING IN STOCKS

A. Stock Splits

B. Buying Stock on Margin

C. Understanding Stock Quotations

learning goal 7

Analyze the opportunities bonds offer as investments.

VII. INVESTING IN BONDS

A. Investing in High-Risk (Junk) Bonds

B. Understanding Bond Quotations

learning goal 8

Explain the investment opportunities in mutual funds and exchange-traded funds (ETFs).

VIII. INVESTING IN MUTUAL FUNDS AND EXCHANGE-TRADED FUNDS

A. Understanding Mutual Fund Quotations

learning goal 9

Describe how indicators like the Dow Jones Industrial Average affect the market.

IX. UNDERSTANDING STOCK MARKET INDICATORS

A. Riding the Market's Roller Coaster

B. Investing Challenges in the 21st-Century Market

X. SUMMARY

lecture outline

Getting to Know MARIA BARTIROMO of CNBC

Emmy Award–winning Maria Bartiromo has been a familiar face on CNBC since the 1990s. She was the first journalist to broadcast directly from the NYSE floor. Quick to show she's more than just another pretty face on television, she's known for her candid interviews and intelligence.

When the price of their stock rises to a certain level, many companies will split the stock (i.e., exchange two shares worth $50 for each original share worth $100) in order to make the stock appear more affordable. However, this company run by America's most successful investor, has never split its stock even when the price of the company's stock reached $150,000 a share. Name that company.

(Students should read the chapter before guessing the company's name : Berkshire Hathaway)

learning goal 1

Explain the role of security markets and of investment bankers.

I. THE FUNCTION OF SECURITIES MARKETS

A. Securities markets are **FINANCIAL MARKET-PLACES** for stocks and bonds.

1. Securities markets serve two **MAJOR FUNCTIONS**:

   a. To help businesses find **LONG-TERM FUNDING**

   b. To provide a place for private investors to **BUY AND SELL SECURITIES (INVESTMENTS)** such as stocks, bonds, and mutual funds

2. Securities markets are divided into **TWO MARKETS:**

   a. **PRIMARY MARKETS** handle the sale of **NEW** securities.

      i. Corporations make money on the sale of

lecture notes

PPT 19-1
Chapter Title

PPT 19-2
Learning Goals

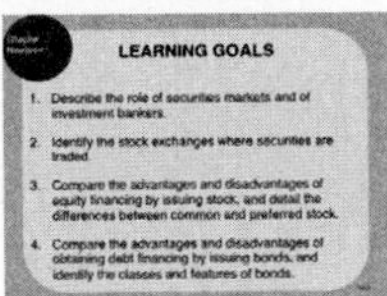

(See complete PowerPoint slide notes on page 19.58.)

PPT 19-3
Learning Goals

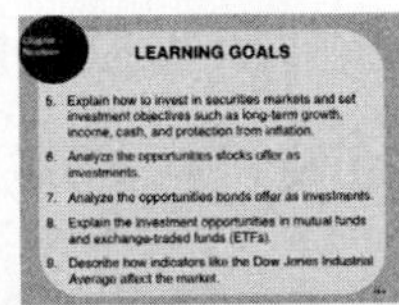

(See complete PowerPoint slide notes on page 19.58.)

PPT 19-4
Maria Bartiromo

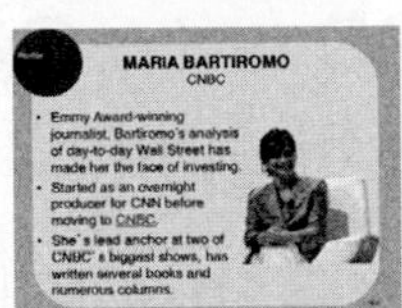

(See complete PowerPoint slide notes on page 19.59.)

PPT 19-5
Name That Company

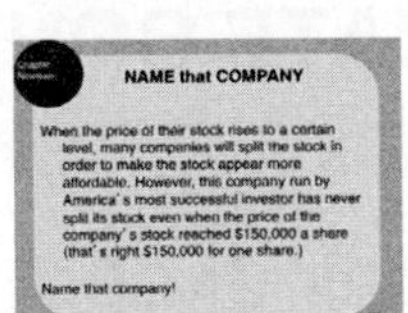

(See complete PowerPoint slide notes on page 19.59.)

PPT 19-6
The Basics of Securities Markets

(See complete PowerPoint slide notes on page 19.59.)

PPT 19-7
Types of Securities Markets

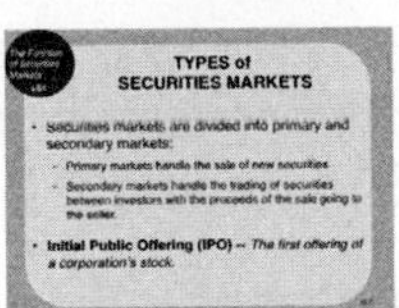

(See complete PowerPoint slide notes on page 19.60.)

their securities **ONLY ONCE**, when they are first sold on the primary market.

ii. An ***INITIAL PUBLIC OFFERING (IPO)*** is the first public offering of a corporation's stock.

b. **SECONDARY MARKETS** handle the trading of securities between investors; the proceeds of the sale go to the investor selling the stock, not to the corporation.

3. **THE IMPORTANCE OF LONG-TERM FUNDING**

   a. Businesses prefer to meet **LONG-TERM FINANCIAL NEEDS** by using **RETAINED EARNINGS** or by **BORROWING** from a lending institution.

   b. If such forms are not available, the company may be able to raise capital by **ISSUING CORPORATE BONDS (DEBT)** or **SELLING STOCK (OWNERSHIP** or **EQUITY).**

   c. These forms of debt or equity financing are not available to all companies.

   d. Getting approval for bond or stock issues requires extensive financial disclosures and scrutiny by the SEC.

B. **THE ROLE OF INVESTMENT BANKERS**

1. ***INVESTMENT BANKERS*** are specialists who assist in the issue and sale of new securities.

2. Investment bankers also **UNDERWRITE NEW ISSUES** of bonds or stocks, buying the entire issue at a discount and then selling the issue to investors.

lecture link 19-1
THE IPO FROM HELL

Google's 2004 IPO didn't go exactly as planned. (See the complete lecture link on page 19.79 in this manual.)

lecture link 19-2
ASIAN IPOS OVERTAKE THE UNITED STATES

In 2010, Asia's number of IPOs eclipsed the competition from the U.S. and Europe. (See the complete lecture link on page 19.80 in this manual.)

critical thinking exercise 19-1
FINANCING GROWTH

This exercise presents a situation in which a company is considering expanding and must decide how to finance the $1 million expansion. (See complete exercise on page 19.85 of this manual.)

PPT 19-8
Investment Bankers and Institutional Investors

(See complete PowerPoint slide notes on page 19.60.)

3. ***INSTITUTIONAL INVESTORS*** are large investors—such as pension funds, mutual funds, and insurance companies—that invest their own funds or the funds of others.
4. Institutional investors are a powerful force in securities markets.

learning goal 2

Identify the stock exchanges where securities are traded.

II. STOCK EXCHANGES

A. A ***STOCK EXCHANGE*** is an organization whose members can buy and sell (exchange) securities for companies and individual investors.

B. **U.S. EXCHANGES**

1. The **NEW YORK STOCK EXCHANGE**, founded in 1792.
   a. The NYSE used to be a **FLOOR-BASED EXCHANGE** but now most trading is done electronically.
   b. In 2005 the NYSE merged with Archipelago.
   c. In 2007 it merged with Europe's Euronext exchange.
   d. In 2008 Euronext acquired the American Stock Exchange (AMEX).
2. **THE OVER-THE-COUNTER (OTC) MARKET**
   a. The ***OVER-THE-COUNTER (OTC) MARKET*** is an exchange that provides a means to trade stocks not listed on the national exchanges.
   b. The ***NASDAQ*** is a nationwide electronic

lecture link 19-3

NYSE'S GERMAN MERGER

In an effort to compete with its rivals, the NYSE merged with the Frankfurt Stock Exchange with hopes they will entice more investors. (See the complete lecture link on page 19.80 in this manual.)

PPT 19-9
Stock Exchanges

(See complete PowerPoint slide notes on page 19.60.)

PPT 19-10
Top Stock Exchanges

(See complete PowerPoint slide notes on page 19.61.)

SPOTLIGHT ON
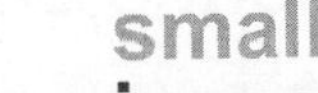
small business
(Text page 525)

PPT 19-11
A Place for Small Companies to Call Home

(See complete PowerPoint slide notes on page 19.61.)

system that links dealers across the nation so that they can buy and sell securities (originally known as the **NATIONAL ASSOCIATION OF SECURITIES DEALERS AUTOMATED QUOTATION SYSTEM**).

c. It is the largest U.S. electronic stock trading market.

d. Originally, the over-the-counter market dealt with small firms, but today, firms such as Intel and Microsoft are traded on the OTC market.

e. The NASDAQ market also handles **CORPORATE AND GOVERNMENT BONDS.**

f. The NASDAQ lists about 3,000 companies.

3. Stocks can be **DELISTED** from an exchange if a company fails to hold up the exchange's minimum requirements.

C. **SECURITIES REGULATIONS AND THE SECURITIES AND EXCHANGE COMMISSION**

1. The **SECURITIES ACT OF 1933** protects investors by requiring full disclosure of financial information by firms selling new stocks or bonds.

2. The ***SECURITIES AND EXCHANGE COMMISSION (SEC)*** is the federal agency that has responsibility for regulating the various exchanges.

   a. Companies trading on the national exchanges must register with the SEC and provide annual updates.

   b. When issuing bonds or stock, companies

lecture link 19-4

THE TOKYO EXCHANGE TYPING ERROR

One erroneous trade cost Mizuho Securities at least 27 billion yen ($225 million). (See the complete lecture link on page 19.81 of this manual.)

PPT 19-12

The Securities and Exchange Commission

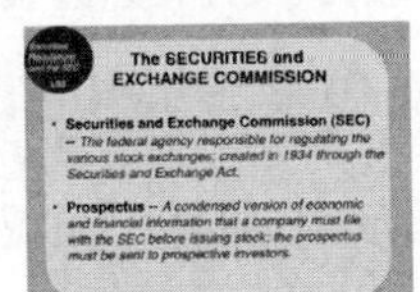

(See complete PowerPoint slide notes on page 19.62.)

must follow established specific guidelines such as filing a **PROSPECTUS**.

3. A ***PROSPECTUS*** is a condensed version of economic and financial information that a company must file with the SEC before issuing stock; the prospectus must be sent to prospective investors.
4. **INSIDER TRADING** involves the use of knowledge or information that individuals gain through their position that allows them to benefit unfairly from fluctuations in security prices.
   a. The key words are **BENEFIT UNFAIRLY.**
   b. The term **INSIDER** has been broadened to include anyone with information about a security not available to the general public.
   c. Penalties for insider trading can include fines or imprisonment.

D. **FOREIGN STOCK EXCHANGES**

1. Stock exchanges operate globally.
2. Investors can now buy securities from companies almost anywhere in the world.
3. Foreign investors can easily invest in U.S. securities through large exchanges such as those in London and Tokyo.
4. Other major exchanges are located in Shanghai, Paris, Sydney, Hong Kong, Sao Paolo, and Toronto.

TEXT FIGURE 19.1
Is It Insider Trading or Not?
(Text page 526)

This figure asks students to test their skill in identifying insider trading.

bonus case 19-1
IS IT TIME FOR AN NYSE CODE OF ETHICS?

Doctors have a code of ethics. Advertisers have a code of ethics. Is it time for the NYSE to enact a code of ethics? (See the complete case, discussion questions, and suggested answers beginning on page 19.91 of this manual.)

progress assessment
(Text page 527)

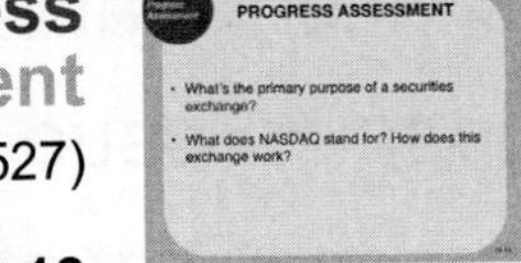

PPT 19-13
Progress Assessment

(See complete PowerPoint slide notes on page 19.62.)

lecture outline

learning goal 3

Compare the advantages and disadvantages of equity financing by issuing stock, and detail the differences between common and preferred stock.

III. HOW BUSINESSES RAISE CAPITAL BY SELLING STOCK

A. LEARNING THE LANGUAGE OF STOCK

1. ***STOCKS*** are shares of ownership in a company.
2. A ***STOCK CERTIFICATE*** is evidence of stock ownership that specifies the name of the company, the number of shares it represents, and the type of stock being issued.
3. **PAR VALUE** is a dollar amount assigned to each share of stock by the corporation's charter.
   a. Some states use par value as a basis for the state's incorporation fees.
   b. Most companies issue **NO-PAR STOCK.**
4. ***DIVIDENDS*** are the part of a firm's profits that may be distributed to shareholders as either cash payments or additional shares of stock.
5. Paying **INTEREST ON BONDS** is a legal obligation; paying **DIVIDENDS ON STOCK** is not.

B. ADVANTAGES AND DISADVANTAGES OF ISSUING STOCK

1. **ADVANTAGES OF ISSUING STOCK INCLUDE:**
   a. As owners of the business, the stockholders' investment never has to be repaid.

PPT 19-14
Learning the Language of Stocks

(See complete PowerPoint slide notes on page 19.62.)

PPT 19-15
Advantages of Issuing Stock

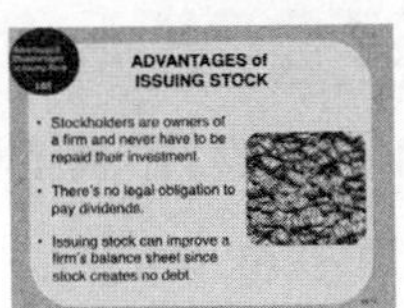

(See complete PowerPoint slide notes on page 19.63.)

b. There is no legal obligation to pay dividends to stockholders.

c. Selling stock can improve the condition of the firm's balance sheet.

2. **DISADVANTAGES OF ISSUING STOCK INCLUDE:**

   a. As owners, stockholders have the **RIGHT TO VOTE** and can alter the direction of the firm.

   b. Dividends are paid out of profit after taxes and are not tax-deductible.

   c. The need to keep stockholders happy can affect management decision making.

C. **ISSUING SHARES OF COMMON STOCK**

1. ***COMMON STOCK*** is the most basic form of ownership in a firm; it confers voting rights and the right to share in the firm's profits through dividends, if approved by the firm's board of directors.

2. Common stock includes the rights:

   a. To **ELECT** a company's board of directors and on important issues.

   b. To **SHARE IN THE FIRM'S PROFITS** through dividends, if approved by the firm's board of directors.

3. With voting rights, common stockholders can influence policy.

4. With **PREEMPTIVE RIGHT**, common

PPT 19-16
Disadvantages of Issuing Stock

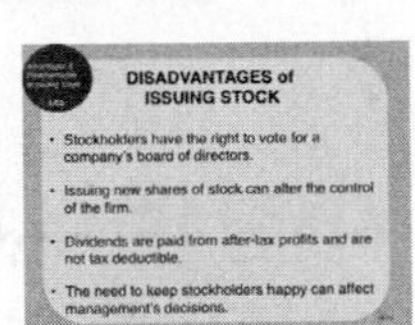

(See complete PowerPoint slide notes on page 19.63.)

PPT 19-17
Two Classes of Stock

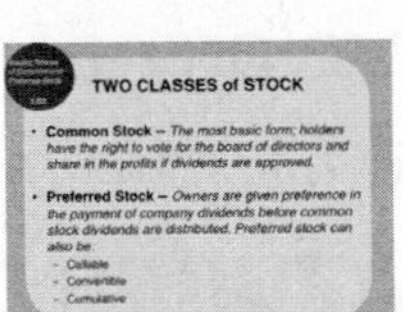

(See complete PowerPoint slide notes on page 19.63.)

stockholders have the first right to purchase any new shares of common stock.

D. **ISSUING SHARES OF PREFERRED STOCK**

1. ***PREFERRED STOCK*** is stock that gives its owners preference in the payment of dividends and an earlier claim on assets than common stockholders if the company is forced out of business and its assets sold. This type of stock doesn't include voting rights.

2. **PREFERRED STOCK DIVIDENDS DIFFER FROM COMMON STOCK DIVIDENDS** in several ways:

   a. The **PAR VALUE** is the basis for the dividend the firm is willing to pay.

   b. Dividends on preferred stock must be paid in full before any common stock dividends can be paid.

3. **SPECIAL FEATURES OF PREFERRED STOCK**

   a. Preferred stock can be **CALLABLE**, meaning a company could require preferred stockholders to sell back their shares.

   b. Preferred stock could also be **CONVERTIBLE** to shares of common stock.

   c. With **CUMULATIVE PREFERRED STOCK,** the missed dividends can be accumulated if they are not paid.

lecture notes

progress assessment
(Text page 529)

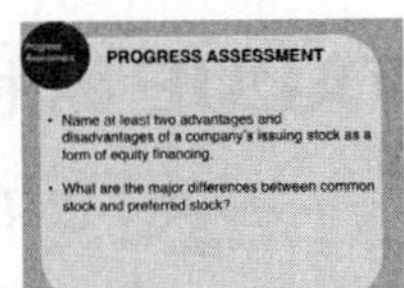

PPT 19-18
Progress Assessment

(See complete PowerPoint slide notes on page 19.64.)

learning goal 4

Compare the advantages and disadvantages of obtaining debt financing by issuing bonds, and identify the classes and features of bonds.

IV. HOW BUSINESSES RAISE CAPITAL BY ISSUING BONDS

A. A ***BOND*** is a corporate certificate indicating that a person has lent money to a firm.

1. A company that issues bonds has a **LEGAL OBLIGATION** to make regular interest payments to investors and to repay the entire bond principal.

B. **LEARNING THE LANGUAGE OF BONDS**

1. The **PRINCIPAL** is the face value of a bond.
2. The ***MATURITY DATE*** is the exact date the issue of a bond must pay the principal to the bondholder.
3. ***INTEREST*** is the payment the issuer of the bond makes to the bondholders to pay for use of the borrowed money.
4. The **BOND'S INTEREST RATE** is also called the bond's **COUPON RATE**, a term from when bonds were issued as bearer bonds.
   a. Today bonds are **REGISTERED**, and changes in ownership are recorded electronically.
   b. The **BOND'S INTEREST RATE VARIES** based on factors such as the state of the economy, the reputation of the company, and the going interest rate for bonds.

PPT 19-19
Learning the Language of Bonds

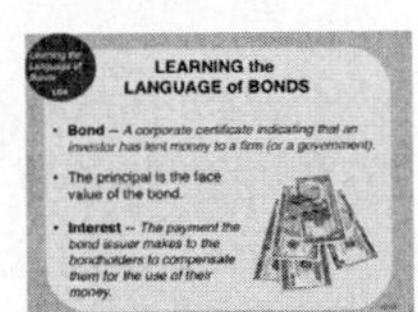

(See complete PowerPoint slide notes on page 19.64.)

TEXT FIGURE 19.2
Types of Government Securities That Compete with Corporate Bonds
(Text page 530)

This text figure lists and describes several types of government bonds that compete in securities markets with corporate bonds.

   c. Once the interest rate is set for a corporate bond issue, it cannot be changed.

5. Bonds are also rated in terms of their **RISK** by independent firms such as Standard & Poor's and Moody's Investor Services.

C. **ADVANTAGES AND DISADVANTAGES OF ISSUING BONDS**

1. **ADVANTAGES OF BONDS INCLUDE:**
   a. **BONDHOLDERS** are creditors, not owners, and seldom have a vote on corporate affairs.
   b. Interest paid on bonds is tax-deductible.
   c. Bonds are a temporary source of funding.
   d. Bonds can be repaid before the maturity date.

2. **DISADVANTAGES OF BONDS INCLUDE:**
   a. Bonds increase debt.
   b. Paying interest on bonds is a legal obligation.
   c. The face value of the bonds must be repaid on the maturity date.

D. **DIFFERENT CLASSES OF BONDS**

1. **UNSECURED BONDS** are not backed by any collateral.
   a. ***<u>DEBENTURE BONDS</u>*** are bonds that are unsecured (i.e., not backed by any collateral such as equipment).
   b. Debenture bonds are issued only by well-respected firms with excellent credit ratings.

lecture notes

PPT 19-20
Advantages of Issuing Bonds

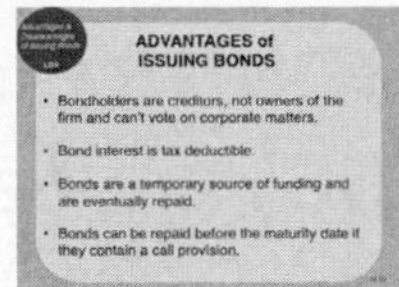

(See complete PowerPoint slide notes on page 19.64.)

PPT 19-21
Disadvantages of Issuing Bonds

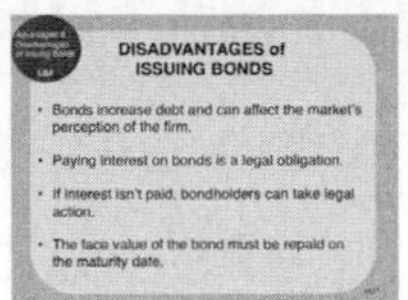

(See complete PowerPoint slide notes on page 19.65.)

TEXT FIGURE 19.3
Bond Ratings: Moody's Investors Service, Standard & Poor's Investor Service, and Fitch Ratings
(Text page 531)

PPT 19-22
Bond Ratings

(See complete PowerPoint slide notes on page 19.65.)

PPT 19-23
Different Classes of Corporate Bonds

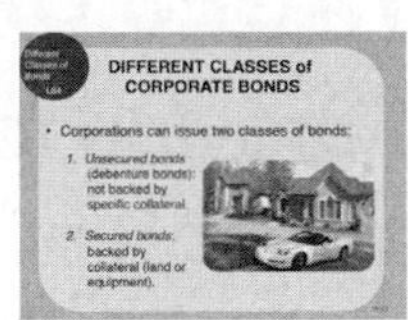

(See complete PowerPoint slide notes on page 19.65.)

2. **SECURED BONDS** (sometimes called **MORTGAGE BONDS)** are backed by some tangible asset (**COLLATERAL**) that is pledged to the bondholder if interest or principal is not paid.

E. **SPECIAL BOND FEATURES**

1. Companies often establish a **RESERVE ACCOUNT** to ensure that funds are available to repay bondholders on the maturity date.
   a. A ***SINKING FUND*** is a reserve account in which the issuer of a bond periodically retires some part of the bond principal prior to maturity so that enough capital will be accumulated by the maturity date to pay off the bond.
   b. **ADVANTAGES OF SINKING FUNDS:**
      i. They provide for an orderly retirement (repayment) of a bond issue.
      ii. They reduce the risk the bond will not be repaid.
      iii. The market price for the bond is supported.
2. A **CALLABLE BOND** is a bond that permits the issuer to pay off the bond principal before its maturity date.
   a. Call provisions must be disclosed when a bond is issued.
   b. Callable bonds give companies some discretion in their long-term forecasting.

PPT 19-24
Special Features in Bond Issues

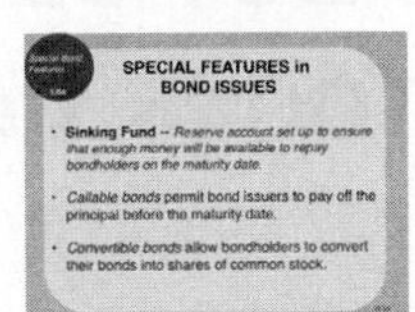

(See complete PowerPoint slide notes on page 19.66.)

3. **CONVERTIBILITY**
   a. A **CONVERTIBLE BOND** is one that can be converted into shares of common stock in the issuing company.
   b. Bondholders must weigh the potential stock profit with the loss of the interest from the bond.

learning goal 5

Explain how to invest in securities markets and set investment objectives such as long-term growth, income, cash, and protection from inflation.

V. HOW INVESTORS BUY SECURITIES

A. HOW TO BUY STOCKS, BONDS, OR OTHER SECURITIES

1. **PROCEDURE:**
   a. The investor must find a ***STOCKBROKER***, a registered representative who works as a market intermediary to buy and sell securities for clients.
   b. The stockbroker places an order with a stock exchange member who goes to the place where the bond or stock is traded and **NEGOTIATES A PRICE**.
   c. The completed transaction is reported to the broker and then to the investor.
   d. Large brokerage firms have **AUTOMATED ORDER SYSTEMS** that allow brokers to instantly place and confirm orders.
2. The broker can also be a source of information about stocks or bonds, but you can learn about and follow stocks or bonds on your own.

lecture notes

progress assessment
(Text page 532)

PPT 19-25
Progress Assessment

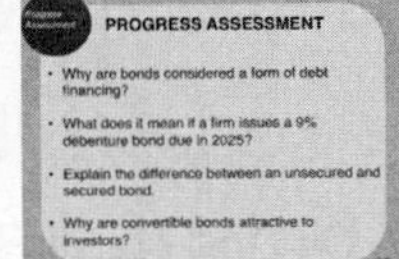

(See complete PowerPoint slide notes on page 19.66.)

PPT 19-26
Buying Securities

(See complete PowerPoint slide notes on page 19.66.)

MAKING ethical decisions
(Text page 533)

PPT 19-27
Money Going Up in Smoke

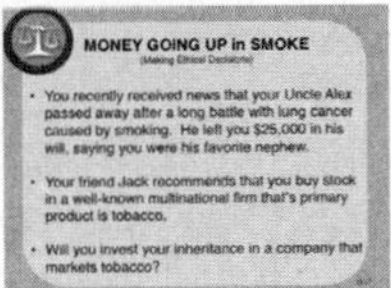

(See complete PowerPoint slide notes on page 19.67.)

B. **INVESTING THROUGH ONLINE BROKERS**

1. Investors can use **ONLINE TRADING SERVICES** to buy and sell stocks and bonds instead of using traditional broker services.
   a. *Examples: Ameritrade, E*Trade, Scottrade*
   b. The **FEES** on these trading services are less than those of regular stockbrokers.
   c. To meet this competition, traditional brokerages have introduced their own online capabilities.
2. These services are targeted primarily at investors willing to do their **OWN RESEARCH** and make their **OWN INVESTMENT DECISIONS.**
   a. The leading online services do provide key market information about companies.
   b. Some online brokers are exploring **OTHER FINANCIAL SERVICES ALTERNATIVES** such as banking services and credit cards.
3. Investing means committing (and risking) money with the expectation of profit—a risky undertaking.
4. The first step in any investment program is to analyze such factors as desired income, cash requirements, level of risk, and so on.

C. **CHOOSING THE RIGHT INVESTMENT STRATEGY**

1. **INVESTMENT OBJECTIVES** change over the course of a person's life.
   a. A young person can afford more high-risk

critical thinking exercise 19-2
PLAYING THE STOCK MARKET

This exercise explores the effect of the stock market ups and downs on an investor. (See complete exercise on page 19.87 of this manual.)

bonus case 19-2
INVESTING AN INHERITANCE

This case explores the investment choices available to an individual with a $30,000 inheritance to invest. (See the complete case, discussion questions, and suggested answers beginning on page 19.93 of this manual.)

investment options than a person nearing retirement.

b. An older person has different objectives, including steady return and additional income.

2. You should consider **FIVE CRITERIA FOR SELECTING AN INVESTMENT VEHICLE:**
   a. **INVESTMENT RISK**, the chance that an investment and its entire yield will be worth less at some future time
   b. **YIELD**, the expected rate of return on an investment, such as interest or dividends
   c. **DURATION**, or the length of time your money is committed
   d. **LIQUIDITY**, how quickly you can get back your invested funds when desired
   e. **TAX CONSEQUENCES**, how the investment will affect your tax situation
3. Investment Strategies
   a. **GROWTH** (choosing stocks you believe will increase in price)
   b. **INCOME** (choosing stocks that pay consistent dividends)
4. Investors need to consider the **RISK/RETURN TRADEOFF.**
5. Investors can read and study the market and make their own decisions or use the services of an investment planner.

D. **REDUCING RISK BY DIVERSIFYING INVESTMENTS**

1. ***DIVERSIFICATION*** means buying several

lecture notes

PPT 19-28
Five Investment Criteria

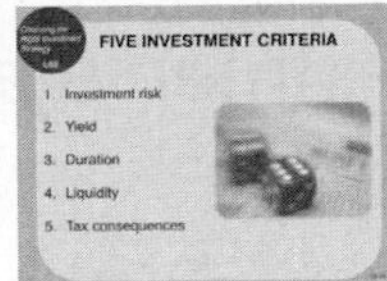

(See complete PowerPoint slide notes on page 19.67.)

PPT 19-29
Investing 101

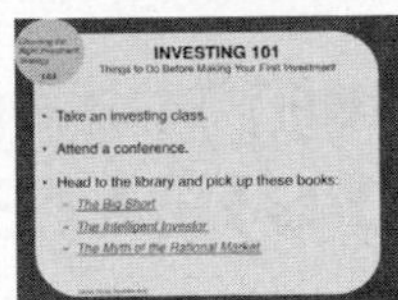

(See complete PowerPoint slide notes on page 19.67.)

PPT 19-30
Average Annual Return of Asset Classes (Since 1926)

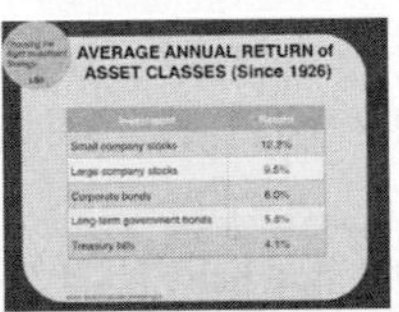

(See complete PowerPoint slide notes on page 19.68.)

PPT 19-31
Diversification

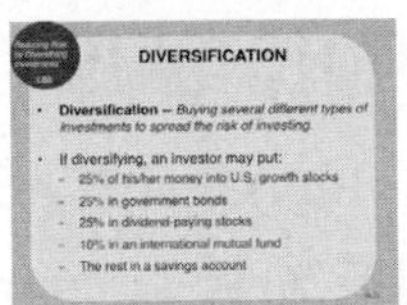

(See complete PowerPoint slide notes on page 19.68.)

lecture link 19-5

THE DOMINICAN NUNS' STOCK PORTFOLIO

The Adrian Dominican Sisters use their standing as stockholders and moral authority as nuns to try to shape policy at some of America's biggest corporations. (See complete lecture link on page 19.81 of this manual.)

REACHING BEYOND
our borders

(Text page 534

PPT 19-32
The Sun Never Sets on Stock Opportunities

(See complete PowerPoint slide notes on page 19.68.)

different investments alternatives to spread the risk of investing.

2. By diversifying, investors decrease the chance of losing everything they have invested.
3. This investment strategy is often called a **PORTFOLIO STRATEGY** or **ALLOCATION MODEL**.

learning goal 6

Analyze the opportunities stocks offer as investments.

VI. INVESTING IN STOCKS

A. **STOCK INVESTMENTS** let investors participate in the success of emerging or expanding companies.

1. As owners, however, stockholders can also **LOSE MONEY** if a company does not do well or if the market is declining, such as the recent market freefall.
2. Stock investors are identified by their perceptions of the market.
   a. **BULLS** are investors who believe that stock prices are going to rise.
   b. When overall stock prices are rising, the market is called a **BULL MARKET.**
   c. **BEARS** are investors who expect stock prices to decline.
   d. When the price of stocks declined, the market is called a **BEAR MARKET.**
3. The market price (and growth potential) of common stock depends heavily on the overall performance of the corporation.

lecture notes

PPT 19-33
Primary Investment Services Consumers Need

(See complete PowerPoint slide notes on page 19.69.)

progress assessment

(Text page 535)

PPT 19-34
Progress Assessment

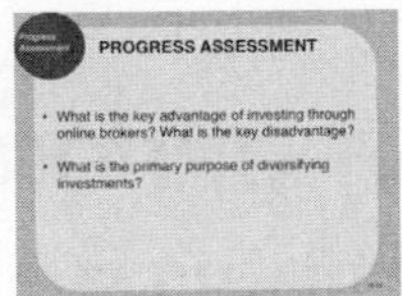

(See complete PowerPoint slide notes on page 19.69.)

PPT 19-35
Perceptions of the Market

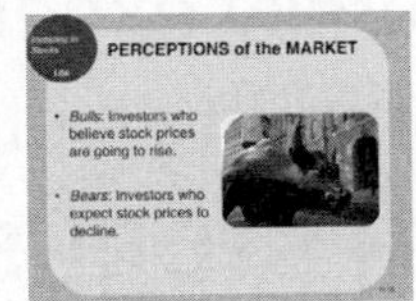

(See complete PowerPoint slide notes on page 19.70.)

PPT 19-36
Bear Market Declines in the S&P 500

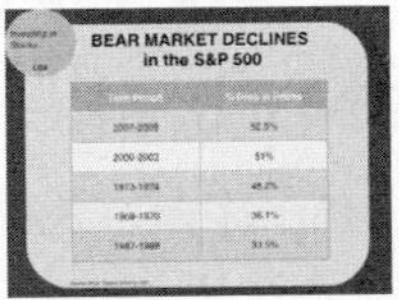

(See complete PowerPoint slide notes on page 19.70.)

PPT 19-37
Selecting Stocks

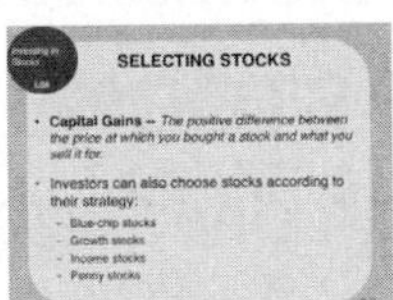

(See complete PowerPoint slide notes on page 19.70.)

a. ***CAPITAL GAINS*** are the positive difference between purchase price of a stock and its sale price.

b. Stocks can be subject to a high degree of risk.

4. **INVESTMENT OPPORTUNITIES IN STOCK**

   a. **BLUE CHIP STOCKS** are stocks of high-quality companies that pay regular dividends and generally experience consistent growth in the company's stock price.

   b. **GROWTH STOCKS** are stocks of corporations whose earnings are expected to grow at a faster rate than those other stocks.

      i. These are often technology-, biotechnology-, or Internet-related firms.

      ii. These stocks are often **RISKY** but offer the potential for **HIGH RETURNS.**

   c. **INCOME STOCKS** are stocks that offer a rather high dividend yield *(e.g., public utilities).*

   d. **PENNY STOCKS** are stocks that sell for less than $2, and are considered very risky investments.

5. **BUYING STOCK: MARKET AND LIMIT ORDERS**

   a. **MARKET ORDERS** are instructions to a broker to buy stock immediately at the best price available.

   b. **LIMIT ORDERS** tell a broker to buy or sell a stock at a specific price, if that price becomes available.

lecture notes

B. **STOCK SPLITS**

1. Companies and brokers prefer to sell stock in **ROUND LOTS**, purchases of 100 shares at a time, although investors can buy stock in **ODD LOTS** (less than 100 shares at a time).
2. A ***STOCK SPLIT*** is an action by a company that gives stockholders two or more shares of stock for each one they own.
3. There is no change in the firm's ownership structure and no change in the investment's value after the stock split.
4. The advantage for shareholders is that the lower price increases demand for the stock.
5. A company cannot be forced to split its stock.

C. **BUYING STOCK ON MARGIN**

1. ***BUYING STOCK ON MARGIN*** is purchasing stocks by borrowing some of the purchase cost from the brokerage firm.
2. **MARGIN** is the amount of money (as a percentage) an investor must invest in the stock; the Federal Reserve sets **MARGIN RATES** (discussed in detail in Chapter 20).
3. However, investors must repay the credit extended, plus interest.
4. If the value of investor's account goes down, the broker will issue a **MARGIN CALL** requiring the investor to come up with more money to cover any losses.
5. If the investor is unable to make the margin call, the broker can legally sell the stock.

PPT 19-38
Stock Splits

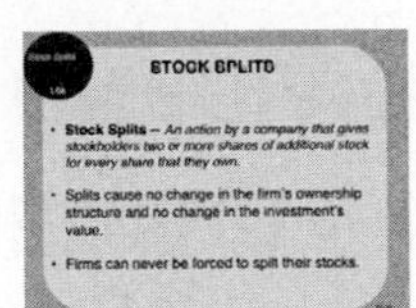

(See complete PowerPoint slide notes on page 19.70.)

PPT 19-39
Buying Stock on Margin

(See complete PowerPoint slide notes on page 19.71.)

D. **UNDERSTANDING STOCK QUOTATIONS**

1. *The Wall Street Journal* lists stock quotations from the OTC markets of New York Stock Exchange, the American Stock Exchange, and the NASDAQ.
2. **Figure 19.4** shows an example of an online stock quotation.
3. **STOCK QUOTES SHOW**:
   a. The **HIGHEST** and **LOWEST PRICE** the stock has sold for over the past 52 weeks
   b. The last **DIVIDEND PER SHARE** paid
   c. The stock's **DIVIDEND YIELD** (annual dividend as a percentage of the price per share)
   d. Important ratios such as the **P/E RATIO** (price to earnings ratio)
   e. **THE NUMBER OF SHARES OUTSTANDING**
   f. The total market capitalization of the firm
4. You can begin to follow stocks with a hypothetical stock portfolio without investing any money.

learning goal 7

Analyze the opportunities bonds offer as investments.

VII. INVESTING IN BONDS

A. Bonds are a relatively **SAFE INVESTMENT.**

1. **U.S. GOVERNMENT BONDS** are backed by the full faith and credit of the federal government.
2. **MUNICIPAL BONDS** offered by local governments often offer **TAX-FREE INTEREST.**
3. **CORPORATE BONDS** are riskier.

TEXT FIGURE 19.4
Understanding Stock Quotations
(Text page 537)

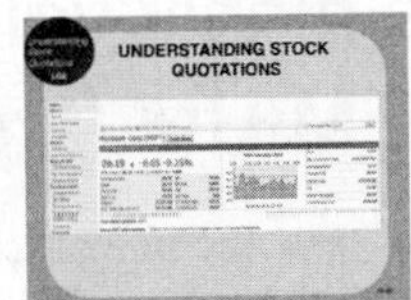

PPT 19-40
Understanding Stock Quotations

(See complete PowerPoint slide notes on page 19.71.)

PPT 19-41
Top Financial News and Research Sites

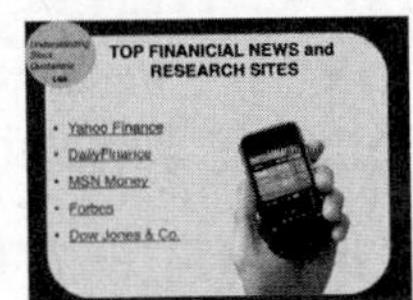

(See complete PowerPoint slide notes on page 19.72.)

PPT 19-42
Important Bond Questions

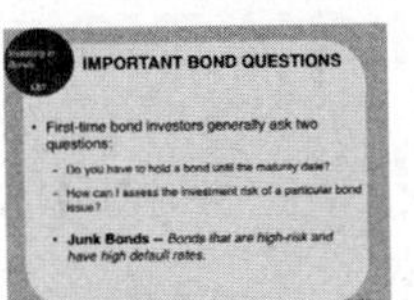

(See complete PowerPoint slide notes on page 19.72.)

B. **BONDS ARE BOUGHT AND SOLD DAILY ON MAJOR SECURITIES EXCHANGES.**

1. You may sell your bond before maturity, but you aren't guaranteed to get the **FACE VALUE** of the bond.
2. If your bond does not have attractive features, you may be forced to sell your bond at a **DISCOUNT**, a price less than the face value.
3. If your bond is highly valued, you may be able to sell it at a **PREMIUM**, a price above the face value.
4. **AS INTEREST RATES GO UP, BOND PRICES FALL, AND VICE VERSA.**
5. Standard & Poor's, Moody's Investors Service, and Fitch Ratings rate the level of risk of many corporate and government bonds.

C. **INVESTING IN HIGH-RISK (JUNK) BONDS**

1. ***JUNK BONDS*** are high-risk, high-interest bonds.
2. Standard & Poor's, Moody's, and Fitch Ratings consider junk bonds as non-investment-grade bonds because of their **HIGH RISK** and **HIGH DEFAULT RATES.**
3. If the company can't pay off the bond, the investor is left with nothing more than paper—in other words, junk.

D. **UNDERSTANDING BOND QUOTATIONS**

1. **BOND PRICE** is quoted as a **percentage of $1,000.**

lecture notes

2. A 9% bond due in 2022 is referred to as "9s of 22."
3. **Figure 19.5** shows simple bond quotations.

learning goal 8

Explain the investment opportunities in mutual funds and exchange-traded funds (ETFs).

VIII. INVESTING IN MUTUAL FUNDS AND EXCHANGE-TRADED FUNDS

A. A ***MUTUAL FUND*** is an organization that buys stocks and bonds and then sells shares in those securities to the public.

1. A mutual fund **POOLS INVESTORS' MONEY** and then buys stocks or bonds in many companies.
2. **TYPES OF MUTUAL FUNDS**
   a. **VERY CONSERVATIVE FUNDS** invest only in government securities or secure corporate bonds.
   b. Others specialize in investments with **GREATER RISK**, *such as high-tech firms, Internet companies, foreign companies, and precious metals.*
3. Beginners can start with a few index funds and diversify.
   a. An **INDEX FUND** may invest in a range of stocks.
   b. Index funds let the investor **DIVERSIFY,** investing in a variety of funds.
   c. A stockbroker, certified financial planner, or banker can help you choose mutual fund investments.

TEXT FIGURE 19.5
Understanding Bond Quotations
(Text page 539)

PPT 19-43
Understanding Bond Quotations

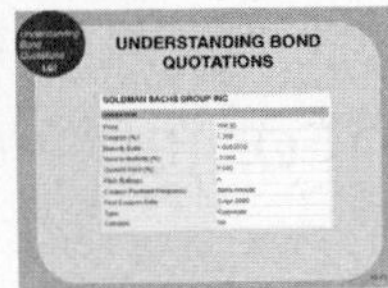

(See complete PowerPoint slide notes on page 19.72.)

PPT 19-44
Investing in Mutual Funds and Exchange-Traded Funds

(See complete PowerPoint slide notes on page 19.73.)

PPT 19-45
What Mutual Funds Can Learn from KaChing

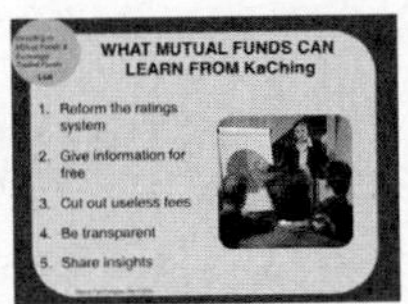

(See complete PowerPoint slide notes on page 19.73.)

PPT 19-46
Percentage of Households Owning Mutual Funds

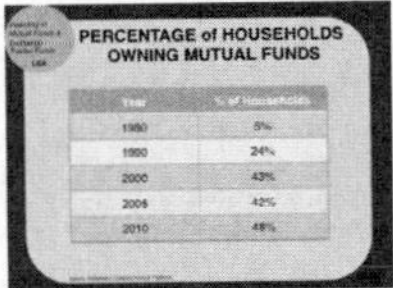

(See complete PowerPoint slide notes on page 19.73.)

d. With mutual funds it is easy to change investment objectives when your financial objectives change.

4. You can **BUY MOST FUNDS DIRECTLY** and save any fees.

   a. A **LOAD FUND** would charge a commission to investors to buy shares in the fund or commissions when the shares are sold.

   b. A **NO-LOAD FUND** is one that charges no commission to buy or sell its shares.

   c. **OPEN-END FUNDS** will accept the investments of any interested investors.

   d. **CLOSED-END FUNDS** offer a specific number of shares; once issued, no further investors can buy into the fund.

5. ***EXCHANGE-TRADED FUNDS (ETFS)*** are collections of stocks that are traded on exchanges but are traded more like individual stocks than like mutual funds.

6. Both mutual funds and ETFs let the small investor **SPREAD THE RISK** of stock ownership.

B. **UNDERSTANDING MUTUAL FUND QUOTATIONS**

1. **Figure 19.7** shows an online listing of mutual funds.

   a. There are many types of funds available to meet investor objectives.

   b. Many companies offer a **VARIETY OF FUND TYPES** within the fund family.

TEXT FIGURE 19.6
Mutual Fund Objectives
(Text page 540)

This text figure shows the wide range of investment categories available for mutual fund investments.

lecture link 19-6
THE DANGERS OF ETFS

ETFs have been a hot item recently. However, as their popularity grows an increasing number of risky ETFs are misleading investors. (See the complete lecture link on page 19.82 of this manual.)

PPT 19-47
Varieties of ETFs

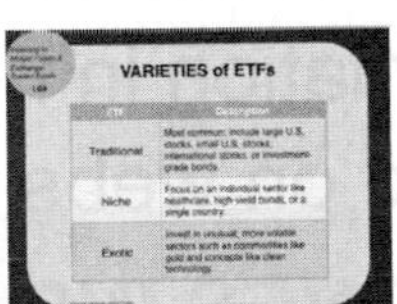

(See complete PowerPoint slide notes on page 19.74.)

2. Today Dow Jones substitutes new stocks in the Dow when it's appropriate.
    a. In 1991 Disney was added.
    b. In 1999 the Dow added Home Depot and the first NASDAQ stocks, Intel and Microsoft.
    c. In 2008, Chevron, Bank of America, and Kraft Foods joined.
    d. In 2009, Travelers and Cisco replaced Citigroup and General Motors.
3. Critics argue that the **SAMPLE IS TOO SMALL** to get a good statistical representation.
4. Stock indexes like the **STANDARD & POOR'S 500** and the **NASDAQ AVERAGE** track a broader mix of stocks.
5. It is important to stay abreast of the market to evaluate investment opportunities.

B. **RIDING THE MARKET'S ROLLER COASTER**

1. The first major crash occurred on **"BLACK TUESDAY,"** October 28, 1929, when the stock market lost almost 13% of its value.
2. The stock market dropped 508 points on October 19, 1987, losing 22% of its value, the **LARGEST ONE-DAY DROP** in history.
3. On October 27, 1997, the Dow fell 554 points due to fears of economic problems in Asian markets.
4. On September 29, 2008, the Dow fell 778 points, the record point drop to that date.
5. From 2000 to 2002, both the S&P and NASDAQ declined significantly in value.

TEXT FIGURE 19.9
The Original Dow and the Current Dow
(Text page 542)

This text figure lists the 12 original Dow stocks and the 30 stocks currently included in the Dow Jones Industrial Average.

PPT 19-52
Market Turmoil

(See complete PowerPoint slide notes on page 19.76.)

lecture link 19-7
THE DAY THEY CALL "BLACK TUESDAY"

The heady expansion of the 1920s came crashing to a halt on October 29, 1929. (See the complete lecture link on page 19.83 in this manual.)

6. Many analysts believe the 1987 crash was due to ***PROGRAM TRADING,*** the process of giving instructions to computers to automatically sell if the price of a stock dips to a certain point to avoid potential losses.
7. As a result, U.S. exchanges created mechanisms to **RESTRICT PROGRAM TRADING** whenever the market rises or drops by a large number of points.
   a. **PROGRAM TRADING CURBS** are put in effect when the Dow moves up or down more than a certain number of points.
   b. A key computer is turned off and trading is halted.
   c. **CIRCUIT BREAKERS**, complete halts in trading, are triggered when the Dow falls 10, 20, or 30% in a day.
   d. Circuit breakers were triggered for the first and only time on October 27, 1997, when the Dow fell 550 points.
   e. The market again collapsed into a deep decline in 2000–2002, largely due to the dot-com bubble bursting.
8. Investor confidence eroded in the early 2000s.
   a. Before 2000, investors believed that the real value of companies was fairly reflected in their financial statements.
   b. Investor trust was shattered by disclosures of **FINANCIAL FRAUD** in companies such as WorldCom, Enron, and Tyco.

PPT 19-53
Turmoil in the 2000s

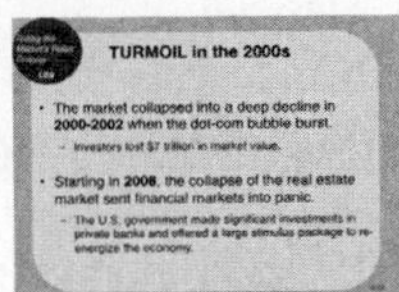

(See complete PowerPoint slide notes on page 19.76.)

PPT 19-54
The Wall Street of Now

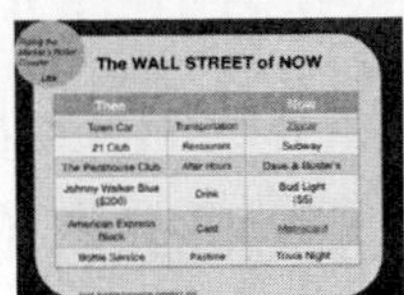

(See complete PowerPoint slide notes on page 19.76.)

PPT 19-55
The Ups and Downs of the Market

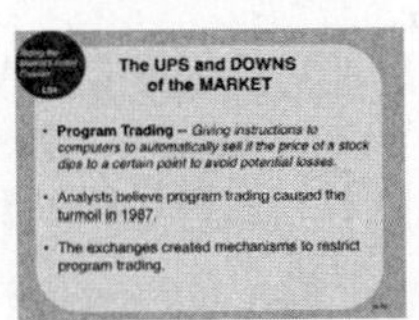

(See complete PowerPoint slide notes on page 19.77.)

PPT 19-56
Who's at Fault for the Economic Crisis?

(See complete PowerPoint slide notes on page 19.77.)

   c. Investment analysts also came under fire for giving companies exaggerated evaluations.

9. The market surged upward again in the mid-2000s.
   a. The Dow set a record high in October 2007.
   b. Prices for housing also improved, increasing 50% from 2000 to 2006.
   c. During the **HOUSING BUBBLE**, financial institutions reduced their lending requirements and buyers overspent.
   d. The government required more mortgages be given to low- and moderate-income buyers, many with weak credit scores.
   e. These **SUBPRIME LOANS** were pooled together and sold to investors through a process.

10. The real estate market collapse caused the economy a combined loss of $8 trillion in housing and commercial property.
    a. Major players such as Lehman Brothers went out of business, and Merrill Lynch was sold to Bank of America.
    b. The federal government bailed out insurer American International Group (AIG).

11. Congress passed an $800 billion financial package to temper the wild market swings.

C. **INVESTING CHALLENGES IN THE 21st-CENTURY MARKET**

1. Markets in the 21st century will probably experience heightened volatility.

bonus case 19-3

THE NEXT GENERATION OF BUBBLES

Rapid inflation led to the bursting of several financial bubbles. Now financial experts are trying to discover what could burst next. (See the complete case, discussion questions, and suggested answers beginning on page 19.95 of this manual.)

legal briefcase

(Text page 545)

PPT 19-57
Cleaning Up the Street

CLEANING UP the STREET

- Congress passed the Dodd-Frank Financial Reform and Consumer Protection Act into law on July 21, 2010.
- Gives the government power to seize and shutter large financial institutions on the verge of collapse in an effort to prevent further bailouts.
- Formed an independent consumer protection agency housed within the Federal Reserve, protecting borrowers against a host of financial abuses ranging from payday loans to mortgages and credit cards.

(See complete PowerPoint slide notes on page 19.78.)

a. The recent financial crisis also reinforced that the world's economies are closely linked.

b. The implosion also affected markets in Europe, Asia, and South America.

2. The basic lessons are to **DIVERSIFY** your investments and **UNDERSTAND THE RISKS** of investing.

X. SUMMARY

lecture link 19-8
INVESTING IN COMMODITIES

Trading in commodities is not for novice investors. (See the complete lecture link on page 19.83 in this manual.)

progress assessment
(Text page 546)

PROGRESS ASSESSMENT

- What does the Dow Jones Industrial Average measure? Why is it important?
- Why do the 30 companies comprising the Dow change periodically?
- Explain program trading and the problems it can create

PPT 19-58
Progress Assessment

(See complete PowerPoint slide notes on page 19.78.)

PowerPoint slide notes

PPT 19-1
Chapter Title

PPT 19-2
Learning Goals

Chapter Nineteen

LEARNING GOALS

1. Describe the role of securities markets and of investment bankers.
2. Identify the stock exchanges where securities are traded.
3. Compare the advantages and disadvantages of equity financing by issuing stock, and detail the differences between common and preferred stock.
4. Compare the advantages and disadvantages of obtaining debt financing by issuing bonds, and identify the classes and features of bonds.

19-3

PPT 19-3
Learning Goals

Chapter Nineteen

LEARNING GOALS

5. Explain how to invest in securities markets and set investment objectives such as long-term growth, income, cash, and protection from inflation.
6. Analyze the opportunities stocks offer as investments.
7. Analyze the opportunities bonds offer as investments.
8. Explain the investment opportunities in mutual funds and exchange-traded funds (ETFs).
9. Describe how indicators like the Dow Jones Industrial Average affect the market.

19-4

PPT 19-4
Maria Bartiromo

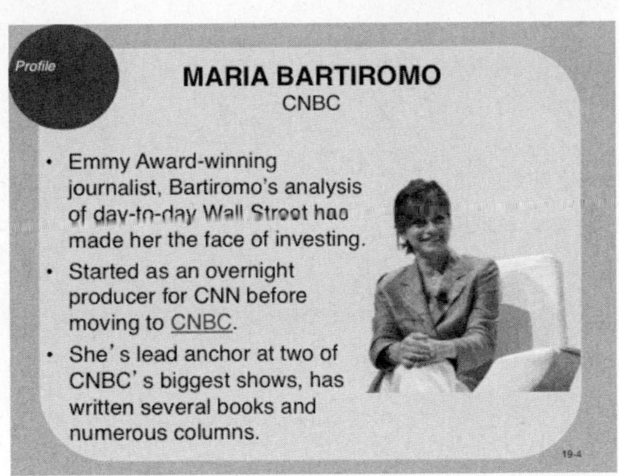

PPT 19-5
Name That Company

Company: Berkshire Hathaway

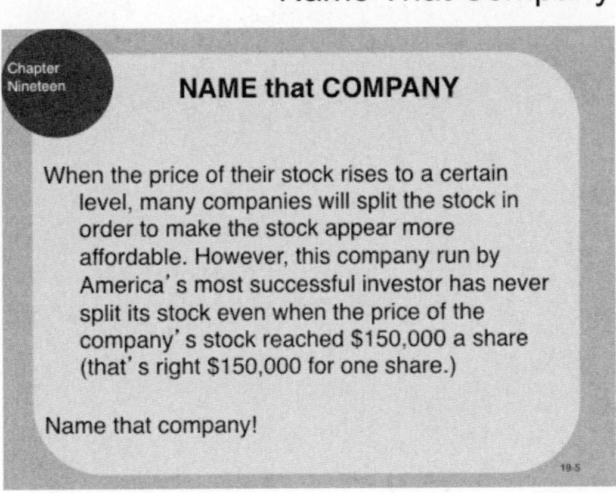

PPT 19-6
The Basics of Securities Markets

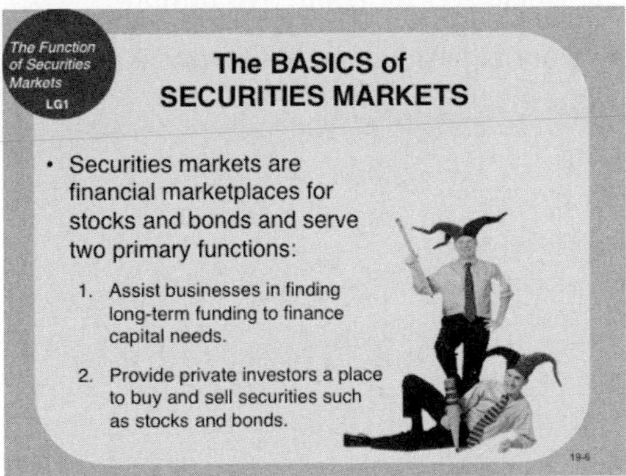

PPT 19-7
Types of Securities Markets

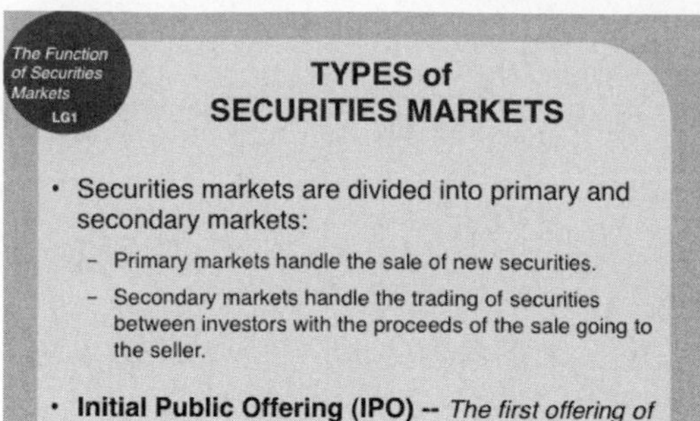

PPT 19-8
Investment Bankers and Institutional Investors

PPT 19-9
Stock Exchanges

1. In 2011, the NYSE Euronext agreed to be acquired by Deutsche Borse AG for about $10 billion.
2. The trading floor is largely symbolic now as most trading is done electronically.

PPT 19-10
Top Stock Exchanges

1. This slide profiles the largest stock exchanges in the world.
2. To be listed on the NYSE, the company must have at least 2,200 shareholders, average daily volume of at least 100,000 shares, a market cap of $750 million, or pretax earnings of $10 million.
3. NASDAQ is an acronym that stands for the National Association of Securities Dealers Automated Quotations.
4. London Exchange merged with the Italian Exchange, both of which have been operating for over 200 years.
5. Tokyo exchange operated a trading floor for 120 years. In 1999, the trading floor was closed as the Tokyo Stock Exchange went to all-electronic trading similar to NASDAQ.
6. The Deutsche Borse is located in Frankfurt, Germany.

PPT 19-11
A Place for Small Companies to Call Home

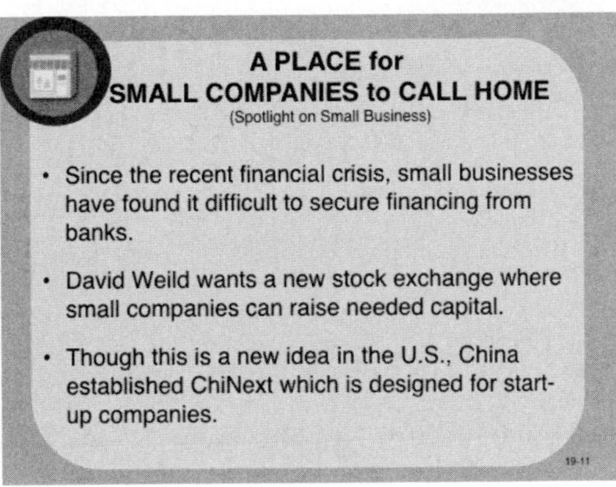

PPT 19-12
The Securities and Exchange Commission

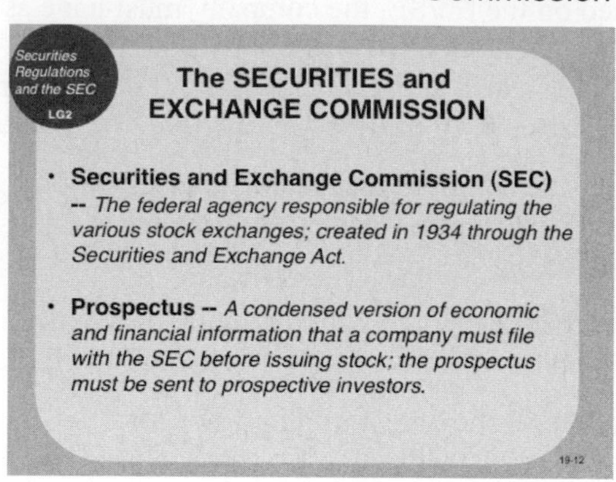

The Securities and Exchange Act also prohibits insider trading by using knowledge or information gained through a person's position in a firm that allows him or her to benefit unfairly.

PPT 19-13
Progress Assessment

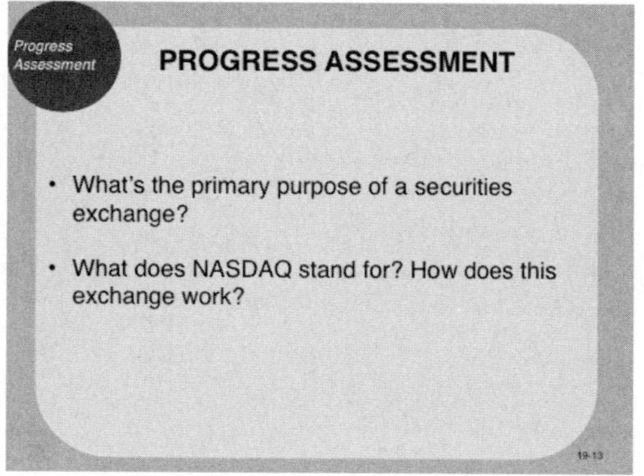

1. The primary purpose of a securities exchange is to allow members of the exchange to buy or sell securities on behalf of investors.
2. NASDAQ stands for National Association of Securities Dealers Automated Quotations. This exchange is completely electronic, allowing for orders to be quickly matched up via computers.

PPT 19-14
Learning the Language of Stocks

PPT 19-15
Advantages of Issuing Stock

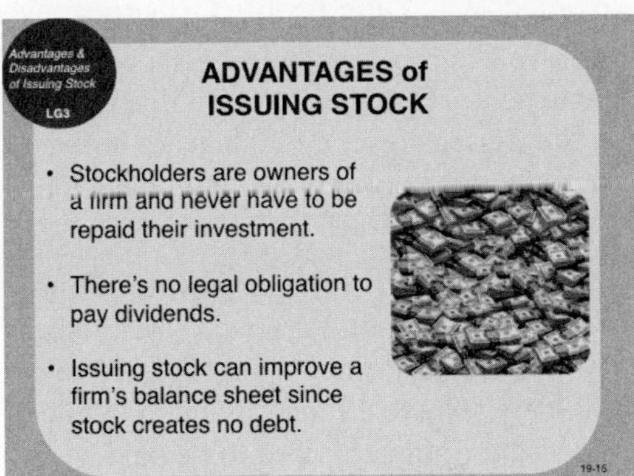

PPT 19-16
Disadvantages of Issuing Stock

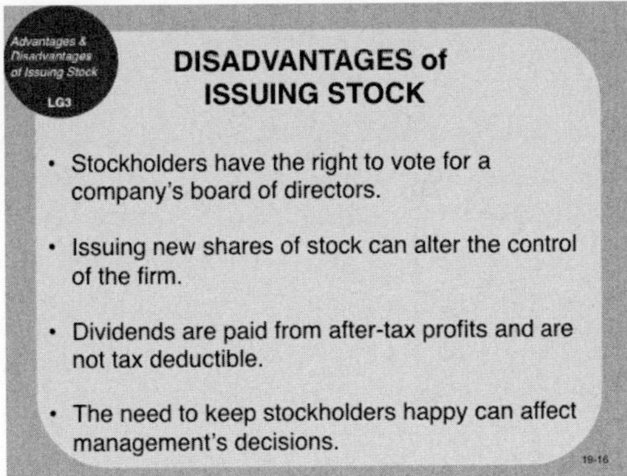

PPT 19-17
Two Classes of Stock

In the event of bankruptcy, the rights of common stockholders are subordinated to preferred stockholders.

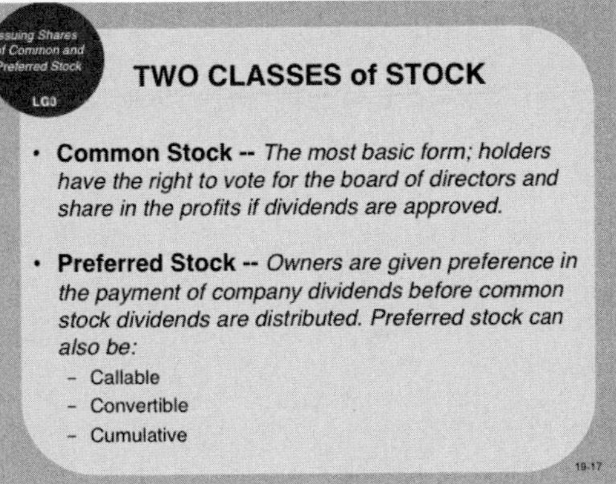

PPT 19-18
Progress Assessment

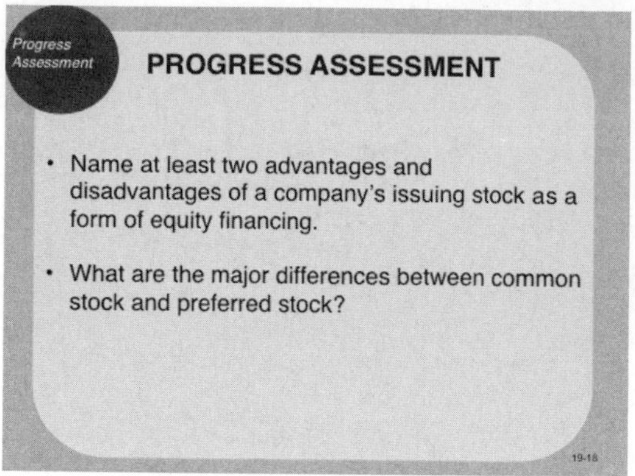

1. Advantages of issuing stock include the following: equity never has to be repaid, the company is under no legal obligation to pay dividends, and selling stock can improve a company's balance sheets since it doesn't create debt. Disadvantages are that equity holders have the right to vote, dividends are not tax-deductible, and the need to keep shareholders happy can affect managers' decisions.
2. Common stockholders have the right to vote, while preferred stockholders do not. Preferred stockholders have rights if the company enters bankruptcy. Preferred stockholders receive a fixed dividend, while common holders are not guaranteed to be paid a dividend.

PPT 19-19
Learning the Language of Bonds

Learning the Language of Bonds
LG4

LEARNING the LANGUAGE of BONDS

- **Bond** -- *A corporate certificate indicating that an investor has lent money to a firm (or a government).*
- The principal is the face value of the bond.
- **Interest** -- *The payment the bond issuer makes to the bondholders to compensate them for the use of their money.*

19-19

Unlike dividends, interest payments are tax-deductible.

PPT 19-20
Advantages of Issuing Bonds

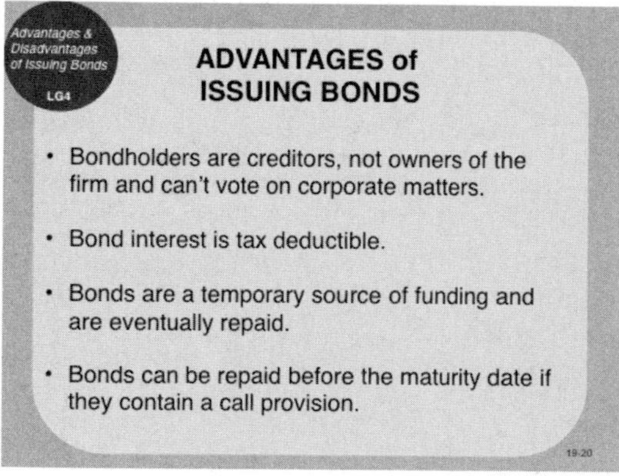

PPT 19-21
Disadvantages of Issuing Bonds

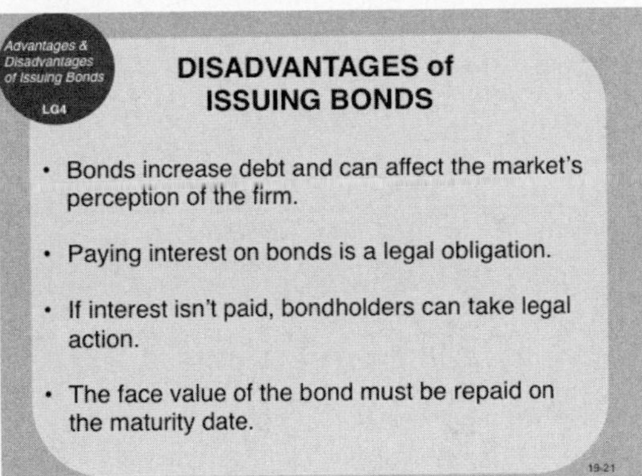

PPT 19-22
Bond Ratings

The rating agencies of Moody's and Standard & Poor's have been under fire for highly rating some of the investment firms that issued mortgage-backed securities. For example, Lehman Brothers received positive ratings within days of its collapse.

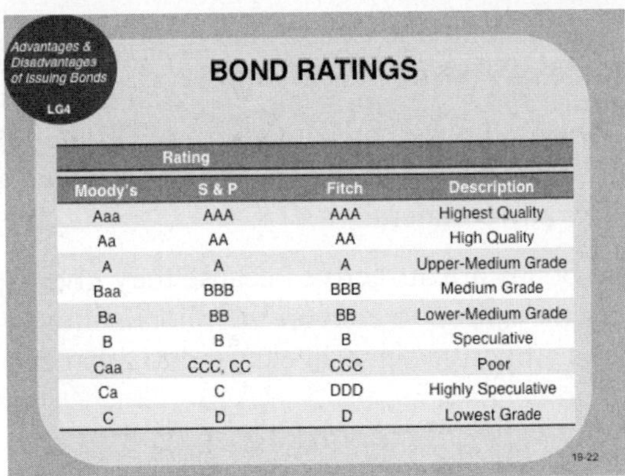

Rating			
Moody's	S & P	Fitch	Description
Aaa	AAA	AAA	Highest Quality
Aa	AA	AA	High Quality
A	A	A	Upper-Medium Grade
Baa	BBB	BBB	Medium Grade
Ba	BB	BB	Lower-Medium Grade
B	B	B	Speculative
Caa	CCC, CC	CCC	Poor
Ca	C	DDD	Highly Speculative
C	D	D	Lowest Grade

PPT 19-23
Different Classes of Corporate Bonds

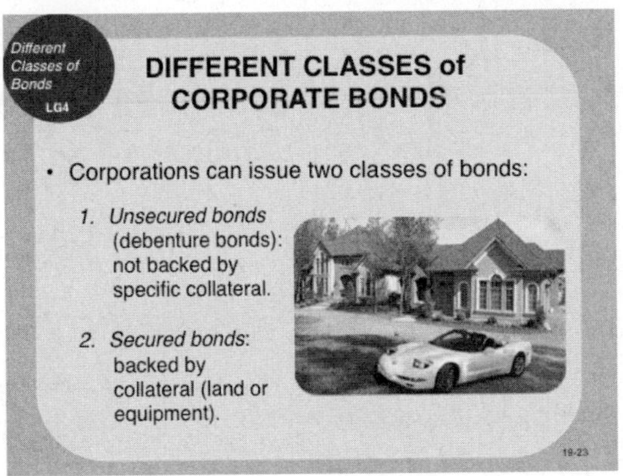

PPT 19-24
Special Features in Bond Issues

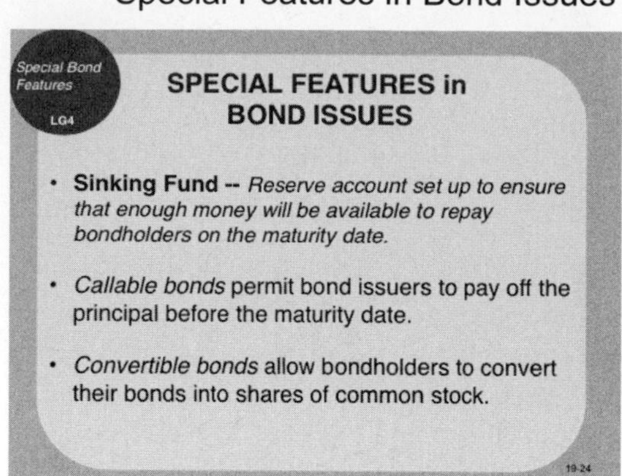

PPT 19-25
Progress Assessment

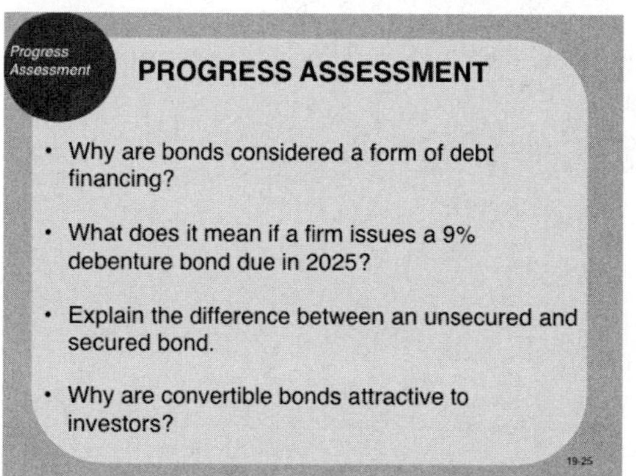

1. Bonds are considered debt financing, since they must be paid back when the bond matures.
2. A 9% debenture bond due in 2025 has a coupon rate or interest rate of 9% and matures in 2025.
3. A secured bond is backed by some form of collateral while an unsecured bond or debenture is not backed or secured by any collateral.
4. Convertible bonds are attractive because they give bondholders the option to convert their bonds into stock. This is attractive since stocks tend to appreciate faster than bonds do.

PPT 19-26
Buying Securities

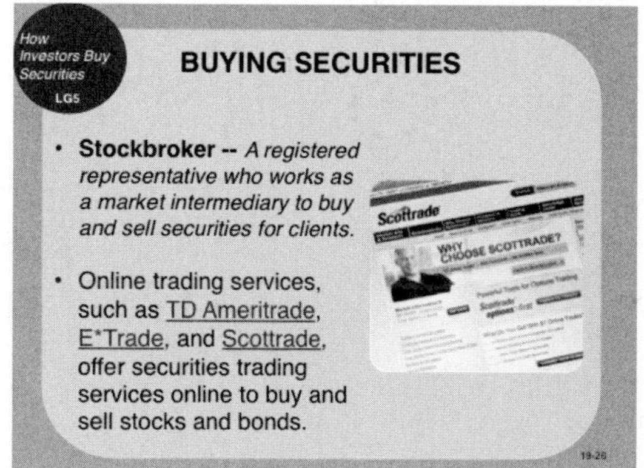

PPT 19-27
Money Going Up in Smoke

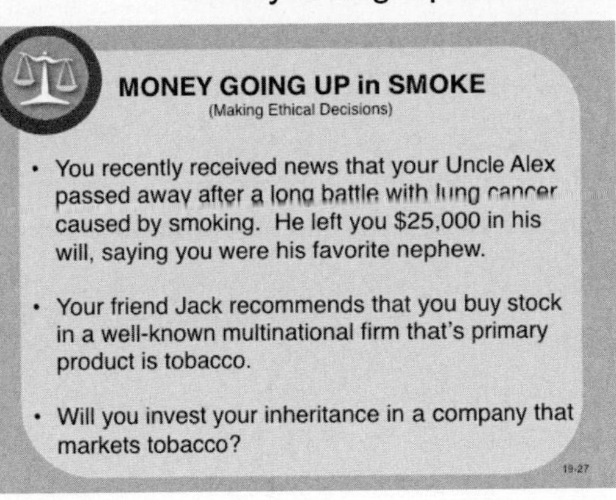

PPT 19-28
Five Investment Criteria

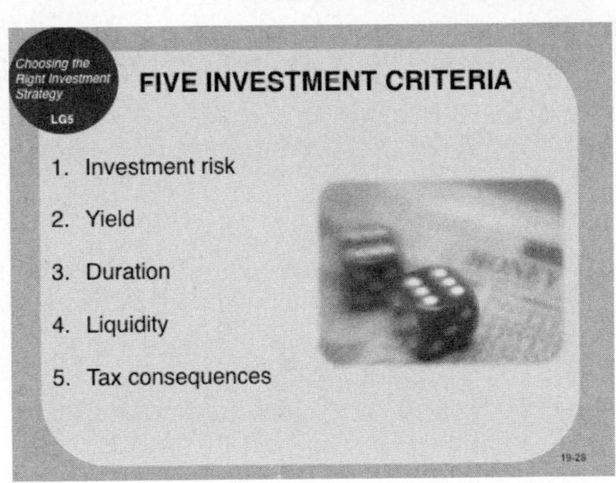

PPT 19-29
Investment 101

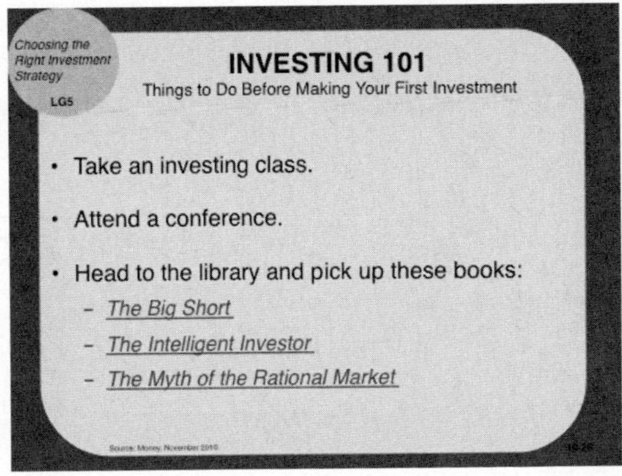

1. Some people want to jump right into an investment.
2. This slide shows three ways to learn about investment strategies.
3. Ask the students, Would you take an investing class or jump straight into the market? Would you know how to do the needed research?

PPT 19-30
Average Annual Return of Asset Classes

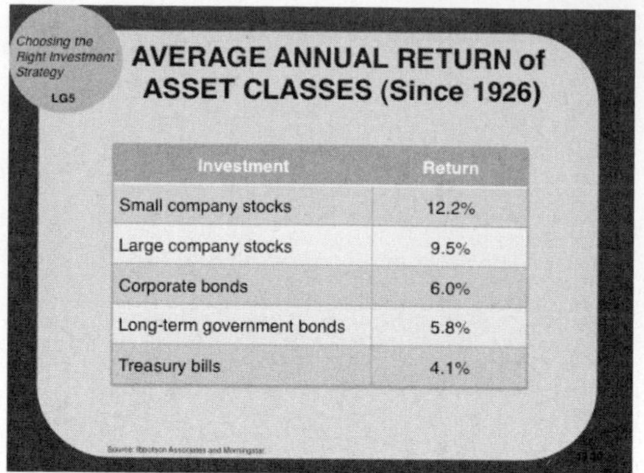

Investment	Return
Small company stocks	12.2%
Large company stocks	9.5%
Corporate bonds	6.0%
Long-term government bonds	5.8%
Treasury bills	4.1%

1. This slide profiles average returns since 1926 for various asset classes.
2. Although the recession since 2008 has been harsh, this chart shows that over the long term, equity is a solid investment.
3. Ask the students, Why do you think small companies have a higher rate of return than any other asset class?

PPT 19-31
Diversification

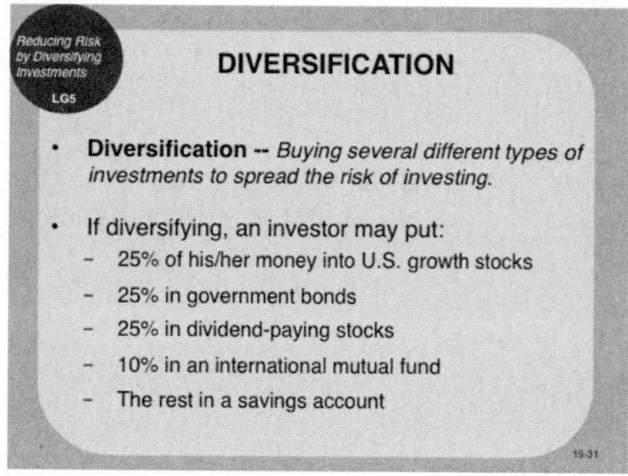

Diversification helps spread risk by buying different types of investments.

PPT 19-32
The Sun Never Sets on Stock Opportunities

PPT 19-33
Primary Investment Services Consumers Need

1. This slide presents the needs of consumers when it comes to financial planning.
2. Today's brokers provide more than simply the buying and selling of stocks and bonds.
3. Companies like Charles Schwab and Fidelity help individuals plan for the future.

PPT 19-34
Progress Assessment

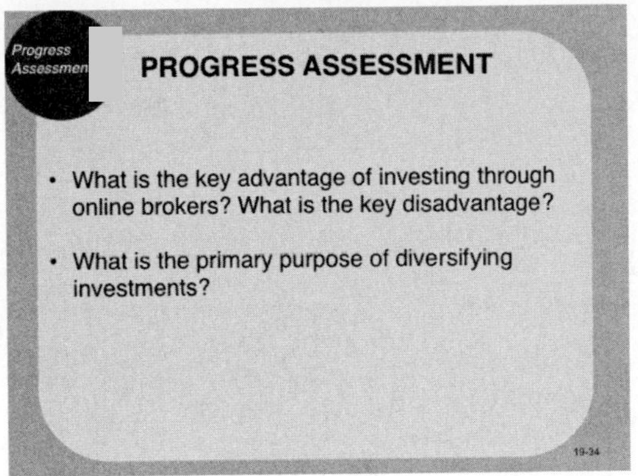

1. The main advantage of investing through online brokers is that the fees charged tend to be lower than traditional brokers. The key disadvantage is that investors must generally do their own research and make their own investment decisions without direct assistance from their broker.
2. The goal of diversification is to reduce the overall risk an investor assumes.

PPT 19-35
Perceptions of the Market

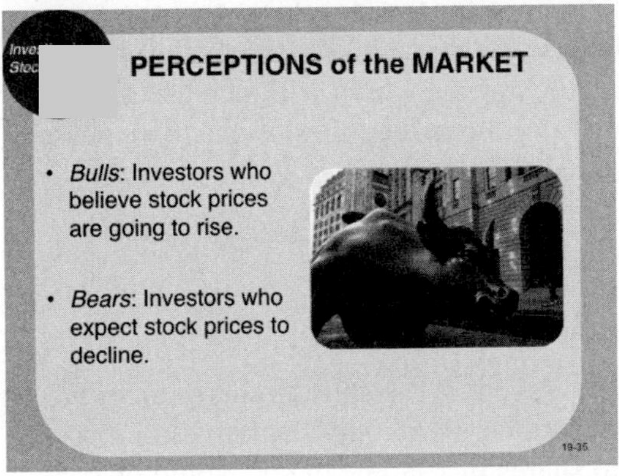

PPT 19-36
Bear Market Declines in the S&P 500

Investing in Stocks
LG6

BEAR MARKET DECLINES in the S&P 500

Time Period	% Drop in Prices
2007-2009	52.5%
2000-2002	51%
1973-1974	48.2%
1968-1970	36.1%
1987-1988	33.5%

1. This slide profiles the bear market declines between 1968 and 2009.
2. The past decade has been abysmal with two significant bear markets.
3. Have students think about the times when bear markets have caused declines in the S&P. What was going on in the country or world at these times? What might have been the causes of these bear markets? What were the effects?

PPT 19-37
Selecting Stocks

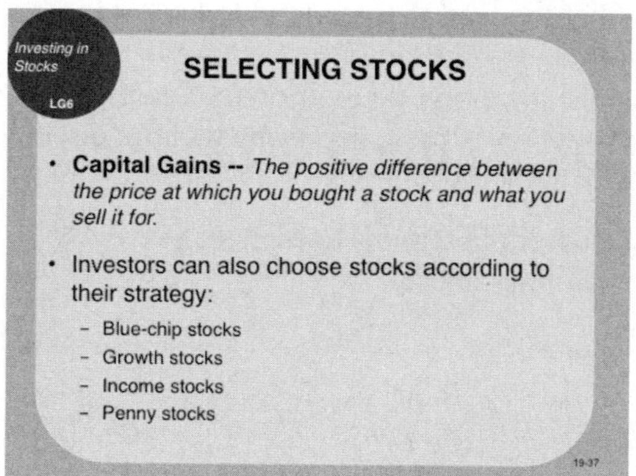

PPT 19-38
Stock Splits

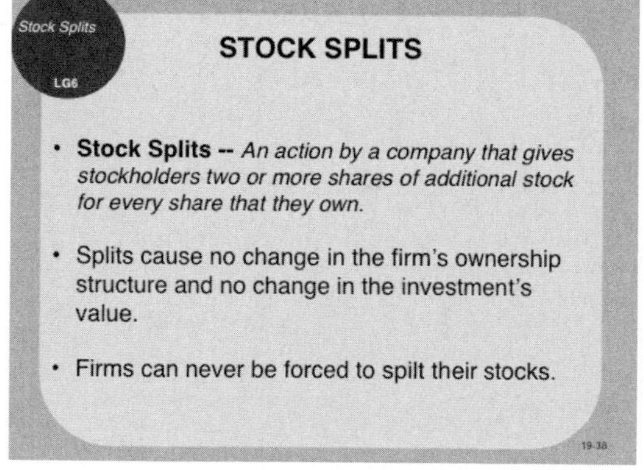

1. An important point to note is investment value does not change immediately after the stock split. The investor has the same original dollar value as before the split. The hope for the investor is that the lower price will cause the demand for the stock to increase, raising the stock price (which will increase the total investment value since the investor has more shares due to the stock split).
2. Dividend rates are also divided according to the degree of split.
3. Most stock splits are two-for-one splits.
4. Since 1975, Wal-Mart has split its shares on eight different occasions. If an individual investor purchased 100 shares in 1980 he or she would own 25,600 shares after adjusting for splits!

PPT 19-39
Buying Stock on Margin

Students should know the risk associated with buying stocks on margin. Investors purchasing on margin are increasing their purchasing power, so they can own more stock without fully paying for it. Margin exposes investors to the following risks:

- You can lose more money than you invested.
- You may have to deposit additional cash or securities in your account on short notice to cover market losses.
- You may be forced to sell some or all of your securities when falling stock prices reduce the value of your securities.
- Your brokerage firm may sell some or all of your securities without consulting you to pay off the loan it made to you.
- Know that your firm charges you interest for borrowing money, which will affect the total return on your investments.

PPT 19-40
Understanding Stock Quotations

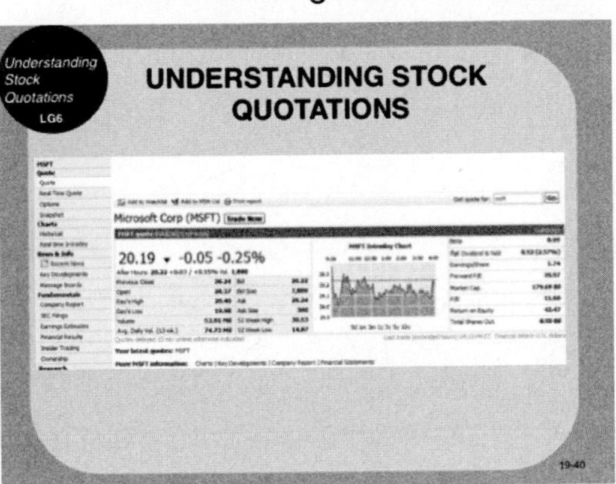

Stock quotations are now readily available on numerous websites.

PPT 19-41
Top Financial News and Research Sites

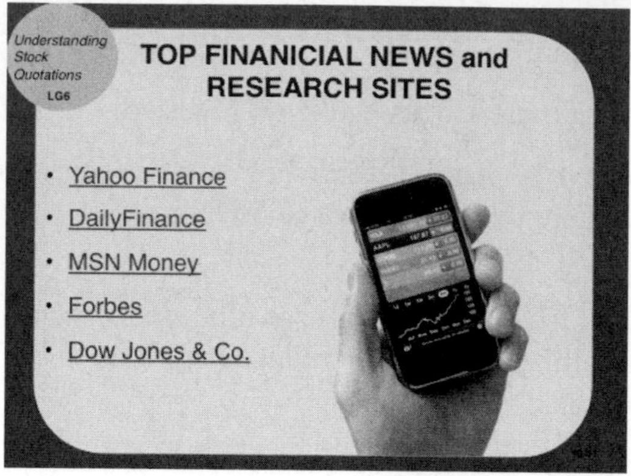

1. Financial information is now readily available online. This slide lists some of the sites where information can be easily gathered.
2. If time allows, encourage students to visit these websites and evaluate their usefulness.
3. Ask the students, Which of these websites was the best? Why would it be a good idea to consult more than one of these sites before deciding to invest?

PPT 19-42
Important Bond Questions

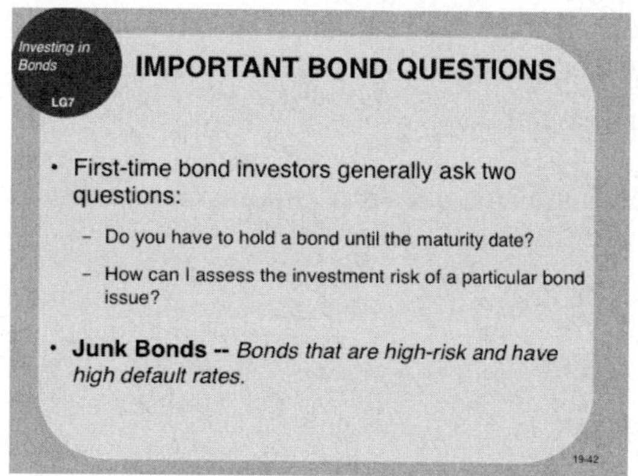

PPT 19-43
Understanding Bond Quotations

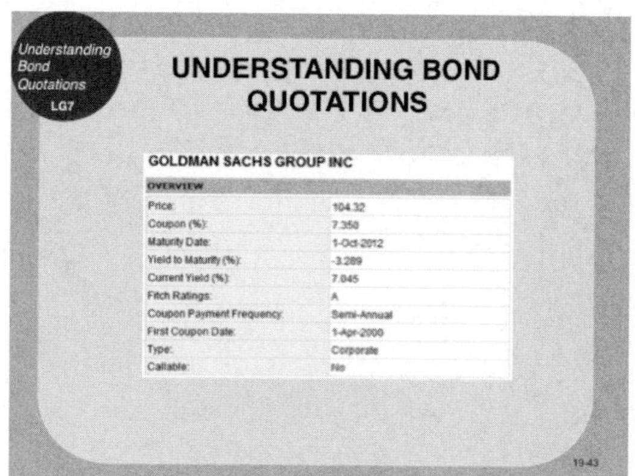

GOLDMAN SACHS GROUP INC

OVERVIEW	
Price:	104.32
Coupon (%):	7.350
Maturity Date:	1-Oct-2012
Yield to Maturity (%):	-3.289
Current Yield (%):	7.045
Fitch Ratings:	A
Coupon Payment Frequency:	Semi-Annual
First Coupon Date:	1-Apr-2000
Type:	Corporate
Callable:	No

A junk bond has a rating of BB or less.

PPT 19-44
Investing in Mutual Funds and Exchange-Traded Funds

PPT 19-45
What Mutual Funds Can Learn from KaChing

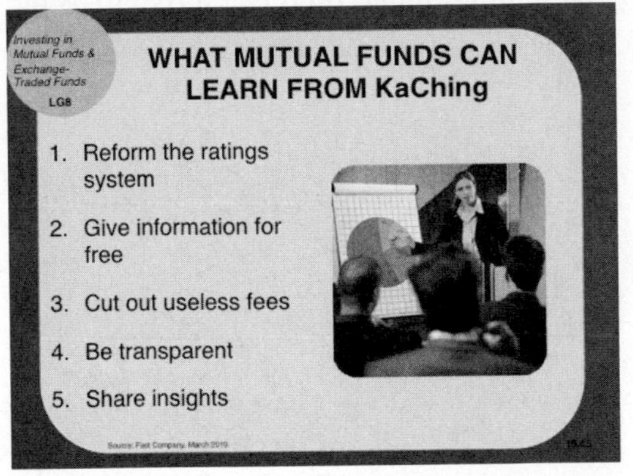

1. KaChing is a website where professional investors share everything about their portfolios.
2. Fast Company shows how KaChing can help investors understand what they're getting into.
3. The magazine uses the example of Morningstar and how most of its portfolio managers didn't invest in their own funds. Potential investors would like to know information like that!

PPT 19-46
Percentage of Households Owning Mutual Funds

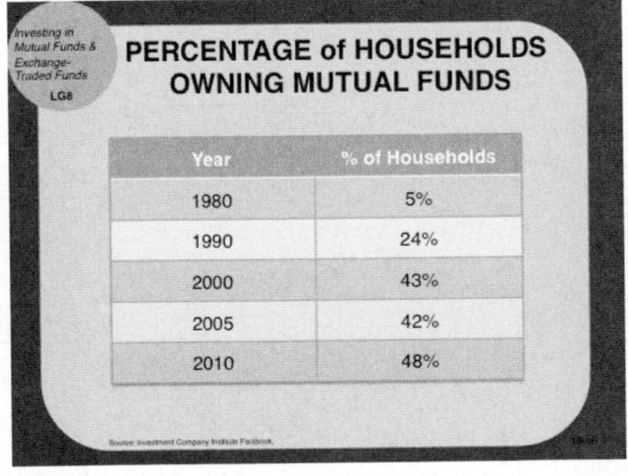

Year	% of Households
1980	5%
1990	24%
2000	43%
2005	42%
2010	48%

1. This slide presents the percentage of U.S. households owning mutual funds between 1980 and 2010.
2. Ask the students, do you or your parents own mutual funds? How did they get involved in purchasing them, and what type of research do they do before buying them? Did they develop investment objectives or was it based on some tip or advice?
3. Point out to the students that people may get into investing for the right reasons and with the right intentions (retirement, savings for college, vacations, home buying, etc.). However, it is very important to maintain discipline. Many people, if not most, deviate from these investment objectives and start to invest based on the so-called hot tip. Mutual funds should be treated as investments that you commit to based on researched information and not hot tip or quick hit gambling.

PPT 19-47
Varieties of ETFs

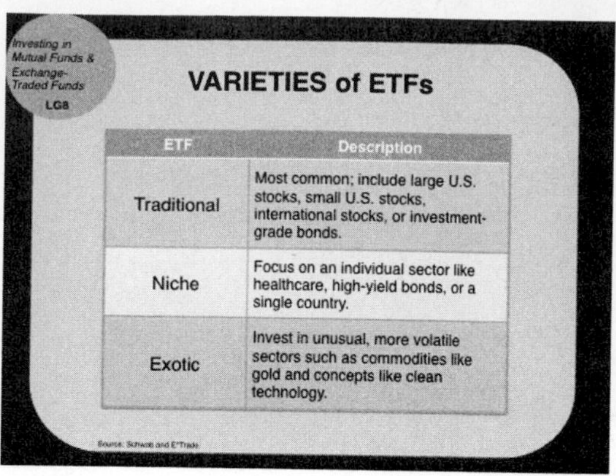

1. This slide lists three varieties of ETFs that are available.
2. ETFs have numerous benefits when compared to mutual funds. If time permits, have students prepare a list of and/or discuss the advantages of ETFs. *(Transparent pricing, lower fees, and returns at least equal to the index that the ETF tracks are just some of the advantages students might discuss.)*
3. Traditional ETFs include SPY, which tracks the S&P 500, and TIP, which tracks inflation-protected government bonds.
4. Niche ETFs include IXJ, which tracks the S&P Global Healthcare Sector.
5. Exotic ETFs include FXA, which tracks the Australian Dollar, and GLD, which tracks the price of gold.

PPT 19-48
Understanding Mutual Fund Quotations

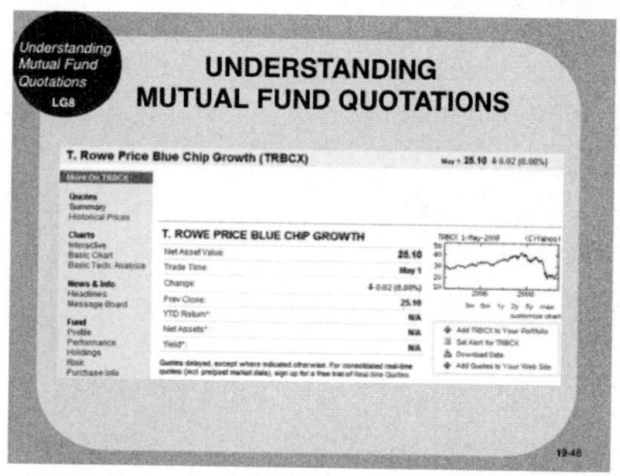

The price per share for a mutual fund is referred to as the net asset value, or NAV.

PPT 19-49
Comparing Investments

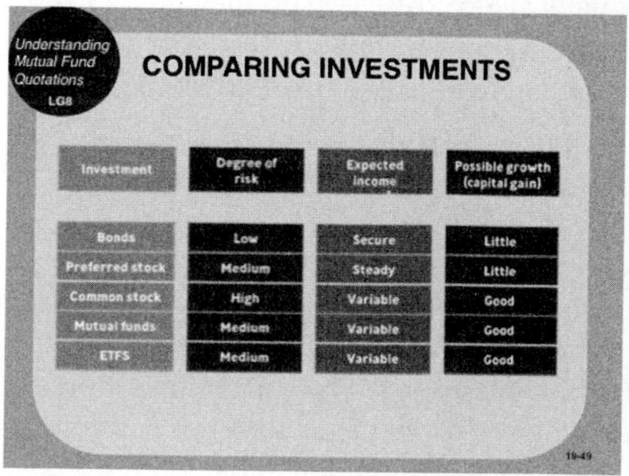

PPT 19-50
Progress Assessment

PROGRESS ASSESSMENT

- What is a stock split? Why do companies sometimes split their stock?
- What does buying stock on margin mean?
- What are mutual funds and ETFs?
- What is the key benefit to investors in investing in a mutual fund or ETF?

19-50

1. When a company splits its stock two-for-one the shareholders receive two shares of stock for each share they own. The current share price is cut in half so the number of shares increases but the total value of the investment remains the same. The board may decide to split a company's stock two-for-one, three-for-two, or any other ratio it determines is appropriate. The reason that a company splits its stock is to reduce the price of the stock, which will hopefully increase the demand for the stock.
2. When an investor buys on margin, he or she uses money borrowed from a broker to purchase stock.
3. A mutual fund is an investment fund that buys stocks and bonds and then sells shares in those securities to the public. The pooling of funds allows small investors to invest in a broader selection of stocks and bonds. Most mutual funds are professionally managed. ETFs are similar to mutual funds, but are traded on exchanges like individual stocks and are passively managed.
4. The key benefit to investing in a mutual fund or ETF is that the investor gets instant diversification.

PPT 19-51
Key Stock Market Indicators

KEY STOCK MARKET INDICATORS

- **Dow Jones Industrial Average --** *The average cost of 30 selected industrial stocks.*
- Critics say the 30-company Dow is too small a sample and suggest following the S&P 500.
- S&P 500 tracks the performance of 400 industrial, 40 financial, 40 public utility, and 20 transportation stocks.

19-51

1. The Dow Jones Industrial Average is the oldest index that was originally created in 1896 by Charles Dow and Edward Jones.
2. The original average had 12 companies, 1 of which, GE, is still in the Dow after all these years.

PPT 19-52
Market Turmoil

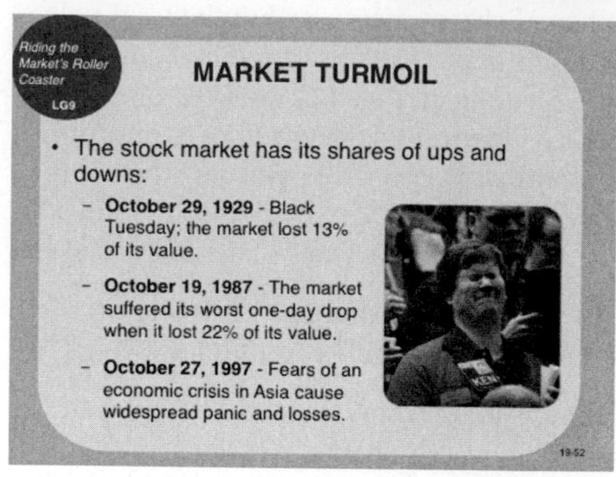

PPT 19-53
Turmoil in the 2000s

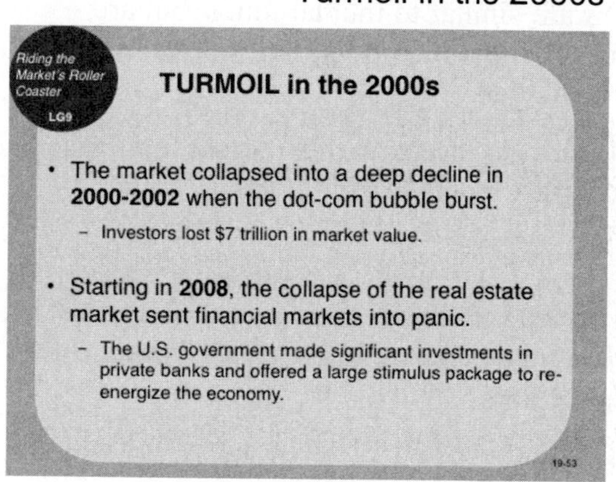

PPT 19-54
The Wall Street of Now

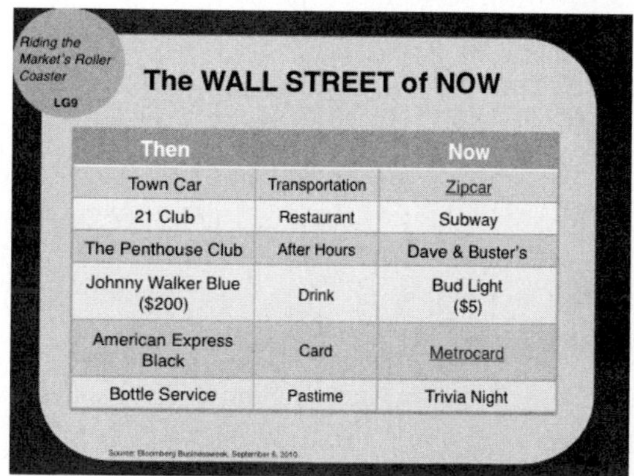

Then		Now
Town Car	Transportation	Zipcar
21 Club	Restaurant	Subway
The Penthouse Club	After Hours	Dave & Buster's
Johnny Walker Blue ($200)	Drink	Bud Light ($5)
American Express Black	Card	Metrocard
Bottle Service	Pastime	Trivia Night

1. Since the economic crisis hit, Wall Street has taken many cuts.
2. This slide shows how Bloomberg Businessweek sees the new way for Manhattan bankers to unwind.

PPT 19-55
The Ups and Downs of the Market

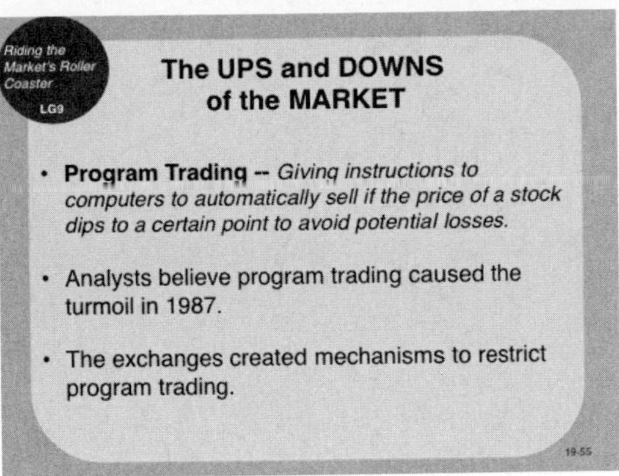

1. The downturn of 1987 prompted the U.S. exchanges to create mechanisms called curbs and circuit breakers to restrict program trading whenever the market moves up or down by a large number of points in a trading day. A key computer is turned off and program trading is halted.
2. If you watch programming on CNBC or MSNBC, you'll see the phrase "curbs in" appear on the screen.

PPT 19-56
Who's at Fault for the Economic Crisis?

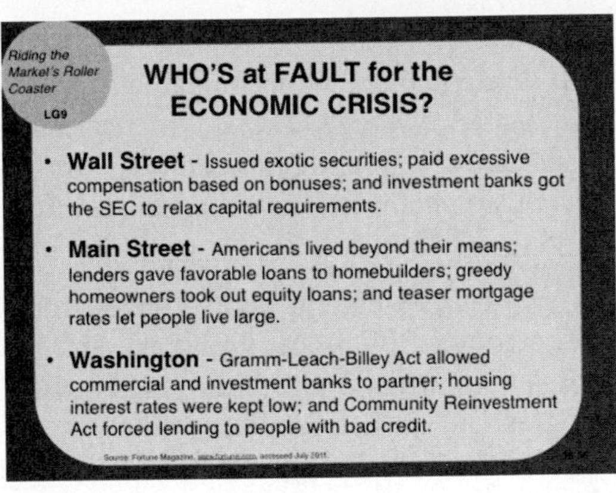

1. This slide reviews some of the players in the economic crisis.
2. Like all complex problems, this crisis was not caused by one group.
3. You could actually include another culprit (not listed on this slide): worldwide saving surplus. Gulf states, China, Japan, and Brazil all reinvested export earnings in U.S.-dominated assets, primarily government bonds. This had the effect of keeping interest low, thus allowing consumers and the U.S. government (as well as many state and local governments) to spend beyond their means, racking up massive consumer and federal debt.
4. To discuss the crisis ask the students, Who's at fault for the economic crisis? (When discussing this highly charged topic it is important to make sure students understand that the fault lies not just with Wall Street and Washington, but with consumers, including themselves.)

PPT 19-57
Cleaning Up the Street

PPT 19-58
Progress Assessment

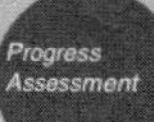

1. The Dow Jones Industrial Average is the average price of 30 specific industrial stocks. It is important because it allows followers of the market to track the general direction of the stock market.
2. The Dow will delete and add new companies to the Dow Jones Industrial Average to reflect increased economic importance of a particular company or industry. Recently, Cisco and Travelers replaced Citi and GM.
3. Program trading occurs when investors give instructions to their computers to execute a sell order if the stock price dips to a certain point. Many attribute the stock market crash of 1987 to program trading as computer sell orders caused many stocks to fall to incredible levels.

lecture links

"Play the game for more than you can afford to lose . . . only then will you learn the game."

Winston Churchill

"You may know where the market is going, but you can't possibly know where it's going after that."

Heisenberg Principle of Investment

"Money is made by discounting the obvious and betting on the unexpected."

George Soros

lecture link 19-1

THE IPO FROM HELL

With its 2004 IPO, Google's reaped $17.5 billion. On the first day of trading, the new shares were quickly bid up from the offering price of $85 to $100. This profitable conclusion, however, came after a very stormy IPO process.

The missteps began almost immediately. When Google announced its plans to go public, it rejected the traditional IPO format in favor of a riskier, but more democratic, auction approach. In the traditional IPO process, the first shares are offered by an investment bank. The shares are hard to get and often underpriced. They are offered to insiders who quickly turn the stock around for a profit. By using the auction approach, the market forces of supply and demand would ultimately set the price of the stock. However, Google's initial share-price estimate ($108 to $135) scared away investors, forcing the company to lower the estimate and reduce the number of shares offered.

More missteps followed. The Securities and Exchange Commission requires company officers to maintain a "quiet period" between the announcement of the IPO and its sale. However, the founders, Larry Page and Sergey Brin, went ahead with a *Playboy* interview. Headlines screamed, "Whiz Kids' Blunders Blacken IPO's Eyes."

The company that started in a dorm room barely six years previously had always rejected the usually corporate culture. Instead of a corporate mission statement, Brin and Page simply promised to "not be evil." Many of Google's most successful products were offered free of charge to any and all users.

Wall Street's traditional philosophy and ways of operation were roundly rejected by Google. In their original prospectus, Brin and Page wrote a self-described "owner's manual" that many investment professionals viewed as heresy. In the document, Brin and Page insisted that their company should be free to operate for the long-term benefit of shareholders, not the quick-buck needs of day-traders and underwriters. No obsessions over quarterly goals. They also claimed that even a public company owes something to the world at large. Google, they warned shareholders, would not trample the common good in an effort to pick up every possible dollar in the soonest possible quarter. Their insistence that corporations should do what they can to help humanity marked them as childishly naïve in the eyes of the street's elite.

When the stock finally opened for trading in August 2004, Brin and Page's approach was vindicated. By the end of the day, the two founders were worth almost $4 billion apiece. Google's $27 billion market value exceeded that of General Motors and almost twice that of Amazon.com.

Six months after the IPO, Google's stock was selling at $425, increasing the company's total market value by roughly 400%. In succeeding years, the stock rose and fell, but eventually stabilized between $300 and $400.[i]

lecture link 19-2

ASIAN IPOS OVERTAKE THE UNITED STATES

As American and European entrepreneurs continue to reel from the recession, Asia's business leaders soldiered on into an unprecedented spurt of economic growth. In 2010, Asia's number of initial public offerings decidedly eclipsed any competition. The continent accounted for 66% of all money raised globally with $134 billion. The United States, meanwhile, sunk to its lowest IPO share in history at 11%.

In 1999 the numbers told a similar story, only the roles were reversed. The United States enjoyed a whopping 75% share of all IPOs while Asia languished at 12%. Times are different now, though, and not just because of the credit crunch. After all, American outsourcing contributed directly to the burgeoning Asian markets that are expanding with capital today. At the top of the heap is America's economic rival China, which attracted $76 billion in investment in 2010. Six Chinese companies' offerings hit the billion-dollar mark, with one IPO for the Agricultural Bank of China selling a world record of $22.1 billion worth of shares. In the United States, no company raised more than $700 million.

While India didn't attain high numbers like China, the nation is nevertheless on pace to shatter its previous annual IPO record of $8.2 billion. Central to India's success was the government's sale of its 10% stake in Coal India, raking in a cool $3.4 billion on the deal. For investors, Asia's appeal lies in its strong growth. Indian and Chinese companies are tapping into relatively untouched markets that could prove to be the most valuable consumer real estate in global business. For the United States, a portion of its future could be based on the success of these foreign companies since six of the 10 biggest IPOs on U.S. exchanges hail from China or India.[ii]

lecture link 19-3

NYSE'S GERMAN MERGER

You've probably seen the photos of the New York Stock Exchange floor jammed with traders in colored jackets, waving arms and shouting orders. What seems like mayhem to us is the natural way of doing business on the NYSE. Or at least it has been up until now. The NYSE has lost considerable market share to electronic platforms that allow faster trading at lower costs.

In an effort to compete with their electronic rivals, in February 2011 the NYSE announced a merger with the Germany's Frankfurt Stock Exchange in a $10 billion deal. The idea is that the new megamarket will entice investors with its access to thousands of stock listings, options, and derivatives from across the United States and Europe. Since Deutche Borse, the union that owns the Frankfurt Exchange, owns 60% of the merged company's operating shares, it will have 10 seats on the new exchange's 17-person board.

The merger has upset several civic and government leaders who fear the deal will undermine New York's role as the world's dominant financial center. But even though the exchange's board will be more than half German, American investors are expected to account for 55% of the company's shareholders. Also, Americans will hold important positions like chief executive officer, chief operating officer, and head of global information technology. All told, the new exchange, which has not released a name yet, will save an estimated $400 million in operating costs annually. These potential savings have made mergers look attractive in other markets, such as one proposed tie-up of the Singapore and Australian exchanges. Nevertheless, Australia's government shares some of the same fears as detractors in America, stalling any deal for the foreseeable future.[iii]

lecture link 19-4

THE TOKYO EXCHANGE TYPING ERROR

Computerized trading systems common on stock exchanges these days have reduced the trade error rate significantly. Yet, the computers' infallibility is only as good as the accuracy of the person entering the information.

In December 2005, the Tokyo Stock Exchange was rocked by an erroneous trade that caused Mizuho Securities to lose at least 27 billion yen ($225 million). The cause of the turmoil was eventually traced to a trader at Mizuho Securities, who meant to sell **1 share** of stock in J-Com Co., a job recruiting company, for 610,000 yen ($5,041). The trader instead entered a trade of **610,000 shares at** 1 yen (less than a penny).

The enormity of the error should have raised red flags through the exchange. The number of shares in the order was 41 times greater than the number of J-Com's shares actually outstanding, but the Tokyo Stock Exchange processed the order anyway. Mizuho says another trader tried to cancel the order three times, but the exchange's policy is not to cancel transactions even if they are executed on erroneous orders. By the end of the day, Mizuho Financial Group had lost at least 27 billion yen.[iv]

lecture link 19-5

THE DOMINICAN NUNS' STOCK PORTFOLIO

The Adrian Dominican Sisters want to make good corporate citizens out of corporations like American Electric Power, Cinergy Corporation, and TXU Corporation. When government environmental agencies fail to keep corporations from spewing out more and more pollution, the Dominican Sisters take their fight into the inner circles of power. The Sisters purchase stock in companies, and then introduce shareholder resolutions that demand corporate reform from within. It doesn't hurt their cause that the order packs a massive portfolio: The Interfaith Center on Corporate Responsibility, which the Sisters represent, has 275 faith-based institutional investors with combined holdings of about $90 billion.

Sister Patricia Daly, executive director of the organization representing the Dominican Order, has introduced shareholder resolutions aimed at the "filthy five," five U.S. utilities viewed as the biggest emitters of carbon dioxide in their business. The resolutions asked investors to agree that the board of directors report to shareholders on "the greenhouse-gas emissions from our company's operations including steps the company can take to reduce emissions of greenhouse gases substantially."

Even if Sister Patricia doesn't win a majority, she'll make her mark. Over the years, her efforts have forced corporations to address many environmental and labor concerns. She stood her ground against some of the biggest egos in business.

The Adrian Dominicans have now spent 30 years as shareholder activists, using their investment portfolio as a means of achieving social change. The move toward "socially responsible investing" in the United States started in the 1960s, as people began to shun companies like Dow Chemical that were profiting from the manufacture of napalm for the Vietnam War. Some investors sold off their "sin stocks," while others used annual shareholder meetings to submit resolutions that called on these companies to stop what they saw as immoral business practices. The Interfaith Center on Corporate Responsibility was founded during this era.

One of its notable efforts was against the textile manufacturer, J. P. Stevens, a flagrant labor-rights violator in the South made infamous by the 1979 film *Norma Rae*. The nuns' decision in 1975 to become activist shareholders came from a need to do more than their direct work in underprivileged communities around the world. So they went behind company lines, using their standing as stockholders and moral authority as nuns to try to shape policy at some of America's biggest corporations.

A division of the National Council of Churches, the group helps coordinate efforts for religious investors. Adrians are revered as much for their willingness to tackle controversial questions as for the many fronts on which they fight social injustice.

The congregation has used its pocketbook to pursue change in many other ways. For example, they developed a $2 million revolving-door fund from which they grant low-interest loans to social service groups. They have also instructed the managers of their multimillion-dollar stock portfolio not to buy shares in tobacco companies. If no women candidates are candidates for the board of directors, the Dominicans refuse to cast a vote.

It is rare that a shareholder resolution they offer passes when voted on by other stockholders. But their concerns generate publicity, which along with dialogue and negotiation have become their most effective tools. They rarely confront an issue—or company—without linking with other groups, usually though ICCR.

The Sisters don't see themselves as enemies of corporations. They are, after all, owner-investors and have a stake in the corporation's success. Most of the money they invest comes from funds set aside for the sisters' retirement, the rest from the congregation's general budget.

Religious investors in the United States have a combined portfolio of about $45 billion. Although they include Protestant churches and their pension funds, most are Roman Catholic groups. Each year religious investors sponsor dozens of shareholder resolutions. In most years, none pass when voted on, and about one-third are withdrawn before annual meetings because negotiations with the companies produced results.

A few months after filing resolutions with the "filthy five" utilities, Sister Daly also filed resolutions with two of the Big Three: General Motors and Ford. They are asking the carmakers to commit to reducing greenhouse gas emissions. According to Sister Daly, "this is not only about what is good for the environment, it is about what is good for GM and Ford Shareholders," by nudging the car giants to focus on their hybrid (gas/electric vehicle) strategy to regain their competitive edge in the United States.[v]

lecture link 19-6

THE DANGERS OF ETFS

It's no secret that the stock market is an unpredictable entity. Nevertheless, every day savvy investors the world over try to find a way to consistently and safely earn money through clever investing. But on the New York Stock Exchange, nothing is assured and even the safest bets have their dark sides. For instance, exchange-traded funds (ETFs) are bundles of stocks, bonds, or other investments that trade like a single stock. Many different companies and funds comprise an ETF, but normally they all fall under one central industry or commodity, such as oil or gold. In this way, ETFs ideally provide an easy and profitable way to diversify a portfolio.

ETFs have been a hot item on the stock market for the past few years, growing at rate of $1.5 billion a week and totaling to an estimated $838 billion overall. But as their popularity grows, Wall Street is increasingly issuing misleading ETFs that contradict the funds' safe reputation. For one, ETFs are closing at an alarming rate, with 140 shutting down since 2008. In the 15 years before then, only 10 had closed. An ETF needs at least $50 million to generate a profit and many disappear due to a lack of investor interest. Although investors don't lose their money once a fund closes, those looking for ETFs as a solid diversification tool instead find themselves saddled with commissions and transfer fees for a new investment.

Sometimes ETFs fail to perform the same way as the indices or products they track. For example, an ETF called the PowerShares FTSE RAFI Emerging Markets Portfolio rose 67% in 2009. A solid return to be sure, except that the collection of stocks it tracked rose 78%. While such tracking errors can occur in some funds from time to time, they're becoming especially common in ETFs, which differ from their indices by an average of 1.25%. So although ETFs are still about as safe a bet as one can make on Wall

Street, their reputation is being polluted by the day thanks to miscalculations and increasingly convoluted bundles of securities.[vi]

lecture link 19-7

THE DAY THEY CALL "BLACK TUESDAY"

October 29, 1929, "Black Tuesday," was the day the boom of the 1920s ended. The market slides of 1987 and 1997 are often compared with this historical watershed.

Few suspected that the go-go era would end so abruptly. Between the spring of 1926 and the spring of 1929, the Dow Jones Industrial Average had more than doubled. During the summer of 1929, it increased another 25%. The national economy, while showing signs of weakness, did not discourage the speculation boom. Investors with as little as 10% cash margin flocked into the market, lured by news of steadily increasing prices. The DJIA reached a peak of 381 on September 3, 1929.

The Federal Reserve Board made a half-hearted attempt to slow down the expansion, jolting prices down briefly during September, but it was not until October 24, a Thursday, that the slide became a crash. On that day, nearly 13 million shares changed hands, 56% more than the previous record. As prices dropped, brokers called investors for more margin, fueling more selling. Only when the nation's top five banks agreed to pool their resources to support the market did the hysteria lessen temporarily.

Monday the selling began again, dropping the Dow by one-day record 38 points, fully 13% of the total market value. There was nothing the banks could do. The next day, Tuesday, October 29, the bottom dropped out. The Dow dropped 31 more points, on a volume of 16.4 million shares. In two days, the market lost almost 25% of its value. Tuesday's volume record stood for nearly four decades. In five trading days, the gains of the previous 16 months were wiped out.

By July, 1932, the DJIA had bottomed out at 41, a reduction of nearly 90% from its peak three years previously. Investors lost more than $74 billion in the collapse. It was not until 1954 that the stock market managed to regain the ground it lost in those three years.

lecture link 19-8

INVESTING IN COMMODITIES

Commodities can be high-risk investments for most investors. Investors willing to speculate in commodities hope to profit handsomely from the rise and fall of prices of items such as coffee, wheat, pork bellies (slabs of bacon), petroleum, and other articles of commerce (commodities) that are scheduled for delivery at a given (future) date. Trading in commodities is not for the novice investor; it demands much expertise. Small shifts in the prices of certain items can result in significant gains and losses. It's estimated, in fact, that 75 to 80% of the investors who speculate in commodities lose money in the long term.

Trading in commodities, however, can also be used as a means of protecting businesspeople, farmers, and others from wide fluctuations in commodity prices and thus for them can be a very conservative investment strategy. A commodity exchange specializes in the buying and selling of precious metals and minerals (e.g., silver, foreign currencies, gasoline) and agricultural goods (e.g., wheat, cattle, sugar). The Chicago Board of Trade (CBOT), with its 60,000-square-foot trading floor, is the largest commodity exchange in terms of floor size. The CBOT is involved with a wide range of commodities, including corn, plywood, silver, gold, and U.S. Treasury bonds.

Commodity exchanges operate much like stock exchanges: Members of the exchange meet on the exchange's floor to transact deals. Yet a commodities exchange looks quite different from a stock exchange, and is interesting to observe. Transactions for a specific commodity take place in a specific trading area, or "pit," that can only be described as an exciting spectacle. Trades result from the meeting of a bid and offer in an open competition among exchange members. The bids and offers are made in a seemingly impossible-to-understand blend of voices, with all participants shouting at once. Today, however, the old color and excitement of the pits are becoming somewhat obsolete. More and more traders and brokers are working electronically at computer screens where millions of contracts are zipping around on global computer networks. In fact, the CBOT has relinquished its long-standing title as the largest trading futures exchange in the world to the Eurex exchange, based in Frankfurt, Germany.

Many companies use commodities markets to their advantage by dealing in the futures market. Futures markets involve the purchase and sale of goods for delivery sometime in the future. Take, for example, a farmer who has corn growing in the field. The farmer is not sure what price the corn will sell for at harvest time. To be sure of a price, the farmer could sell the corn on the commodity floor for delivery in the future at a fixed price. Since the price is now fixed, the farmer can plan the farm's budget and expenses accordingly. In contrast, as the owner of Very Vegetarian, you may be worried about the possibility that corn prices will rise. If you buy the corn in the futures market, you know what you will have to pay and, like the farmer, can also plan accordingly. All of this is possible because of commodity exchanges.

critical thinking exercises

Name: ______________________

Date: ______________________

critical thinking exercise 19-1

FINANCING GROWTH

You've owned a tool and die company for the last five years. Even during the recession, you have been earning a net profit of 30% on your investment and have been able to pay yourself a reasonable salary. You are feeling so confident that you are considering expanding. You believe that your profit potential can improve greatly if you could expand your product line with newer high-tech equipment. You estimate that you will need $1 million for the expansion.

1. What are your financing alternatives?

2. Would you consider selling bonds if you had to pay 12% interest?

3. What are the major advantages of using issuing bonds?

4. What are the major disadvantages of using issuing bonds?

notes on critical thinking exercise 19-1

1. *What are your financing alternatives?*

   You could raise the money by selling more stock or by borrowing money through the sale of bonds.

2. *Would you consider selling bonds if you had to pay 12% interest?*

   Probably not. You have been realizing a return higher than that, but 12% is simply too much to pay in the long run. Business could slow and you would be stuck paying 12% to bondholders for a long time.

3. *What are the major advantages of using issuing bonds?*

   You maintain control over the firm and you don't dilute the ownership.

4. *What are the major disadvantages of using issuing bonds?*

   You have to pay back the debt even if you don't have the revenues to do so. Debt weakens the financial base of the firm and makes it harder to sell stock

Name: ______________________

Date: ______________________

critical thinking exercise 19-2

PLAYING THE STOCK MARKET

Suppose you are a stockbroker, who has just sold a new client 500 shares of a stock your brokerage recommends. The very next day after the sale, the price of the stock drops $3. The client calls you as soon as he's looked in *The Wall Street Journal.* He's obviously upset that he "lost" $1,500 in only one day. Although you assure him that your researchers rate the stock highly and that the stock market as a whole had a low day yesterday, the client still threatens to sell his shares and take his business elsewhere.

1. Why would a good stock drop $3 in one day?

2. What do you tell your client if the market drops again tomorrow and his stock drops with it?

3. Are some people emotionally unsuited to handle the stresses of the ups and downs of the stock market? Should such people stay out of the stock market? If so, what are their investment alternatives?

notes on critical thinking exercise 19-2

1. *Why would a good stock fall $3 in one day?*

   The price of a stock depends on the supply and demand for that stock. It can easily fall $3 if a major brokerage house tells its customers that the stock is no longer a recommendation. This does not mean the company has changed in any way. It means only that this brokerage has changed its views. An announcement by the government of a change in fiscal or monetary policy could also cause such a drop.

2. *What do you tell your client if the market drops again tomorrow and his stock drops with it?*

   If you want to minimize your losses in a stock, put in a stop loss order when you buy it. This means that the stock is sold automatically if it falls a certain amount. This gets you out before the stock falls further than you want. However, it is not always a good idea to sell when a stock drops a few points. The situation may be temporary and the market hasn't recognized the potential of the firm yet. If you can't take the ups and downs of individual stocks, it is best to invest in a mutual fund.

3. *Are some people emotionally unsuited to handle the stresses of the ups and downs of the stock market? Should such people stay out of the stock market? If so, what are their investment alternatives?*

   Yes, some are. They are better off investing in money market funds or putting their money in a bank. They may lose part of their money that way anyway because of inflation, but they would be less concerned about it in the short run. If people are just a little nervous, they can invest in conservative mutual funds or bond funds.

Name: ____________________

Date: ____________________

critical thinking exercise 19-3

DOW JONES COMPONENTS

Go to the Dow Jones Indexes website (www.djindexes.com.) (Sometimes the Web address for a location changes. You might need to search to find the exact location mentioned.) Using the information about the Dow Jones Industrial Average given on the site, answer the following questions:

1. What is the Dow Jones Industrial Average Index value at the end of yesterday's trading?

2. What is the percentage change in the index in the year to date?

3. The website contains information about the composition of the DJIA index. Use this information to answer the following questions:

   a. In what year was the DJIA index expanded to twelve stocks?

   b. In what year was General Motors added to the index?

   c. In what year was Microsoft added to the index?

4. Choose one of the stocks included in the DJIA today and trace its history.

critical thinking exercise 19-3 (continued)

5. The website includes a chart showing what happened to the Dow Jones Industrial Average after major world events.

    a. After the Oklahoma City bombing in 1995, what was the one-day effect on the Dow Jones Industrial Average? What was the effect one year later?

    b. After the September 11, 2001, terrorist attacks, what was the one-day effect on the Dow Jones Industrial Average? What was the effect one year later?

    c. After Hurricane Katrina hit the Gulf Coast in August 2005, what was the one-day effect on the Dow Jones Industrial Average? What was the effect one year later?

bonus cases

bonus case 19-1

IS IT TIME FOR AN NYSE CODE OF ETHICS?

Doctors have the Hippocratic Oath. Pharmacists, mathematicians, advertisers, even football coaches all have codes of ethics. Not investment bankers.

Investment banking would be a complicated area to police. Bankers dole out loans, hammer out contracts, counsel companies on the sensitive topics of mergers and acquisitions. However, it is in these areas that ethical lapses can occur. Investment bankers and stock brokerages have been known to downplay the drawbacks of a particular investment to score a big commission. There have been many examples in recent years of brokers shading the truth or engaging in outright unethical behavior.

A group of investment professionals, including investment banker Felix Rohatyn, mergers lawyer Marty Lipton, and New York Stock Exchange chair John Reed, has proposed that bankers, brokers, and analysts adopt an industry-wide code of ethics. Instead of trying to create a rule for every ethical decision, the suggested code would contain basic principles about whom the investment community is accountable to and what priorities should exist between banker, client, and regulator.

A professional ethics code would be different from a company ethics code. Many analysts are skeptical about individual corporate codes, pointing to the carefully crafted code of ethics established (and ignored) at Enron. A professional code, in contrast, could be used as justification for bankers and brokers who want to do the right thing when their company demands otherwise.

The group advocating a professional code is trying to distill universal statements or principles. A code could include principles for handling conflicts of interest, behavioral guidelines for dealing with clients and competitors, and some recognition of a broker's duty to society at large.[vii]

discussion questions for bonus case 19-1

1. Many in the investment company were implicated in the accounting/underwriting scandals involving Enron, WorldCom, and Arthur Andersen. Would a code of ethics have discouraged or prevented these unethical situations?

2. Suppose you were a stockbroker and recognized a profitable, but questionably ethical investment opportunity. The investment would significantly benefit the major corporate directors and generate commission income for you and your brokerage. What is your obligation to other stockholders, regulators, and society in general?

3. Does a broker have a duty to make as much money for his or her clients as possible? Does the wide separation in wealth between rich and poor create a situation where brokers should stop making as much money as possible for rich people?

notes on discussion questions for bonus case 19-1

1. *Many in the investment company were implicated in the accounting/underwriting scandals involving Enron, WorldCom, and Arthur Andersen. Would a code of ethics have discouraged or prevented these unethical situations?*

   It may have discouraged such behavior, but not stopped it entirely. People are always searching for ways to get around rules, and ethical rules are no exception. On the other hand, we should do everything possible to have them comply.

2. *Suppose you were a stockbroker and recognized a profitable, but questionably ethical investment opportunity. The investment would significantly benefit the major corporate directors and generate commission income for you and your brokerage. What is your obligation to other stockholders, regulators, and society in general?*

   It depends entirely on what is meant by "questionably ethical." Does that mean questionably legal as well? In that case, there is no debate. It is wrong to do. Period. If it means that people might have some question as to why you did something, you have to judge each case by its merits. Things may "look" unethical, but be clearly ethical to others. One has to use his or her own conscience as a guide. Such a question may create lively class discussion as students bring up practices for examples.

3. *Does a broker have a duty to make as much money for his or her clients as possible? Does the wide separation in wealth between rich and poor create a situation where brokers should stop making as much money as possible for rich people?*

   Brokers should not be deciding who deserves to become richer and who does not. Their job is to help people of all classes become richer. The way that poor people become rich is by investing, and brokers are there to help.

bonus case 19-2

INVESTING AN INHERITANCE

Jason Heimberg's grandmother died and left him $30,000. Jason needed $5,000 of the inheritance to finish his last year at County Community College. He had $25,000 left to invest. Jason investigated several stocks that he felt were likely to grow rapidly. Most were high-tech stocks in industries such as gene splicing and robotics. Jason's stockbroker encouraged him to diversify his investments by buying stock in two mutual funds. One was a fund that specializes in smaller-growth companies. Another specialized in bonds.

A broker Jason met at a party suggested that he really need not use a broker at all. Her suggestion was to keep some funds in the bank for his use in an emergency. Other funds could be invested in several different mutual funds that were managed by one firm. She called them no-load mutual funds and explained that they could be bought for no brokerage fee. She said the funds have an NL notation in the various mutual fund quotations, as found in *The Wall Street Journal.*

A financial adviser has suggested that Jason buy insurance first, even though he is not married. The idea was to buy a policy that would invest money for Jason at what looked like a reasonable return. Any excess funds would be placed in a bank (for emergencies) and in mutual funds that the adviser would recommended.

discussion questions for bonus case 19-2

1. What are the criteria Jason should use in evaluating investment alternatives?

2. Look up no-load mutual funds in a newspaper or magazine that lists them. Do you understand what is available? What are the advantages and disadvantages of buying a mutual fund through a broker?

3. What questions does this case raise that you need to have answered before you can invest your funds more intelligently? Where could you find answers to such questions?

notes on discussion questions for bonus case 19-2

1. *What are the criteria Jason should use in evaluating investment alternatives?*

   The investment criteria mentioned in the text include risk, yield, duration, liquidity, and tax consequences. Another important consideration is diversification. By putting some money into the bank and buying a couple of mutual funds, Jason could diversify his investment, get a good yield, remain relatively liquid, and keep his taxes at a reasonable rate. It is a good idea to buy into a no-load mutual fund to save the sales commission. Jason does not need much, if any, insurance at this time. He may want to have some term insurance to cover funeral expenses if he feels the need.

2. *Look up no-load mutual funds in a newspaper or magazine that lists them. Do you understand what is available? What are the advantages and disadvantages of buying a mutual fund through a broker?*

   No-load mutual funds offer a full range of types, from growth funds to international funds and more. If you cannot understand the symbols, call a couple of the more diverse funds and ask them to send you descriptions of the various funds. One advantage of buying mutual funds through brokers is that they can pick the best funds to meet your needs, if they are qualified. The disadvantage is that you lose 8% or so in commission fees by going through a broker instead of buying a no-load fund.

3. *What questions does this case raise that you need to have answered before you can invest your funds more intelligently? Where could you find answers to such questions?*

   A good broker can answer most of your investment questions. It is also a good idea to read *Money* magazine and other business periodicals to learn more about investments. Television programs like *Wall Street Week* answer viewer questions every week. If you watch such programs for a while, you will learn much about investment strategy and some specific stocks or mutual funds to consider.

bonus case 19-3

THE NEXT GENERATION OF BUBBLES

For more than a decade the rapid inflation and subsequent bursting of several bubbles have defined the American economy. From dot-coms to the subprime crisis, optimistic financial forecasts combined with overeager investors worked to create moments of economic euphoria before the bottom eventually dropped out. In the case of the 2008 meltdown, the bursting of the American real estate bubble incurred consequences that reverberated around the globe. Three years later, some economists worry that the world's financial leaders have still not learned their lesson.

Analysts have outlined a number of areas where price increases don't mirror economic fundamentals. For instance, the price of gold has risen 464% since 2001 thanks to the increasing prominence of a trust that allows investors to speculate on the commodity. Some parts of the tech world also appear to be inflating disproportionately. The movie streaming service Netflix saw its stock price skyrocket 304% over 2010 and 2011, 79 times larger than the earnings per share over the same time period. Economists worry about social media companies most of all, however. After all, Facebook makes almost all of its money on clickable ads, which some don't think translates into a venture worth $65 billion.

Worried financial pundits point the blame at the Federal Reserve for fostering a bubble culture due to their ultralow interest rates. While the Fed remains committed to keeping rates low while the economy bounces back, some see the flood of money as little more than fuel for the bubble fire. Even China has requested an interest rate increase from the Fed in order to relieve its growing inflation problem. Others have blamed the organization for inciting the recent jump in commodities costs that has led to price increases on oil and food worldwide. The Fed cited "rising global demands and disruptions in global supply" in response. While the Fed may be correct on that point, it has still not addressed the alleged presence of new bubbles in the world economy. Only time will tell if its inaction will have global repercussions or if the world's outspoken economists are incorrectly convinced that the sky is falling.

discussion questions for bonus case 19-3

1. What key economic principles can we learn from "bubbles"?

2. Is it time for the Federal Reserve to increase interest rates?

notes on discussion questions for bonus case 19-3

1. *What key economic principles can we learn from "bubbles"?*

   From the tulip bubble, to the dot-com bubble, to the real estate bubble, it's important to note that economic principles teach us that products have fundamental values and their prices cannot increase forever. We should keep in mind the adage that if something sounds too good to be true, it probably is.

2. *Is it time for the Federal Reserve to increase interest rates?*

   Ask 100 economists this question and you'll likely get a split verdict. Many support the Fed's position that interest rates need to remain ultralow due to the painfully slow recovery. Others feel the Fed is creating a global bubble ready to explode with its cheap money policy.

endnotes

---

[i] *Sources:* Steven Levy, "Surviving the IPO from Hell," *Newsweek*, August 20, 2004; "Google Stock Bargain or Bubble?" *The Clarion-Ledger*, Associated Press, December 4, 2004.

[ii] *Source:* Michael Tsang and Lee Spears, "Asia Trounces the World in IPOS," *Bloomberg Businessweek*, November 4, 2010.

[iii] *Source:* Michael J. de la Merced, "New York and German Exchanges to Merge in $10 Billion Deal," DealBook, February 15, 2011.

[iv] *Source:* "Typing Error Causes Japan Stock Confusion," *The Clarion Ledger,* Associated Press, December 10, 2005.

[v] *Sources:* Marilyn Berlin Snell, "Sister Action: The Almighty Dollar Meets Its Match in a Dominican Nun," *Sierra*, May 1, 2003; Tom Murphy, "Lilly Faction Seeks Split of Exec Roles," *Indianapolis Business Journal,* March 21, 2005; Sarah A. Webster, "Stockholders Support Ford Leadership: Few at Annual Meeting Criticize Chairman's Work," *Detroit Free Press,* May 12, 2006

[vi] *Source:* J. Alex Tarquinio, "The New ETF Pitfalls," *SmartMoney*, October 10, 2010.

[vii] *Sources:* Dennis K. Berman, "Does Wall Street Finally Need an Ethics Code?" *The Wall Street Journal,* March 10, 2005.

Money, Financial Institutions, and the Federal Reserve

chapter **20**

what's new in this edition

additions to the 10th edition:

- Name That Company: Mango
- Discussion of Bitcoin added to subsection What Is Money?
- Spotlight on Small Business: Rise of the Nonbank
- Social Media in Business: Banking on Social Media
- Reaching Beyond Our Borders: New Issues Facing the World Bank and the IMF
- Video case

revisions to the 10th edition:

- Text was revised to eliminate redundancy and tighten discussions.
- Statistical data and examples throughout the chapter were updated to reflect current information.
- Getting to Know Ben Bernanke, Chairman of the Federal Reserve

deletions from the 9th edition:

- Name That Company: Credit Unions
- Spotlight on Small Business
- Reaching Beyond Our Borders

brief chapter outline and learning goals

chapter 20

Money, Financial Institutions, and the Federal Reserve

Getting To Know BEN S. BERNANKE, CHAIRMAN of the FEDERAL RESERVE

learning goal 1

Explain what money is and what makes money useful.

I. WHY MONEY IS IMPORTANT

A. What Is Money?

learning goal 2

Describe how the Federal Reserve controls the money supply.

B. What Is the Money Supply?

C. Managing Inflation and the Money Supply

D. The Global Exchange of Money

II. CONTROL OF THE MONEY SUPPLY

A. Basics about the Federal Reserve

B. The Reserve Requirement

C. Open-Market Operations

D. The Discount Rate

E. The Federal Reserve's Check-Clearing Role

learning goal 3

Trace the history of banking and the Federal Reserve System.

III. THE HISTORY OF BANKING AND THE NEED FOR THE FED

A. Banking and the Great Depression

learning goal 4

Classify the various institutions in the U.S. banking system.

IV. THE U.S. BANKING SYSTEM

A. Commercial Banks

B. Services Provided by Commercial Banks

C. Services to Borrowers

D. Savings and Loan Associations (S&Ls)

E. Credit Unions

F. Other Financial Institutions (Nonbanks)

learning goal 5

Briefly trace the causes of the banking crisis starting in 2008 and explain how the government protects your funds during such crises.

V. THE RECENT BANKING CRISIS AND HOW THE GOVERNMENT PROTECTS YOUR MONEY

A. Protecting Your Funds

B. The Federal Deposit Insurance Corporation (FDIC)

C. The Savings Association Insurance Fund (SAIF)

D. The National Credit Union Administration (NCUA)

learning goal 6

Describe how technology helps make banking more efficient.

VI. USING TECHNOLOGY TO MAKE BANKING MORE EFFICIENT

A. Online Banking

learning goal 7

Evaluate the role and importance of international banking, the World Bank, and the International Monetary Fund.

VII. INTERNATIONAL BANKING AND BANKING SERVICES

A. Leaders in International Banking

B. The World Bank and the International Monetary Fund (IMF)

VIII. SUMMARY

lecture outline

Getting to Know BEN S. BERNANKE, Chairman of the FEDERAL RESERVE

Ben Bernanke earned a PhD from MIT and then moved up through government economics and monetary organizations. He served as chair of the President's Council of Economic Advisors, then was a member of the Board of Governors of the Federal Reserve from 2002 through 2005. He was appointed by former president George W. Bush to replace Alan Greenspan as chair of the Federal Reserve system, one of the most powerful positions in the United States. Bernanke's job became even more difficult starting in 2008 when the credit crunch and market meltdown began.

This banklike store in Austin, Texas, was designed to serve low-income clients who don't have traditional bank accounts. Customers pay a one-time $10 fee that allows them to cash checks and put the money onto debit cards. Name that company.

(Students should read the chapter before guessing the company's name: Mango)

learning goal 1

Explain what money is and how its value is determined.

I. WHY MONEY IS IMPORTANT

A. Economic growth and creation of jobs depends on money—its availability and its value relative to other currencies.

1. The recent banking crisis has focused attention on the Federal Reserve.
2. Money is so important that many institutions have evolved to manage money and to make it available to you when you need it.
3. The flow of money from country to country is as free as the flow **FROM STATE TO STATE**.
4. Each day about $4 trillion is exchanged in world markets.

lecture notes

PPT 20-1
Chapter Title

PPT 20-2
Learning Goals

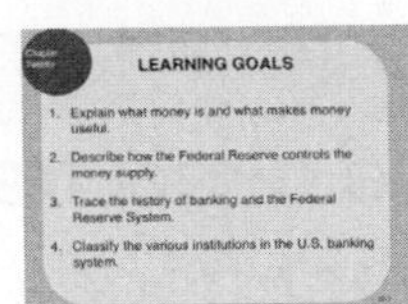

(See complete PowerPoint slide notes on page 20.52.)

PPT 20-3
Learning Goals

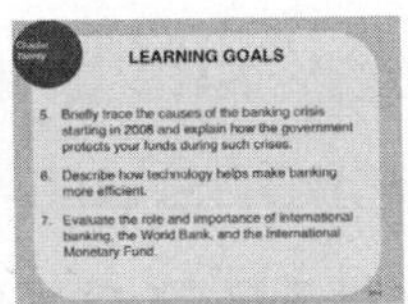

(See complete PowerPoint slide notes on page 20.52.)

PPT 20-4
Ben Bernanke

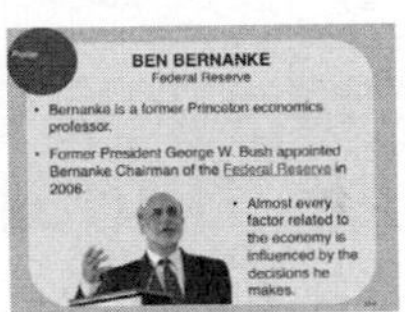

(See complete PowerPoint slide notes on page 20.53.)

PPT 20-5
Name That Company

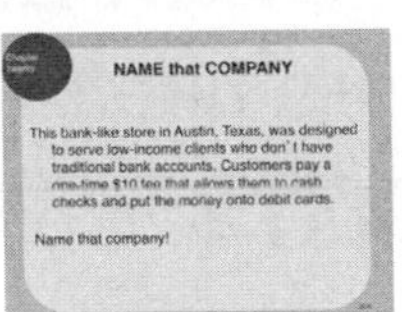

(See complete PowerPoint slide notes on page 20.53.)

lecture link 20-1

FIXED ASSETS, OR WHY A LOAN IN YAP IS HARD TO ROLL OVER

The traditional money supply in the Yap Islands consists of enormous stone wheels. (See the complete lecture link on page 20.66 in this manual.)

5. What happens to any major country's economy has an effect on the U.S. economy, and vice versa.

B. **WHAT IS MONEY?**

1. ***MONEY*** is anything that people generally accept as payment for goods and services.
2. ***BARTER*** is the direct trading of goods and services for other goods and services.
   a. Many people have discovered the benefits of bartering online.
   b. Others today still barter goods and services, but transactions are difficult.
   c. Today **BARTER EXCHANGES** let people put goods and services into the system and get credits for other goods and services.
   d. People need some form of currency that is **PORTABLE, DIVISIBLE, DURABLE, AND STABLE** so that they can trade without having to carry the actual goods.
3. **COINS AND PAPER BILLS** meet all the standards for a more useful money:
   a. **PORTABILITY**: Coins are easier to take to market than goods.
   b. **DIVISIBILITY**: Different-sized coins can be made to represent different values.
   c. **STABILITY**: When everybody agrees on the value of coins, the value of money is relatively stable.
   d. **DURABILITY**: Coins last for thousands of years.

PPT 20-6
What's Money?

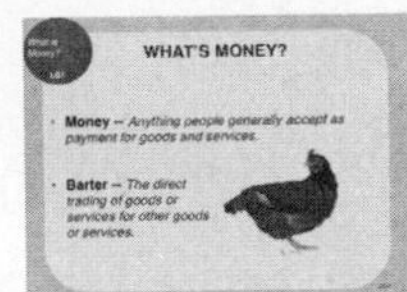

(See complete PowerPoint slide notes on page 20.53.)

critical thinking exercise 20-1
BARTERING: BUYING A PAIR OF JEANS

This exercise explores how bartering would work using the example of a pair of jeans (See complete exercise on page 20.74 of this manual.)

PPT 20-7
Standards for a Useful Form of Money

(See complete PowerPoint slide notes on page 20.54.)

lecture link 20-2
THE FATE OF THE PENNY

The lowly penny can buy very little. Should the coin be phased out? (See the complete lecture link on page 20.67 in this manual.)

e. **UNIQUENESS:**
   i. The government has had to go to extra lengths to make real dollars readily identifiable.
   ii. The new paper money has many security enhancements, including blue, peach, and green color inks.

4. Coins and paper money thus became **UNITS OF VALUE**, simplifying exchanges.
   a. Most countries have their own coins and paper that they use as money.
   b. However, they are not always equally stable.

5. **ELECTRONIC CASH (E-CASH)** is the latest form of money.
   a. You can pay bills online.
   b. You can also e-send e-cash to anyone using services such as PayPal.

learning goal 2

Describe how the Federal Reserve controls the money supply.

C. **WHAT IS THE MONEY SUPPLY?**

1. Control of the money supply involves two questions:
   a. What is the money supply?
   b. Why does it need to be controlled?

2. The ***MONEY SUPPLY*** is the amount of money the Federal Reserve Bank makes available for people to buy goods and services.

lecture link 20-3
EURO PORTRAITS

Ten years after the introduction of the euro, the European Union is honoring the original 10 adopters. (See the complete lecture link on page 20.67 in this manual.)

lecture link 20-4
DIRTY MONEY

"Dirty money" usually means money tainted by corruption, but in the Republic of the Congo, it could be literally true. (See the complete lecture link on page 20.68 of this manual.)

lecture link 20-5
CURRENCY FOR CONSUMERS WITH VISUAL IMPAIRMENTS

The United States is one of the few nations that have taken no actions to make denominations of paper money legible to individuals who are blind. (See complete lecture link on page 20.68 of this manual.)

PPT 20-8
The Money Supply

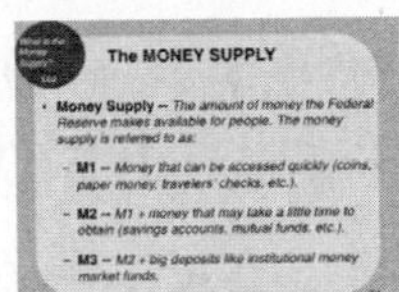

(See complete PowerPoint slide notes on page 20.54.)

3. There are several **CLASSIFICATIONS OF THE MONEY SUPPLY** (M-1, M-2, and so on).
   a. ***M-1*** is money that can be accessed quickly and easily *(coins and paper bills, checks, traveler's checks, etc.).*
   b. ***M-2*** is money included in M-1 plus money that may take a little more time to obtain *(savings accounts, money market accounts, mutual funds, certificates of deposit, and the like).*
   c. M-2 is the most commonly used definition of money.
   d. ***M-3*** is M-2 plus big deposits like institutional money market funds.

D. **MANAGING INFLATION AND THE MONEY SUPPLY**
   1. If **TOO MUCH MONEY** is available, prices go up: **INFLATION** (too much money chasing too few goods).
   2. If **TOO LITTLE MONEY** is available, prices would go down: **DEFLATION**.
   3. The prices of goods and services can be managed somewhat by controlling the amount of money available in the economy.

E. **THE GLOBAL EXCHANGE OF MONEY**
   1. **FALLING DOLLAR** means that the amount of goods and services you can buy with a dollar **GOES DOWN.**
   2. **RISING DOLLAR** means that the amount of goods and services you can buy with a dollar **GOES UP.**

lecture link 20-6
MONEY FACTS

Why do some coins have grooved edges? How much gold is in Fort Knox? (See the complete lecture link on page 20.69 of this manual.)

critical thinking exercise 20-2
TEST YOUR KNOWLEDGE OF MONEY

This exercise is a brief test of the student's knowledge of money. (See complete exercise on page 20.76 of this manual.)

PPT 20-9
New Money

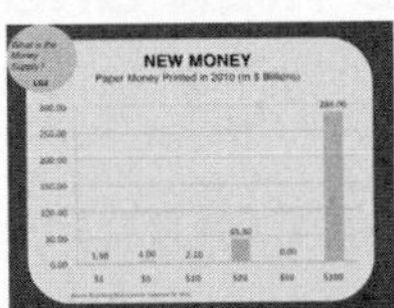

(See complete PowerPoint slide notes on page 20.54.)

PPT 20-10
How Long Does Paper Money Last?

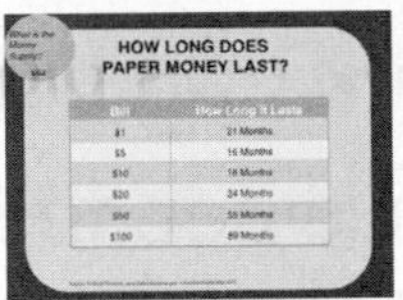

(See complete PowerPoint slide notes on page 20.55.)

PPT 20-11
Money Milestones

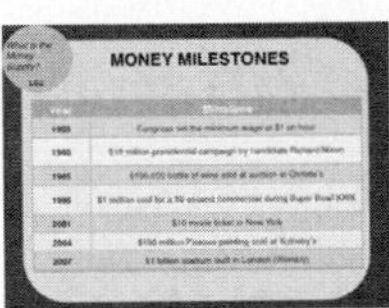

(See complete PowerPoint slide notes on page 20.55.)

PPT 20-12
Money Facts

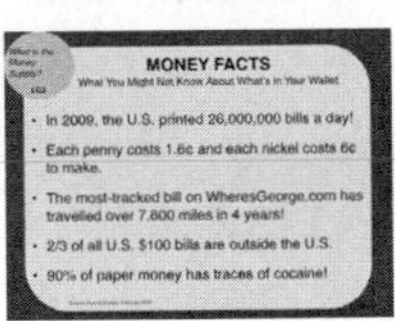

(See complete PowerPoint slide notes on page 20.55.)

PPT 20-13
Exchanging Money Globally

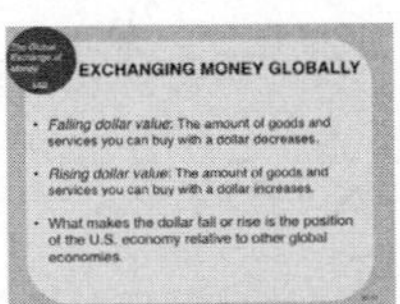

(See complete PowerPoint slide notes on page 20.56.)

3. *For example, a strong euro would drive up the cost of cars from Germany.*
4. What makes the dollar weak or strong is the **POSITION OF THE U.S. ECONOMY** relative to other economies.
    a. In a **STRONG ECONOMY**, the demand for dollars is high and the value of the dollar rises.
    b. When the country's economy is perceived as **WEAKENING**, the demand for the dollar declines and the value of the dollar falls.

II. CONTROL OF THE MONEY SUPPLY

A. An organization is needed that **CONTROLS THE MONEY SUPPLY** to try to keep the U.S. economy from growing too fast or too slowly.
   1. The organization in charge of monetary policy is the **FEDERAL RESERVE SYSTEM (THE FED).**

B. **BASICS ABOUT THE FEDERAL RESERVE**
   1. The Federal Reserve System consists of five major parts:
      a. The **BOARD OF GOVERNORS** administers and supervises the 12 Federal Reserve System banks.
         i. Seven members are appointed by the president and confirmed by the senate.
         ii. The primary function is to set monetary policy.
      b. The **FEDERAL OPEN MARKET COMMIT-TEE** has 12 voting members and is the policy-making body.

lecture notes

critical thinking exercise 20-3

CURRENCY TRADING

This exercise asks the student to research currency values and calculate several currency conversions. (See complete exercise on page 20.81 of this manual.)

PPT 20-14

The Impact of a Falling Dollar

(See complete PowerPoint slide notes on page 20.56.)

bonus case 20-1

KEEPING AHEAD OF COUNTERFEITERS

This case involves the U.S. Treasury's continuous battle to keep ahead of counterfeiters. (See the complete case, discussion questions, and suggested answers beginning on page 20.83 of this manual.)

PPT 20-15

Five Major Parts of the Federal Reserve System

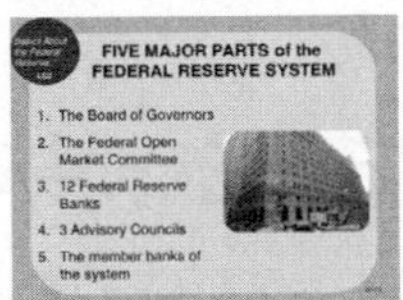

(See complete PowerPoint slide notes on page 20.56.)

PPT 20-16

The 12 Federal Reserve District Banks

TEXT FIGURE 20.1

The Federal Reserve District Banks

(Text page 558)

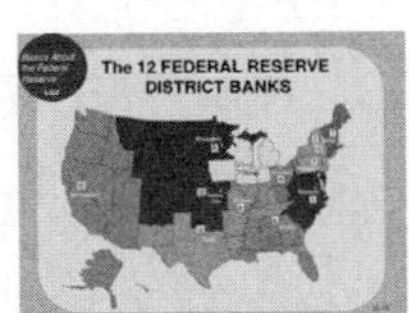

(See complete PowerPoint slide notes on page 20.57.)

c. The **12 FEDERAL RESERVE BANKS**

d. **THREE ADVISORY COUNCILS**

e. The **MEMBER BANKS** of the system

2. The **FEDERAL RESERVE:**

a. Buys and sells foreign currencies

b. Regulates various types of credit

c. Supervises banks

d. Collects data on the money supply and other economic activities

3. The **TOOLS USED TO REGULATE THE MONEY SUPPLY** include reserve requirements, open-market operations, and the discount rate.

C. **THE RESERVE REQUIREMENT**

1. The ***RESERVE REQUIREMENT*** is a percentage of commercial bank's checking and savings accounts that must be physically kept in the bank *(for example, as cash in the vault)* or a non-interest-bearing deposit at the local Federal Reserve district bank.

2. Changing the reserve requirement is one of the Fed's most powerful tools.

3. When the Fed **INCREASES THE RESERVE REQUIREMENT:**

a. Banks have **LESS MONEY FOR LOANS** and make fewer loans, which reduces inflation.

b. The money supply would be **REDUCED** and prices would likely fall.

TEXT FIGURE 20.2
How the Federal Reserve Controls the Money Supply
(Text page 558)

This text figure shows how the Federal Reserve System uses its four tools to control the money supply.

critical thinking exercise 20-4
RESEARCHING THE FEDERAL RESERVE'S TOOLS

This exercise asks the student to go online and obtain up-to-date information about the Fed's money supply management tools. (See complete exercise on page 20.82 of this manual.)

lecture link 20-7
WRENCHING INFLATION OUT OF THE ECONOMY

The U.S. inflation rate in 1979 was almost 15%. Then Federal Reserve chair Paul Volcker was appointed in 1980 with a mandate to bring inflation under control. (See the complete lecture link on page 20.70 in this manual.)

bonus case 20-2
BERNANKE'S BIG GAMBLE

The U.S. economy is slowly expanding and Ben Bernanke has announced his intention to invest $600 billion in Fed money. (See the complete case, discussion questions, and suggested answers beginning on page 20.85 of this manual.)

4. When the Fed **DECREASES THE RESERVE REQUIREMENT**:

    a. Banks have **MORE MONEY AVAILABLE FOR LOANS** and make more loans.

    b. An increase in the money supply **STIMULATES THE ECONOMY** for higher growth, but it can also create inflationary pressures.

D. **OPEN-MARKET OPERATIONS**

1. The most commonly used tool is ***OPEN-MARKET OPERATIONS***, the buying and selling of U.S. government bonds by the Fed with the goal of regulating the money supply.

2. When the Fed wants to **DECREASE THE MONEY SUPPLY**, it **SELLS GOVERNMENT SECURITIES** to the public.

3. When the Fed wants to **INCREASE THE MONEY SUPPLY**, it **BUYS GOVERNMENT SECURITIES** from individuals, corporations, or organizations willing to sell.

E. **THE DISCOUNT RATE**

1. The Fed is called the **BANKER'S BANK.**

2. Member banks can borrow money from the Fed and then pass it on to their customers.

3. The ***DISCOUNT RATE*** is the interest rate that Fed charges for loans to member banks.

4. **INCREASING THE DISCOUNT RATE** discourages banks from borrowing and consequently reduces the number of available loans, resulting in a **DECREASE IN THE MONEY SUPPLY.**

PPT 20-17
Managing the Money Supply

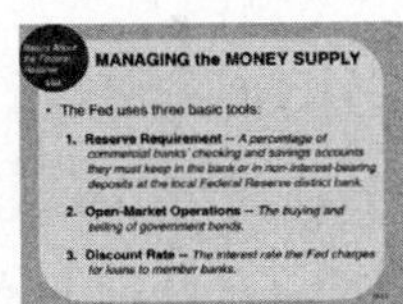

(See complete PowerPoint slide notes on page 20.57.)

5. **LOWERING THE DISCOUNT RATE** encourages bank borrowing and increases the amount of funds available for loans, resulting in an **INCREASE IN THE MONEY SUPPLY.**
6. The Fed also sets the **FEDERAL FUNDS RATE**, the rate that banks charge each other.

F. **THE FEDERAL RESERVE'S CHECK-CLEARING ROLE**

1. One of the functions of the Federal Reserve System is to help **PROCESS YOUR CHECKS.**
2. When a check is presented at another bank, a complicated process (shown in **Figure 20.3**) transfers funds from one's home bank.
3. This process is costly, so banks try to **LESSEN THE USE OF CHECKS** through use of credit cards, debit cards, and electronic transfer of money.

G. The **WHOLE ECONOMY** is affected by actions taken by the Federal Reserve System.

learning goal 3

Trace the history of banking and the Federal Reserve System.

III. THE HISTORY OF BANKING AND THE NEED FOR THE FED

A. **EARLY BANKING HISTORY**

1. There were **NO BANKS IN EARLY COLONIAL AMERICA.**
   a. Strict laws limited the number of coins that could be brought to the colonies.
   b. Colonists were forced to barter for goods.

PPT 20-18
Check-Clearing Process through the Federal Reserve

TEXT FIGURE 20.3
Check-Clearing Process through the Federal Reserve Bank System
(Text page 560)

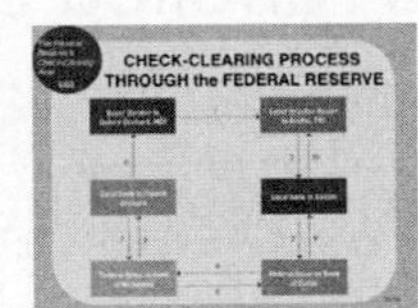

(See complete PowerPoint slide notes on page 20.57.)

progress assessment
(Text page 561)

PPT 20-19
Progress Assessment

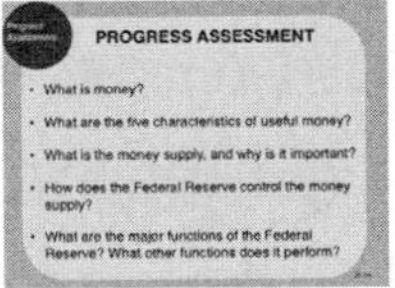

(See complete PowerPoint slide notes on page 20.58)

2. **MASSACHUSETTS** issued its own **PAPER MONEY** in 1690, and soon other colonies did as well.
   a. But **CONTINENTAL MONEY**, the first paper money printed in the U.S., became worthless because people didn't trust its value.
   b. **LAND BANKS** were established to make loans to farmers, but England stopped these practices by 1741.
   c. Colonies rebelled against these restrictions, and a new bank was formed during the American Revolution.
3. **ALEXANDER HAMILTON** convinced Congress to form a **CENTRAL BANK** in 1791.
   a. The bank had so much opposition that it closed in 1811.
   b. An attempt to replace the bank in 1816 caused conflict between the Second (Central) Bank and state banks.
   c. The bank was closed in 1836.
4. By the time of the **CIVIL WAR**, banking was a mess.
   a. Different banks issued **DIFFERENT CURRENCIES.**
   b. Often the **COINS** were worth more as gold or silver than as coins.
   c. Many people became nervous about their money and caused runs on banks; **TRUST IN BANKING DECLINED**.

lecture link 20-8
GOLDSMITH BANKING

Economists believe that modern money and banking have their roots in medieval Europe with the village goldsmith. (See the complete lecture link on page 20.71 in this manual.)

5. The cash shortage problems of 1907 led to the formation of the **FEDERAL RESERVE SYSTEM**, designated as a **"LENDER OF LAST RESORT."**
    a. All federally chartered banks **MUST** join; state-chartered banks **MAY** join.
    b. The Federal Reserve became the **BANKERS' BANK.**

B. **BANKING AND THE GREAT DEPRESSION**
1. The **STOCK MARKET CRASH OF** 1929 led to bank failures in the early 1930s.
2. People rushed to take money out of banks; **BANKS RAN OUT OF MONEY** and closed.
3. Franklin D. Roosevelt extended these bank closings in 1933 to gain time for a solution.
4. In 1933 and 1935, the federal government passed **LAWS** to strengthen the banking system.
5. The government also started an insurance program to protect depositors from bank failures.

learning goal 4

Classify the various institutions in the U.S. banking system.

IV. THE U.S. BANKING SYSTEM

A. The **U.S. BANKING SYSTEM** consists of commercial banks, savings and loan associations, credit unions, mutual savings banks, and nonbanks.

B. **COMMERCIAL BANKS**
1. A ***COMMERCIAL BANK*** is a profit-making organization that receives deposits from

PPT 20-20
The Establishment of the Federal Reserve System

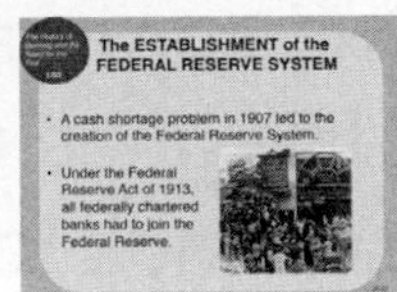

(See complete PowerPoint slide notes on page 20.58.)

bonus case 20-3
WHEN MONEY LOSES ITS MEANING

This case explores what happens when hyperinflation erodes the value of a country's money. (See the complete case, discussion questions, and suggested answers beginning on page 20.87 of this manual.)

PPT 20-21
Largest Bank Failures

(See complete PowerPoint slide notes on page 20.59.)

lecture link 20-9
RESPONSIBLE BANKING WITH CDFIS

As small-business owners have struggled to find loans from commercial banks, they've started turning to CDFIs. (See the complete lecture link on page 20.71 in this manual.)

PPT 20-22
The U.S. Banking System

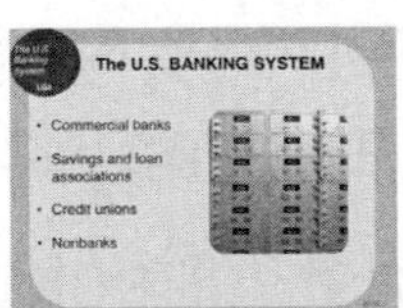

(See complete PowerPoint slide notes on page 20.59)

individuals and corporations in the form of checking and savings accounts and then uses some of these funds to make loans.

2. Commercial banks have two types of customers: **DEPOSITORS** and **BORROWERS.**
3. Commercial banks make a profit if the revenue generated by loans exceeds the interest paid to depositors.

C. **SERVICES PROVIDED BY COMMERCIAL BANKS**

1. Individuals and corporations that deposit money in a checking account can write personal checks to pay for almost any transaction.
2. A ***DEMAND DEPOSIT*** is the technical name for a checking account; the money in a demand deposit can be withdrawn anytime on demand from the depositor.
    a. Banks impose a service charge for check writing, and may charge a handling fee.
    b. In the past, checking accounts paid no interest, but interest-bearing checking accounts have grown in recent years.
3. A ***TIME DEPOSIT*** is the technical name for a savings account; the bank can require prior notice before the owner withdraws money from a time deposit.
    a. A ***CERTIFICATE OF DEPOSIT (CD)*** is a time-deposit (savings) account that earns interest to be delivered at the end of the certificate's maturity date.

lecture notes

PPT 20-23
Commercial Banks

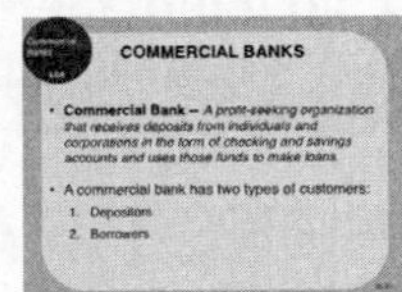

(See complete PowerPoint slide notes on page 20.59.)

PPT 20-24
Commercial Banks' Services

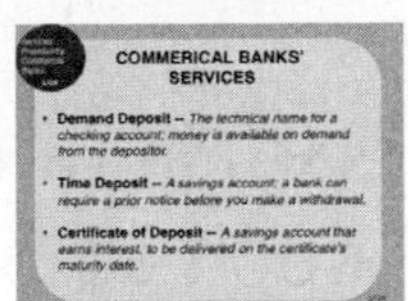

(See complete PowerPoint slide notes on page 20.60.)

social media in business
(Text page 564)

PPT 20-25
Banking on Social Media

(See complete PowerPoint slide notes on page 20.60.)

MAKING ethical decisions
(Text page 565)

PPT 20-26
What to Tell the Teller

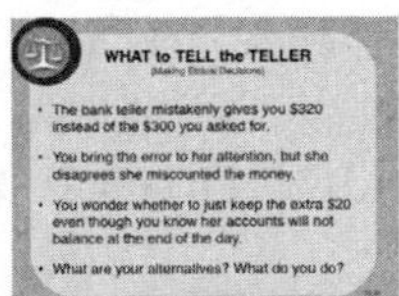

(See complete PowerPoint slide notes on page 20.60.)

b. The CD cannot be withdrawn without penalty until the **MATURITY DATE.**

c. The **INTEREST RATE** depends on the length of the period, the economic conditions, and the prime rate at the time of deposit.

4. Commercial banks may also offer **OTHER SERVICES**, such as credit cards, brokerage services, financial counseling, automatic payment of bills, safe deposit boxes, tax-deferred IRAs, travelers' checks, and overdraft privileges.

5. **AUTOMATED TELLER MACHINES (ATMs)** give customers the convenience of 24-hour banking.

D. **SERVICES TO BORROWERS**

1. Loans are generally given on the basis of the recipient's **CREDITWORTHINESS.**

2. Banks are supposed to screen loan applicants carefully to make sure that the loan plus interest will be paid back on time.

E. **SAVINGS AND LOAN ASSOCIATIONS (S&Ls)**

1. A ***SAVINGS AND LOAN ASSOCIATION (S&L)*** is a financial institution that accepts both savings and checking deposits and provides home mortgage loans.

a. S&Ls are often known as **THRIFT INSTITUTIONS** since their original purpose was to promote consumer thrift and home ownership.

PPT 20-27
Savings and Loan Associations

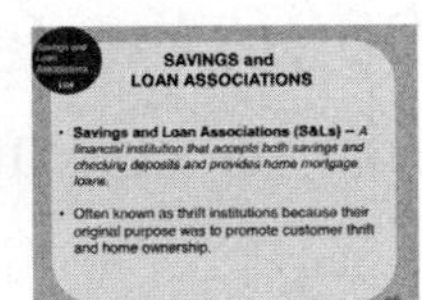

(See complete PowerPoint slide notes on page 20.61.)

   b. Thrifts were permitted to offer slightly higher interest rates to attract funds.
   c. These funds were then used to offer **LONG-TERM FIXED RATE MORTGAGES.**
   d. S&Ls no longer offer better rates than banks.
2. In the early 1980s, S&Ls ran into trouble; 20% of the nation's S&Ls failed.
   a. The biggest reason was that **CAPITAL GAINS** taxes were raised, making investments in real estate less attractive.
   b. S&Ls were left with property that was worth less than the money they had lent to investors.
   c. In the 1980s, the federal government has stepped in to strengthen S&Ls, allowing them to:
      i. Offer **HIGHER INTEREST RATES**
      ii. Allocate up to 10% of their funds to **COMMERCIAL LOANS**
      iii. Offer mortgage loans with **ADJUSTABLE INTEREST RATES**
   d. Savings and loans have become very similar to commercial banks.

F. **CREDIT UNIONS**

1. ***CREDIT UNIONS*** are nonprofit, member-owned financial cooperatives that offer the full variety of banking services to their members, including:
   a. Interest-bearing checking accounts at relatively high rates

PPT 20-28
Credit Unions

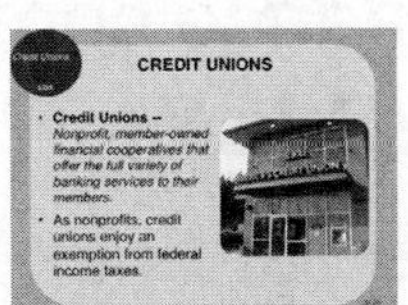

(See complete PowerPoint slide notes on page 20.61.)

   b. Short-term loans at relatively low rates
   c. Financial counseling
   d. Life insurance
   e. Home mortgage loans
2. As not-for-profit institutions, credit unions enjoy an exemption from federal income taxes.

G. **OTHER FINANCIAL INSTITUTIONS (NONBANKS)**

1. ***NONBANKS*** are financial organizations that accept no deposits but offer many of the services provided by regular banks.
   a. **NONBANKS** include life insurance companies, pension funds, brokerage firms, commercial finance companies, and corporate financial services.
   b. Nonbanks cut back their lending during the recent banking crisis.
   c. Competition between banks and nonbanks has increased making the difference between them less apparent.
   d. In response to the diverse investment alternatives offered by nonbanks, banks expanded their services.
   e. Some banks have merged with brokerage firms.
2. **LIFE INSURANCE COMPANIES** provide financial protection for policyholders who periodically pay premiums.

lecture link 20-10

CONTROVERSIAL CREDIT UNION LOANS

Some new loans issued by credit unions are almost identical to those issued by suspicious organizations. (See the complete lecture link on page 20.55 of this manual.)

PPT 20-29
Nonbanks

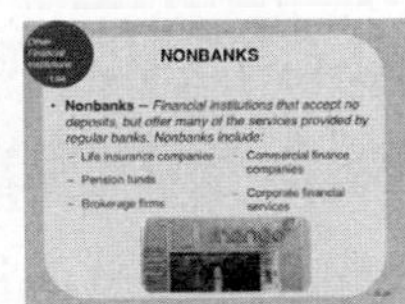

(See complete PowerPoint slide notes on page 20.61.)

SPOTLIGHT ON
small business
(Text page 567)

PPT 20-30
The Rise of the Nonbank

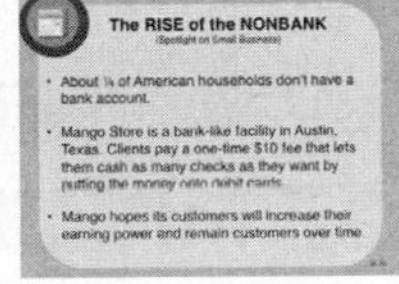

(See complete PowerPoint slide notes on page 20.62.)

PPT 20-31
What Attracts Customers to Online Banking

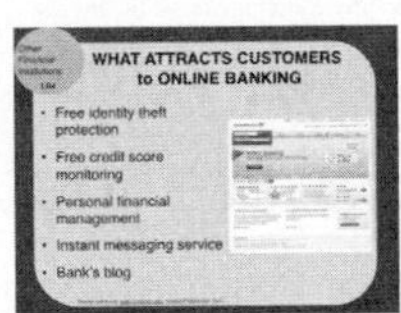

(See complete PowerPoint slide notes on page 20.62.)

3. ***PENSION FUNDS*** are amounts of money put aside by corporations, nonprofit organizations, or unions to cover part of the financial needs of members when they retire.
   a. Contributions to pensions are made by employees, employers, or both.
   b. Pension funds typically invest in low-return, but safe, corporate stocks or government securities.
   c. Many large pension funds are becoming forces in U.S. financial markets.
4. **BROKERAGE FIRMS** traditionally offered investments in stock exchanges, but now offer services such as high-yield checking/savings accounts and loans.
5. **COMMERCIAL AND CONSUMER FINANCE COMPANIES** are institutions that offer short-term loans to businesses and individuals with higher credit risks.
   a. Interest rates are higher than regular banks.
   b. Use caution when borrowing from such institutions because the **INTEREST RATES CAN BE QUITE HIGH.**

learning goal 5

Briefly trace the causes of the banking crisis starting in 2008 and explain how the government protects your funds during such crises.

V. THE RECENT BANKING CRISIS AND HOW THE GOVERNMENT PROTECTS YOUR MONEY

A. THE RECENT BANKING CRISIS

1. Who is responsible?

progress
assessment
(Text page 566)

PPT 20-32
Progress Assessment

PROGRESS ASSESSMENT

- Why did the U.S. need a Federal Reserve Bank?
- What is the difference between a bank, a savings and loan association, and a credit union?
- What is a consumer finance company?

(See complete PowerPoint slide notes on page 20.63.)

a. The Federal Reserve, in keeping cost of borrowing low

b. Congress, in creating more affordable housing

c. The Community Reinvestment Act, further encouraged loans with families with questionable ability to repay

2. Banks made risky loans and then divided their portfolios of mortgages up into **MORTGAGE-BACKED SECURITIES (MBSs)** and sold to other organizations.

    a. Banks sold more and more MBSs to consumers.

    b. The Fed and the SEC failed to provide sufficient oversight and regulatory functions.

    c. House values plummeted and people lost their homes.

3 Bank profit dropped; this led to the banking crisis.

4. Toward the end of George W. Bush's presidency, the Treasury Department created a $700 billion "bailout" package, known as the **TROUBLED ASSETS RELIEF PROGRAM (TARP),** but the program did not work as anticipated.

5. Under President Barack Obama's administration, Congress passed another $800 billion spending program to stimulate the economy.

bonus case 20-4
REFORMING WALL STREET

After the recent recession, Washington is trying to do its part in preventing another widespread collapse. (See the complete case, discussion questions, and suggested answers beginning on page 20.89 of this manual.)

B. **PROTECTING YOUR FUNDS**

1. As a result of the depression of the 1930s, several organizations evolved to protect your money.
2. Three organizations protect your money: the Federal Deposit Insurance Company (FDIC), the Savings Association Insurance Fund (SAIF), and the National Credit Union Administration (NCUA).

C. The ***FEDERAL DEPOSIT INSURANCE CORPORATION (FDIC)*** is an independent agency of the U.S. government that insures bank accounts.

1. If a bank were to be in serious danger, the FDIC would arrange to have its accounts transferred to another bank or pay off depositors up to $250,000 per account.
2. The goal is to maintain **CONFIDENCE IN BANKS** so that if one falls others don't.
3. The FDIC covers about 13,000 institutions, mostly commercial banks.

D. The ***SAVINGS ASSOCIATION INSURANCE FUND (SAIF)*** insures holders of accounts in savings and loan associations.

1. It was originally called the Federal Savings and Loan Insurance Corporation).
2. During the Great Depression, some 1,700 bank and thrift institutions failed, and people lost confidence in them.
3. The FDIC and FSLIC were designed to **CREATE MORE CONFIDENCE** in banking institutions.
4. In the 1980s, the FSLIC was placed under the FDIC (and renamed) to better control banking.

PPT 20-33
Protecting Depositors' Money

(See complete PowerPoint slide notes on page 20.63.)

E. The **NATIONAL CREDIT UNION ADMINISTRATION (NCUA)**

1. The NCUA provides up to $250,000 coverage per depositor.
2. Additional protection can be obtained by holding accounts jointly or in trust.

learning goal 6

Describe how technology helps make banking more efficient.

VI. USING TECHNOLOGY TO MAKE BANKING MORE EFFICIENT

A. Banks have long looked for ways to make the system more efficient.

1. **CREDIT CARDS** reduce the flow of checks but have their own costs.
   a. There will be more electronic rather than physical exchange of money in the future.
   b. If you must use a credit card, look for one that offers the best deal for you.
2. ***ELECTRONIC FUNDS TRANSFER (EFT) SYSTEM*** is a computerized system that electronically performs financial transactions such as making purchases, paying bills, and receiving paychecks.
   a. EFT tools include electronic check conversion, debit cards, smart cards, direct deposits, and direct payments.
   b. The latest technology is the **GO-TAG**, a chip with a radio transmitter inside that can stick to a cell phone and make payments fast and easy.

PPT 20-34
Technological Advancements in Banking

(See complete PowerPoint slide notes on page 20.63)

lecture link 20-11
THE FUTURE OF TRANSFERRING MONEY

The days of credit card company dominance may be coming to a close as PayPal and other companies are changing the cashless industry. (See the complete lecture link on page 20.72 of this manual.)

3. Debit cards **ELIMINATE THE PAPER-HANDLING COSTS** of using checks.
    a. A ***DEBIT CARD*** is an electronic funds transfer tool that serves the same function as checks; it withdraws funds from a checking account.
    b. Your spending is limited to the amount that is in your account.
    c. A debit card is swiped at a point-of-sale terminal signaling the bank to immediately transfer funds.
    d. Some companies use **PAYROLL DEBIT CARDS** to reduce paper processing.
4. A ***SMART CARD*** is an electronic funds transfer tool that is a combination credit card, debit card, phone card, driver's license card, and more.
    a. The magnetic strip on a credit card is replaced with a microprocessor.
    b. The card can store a variety of information, including the bank balance.
    c. Some smart cards have embedded radio-frequency chips.
5. **AUTOMATIC TRANSFERS**
    a. A **DIRECT DEPOSIT** is a credit made directly to a checking or savings account, such as automatically deposited paychecks.
    b. A **DIRECT PAYMENT** is a preauthorized electronic payment.

PPT 20-35
Smart Cards

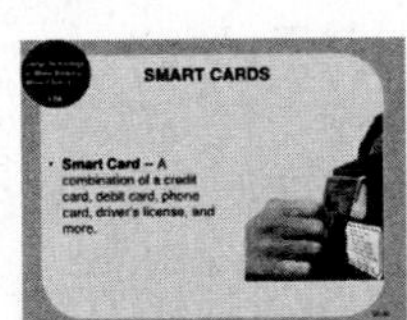

(See complete PowerPoint slide notes on page 20.64.)

B. **ONLINE BANKING**

1. Using online banking, you can complete all your financial transactions from home on your computer:
   a. Transfer funds from one account to another.
   b. Pay bills.
   c. Check account balances.
   d. Apply for a car loan or mortgage.
   e. Buy and sell stocks and bonds.
2. Internet banks such as E*Trade Bank offer online banking only, not physical branches.
   a. They can offer higher interest rates and lower fees.
   b. Some people are nervous about online security and fear putting their money into online banks.
   c. Others want to talk to a banking professional in person.
3. The future seems to be with traditional banks that offer both online services and brick-and-mortar facilities.

learning goal 7

Evaluate the role and importance of international banking, the World Bank, and the International Monetary Fund.

VII. INTERNATIONAL BANKING AND BANKING SERVICES

A. Banks help businesses conduct business in other countries by providing three services.

PPT 20-36
Making Transactions in Other Countries

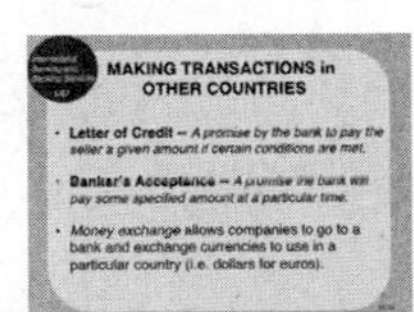

(See complete PowerPoint slide notes on page 20.64.)

1. A ***LETTER OF CREDIT*** is a promise by the bank to pay the seller a given amount if certain conditions are met.
2. A ***BANKER'S ACCEPTANCE*** is a promise that the bank will pay some specified amount at a particular time.
3 **CURRENCY EXCHANGE** is the exchange of one country's currency for another country's currency.
4. ATMs now may provide foreign currency.

B. **LEADERS IN INTERNATIONAL BANKING**

1. In the future, many crucial financial issues will be international in scope.
2. Today's money markets form a **GLOBAL MARKET SYSTEM.**
   a. Large international banks make investments in any country where they can earn maximum return.
   b. World economies are linked into **ONE INTERRELATED SYSTEM** with **NO REGULATORY CONTROL.**
   c. American firms must compete for funds with firms all over the world.
3. Banking is no longer a domestic issue—it is an international issue.
4. The world economy has evolved, financed by international banks.

lecture notes

C. **THE WORLD BANK AND THE INTERNATIONAL MONETARY FUND (IMF)**

1. The World Bank and the IMF are twin intergovernmental pillars that support the structure of the world's banking community.
2. The ***WORLD BANK*** is the bank primarily responsible for financing economic development; it is also known as the **INTERNATIONAL BANK FOR RECONSTRUCTION AND DEVELOPMENT.**
   a. Today, most of the money is lent to developing nations to raise productivity and raise the standard of living.
   b. Recently, the World Bank has received considerable criticism regarding human rights, AIDS, and the environment.
   c. Some want the bank to forgive the debts of less developed countries or stop making loans until the country makes economic reforms.
3. The ***INTERNATIONAL MONETARY FUND (IMF)*** is an organization that assists the smooth flow of money among nations.
   a. About 185 countries are voluntary members of the IMF.
   b. It requires members to allow their own money to be exchanged for foreign currencies freely and keep the IMF informed about changes in monetary policy.

PPT 20-37
Leading Institutions in International Banking

(See complete PowerPoint slide notes on page 20.64.)

REACHING BEYOND
our borders
(Text page 573

PPT 20-38
New Issues Facing the World Bank and the IMF

(See complete PowerPoint slide notes on page 20.65.)

c. The IMF is not primarily a lending institution, rather an **OVERSEER** of member countries monetary and exchange rate policies.

d. The IMF has allowed some countries like Brazil, South Korea, and Turkey to put up barriers to protect their currencies from inflation.

VIII. SUMMARY

progress
assessment
(Text page 573)

PPT 20-39
Progress Assessment

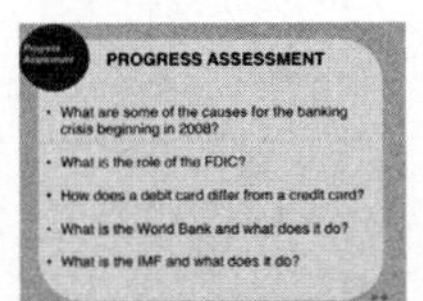

(See complete PowerPoint slide notes on page 20.65.)

PowerPoint slide notes

PPT 20-1
Chapter Title

PPT 20-2
Learning Goals

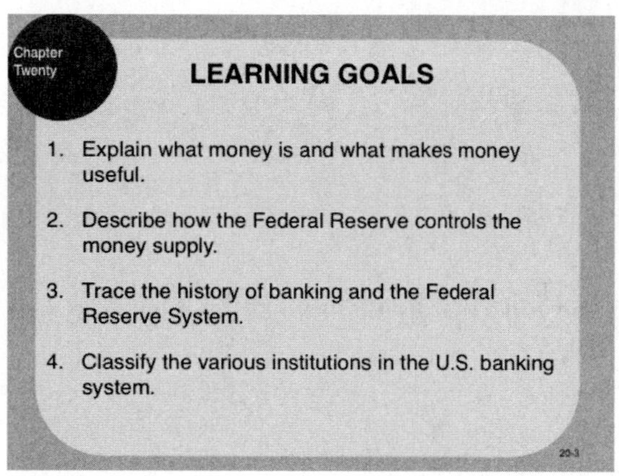

PPT 20-3
Learning Goals

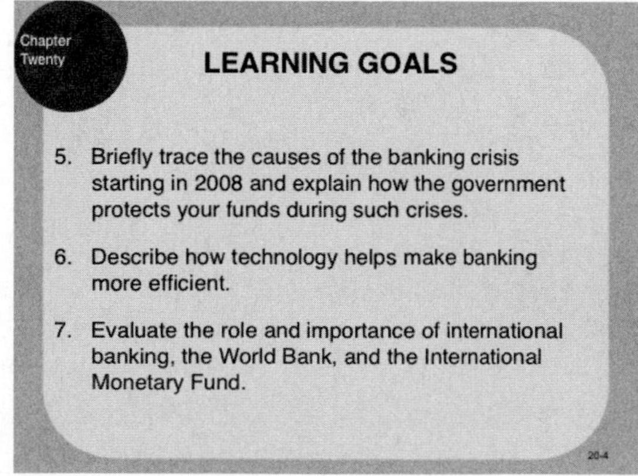

PPT 20-4
Ben Bernanke

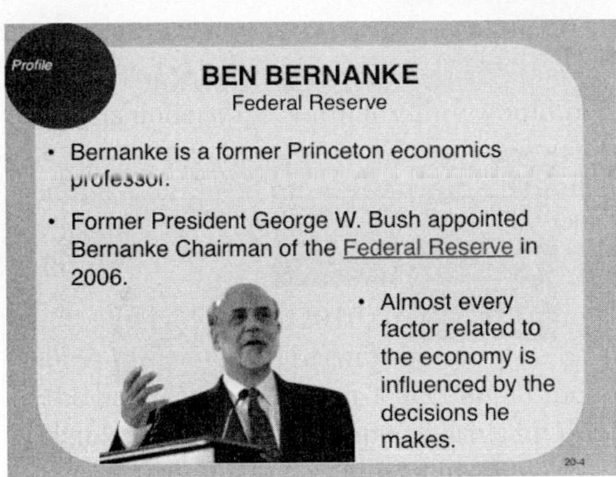

PPT 20-5
Name That Company

Company: Mango

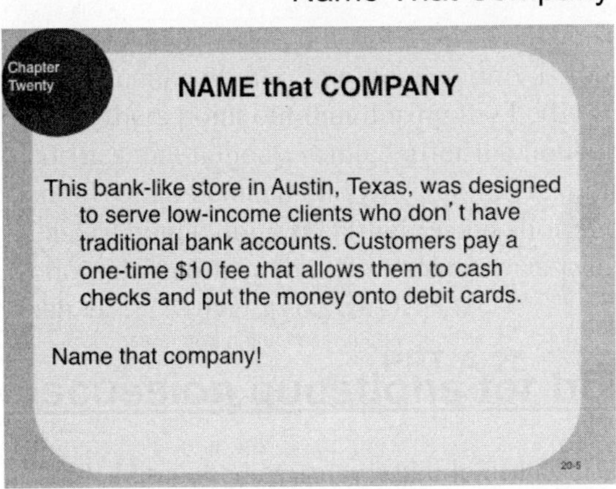

PPT 20-6
What's Money?

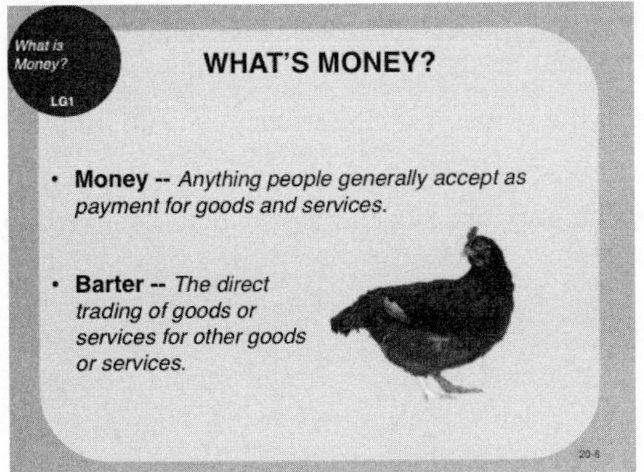

PPT 20-7
Standards for a Useful Form of Money

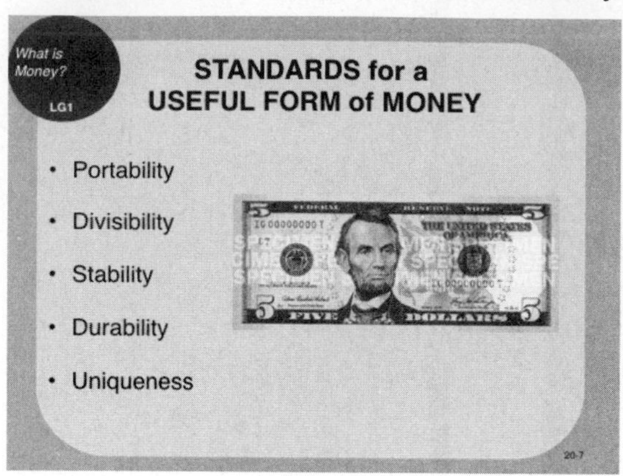

The new $100 bill has features like a 3-D ribbon, as well as ink with microscopic flakes that shift color.

PPT 20-8
The Money Supply

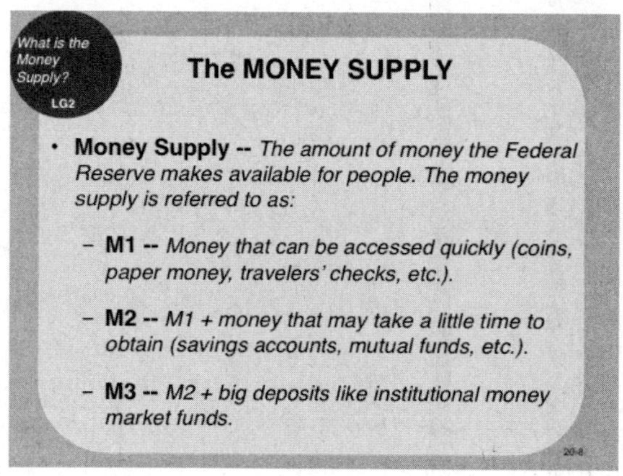

PPT 20-9
New Money

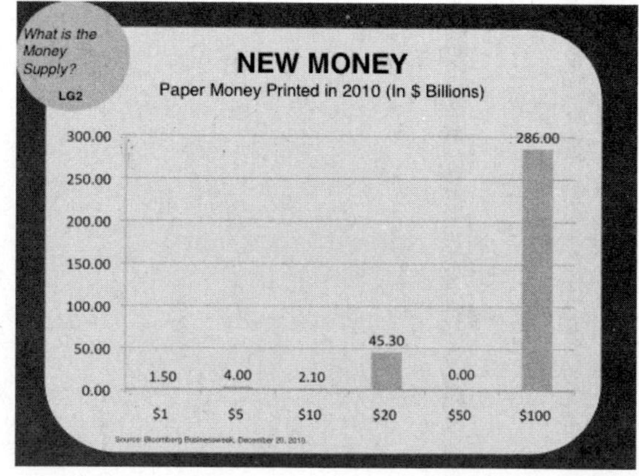

1. This slide shows the value of different bills printed in 2010.
2. In 2010 over 1 billion $1 bills, 2 billion $20 bills, and over 2 billion $100 bills were printed.
3. Most of the value of U.S. currency is $100 bills.
4. In 2010 the United States printed more bills in every category but $1s and $50s when compared to 2009.

PPT 20-10
How Long Does Paper Money Last?

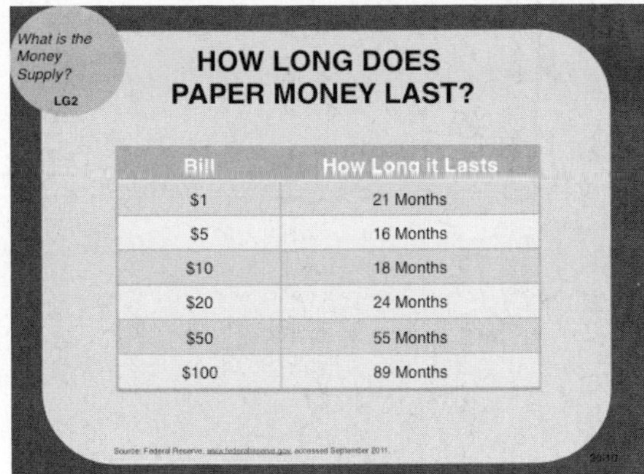

Bill	How Long it Lasts
$1	21 Months
$5	16 Months
$10	18 Months
$20	24 Months
$50	55 Months
$100	89 Months

1. This slide gives the students an idea of the life span of paper money in circulation.
2. The largest denomination ever printed was a $100,000 gold certificate.
3. Share with students some interesting facts regarding U.S. currency:
   - Originally, U.S. currency included denominations of $500, $1,000, $5,000, and $10,000. No currency printed today is greater than $100.
   - The percentage of U.S. counterfeit currency in circulation is estimated to be .02%.
   - U.S. currency bills are 2.61 inches wide, 6.14 inches long, and .0043 inch thick, and weigh 1 gram.
   - It costs 4.2 cents to produce a U.S. bill.

PPT 20-11
Money Milestones

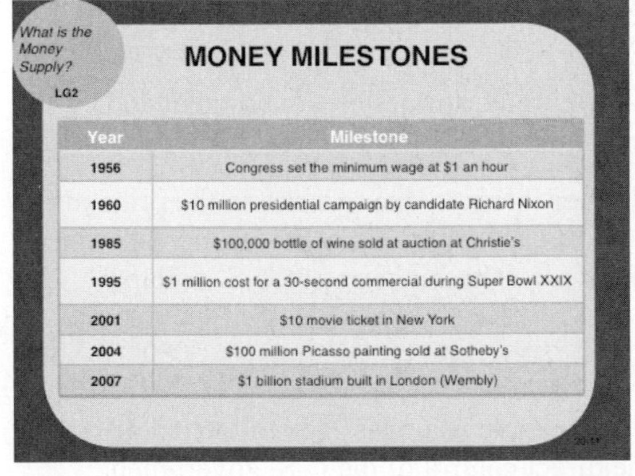

Year	Milestone
1956	Congress set the minimum wage at $1 an hour
1960	$10 million presidential campaign by candidate Richard Nixon
1985	$100,000 bottle of wine sold at auction at Christie's
1995	$1 million cost for a 30-second commercial during Super Bowl XXIX
2001	$10 movie ticket in New York
2004	$100 million Picasso painting sold at Sotheby's
2007	$1 billion stadium built in London (Wembly)

1. This slide illustrates some interesting dates regarding U.S. money.
2. Have students look through the dates. Which do they find most interesting or surprising and why?
3. Ask the students, How do some of the amounts listed compare to today?

PPT 20-12
Money Facts

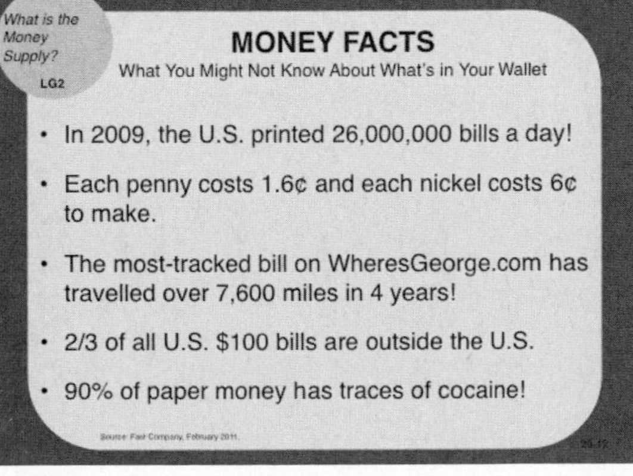

PPT 20-13
Exchanging Money Globally

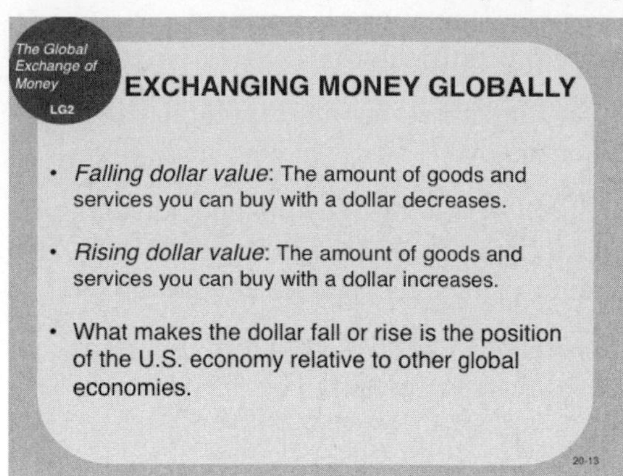

Since the United States abandoned the gold standard, the U.S. dollar has depreciated by approximately 90%.

PPT 20-14
The Impact of a Falling Dollar

1. This slide highlights some of the issues related to a falling dollar.
2. While these points are positive, the long-term implications of a falling dollar are more serious.
3. A declining dollar will eventually result in the following:
    - Higher interest rates on government and consumer debt.
    - Higher inflation due to a rise in the price of imports, and commodity prices increase since most are priced in terms of U.S. dollars.

PPT 20-15
Five Major Parts of the Federal Reserve System

Basics About the Federal Reserve
LG2

FIVE MAJOR PARTS of the FEDERAL RESERVE SYSTEM

1. The Board of Governors
2. The Federal Open Market Committee
3. 12 Federal Reserve Banks
4. 3 Advisory Councils
5. The member banks of the system

20-15

The Federal Reserve is a quasi-governmental agency not under the direct control of the U.S. government.

PPT 20-16
The 12 Federal Reserve District Banks

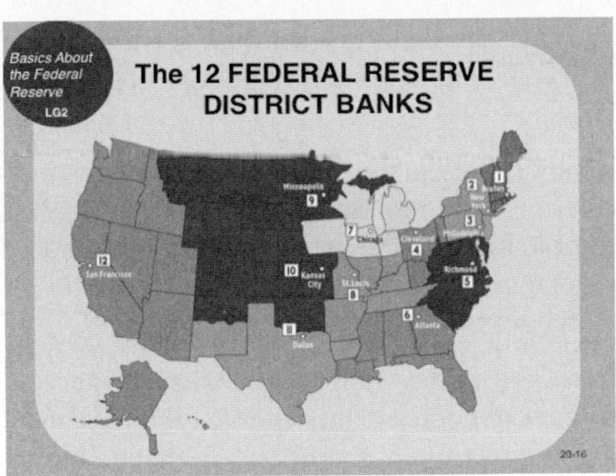

PPT 20-17
Managing the Money Supply

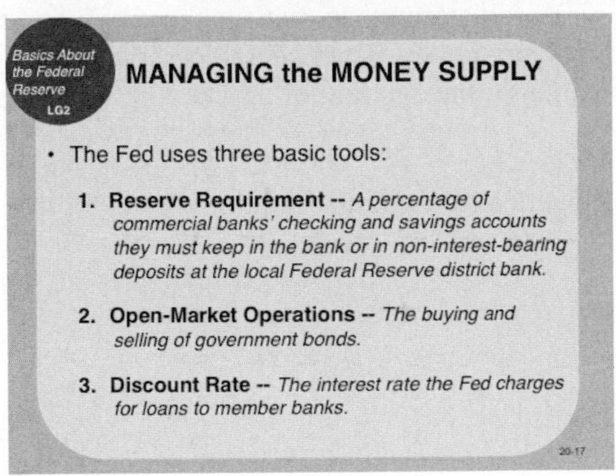

PPT 20-18
Check-Clearing Process through the Federal Reserve

See Figure 20.3 in the text for further information.

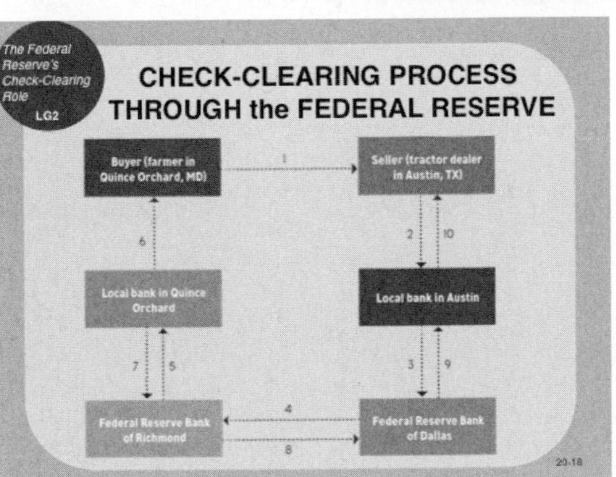

PPT 20-19
Progress Assessment

PROGRESS ASSESSMENT

Progress Assessment

- What is money?
- What are the five characteristics of useful money?
- What is the money supply, and why is it important?
- How does the Federal Reserve control the money supply?
- What are the major functions of the Federal Reserve? What other functions does it perform?

20-19

1. Money can be anything that people accept as payment for goods and services.
2. The five characteristics of useful money are portability, divisibility, stability, durability, and uniqueness.
3. The money supply is the amount of money available for people to buy goods and services. It is important to manage the money supply, since too much money could cause inflation and too little money may cause deflation.
4. To control the money supply the Federal Reserve can increase or decrease the reserve requirement, buy or sell government securities, or change the discount rate.
5. The Federal Reserve is responsible for creating an environment that fosters stable prices and full employment. It attempts to manage these two goals with monetary policy. The Federal Reserve is also responsible for the clearing of checks.

PPT 20-20
The Establishment of the Federal Reserve System

The ESTABLISHMENT of the FEDERAL RESERVE SYSTEM

The History of Banking and the Need for the Fed
LG3

- A cash shortage problem in 1907 led to the creation of the Federal Reserve System.
- Under the Federal Reserve Act of 1913, all federally chartered banks had to join the Federal Reserve.

20-20

State banks were also permitted to join.

PPT 20-21
Largest Bank Failures

1. This slide highlights the largest bank failures in U.S. banking history.
2. Three of these failures are a direct result of the financial crisis that started in 2008.
3. Ask the students, Why didn't the Washington Mutual and IndyMac Bank failures create a total loss of confidence in the U.S. banking system like we saw during the Great Depression? *(Students should be able to recognize the stepped-up role of the U.S. government including the creation of the FDIC insurance program and the increase in FDIC coverage from $100,000 to $250,000.*

PPT 20-22
The U.S. Banking System

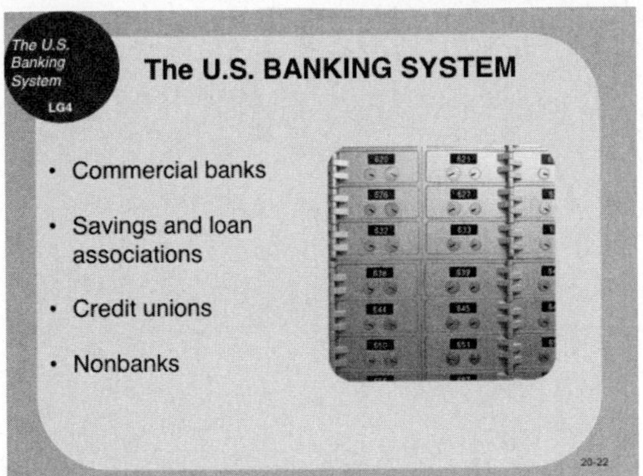

PPT 20-23
Commercial Banks

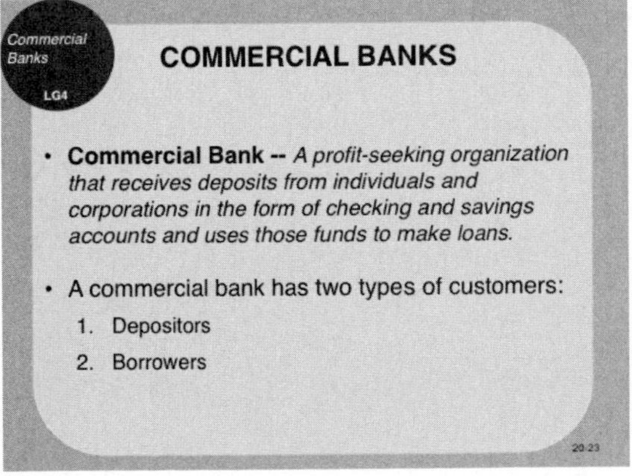

PPT 20-24
Commercial Banks' Services

Commercial banks also offer credit cards, financial counseling, automatic payment of bills, brokerage services, safe-deposit boxes, travelers' checks, and individual retirement accounts (IRAs).

PPT 20-25
Banking on Social Media

PPT 20-26
What to Tell the Teller

PPT 20-27
Savings and Loan Associations

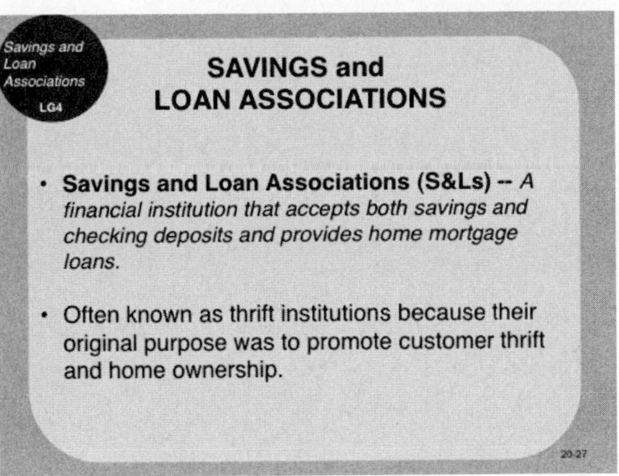

PPT 20-28
Credit Unions

Due to their exemption from federal income taxes, credit unions' fees are typically less and the interest rates paid on deposits are often higher.

PPT 20-29
Nonbanks

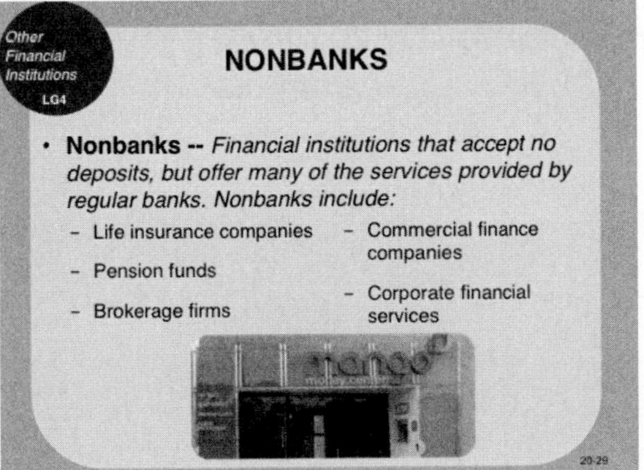

PPT 20-30
The Rise of the Nonbank

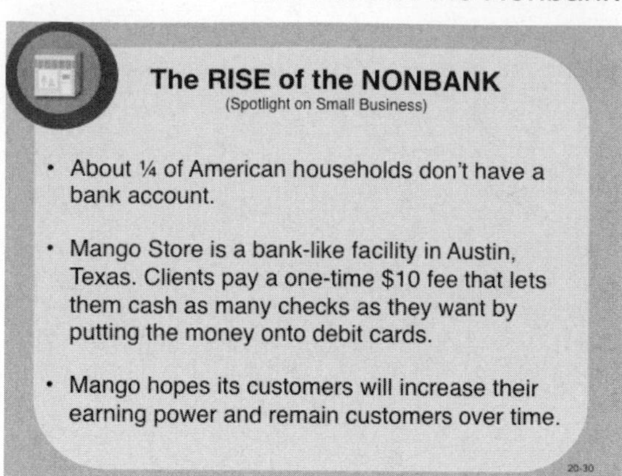

PPT 20-31
What Attracts Customers to Online Banking

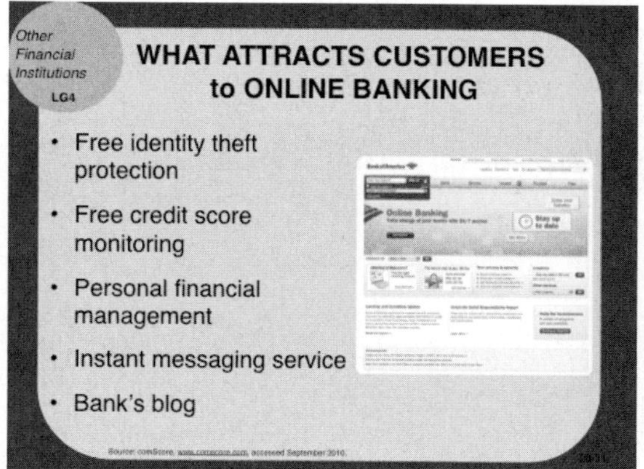

1. This slide illustrates what attracts customers to online banking.
2. Households increased their use of online banking from approximately 8 million households to 51 million households in 2009.
3. Leading the growth of online banking are California, Florida, and Texas. Combined, these states made up more than 40% of the growth in online banking. Others in the top 10 for growth were Washington, Georgia, Arizona, North Carolina, Missouri, and Maryland.
4. More than 71% of online banking customers report they are highly satisfied with their online banking experience.
5. According to ComScore, the adoption of online banking is rising at a rate of 13% each year. And in 2011, 76 million households will bank online compared with 51 million in 2009.

PPT 20-32
Progress Assessment

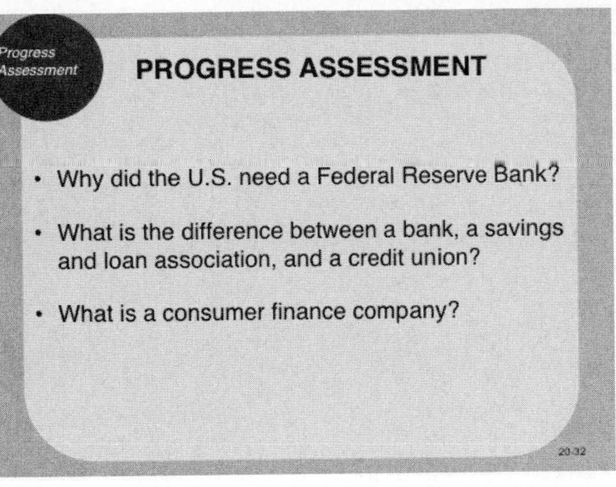

1. The Federal Reserve emerged after the banking crisis of 1907 and was organized originally to be a lender of last resort.
2. After bank deregulation, the services offered by banks and S&Ls are now similar. They both offer many of the same services. Credit Unions are tax-exempt member-owned cooperatives that operate like banks.
3. Consumer finance companies offer short-term loans to those who cannot meet the credit requirements of regular banks.

PPT 20-33
Protecting Depositors' Money

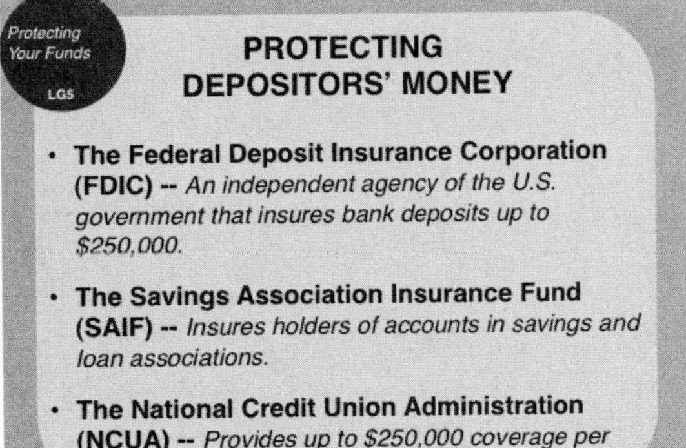

The amount of depositors' insurance was increased to $250,000 to create confidence in the banking system.

PPT 20-34
Technological Advancements in Banking

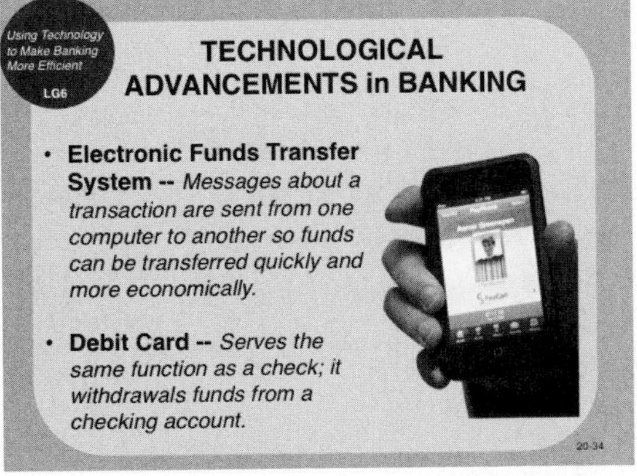

PPT 20-35
Smart Cards

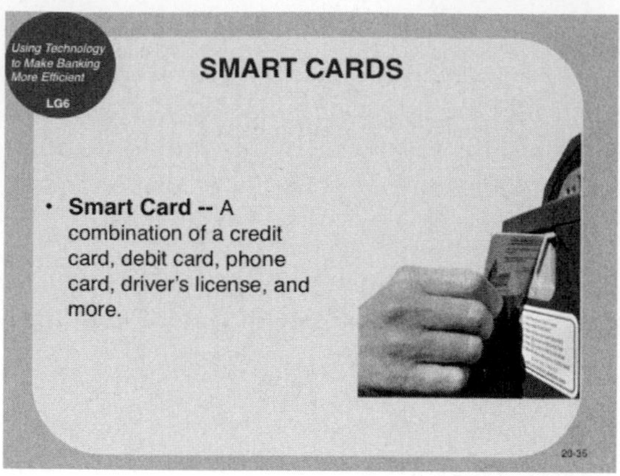

PPT 20-36
Making Transactions in Other Countries

PPT 20-37
Leading Institutions in International Banking

Both the World Bank and the IMF were created to rebuild the world economy after World War II.

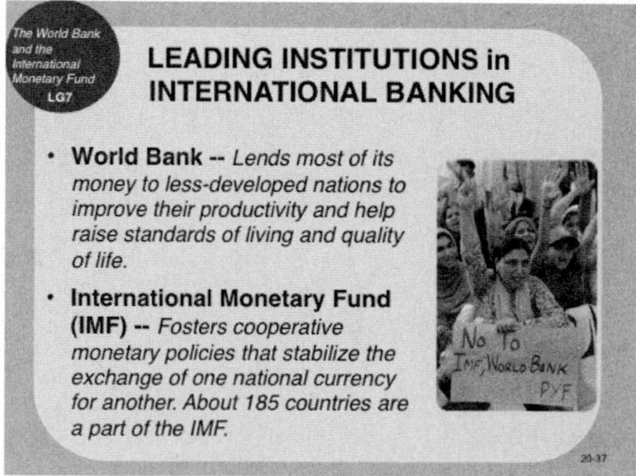

PPT 20-38
New Issues Facing the World Bank and the IMF

NEW ISSUES FACING the WORLD BANK and the IMF
(Reaching Beyond Our Borders)

- A debt crisis in Europe; Japan trying to recover from its earthquake and tsunami; major disruptions in the Middle East; China and Brazil are having problems with high inflation; and rising food prices are happening all over the planet.
- Poorer nations are having a particularly hard time because of the high food prices.
- The IMF and the World Bank are both trying to come up with answers to the global issues that have become very serious.

20-38

PPT 20-39
Progress Assessment

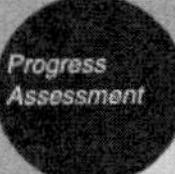

PROGRESS ASSESSMENT

- What are some of the causes for the banking crisis beginning in 2008?
- What is the role of the FDIC?
- How does a debit card differ from a credit card?
- What is the World Bank and what does it do?
- What is the IMF and what does it do?

20-39

1. After the Internet bubble of the late 1990s, the Federal Reserve lowered interest rates creating a situation in which mortgage rates were low thus fueling a housing boom. Banks relaxed their underwriting standards and created mortgage-backed securities and sold them to organizations throughout the world. The government did not regulate these transactions well and banks collapsed as housing values fell and individuals defaulted on their loans.
2. The role of the FDIC is to insure bank deposits if a bank were to fail. Bank deposits are currently insured up to $250,000.
3. Unlike a credit card, a debit card functions as a check, withdrawing funds directly from a checking account. The debit card allows you to spend only money that is in your account; once the balance is zero the card cannot be used. If the card is used with a zero balance, it will result in overdrafts.
4. The World Bank, also called the International Bank for Reconstruction and Development, is responsible for financing economic development.
5. The IMF was established to assist the smooth flow of money among nations. Nations must join the IMF and allow for flexible exchange rates, inform the IMF of changes in a country's monetary policy, and modify policies on the advice of the IMF.

lecture links

"Money is power, freedom, a cushion, the root of all evil, the sum of all blessings."
Carl Sandburg

"A fool and your money are soon partners."
Mark's Law of Monetary Equalization

lecture link 20-1

FIXED ASSETS, OR WHY A LOAN IN YAP IS HARD TO ROLL OVER

On the tiny South Pacific island of Yap, Micronesia, life is easy and the currency is hard. Elsewhere, the world's troubled monetary system creaks along, and devaluations are commonplace. But on Yap, the currency is as solid as a rock. In fact, it is rock—limestone, to be precise.

For nearly 2,000 years, the Yapese have used large stone wheels to pay for major purchases, such as land, canoes, and permission to marry. Yap is a U.S. trust territory, and the dollar is used in grocery stores and gas stations. But reliance on stone money, called rai stones, continues.

The people of Yap have been using stone money ever since a Yapese warrior named Anagumang first brought the huge stones over from limestone caverns on neighboring Palau, some 1,500 to 2,000 years ago. Inspired by the moon, he fashioned the stones into large circles. The residents of Palau required Yapese to pay in beads, coconuts, and copra for the privilege of quarrying. Yap has no limestone, and it was viewed by the Yapese as an exotic luxury, much like gold and diamonds are to the rest of the world. Every village chief wanted a bigger stone than his rivals.

The discs took years to carve, and the journey to bring such massive objects back to Yap, in wooden canoes through rough seas, was an extremely dangerous one. Many boats sank. Sailors drowned, and hundreds of enormous rocks sunk to the ocean floor.

Human nature being what it is, the danger only increased the demand. The worth of stone money doesn't depend on size. Instead, the pieces are valued by how hard it was to get them to the island. The earliest stones, brought by war canoe by Anagumang and his descendants, are the most precious because they cost so many lives to bring in. Although the heavily laden Yapese canoes were fitted with outriggers, they often capsized during the 280-mile ocean voyage from Palau.

Next in value are some stones cut on Palau in the 1870s by David Dean O'Keffe, a shipwrecked American sailor who escaped from the island and returned later with a Chinese junk. O'Keffe, who helped transport the boulders in return for Yapese help in processing dried coconut, ultimately ran the island as a self-styled emperor. Finally, there are a few mechanically chiseled stone wheels brought in without problems by German traders in the late 1800s and early 1900s. But the value of these is much lower than the older stones. The Yapese can tell the difference—many of the stones had (and still have) individual names.

Rai stones are used in social transactions like marriages, inheritance, political deals, even ransom in battle. The largest are 10 feet in diameter and weigh 4 tons. Some of the smaller stones are about the size of a saucer. These smaller "coins" are everyday money, used to buy fish and pigs.

Yapese lean the stone wheels against their houses or prop up rows of them in village "banks." Each has a hole in the center so it can be slipped onto a tree trunk and carried. It takes 20 people to lift some wheels.

By custom, the stones are worthless when broken. Rather than risk a broken stone, Yapese tend to leave the larger stones where they are and make a mental accounting that the ownership has been transferred—much as gold bars used in international transactions change hands without leaving the vault of the New York Federal Reserve Bank.

There are some decided advantages to using massive stones for money. They are immune to black-market trading, are impossible to counterfeit, and pose formidable obstacles to pickpockets. With only about 6,600 stone wheels remaining on the island, the money supply stays level. Stone wheels don't make good pocket money, so for small transactions, Yapese use other forms of currency. In addition to U.S. dollars, beer is widely used for trading.

Stone money has its limits. Most of the island's few retail stores won't accept it for general merchandise. But stone money remains and important part of Yapese traditions. There are instances in Yap where you cannot use U.S. money. One is the settling of disputes. If a Yapese wants to settle an argument, he brings his adversary stone money as a token. The apology is accepted without question.

Stone money even figured in international diplomacy. Micronesia president Tosiho Nakayama brought a stone disk when he visited the United States in 1984. Officials say Nakayama intended the stone as Micronesia's symbolic contribution toward reducing the U.S. budget deficit.

lecture link 20-2

THE FATE OF THE PENNY

The lowly penny gets no respect. In early American, a penny bought a loaf of bread, but it is now sliding into obsolescence due to inflation. Fifty-eight percent of Americans say they stash pennies in piggy banks, jars, and drawers instead of spending them like other coins. Stray pennies turn up everywhere: in streets, cars, sofas, beaches, even landfills.

The U.S. Mint is the money-making government operation in more ways than one. Pennies have traditionally been moneymakers for the government. In 2005, the Mint made $730 million in profits. However, it now costs the U.S. Mint more than 1 cent to make a penny. Higher prices for component metals have raised the basic cost of a penny to 1.4 cents. Multiply that by 7 or 8 billion pennies made each year, and it comes to a $20 million loss. This imbalance is a milestone for the Mint because coins have historically cost less to produce than the face value.

Some people think this expense is ridiculous and are petitioning the government to retire the penny. However, Gallup polling has shown that two-thirds of Americans want to keep the penny coin. There's even a pro-penny lobby called Americans for Common Cents. The push to retire the penny gained traction in 1989 with a bill in Congress to round off purchases to the nearest nickel. Although that bill failed, there is again pressure to eliminate the money-losing coin. The same Gallup poll found that 2% of Americans admit to just throwing pennies out.

Others view the penny as a reassuring symbol of tradition and hesitate to abandon it. Some also argue that eliminating the penny would hurt the poor. A study by a former Federal Reserve economist shows that rounding hurts lower-income citizens most because only cash transactions would have to be rounded up.[i]

lecture link 20-3

EURO PORTRAITS

The euro is the currency of 15 European Union nations, but each country is able to customize one side of the coins that they circulate. The images described below are on the 1-euro coin of the first 11 EU countries:

- *Austria:* Shows Mozart, who was born and raised in Salzburg
- *Belgium:* Shows Albert II, king of the Belgians since 1993
- *Finland:* Shows the whooper swan, the national bird of Finland
- *France:* Features the motto "liberté, égalité, fraternité"
- *Germany:* Features the eagle, an ancient symbol of the German state
- *Ireland:* Shows a harp, which has been an Irish icon since medieval times
- *Italy:* Shows Da Vinci's Vitruvian Man, used to map proportion
- *Luxembourg:* Shows Grand Duke Henri, ruler of the world's last grand duchy
- *Netherlands:* Shows Queen Beatrix, who succeeded her mother in 1980
- *Portugal:* Shows the royal seal used by Portugal's first king in 1144
- *Spain:* Features King Juan Carlos, Franco's successor

lecture link 20-4

DIRTY MONEY

"Dirty money" is usually considered money tainted by corruption. In the Democratic Republic of the Congo (formerly Zaire) the meaning can be literal. Bills have become filthy; some are even contaminated with diseases.

The Congolese franc first came into circulation in 1998 when Laurent Kabila overthrew the government then in power. Kabila gave the country its new name and issued a new, more stable currency. Unfortunately, the political situation continued to deteriorate. As the Civil War continued, the government began printing more and more money, devaluing the value of the Congolese franc. Soon the cost of printing bills was prohibitive, so francs remained in circulation long past their prime.

Unsanitary handling practices contribute to the deterioration of the bills. Congolese don't use wallets; instead, they carry their money against their bodies. The deteriorating bills soon became known as *blessés de guerre*, or casualties of war.

Some degree of stability has been restored by Joseph Kabila, who took power after his father's assassination in 2001. The country has been able to secure international loans, and the worn-out francs are slowly being retired.[ii]

lecture link 20-5

CURRENCY FOR CONSUMERS WITH VISUAL IMPAIRMENTS?

The American Council of the Blind scored a victory in 2006 when a federal district judge ruled that American currency violates the Federal Rehabilitation Act because denominations are not easily distinguishable by blind people. Since 1983 the advocacy group has been urging U.S. Treasury officials to make paper money easier for individuals who are blind to use.

Blind people typically determine the denominations of paper money by using bill-reading machines or by asking sighted people a bill's value and then folding the various denominations in different ways. The November 2006 district court decision ruled that if blind people "cannot accurately identify paper money without assistance" they are being illegally denied "meaningful access" to the currency, in violation of the law.

Fixing the U.S. currency could be expensive. The costliest option—adopting different-sized bills for different denominations—would require an initial investment of about $225 million for new presses and plates, according to the U.S. Treasury. Other options suggested include microperforations in the bills or raised intaglio printing. Advocates for people with visual impairments point out that the Treasury's budget of $4.2 billion over the past 10 years has incorporated major currency revisions—color-shifting ink, microprinting, and plastic security threads—in 1996 and 2004.

Of the 180 nations using paper currency today, the United States is the only one currently taking no steps to make denominations legible to people who are blind.[iii]

lecture link 20-6

MONEY FACTS

WHAT ARE PENNIES MADE OF?

Contrary to popular opinion, pennies are no longer made of pure copper. From 1793 to 1837 pennies were indeed pure copper. In 1837, the Mint added 5% tin and zinc to create bronze pennies. In 1962, the cent's tin content was removed, leaving 95% copper and 5% zinc. To further reduce the cost of component metals, the composition was changed to 97.5% zinc and 2.5% copper in 1982.

WHY DO SOME COINS HAVE GROOVES ON THE EDGES?

The dollar, half-dollar, quarter, and 10-cent coins were originally produced from precious metals (gold and silver). Grooved, or "reeded," edges were added to deter counterfeiting and stop the filing down of the edges to recover the precious metals. The 1-cent and 5-cent pieces are considered "minor" coins, and have never contained precious metals. Although none of the coins produced for circulation today contain precious metals, the reeded edges are still incorporated. The edges are useful to users who are visually impaired. The 10-cent and the 1-cent coins are similar in size; the reeding of the 10-cent coin makes it easy to identify by touch.

WHY ARE CERTAIN PRESIDENTS CHOSEN FOR CERTAIN COINS?

The presidents who appear on the front side of circulating coins are all selected by Congress in recognition of their service to the country. The Lincoln cent was issued in 1909 to commemorate the 100th anniversary of Abraham Lincoln's birth. The image on the nickel is Thomas Jefferson. The portrait was chosen in 1938 in a design competition among 390 artists. One year after Franklin Roosevelt's death, his portrait was added to the dime and released to the public on January 20, 1947, FDR's birthday. The portrait of George Washington on the quarter was selected to commemorate the 100th anniversary of his birth. Following President John Kennedy's assassination in 1963, the Treasury issued a new 50-cent piece bearing his portrait in February 1964.

HOW MANY COINS ARE MINTED EACH YEAR?

The total number of coins minted in 2005 is given below:

- 1¢ 7,700,050,500
- 5¢ 1,741,200,000
- 10¢ 2,85,5000,000
- 25¢ 3,013,600,000
- 50¢ 7,300,000
- $1 5,040,000

HOW MUCH GOLD IS STORED IN FORT KNOX?

The U.S. Bullion Depository at Fort Knox, Kentucky, currently holds 147.3 million ounces. The highest gold holdings occurred in December 1941—649.6 million ounces. The only gold that is ever removed is a small sample used to test the purity of the gold in routine audits. The gold is held as an asset of the United States and has a book value of $42.22 per ounce. Each gold bar is 7 inches by 3 5/8 inches by 1 ¾ inches, and weighs approximately 400 ounces (27.5 pounds). In addition to the stored gold, the Fort Knox Depository has in the past stored the Declaration of Independence, the U.S. Constitution, the Articles of Confederation, Lincoln's Gettysburg Address, three volumes of the Gutenberg Bible, and Lincoln's second inaugural address. The Mint has also stored valuable items for other government agencies. The Magna Carta was once stored there, as was the crown, sword, scepter, orb, and cape of St. Stephen, King of Hungary. These items were returned to the government of Hungary in 1978.[iv]

(**Critical Thinking Exercise 20-2,** "Test Your Knowledge of Money," on page 20.76 also deals with this topic.)

lecture link 20-7

WRENCHING INFLATION OUT OF THE ECONOMY

The Federal Reserve's primary function is to control the money supply. It uses its tools to increase or decrease the money supply in response to changing economic conditions. When the economy is slowing, the Fed increases the money supply, which results in lower interest rates and more investment. When the economy is overheated, the Fed takes money out of circulation, driving up interest rates.

But during the late 1970s, the economic conditions were more complicated. The economy was less than robust—the decade saw a series of economic dips—but at the same time, inflation was driving up prices at an alarming rate. The combination became known as "stagflation." In 1979, the inflation rate was 14.6%. A dollar at the beginning of the year would be worth less than 85 cents by the end of the year. Prices increased rapidly, followed by wages. Because of the declining value of money, consumers rushed out to buy products before prices increased. More money chasing a fixed amount of goods drove inflation up still further.

During the 1970s, the Fed managed the economy with an eye on interest rates. If interest rates increased, the Fed put more money into circulation. The goal was a stable interest rate to provide equilibrium in nation's economy.

In 1980, President Jimmy Carter appointed Paul Volcker as chair of the Federal Reserve with a mandate to stabilize inflation. Volcker brought a radical new philosophy to the Fed leadership. Instead of using interest rates to control the economy, he believed that the only hope for stopping inflation was to control inflation's fuel—the money in circulation.

The Fed immediately put the brakes on the money supply. Then it relied on basic laws of supply and demand to set the price of the fixed amount of money in circulation. With less money created, the existing money in circulation became more valuable. In order to secure financing, businesses had to pay more for the money they needed and the cost of money (the interest rate) soared.

By 1981, the prime interest rate peaked at 21.5%. The high interest rate dramatically affected all businesses activity, but the housing market was hit especially hard. The difference between a mortgage at 8% and a mortgage at 14% amounted to hundreds of dollars a month in increased mortgage expense. Realtors and homeowners scrambled to find creative financing options to move property. The high interest rates also brought business expansion to a halt, throwing the economy into recession.

Volcker's Fed held fast to its fixed money philosophy. By 1982, it succeeded in reducing the inflation rate to 3.9%, but the cost was high. The U.S. unemployment rate that year climbed to 9.7%. Almost 1 in 10 workers was out of a job.

The economy gradually stabilized, and interest rates dropped steadily. The public had learned the lesson—they no longer expected prices to soar, and pressure on wages gradually decreased. Although President Reagan has been credited with reining in inflation, the true credit goes to Fed chair Paul Volcker, appointed by the previous Democratic president.

lecture link 20-8

GOLDSMITH BANKING

Many economists believe that modern money and banking have their roots in medieval Europe. Toward the end of the Middle Ages, Europe was a dangerous place to live, especially if one had gold and silver coins so attractive to bandits. Most villages had only one institution that could safely store precious metal—the village goldsmith. The goldsmiths, makers and sellers of plate and jewelry, flourished in the 1500s after the monasteries were dissolved, increasing the available supplies of gold.

Many goldsmiths developed strong connections with the monarchy, and most began to take in valuables for safekeeping in their vaults. The locals also brought their gold and silver to the goldsmith's vault. In exchange, the goldsmith would write a receipt stating that Joe Nobleman had 15 gold coins on deposit. When local sales transactions were made, the villager and merchant would go to the goldsmith shop and withdraw the needed amount of coins. Often, the merchant would turn around and leave the same coins with the goldsmith for safety.

Inevitably, the inconvenience of meeting and physically exchanging gold coins led villagers to trade not coins, but rather the *receipts* for coins from the goldsmith. These receipts circulated in the area, with all buyers and sellers aware that the paper could be traded at any time for the underlying precious metal. Some enterprising goldsmith eventually noticed that the gold he had in storage rarely left the vault, and one gold coin was like every other gold coin. From that point, it was a simple step to loan part of the gold in storage to others, for a fee. In its earliest form, we have the first paper money and the first bank loan with interest.

By 1677, there were 44 goldsmith bankers in London. Two of the oldest surviving banks, Coutts & Co and Child & Co, which originated as goldsmith bankers, continue to operate as part of The Royal Bank of Scotland Group today.

Incidentally, paper money was not developed first in Europe, but in China, probably during the 600s A.D. The Italian trader Marco Polo traveled to China in the 1200s and was amazed to see the Chinese using paper money instead of coins.[v]

lecture link 20-9

RESPONSIBLE BANKING WITH CDFIS

A common complaint among small-business owners these days is that banks have been too reluctant to lend since the financial meltdown. As a result, some companies seek assistance from local sources like community development financial institutions (CDFIs). Originally founded by socially motivated investors and faith-based groups, CDFIs provide loans and financial education to small businesses in impoverished areas. And ironically enough, most new capital for CDFIs comes from large commercial banks, with over $1 billion in investment in 2010 coming from Citi, Goldman Sachs, and others.

So why fund CDFIs while remaining stingy lending through traditional banks? For one, CDFIs operate in a far more disciplined fashion than most commercial banks. If borrowers fail to pay back loans, the CDFI itself takes the financial hit, not the investors. To combat delinquency, CDFIs take an active interest in securing their loans, going so far as to knock on a borrower's door even if a payment is one day late. Most importantly, though, CDFIs offer their clients a wealth of educational services. After all, keeping the borrower's business alive is a sure way to sustain their loan payments, so CDFIs help businesses with everything from bookkeeping to business strategy.

Large commercial banks focused on maximizing profit simply can't afford to tend to their clients so closely. Nor can they match CDFIs' abilities to substantially impact depressed communities in a positive way. CDFIs are unique in that when the economy contracts, their market expands. And in the wake of a banking crisis coupled with a decades-long exodus of industrial interests, CDFIs like local credit unions and loan and equity funds can be the sole financial lifeline for otherwise isolated communities. All told, CDFIs manage a staggering $30 billion in assets, and their methods are attracting attention from high places. First Lady Michelle Obama, for instance, based the Obama administration's Healthy Food Financing Initiative on a Pennsylvania CDFI that has financed more than 85 health food stores across the state.[vi]

lecture link 20-10

CONTROVERSIAL CREDIT UNION LOANS

For millions of Americans, credit unions serve as a safe haven from profit-driven banks and predatory payday lenders. As a result, members are more prone to trust their credit union than other financial institutions. But recent regulation changes may crush that confidence for some. Due to the National Credit Union Administration's increase of the interest rate cap on short-term loans, some credit unions are now in direct competition with slippery payday lenders.

Some new loans issued by credit unions are almost identical to those issued by suspicious street corner outlets. The NCUA's rate hike allows credit unions to charge as much as 28% interest on small loans that give borrowers at least one month to pay. Sky-high interest rates don't tell the whole story, though. Credit unions are also allowed to charge an application fee for each new loan, which subsequently inflates the overall rate to astronomical proportions. For instance, a two-month $200 loan with a $20 application fee translates into an annual interest rate of more than 100%. Lenders can charge even more if they sell loans in states that need not operate inside the federal program. At one credit union in Utah, a $12 fee attached to its five-day $100 "MyInstaCash" loan kicks the annual rate up to 876%.

It may seem strange that more than 500 federally insured credit unions would choose to offer payday loans in these days of widespread financial mistrust. After all, who can consumers count on if not nonprofit institutions? Unfortunately, many of the nation's credit unions are tilting into the red, with 7% of about 4,600 firms designated by the NCUA as "serious supervisory concerns" or at high risk of failure. Given that their nonprofit nature prevents credit unions from raising capital investment, short-term loans present an appealing path toward profitability for many firms. While some credit unions continue to tout these loans as "alternatives" to payday lenders, the National Consumer Law Center has called for regulators to put a halt to this practice. In the meantime, potential borrowers are advised, as always, to read the fine print and find out exactly what they're getting into when they sign on the dotted line.[vii]

lecture link 20-11

THE FUTURE OF TRANSFERRING MONEY

When credit cards first came on the scene in the early 1960s, card issuers maintained expensive and technologically advanced infrastructures in order to provide customers with a convenient way to spend money. Companies levied fees on each transaction in order to offset costs. Now transferring money electronically is a streamlined and relatively inexpensive process, but somehow the fees have gotten much higher. In 1991, MasterCard had only four fees, with the highest one clocking in at 2.08%. Today it has 243 separate fees, including one that tops out to more than 3%. For retailers, the fees are a necessary evil given the prevalence of credit cards in this day and age.

But the days of credit card company dominance could be numbered. Since 1998, the eBay-owned online money transfer system PayPal has been finding ways to circumvent the exorbitant fees incurred on vendors by card companies. PayPal cuts out intermediaries by dealing in direct bank deposits and automatic bill payment systems rather than give a cut to banks and card issuers. The business is no doubt a success, transacting $47 billion last year alone. However, that number is a pittance compared to the $2 trillion in credit card transactions and $1.3 trillion in debit transactions handled by the credit card industry in 2009.

However, in November 2009 PayPal did something that could change the industry. The company opened its code to the public, allowing any programmer to build on and change the PayPal model. So far, 15,000 developers created new payment systems built on PayPal. Some of these new companies are using the code to eliminate needless fees. TwitPay, for example, allows users to instantly transfer cash using their Twitter account. Another company, Square, allows vendors to accept physical credit card payments without using an expensive (and fee-inducing) card swipe reader. These "alternative payment systems" already account for 20% of all online transactions, with experts predicting it will grow to 30% by 2013.[viii]

critical thinking exercises

Name: ______________________________

Date: ______________________________

critical thinking exercise 20-1

BARTERING: BUYING A PAIR OF JEANS

As the text notes, bartering was used rather than money in early commerce. In fact, countries suffering from hyperinflation have resorted to bartering in more recent years. Let's see how cumbersome bartering can become and how difficult it is to get your needs met in a barter economy.

Suppose you live in a barter economy and you need to buy pair of jeans. Listed below are six people who live in your community. Each person has goods or services that he or she can trade to satisfy a particular need. You must figure out how to barter so that you get that pair of jeans. Be sure to indicate how much of each good or service is traded. Does everyone get his or her need met? Why? (This exercise is more fun if it is done in groups, with each person playing a specific role.)

YOU:

Have: Artistic talent and advertising experience

Need: Pair of jeans

GREAT VALUE STORE:

Has: Pair of jeans

Needs: Shelves stocked

BUBBLES AND BOWS:

Has: Facilities to clean and mend clothes

Needs: Flyers to advertise opening of new store

SLY SLIVERBOTTOM:

Has: Two tickets to the Falling Rock concert

Needs: Music video by the Royal Paynes

MAC CANNICK:

Has: A gas station

Needs: Clothes cleaned

CLARK CLERK:

Has: Time and ability to stock shelves

Needs: Gas for his pickup truck

notes on critical thinking exercise 20-1

Students must decide how much of each good or service (represented by the Xs below) are involved in each transaction. Students will disagree on the worth of each good or service. This disagreement is one of the problems of a barter economy.

The solution is:

First, you must trade X number of flyers for X loads of clothes cleaning with Bubbles and Bows.

Second, you must trade X loads of clothes cleaning for X gallons of gas with Mac Cannick.

Third, you must trade X gallons of gas for X hours of stock shelving with Clark Clerk.

Fourth, you must trade X hours of stock shelving for X pairs of jeans with Great Value Store.

Sly Sliverbottom doesn't seem to get his video since no one needs his concert tickets. That's one of the problems in a barter economy: some people have nothing to trade.

This exercise emphasizes how awkward and cumbersome a barter economy is and how important money is in facilitating exchange of goods and services. Ask your students to identify the problems of a barter economy.

Name: ____________________

Date: ____________________

critical thinking exercise 20-2

TEST YOUR KNOWLEDGE OF MONEY

ANSWER THE FOLLOWING QUESTIONS ABOUT MONEY.

1. Where is the U.S. stock of gold and silver bullion stored? What is the value of these assets?

2. Whose signature appears on U.S. currency?

3. What is the largest denomination bill issued today?

4. When is it legal to reproduce a U.S. dollar note?

5. How many commercial banks are there in the United States?

MATCH THE PORTRAIT THAT APPEARS ON THE FRONT OF U.S. CURRENCY WITH THE DENOMINATION OF THAT BILL.

_______ 6. Benjamin Franklin

_______ 7. Ulysses S. Grant

_______ 8. Andrew Jackson

_______ 9. George Washington

_______ 10. Abraham Lincoln

critical thinking exercise 20-2 (continued)

_______ 11. Thomas Jefferson

_______ 12. Alexander Hamilton

a. $1

b. $2

c. $5

d. $10

e. $20

f. $50

g. $100

MATCH THE NAME OF THE CURRENCY WITH THE COUNTRY THAT ISSUES IT.

_______ 13. Dollar

_______ 14. Rupee

_______ 15. Peso

_______ 16. Dinar

_______ 17. Pound

_______ 18. Baht

_______ 19. Rand

_______ 20. Franc

_______ 21. Yen

_______ 22. Krona

a. Sweden

b. Japan

c. South Africa

d. Iraq

critical thinking exercise 20-2 (continued)

e. New Zealand

f. Thailand

g. Pakistan

h. United Kingdom

i. Switzerland

j Argentina

MARK EACH STATEMENT EITHER TRUE OR FALSE.

_______ 23. A retailer is required by law to accept any U.S. coins in payment for goods.

_______ 24. U.S. dollars are backed by the country's gold and silver assets.

_______ 24. U.S. quarters and dimes have no silver content.

_______ 26. The U.S. government plans to recall all currency and replace it with the newly designed currency.

_______ 27. It costs the U.S. Mint more than 1 cent to mint a penny.

_______ 28. The $1 bill makes up 20% of the currency printed by the U.S. Mint.

notes on critical thinking exercise 20-2

1. *Where is the U.S. stock of gold and silver bullion stored? What is the value of these assets?*

   The U.S. stock of gold and silver is stored at Fort Knox, Kentucky. The second part of this question is harder to answer. As of 2008, the United States had 147.7 million ounces of bullion stored at Fort Knox. The U.S. gold stock is listed at a "standard value" set at $42.2222 per ounce. Using this price, the value of the bullion is over $6 trillion. However, gold on the open market trades at significantly higher prices. Recently, an ounce of gold traded at a historic high of $928. If the U.S. gold stock were stated at market value, the total valuation would be over $137 trillion. (Interestingly, the gold stored in Fort Knox has not been inventoried since the 1950s, so the actual amount of bullion is the subject of some controversy.)

2. *Whose signature appears on U.S. currency?*

   The signature on all U.S. currency is that of the secretary of the treasury. From 2003 to 2006, the secretary of the treasury was John W. Snow. In 2009, Henry M. Paulson became treasury secretary. President Barack Obama appointed Timothy Geithner as treasury secretary in 2009.

3. *What is the largest denomination bill issued today?*

   Today the largest denomination bill is $100. There have been $500 notes, $1,000 notes, even $100,000 notes, but they were phased out beginning in 1946 as checks became more widely used for large debts.

4. *When is it legal to reproduce a U.S. dollar note?*

   It is illegal to reproduce a U.S. dollar note at 100% of its size. It is not illegal to reproduce a note if it is less than three-fourths or more than one and one-half the size of the original.

5. *How many commercial banks are there in the United States?*

   In 2005, there were 7,527 commercial banks.

MATCHING

Denominations:

6. Benjamin Franklin—g ($100)
7. Ulysses S. Grant—f ($50)
8. Andrew Jackson—e ($20)
9. George Washington—a ($1)
10. Abraham Lincoln—c ($5)
11. Thomas Jefferson—b ($2)
12. Alexander Hamilton—d ($10)

Currencies:

13. Dollar—e (New Zealand)

14. Rupee—g (Pakistan)

15. Peso— j (Argentina)

16. Dinar—d (Iraq)

17. Pound—h (United Kingdom)

18. Baht—f (Thailand)

19. Rand—c (South Africa)

20. Franc—i (Switzerland)

21. Yen—b (Japan)

22. Kronor—a (Sweden)

TRUE OR FALSE

23. *A retailer is required by law to accept any U.S. coins in payment for goods.*

    False. There is no federal law that mandates that a person must accept currency or coins as payment for goods or services *not yet provided.* For example, a bus line may prohibit payment of fares in pennies or dollar bills. Some gas stations as a matter of policy may refuse to accept currency of a large denomination, such as notes above $20, as long as the notice is posted and a transaction has not already been completed.

24. *U.S. dollars are backed by the country's gold and silver assets.*

    False. In the past, the U.S. Treasury issued notes backed by precious metals. You can still occasionally find a "silver certificate" that is backed by silver. Today's currency is almost exclusively "Federal Reserve Notes," backed only by our faith in the U.S. economy.

25. *U.S. quarters and dimes have no silver content.*

    True. U.S. quarters and dimes are now minted using 75% copper and 25% nickel.

26. *The U.S. government plans to recall all currency and replace it with the newly designed currency.*

    False. The new currency will gradually replace older bills in circulation, but the U.S. government will NOT recall older currency.

27. *It costs the U.S. Mint more than 1 cent to mint a penny.*

    True. In 2006, it cost 1.4 cents to produce one penny.

28. *The $1 bill makes up 20% of the currency printed by the U.S. Mint.*

    False. The $1 bill makes up about 47% of our currency. (It costs only 4 cents to produce a dollar bill.)

Name: ______________________________

Date: ______________________________

critical thinking exercise 20-3

CURRENCY TRADING

Currencies of various nations are valued by the market in relation to other currencies. The rates are available daily in *The Wall Street Journal* (in the "Currency Markets" chart in the "Money and Investing" section). They are also available on many websites, such as the Universal Currency Converter (www.xe.com/ucc),[ix] CNNMoney (http://money.cnn.com/markets/currencies/), or Yahoo Finance (www.finance.yahoo.com). (Sometimes the Web address for a location changes. You might need to search to find the exact location mentioned.) Using one of these sources, determine the following:

1. What is the value in United Kingdom pounds of 100 U.S. dollars?

2. How many Canadian dollars will 20 U.S. dollars buy?

3. What is the value in Euros of 100 United Kingdom pounds?

4. How many Euros will 1,000 Japanese yen buy?

5. What is the value in Mexican pesos of 100 Canadian dollars?

6. How many Japanese yen will 500 United Kingdom pounds buy?

7. How many U.S. dollars would it take to buy $1,000 in Canadian dollars?

8. What is the value in Japanese yen of 1,000 Deutsche marks?

Name: ______________________

Date: ______________________

critical thinking exercise 20-4

RESEARCHING THE FEDERAL RESERVE'S TOOLS

The purpose of this exercise is to encourage students to find up-to-date information about the money management tools used by the Federal Reserve System. The information can be obtained by visiting the Federal Reserve Board website at www.federalreserve.gov.[x] (Sometimes the Web address for a location changes. You might need to search to find the exact location mentioned.)

1. What is the current federal funds percentage rate? How has this rate changed in the past year?

2. What is the current reserve requirement for banks? Is the reserve requirement the same for all banks ("depository institutions")?

3. What is the primary concern of the Fed Open Market Committee now—inflation or recession?

4. Look back at the Open Market Committee actions for previous years. Compare the actions of the Federal Reserve today with those two years ago. How has the emphasis changed?

bonus cases

bonus case 20-1

KEEPING AHEAD OF COUNTERFEITERS

Counterfeiting used to be very straightforward. Crooks just found the best engraver who painstakingly attempted to reproduce the details in U.S. currency notes. The Department of Treasury tried to keep one step ahead by adding anticounterfeit measures to the currency. A sweeping change to the appearance of all paper money occurred in 1929. All currency was reduced in size by about 30%, and designs were standardized for each denomination, making it easier for the public to distinguish between genuine and counterfeit notes.

In the 1990s, advanced reprographic technology made it possible to reproduce the colors and details of security documents and currency. In the face of digital scanners, sophisticated copiers, and computer software, the security of the U.S. currency became inadequate. In 1990, a security thread and microprinting were introduced to deter counterfeiting by this advanced equipment. The note's denomination is printed on the threads in bills larger than $1. Since it is visible to transmitted light, not reflected light, the thread is difficult to copy with a color copier. Each denomination has a unique thread position to guard against counterfeit techniques such as bleaching a lower denomination bill and using the paper to "reprint" the bill as a higher valuation. The thread in each denomination glows a different color under ultraviolet light. The $5 note glows blue, the $10 note glows orange, the $20 note glows green, the $50 note glows yellow, and the $100 note glows red.

Microprinting appears as a thin line to the naked eye, but the lettering is easily read using a low-power magnifier. The resolution of most current copiers is not adequate to copy such fine print.

The first sweeping design change in 67 years occurred in 1996 when U.S. currency was redesigned to further deter counterfeiting. Color-shifting inks were added. The ink appears green when viewed directly and changes to black when the note is tilted. A watermark was added by varying paper density in a small area during the papermaking process. The image is visible as darker and lighter areas when held to the light. Since the watermark does not copy on color copiers or scanners, it is a good way to authenticate the note. The note's portrait was also shifted off-center and enlarged. The larger portrait incorporated more detail, making it easier to recognize and harder to counterfeit.

In 2003, the currency was again changed to make it harder to fake. Subtle green, peach, and blue colors were added to the background. Different colors are used for different denominations. These additions added complexity to the notes, making counterfeiting even more difficult.

It is impossible to completely prevent ingenious crooks from attempting to counterfeit U.S. currency. The U.S. Treasury is continually evaluating new reproduction technology to identify future threats. Digital technology represents the greatest threat. In 1995, less than 1% of counterfeit notes detected in the United States were digitally produced. By 2005, that number was nearly 40%.

discussion questions for bonus case 20-1

1. Coins are more durable than bills and cost less to produce. But in recent years the Treasury has twice introduced one-dollar coins—the Susan B. Anthony coin and the Sacagawea coin—that have not been accepted by the public. Why do you think people resist using these dollar coins?

2. Some European currencies use bright-colored inks for different denominations. Do you think the American consumer would accept "orangebacks" or "bluebacks" as replacements for today's "greenbacks"? Why or why not?

3. To make different denominations of currency easier to identify, some people have suggested that each denomination's size be different. What changes in the economy would be necessary if higher denomination bills were physically larger?

notes on discussion questions for bonus case 20-1

1. *Coins are more durable than bills and cost less to produce. But in recent years the Treasury has twice introduced one-dollar coins—the Susan B. Anthony coin and the Sacagawea coin—that have not been accepted by the public. Why do you think people resist using these dollar coins?*

   One reason the coins were not accepted was their size—only slightly larger than a quarter. Many complained that the dollar coin and the quarter were easily confused. There is also something inherently reassuring about a dollar bill—the symbol of the American economy. If students have any insights on this issue, the Treasury would be interested.

2. *Some European currencies use bright-colored inks for different denominations. Do you think the American consumer would accept "orangebacks" or "bluebacks" as replacements for today's "greenbacks"? Why or why not?*

   Americans seem to have accepted the new multicolor $10, $20, and $100 bills. Students can express their opinions one way or the other.

3. *To make different denominations of currency easier to identify, some people have suggested that each denomination's size be different. What changes in the economy would be necessary if higher denomination bills were physically larger?*

   Vending machines would have to be adapted to accept different sizes. Wallets would need to be larger. Bank teller cash drawers and ATMs would have to be redesigned. (But, as discussed in **Lecture Link 20-5,** "Currency for Consumers with Visual Impairments?" on page 20.68, different-sized denominations for bills would make using currency easier for consumers who are visually impaired.)

bonus case 20-2

BERNANKE'S BIG GAMBLE

In a technical sense, the recession is over. The overall economy has ceased to contract and a recovery is underway. Normally this would be good news, but the economy is expanding at a snail's pace. Its current rate of growth isn't strong enough to combat a sizeable unemployment rate and a crippled real estate market. In an effort to incite economic expansion, Fed chair Ben Bernanke has set interest rates as low as they can go and purchased nearly $1.5 trillion in assets since 2008. Nevertheless, recovery remains slothful.

In November 2010, Bernanke announced his intention to invest another $600 billion of Fed money, this time in Treasury bonds. The cash for this mammoth investment will be created by marking up the balance in the seller's account at the Fed, essentially the electronic equivalent of printing money. Bernanke and company hope to drive up demand for bonds with this mass purchase, thus increasing their price and driving down their yields. Once Treasury bonds become unappealing to investors, Bernanke posits they'll turn their attention to higher-yield items like fixed-income securities. After greater demand drives down yields for those, interest rates will fall accordingly, stimulating economic growth.

By all accounts Bernanke's taking a big gamble. Critics worry that the Fed's latest round of money creation could flood the economy with cash and spark heavy inflation. In normal times this would be true, Bernanke argues, but the economy is too weak to drive the value of the dollar down to an alarming level. Others point out that during the Fed's first bond buying spree they purchased mortgage-backed securities that nobody wanted after the housing crisis. Acquiring so many unwelcome assets en masse then drove up demand and lowered interest rates as expected. This time, though, the Fed is buying up Treasury bonds, for which there is no shortage of demand already. Still, if all goes according to plan, economists estimate that Bernanke's massive bond investment could boost the size of the economy by as much as 1.2% over two years.[xi]

discussion questions for bonus case 20-2

1. What is the key role the Federal Reserve plays in the U.S. economy?

2. Why are critics of the Fed's action concerned about inflation?

notes on discussion questions for bonus case 20-2

1. *What is the key role the Federal Reserve plays in the U.S. economy?*

   The key role of the Fed is to add or subtract money from the economy through monetary policy. Monetary policy is the management of the nation's money supply and control of interest rates to stimulate growth in the U.S. economy.

2. *Why are critics of the Fed's action concerned about inflation?*

   Inflation, you may recall, is "too many dollars chasing too few goods." Critics of the Fed's current plan worry that pumping too much money in the economy can cause inflation to rise with prices eventually getting out of hand.

bonus case 20-3

WHEN MONEY LOSES ITS MEANING

When money decreases in value because of inflation, people tend to place less trust in it as a method of storing value, and look for alternative means of storing their wealth that would be more efficient. Hyperinflation—extremely high inflation that can range from 100 to 10,000% annually—makes money particularly unstable. In fact, hyperinflation makes money meaningless. That is what happened in Germany during the 1920s. A pack of cigarettes, for example, had a price tag of 200 trillion marks. As a result, people ceased to use the official, but worthless, currency and resorted to using other objects as money (such as clothes, appliances, jewelry, antiques, diamonds, silver, and gold). These objects effectively became money. Subsequently, the German economy collapsed, setting the stage for the rise of Nazism.

Hyperinflation in post–World War I Germany is one of the worst such cases in this century. Nevertheless, there are numerous recent examples of hyperinflation. In the South American country of Bolivia, for example, prices during 1984 rose at an annual rate of 10,000%. A hamburger cost 1 million pesos, a loaf of bread sold for 300,000 pesos, and one night's lodging in a good hotel cost 35 million pesos. Hyperinflation in Bolivia skyrocketed to the point where the peso was virtually worthless.

The most severe known incident of inflation was in Hungary after the end of World War II when prices rose at a rate of 4.19×10^{16}% per month (prices doubled every 15 hours). More recently, Yugoslavia suffered 5×10^{15}% inflation per month (prices doubled every 16 hours) between October 1993 and January 1994.

discussion questions for bonus case 20-3

1. Why did official money lose its meaning in Germany during the 1920s?

2. Do you believe that the United States could be facing a hyperinflation problem in the foreseeable future? Why or why not?

3. How can we deal with hyperinflation? What is the role of the Federal Reserve in controlling inflation? How does it perform this function?

notes on discussion questions for bonus case 20-3

1. *Why did official money lose its meaning in Germany during the 1920s?*

   When a government gets into financial trouble, one of the ways to finance those problems is through inflation. If the government owes people money, that debt is lessened considerably if money is worth less and less. A government can also print money to pay its bills. The more money pumped into an economy, though, the higher inflation becomes. The principle, again, is too much money chasing too few goods. When a government is preparing for war, it often prints lots of money to pay for war materials. This is very inflationary, and has resulted in inflation in many countries.

2. *Do you believe that the United States could be facing a hyperinflation problem in the foreseeable future? Why or why not?*

   The economy of the United States steadily grew throughout the early 2000s, and inflation was down from double-digit levels of a decade ago. Many felt that inflation was under control. But by early 2008, producer prices shot up rapidly, raising inflation fears. Any threat of war or collapse in the banking system could further fuel inflationary pressure. The Federal Reserve plays a pivotal role in all this by controlling the money supply.

3. *How can we deal with hyperinflation? What is the role of the Federal Reserve in controlling inflation? How does it perform this function?*

   The Fed has three tools for managing the money supply: (1) reserve requirements, which keep money out of circulation; (2) open-market operations that manage the money supply by the purchase and sale of securities; and (3) the discount rate (the rate charged banks for borrowing funds from the Fed). By keeping the money supply in balance, the Fed can lessen pressures for inflation. Too tight a policy can result in another depression, whereas too loose a policy could result in hyperinflation.

bonus case 20-4

REFORMING WALL STREET

Though the United States has certainly learned its share of lessons from the economic meltdown of 2008, the financial institutions that helped cause it remain largely intact and unrestrained. For legislators in Washington, writing regulations to prevent another widespread collapse is a slippery slope. For instance, Democratic leaders in the House and Senate called for a consumer protection agency to serve as a watchdog over Wall Street's biggest banks. As with every political issue, the idea is not universally supported. Opposition from Republicans and disagreement over the autonomy of the agency has delayed its implementation for the time being.

Ideally, the consumer protection agency would act like the FDIC: If a bank goes belly up, it won't take its customer base or the whole financial system down with it. Regulators are searching for an elusive middle ground that would allow an ailing bank to fail smoothly without causing a Lehman Brothers–level panic or another controversial bailout. The Senate's version of the financial regulation bill includes provisions that would make banks easier to break apart should they fail. But the crux of the bill lies in the consumer protection agency, which would help prevent banks from failing in the first place by keeping a close eye on them.

Nevertheless, the United States is a free market that needs healthy financial institutions to support a stable economy. Too much oversight on banks' lending practices could hamper their day-to-day operations. Still, it's hard to forget that the reason why the Great Recession has been so severe is because of the toxic assets banks bundled together and pushed around to each other. It's true that banks aren't solely responsible for the economic collapse: foreclosures by debt-ridden consumers triggered the initial panic. But perhaps the whole ordeal could have been avoided if something had prevented banks from offering such bad loans in the first place. In the end, the leverage of banks to deal in debt so freely played a major role in the financial meltdown. Simple solutions like raising reserve requirements wouldn't work due to the adverse effect they'd have on recovering businesses. A more sweeping change is needed, and hopefully it will come in the form of sound and fair reform.[xii]

discussion questions for bonus case 20-4

1. Would banking reform threaten the U.S. free-market economy?

2. Do we really need reform in the banking industry?

notes on discussion questions for bonus case 20-4

1. *Would banking reform threaten the U.S. free-market economy?*

   It's doubtful the U.S. free-market economy would be in jeopardy. The passage of legislation and the creation of a consumer protection agency is based on political compromise that we suspect would put limits on any oversight of the U.S. free-market banking system.

2. *Do you believe that the United States could be facing a hyperinflation problem in the foreseeable future? Why or why not?*

   Ask 10 economists and you would likely get 10 different answers. However, what most analysts, economists, and consumers want to ensure is that we do not go through the trying and painful economic meltdown again we felt in 2008. Best guess is that we need some reform.

endnotes

---

[i] *Sources:* Associated Press, "Is the Penny Worth It? Rising Cost May Mean End to Coin," *The Clarion-Ledger*, July 2, 2006; Brian Wilson, "Bad Penny! Lawmakers Consider Elimination of Least-Valued U.S. Currency," *Fox News*, July 20, 2006; "The Composition of the Cent," The United States Mint, www.usmint.gov

[ii] *Source:* Whitney Dangerfield, "Casualties of War," *National Geographic,* March 2005.

[iii] *Source:* Robert Parloff, "The Blind Undercutting the Blind," *Fortune*, January 22, 2007.

[iv] *Source:* The United States Mint, U.S. Department of the Treasury, www.usmint.gov.

[v] *Sources:* "A History of British Banking," The Royal Bank of Scotland Group, www.rbs.com; "The Goldsmith Era of Banking," The Federal Debt Relief System, www.fdrs.org.

[vi] *Source:* Mark Pinsky, "Help for Small Businesses: Loans Are Just the Start," *Bloomberg Businessweek*, October 21, 2010.

[vii] *Source:* Ben Hallman, "Credit Unions Increasingly Offer High-Rate Payday Loans," *The Washington Post,* May 27, 2011.

[viii] *Source:* Daniel Roth, "The Future of Money," *Wired*, February 22, 2010.

[ix] The Internet is a dynamic, changing information source. Web links noted of this manual were checked at the time of publication, but content may change over time. Please review the website before recommending it to your students.

[x] The Internet is a dynamic, changing information source. Web links noted of this manual were checked at the time of publication, but content may change over time. Please review the website before recommending it to your students.

[xi] *Sources:* Jon Hilsenrath, "Fed Fires $600 Billion Stimulus Shot," *The Wall Street Journal,* November 4, 2010; Peter Coy, "The Bernanke Code," *Bloomberg Businessweek,* November 4, 2010.

[xii] *Sources:* Roger Lowenstein, "First, Slap Limits on Bank Leverage," *Bloomberg Businessweek,* March 11, 2010; "In Praise of Doddery," *The Economist,* March 18, 2010.

Working within the Legal Environment

bonus chapter **A**

what's new in this edition

additions to the 10th edition:

- Getting to Know Kenneth C. Frazier, CEO of Merck
- Name That Company: Toyota
- Credit Card Act of 2009 was added to Figure A.4 Consumer Protection Laws
- Video case

revisions to the 10th edition:

- Text was revised to eliminate redundancy and tighten discussions.
- Statistical data and examples throughout the chapter were updated to reflect current information.

deletions from the 9th edition:

- Getting to Know David Boies, Corporate Attorney
- Name That Company: McDonald's
- Figure: Major Product Liability Cases

brief chapter outline and learning goals

bonus chapter A

Working within the Legal Environment

Getting To Know KENNETH C. FRAZIER, MERCK

learning goal 1

Define business law, distinguish between statutory and common law, and explain the role of administrative agencies.

I. THE CASE FOR LAWS

A. Statutory and Common Law

B. Administrative Agencies

learning goal 2

Define tort law and explain the role of product liability in tort law.

II. TORT LAW

A. Product Liability

learning goal 3

Identify the purposes and conditions of patents, copyrights, and trademarks.

III. LEGALLY PROTECTING IDEAS: PATENTS, COPYRIGHTS, AND TRADEMARKS

learning goal 4

Describe warranties and negotiable instruments as covered in the Uniform Commercial Code.

IV. SALES LAW: THE UNIFORM COMMERCIAL CODE

A. Warranties

B. Negotiable Instruments

learning goal 5

List and describe the conditions necessary to make a legally enforce-able contract, and describe the possible consequences if such a contract is violated.

V. CONTRACT LAW

A. Breach of Contract

learning goal 6

Summarize several laws that regulate competition and protect consumers in the United States.

VI. PROMOTING FAIR AND COMPETITIVE BUSINESS PRACTICES

A. The History of Antitrust Legislation

VII. LAWS TO PROTECT CONSUMERS

learning goal 7

Explain the role of tax laws in generating income for the government and as a method of discouraging or encouraging certain behaviors among taxpayers.

VIII. TAX LAWS

learning goal 8

Distinguish among the various types of bankruptcy as outlined by the Bankruptcy Code.

IX. BANKRUPTCY LAWS

learning goal 9

Explain the role of deregulation as a tool to encourage competition.

X. DEREGULATION VERSUS REGULATION

XI. SUMMARY

lecture outline

Getting to Know KENNETH C. FRAZIER, MERCK

Before rising to the CEO position at Merck, Frazier was general counsel for the pharmaceutical firm. He was in the defendant's position when Merck's popular drug, Vioxx, had a sea of lawsuits against it. Frazier's goal as CEO is to prevent another situation like Vioxx's and to make drug research a priority

This automaker sells more cars in the United States than any other auto producer. In 2010–2011, however, the company was forced to recall 3 million cars due to sudden accelerator incidents. It's likely the company will face years of litigation from customers who were affected by the product problem. Name that company

(Students should read the chapter before guessing the company's name : Toyota)

learning goal 1

Define business law, distinguish between statutory and common law, and explain the role of administrative agencies.

I. THE CASE FOR LAWS

A. Laws are an essential part of a civilized nation.

1. Over time, the body of law changes to reflect the needs and changes in society.
2. The ***JUDICIARY*** is the branch of government chosen to oversee the legal system through the court system.
3. The **COURT SYSTEM** in the U.S. is organized at the federal, state, and local levels.
   a. **TRIAL COURTS** hear cases involving criminal and civil law.
   b. **CRIMINAL LAW** defines crimes, establishes punishment, and regulates prosecution.
   c. **CIVIL LAW** involves legal proceedings that do not involve criminal acts.

PPT A-1
Chapter Title

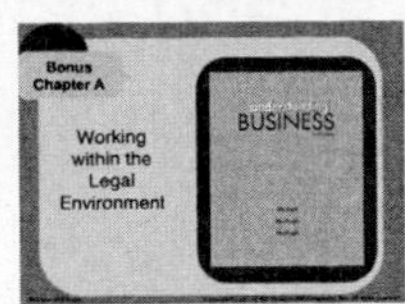

PPT A-2
Learning Goals

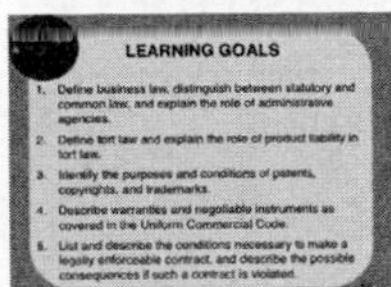

(See complete PowerPoint slide notes on page A.44.)

PPT A-3
Learning Goals

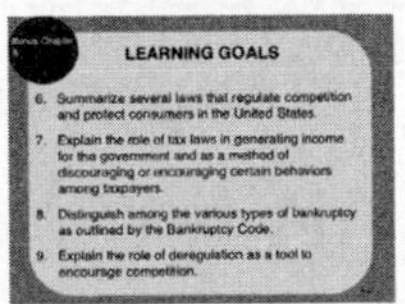

(See complete PowerPoint slide notes on page A.44.)

PPT A-4
Kenneth Frazier

(See complete PowerPoint slide notes on page A.45.)

PPT A-5
Name That Company

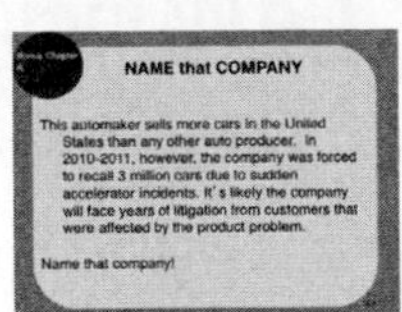

(See complete PowerPoint slide notes on page A.45.)

PPT A-6
The Need for Laws

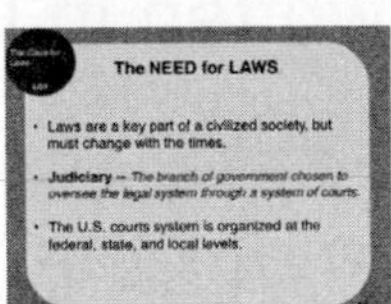

(See complete PowerPoint slide notes on page A.45.)

PPT A-7
Types of Court

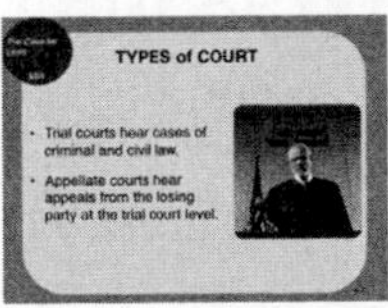

(See complete PowerPoint slide notes on page A.46.)

   d. Both federal and state systems have **APPELLATE COURTS** to hear appeals of trial court decisions.

4. The judiciary also governs the activities and operations of a business.

5. Government has stepped in to make **LAWS** governing behavior because the U.S. business community has been perceived as not implementing acceptable practices fast enough.

6. ***BUSINESS LAW*** are the rules, statutes, codes, and regulations that are established to provide a legal framework within which business may be conducted and that are enforceable by court action.

B. **STATUTORY AND COMMON LAW**

1. ***STATUTORY LAW*** includes state and federal constitutions, legislative enactments, treaties of the federal government, and ordinances—in short, *written laws.*
   a. Laws are written in legal terminology and are difficult to read.
   b. There are more than 1.1 million lawyers in the U.S.

2. ***COMMON LAW*** is the body of the law that comes from decisions handed down by judges; also referred to as *unwritten law.*
   a. ***PRECEDENT*** involves decisions judges have made in earlier cases that guide the handling of new cases.

PPT A-8
Types of Law

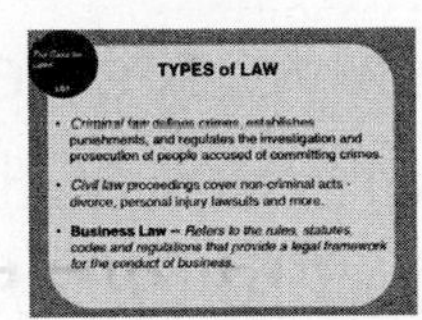

(See complete PowerPoint slide notes on page A.46.)

PPT A-9
Major Areas of Law

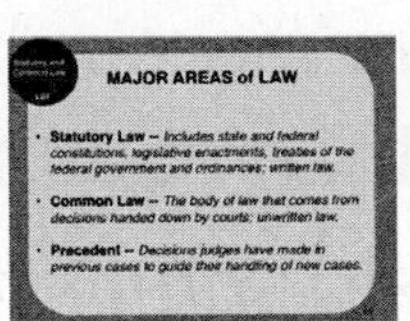

(See complete PowerPoint slide notes on page A.46.)

b. Lower courts must abide by the precedents set by higher courts.

C. **ADMINISTRATIVE AGENCIES**

1. ***ADMINISTRATIVE AGENCIES*** are federal or state institutions and other government organizations created by Congress or state legislatures with delegated power to pass rules and regulations within their mandated area of authority.
2. Administrative agencies hold quasi-legislative, quasi-executive, and quasi-judicial powers.
   a. The agency is allowed to pass regulations within its area of authority, conduct investigations, and hold hearings when rules and regulations have been violated.
   b. They issue more rulings and settle more disputes than courts do.
3. **Figure A.1** lists some of these administrative agencies.

learning goal 2

Define tort law and explain the role of product liability in tort law.

II. TORT LAW

A. A ***TORT*** is a wrongful act that causes injury to another person's body, property, or reputation.

1. An **INTENTIONAL TORT** is a willful act purposely inflicted that results in injury.
2. ***NEGLIGENCE***, in tort law, is behavior that causes unintentional harm or injury.
3. Product liability is one of the more controversial areas of tort law.

PPT A-10
Administrative Agencies

(See complete PowerPoint slide notes on page A.47.)

TEXT FIGURE A.1
Examples of Federal, State, and Local Administrative Agencies
(Text page A-4)

This text figure lists and describes the powers and functions of several administrative agencies at the federal, state, and local levels of government.

progress assessment
(Text page A-3)

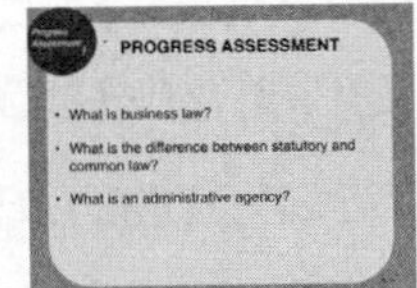

PPT A-11
Progress Assessment

(See complete PowerPoint slide notes on page A.47.)

PPT A-12
What Is Tort Law?

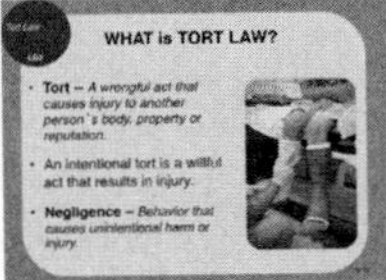

(See complete PowerPoint slide notes on page A.47.)

B. PRODUCT LIABILITY

1. ***PRODUCT LIABILITY*** is the part of tort law that holds businesses liable for harm that results from production, design, sale, or use of products it markets.
2. At one time, the legal standard for liability was **KNOWINGLY** placing a product on the market.
   a. Today, many states have extended liability to the level of ***STRICT PRODUCT LIABILITY***, the legal responsibility for harm or injury caused by a product regardless of fault.
   b. The company may be held liable even if the company did not know of the defect at the time of sale.
3. The rule of **STRICT LIABILITY** has caused serious problems for manufacturers of some products, such as asbestos and lead-based paint.
   a. *Manufacturers of chemicals and drugs are also susceptible to lawsuits.*
   b. *Toyota recalled 3 million cars in 2010 and 2011; the company now faces years of litigation.*
   c. *Pharmaceutical giant, Merck, reached settlements to end thousands of lawsuits filed regarding its drugs.*
   d. *The gun industry has been accused of damages under the rules of strict product liability.*
   e. *Fast-food companies are facing liability suits charging that their food causes obesity and other health concerns.*

PPT A-13
Product Liability Laws

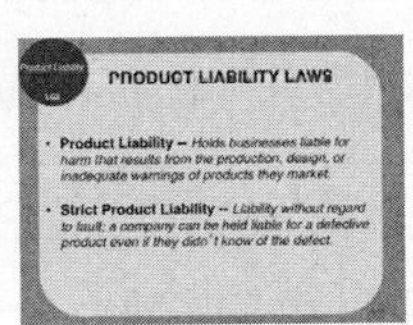

(See complete PowerPoint slide notes on page A.48.)

PPT A-14
Major Product Liability Cases

TEXT FIGURE A.2
Major Product Liability Cases
(Text page A-5)

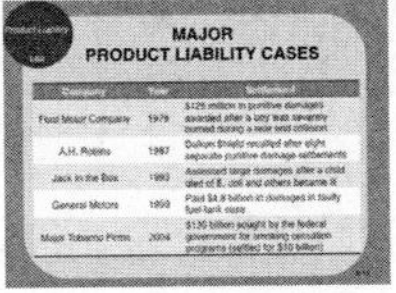

(See complete PowerPoint slide notes on page A.48.)

4. Businesses and insurance companies have called for meaningful **TORT REFORM** from huge losses in strict product liability suits.

5. Congress passed the **CLASS ACTION FAIRNESS ACT**, a first step in tort reform.

learning goal 3

Identify the purposes and conditions of patents, copyrights, and trademarks.

III. LEGALLY PROTECTING IDEAS: PATENTS, COPYRIGHTS, AND TRADEMARKS

A. A ***PATENT*** is a document that gives inventors exclusive rights to their inventions for 20 years.

1. Filing a patent with the U.S. Patent Office requires a **SEARCH** to ensure the patent is truly unique, followed by the **FILING OF FORMS**.

2. There are 6,200 examiners in the U.S. Patent and Trademark Office that review patents.

   a. The examiners review about 350,000 patent requests each year and grant more than 150,000.

   b. Because of a huge backup, the Supreme Court imposed stricter standards on the process.

   c. A patent cannot be granted for an invention that is an obvious extension of an existing product.

3. Patent owners may **SELL OR LICENSE** the use of the patent to others.

4. **PENALTIES** for violating a patent can be severe.

PPT A-15
Patents, Copyrights, and Trademarks

(See complete PowerPoint slide notes on page A.48.)

lecture link A-1

THE DIFFERENCES BETWEEN PATENTS, COPYRIGHTS, AND TRADEMARKS

Although patents, copyrights, and trademarks are similar legal concepts, each has a very specific definition. (See the complete lecture link on page A.58 in this manual.)

PPT A-16
Patent Facts

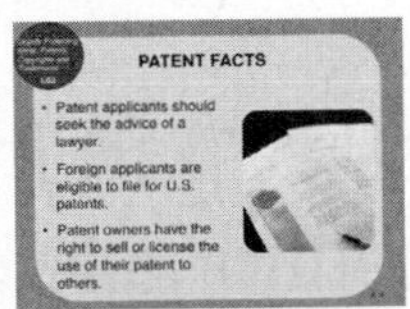

(See complete PowerPoint slide notes on page A.49.)

PPT A-17
Patent Leaders in 2010

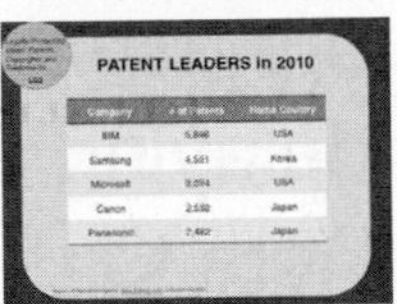

(See complete PowerPoint slide notes on page A.49.)

a. Defending of patent rights is solely the job of the patent holder.

b. *Dr. Gary Michelson received a settlement of $1.35 billion from Medtronic Inc. to end litigation and license patents.*

B. The **AMERICAN INVENTION PROTECTION ACT** requires patent applications to be made public after 18 months.

1. It was passed in part in response to some inventors intentionally dragging out the patent application.

2. Some inventors use a **SUBMARINE PATENT**, intentionally delaying a patent application and waiting for others to develop the technology.

3. Technology companies also defend themselves against patent infringement suits by joining Allied Security Trust, a firm that acquires intellectual property of interest to its members.

C. A ***COPYRIGHT*** is a document that protects a creator's rights to materials such as books, articles, photos, and cartoons.

1. Copyrights are filed with the **LIBRARY OF CONGRESS**.

2. They involve a minimum of paperwork and last for the lifetime of the author or artist plus 70 years.

3. The Copyright Act of 1978 gives a special term of 75 years for publication to works published before January 1, 1978.

lecture notes

lecture link A-2

NORTEL'S PATENT AUCTION

As Nortel Communications filed for bankruptcy, it hired a company to help sell its powerful patent portfolio. (See the complete lecture link on page A.59 in this manual.)

4. The holder of an **EXCLUSIVE COPYRIGHT** may charge a fee to anyone who wishes to use the material.
5. If a work is created by an employee in the normal course of a job, the copyright belongs to the employer.

D. A **TRADEMARK** is a legally protected name, symbol, or design (or combination of these) that identifies the goods or services of one seller and distinguishes them from those of competitors.

1. Generally, trademarks belong to the owner forever.
2. *Examples include the Aflac duck, Disney's Mickey Mouse, the Nike swoosh, and McDonald's Golden Arches.*
3. Like a patent, a trademark is protected from infringement.

learning goal 4

Describe warranties and negotiable instruments as covered in the Uniform Commercial Code.

IV. SALES LAW: THE UNIFORM COMMERCIAL CODE

A. The ***UNIFORM COMMERCIAL CODE (UCC)*** is a comprehensive commercial law, adopted by every state in the United States, that covers sales laws and other commercial laws.

1. The **11 ARTICLES** of the **UCC** cover sales; commercial paper; bank deposits and collections; letters of credit; bulk transfers; warehouse receipts, bills of lading, and other

lecture link A-3
PIRACY MAY KO UFC

As online streaming has advanced, UFC has to work to combat copyright infringement of its pay-per-view fights. (See the complete lecture link on page A.60 in this manual.)

progress assessment
(Text page A-7)

PROGRESS ASSESSMENT
- What is tort law?
- What is product liability? What is strict product liability?
- How many years is a patent protected from infringement?
- What is a copyright?

PPT A-18
Progress Assessment

(See complete PowerPoint slide notes on page A.49.)

PPT A-19
What Is the Uniform Commercial Code?

(See complete PowerPoint slide notes on page A.50.)

documents of title; investment securities; and secured transactions.

2. The text discusses two of these articles: **ARTICLE 2 (WARRANTIES)** and **ARTICLE 3 (NEGOTIABLE INSTRUMENTS).**

B. **WARRANTIES**

1. A **WARRANTY** guarantees that the product sold will be acceptable for the purpose for which the buyer intends to use it.
2. ***EXPRESS WARRANTIES*** are specific representations by the seller that buyers rely on regarding the goods they purchase.
3. ***IMPLIED WARRANTIES*** are guarantees legally imposed on the seller.
4. A **FULL WARRANTY** requires a seller to replace or repair a product at no charge if the product is defective.
5. **LIMITED WARRANTIES** typically limit the defects or mechanical problems that are covered.
6. The rights of buyers are spelled out in Article 2 of the UCC.

C. **NEGOTIABLE INSTRUMENTS**

1. ***NEGOTIABLE INSTRUMENTS*** are forms of commercial paper (such as checks) that are transferable among businesses and individuals and represent a promise to pay a specified amount.
2. Article 3 of the UCC requires that **NEGOTIABLE INSTRUMENTS**:

PPT A-20
Understanding Warranties

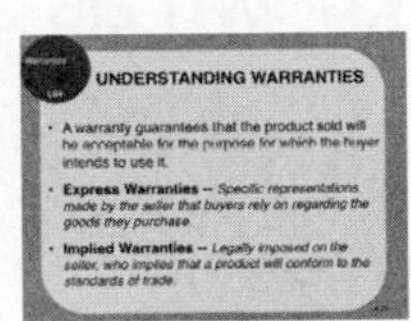

(See complete PowerPoint slide notes on page A.50.)

PPT A-21
Negotiable Instruments

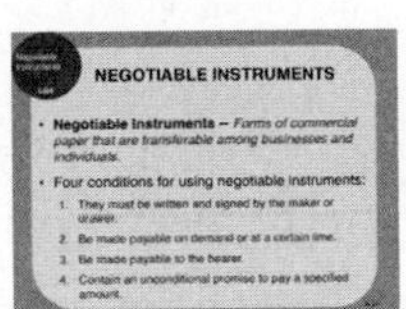

(See complete PowerPoint slide notes on page A.50.)

a. Be **WRITTEN** and **SIGNED** by the maker

b. Be made **PAYABLE ON DEMAND** or at a certain time

c. Be made **PAYABLE TO THE BEARER** or to specific order

d. Contain an **UNCONDITIONAL PROMISE** to pay a specified amount of money

3. Checks or other forms of negotiable instruments are transferred when the payee signs the back of the check, known as an **ENDORSEMENT**.

learning goal 5

List and describe the conditions necessary to make a legally enforceable contract, and describe the possible consequences if such a contract is violated .

V. CONTRACT LAW

A. TERMINOLOGY

1. A ***CONTRACT*** is a legally enforceable agreement between two or more parties.

2. ***CONTRACT LAW*** is the set of laws that specify what constitutes a legally enforceable agreement.

B. A contract is **LEGALLY BINDING** if the following conditions are met:

1. An **OFFER** is made

2. There is a **VOLUNTARY ACCEPTANCE** of the offer

3. Both parties give **CONSIDERATION**

a. ***CONSIDERATION*** is something of value; it is one of the requirements of a legal contract.

lecture link A-4

NEGOTIABLE INSTRUMENT FORGERY AND THE UNIFORM COMMERCIAL CODE

Frank Abagnale seems an unlikely person to work with the FBI's Financial Crimes Unit, but he does. Thirty years ago he created and passed millions of dollars of bad checks. (See the complete lecture link on page A.60 of this manual.)

PPT A-22
Contract Law

(See complete PowerPoint slide notes on page A.51.)

PPT A-23
Contract Requirements

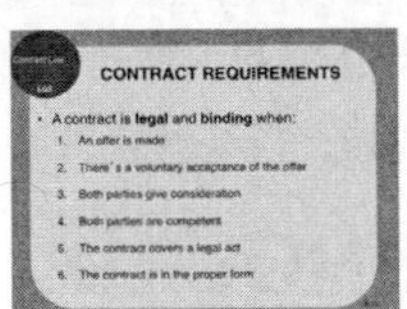

(See complete PowerPoint slide notes on page A.51.)

4. Both parties are **COMPETENT.**
5. The contract act must be **LEGAL.**
6. The contract is in a **PROPER FORM**—some contracts must be written.

C. **BREACH OF CONTRACT**

1. ***BREACH OF CONTRACT*** occurs when one party fails to follow the terms of the contract.
2. **CONSEQUENCES** of a breached contract are:
    a. **SPECIFIC PERFORMANCE:** The person violating contract may be required to live up to the agreement if no monetary award is adequate.
    b. **PAYMENT OF *DAMAGES***, the monetary settlement awarded to a person who is injured by a breach of contract
    c. **DISCHARGE OF OBLIGATION**, agreeing to drop the matter

D. **A CONTRACT SHOULD:**

1. Be in writing
2. Specify mutual consideration
3. Be clearly offered and accepted

learning goal 6

Summarize several laws that regulate competition and protect consumers in the United States.

VI. PROMOTING FAIR AND COMPETITIVE BUSINESS PRACTICES

A. The legislature passes laws to enforce a competitive atmosphere among businesses.

PPT A-24
Breached Contracts

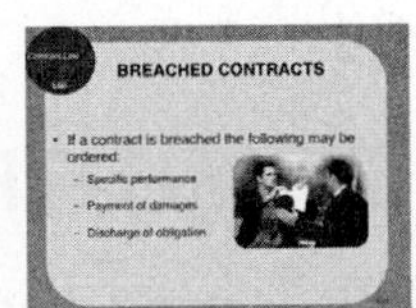

(See complete PowerPoint slide notes on page A.51.)

progress
assessment
(Text page A-10)

PPT A-25
Progress Assessment

PROGRESS ASSESSMENT
• What is the purpose of the Uniform Commercial Code (UCC)?
• Compare express and implied warranties.
• What are the four elements of a negotiable instrument specified in the UCC?
• What are the six conditions for a legally binding contract? What could happen if it's breached?

(See complete PowerPoint slide notes on page A.52.)

1. The Justice Department's antitrust division serves as watchdog.
2. The scope of government is broad and extensive.
3. The department's antitrust division has prosecuted giant companies such as Microsoft, Apple, Visa, and Google.
4. Businesses were once (but no longer) able to drive smaller competitors out of business with little resistance.

B. **THE HISTORY OF ANTITRUST LEGISLATION**

1. In the late 19th century, big industrial firms dominated the U.S. economy.
    a. Congress passed the **SHERMAN ANTI-TRUST ACT** in 1890.
    b. The act was designed to prevent large organizations from stifling the smaller competitors.
2. The **SHERMAN ACT** forbids:
    a. Contracts, combinations, or conspiracies in restraint of trade
    b. Actual monopolies or attempts to monopolize any part of trade or commerce
3. Later laws clarified the legal concepts of the Sherman Act.
    a. The **CLAYTON ACT OF 1914** prohibits exclusive dealing, tying contracts, interlocking directorates, and buying large amounts of stock in competing corporations.

lecture notes

PPT A-26
The Clayton Act of 1914

(See complete PowerPoint slide notes on page A.52.)

i. **EXCLUSIVE DEALING** is selling goods with the condition that the buyer will not buy goods from a competitor.

ii. A **TYING CONTRACT** requires a buyer to purchase unwanted items in order to purchase desired items.

iii. An **INTERLOCKING DIRECTORATE** occurs when a board of directors includes members of the board of competing corporations.

b. The **FEDERAL TRADE COMMISSION ACT OF 1914** prohibits unfair methods of competition in commerce and created the Federal Trade Commission.

i. This legislation set up the five-member **FEDERAL TRADE COMMISSION (FTC)** to enforce compliance with this act.

ii. The FTC regulates activities ranging from misleading advertising to price disclosure for funeral homes.

iii. The **WHEELER-LEA AMENDMENT** in 1938 gave the FTC additional jurisdiction over false or misleading advertising.

c. The **ROBINSON-PATMAN ACT OF 1936** prohibits price discrimination.

i. It applies to both sellers and buyers who "knowingly" induce unlawful discrimination in price.

ii. The law outlaws price differences that "substantially" weaken competition

PPT A-27
Antitrust Legislation

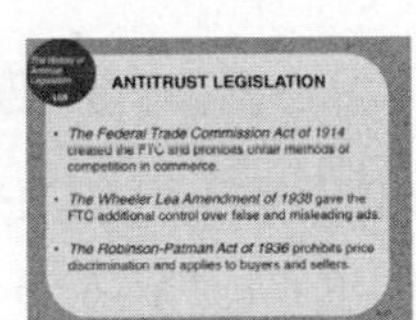

(See complete PowerPoint slide notes on page A.53.)

PPT A-28
History of High-Profile
.Antitrust Cases

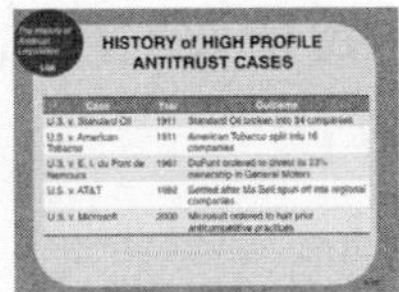

TEXT FIGURE A.3
History of High-Profile
.Antitrust Cases
(Text page A-11)

(See complete PowerPoint slide notes on page A.53.)

unless these differences can be justified by lower selling costs.

iii. This act applies to business-to-business transactions and does not apply to consumers in business transactions.

4. **MICROSOFT'S COMPETITIVE PRACTICES** have been criticized as being unfair competition.
   a. Microsoft was accused of hindering competition in its dealings with computer manufacturers.
   b. The case broadened the definition of anticompetitive behavior.
   c. The NASDAQ OMX and Intercontinental Exchange Inc withdrew their bid for NYSE Euronext when an antitrust suit was threatened in 2011.

VII. LAWS TO PROTECT CONSUMERS

A. ***CONSUMERISM*** is a social movement that seeks to increase and strengthen the rights and powers of buyers in relation to sellers.

1. Consumerism has taken on new vigor in the wake of the Enron and WorldCom scandals.
2. The **PUBLIC COMPANY ACCOUNTING REFORM AND INVESTOR PROTECTION ACT** (Sarbanes-Oxley Act) requires CEOs to verify the accuracy of their firms' financial statements to the SEC.
3. The market meltdown raised consumer anger at the lack of oversight of the securities market.

PPT A-29
Consumer Protections

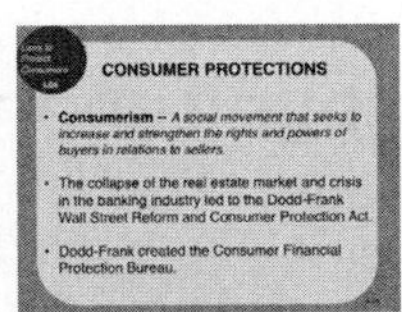

(See complete PowerPoint slide notes on page A.53.)

PPT A-30
Number of Identity Theft Complaints

(See complete PowerPoint slide notes on page A.54.)

TEXT FIGURE A.4
Consumer Protection Laws
(Text page A-13)

This text figure lists several major consumer protection laws and their purpose.

4. The **DODD-FRANK ACT** created the **Consumer Financial Protection Bureau** that provides government oversight involving consumers.

B. **Figure A.4** lists major consumer protection laws.

learning goal 7

Explain the role of tax laws in generating income for the government and as a method of discouraging or encouraging certain behaviors among taxpayers.

VIII. TAX LAWS

A. ***TAXES*** are how government (federal, state, and local) raises money.

B. Governments use taxes to:

1. **FUND** government operations
2. **DISCOURAGE** citizens from doing what it considers harmful *(for example, sin taxes on cigarettes and alcohol)*
3. **ENCOURAGE** businesses to hire new employees or purchase new equipment by offering a **TAX CREDIT**

C. Taxes are levied from a variety of **SOURCES**.

1. **INCOME, SALES,** and **PROPERTY** are the major bases of tax revenue.
2. States and local communities often make extensive use of **SALES TAXES.**
3. Businesses take the tax policies of states and cities into consideration when deciding where to locate operations.

D. A key tax issue in the next few years involves **INTERNET TAXATION**, especially e-commerce.

lecture notes

PPT A-31
Taxes

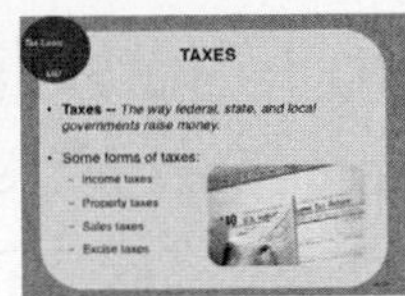

(See complete PowerPoint slide notes on page A.54.)

PPT A-32
Sin Taxes

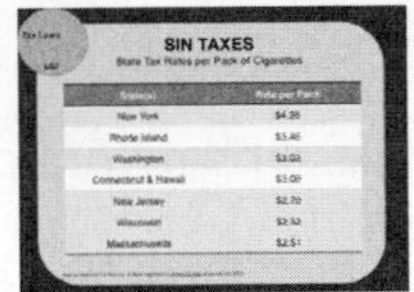

(See complete PowerPoint slide notes on page A.54.)

PPT A-33
Do the Rich Pay Taxes?

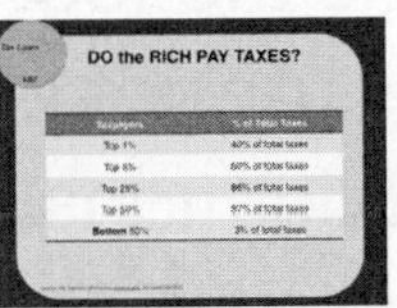

(See complete PowerPoint slide notes on page A.55.)

TEXT FIGURE A.5
Types of Taxes
(Text page A-14)

This text figure highlights the primary types of taxes levied on individuals and businesses.

1. States claim to lose billions in sales tax as a result of e-commerce.
2. The European Union already levies certain Internet taxes.

learning goal 8

Distinguish among the various types of bankruptcy as outlined by the Bankruptcy Code.

IX. BANKRUPTCY LAWS

A. ***BANKRUPTCY*** is the legal process by which a person, business, or government entity, unable to meet financial obligations, is relieved of those obligations by a court that divides any assets among creditors, allowing creditors to get at least part of their money and freeing the debtor to begin anew.
   1. The court divides any assets among creditors.
   2. The Constitution gives Congress the power to establish bankruptcy laws.

B. **AMENDMENTS TO THE BANKRUPTCY LAW**
   1. The **BANKRUPTCY AMENDMENTS OF 1984** allow a person who is bankrupt to keep part of the equity in a house.
   2. The **BANKRUPTCY REFORM ACT OF 1994** creates reforms that speed up and simplify the process.
   3. The **BANKRUPTCY REFORM ACT OF 2005** made it harder for individuals to eliminate most debts from a bankruptcy.

C. It's expected in 2011 an average of **1.5 MILLION AMERICANS** will file for bankruptcy.

lecture link A-5
GOOGLE'S TAX TACTICS

Tax havens are used by multinationals, including Google. (See complete lecture link on page A.62 of this manual.)

PPT A-34
Bankruptcy Laws

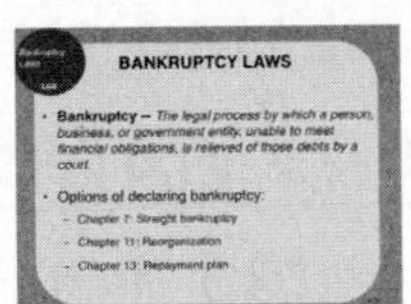

(See complete PowerPoint slide notes on page A.55.)

lecture link A-6
BAD TIMING FOR BANKRUPTCY LAW CHANGES

The 2005 Bankruptcy Act took effect in October 2005, bad timing for residents of the Gulf Coast recently hit by Hurricane Katrina. (See the complete lecture link on page A.62 of this manual.)

1. The number of bankruptcies increased in the 1980s and 1990s.
2. The **2005 BANKRUPTCY LEGISLATION** makes it more difficult for people to escape debt from credit cards, medical bills, student loans, or other unsecured loans.
3. Filings dropped to 600,000 in 2006.
4. Over 90% of filings each year are by individuals.

D. Bankruptcy can be either **VOLUNTARY** or **INVOLUNTARY**.

1. ***VOLUNTARY BANKRUPTCY*** involves legal procedures initiated by a debtor.
2. ***INVOLUNTARY BANKRUPTCY*** involves bankruptcy procedures filed by a debtor's creditors.

E. Bankruptcy procedures are filed under one of the following **SECTIONS OF THE BANKRUPTCY CODE:**

1. **CHAPTER 7**: "Straight bankruptcy" or liquidation (used by businesses and individuals)
2. **CHAPTER 11**: Reorganization (used by businesses and some individuals)
3. **CHAPTER 13**: Repayment (used by individuals)

F. **CHAPTER 7** calls for **"STRAIGHT BANKRUPTCY,"** which requires the sale of nonexempt assets of debtors.

1. Up to $21,625 of equity in a home and $3,225 equity in a car are protected.
2. Cash from the sale is divided among creditors
3. First, creditors with **SECURED CLAIMS** are paid, and then the unsecured claims are paid.

PPT A-35
Chapter 7 Bankruptcy

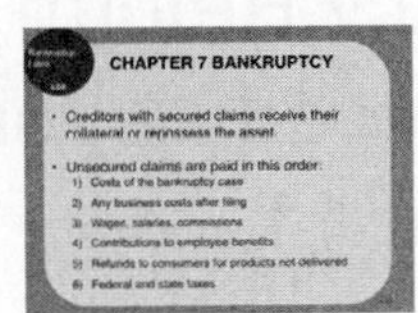

(See complete PowerPoint slide notes on page A.56.)

PPT A-36
How Assets Are Divided in Bankruptcy

TEXT FIGURE A.6
How Assets Are Divided in Bankruptcy
(Text page A-16)

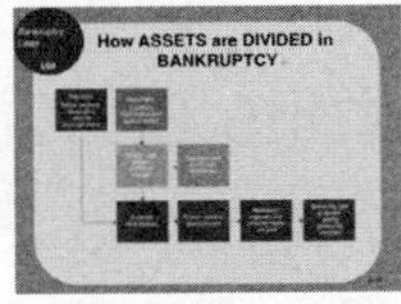

(See complete PowerPoint slide notes on page A.56.)

4. Chapter 7 is the most popular form of bankruptcy.
5. **Text Figure A.6** lists the order that **UNSECURED CLAIMS** are paid.

G. **CHAPTER 11**

1. Under Chapter 11 a company **CONTINUES TO OPERATE**, but has court protection against creditors' lawsuits while it tries to work out a debt repayment plan.
2. Less than 33% of Chapter 11 companies survive.
3. The Bankruptcy Reform Act of 1994 extends a "fast track" procedure for small businesses filing under Chapter 11.
4. Individuals have the right to file bankruptcy under Chapter 11, but it is uncommon.

H. **CHAPTER 13** permits individuals, including small-business owners, to **PAY BACK CREDITORS OVER A THREE-TO-FIVE-YEAR PERIOD**.

1. **CHAPTER 13** proceedings are less complicated than Chapter 7 proceedings.
2. The debtor files a proposed plan for paying off debts to the court.

learning goal 9

Explain the role of deregulation as a tool to encourage competition.

X. DEREGULATION VERSUS REGULATION

A. ***DEREGULATION*** is government withdrawal of certain laws and regulations that seem to hinder competition.

B. Deregulation has had a huge impact on the airline and telecommunication industries.

lecture notes

PPT A-37
Going, Going, Gone

(See complete PowerPoint slide notes on page A.56.)

PPT A-38
Deregulating Commerce

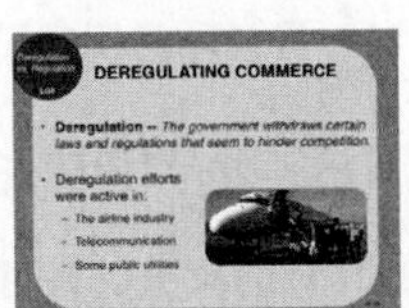

(See complete PowerPoint slide notes on page A.56.)

lecture outline

1. When restrictions on routes were lifted under the Deregulation Act of 1978, airlines began competing for routes and lowering prices.
2. Today, some feel more government intervention is needed since passenger services have decreased and delays or cancellations have increased.
3. Similar deregulation in telecommunication occurred after the passage of the **TELECOMMUNICATIONS ACT OF 1996.**
4. Deregulation efforts have also been attempted in the electric power industry.
    a. California was the first state to deregulate power and experienced significant problems.
    b. Time will tell whether utility deregulation will survive and prosper.
5. New regulations in the banking and investments industries changed the nature of financial markets and created huge problems.
    a. The Federal Reserve was reluctant to toughen mortgage regulations, contributing to the collapse of the real estate market.
    b. The failure of huge financial institutions also angered consumers.
6. The electric power industry has also been the target of deregulation, with disastrous results in California; other states dropped deregulation plans.
7. In 2010, the Patient Protection and Affordable Care Act introduced a comprehensive system of

PPT A-39
Hamburger Regulations

TEXT FIGURE A.7
Hamburger Regulations
(Text page A-18)

(See complete PowerPoint slide notes on page A.57.)

mandated health insurance for 32 million Americans and increased government regulation of the insurance industry.

C. Some regulation of business is necessary to assure fair and honest dealings with the public.

   1. The scandals of the early 2000s and the financial market collapse led to a further demand for better government regulation and oversight.

   2. With global competition increasing, businesses and government need to continue to work together to create a competitive environment that is fair and open.

XI. SUMMARY

progress
assessment
(Text page A-19)

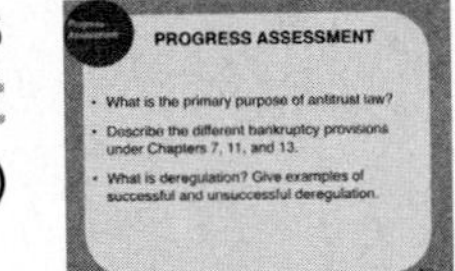

PPT A-40
Progress Assessment

(See complete PowerPoint slide notes on page A.57.)

PowerPoint slide notes

PPT A-1
Chapter Title

PPT A-2
Learning Goals

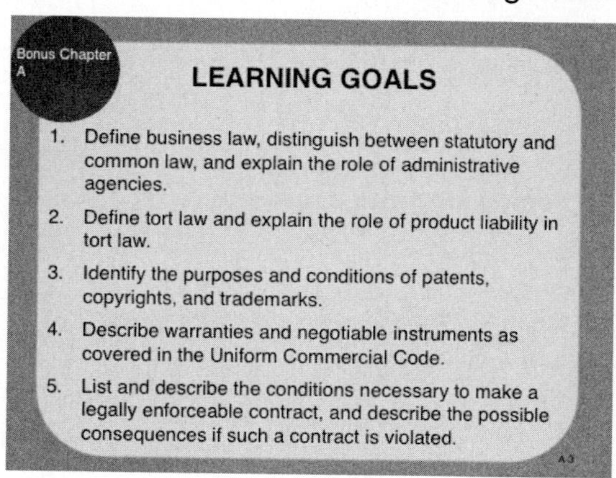

PPT A-3
Learning Goals

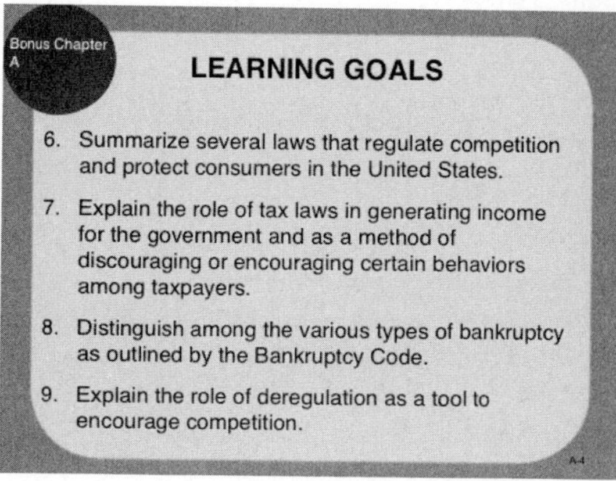

PPT A-4
Kenneth Frazier

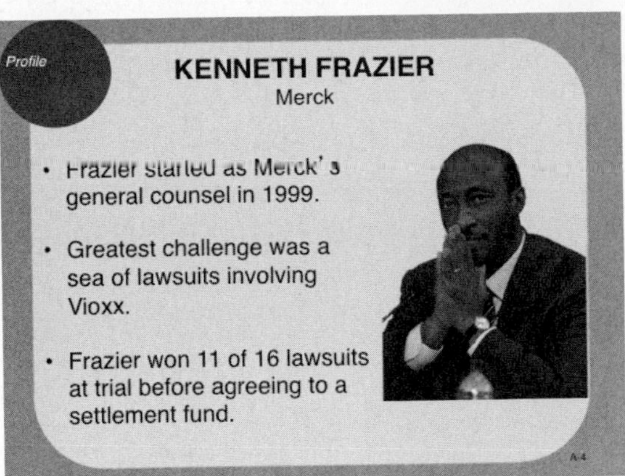

PPT A-5
Name That Company

Company: Toyota

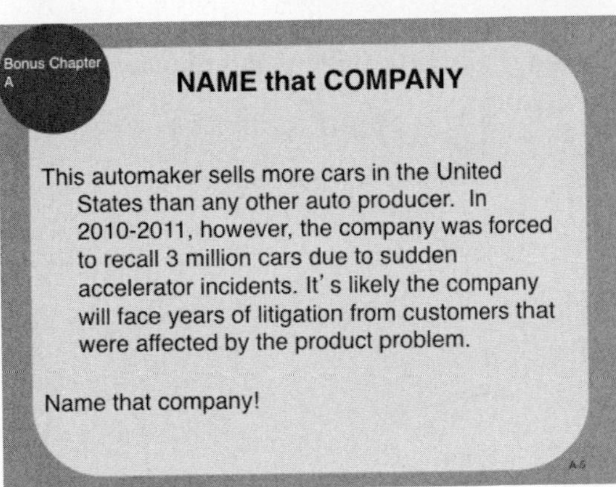

PPT A-6
The Need for Laws

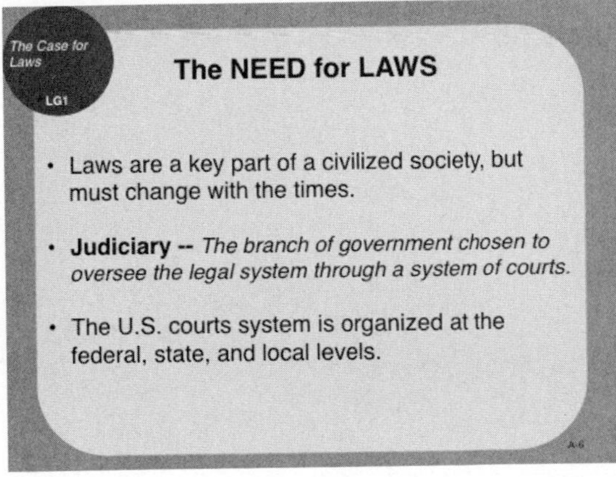

PPT A-7
Types of Court

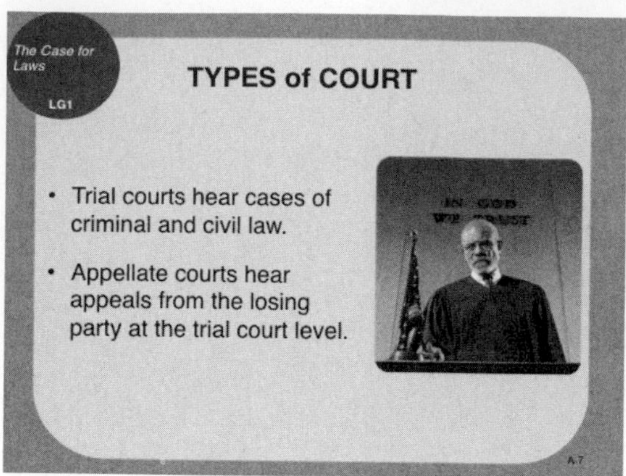

PPT A-8
Types of Law

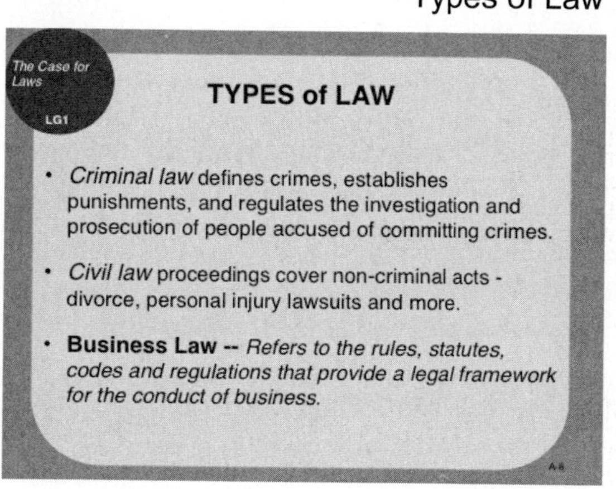

It is important for students to understand that as businesspeople they must have knowledge of business law. Business law provides a framework in which business must be conducted. Failure to understand the law could have dire consequences.

PPT A-9
Major Areas of Law

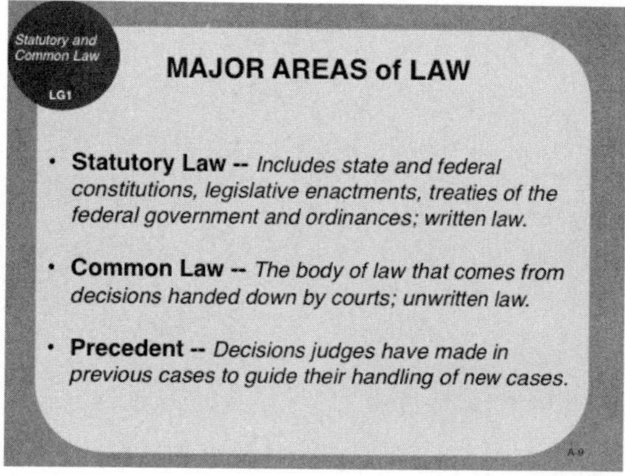

PPT A-10
Administrative Agencies

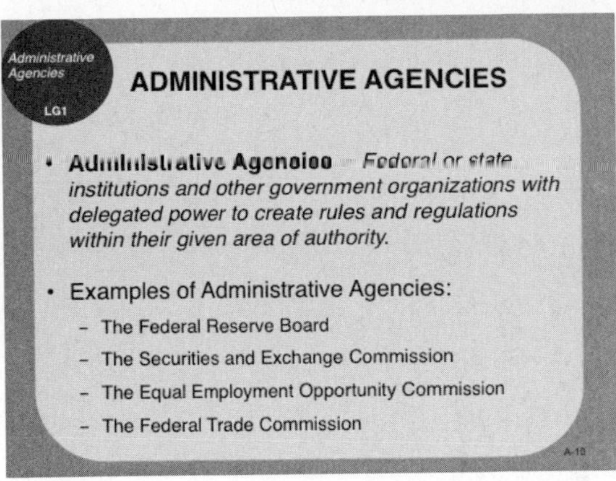

In addition to following the law, businesses must also follow regulations set by administrative agencies.

PPT A-11
Progress Assessment

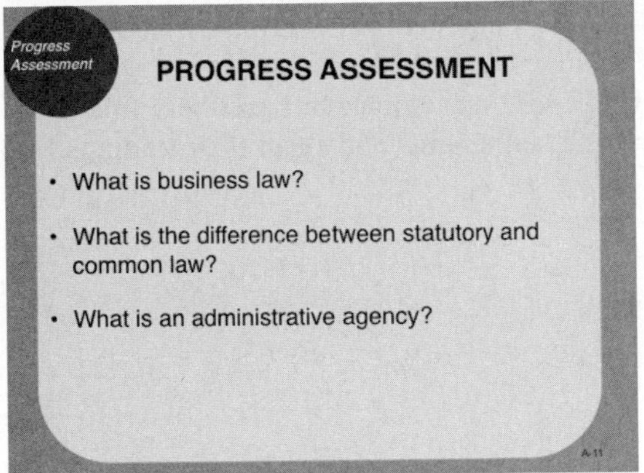

1. Business law refers to the rules, statutes, codes, and regulations that provide a legal framework for the conduct of business and that are enforceable.
2. Statutory law includes state and federal constitutions, legislative enactments, treaties of the federal government, and ordinances or written law. Common law is the body of law that comes from decisions handed down by courts. Common law is often referred to as precedent.
3. Administrative agencies are federal and state institutions and other government organizations created by Congress or state legislatures with delegated power to create rules and regulations within their given area of authority.

PPT A-12
What Is Tort Law?

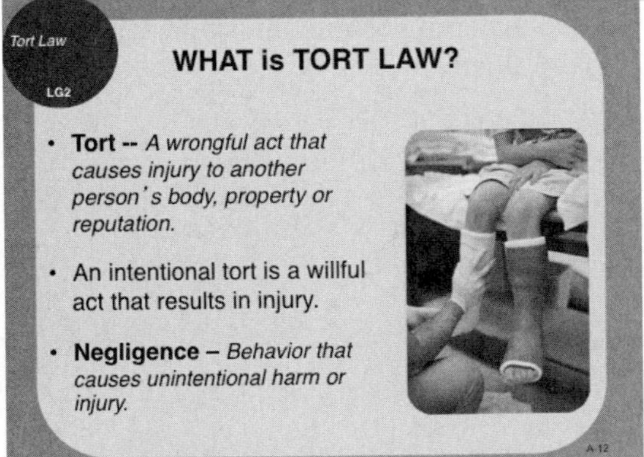

PPT A-13
Product Liability Laws

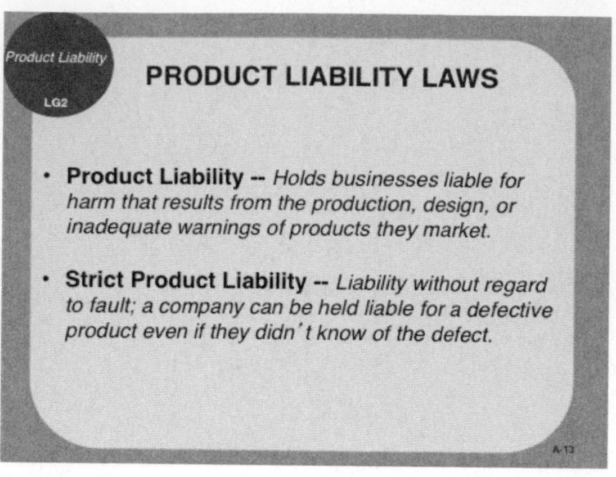

Toyota Motors recalled 3,000,000 cars in 2010 and 2011 due to sudden accelerator incidents. The company now faces a year of litigation.

PPT A-14
Major Product Liability Cases

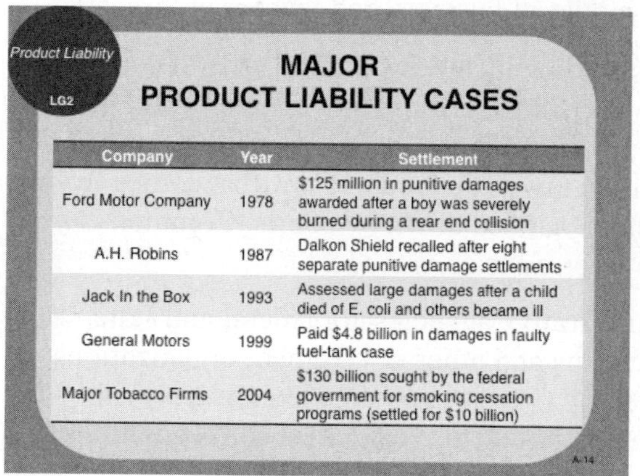

Company	Year	Settlement
Ford Motor Company	1978	$125 million in punitive damages awarded after a boy was severely burned during a rear end collision
A.H. Robins	1987	Dalkon Shield recalled after eight separate punitive damage settlements
Jack In the Box	1993	Assessed large damages after a child died of E. coli and others became ill
General Motors	1999	Paid $4.8 billion in damages in faulty fuel-tank case
Major Tobacco Firms	2004	$130 billion sought by the federal government for smoking cessation programs (settled for $10 billion)

1. This slide is based on Figure A.2.
2. This slide outlines major product liability cases with large settlements from well-known companies. If time allows, have students research the details of these settlements or have them find other large settlements and share their findings with the class.

PPT A-15
Patents, Copyrights, and Trademarks

1. Copyright law is becoming more and more important with the increase in publication using various media.
2. Copyrighted material is sometimes referred to as intellectual property.

PPT A-16
Patent Facts

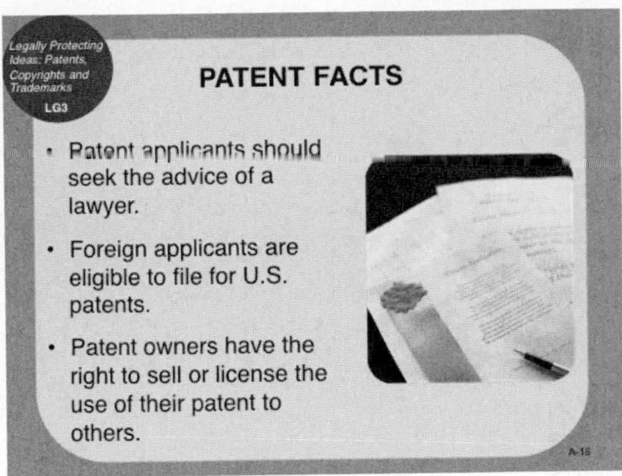

PPT A-17
Patent Leaders in 2010

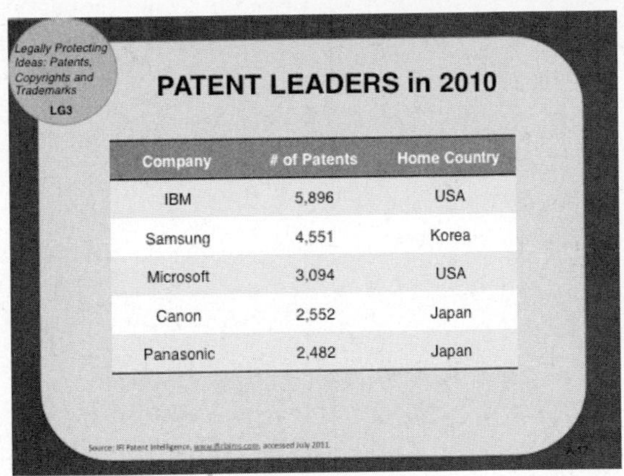

1. This slide presents the top patent recipient companies in 2010.
2. IBM, for the 18th straight year, was the top company granted the most patents by the U.S. Patent and Trademark Office.
3. *Source:* IFI Patent Intelligence.

PPT A-18
Progress Assessment

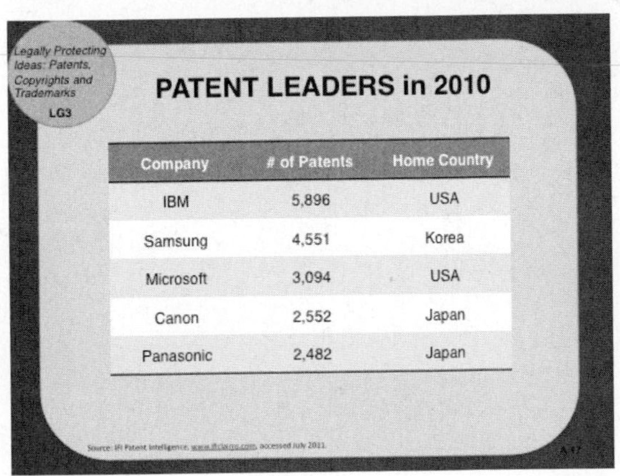

1. Tort law is a wrongful act that causes injury to another person's body, property, or reputation.
2. Product liability holds businesses liable for harm that results from production, design, or inadequate warnings of products they market. Strict product liability means having liability without regard to fault.
3. A patent is protected from infringements for 20 years.
4. A copyright protects a creator's rights to materials, such as books, articles, photos, paintings, and cartoons.

PPT A-19
What Is the Uniform Commercial Code?

PPT A-20
Understanding Warranties

Warranties can be full or limited.

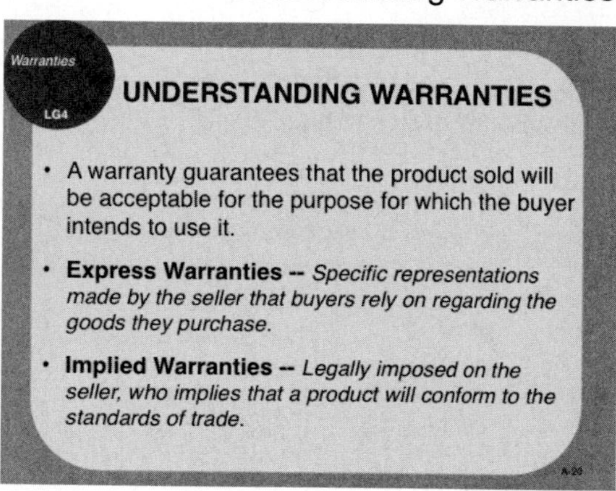

PPT A-21
Negotiable Instruments

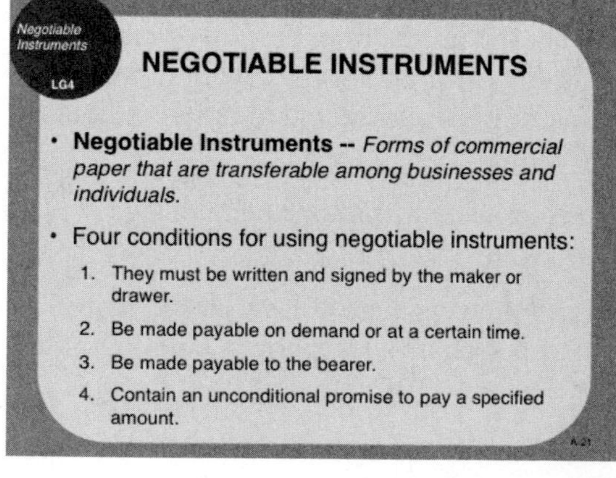

PPT A-22
Contract Law

PPT A-23
Contract Requirements

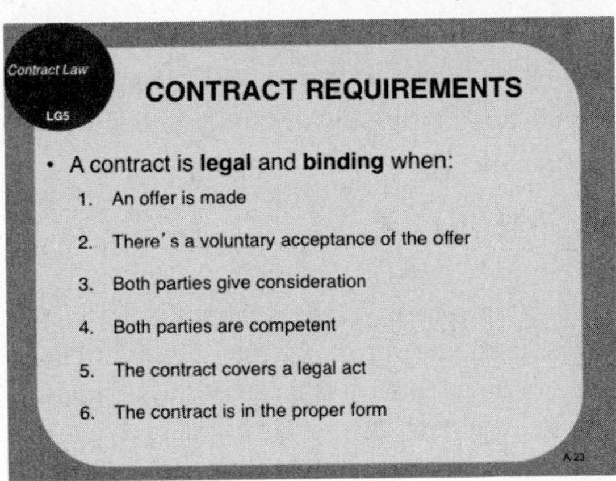

PPT A-24
Breached Contracts

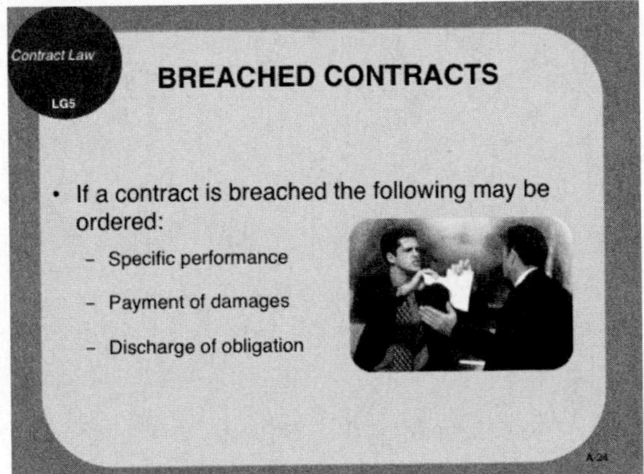

PPT A-25
Progress Assessment

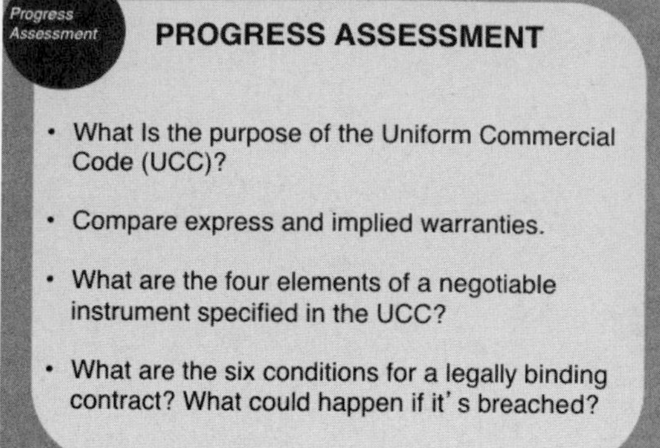

1. UCC is a comprehensive commercial law that covers sales laws and other commercial laws. The goal of the UCC is to simplify commercial transactions across state lines.
2. Express warranties are specific representations by the seller that buyers rely on regarding the goods they purchase. The warranty you receive in the box when you buy a new TV or mobile phone is an express warranty. Implied warranties are legally imposed on the seller, who implies that a product will conform to the customary standards of the trade or industry in which it competes.
3. The four elements of a negotiable instrument specified in the UCC are (1) be written and signed by the maker or drawer, (2) be made payable on demand or at a certain time, (3) be made payable to the bearer to specific order, and (4) contain an unconditional promise to pay a specified amount of money.
4. The six conditions for a legally binding contract are (1) an offer is made, (2) there is voluntary acceptance of the offer, (3) both parties give consideration, (4) both parties are competent, (5) the contract covers a legal act, and (6) the contract must be in proper form. If the contract is breached specific performance may be required, payment of damages or discharge of the obligation may be ordered.

PPT A-26
The Clayton Act of 1914

The Clayton Act of 1914 was intended to deal with price discrimination.

PPT A-27
Antitrust Legislation

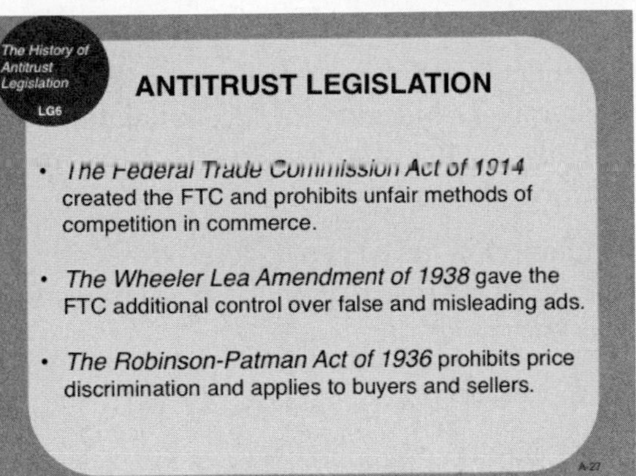

PPT A-28
History of High-Profile Antitrust Cases

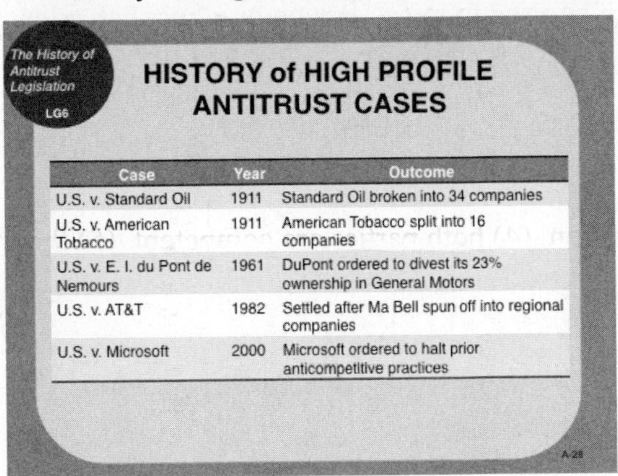

Case	Year	Outcome
U.S. v. Standard Oil	1911	Standard Oil broken into 34 companies
U.S. v. American Tobacco	1911	American Tobacco split into 16 companies
U.S. v. E. I. du Pont de Nemours	1961	DuPont ordered to divest its 23% ownership in General Motors
U.S. v. AT&T	1982	Settled after Ma Bell spun off into regional companies
U.S. v. Microsoft	2000	Microsoft ordered to halt prior anticompetitive practices

PPT A-29
Consumer Protections

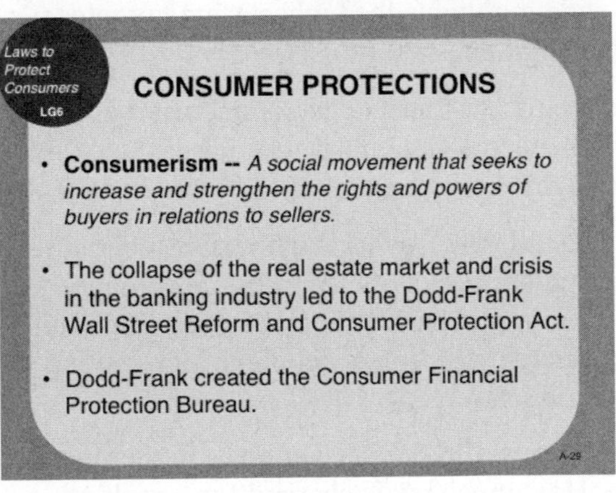

PPT A-30
Number of Identity Theft Complaints

1. This slide highlights the rise in the number of identity theft complaints according to the Federal Trade Commission.
2. Ask the students, What has given rise to the growing number of identity theft complaints? Do you know anyone who has experienced identity theft?
3. If you believe you have been a victim of identity theft, the Federal Trade Commission advises you to do the following:
   - File a police report.
   - Check your credit reports.
   - Notify creditors and dispute any unauthorized transactions.

PPT A-31
Taxes

Tax Laws
LG7
TAXES
- **Taxes** -- *The way federal, state, and local governments raise money.*
- Some forms of taxes:
  - Income taxes
  - Property taxes
  - Sales taxes
  - Excise taxes

A-31

Taxes can be used to raise revenue or adjust behavior.

PPT A-32
Sin Taxes

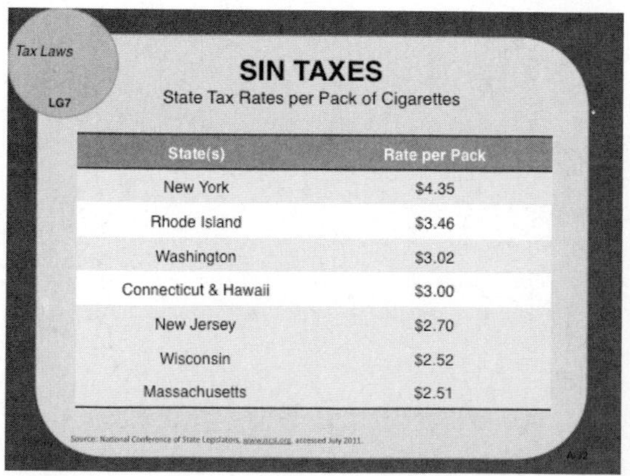

1. This slide highlights the highest state tax rates per pack on cigarettes.
2. Since the recent financial crisis, increasing sin taxes has become a popular way for cash-starved states to raise revenue.
3. Ask the students, How do high taxes on certain items, such as packs of cigarettes, discourage people from purchasing them? Do you think this is an effective way to get people to stop buying these products?
4. Have students investigate sin taxes in their own states. How much tax is charged for a pack of cigarettes, alcohol, and so on? Have sales been affected by the increase in these taxes?

PPT A-33
Do the Rich Pay Taxes?

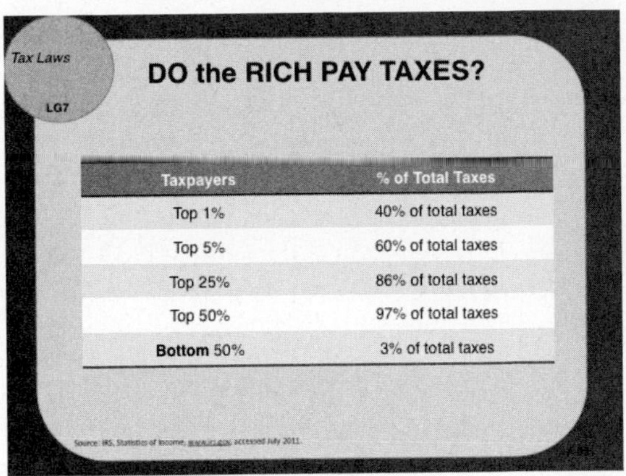

1. This slide illustrates the tax burden on various earnings groups.
2. Most students will be surprised to learn that 97% of total taxes are paid by the top 50% of taxpayers; in fact, the top 5% pay more than half the total taxes.
3. Ask the students, Should the rich pay more or less than they do now? Why? Should there be a flat tax rate, where all earners pay the same percentage of income regardless of how much money they earn overall? *(These questions should start a healthy debate among class members.)*

PPT A-34
Bankruptcy Laws

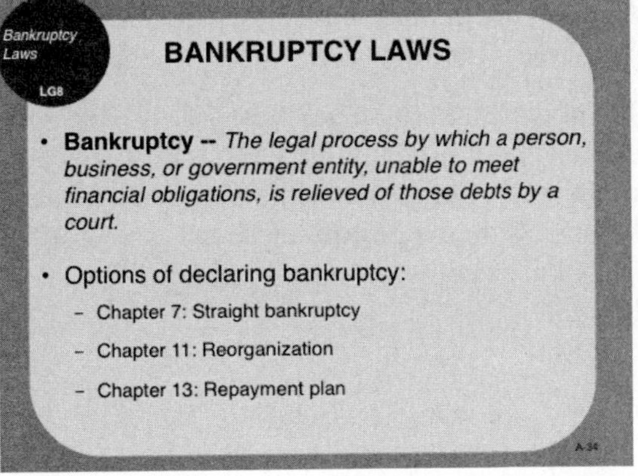

1. Chapter 7 is the most popular form of bankruptcy among individuals.
2. The recent financial crisis has pushed the number of bankruptcies to over a million. Bankruptcies are expected to reach almost 1.5 million in 2011.

PPT A-35
Chapter 7 Bankruptcy

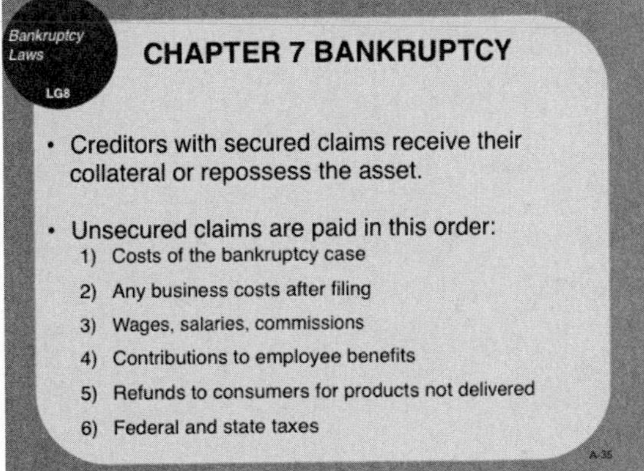

PPT A-36
How Assets Are Divided in Bankruptcy

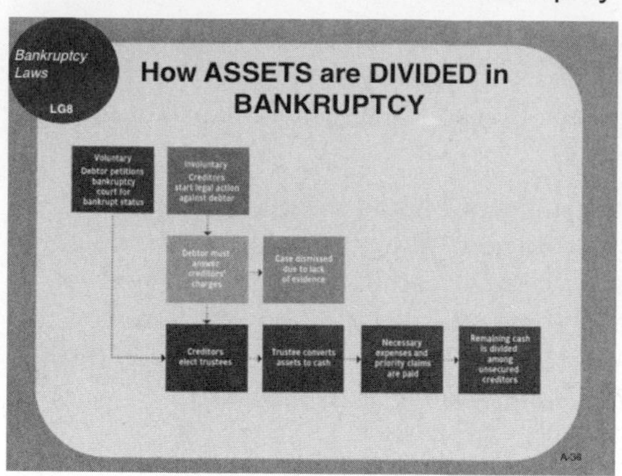

PPT A-37
Going, Going, Gone

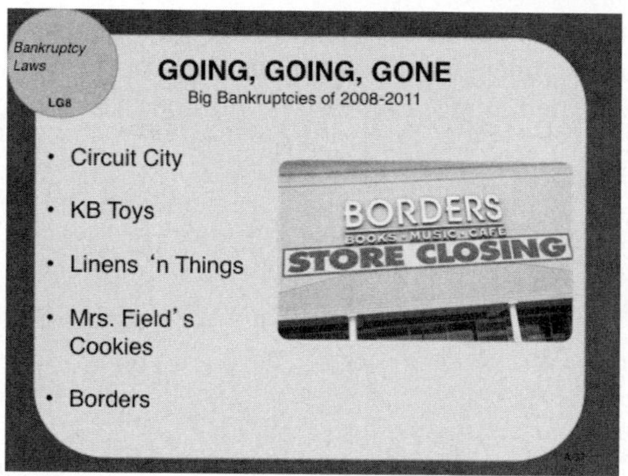

1. This slide profiles the bankruptcies of 2008–2011.
2. Have students research the companies listed in the slide. Why did these businesses go bankrupt instead of their competitors?
3. Ask the students, Is there a pattern of why businesses survive or go bankrupt? What mistakes do failed businesses make that others do not? What are the effects on the consumer when businesses fail? What are the effects on the economy as a whole?

PPT A-38
Deregulating Commerce

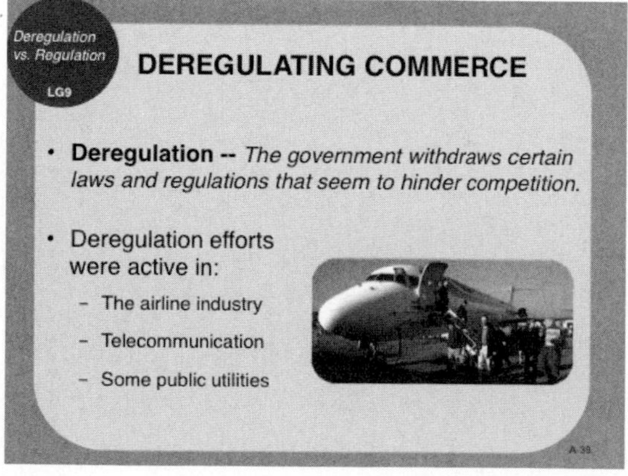

Today some believe the airline industry could use more government regulation since passenger services have decreased, delays and flight cancellations have increased, and charges such as baggage fees have become common.

PPT A-39
Hamburger Regulations

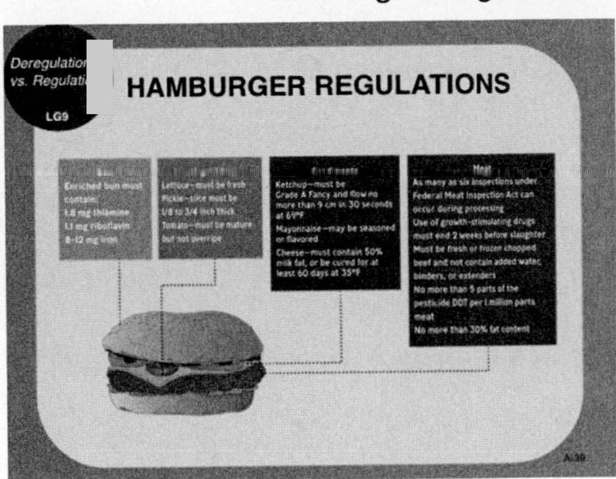

PPT A-40
Progress Assessment

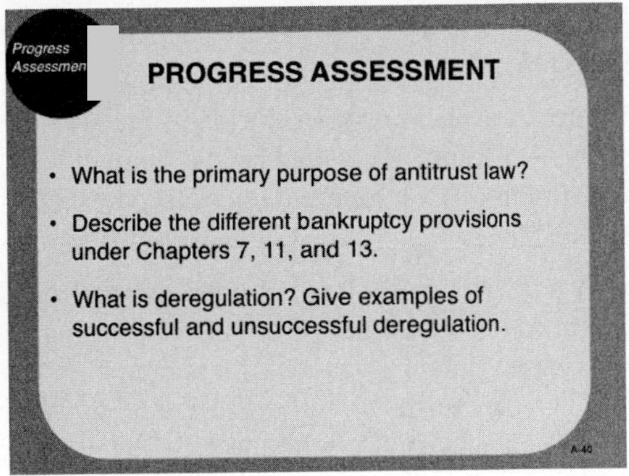

1. The purpose of antitrust law is to foster competition in the free market.
2. Describe bankruptcy provisions under Chapters 7, 11, and 13.
   - *Chapter 7— liquidation of nonexempt assets used by business and individuals.*
   - *Chapter 11—reorganizations of firms assets used by businesses*
   - *Chapter 13—allows small businesses and individuals to pay back creditors over a three- to five-year time period*
3. Deregulation occurs when the government withdraws certain laws and regulations that seem to hinder competition. Examples of deregulation include telecommunications and the airline industry. Deregulation of the banking and investment industries has not been successful.

lecture links

"Take calculated risks. That is quite different from being rash."
George S. Patton

"The minute you read something that you can't understand, you can almost be sure it was drawn up by a lawyer."
Will Rogers

"To win without risk is to triumph without glory."
Pierre Corneille

lecture link A-1

THE DIFFERENCES BETWEEN PATENTS, COPYRIGHTS, AND TRADEMARKS

Patent is the abbreviated term for *letters patent*. The Constitution gives Congress the power to enact laws relative to patents in Article I, section 8. The first Patent Law was enacted in 1790. The most recent revision was the American Inventors Protection Act of 1999. Patents are issued by the United States Patent and Trademark Office (USPTO) of the U.S. Department of Commerce. Generally, the term of a patent is 20 years from the date on which the patent was filed.

A **patent** is a grant of a property right to the inventor of a device, process, or composition of matter. Specifically, the right conferred by a patent grant is "the right to exclude others from making, using, offering for sale, or selling" the invention in the United States. Once a patent is issued, the patentee is responsible for enforcing the patent, without the aid of the USPTO. The terms *patent pending* and *patent applied for* are used to inform the public that an application for a patent is on file with the USPTO.

In the words of the statute, any person who "invents or discovers any new and useful process, machine, manufacture, or composition of matter, or any new and useful improvement thereof, may obtain a patent." Utility patents are granted for new processes, machines, or articles of manufacture. Design patents are granted for new, original, and ornamental designs for an article of manufacture; a new design for a telephone might be an example. Plant patents are granted for new and distinct, asexually reproduced plants; examples would include corn hybrids.

A **trademark** is a word, name, symbol, or device that is used in trade with goods to identify the source of the goods and to distinguish them from others. A **service mark** is the same as a trademark but it identifies the source of a service rather than a product. A real estate agency or a financial consultant might use a service mark.

Trademarks may be used to prevent others from using a confusingly similar mark but not to prevent others from manufacturing the same product or providing similar services. Names of types of products or devices, such as television or radio, cannot be trademarks; but some product names, intended by their manufacturers to be trademarks, have lost their legal status as trademarks by virtue of their use by customers to identify products rather than a specific brand. Some examples are the terms *aspirin, cellophane,* and *escalator*. While many people still accept Pepsi or RC, when they say "I'd like a coke" "Coke" is still a registered trademark.

While registering a trademark with the USPTO gives the holder some advantages, registration is not necessary to establish legal rights. In fact, the symbols *TM* or *SM* may be used with a person's mark to inform the public of his or her claims. However, the "R in a circle" mark can be used only after the

USPTO actually registers it. Also, a mark cannot be registered unless it had been used "in commerce" or unless the applicant files an "intent to use" application.

Copyright is a form of protection provided by the laws of the United States to the authors of "original works of authorship," including literary, dramatic, musical, artistic, and certain other intellectual works. Copyright gives the owner exclusive rights to do and to authorize others to do the following:

Reproduce the work or phonorecord

Prepare derivative works

Distribute copies by sale or rent

Perform the work publicly or, in the case of records, to play the work publicly

Display the work

Copyright protection begins at the time the work is created in fixed form, whether written, or notated (as in music or choreography), or saved to a computer disk. Works created after 1978 are protected by copyright during the author's lifetime plus 70 years. For works whose rights are owned by a corporation, the duration of copyright is 95 years from publication or 120 years from creation, whichever is shorter.

Copyright begins automatically when a work is created and it is "created" when it is fixed in a copy or phonorecord for the first time. If a work is prepared over a period of time, the portion that is fixed on a particular date is protected from that date. Under the 1976 Copyright Act, publication is no longer the key to obtaining copyright protection.

For works created after March 1, 1989, notice of copyright is not required, but it is beneficial. Notice of copyright is made by using the word *copyright*, the abbreviation *copyr*, or the symbol of a "c in a circle" (a "p in a circle" for recordings) with the year of publication and the name of the owner of the copyright. For example,

Copyright 2012 John Doe

Copyrights are registered by the Copyright Office of the Library of Congress.

lecture link A-2

NORTEL'S PATENT AUCTION

In early 2009, the telecommunications company Nortel Networks filed for Chapter 11 bankruptcy in Delaware, Canada, and Europe. In order to cover some of the costs of its financial downfall, the company hired a small law firm specializing in intellectual property to help sell its cache of patents. While a patent auction may not carry the same glitz as priceless paintings or jewelry on the block, their value far exceeds that of any standard trinket sell-off. Analysts estimate the patent portfolio will sell for no less than several billion dollars.

Whoever ends up in possession of the patents will hold a powerful position in the wireless world. First of all, the patents could provide integral assistance for some companies wanting to expand their telecommunications presence. More than that, though, the patents could prove to be a fierce legal weapon in the highly litigious wireless industry. This point has regulators at the U.S. Justice Department worried that tech giants like Apple or Google could use the patents to stifle competition by extracting huge licensing fees from rivals.

In the R&D–obsessed world of tech, patents have become something of a prized possession. Entire companies exist these days solely to purchase patents. Meanwhile, a whole industry of brokers, lawyers, and engineers has developed just to figure out exactly how much these things are worth. After all, a patent is little more than "an exclusive right to develop an invention for a certain period of time." The U.S. Patent Office doesn't attach a price tag to it following approval. In the case of the Nortel cache, Google's opening offer of $900 million will provide the starting point for bidding. Originally scheduled for June 20, 2011, a "significant level of interest" in the auction necessitated a one-week delay. The bidding commenced behind the closed doors of an unnamed New York law firm on June 27, 2011, although the matter is expected to continue for some time after that.[i]

lecture link A-3

PIRACY MAY KO UFC

For years, sports leagues have been free of the piracy that has plagued music and movies. Fans typically like to watch games as they happen, making piracy of a baseball game less appealing to downloaders than a film or a song. But as online streaming technology advanced, so too have the pirates' efforts to get entertainment for free. Thousands of game feeds from the NFL to the UFC now leak onto the Internet every day. Although company watchdogs constantly scour the Web looking for infringers, the sheer number of sites involved makes it almost impossible to shut them all down.

Mainstream professional sports leagues earn billions of dollars from exclusive broadcast contracts with networks and pricey stadium seats. When those games are pirated, though, their brands are undermined. The situation is even worse for up-and-coming organizations like the mixed martial arts league UFC. Given the company's reliance on $45-a-pop pay-per-view sales, illegal online streams don't just damage their brand, they take money directly out of the company's pockets.

To combat infringement, UFC, as well as the federal government, is taking streaming sites to court. In January 2011 UFC's parent company Zuffa sued Justin.tv, a live video streaming service. That same month, federal investigators seized 10 domain names that broadcast pirated game feeds. Nevertheless, even direct litigation might not be enough to stop infringers. Zuffa's suit against Justin.tv is much like Viacom's unsuccessful lawsuit against YouTube. Justin.tv's assertion that it removed infringing videos when prompted by copyright owners is almost identical to YouTube's winning defense. Also, despite the government's wide reach, the servers of many illegal streaming sites are located in other countries with lax copyright laws and a disinclination to cooperate with American authorities.[ii]

lecture link A-4

NEGOTIABLE INSTRUMENT FORGERY AND THE UNIFORM COMMERCIAL CODE

Frank W. Abagnale was the main speaker at a seminar on document fraud. He is an unlikely expert, having spent time in French, Swedish, and U.S. prisons 30 years ago for creating and passing millions of dollars of bad checks. Interpol, Abagnale said, dubbed him a "master forger," a badge of honor of sorts, as Abagnale began his career when he was 16 years old and concluded it at age 21 with a stint in a French lockup. After serving his time there, he was extradited to Sweden and finally to the United States, doing 12 years. He was released early on the condition that he assist the U.S. government in its battle against forgers. (The film *Catch Me If You Can* is based on Abagnale's career as a forger.)

Now he's a "senior advisor" to the FBI's Financial Crimes Unit. In that role, he assisted in designing the new $100 bill. He also provides consulting services to financial institutions and companies worldwide.

Abagnale cited a *BusinessWeek* study, which concluded that $12.6 billion is lost annually to check forgery. Bank robbers may grab the headlines, but they net only about $68 million yearly, he said. That's $50 for every man, woman, and child nationwide lost to check fraud compared to 27 cents per American taken at gunpoint. Embarrassed companies do not report many frauds, so the $12.6 billion figure is conservative, Abagnale said.

Lack of publicity about the problem has helped put the document fraud industry where it is today, Abagnale said. Politicians, prosecutors, and judges don't concentrate on stopping fraud. Consequently, punishments are lower for forgery, assuming someone is arrested, which is rare. "Nobody ever ran for office promising 'I'll clear the streets of check writers if you elect me,'" he said.

Advances in modern technology also have made the forger's job easier. When Abagnale was practicing his former trade, a four-color printer was the size of a large room and cost $250,000. Now, he said, $5,000 worth of computer equipment provides a superior and portable alternative.

Disputes over who is liable for bad checks often end up in court. These matters are governed by the Uniform Commercial Code, or UCC, a set of model statutes designed by legal experts to be used by all states in order to provide a level playing field for commerce. It is not an all encompassing federal law, but rather a guideline for laws to be adopted by the states individually.

States can adopt a provision of the UCC or not. For example, the portion of the UCC concerning liability in document frauds was amended in 1990. Connecticut adopted the amendment in 1991, but New York State has not yet done so.

What can a company do to make itself less vulnerable? One powerful weapon is known as "positive pay." A customer keeps an electronic list of all checks written and downloads it into the bank's computer at the end of the day. If a check shows up that is not on the list, it is flagged as a forgery, and the bank doesn't honor it. Most banks have positive pay programs, said Abagnale.

An alternative for smaller businesses that may lack the sophisticated computer software necessary to create a daily list is "reverse positive pay." In this case, a bank sends a list to the business owner of checks drawn upon the company's account each day. The owner then compares his or her records with the bank's list and notifies the bank if there are any discrepancies.

Companies should stay up to date in reconciling bank statements since the UCC allows only 30 days to report a fraudulent instrument.

Banking procedures are not the only defense. Corporate officers who proudly affix their John Hancocks to annual reports or Security and Exchange Commission filings are a forger's delight. For a signature that will pass muster, the forger can just scan it off the report. Abagnale recommends that the lawyers who draft these reports sign them as opposed to officers whose signatures may appear on checks.

Checks turned out by high-speed laser printers allow forgers to lift the toner off the check with tools as sophisticated as scotch tape and substitute dollar numbers—usually with several extra zeros. Abagnale said that "toner anchorage," a chemical injected into the paper, causes the toner and the paper to fuse, preventing the writing from being lifted and changed. Also, chemicals can be added to checks so they change color upon being exposed to materials, such as bleach, which are used to erase the original writing.

The dollar amounts printed on checks should be in a unique font, or type style. Additionally, the numbers themselves should have writing incorporated into them. This prevents adding, say, three zeroes to a $20 check and turning it into $20,000.

Because blank check paper is readily available through mail-order vendors, prudent companies should arrange with their printer for a unique type of paper with security features built in. One such feature involves microprinting, used in the new $100 bill. Those lines along Ben Franklin's collar actually say something when held under a magnifying glass. Scanners and copiers are not sufficiently sensitive, so they can't reproduce the microprinting. The signature line of the check is a good place to use microprinting.

What scanners and copiers will catch is a "void pantograph." Scanners reproduce patterns of large dots before they reproduce patterns of small ones. A series of large dots spelling out the word "void" should be hidden in a secure check. This pattern may not be visible to the naked eye, but should the document be scanned or copied, up pops "void," thereby ruining the forger's work.

Warning labels should indicate other security features, such as watermarks, and state clearly that if the check does not have a watermark, "do not cash," Abagnale said.

Generally, the more difficult a company makes forgery, the less likely it is to be a victim. Forgers, Abagnale said, look for easy targets, of which there are too many. "We make it so easy for people to steal from us, that people do. People steal from us because we let them," Abagnale said.

lecture link A-5

GOOGLE'S TAX TACTICS

Tax havens have long been used by multinationals to skirt the stringent corporate tax laws of their home countries. But for many in and outside the business world, the abundance of tax havens by no means justifies the revenue they deprive deserving states. Unfortunately, not only is tax sheltering common, in most cases it is legal. Google, for instance, earned $12.5 billion overseas since 2007, only 2.4% of which was taxed. Google's clever, entirely legal money funneling saved the company $3.1 billion and boosted 2009's earnings by 26%.

The system starts in Dublin at Google's international headquarters. All the money from ad sales outside the United States finds its way to Google Ireland, where corporate profits are taxed at 12.5%. The company's ultimate goal is to send its earnings to Bermuda, where there's no corporate income tax at all. But sending the money directly to the Caribbean would incur a large fee according to Irish law. To circumvent this, the money is sent to Google Netherlands Holdings, a shell company with no employees. Ireland doesn't tax payments to companies in other European Union states, ensuring that Google's money can take advantage of the Netherlands' lax tax laws. From there, 99.8% of the money that hits Holland's shores goes off to Bermuda.

Google also eliminates a portion of its domestic taxes by licensing its search and advertising technology through Google Ireland, even though most of the development is performed in the United States. In total, tax avoidance from corporations costs the U.S. government as much as $60 billion annually. And though Google is certainly not alone in its tax control techniques, no other tech company has managed to manipulate its overseas tax rate quite as low as the search giant. From a legal standpoint, the company has done no wrong, but some believe Google has violated its famous "Don't be evil" motto. However, such a statement ignores the popular belief that businesses have an obligation to its shareholders to minimize its taxes and other costs legally. Whether ethically or unethically, Google has certainly accomplished that task.[iii]

lecture link A-6

BAD TIMING FOR BANKRUPTCY LAW CHANGES

In October 2005, the U.S. Bankruptcy Code was changed to make it harder for individuals to file for bankruptcy. The code sets new limits on personal bankruptcy filing and requires people to get professional credit counseling before they file petitions. It prohibits most middle-income filers from filing Chapter 7 petitions, which would allow debts to be erased. Instead, if people judged to have at least $100 a month left over after paying certain debts, they must submit a five-year repayment plan under the more restrictive rules. During the months leading up to the October transition, bankruptcy petitions hit a record high.

For residents of the south-central Gulf Coast, the timing could not have been any worse. Hurricane Katrina had swept through the area just five weeks before, causing over $80 billion in destruction.

These figures represent lives changed forever. Not only were homes destroyed, but also jobs, relationships, religious communities, and dreams. For many the cost impact was doubled—when a home was lost to wind damage, insurers were required to pay the amount of the homeowner's policy. However, when any part of the damage was due to water, insurers generally refused to cover most loses. After the storm, homeowners found that although their homes and businesses were damaged beyond repair with no insurance reimbursement, mortgage holders still expected to be paid. For many families and small businesses, the storm's devastation was not to be fully felt for weeks or months—until they faced the crippling financial consequences of lost property, lost wages, and lost jobs. They may have lost the house and the car, but the obligation to pay for them didn't expire.

Most people who file for bankruptcy do so only when a major life disruption occurs. Almost 80% of bankruptcy filings occur due to death of a spouse, huge medical expenses, breakup of a family, job loss, or natural disaster.

A study of bankruptcy filing shows that following the biggest hurricanes of the past 30 years bankruptcy filings were about 50% higher in states that suffered a direct hit. When storms hit areas with less expensive buildings (rather than expensive beachfront condos), the increase in bankruptcy rates goes even higher. The highest increase in bankruptcy filings occurred when Hurricane Elena hit Mississippi in 1985.

Once the new bankruptcy bill went into effect, everyone—regardless of income and regardless of the reason for filling—was required to file extensive new paperwork and meet the new procedural requirements. The new rules demand more payments for car lenders and credit card issuers. Many workers discovered that the bankruptcy court may believe they have phantom income for repayment—money from jobs they held before the storm. The court may presume they still have income even when those jobs are gone.

What happens to small businesses is even worse. They new Chapter 11 provisions target smaller businesses for special treatment. Unlike major corporations, small businesses face a shutdown if they cannot confirm a plan of reorganization within 300 days. Under the new law, small businesses—and only small businesses—will be required to submit a stack of new forms for more extensive examination by bankruptcy judges. Just when the Gulf Coast region needs its entrepreneurs most, fewer of them will get the chance to recover from the devastation and start their businesses again.

The Justice Department has acknowledged the problems but has not changed the rules or guaranteed expedited treatment. When the stunned and exhausted victims of Hurricane Katrina finally arrive in bankruptcy courts, they will find that the bankruptcy laws now offer less relief than before the storms struck.[iv]

endnotes

[i] *Sources:* Ameet Sachdev, "Nortel Networks' Patent Portfolio Up for Auction," *Chicago Tribune*, June 7, 2011; Hugo Miller, "Nortel Delays Auction to June 27 on 'Significant' Interest." *Bloomberg Businessweek*, June 16, 2011.

[ii] *Source:* Brad Stone, "Unpaid Per View," *Bloomberg Businessweek*, February 28, 2011.

[iii] *Source:* Jesse Drucker, "The Tax Haven That's Saving Google Billions," *Bloomberg Businessweek*, October 21, 2010.

[iv] *Sources:* Elizabeth Warren, "Those Swamped by Katrina Face Tougher Bankruptcy Law," *The Clarion-Ledger*, October 16, 2005; "Many Dash to Court to Dump Debt, Dodge Law," *The Clarion-Ledger*, October 15, 2005; Associated Press, "Bankruptcies Hit Record High," *The Clarion-Ledger*, March 25, 2006.

Using Technology to Manage Information

bonus chapter **B**

what's new in this edition

additions to the 10th edition:

- Getting to Know Chris Hughes, Co-founder of Facebook
- Name That Company: 4food
- Subsection Web 3.0 with discussion of Web 3.0, Semantic Web, and Mobile Web
- Term **Web 3.0** added to Key Terms and Glossary
- New title Mobile Devices with new discussion of smartphones and tablet computers added to deleted subsection titled Cutting the Cords: Wireless Information Appliances
- Discussion of advantages and disadvantages of cloud computing added to subsection Cloud Computing
- Discussion of apps added to subsection Software
- Figure: Taming E-Mail Interruptions
- Figure: Tips for Using Social Media to Partner with Customers
- Video case

revisions to the 10th edition:

- Text was revised to eliminate redundancy and tighten discussions.
- Statistical data and examples throughout the chapter were updated to reflect current information.
- Discussion of business intelligence moved to new subsection Evolution from Data Processing to Business Intelligence from deleted subsection The Move toward Business Intelligence.
- Subsection titled The Front Door: Enterprise Portals was deleted; discussion of enterprise portals remains
- Subsection title changed to Social Media and Web 2.0; expanded with discussion of uses of Facebook and Twitter in business

deletions from the 9th edition:

- Getting to Know David Steward, CEO of World Wide Technology
- Name That Company: Wal-Mart
- Subsection Green IT

brief chapter outline and learning goals

bonus chapter B

Using Technology to Manage Information

Getting To Know CHRIS HUGHES, CO-FOUNDER of FACEBOOK

learning goal 1

Outline the changing role of business technology.

I. THE ROLE OF INFORMATION TECHNOLOGY

A. Evolution from Data Processing to Business Intelligence

B. How Information Technology Changes Business

learning goal 2

List the types of business information, identify the characteristics of useful information, and discuss how data are stored and mined.

II. TYPES OF INFORMATION

A. Managing Information

B. Organizing E-Mail and Electronic Files

C. Storing and Mining Data

learning goal 3

Compare the scope of the Internet, intranets, extranets, and virtual private networks and explain how broadband technology enabled the evolution to Web 2.0 and 3.0.

III. THE HEART OF KNOWLEDGE MANAGEMENT: THE INTERNET

A. Broadband Technology

B. Social Media and Web 2.0

C. Web 3.0

learning goal 4

Review the computer hardware most frequently used in business.

IV. THE ENABLING TECHNOLOGY: HARDWARE

A. Mobile Devices

B. Computer Networks

C. Virtualization and Cloud Computing

learning goal 5

Classify the types of computer software most frequently used in business.

V. SOFTWARE

learning goal 6

Evaluate the human resource, security, privacy, and stability issues in management that are affected by information technology.

VI. EFFECTS OF INFORMATION TECHNOLOGY ON MANAGEMENT

A. Human Resource Issues

B. Security Issues

C. Privacy Issues

D. Stability Issues

VII. TECHNOLOGY AND YOU

VIII. SUMMARY

lecture outline

Getting to Know CHRIS HUGHES, of FACEBOOK

Hughes joined Facebook early, but not as a code writer. He developed the brand and examined the features that bring people closer together. Hughes helped grow the site from Harvard-only to a global phenom. After making a name at Facebook, Hughes joined President Obama's campaign and worked with staff to create Obama's huge on-line presence.

This company used social media to build its business. Its customers design new products, name them, and enter them in the company's database. Customers may even make You-Tube commercials that are featured on the company's video wall. If other customers buy the new product, the creator gets a small store credit.

(Students should read the chapter before guessing the company's name : 4food)

learning goal 1

Outline the changing role of business technology.

I. THE ROLE OF INFORMATION TECHNOLOGY

A. Business technology is continuously **CHANGING NAMES** and **CHANGING ROLES**.

B. **EVOLUTION FROM DATA PROCESSING TO BUSINESS INTELLIGENCE**

1. ***DATA PROCESSING (DP)*** is the name for business technology in the 1970s; included technology that supported an existing business and was primarily used to improve the flow of financial information.

   a. **DATA** are raw, unanalyzed, and unorganized facts and figures.

   b. **INFORMATION** is the processed and organized data that can be used for managerial decision making.

lecture notes

PPT B-1
Chapter Title

PPT B-2
Learning Goals

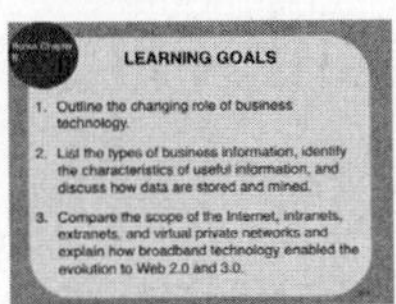

(See complete PowerPoint slide notes on page B.48.)

PPT B-3
Learning Goals

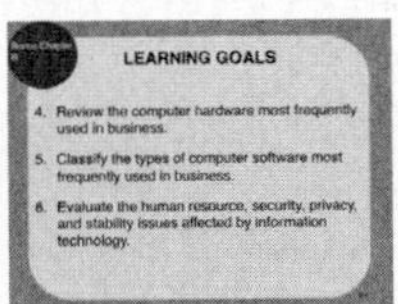

(See complete PowerPoint slide notes on page B.48.)

PPT B-4
Chris Hughes

(See complete PowerPoint slide notes on page B.49.)

PPT B-5
Name That Company

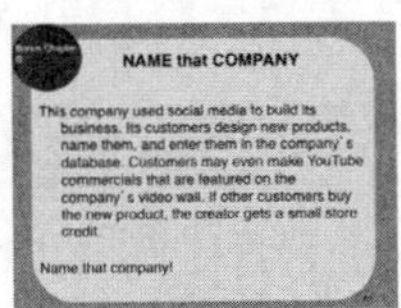

(See complete PowerPoint slide notes on page B.49.)

lecture link B-1
WHY WE TYPE THIS WAY

The modern office has a 19th century bottleneck—the computer keyboard. (See the complete lecture link on page B.64 in this manual.)

PPT B-6
Technology in the 1970s

(See complete PowerPoint slide notes on page B.49.)

   c. **DATA PROCESSING** was used to support and improve an existing business by improving the flow of financial information.

2. In the 1980s, business technology became known as **INFORMATION SYSTEMS (IS).**
   a. An ***INFORMATION SYSTEMS (IS)*** is technology that helps companies do business; includes such tools as automated teller machines (ATMs) and voice mail.
   b. Its role was changed from **SUPPORTING** business to **DOING** business *(for example, ATMs and voice mail).*
   c. As business used technology more, it became more dependent on it.

3. Until the late 1980s business technology involved using **NEW TECHNOLOGY** on **OLD METHODS.**
   a. Then business shifted to using **NEW TECHNOLOGY** on **NEW METHODS**.
   b. ***INFORMATION TECHNOLOGY (IT)*** is technology that helps companies change business by allowing them to use new methods.
   c. The role of the IT staff has changed and increased in importance.
   d. Today, the CIO helps business technology communicate better while offering better services and lower costs.

4. **KNOWLEDGE** is information charged with enough intelligence to make it relevant and useful.

PPT B-7
Technology in the 1980s

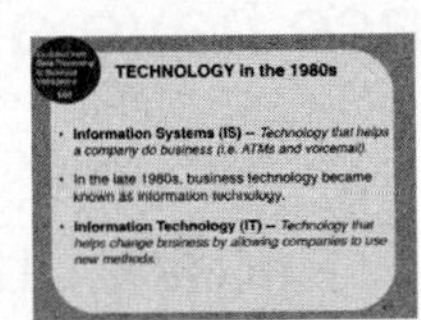

(See complete PowerPoint slide notes on page B.50.)

5. A new sophisticated form of IT is ***BUSINESS INTELLIGENCE (BI)***, any variety of software applications that analyze an organization's raw data and take out useful insights from it.
6. Business intelligence changes the traditional flow of information.
7. BI provides the right information to the right person at the right time.
8. Maintaining **FLEXIBILITY** to deal with future changes is critical to business survival.

C. **HOW INFORMATION TECHNOLOGY CHANGES BUSINESS**

1. Time and place have always been at the center of business.
   a. Today, IT allows businesses to delivery products and services whenever and wherever it is convenient for the **CUSTOMER**.
   b. *The text uses the entertainment industry to illustrate the changes created by new technologies.*
   c. As IT breaks time and location barriers, it creates organizations and services that are **INDEPENDENT OF LOCATION.**
   d. NASDAQ, an electronic stock exchange without a trading floor, allows buyers and sellers to make trades by computer.
2. When companies increase their technological capabilities, it changes the way people do business.

PPT B-8
Technology in the Early 2000s

(See complete PowerPoint slide notes on page B.50.)

PPT B-9
Further Evolution

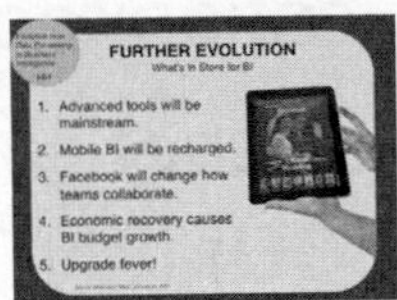

(See complete PowerPoint slide notes on page B.50.)

PPT B-10
Technology Brings Change

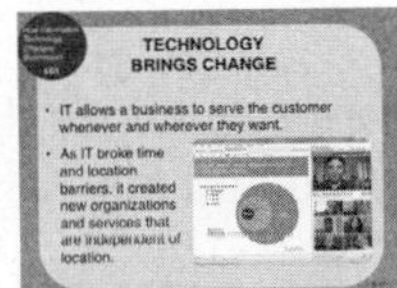

(See complete PowerPoint slide notes on page B.51.)

TEXT FIGURE B.1
The 7 Worst Tech Predictions of All Time
(Text page B-4)

This text figure gives a few quotes from technology leaders who got it wrong—very wrong.

TEXT FIGURE B.2
How Information Technology Is Changing Business
(Text page B-5)

This text figure shows a few of the ways that information is changing businesses, their employees, suppliers, and customers.

PPT B-11
Top U.S. Cities by High-Tech Employment

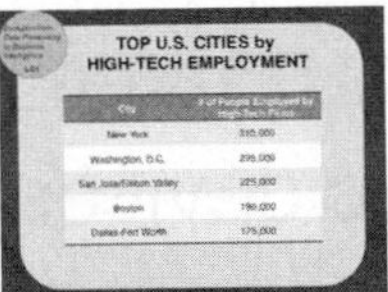

(See complete PowerPoint slide notes on page B.51.)

a. **E-MAIL** is far faster than paper-based correspondence.

b. **TEXTING AND INSTANT MESSAGING (IM)** has become a favorite business real-time communication tool.

3. Internet and intranet communication using **SHARED DOCUMENTS** lets contributors work on a common document without meeting in person.

learning goal 2

List the types of business information, identify the characteristics of useful information, and discuss how data are stored and mined.

II. TYPES OF INFORMATION

A. TYPES OF INFORMATION THAT ARE AVAILABLE:

1. **BUSINESS PROCESS INFORMATION**, such as information about sales, enterprise resource planning, supply chain management, and customer relationship management systems
2. **PHYSICAL-WORLD OBSERVATIONS** from devices such as RFID devices, web cams, global positioning systems, and sensor technology
3. **BIOLOGICAL DATA,** including fingerprinting and biometric devices
4. **PUBLIC DATA,** including electronic traces that people leave when surfing the Internet
5. Data that indicate **PERSONAL PREFERENCE OR INTENTIONS** such as the trail of information that Internet shoppers leave.

progress assessment
(Text page B-5)

PROGRESS ASSESSMENT
- How has the role of information technology changed since the days when it was known as data processing?
- How has information technology changed the way we do business?

PPT B-12
Progress Assessment

(See complete PowerPoint slide notes on page B.51.)

PPT B-13
Key Types of Business Information Available

(See complete PowerPoint slide notes on page B.52.)

PPT B-14
Four Characteristics That Make Information Useful

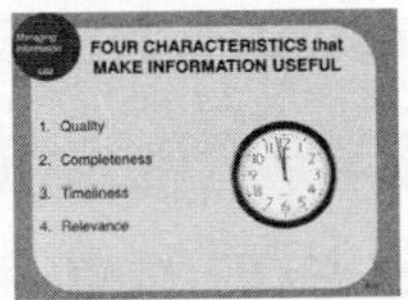

(See complete PowerPoint slide notes on page B.52.)

PPT B-15
Top Sites to Keep You Connected

(See complete PowerPoint slide notes on page B.52.)

B. **MANAGING INFORMATION**

1. To find what they need, managers have to sift through mountains of information.
2. Businesspeople refer to all this information overload as **"INFOGLUT."**
3. **IDENTIFYING THE FOUR OR FIVE KEY GOALS** helps eliminate unnecessary information.
4. **USEFULNESS** of management information depends on four characteristics:
   a. **QUALITY**: The information must be accurate and reliable.
   b. **COMPLETENESS**: There must be enough data to make a decision, but not too much to confuse the issue.
   c. **TIMELINESS**:
      i. Information must reach managers quickly.
      ii. Technologies such as e-mail, texting, and instant messaging increase information timeliness.
   d. **RELEVANCE**: Managers must know the questions to ask to get the answers they need.
5. It is impossible to understand all the information available, so priorities must be established.

C. **ORGANIZING E-MAIL AND ELECTRONIC FILES**

1. Use your e-mail program's organizing tools and create folders for specific topics, projects, or clients.

TEXT FIGURE B.3
Taming E-Mail Interruptions
(Text page B-7)

This text figure shows a few of the ways workers can reduce the number of e-mail distractions.

PPT B-16
Effectively Using Your Electronic Files

(See complete PowerPoint slide notes on page B.53.)

2. Use consistent file names.
3. Use online backup services.
4. Use desktop search software, such as Google Desktop.

D. **STORING AND MINING DATA**

1. The goals in managing information are storing, sorting, and getting useful information to the **RIGHT PEOPLE** at the **RIGHT TIME.**
2. Many companies use a **DATA WAREHOUSE**, a store of data on a single subject over a specific period of time.
3. **DATA MINING,** looking for hidden patterns in a data warehouse, has led to a new science of tracking what's selling where and who's buying it.
4. *The text uses the example of Wal-Mart's successful data mining to customize its store offerings.*

learning goal 3

Compare the scope of the Internet, intranets, extranets, and virtual private networks and explain how broadband technology enabled the evolution to Web 2.0 and 3.0.

III. THE HEART OF KNOWLEDGE MANAGEMENT: THE INTERNET

A. The **INTERNET** is a network of computer networks.

1. It has evolved into a one-to-many broadcast communication tool and is the heart of **KNOWLEDGE MANAGEMENT.**
2. An ***INTRANET*** is a companywide network closed to public access, that uses Internet-type technology.

lecture link B-2

E-MAIL RULES

Writing an e-mail is not like writing a letter—some suggestions for better electronic communication. (See the complete lecture link on page B.65 in this manual.)

PPT B-17

How Do You Organize Data Glut?

(See complete PowerPoint slide notes on page B.53.)

lecture link B-3

THE ELITE WORLD OF DATA MINING

Data mining is big business. Palantir is quickly becoming Silicon Valley's most exclusive employers. (See the complete lecture link on page B.66 in this manual.)

progress assessment

(Text page B-8)

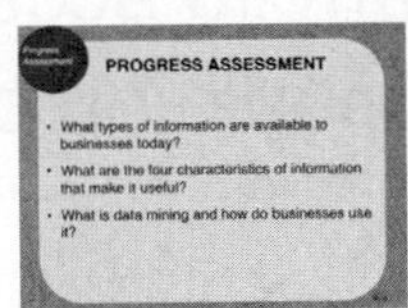

PPT B-18

Progress Assessment

(See complete PowerPoint slide notes on page B.53.)

   a. To prevent unauthorized access by outsiders, companies use a **FIREWALL** consisting of hardware, software, or both, that allows only authorized users to access the intranet.
   b. Some companies use intranets only to publish information for employees.
   c. Others create interactive intranets, allowing employees to input information.
3. An ***EXTRANET*** is a semiprivate network that uses Internet technology and allows more than one company to access the same information or allows people on different servers to collaborate.
   a. Extending an intranet to outside customers is a common use of extranets.
   b. Almost all companies can use extranets for **ELECTRONIC DATA INTERCHANGE (EDI)** to share data and process orders.
4. Since an extranet does use public lines, **HACKERS** can gain unauthorized access.
   a. One solution is to use **DEDICATED LINES**, but this is expensive and limits use to computers directly to those lines.
   b. This solution is expensive and limits use of computers.
5. ***A VIRTUAL PRIVATE NETWORK (VPN)*** is a private data network that creates secure connections, or "tunnels," over regular Internet lines.

PPT B-19
Beyond the Internet

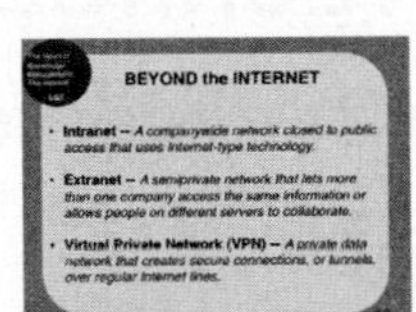

(See complete PowerPoint slide notes on page B.54.)

   a. Companies no longer need dedicated lines, but can use the public lines securely.
   b. VPNs make sharing of public resources for data more secure.
6. An **ENTERPRISE PORTAL** serves as entry point to a variety of resources.
   a. Portals identify users and allow them access to areas of the intranet according to their roles.
   b. The challenge is to integrate resources so that they appear seamless to the user.

B. **BROADBAND TECHNOLOGY**

1. As traffic on the Internet increases, the connection becomes slower.
2. ***BROADBAND TECHNOLOGY*** is a technology that offers users a continuous connection to the Internet and allows them to send and receive mammoth files that include voice, video, and data much faster than ever before.
3. As people use more and more bandwidth, ISPs have been placing caps on how much consumers can use.
4. The **TRAFFIC ON THE INTERNET** has become so intense that some users like scientists and scholars need a faster solution.
   a. One answer is to create another Internet, reserved for research purposes only.

PPT B-20
Increasing Internet Power

(See complete PowerPoint slide notes on page B.54.)

PPT B-21
Broadband Caps

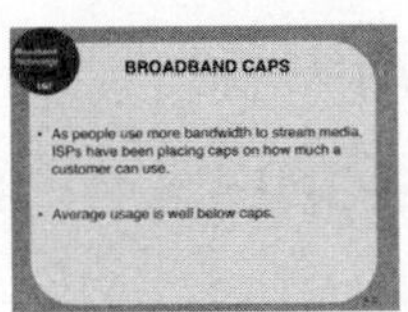

(See complete PowerPoint slide notes on page B.54.)

b. ***INTERNET2*** is the private Internet system that links government supercomputer centers and a select group of universities; it runs more than 22,000 times faster than today's public infrastructure and supports heavy-duty applications.

c. A key element is a network called **vBNS**, or **VERY HIGH SPEED BACKBONE NETWORK SERVICE**, set up in 1995 to link government supercomputer centers and a select group of universities.

d. There are more than 400 member universities.

e. Users who pay more can use more bandwidth.

f. The designers of Internet2 are planning to filter out Internet2 technology in such a way that there is plenty of room for everyone.

C. **SOCIAL MEDIA AND WEB 2.0**

1. Social media are providing opportunities and challenges to today's businesses.

   a. Companies can collaborate with customers on products, service, and promotion.

   b. It's believed that if businesses don't have a social media presence in the next three to five years, they won't survive.

   c. Employees' productivity may go down as they use social media.

   d. Also, the company cannot control all the content.

PPT B-22
Social Media

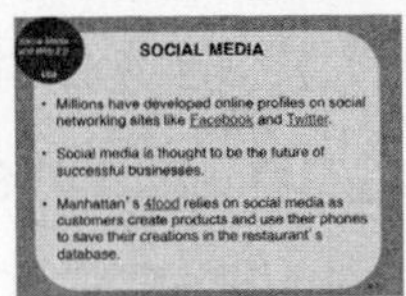

(See complete PowerPoint slide notes on page B.55.)

TEXT FIGURE B.4
Tips for Using Social Media to Partner with Customers
(Text page B-11)

This text figure gives some tips on how to enhance your brand through social media efforts.

PPT B-23
Web 2.0

(See complete PowerPoint slide notes on page B.55.)

3. ***WEB 2.0*** is the set of tools that allow people to build social and business connections, share information, and collaborate on projects online (including blogs, wikis, social networking sites, and other online communities, and virtual worlds).
   a. YouTube and Twitter are among the largest Web 2.0 businesses.

D. **WEB 3.0**

1. The Internet is evolving into a new generation that learns about you and pushes information it "thinks" you might like.
2. ***WEB 3.0*** is a combination of technologies that adds intelligence and changes how people interact with the Web; includes the semantic Web, mobile Web, and immersive Internet.
   a. **The semantic Web** refers to powerful intelligent decision-making applications.
   b. **The mobile Web** allows users to use the Internet wherever they want.
   c. **The immersive Internet** includes virtual worlds, augmented reality, and 3-D environments.

learning goal 4

Review the computer hardware most frequently used in business.

IV. THE ENABLING TECHNOLOGY: HARDWARE

A. What is powerful today in computer hardware may be obsolete by the time you study this.

lecture notes

PPT B-24
Americans and Social Networks

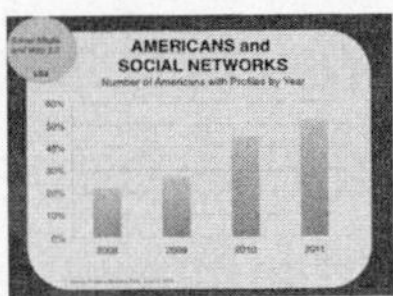

(See complete PowerPoint slide notes on page B.55.)

PPT B-25
Americans and Social Networks

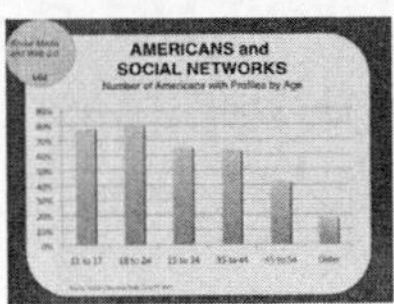

(See complete PowerPoint slide notes on page B.56.)

PPT B-26
Web 3.0

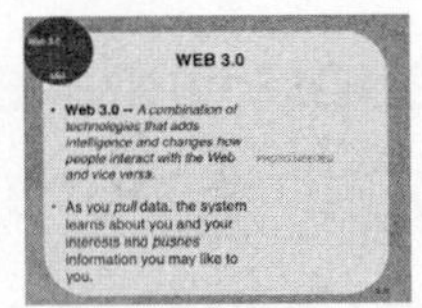

(See complete PowerPoint slide notes on page B.56.)

PPT B-27
Components of Web 3.0

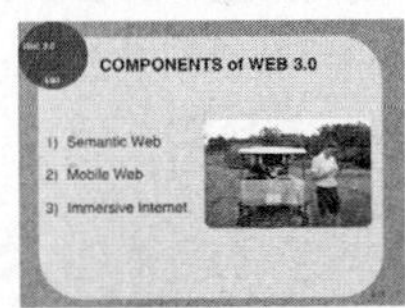

(See complete PowerPoint slide notes on page B.57.)

progress assessment
(Text page B-13)

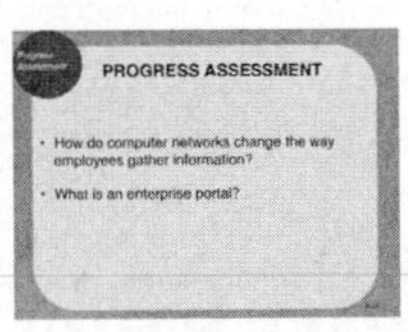

PPT B-28
Progress Assessment

(See complete PowerPoint slide notes on page B.57.)

lecture link B-4
REVISING MOORE'S LAW

In the mid-1970s Gordon Moore, former chair of Intel Corporation, predicted that the capacity of computer chips would double every year or so. (See the complete lecture link on page B.66 of this manual.)

1. Gordon Moore, former chair of Intel Corporation, said that the capacity of computer chips would double every year or so (**MOORE'S LAW**).
2. This chapter will be a simple overview of the current computer technology.

B. **MOBILE DEVICES**

1. **SMARTPHONES** are designed to connect people to the Internet and to e-mail.
2. Standardization of wireless technology has made computing more portable.
3. Wireless networks use a technology called **WI-FI**, from the term **WIRELESS FIDELITY**.
4. Smartphones account for nearly 50% of mobile devices in the U.S.

C. **COMPUTER NETWORKS**

1. Mainframe computer processing has moved **TOWARD NETWORK SYSTEMS** that allow many users to access information at the same time.
   a. ***NETWORK COMPUTING SYSTEMS (CLIENT/SERVER COMPUTING)*** are computer systems that allow personal computers (*clients*) to obtain needed information from huge databases in a central computer (the *server*).
   b. Networks connect people to people and people to data.

lecture notes

lecture link B-5

JOHN ATANASOFF'S COMPUTER

Dr. John V. Atanasoff built the first digital computer over half a century ago, but his contribution to computing was nearly lost to history. (See complete lecture link on page B.67 of this manual.)

PPT B-29

Moving from a Computer. Dominant Environment

(See complete PowerPoint slide notes on page B.57.)

PPT B-30

Fastest-Growing Cell Phone Activities

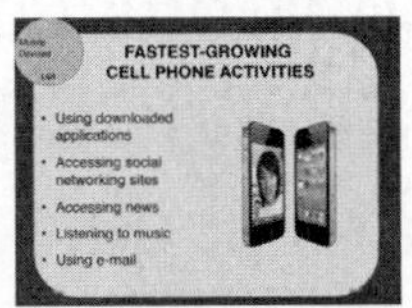

(See complete PowerPoint slide notes on page B.58.)

PPT B-31

The Intelligence of Apps

(See complete PowerPoint slide notes on page B.58.)

PPT B-32

Computer Networks

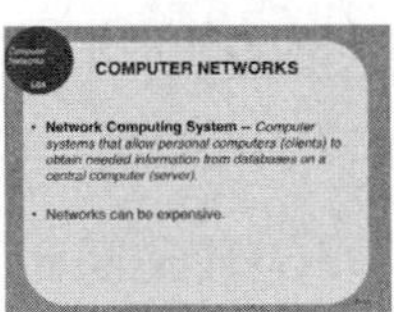

(See complete PowerPoint slide notes on page B.58.)

2. Networks have their **DRAWBACKS** also.
   a. Maintaining a system of desktop PCs can be expensive.
   b. System and hardware upgrades can be disruptive and expensive.
3. One option to reduce costs was to **RENT** software and hardware access by way of the Internet as needed.
   a. In the Web boom, companies called **APPLICATION SERVICE PROVIDERS (ASPs)** ran software at data centers and rented access to these functions to customers.
   b. Most ASPs failed because customers had little faith in their **DATA SECURITY**.
   c. Some companies, such as IBM, still offer these services.

D. **VIRTUALIZATION AND CLOUD COMPUTING**

1. ***VIRTUALIZATION*** is a process that allows networked computers to run multiple operating systems and programs through one central computer at the same time.
   a. This gives companies ready access to update system software and fix problems.
   b. Virtual desktops are also safer from thieves and hackers.
2. ***CLOUD COMPUTING*** is a form of virtualization in which a company's data and applications are stored at offsite data centers that are accessed over the Internet (the **CLOUD**).

PPT B-33
Virtualization and Cloud Computing

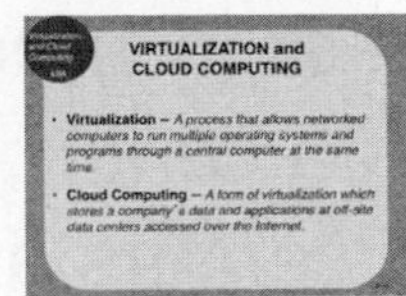

(See complete PowerPoint slide notes on page B.59.)

PPT B-34
Advantages of Cloud Computing

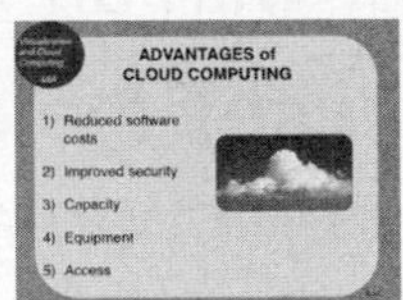

(See complete PowerPoint slide notes on page B.59.)

PPT B-35
Disadvantages of Cloud Computing

(See complete PowerPoint slide notes on page B.60.)

PPT B-36
Clouds in the Office

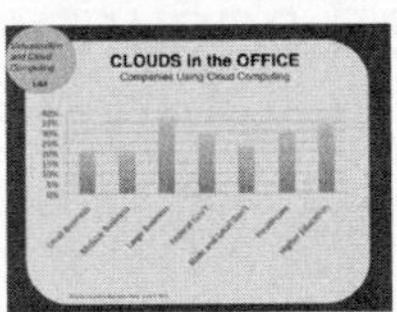

(See complete PowerPoint slide notes on page B.60.)

a. The data aren't necessarily stored in a single data center; portions could be in a series of centers anywhere.

b. The data are easily accessible from any computer with an Internet connection.

c. *The text uses the example of storing a school project on a cloud to work on it at multiple locations.*

3. There are **THREE TYPES OF CLOUD COMPUTING:** (1) private, (2) public, and (3) hybrid clouds.

4 The **ADVANTAGES** of cloud computing are:

a. Reduced software costs

b. Improved security

c. Capacity

d. Equipment

e. Access

learning goal 5

Classify the types of computer software most frequently used in business.

V. SOFTWARE

A. **COMPUTER SOFTWARE** provides the instructions that enable you to tell the computer what to do.

1. Some, but not all, software is **DISTRIBUTED COMMERCIALLY** through suppliers.

2. ***SHAREWARE*** is software that is copyrighted but distributed to potential customers free of charge; users pay a fee if the program meets their needs.

lecture notes

PPT B-37
Top Cloud Applications

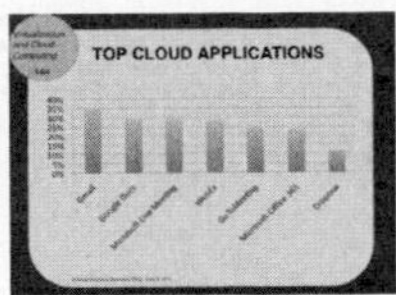

(See complete PowerPoint slide notes on page B.60.)

lecture link B-6
APPLE TAKES TO THE ICLOUD

In the summer of 2011, the late Steve Jobs introduced one of the most anticipated consumer cloud storage systems. (See the complete lecture link on page B.68 of this manual.)

PPT B-38
Software: Telling the Computer What to Do

(See complete PowerPoint slide notes on page B.60.)

lecture link B-7
SHARING IN SILICON VALLEY

In most industries, competitors don't share their intel. That's what makes Silicon Valley a bit different—but not everyone is willing to release their information. (See the complete lecture link on page B.68 in this manual.)

3. ***PUBLIC DOMAIN SOFTWARE (FREEWARE)*** is software that is free for the taking.

B. Businesspeople most frequently use software for **SIX MAJOR PURPOSES**:

1. **WRITING** (word processors)
2. **MANIPULATING NUMBERS** (spreadsheets)
3. **FILING AND RETRIEVING DATA** (databases)
4. **PRESENTING INFORMATION VISUALLY** (graphics)
5. **COMMUNICATING** (e-mail and instant messaging)
6. **COLLABORATING**
7. **ACCOUNTING**

C. Many of these functions have been combined into **INTEGRATED SOFTWARE** or **SUITES**.

learning goal 6

Evaluate the human resource, security, privacy, and stability issues in management that are affected by information technology.

VI. EFFECTS OF INFORMATION TECHNOLOGY ON MANAGEMENT

A. HUMAN RESOURCE ISSUES

1. Because it replaces many bureaucratic functions, technology makes the work process more efficient.
   a. One challenge for human resource managers is to **RECRUIT EMPLOYEES** who know how to use the new technology or **TRAIN** those who already work in the company.
   b. Some companies **OUTSOURCE** technical training.

progress assessment
(Text page B-16)

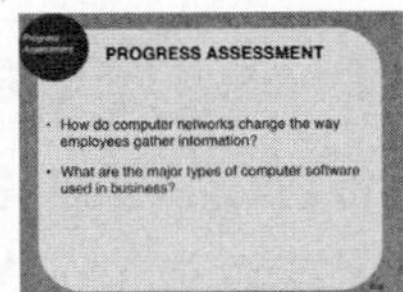

PPT B-39
Progress Assessment

(See complete PowerPoint slide notes on page B.61.)

PPT B-40
Contemporary Issues in Technology

(See complete PowerPoint slide notes on page B.61.)

2. Mobile employees can transmit their work from anywhere (**TELECOMMUTING**).
3. **ADVANTAGES OF TELECOMMUTING:**
   a. Telecommuting involves **LESS TRAVEL TIME** and costs, and often increases productivity.
   b. It helps companies **SAVE MONEY** by retaining valuable employees and by tempting experienced employees out of retirement.
   c. Companies can get by with **SMALLER, LESS EXPENSIVE OFFICE SPACE.**
   d. Telecommuting enables men and women to stay home with small children and is a boon for **WORKERS WITH DISABILITIES.**
   e. Telecommunication is most successful among workers:
      i. Who are self-starters
      ii. Who don't have home distractions
      iii. Whose work doesn't require face-to-face interaction with coworkers
4. **DISADVANTAGES OF TELECOMMUTING:**
   a. Extended long-distance work can give workers a **DISLOCATED FEELING** of being left out of the office loop.
   b. Some feel a **LOSS OF ENERGY** that comes through social interaction.
   c. Often people working from home don't know **WHEN TO TURN OFF THE WORK.**

TEXT FIGURE B.5
When Information Technology Alters the Workplace
(Text page B-19)

This text figure illustrates how information technology changes the way managers and workers interact.

   d. Some companies are using telecommuting as a **PART-TIME ALTERNATIVE.**

   e. The industry defines **TELECOMMUTING** as working at home a minimum of two days a week.

5. A new class of mobile worker has emerged: nearly autonomous, not in the office, doing business in his or her own time staff (or **NANOBOTS**).

   a. The most successful workers are highly skilled high achievers who meet the organization's goals in their own way.

   b. They must have personal networks, knowledge, and experience to handle tasks, situations, and problems.

   c. Managers have found that it is best to "macro manage" nanobots, setting goals without telling them specifically how to achieve them.

6. Electronic communication **CAN NEVER REPLACE HUMAN COMMUNICATION** for creating enthusiasm and esprit de corps.

B. **SECURITY ISSUES**

1. Web-enabled smartphones and the 3G networks they run on, social networks, online games, and USB storage devices have become hackers' targets.

2. "Secure" information is typically stolen by

   a. Hackers who break into companies' networks

   b. Employees who steal it

   c. Companies that lose it through negligence

lecture link B-8
PASSWORD OVERLOAD

Passwords protect information, but too many passwords can lead to decreased security. (See the complete lecture link on page B.69 in this manual.)

PPT B-41
Viruses and Phishing

(See complete PowerPoint slide notes on page B.61.)

3. Computer security today is more complicated than in the past.
    a. When information was processed in a mainframe environment, the **SINGLE DATA CENTER** was **EASIER TO CONTROL**.
    b. Today computers are accessible in all areas of the company and with other companies.
4. A ***VIRUS*** is a piece of programming code inserted into other programming to cause some unexpected and, for the victim, usually undesirable event.
    a. Viruses are spread by **DOWNLOADING INFECTED PROGRAMMING** over the Internet or by sharing an infected USB drive.
    b. Some viruses are playful, but some can erase data or crash a hard drive.
    c. Software programs such as Norton's AntiVirus **"INOCULATE"** the computer so that it doesn't catch a known virus.
    d. It is important to keep your **ANTIVIRUS PROTECTION PROGRAM UP-TO-DATE** and practice "safe computing."
7. Another online security threat is **PHISHING,** in which a scammer sends an e-mail with a stolen logo that makes the message look authentic.
    a. Phishers use messages like "account activation required" to lure users.
    b. Recipients who click on the link in the message are sent to a phony site that tries to gather personal information.

PPT B-42
How to Protect Yourself Against Phishing

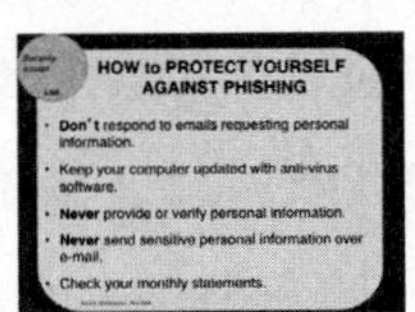

(See complete PowerPoint slide notes on page B.62.)

lecture link B-9
WEB SHOPPING SAFELY

Here are a few tips to shop safely. (See the complete lecture link on page B.69 in this manual.)

   c. To avoid phishing scans, **NEVER ACCESS A WEBSITE THROUGH A LINK** in an e-mail message.

8. **EXISTING LAWS** do not address some Internet issues such as:
   a. Copyright and pornography laws
   b. Intellectual property and contract disputes
   c. Online sexual and racial harassment
   d. Crooked sales schemes
9. After September 11, 2001, security officers are most concerned about **CYBERTERRORISM.**
   a. An electronic attack on critical computers could cripple the Internet.
   b. Such an attack in 2002 demonstrated the Internet's vulnerabilities.
10. The Critical Infrastructure Protection Board was created to **IMPROVE THE SECURITY** of America's critical infrastructure.
    a. In order to do this, the agency needs the cooperation of businesses.
    b. However, many CIOs are reluctant to cooperate and reveal security breaches.
    c. To encourage sharing of information, **CONGRESS PASSED THE CRITICAL INFRASTRUCTURE INFORMATION ACT OF 2002** that makes critical infrastructure information exempt from disclosure.

PPT B-43
Laws and the Internet

(See complete PowerPoint slide notes on page B.62.)

PPT B-44
Cyberterrorism

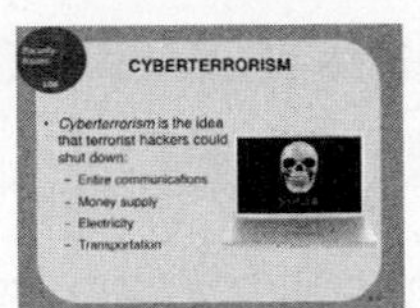

(See complete PowerPoint slide notes on page B.62.)

lecture link B-10
E-MAIL NEVER GOES AWAY

When it comes to the Internet, nothing is ever really forgotten and everything leaves a trail. (See the complete lecture link on page B.51 of this manual.)

C. **PRIVACY ISSUES**

1. Your **E-MAIL** is no more private than a postcard.
   a. Many U.S. companies legally scan employee e-mail regularly.
   b. Most e-mail travels over the Internet in **UNENCRYPTED PLAIN TEXT.**
   c. Some e-mail systems can **ENCRYPT** messages to keep them private.
2. As more and more **PERSONAL INFORMATION** is stored in computers, people are able to access those data legally and illegally, creating a privacy nightmare.
   a. The Internet allows Web surfers to access all sorts of information about you.
   b. Civil libertarians fight to keep certain kinds of information available to the public.
   c. Privacy advocates disagree and argue that the Internet makes obtaining personal information too easy.
3. Websites have gotten downright nosy by secretly **TRACKING USERS' MOVEMENTS** online.
   a. Web surfers seem willing to swap personal details for free access to online information.
   b. Websites often send **COOKIES** to your computer that stay on your hard drive.
   c. ***<u>COOKIES</u>*** are pieces of information, such as registration data or user preferences, sent by a website over the Internet to a

PPT B-45
Privacy Issues in Technology

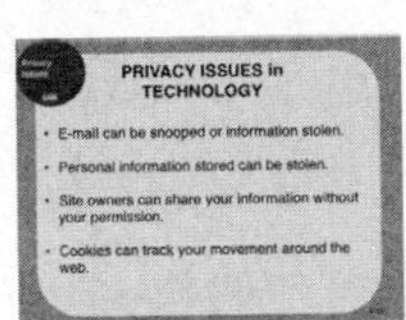

(See complete PowerPoint slide notes on page B.63)

critical thinking exercise B-1
SPAM STATISTICS

A growing problem with electronic communication is spam, unwanted e-mail messages. (See complete exercise on page B.72 of this manual.)

Web browser that the browser software is expected to save and send back to the server whenever the user returns to that site.

d. Some contain only your name and password.

e. Others **TRACK YOUR MOVEMENTS** around the Web, letting companies blend that information with their databases and tailor the ads you receive accordingly.

f. Some software, known as **SPYWARE**, can be installed on your computer without your knowledge and infect your system.

g. Tim Berners-Lee, the researcher who invented the World Wide Web, developed a way to prevent you from receiving cookies without your permission.

h. His **PLATFORM FOR PRIVACY PREFERENCES (P3)** lets you decide how much information about yourself you are willing to give away.

D. **STABILITY ISSUES**

1. **INSTABILITY** in technology also has a significant impact on business.
2. *The text uses the example of Hershey and the disruptions to its Halloween candy delivery caused by a computer system failure.*
3. The blame for such problems is a combination of computer error, human error, malfunctioning software, and overly complex systems.

critical thinking exercise B-2
EDUCATION ONLINE

Can't afford to go to MIT? Try the free website. (See complete exercise on page B.73 of this manual.)

VII. TECHNOLOGY AND YOU

A. It may be occupational suicide to **BE COMPUTER ILLITERATE** since most workers come in contact with computers to some degree.

B. Information technology eliminates old jobs while creating new ones.

C. It is up to you to learn the skills you need to be certain you aren't left behind.

VIII. SUMMARY

progress
assessment
(Text page B-22)

PPT B-46
Progress Assessment

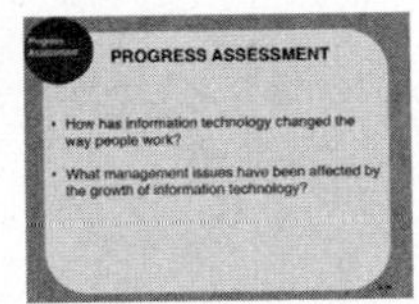

(See complete PowerPoint slide notes on page B.63.)

PowerPoint slide notes

PPT B-1
Chapter Title

PPT B-2
Learning Goals

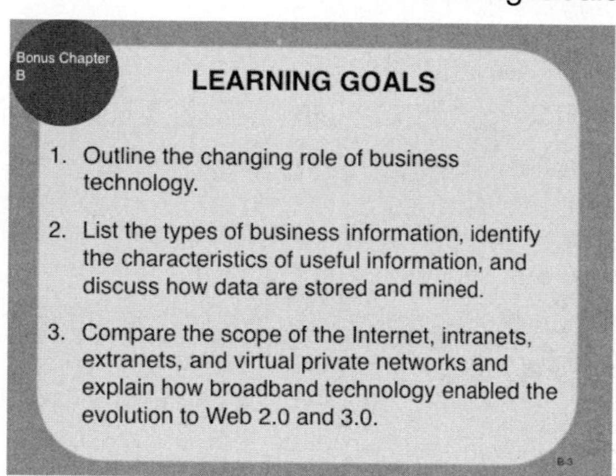

PPT B-3
Learning Goals

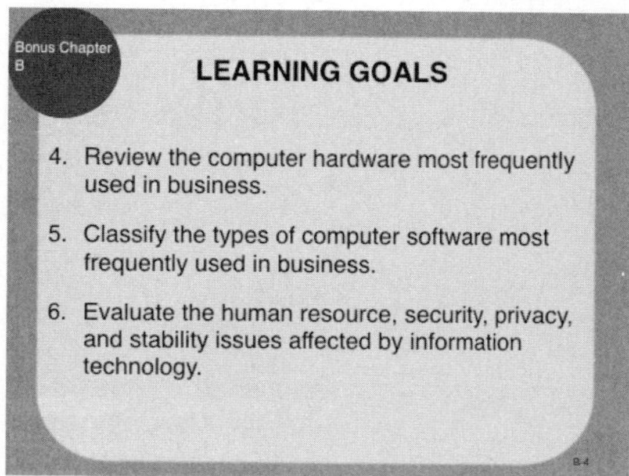

PPT B-4
Chris Hughes

PPT B-5
Name That Company

Company: 4food

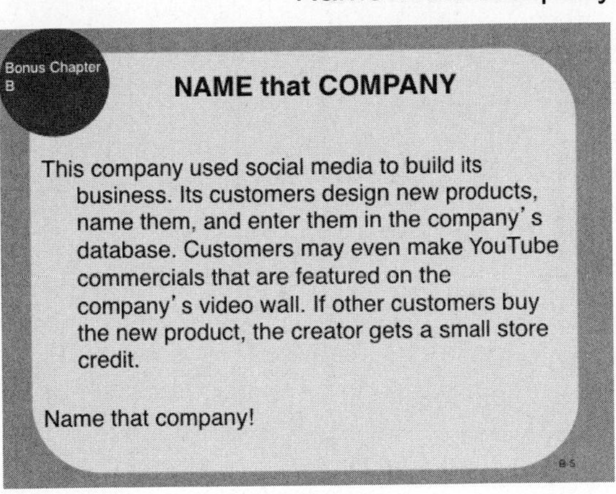

PPT B-6
Technology in the 1970s

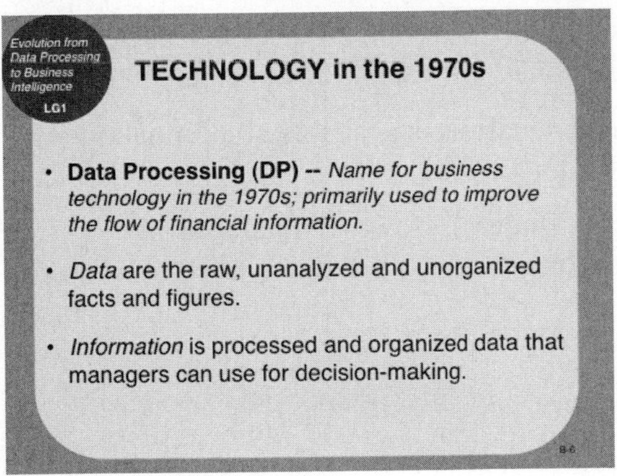

PPT B-7
Technology in the 1980s

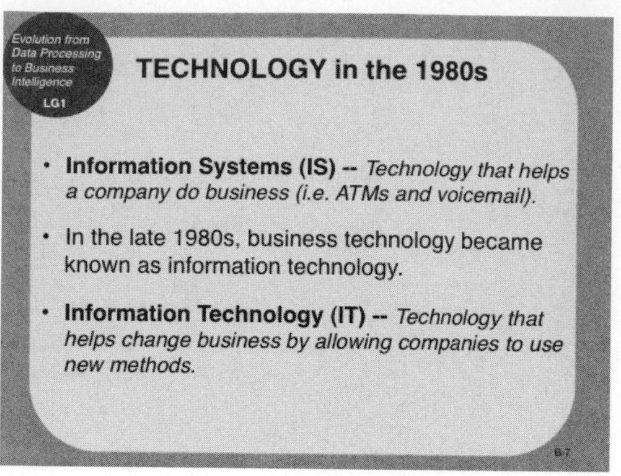

PPT B-8
Technology in the Early 2000s

Companies such as SAS, Oracle, and IBM are leaders in business intelligence software.

PPT B-9
Further Evolution

1. This slide shows what some believe will happen to BI in the future.
2. The introduction of tablets and more advanced smartphones will change business intelligence.
3. A longer analysis is available at information-week.com/1289/bi.
4. Ask the students, How will platforms like Facebook change collaboration efforts?

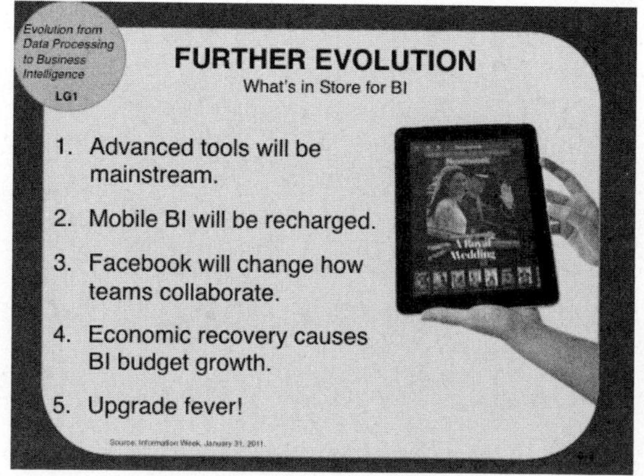

PPT B-10
Technology Brings Change

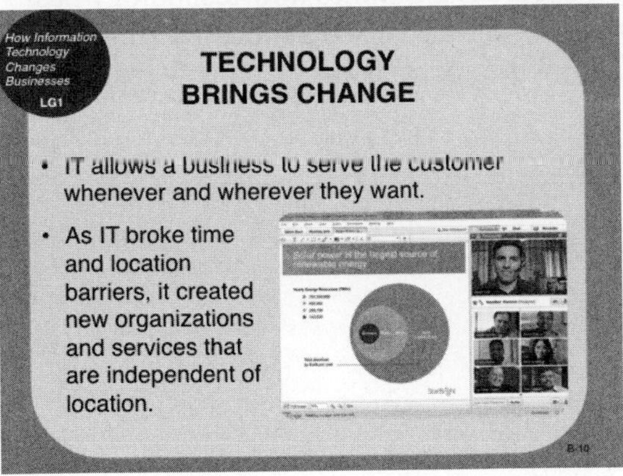

1. You can instantly rent a movie, do research on mortgage rates, and make stock trades all from home.
2. The NASDAQ is an electronic stock exchange without trading floors where buyers and sellers make trades using computers.
3. The independence created by smartphones, laptops, and tablets allows work to go to people instead of people to work.

PPT B-11
Top U.S. Cities by High-Tech Employment

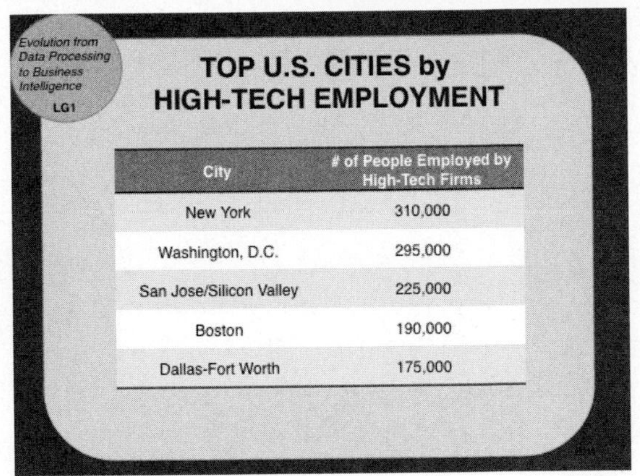

City	# of People Employed by High-Tech Firms
New York	310,000
Washington, D.C.	295,000
San Jose/Silicon Valley	225,000
Boston	190,000
Dallas-Fort Worth	175,000

1. This profiles the cities with the largest number of high-tech jobs.
2. While Silicon Valley gets all of the publicity, the eastern shore of the United States—New York, Boston, and Washington, DC—has a large concentration of high-tech jobs.
3. These jobs are sought after due to high average salaries:
   - Software engineer, 2009 average salary range: $72,000 to $108,000
   - System administrator, 2009 average salary range: $52,000 to $82,000
   - Database manager, 2009 average salary range: $91,000 to $126,000

   (*Source:* Datamation.)

PPT B-12
Progress Assessment

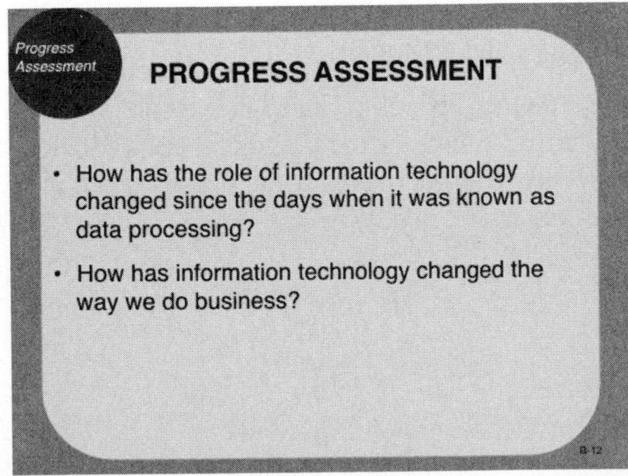

1. The role of information technology changed from backroom activities that simply processed data in the 1970s, to the center of the business in the 1980s. In the 1980s, technology was just an addition to the existing way of doing business (applying new technology on old methods). Things started to change when businesses applied new technology to new methods (information technology). By the early 2000s, technology become more sophisticated and became known as business intelligence (or analytics). BI includes activities such as data mining, online analytical process, querying, and reporting.

(continued

PPT B-12
Progress Assessment
(continued)

2. Information technology has broken the time barriers of business, allowing businesses to provide goods and services to customers anytime, anywhere. Figure B.2 outlines how technology has changed organizations, operations, staffing, new products, customer relations, and new markets.

PPT B-13
Key Types of Business
Information Available

PPT B-14
Four Characteristics That Make
Information Useful

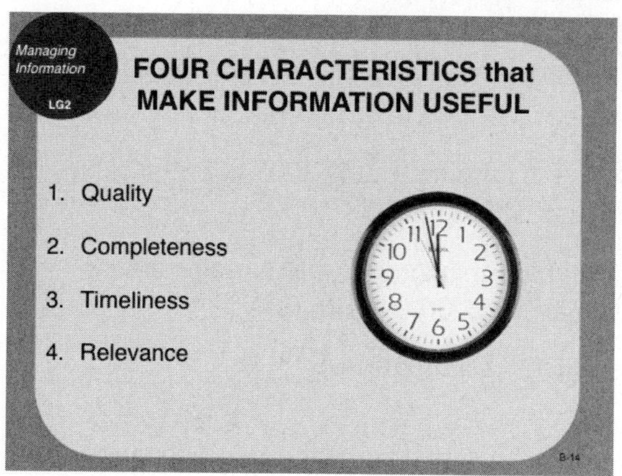

PPT B-15
Top Sites to Keep You Connected

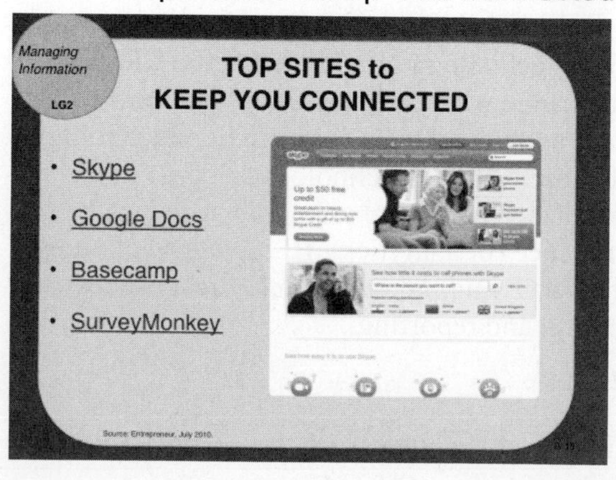

1. This slide lists the top sites for keeping connected to your vendors and customers.
2. Ask the students, Which of these brands are you familiar with? Which of the brands on the slide do you use? Why? What makes some brands more popular than others?

PPT B-16
Effectively Using Your Electronic Files

PPT B-17
How Do You Organize Data Glut?

If people can suffer from information overload, so can organizations. Data mining can help manage data.

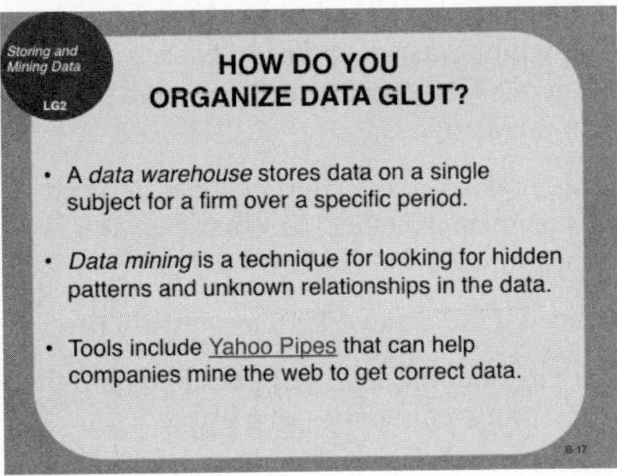

PPT B-18
Progress Assessment

1. Today there are five types of information available to businesses: (1) business process information, (2) physical-world observations, (3) biological data, (4) public data, and (5) data that indicate personal preferences.
2. The four characteristics of information that make it useful are quality, completeness, timeliness, and relevance.
3. Data mining seeks hidden patterns and relationships among data in a data warehouse. Companies use this information in an effort to provide better service to customers and gain a competitive advantage over rivals.

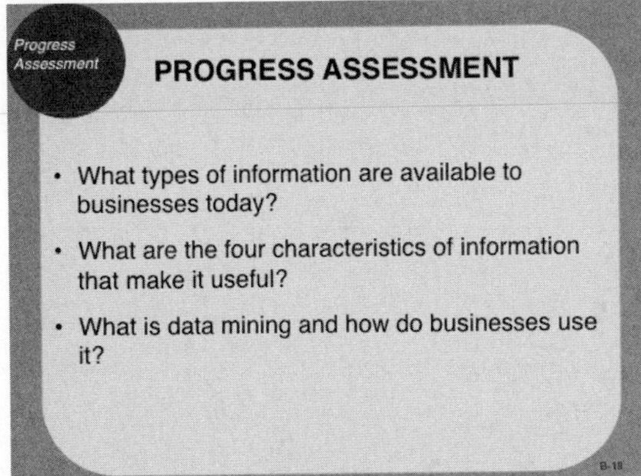

PPT B-19
Beyond the Internet

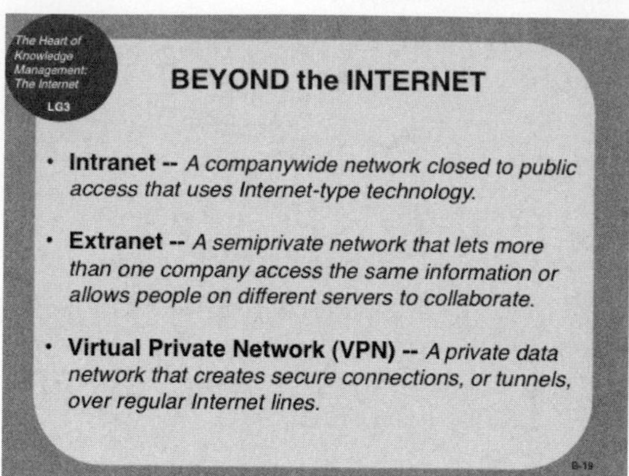

If you don't have access to a corporate VPN, you can easily set up an account at a public VPN provider like WiTopia or StrongVPN.

PPT B-20
Increasing Internet Power

1. A key element of Internet2 is a network called very-high-speed backbone network service (vBNS), which was set up in 1995 as a way to link government supercomputer centers and a select group of universities.
2. There are now more than 400 member universities, government agencies, corporations, and laboratories in over 50 countries.
3. Users pay for the bandwidth they actually use.
4. Plans are to filter out Internet2 technology to the wider Internet community—at a price.

PPT B-21
Broadband Caps

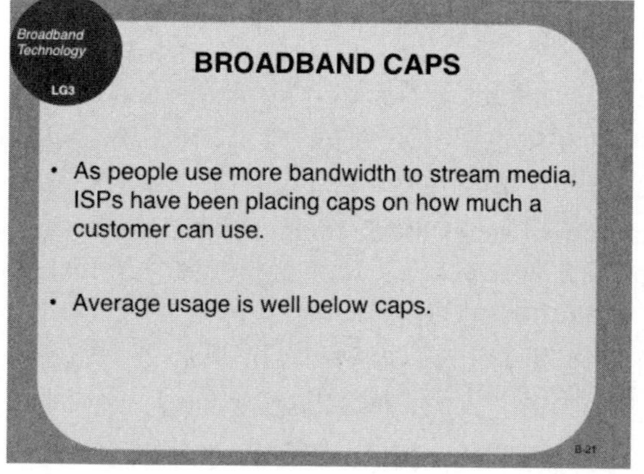

PPT B-22
Social Media

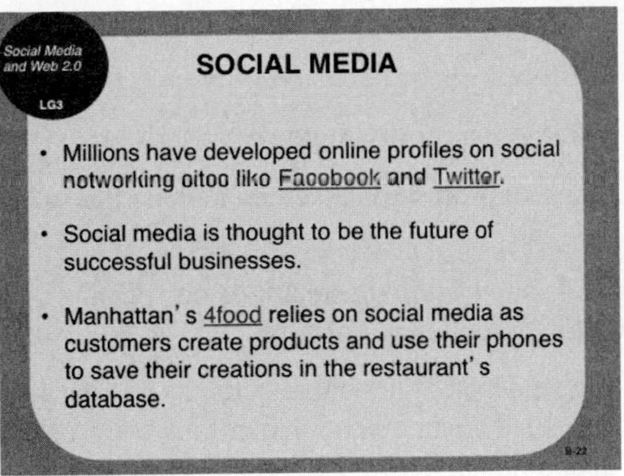

PPT B-23
Web 2.0

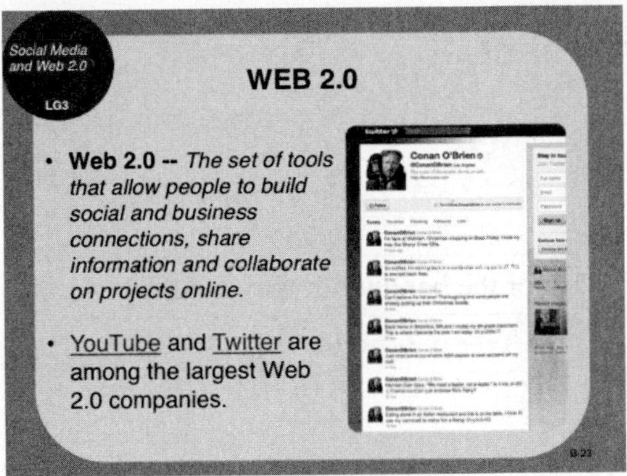

PPT B-24
Americans and Social Networks
(Profiles by Year)

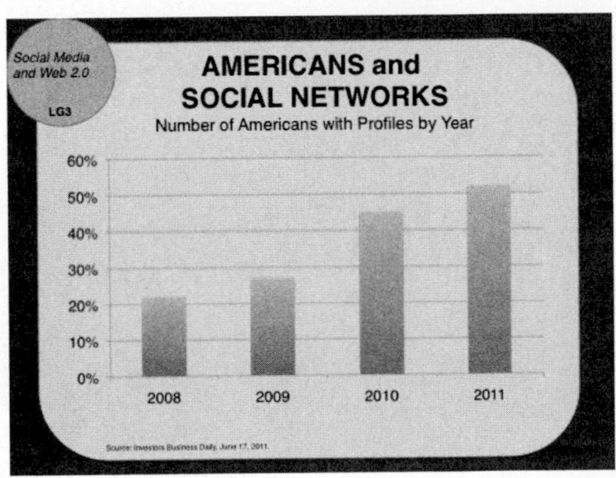

1. This slide shows the growth of social networking sites since 2008.
2. The irony is that as people talk about privacy, they are posting more and more intimate details about their lives online.
3. According to careerbuilder.com employers are checking social networking sites like the ones mentioned in this slide to look for information about job applicants.
4. In a survey conducted by careerbuilder.com, 35% of employers say they have dropped a candidate because of something they discovered during a search of social networking sites.
5. From Buzzle.com, here are top reasons given by employers for not hiring someone based on an Internet search:

(continued)

PPT B-24
Americans and Social Networks
(Profiles by Year)
(continued)

- Lying about job qualifications (31%)
- Poor communication skills (25%)
- Links to criminal behavior (24%)
- Trash-talking previous employers (19%)
- Posting inappropriate photographs (11%)
- Using unprofessional screen names (8%)

PPT B-25
Americans and Social Networks
(Profiles by Age)

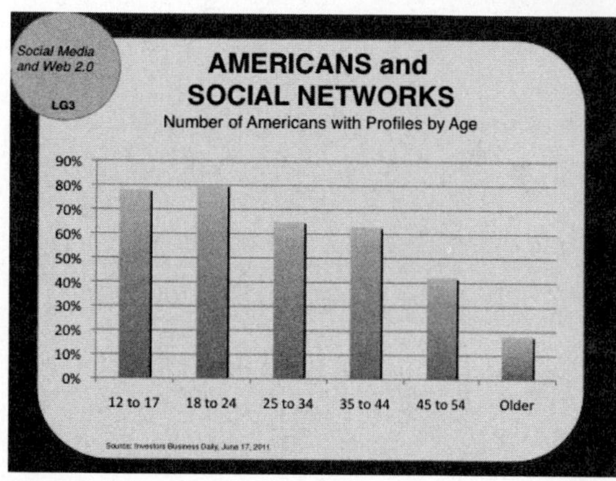

1. This slide shows who has profiles on social networks, based on age groups.
2. Ask the students, What enhancements to your life do these sites create? Who doesn't have a profile on Facebook, LinkedIn, and so on? How much time do you spend on these sites daily?

PPT B-26
Web 3.0

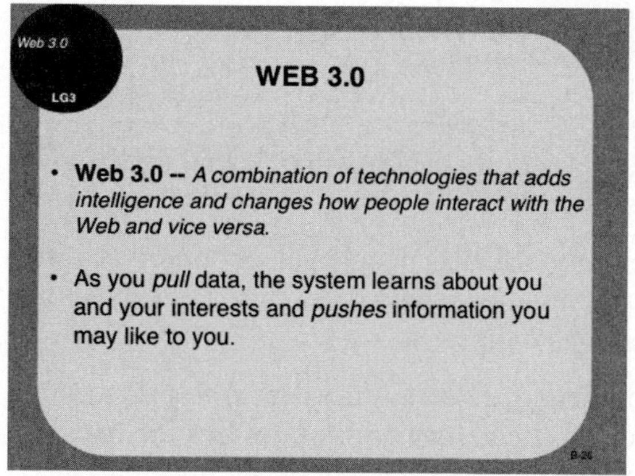

PPT B-27
Components of Web 3.0

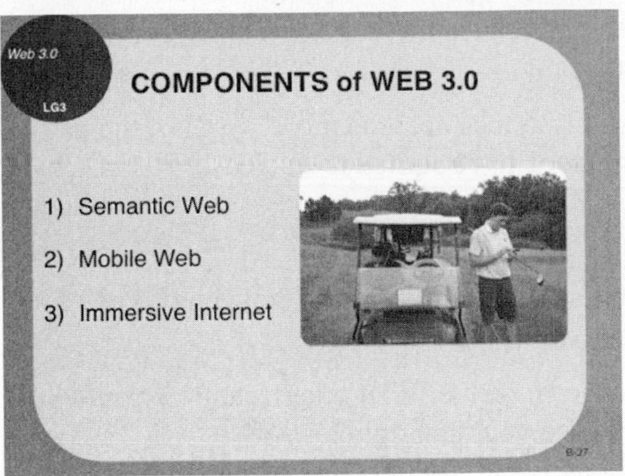

1. The semantic Web refers to powerful intelligent decision-making applications. For example, Amdocs combines information from a variety of sources in real time to anticipate the reasons for a customer's call. Response can be made 30% faster, making customers happy.
2. The mobile Web allow users to use the Web as they move from one device to another and one location to another. This includes location-based services.
3. The immersive Internet includes virtual worlds, augmented reality, and 3-D environments.

PPT B-28
Progress Assessment

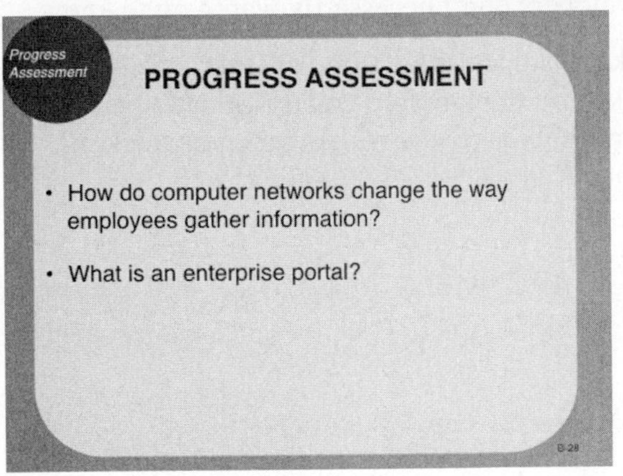

1. Computer networks save time and money, provide easy links across functional boundaries, and allow employees to see complete information.
2. The enterprise portal centralizes information and transactions and serves as an entry point to a variety of resources, such as e-mail, financial records, schedules, and employment and benefits files.

PPT B-29
Moving from a Computer-Dominant Environment

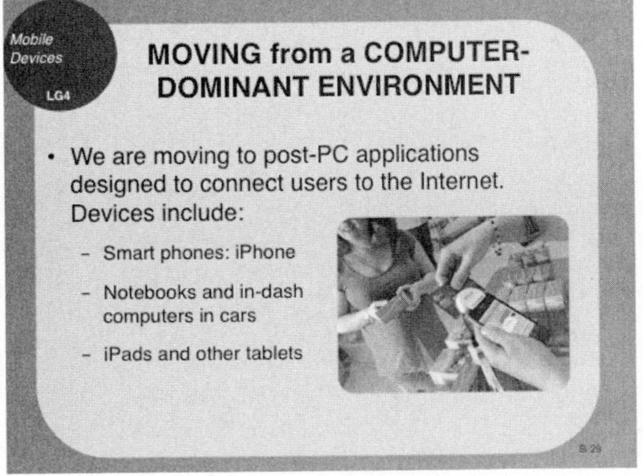

PPT B-30
Fastest-Growing Cell Phone Activities

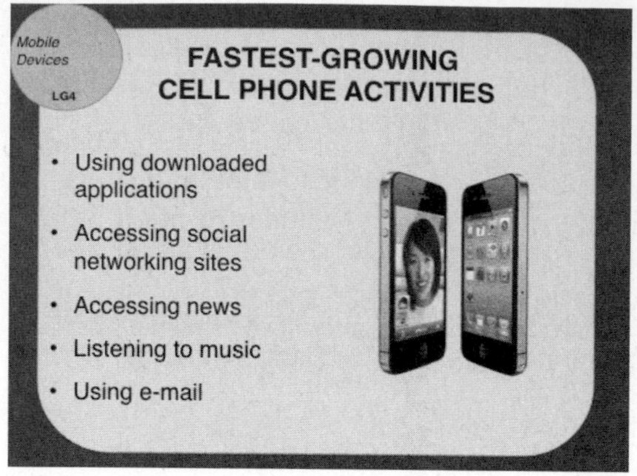

1. This slide illustrates some of the fast-growing cell phone activities.
2. The cell phone is no longer used just for making phone calls.
3. As smartphones become more popular, the price of the units have started to decrease. A study by NPD Group showed the price of the smartphone is now $174, a decline of 26%.
4. Apple has sold millions of iPhone and iPad units that blend laptop and phone.
5. Ask the students, What other features would you like to see your smartphone do?

PPT B-31
The Intelligence of Apps

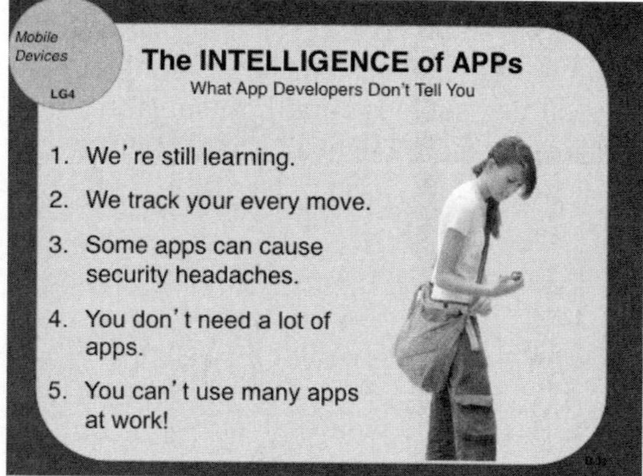

1. This slide shows some of the things app developers don't necessarily want you to know.
2. Ask the students, Do some of these statements make you think before you download? How comfortable are you with developers tracking your activity?

PPT B-32
Computer Networks

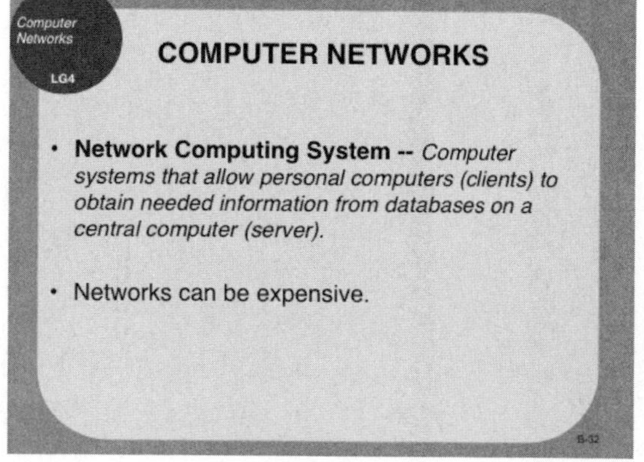

PPT B-33
Virtualization and Cloud Computing

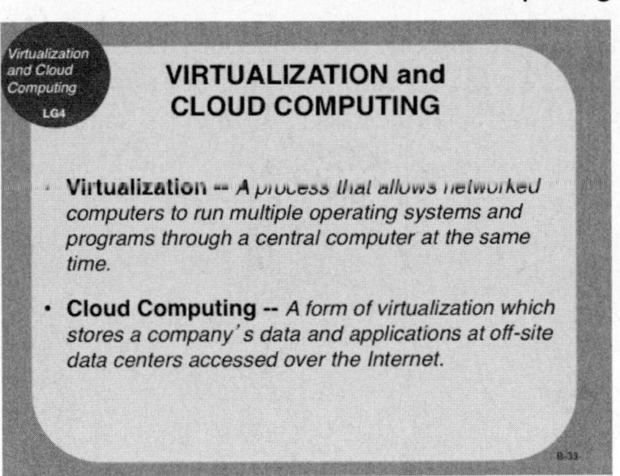

Companies like VM Ware and Virtual Iron have revolutionized virtualization, thus reducing many companies' need for multiple new servers.

PPT B-34
Advantages of Cloud Computing

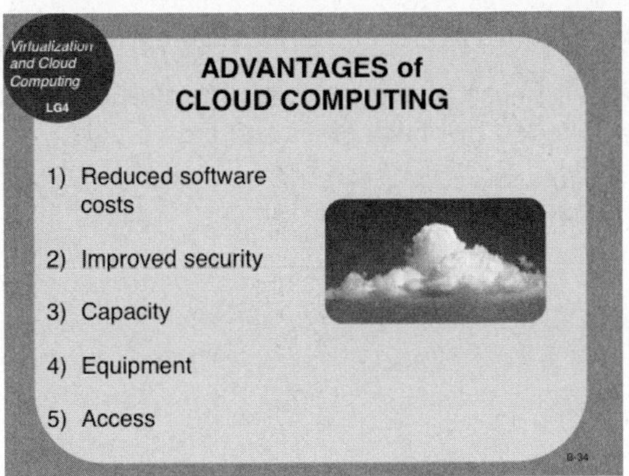

PPT B-35
Advantages of Cloud Computing

An outage on Amazon caused customers to lose data. Other companies have misled users about their security levels.

PPT B-36
Clouds in the Office

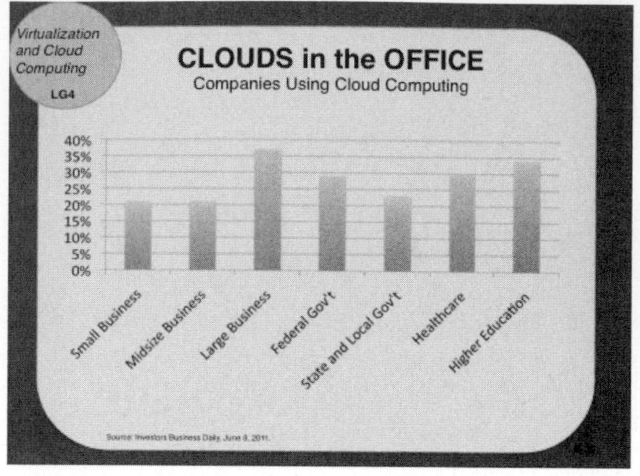

1. More and more companies are using the cloud to work efficiently without borders.
2. Cloud computing can be helpful in your school career as well. You can work on your papers and projects from anyplace you get Internet access.

PPT B-37
Top Cloud Applications

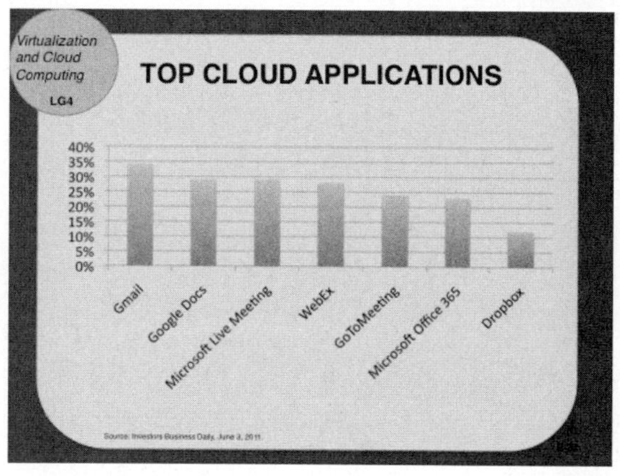

1. This slide highlights some of the most successful clouds for businesses.
2. These can also be beneficial to students now.
3. Navigate to one of these clouds sites to show what they have to offer businesses and individuals.

PPT B-38
Software: Telling the Computer What to Do

PPT B-39
Progress Assessment

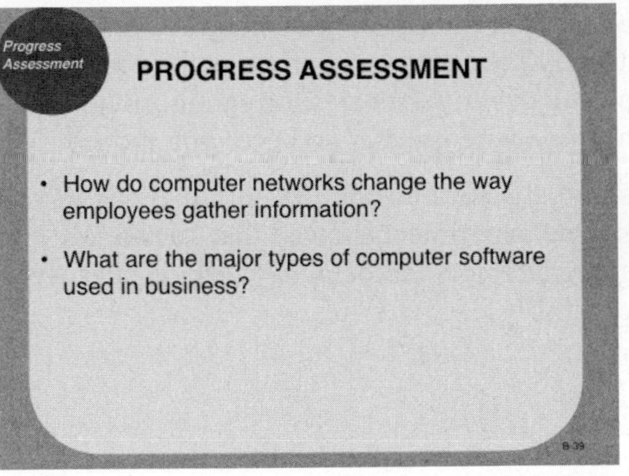

1. Computer networks save time and money, provide easy links across functional boundaries, and allow employees to see complete information.
2. The major types of computer software used in business are word processors, spreadsheets, databases, graphics, communicating, and accounting.

PPT B-40
Contemporary Issues in Technology

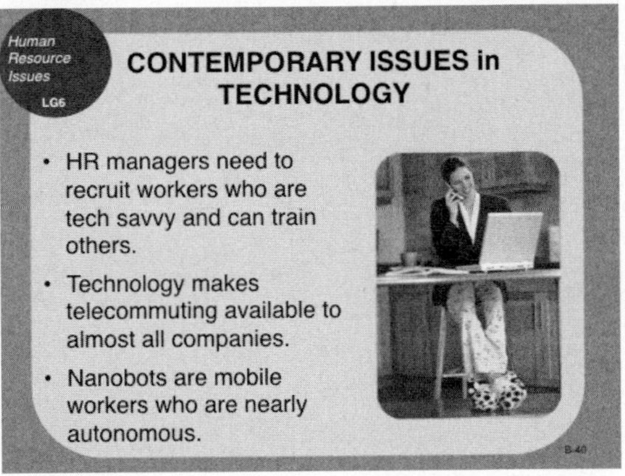

PPT B-41
Viruses and Phishing

Security Issues
LG6
VIRUSES and PHISHING
• **Virus** -- *A piece of programming code inserted into other programming that usually lies dormant until triggered; then causes unexpected, undesired events.*
• *Phishing* attempts to trick victims into giving important information to a bogus website.

As technology becomes a more important part of everyday life, the number of phishing attempts and computer viruses has grown.

PPT B-42
How to Protect Yourself Against Phishing

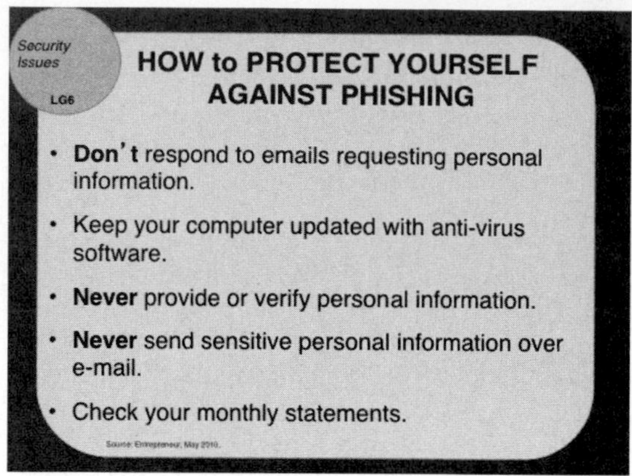

1. This slide highlights some of the ways people can protect themselves against phishing.
2. One common example of phishing that many students may have received is from an African prince who needs your personal information, so he can complete a wire transfer and give you money.
3. Phishing attacks are common on social networking sites. One experiment showed that 70% of all phishing attempts on social networking sites were successful.

PPT B-43
Laws and the Internet

PPT B-44
Cyberterrorism

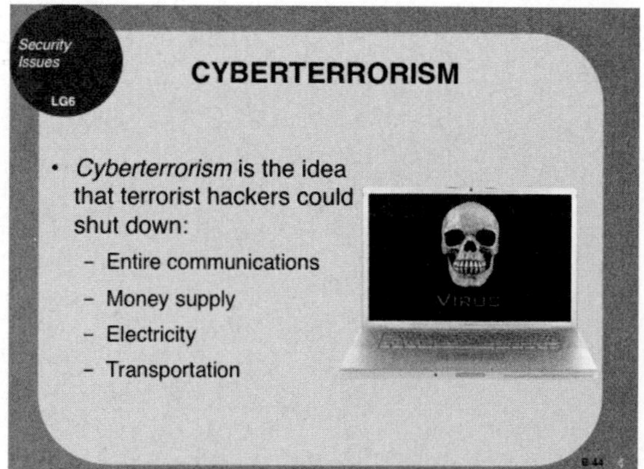

PPT B-45
Privacy Issues in Technology

PPT B-46
Progress Assessment

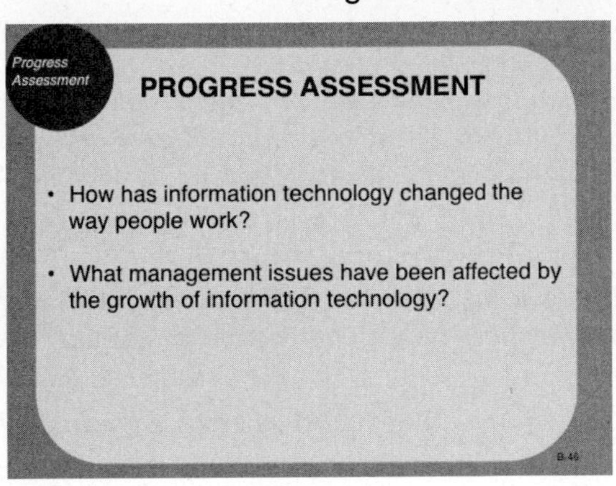

1. Information technology has allowed workers to telecommute. Using computers and the Internet, the employee links to the company's network to transmit his or her work to the office from anywhere in the world.
2. Four major issues that have affected management are human resource changes, security threats, privacy concerns, and stability.

lecture links

"Never trust a computer you can't throw out the window."
Steve Wozniak

"Computers make very fast, very accurate mistakes."
Murphy's Law

"Knowledge is a process of piling up facts; wisdom lies in their simplification."
Alexander Graham Bell

"You can give people responsibility and authority, but without information they are helpless."
Bill Gates

"To err is human, but to really foul up requires a computer."
Anonymous

"Programming today is a race between software engineers striving to build bigger and better idiot-proof programs, and the Universe trying to produce bigger and better idiots. So far, the Universe is winning."
Rich Cook

"Where a calculator on the ENIAC is equipped with 18,000 vacuum tubes and weighs 30 tons, computers in the future may have only 1,000 vacuum tubes and perhaps weigh 1½ tons."
Popular Mechanics, *March 1949*

lecture link B-1

WHY WE TYPE THIS WAY

The modern office is likely to be equipped with personal computers linked through local area networks to each other, to the Internet, and to a host of specialized equipment, from laser printers to scanners to databases storing millions of customer records. Within this state-of-the-art system is a 19th-century bottleneck—the computer keyboard.

The computer keyboard is simply a transplanted typewriter keyboard, the same keyboard that has been used since the 1870s. The first practical modern typewriter was patented in 1868 by Christopher Sholes, who invented the device with partners S. W. Soule and G. Glidden.

When Sholes invented the first typewriter, keys were arranged alphabetically (vestiges of this arrangement can be seen on the second row of keys—D F G H J K L). Printing bars were mechanically pushed against the paper by the pressure on the keys. Typists soon became proficient enough to cause jams as they typed faster than the mechanical bars could move.

Typewriter manufacturers went back to the drawing board and designed a new keyboard to slow typists down to speeds within the limits of the crude mechanism. The resulting keyboard is referred to as "Qwerty," named for the first six keys of the top row. Keys were placed awkwardly to force slower typing. The "A," for instance, one of the most frequently used keys, was placed under a typist's left-hand little finger, the weakest finger on the hand. "E" required an awkward reach using the middle finger of the left hand. Results were encouraging—typing speeds declined.

Today mechanical keys have been replaced by electronic ones, but the keyboard arrangement has remained unchanged. While the arrangement of keys is familiar, it is far from efficient. In the 1930s, Washington State University Professor August Dvorak designed a better keyboard that groups the most frequently used letters on the home row and eliminates many awkward reaches. The Dvorak system is faster to learn, easier to type, less tiring, and less likely to cause errors than Qwerty. Using it increases typing speed by more than 20%. Yet the system never caught on—typists did not want to learn a new system when their typewriters all used Qwerty, and manufacturers did not want to produce Dvorak typewriters as long as typists used Qwerty.

lecture link B-2

E-MAIL RULES

The most-used Internet application by volume is e-mail. Although e-mail has become a necessary part of our modern lives, it is often misused.

In your early education, you were taught how to write a letter. You probably learned how to write business and casual headings and salutations, state your purpose, make a request, ask for a response, and wrap it up with "Sincerely yours."

But an e-mail is not a letter, and the days of graceful formal communication are fading away. Short is in, "yours truly" is out. Some guidelines:

KEEP IT SHORT. Short e-mails get attention. If you receive an e-mail that's several pages long, you have to make some decisions. Do I have time to handle this now? Is it important enough to come back to? If the answer is no, that e-mail won't be read, no matter how carefully written. Supporting material can be sent as an attachment, but give the reader a clear, concise message in the e-mail body.

KEEP IT IN CONTEXT. Our inboxes are flooded with dozens of legitimate messages each day, not to mention the mountains of spam that may or may not get through spam filters. When you send a message to someone you don't usually communicate with, include some mention of your identity. "I met you at the conference last week" or "Jim suggested I contact you regarding this issue." If you are responding to an earlier message, include the previous thread. Nothing is as confusing as an e-mail saying, "What do you mean?" or "Not really" when you have no idea what you're supposed to understand.

GIVE IT A SUBJECT. The subject line is there for a reason. It tells your recipients what you want to communicate. Some very important e-mails get overlooked with blank subject lines or topics like "Important" or "RE: RE: RE: RE: RE:" If the topic changes, change the subject line. Remember that on the recipients' screens, your subject competes with a large number of others for their attention.

KEEP THE THREAD. Some e-mail users routinely trim everything out of the body of the e-mail except their replies. Don't do this. For example, if you are responding to a request for an opinion, don't just say "I agree" and cut out the thread. Let your reader browse through the background for your response. A slightly longer e-mail isn't going to bog down the server—the thousands of spam messages are doing that just fine.

MAKE YOUR REQUESTS CLEAR. You should set your requests apart from the rest of the message by trimming them down to one sentence or series of bullet points. Close-ended questions (yes or no) are more readily answered. Open-ended questions can get long and involved, and reduce the likelihood that you'll get a reply.

DON'T BE AFRAID OF DEADLINES. If you need the information by Friday, let the reader know. Then if he or she can't meet the timetable, the reader can let you know in time for you to find another source. If you've requested something that has not been delivered, it is acceptable to send a cordially worded reminder. But just one. Daily reminders suggest to recipients that they're being bossed around. They may be too busy, away on vacation, or actually working on your last request.

REMEMBER TO SAY "THANK YOU." Not only is it polite, but it also lets the sender know you've received the message and gives the subject closure. Remember, you'll probably need their good will at some time in the future.

lecture link B-3

THE ELITE WORLD OF DATA MINING

Today's tech giants like Facebook and Google have become household names as people around the world rely on them every day to navigate the Net. Silicon Valley is home to a number of other mighty companies that could someday be worth billions as well. One of these elite few is Palantir, a data-mining company that is quickly becoming one of Palo Alto's most exclusive employers.

If one thing is certain about the technological surge of the last two decades, it's that the sum of all these digital endeavors has led to an immense amount of data. Google alone facilitates millions of gigabytes' worth of information every day. As a result, detecting weak spots or potential infiltration by hackers becomes much more difficult, if not impossible, for even the savviest organizations. That's where Palantir comes in. The company's band of computer whizzes creates highly sophisticated interfaces that can parse enormous streams of data. This allows its clientele, ranging from the CIA to major banks, to search for and pinpoint any signs of unlawful access.

Ironically, some of Palantir's employees are former hackers themselves. But despite their pasts, every staffer at the company is the best of the best. They see their work as a matter of good against evil. However, the staggering abilities and independence of the Palantir staff can lead to trouble. In February the company's name was found on a series of e-mails that laid out a plan to sabotage the whistleblowing organization Wikileaks as well as ThinkProgress.com. Amateur hackers and tech enthusiasts across the Web blasted Palantir as traitors against their mission statement to defend rather than attack sites. Although Palantir's CEO traced the e-mails to a single employee and placed him on leave, the company's reputation within the tech community may have suffered irreparable damage. Still, Palantir could be the next multibillion-dollar behemoth, according to the company's chief investor Peter Thiel. A founder of PayPal and one of the first investors in Facebook, Thiel says Palantir has the potential to rival both of those companies. And with the company valued at $735 million already, he could very well be correct.[i]

lecture link B-4

REVISING MOORE'S LAW

Sixty years after transistors were invented the tiny on–off switches are starting to show their age. The devices have been shrunk so much that the day is approaching when it will be physically impossible to make them even smaller.

In the mid-1970s the chair of Intel Corporation, Gordon E. Moore, predicted that the capacity of computer chips would double every year or so. This has since been called "Moore's law." The million-dollar vacuum tube computers that awed people in the 1950s couldn't keep up with a pocket calculator today. In fact, a greeting card that plays "Happy Birthday" contains more computing power than existed before 1950.

The transistor was invented by scientists William Shockley, John Bradeen, and Walter Brattain to amplify voices in telephones for a Bell Labs project, for which they later shared the Nobel Prize in physics. Transistors' ever-decreasing size and low power consumption made them an ideal candidate to replace the bulky vacuum tubes then used to amplify electrical signals. Transistors eventually found their way into portable radios and other electronics devices and became the foundation of microprocessors, memory chips, and other semiconductor devices.

The pace of innovation gained further momentum after the invention of the integrated circuit in the late 1950s. The integrated circuit was invented by Texas Instruments' Jack Kilby and future Intel co-founder Robert Noyce.

The number of transistors on microprocessors—the brains of computers—has leaped from just several thousand in the 1970s to nearly a billion today. Although Moore has qualified his capacity-doubling prediction in the last decade, he thinks the transistor is going to be around for a long time. "There have been ideas about how people are going to replace it," he says, "but I don't see anything coming along that would really replace the transistor."

The density of transistors, however, is reaching the physical limits of the technology. Once chip makers can't squeeze any more transistors into the same-sized slice of silicon, the dramatic performance gains and cost reductions could suddenly slow. One problem has been trying to prevent too much heat from escaping from thinner and thinner components. Chip companies are avidly looking for new materials and other ways to improve performance.

lecture link B-5

JOHN ATANASOFF'S COMPUTER

Dr. John Vincent Atanasoff built the first digital computer over half a century ago, but his contribution to computing was nearly lost to history. Atanasoff worked on his machine during the 1930s at Iowa State University. After hours of work one night in 1937, he found that he was stumped by a basic problem of electronic design. In exhaustion, Atanasoff drove 170 miles over the state line to a roadhouse in Illinois. ("There wasn't any place to get a drink in Iowa," he recalls.) In the Illinois tavern, he saw things from a new perspective and solved some of the thorny problems that had plagued him. The computer would be a digital device, unlike the analog devices that were then in use. It would use vacuum tubes and have an on–off configuration. The computer would also have memory and be based on the base-two number system. Finally, it would have a "jogging" function to refresh the computer memory and prevent loss of information.

With his assistant, Clifford Berry, Atanasoff finally built his machine—the "ABC" (Atanasoff Berry Calculator). Atanasoff signed over his rights to the invention to the Iowa State College Research Foundation in exchange for a $5,330 grant, assuming that the college would patent the invention. World War II intervened, however, and no one followed up. Later, personnel in charge apparently did not realize the significance of the device, and no patent was ever obtained.

Meanwhile, Drs. John Mauchly and J. Presper Eckert of the Moore School of Electrical Engineering at University of Pennsylvania were working on a computing machine for the U.S. Army. ENIAC, the machine they developed, was completed in 1946 and has been widely referred to as the first modern computer. They applied for and received two patents, one for ENIAC and one for the "jogging" memory function they used. Mauchly and Eckert assigned their patents to the Sperry Rand Corporation, for which they later went to work. Sperry collected royalties from other computer companies for all computers using the technology developed in ENIAC, which, over the years, has been estimated to total over $1 billion.

It was not until 1967 that another computer company, Control Data Corporation, found an obscure reference to Atanasoff's machine. CDC, along with several other companies, sued and won release from the royalties, largely on the basis of Atanasoff's testimony. The court ruled that the patents had wrongly been issued and that the original theory was Dr. Atanasoff's. However, neither Iowa State nor Atanasoff has received any financial reward from the decision.

lecture link B-6

APPLE TAKES TO THE ICLOUD

For years the term *cloud computing* functioned as a buzzword for the future of digital storage but offered little in the way of practical use for consumers. All that has changed over the last year as companies like Google and Amazon have introduced new digital storage systems. However, no other announcement captured the press's attention quite like the late Steve Jobs's unveiling of the new Apple iCloud system.

One reason for all the excitement has to do with Jobs's prediction of the personal computer's fading future. Along with Bill Gates and Microsoft, Jobs and Apple helped spearhead a technological revolution that led to the presence of a computer in most American homes. But according to Jobs, the computer's days as the center of consumer technology are just about over, and the future now rests in the clouds. With iCloud, every item in a person's digital library (e.g., documents, music, videos, photos, etc.) will be accessible to them from their phones, tablets, and other devices so long as they have an Internet connection. Under the new system, the PC will be nothing more than just another device.

As the emergence of cloud-based technology theoretically spells doom for PCs, it places additional pressure on lagging tech giants like Microsoft and Dell. While the former may have the financial resources to branch out, Dell has struggled to redefine itself over the years as the PC's presence has waned. Founder Michael Dell reportedly went on a rehiring spree in order to craft a response to his competitors' forays into the cloud. Nevertheless, Apple is not assured prosperity in the clouds just yet, no matter what its recent run of successes might imply. Cloud systems are susceptible to crashes that reverberate across other sites. For instance, a recent outage at one of Google's cloud servers caused thousands of Gmail users to temporarily lose e-mails. In the meantime, the Apple team is setting iCloud apart from the pack by highlighting how his relationships with record companies will allow users to instantly access their iTunes libraries.[ii]

lecture link B-7

SHARING IN SILICON VALLEY

In most industries, companies don't share their most valuable information with competitors. For example, the business community would consider Coca-Cola crazy if it shared its secret recipe with Pepsi. In Silicon Valley, however, sharing information with the world, including rivals, is an everyday practice. For instance, Google dedicates an entire team of engineers exclusively to the practice of moving data into a format understood by their competitors' programs in case a client wants to switch companies. Former CEO Eric Schmidt said that the free service is meant to ensure that no users feel trapped in Google's networks should something go wrong.

Just as the tech industry started to boom in the 1990s, a landmark California court decision refused to uphold noncompete clauses commonly found in East Coast firms. With no barriers between them, engineers and developers were free to jump from company to company. This created a sense of community and fellowship in Silicon Valley unlike anywhere else in the business world. Sometimes collaborating with a competitor just makes good sense financially. Facebook is the prime example of a tech giant whose dominance is feared by some companies, but at the same time makes them impossible not to do business with. That's why Google-owned YouTube videos can be embedded on Facebook and why nearly every major website includes a linkable tag to the social network on all their pages.

Not every company plays the sharing game, though. Apple is notoriously unwilling to release its code to either users or companies. It also subjects any developers looking to list a program on the App Store to a rigorous approval process. Google, on the other hand, allows its mobile operating system Android to be adapted by rival companics and provides its app developers with relatively free reign.

Right now it's difficult to tell which strategy is winning since both the iPhone and the many Android-powered devices are each wildly popular. Only time will tell if Silicon Valley's culture of sharing is sustainable in the long term.[iii]

lecture link B-8

PASSWORD OVERLOAD

Using a password can protect information and improve security. Using multiple passwords, paradoxically, can make data less secure.

PricewaterhouseCoopers consulting firm conducted a study for the British Department of Trade and Industry to estimate the cost of security breaches from computer viruses, spyware, hacker attacks, and equipment theft. It found that these breaches cost British industry $18 billion in 2005.

One concern for security is the increasing number of user IDs/passwords that employees must deal with. The study found that employees have to remember three different user IDs/passwords on average. Two percent had to recall 10 different IDs.

The more IDs and passwords that users have to remember, the more likely the business is to have unauthorized access. The human memory is not programmed to remember this many numbers, letters, and combinations. Users are more likely to choose passwords that are personally memorable—pet names, birthdays, hometowns—terms that are easier for hackers to guess.[iv]

lecture link B-9

WEB SHOPPING SAFELY

E-commerce is exploding. Whether you're ordering a book from Amazon.com or downloading a tune from iTunes, online shopping is easy and convenient. But this convenience comes with a price. You don't get to examine an item closely, and entering your credit card number on an unknown site can take some courage.

According to Lauren Weinstein, co-founder of People for Internet Responsibility, "With the Internet, you don't know if that flashy Web site you're looking at is a multinational organization or some kid in a garage somewhere." Even official seals of approval from TRUSTe, VeriSign, and the Better Business Bureau are no guarantee that you're dealing with a reputable company. Those symbols can easily be reproduced, and they may not connect you as they should to the official sites of the certifying organization.

Scammers aren't the only problem. Many high-volume brick-and-mortar retailers that operate online impose different policies for Web purchases than they do for purchases in the physical store. For example, you have fewer protections shopping at Circuitcity.com than at a Circuit city store.

A few tips to make online shopping safer:

1. **FIND THE GOTCHAS.** A site's "terms and conditions" detail the existing protections—for the retailer, that is. You might discover that you must abide by rules of a distant state, where you agree to go if you sue. At Target.com, the purchaser agrees to assume the risk of loss or damage to merchandise when the shipping firm picks it up, not after delivery. When *Consumer Reports* tested Internet shopping sites, nearly every one, including Amazon.com and Walmart.com, disclaimed "implied warranties," unwritten assurances that products will work properly and last a reasonable amount of time.

2. **CHECK RETURN POLICIES.** Some sites charge restocking fees as high as 25%, and others don't accept returns of opened merchandise. *Consumer Reports* found some smaller sites that wouldn't even take returns of some defective products. Also, if you return items that came with free shipping, you

probably will have to pay the cost for the return postage. Some retailers deduct the original free shipping charges from your refund or charge you for shipping costs even if the product is defective.

3. **GUARD YOUR PRIVACY AND SECURITY**. Read a site's privacy policy. Some sites sell your customer data, which means you'll get tons of spam. One suggestion is to set up an e-mail account exclusively for buying online. Most ISPs will let you set up multiple accounts. If not, services such as Hotmail and Yahoo offer free e-mail service. For security, make sure that you see a security icon (such as a closed padlock) when you open the Web page. This indicates a secure connection to transmitting financial data, but doesn't guarantee that the site is legitimate.

4. **PAY WITH THE RIGHT PLASTIC.** When you pay by credit card, your liability for unauthorized purchase is capped at $50. Credit cards also let you dispute charges for items that arrive broken or not as ordered. Debit cards may not cover fraudulent charges if you don't act fast enough. Another suggestion is to investigate use of a "virtual" card number. Card issuers such as Citibank offer disposable numbers, which limit how much retailers can charge your account.

5. **DON'T DO BUSINESS WITH A SITE IF IT DOESN'T LIST THE OWNER'S NAME, ADDRESS, OR PHONE NUMBER**, or if it is full of spelling errors.

6. **USE SHOPPING-COMPARISON SITES** such as Shopping.com and Bizrate.com for ratings and user feedback on Web retailers.[v]

lecture link B-10

E-MAIL NEVER GOES AWAY

When it comes to the Internet, nothing is ever really forgotten and everything leaves a trail. This can be good or bad for business. These data trails can be used by companies to find who has been stealing their trade secrets—or to bust you if you are the thief. They can show who is working and who is goofing off. They can tell vendors who their online customers are and allow them to make better decisions and more money. This information is extraordinarily valuable, and there are laws that require companies to produce it, and do it right now.

In the pre-Enron, pre-WorldCom, pre-Tyco days, the legal rules for retaining communication records said only that a company had to be consistent. A company couldn't, for example, keep all e-mails except those having to do with a hostile takeover or a case under litigation. If the company's policy was to erase all old e-mails once a year or once a month, that was okay, as long as the policy was in writing and was strictly followed. Enron, for example, wiped its e-mail slate clean every 72 hours, which is hardly a surprise.

Today the rules have changed. Public and many private companies have to keep a copy of written communication of every type (letters, e-mails, even Internet instant messages) for up to seven years. These copies have to be kept in a form that allows their authenticity to be verified, whatever that means. Not only that, but companies must keep a second copy of every message in a different location in case of fire or natural disaster. The second copies must be on nonerasable storage media, such as optical disks. And if the SEC asks you to provide a copy of any given document or every given document, you have until close of business today to do it.

If the organization is a health care organization, an insurance company, or even a human resources department, the rules are even stricter. If a client asks for a list of every person or organization who has shared his or her medical records, the Health Insurance Portability and Accountability Act of 1996 (HIPAA) requires that the organization provide that list—on the spot.

Companies that aren't a public company, don't engage in health care, or have no human resources department aren't off the hook, because these requirements are becoming the accepted standards for all companies. If companies still dump e-mail every 72 hours and end up in court, they are effectively guilty as charged. Currently penalties for noncompliance are mild, but will get stronger in the future, right up to sending people to jail. New SEC regulations, for example, hold the CEO personally responsible for record retention, meaning he or she, not some nerd in the computer room, will be doing time. Then there are the civil penalties that will come from the inevitable lawsuits.

Every hospital and clinic in America is vulnerable, because they are all in violation. Most companies don't have the technology to comply with laws already on the books, much less the even stricter ones likely to follow. Faced with the huge costs of complying with the SEC regulations, many companies might be tempted to just take the fine—except for that little part about the CEO going to jail.vi

critical thinking exercises

Name: ______________________

Date: ______________________

critical thinking exercise B-1

SPAM STATISTICS

A growing problem with electronic communication over the Internet is spam, unwanted e-mail messages. The percentage of spam for most consumers is over 75%. In late 2007 the Internet security firm Postini found that 87% of e-mail messages were spam.

Go to Postini's website (www.Postini.com)[vii] and find the statistics in the online resource center. (Sometimes the Web address for a location changes. You might need to search to find the exact location mentioned.)

1. How many e-mail messages were processed in the last 24 hours? What percentage of these messages was spam?

2. How do spammers get your e-mail address?

3. Postini's resource center also tracks the number of messages that contain viruses, malicious worms, and Trojan horses. In the last 24 hours, what percentage of e-mail messages were virus infected?

4. Do you think that spam is a real problem for organizations? Why or why not? Will spam change American business reliance on e-mail communication in the future?

Name: ______________________________

Date: ______________________________

critical thinking exercise B-2

EDUCATION ONLINE

The Massachusetts Institute of Technology is one of several elite schools that are now putting their course materials online. The MIT initiative, called OpenCourseWare, makes virtually all the school's courses available online for free.

Go to the MIT OpenCourseWare website (http://ocw.mit.edu). Choose one of the classes available, open the course's Web page, and research the course.

1. Go to the course syllabus and summarize the course description.

2. What are the requirements for the course?

3. What text is used for the course? Also list any suggested readings.

4. Do you think you would learn as much through an online course as through a live lecture course? Why or why not?

endnotes

[i] *Source:* Oliver Chiang, "Super Crunchers," *Forbes*, March 14, 2011.

[ii] *Source:* Elizabeth Flock and Hayley Tsukayama, "iCloud, Cloud Computing Services Promise to Change the Way We Use Computers," *The Washington Post*, June 6, 2011.

[iii] *Sources:* Greg Ferenstein, "In a Cutthroat World, Some Tech Giants Thrive by Sharing," *The Washington Post*, February 19, 2011; Geoffrey A. Fowler, "Facebook's Web of Frenemies," *The Wall Street Journal*, February 15, 2011.

[iv] *Source:* "Password Overload Hurts Security, Survey Finds," *Reuters/ZDnet.com*, April 25, 2006.

[v] *Source:* "Web Shopping: 4 Ways to Protect Yourself," *Consumer Reports*, May 2006; "One in Four Credit Reports Contain Serious Mistakes," Associated Press, *The Clarion-Ledger,* June 20, 2004; "Prevent Identity Theft by Avoiding These Seven Common Mistakes," *TechRepublic.com*, May 17, 2007; "CR Investigates: The End of Privacy?" *Consumer Reports*, June 2006; "CR Investigates: Your Privacy for Sale," *Consumer Reports*, June 2006; Identity Theft Center, www.idtheftcenter.org, February 14, 2007.

[vi] *Source*: Robert X. Cringely, "What's Next: Data Disasters," *Inc. Magazine*, November 2003, p. 47.

[vii] The Internet is a dynamic, changing information source. Web links noted of this manual were checked at the time of publication, but content may change over time. Please review the website before recommending it to your students.

Managing Risk

bonus chapter C

what's new in this edition

additions to the 10th edition:

- Getting to Know Joaachim Oechslin of Munich Re
- Video case

revisions to the 10th edition:

- Text was revised to eliminate redundancy and tighten discussions.
- Statistical data and examples throughout the chapter were updated to reflect current information.
- Discussion of recent health care issues in subsection Health Insurance

deletions from the 9th edition:

- Getting to Know Richard Ward, CEO of Lloyds

brief chapter outline and learning goals

bonus chapter C

Managing Risk

Getting To Know JOACHIM OECHSLIN, of Munich Re

learning goal 1

Identify the environmental changes that have made risk management important.

I. **UNDERSTANDING BUSINESS RISKS**

   A. **How Rapid Change Affects Risk Management**

learning goal 2

Explain the four ways of managing risk, and distinguish between insurable and uninsurable risk.

II. **MANAGING RISK**

   A. **Reducing Risk**

   B. **Avoiding Risk**

   C. **Self-Insurance**

   D. **Buying Insurance to Cover Risk**

learning goal 3

Define insurance policies and explain the law of large numbers and the rule of indemnity.

III. **UNDERSTANDING INSURANCE POLICIES**

   A. **Rule of Indemnity**

   B. **Types of Insurance Companies**

learning goal 4

Discuss the various types of insurance businesses can buy to manage risk.

IV. **INSURANCE COVERAGE FOR VARIOUS KINDS OF RISK**

   A. **Health Insurance**

   B. **Disability Insurance**

   C. **Workers' Compensation**

   D. **Liability Insurance**

E. **Life Insurance for Businesses**

F. **Insurance Coverage for Home-Based Businesses**

G. **The Risk of Damaging the Environment**

V. SUMMARY

Getting to Know JOACHIM OECHSLIN, of MUNICH RE

Oechslin is chief risk officer of Munich Re and is known for his holistic approach to risk management. Knowing that the damage of a disaster isn't limited to its direct aftermath, it also spreads through the supply chain; he evaluates financial market risks as well as insurance risks.

Every business faces risks that can affect the health of the company. When the government suspected some of our hens had been exposed to bird flu, we killed and buried some 15,000 hens in northwestern Arkansas. Who are we?

(Students should read the chapter before guessing the company's name : Tyson)

learning goal 1

Identify the environmental changes that have made risk management more important.

I. UNDERSTANDING BUSINESS RISKS

A. **RISK MANAGEMENT** is a major issue for businesses.

1. Given natural disasters, hackers, identity theft, and other catastrophes, risk management is getting more attention.
2. In some states, insurance is not available or too expensive for some businesses.
3. Some states have passed legislation to let companies obtain insurance coverage again at a reasonable price.
4. When events involve loss, businesses must pay to restore the property and compensate those who are injured.
5. More than 90% of executives are building **ENTERPRISE RISK MANAGEMENT (ERM)** into their organization.

lecture notes

PPT C-1
Chapter Title

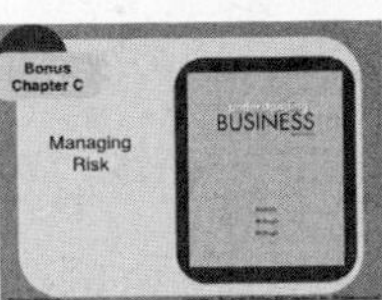

PPT C-2
Learning Goals

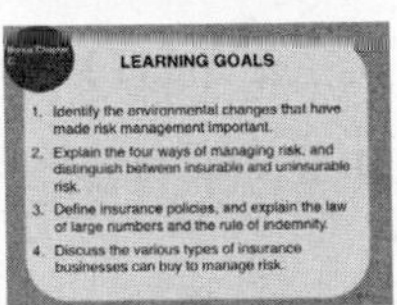

(See complete PowerPoint slide notes on page C.28.)

PPT C-3
Joachim Oechslin

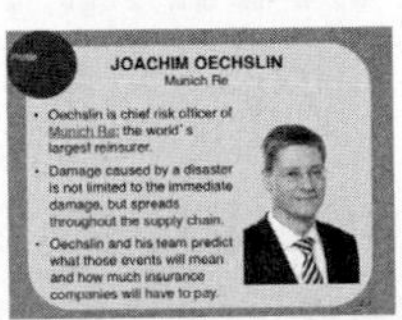

(See complete PowerPoint slide notes on page C.28.)

PPT C-4
Name That Company

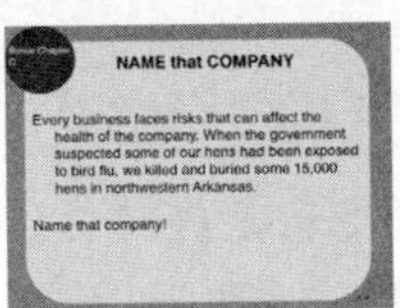

(See complete PowerPoint slide notes on page C.29.)

PPT C-5
What's Enterprise Risk Management?

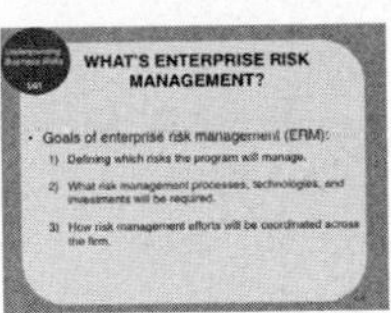

(See complete PowerPoint slide notes on page C.29.)

6. An ERM program should have well-defined goals, such as defining:
   a. Which risks the program will manage
   b. What risk management process, technologies, and investments will be required
   c. How these efforts will be coordinated

B. **HOW RAPID CHANGE AFFECTS RISK MANAGEMENT**

1. Changes are occurring so fast that it is difficult to keep up with the new risks involved.
2. Recent changes include Internet selling, currency fluctuations, global warming, threat of new terrorist attack, a possible flu epidemic, and financial collapse.

learning goal 2

Explain the four ways of managing risk, and distinguish between insurable and uninsurable risk.

II. MANAGING RISK

A. ***RISK*** refers to the chance of loss, the degree of probability of loss, and the amount of possible loss.

1. There are two different kinds of risk.
   a. ***SPECULATIVE RISK*** involves a chance of either profit or loss.
      i. Buying new machinery may bring extra revenue, but it also involves risk.
      ii. An entrepreneur takes speculative risk on the chance of making a profit.
   b. ***PURE RISK*** is the threat of loss with no chance for profits.

PPT C-6
What's Risk?

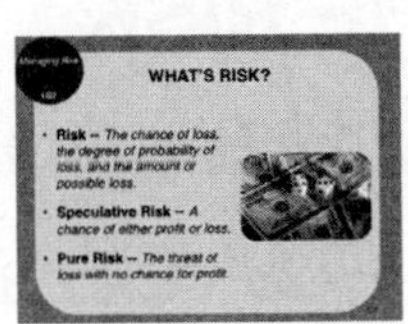

(See complete PowerPoint slide notes on page C.29)

lecture link C-1
THE FOUR FACETS OF RISK

Businesses are becoming much better at managing hazard risk, financial risk, and operational risk, but most have failed to appreciate the impact of the more dangerous risk, strategic risk. (See the complete lecture link on page C.37 in this manual.)

i. Pure risk involves the threat of fire, accident, or loss.

ii. If such events occur, a company loses money; but if the events do not occur, the company gains nothing.

2. **PURE RISK** threatens the very existence of firms.

3. Once such risks are identified, firms can:

   a. **REDUCE THE RISK**

   b. **AVOID THE RISK**

   c. **SELF-INSURE** against the risk

   d. **BUY INSURANCE** against the risk

B. **REDUCING RISK**

1. A firm can reduce risk by establishing **LOSS-PREVENTION PROGRAMS.**

2. *Examples:*

   a. *Fire drills, health education, safety inspections, equipment maintenance, accident prevention programs can reduce risk.*

   b. *Retail stores use mirrors and cameras to reduce shoplifting.*

   c. *Industries have safety devices to protect workers against accidents and injury.*

3. **COMPANIES** can also reduce risk.

   a. *Tyson killed and buried 15,000 hens because the government suspected they had been exposed to bird flu.*

   b. *Firestone and Ford recalled thousands of tires when 400 deaths were linked to faulty tires.*

lecture link C-2

RISK PERCEPTION: ANALYTICAL VERSUS INTUITIVE

Perceived risk involves two elements—the logical and analytical component and the intuitive and emotional component. (See the complete lecture link on page C.38 in this manual.)

PPT C-7

How to Deal with Pure Risk

(See complete PowerPoint slide notes on page C.30.)

PPT C-8

Most Costly Disasters

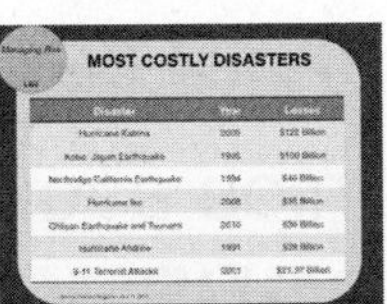

(See complete PowerPoint slide notes on page C.30.)

lecture link C-3

THE ECONOMIC IMPACT OF A CATASTROPHE

After the devastating 2011 earthquake and tsunami that hit Japan, the country's economic outlook is uncertain. (See the complete lecture link on page C.38 in this manual.)

4. Employees can reduce risk by wearing protective gear.
5. An **EFFECTIVE RISK MANAGEMENT STRATEGY** starts with a good loss-prevention program.
6. High insurance rates have forced some people to avoid risks, and in extreme cases go out of business.

C. **AVOIDING RISK**

1. Many risks cannot be avoided.
2. Some companies avoid risk by **NOT ACCEPTING HAZARDOUS JOBS** and by outsourcing certain functions.
3. Due to lack of liability insurance, some companies are losing outside members of boards of directors.

D. **SELF-INSURANCE**

1. ***SELF-INSURANCE*** is the practice of setting aside money to cover routine claims and buying only "catastrophe" policies to cover big losses.
2. Self-insurance is most appropriate when a firm has several widely distributed facilities, where one catastrophe will not destroy the whole operation.
3. Some companies are using a risky strategy for self-insurance called **"GOING BARE,"** paying claims straight out of the budget.
4. A less risky alternative is the forming of **RISK RETENTION GROUP-INSURANCE POOLS** that share similar risks.

PPT C-9
What's Self Insurance?

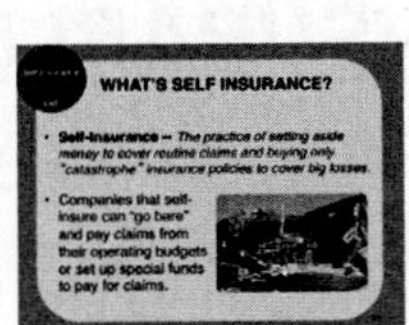

(See complete PowerPoint slide notes on page C.30.)

E. **BUYING INSURANCE TO COVER RISK**

1. Well-designed, consistently enforced risk-prevention programs **REDUCE THE PROBABILITY OF CLAIMS**, but accidents do happen.
    a. Spending by business and nonprofits on insurance makes up 10% of the GDP.
    b. The federal government provides some insurance protection.
    c. Most risks must be covered by individuals and businesses on their own.
2. **WHAT RISKS ARE UNINSURABLE?**
    a. An ***UNINSURABLE RISK*** is a risk that no insurance company will cover.
    b. You cannot insure market risks, political risks, some personal risks, and some operational risks.
3. **WHAT RISKS ARE INSURABLE?**
    a. An ***INSURABLE RISK*** is a risk that the typical insurance company will cover.
    b. Insurance companies use these guidelines:
        i. The policyholder must have an ***INSURABLE INTEREST***, the possibility of the policyholder to suffer a loss.
        ii. The loss should be **MEASURABLE.**
        iii. The **CHANCE OF LOSS** should be measurable.
        iv. The **LOSS** must be **ACCIDENTAL.**

lecture notes

TEXT FIGURE C.1
Public Insurance
(Text page C-5)

This text figure shows some types of insurance protection provided by the federal government.

PPT C-10
What Risks Are Uninsurable?

(See complete PowerPoint slide notes on page C.31.)

PPT C-11
What Risks Are Insurable?

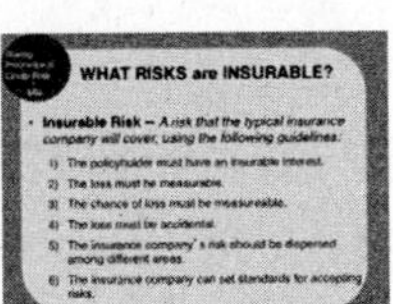

(See complete PowerPoint slide notes on page C.31)

v. The risk should be **DISPERSED**, spread among different geographic areas.

vi. The insurance company can **SET STANDARDS FOR ACCEPTING RISK.**

learning goal 3

Define insurance policies, and explain the law of large numbers and the rule of indemnity.

III. UNDERSTANDING INSURANCE POLICIES

A. An ***INSURANCE POLICY*** is a written contract between the insured and an insurance company that promises to pay for all or part of a loss.

1. A ***PREMIUM*** is the fee charged by the insurance company for an insurance policy.
2. A ***CLAIM*** is statement of loss that the insured sends to the insurance company to request payment.
3. The object of an insurance company is to make a profit.
4. The **LAW OF LARGE NUMBERS** makes the acceptance of risk possible.
5. The ***LAW OF LARGE NUMBERS*** is the principle that if a large number of people are exposed to the same risk, a predictable number of losses will occur during a given period of time.
   a. These figures are used to determine the appropriate premiums to assume the risk.
   b. Many insurance companies charge high premiums anticipating costs of more court cases and higher damage awards.

lecture notes

progress assessment

(Text page C-6)

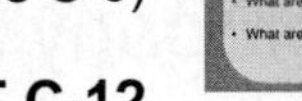

PPT C-12

Progress Assessment

(See complete PowerPoint slide notes on page C.31.)

PPT C-13

Insurance Policies

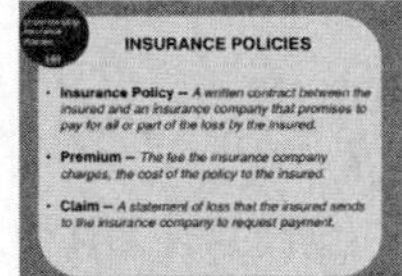

(See complete PowerPoint slide notes on page C.32.)

PPT C-14

Basics of Insurance Policies

(See complete PowerPoint slide notes on page C.32.)

B. **RULE OF INDEMNITY**

1. The ***RULE OF INDEMNITY*** says that an injured person or organization cannot collect more than the actual loss from an insurable risk.
2. One cannot gain from risk management; one can only **MINIMIZE LOSES**.

C. **TYPES OF INSURANCE COMPANIES**

1. A ***STOCK INSURANCE COMPANY*** is a type of insurance company owned by stockholders.
2. A ***MUTUAL INSURANCE COMPANY*** is a type of insurance company owned by its policyholders.
   a. A mutual insurance company does not earn profits for its owners.
   b. It is a nonprofit organization, and any excess funds go to the policyholder in the form of dividends or premium reduction.

learning goal 4

Discuss the various types of insurance businesses can buy to manage risk.

IV. INSURANCE COVERAGE FOR VARIOUS KINDS OF RISK

A. There are many types of insurance that cover various losses.

1. **PROPERTY LOSSES** result from fires, accidents, theft, or other perils.
2. **LIABILITY LOSSES** result from property damage or injuries suffered by others for which the policyholder is held responsible.

PPT C-15
Types of Insurance Companies

(See complete PowerPoint slide notes on page C.32.)

PPT C-16
Stock and Mutual Insurance Companies

(See complete PowerPoint slide notes on page C.33.)

progress assessment
(Text page C-7)

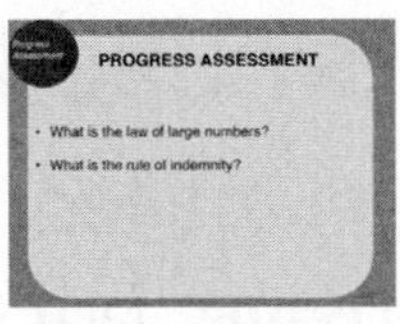

PPT C-17
Progress Assessment

(See complete PowerPoint slide notes on page C.33.)

B. **HEALTH INSURANCE**

1. The U.S. is going through major changes in health insurance as the government is now more involved.
2. We are likely to see many variations of health coverage in the future.
3. Organizations can offer their employees an array of health care benefits to choose from.
4. ***HEALTH MAINTENANCE ORGANIZATIONS (HMOs)*** are health care organizations that require members to choose from a restricted list of doctors.
   a. HMOs offer a full range of health care benefits with emphasis on helping members to **STAY HEALTHY.**
   b. HMOs employ or contract with doctors, hospitals, and other systems; and **MEMBERS MUST USE THOSE PROVIDERS.**
   c. This system, called **"MANAGED CARE,"** is less expensive, but members aren't able to choose doctors.
   d. Doctors also complain that they lose freedom to treat patients as they see fit.
   e. To save money, HMOs usually must approve treatment before it is given.
3. ***PREFERRED PROVIDER ORGANIZATIONS (PPOs)*** are health care organizations similar to HMOs except that they allow members to choose their own physicians (for a fee).

PPT C-18
Health Insurance Changes

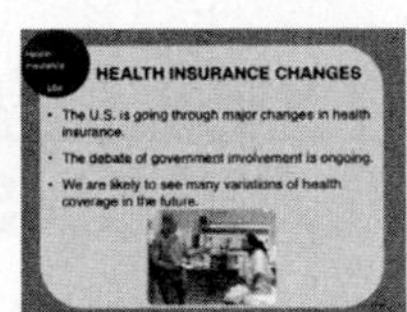

(See complete PowerPoint slide notes on page C.33.)

PPT C-19
Employer Health Insurance Options

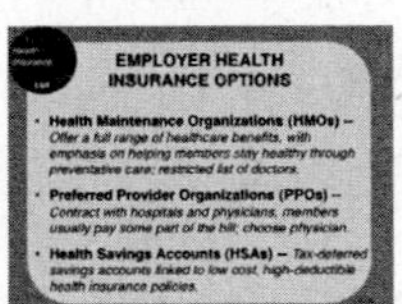

(See complete PowerPoint slide notes on page C.34.)

TEXT FIGURE C.2
Private Insurance
(Text page C-8)

This text figure shows some types of insurance coverage not provided by private insurance companies.

a. PPOs also contract with hospitals and physicians, but, unlike HMOs, **YOU DO NOT HAVE TO GO TO THOSE PHYSICIANS.**

b. Members usually have to pay a **DEDUCTIBLE** before the PPO will pay any bills.

c. The benefit of such plans is that you can choose your own physician.

d. Both HMOs and PPOs can cost 80% less than comprehensive individual health insurance policies.

4. ***HEALTH SAVINGS ACCOUNTS (HSAs)*** (formerly called **MEDICAL SAVINGS ACCOUNTS**) are tax-deferred accounts linked to low-cost, high-deductible health insurance policies.

   a. Employees put part of their salary into an HSA, which is used to cover major medical expenses.

   b. The use of HSAs may lower overall health costs.

   c. If you don't spend the money in your account in any one year, you can save the money for future medical expenses.

C. **DISABILITY INSURANCE**

1. Disability insurance replaces part of your income if you become disabled and unable to work.

2. Experts recommend this type of insurance: the chances of becoming disabled are much higher than the chance of dying.

PPT C-20
Other Types of Insurance

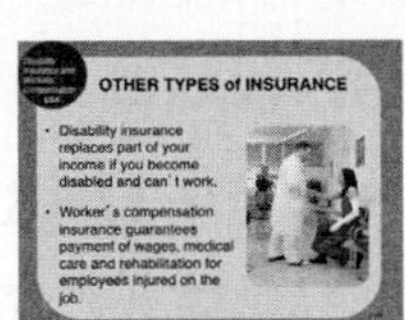

(See complete PowerPoint slide notes on page C.34.)

PPT C-21
Getting the Most out of Life Insurance

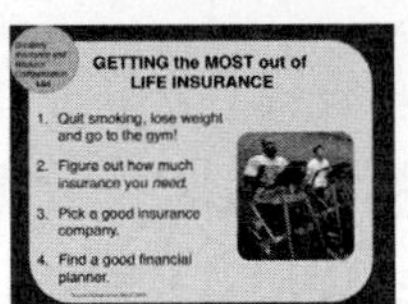

(See complete PowerPoint slide notes on page C.34.)

D. **WORKERS' COMPENSATION**

1. **WORKERS' COMPENSATION INSURANCE** guarantees payment of wages, medical care, and rehabilitation services (e.g., retraining) for employees who are injured on the job, regardless of fault.
2. Employers in all 50 states are required to provide this insurance.
3. The cost of insurance varies by the company's safety record, its payroll, and the types of hazards faced by workers.

E. **LIABILITY INSURANCE**

1. **PROFESSIONAL LIABILITY INSURANCE,** also called **MALPRACTICE INSURANCE**, covers people who are found liable for professional negligence.
2. Many professionals, not just doctors, buy this type of insurance in the face of increasing lawsuits.
3. **PRODUCT LIABILITY INSURANCE** provides coverage against liability arising out of products sold.

F. **LIFE INSURANCE FOR BUSINESSES**

1. Bonus Chapter D, "Managing Personal Finance," discusses life insurance.
2. All the concepts discussed there apply to businesses also.
3. The best coverage for most individuals is **TERM INSURANCE.**

PPT C-22
Liability Insurance

(See complete PowerPoint slide notes on page C.35.)

G. **INSURANCE COVERAGE FOR HOME-BASED BUSINESSES**

1. Homeowner's policies usually don't provide adequate protection for a home-based business.
2. For more coverage, you may need an **ENDORSEMENT** (sometimes called a **RIDER**) to your homeowner's insurance.
3. You may also need **HOME OFFICE INSURANCE** if you have visitors in your house.
4. For businesses that are more elaborate a **BUSINESS OWNER POLICY** may be needed.

H. **THE RISK OF DAMAGING THE ENVIRONMENT**

1. **RISK MANAGEMENT** now goes far beyond the protection of individuals, businesses, and nonprofit organizations from known risks.
2. Organizations must prioritize these risks so funds can be spent were they can do the most good.
3. No insurance company can protect humanity from such risks.
4. 94% of all consumers prefer to do business with companies that demonstrate that they care about the environment.

V. SUMMARY

PPT C-23
Home-Based Businesses

(See complete PowerPoint slide notes on page C.35.)

PPT C-24
Home Matters

(See complete PowerPoint slide notes on page C.35.)

lecture link C-4

RECONSIDERING FLOOD INSURANCE

As Gulf residents have learned, most insurance covers wind damage, but not flood damage. A federal program exists to provide low-cost flood insurance, but few vulnerable homeowners use it. (See the complete lecture link on page C.39 of this manual.)

progress assessment

(Text page C-11)

PPT C-25
Progress Assessment

PROGRESS ASSESSMENT
- Why should someone buy disability insurance?
- How many different kinds of private insurance can you name?

(See complete PowerPoint slide notes on page C.36.)

PowerPoint slide notes

PPT C-1
Chapter Title

PPT C-2
Learning Goals

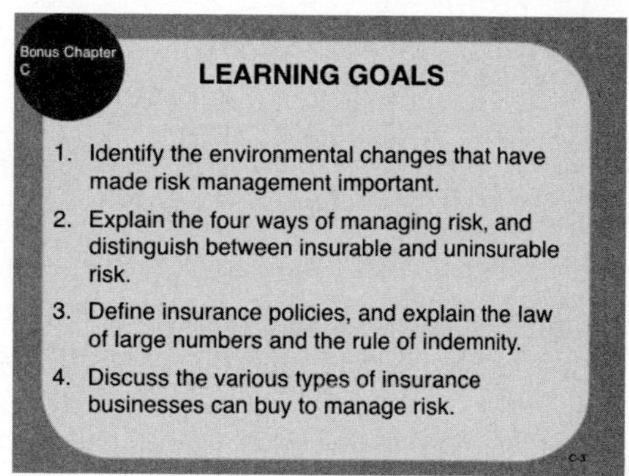

PPT C-3
Joachim Oechslin

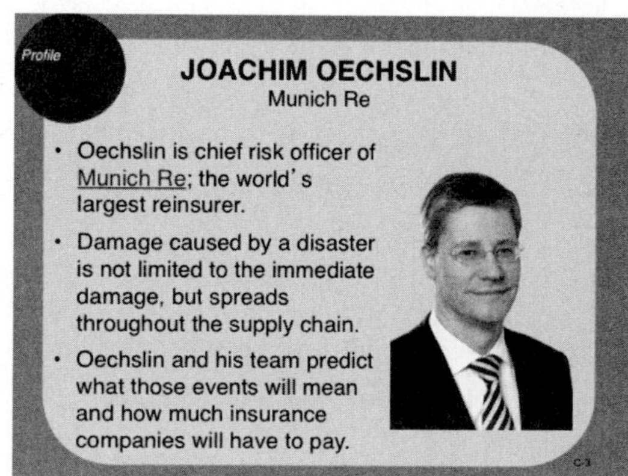

PPT C-4
Name That Company

Company: Tyson

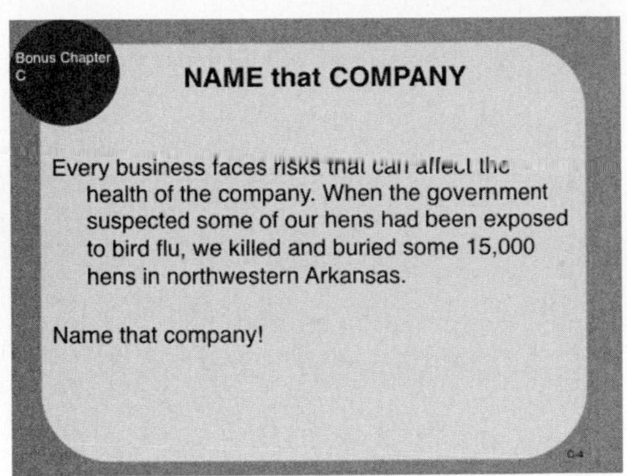

PPT C-5
What's Enterprise Risk Management?

The risk management function of large corporations plays an important role in the organization's success.

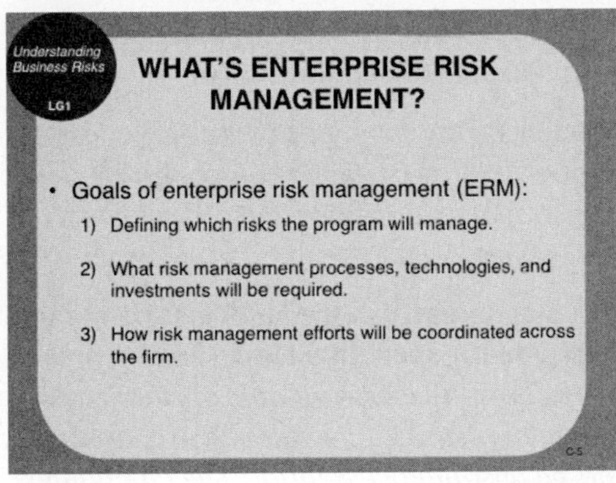

PPT C-6
What's Risk?

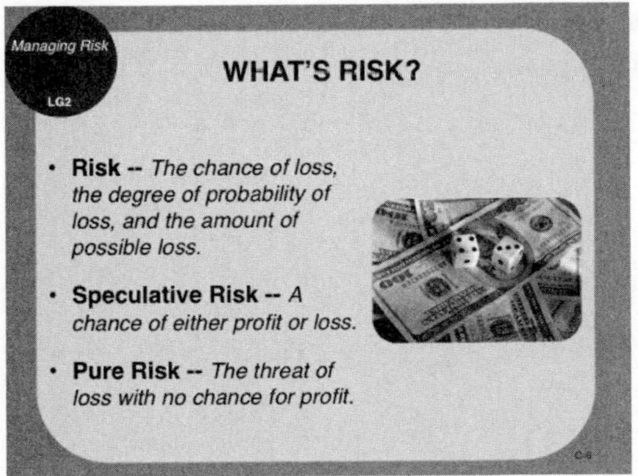

PPT C-7
How to Deal with Pure Risk

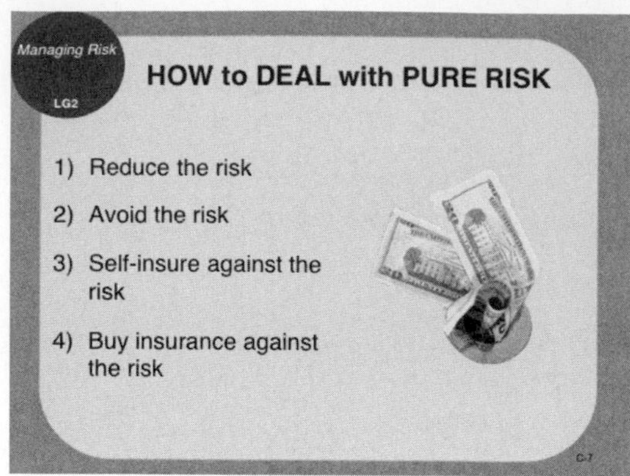

PPT C-8
Most Costly Disasters

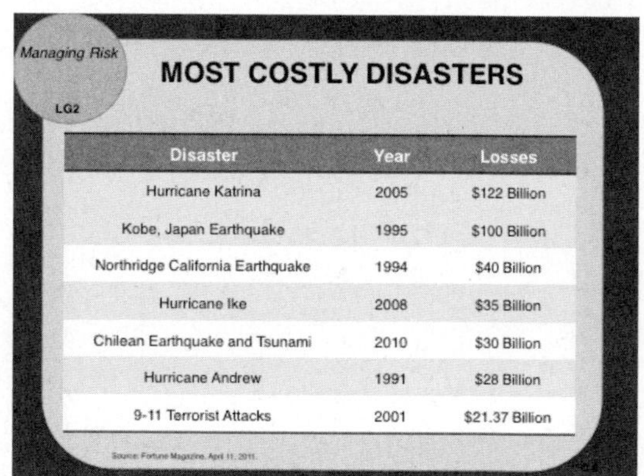

Disaster	Year	Losses
Hurricane Katrina	2005	$122 Billion
Kobe, Japan Earthquake	1995	$100 Billion
Northridge California Earthquake	1994	$40 Billion
Hurricane Ike	2008	$35 Billion
Chilean Earthquake and Tsunami	2010	$30 Billion
Hurricane Andrew	1991	$28 Billion
9-11 Terrorist Attacks	2001	$21.37 Billion

Source: Fortune Magazine, April 11, 2011.

1. This slide presents the costliest disasters in billions of dollars.
2. We don't yet know the economic impact of the 2011 earthquake and tsunami in Japan.
3. Ask the students, How many of these disasters do you remember? *(Most of them should identify the 9/11 terrorist attacks and Hurricane Katrina as the most talked-about events.)*
4. From a risk standpoint, ask the students, How can a business prepare for such disasters? *(Taking precautionary actions by ensuring appropriate types and coverage of insurance, employee preparedness, etc. should be absolutely essential. The companies need to protect their people, property, data and information, and finances.)*

PPT C-9
What's Self Insurance?

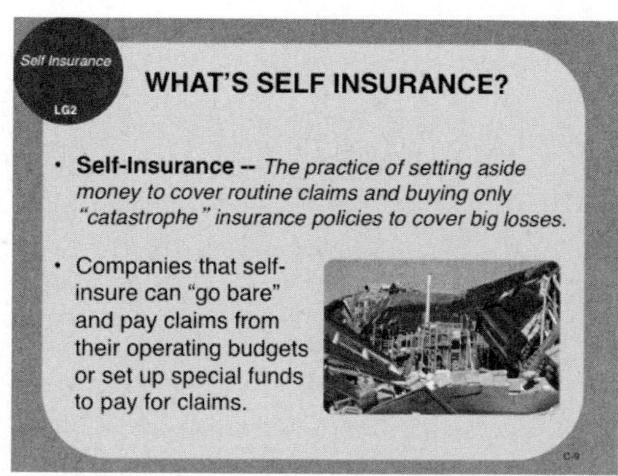

Many large companies use self-insurance as a means of risk management.

PPT C-10
What Risks Are Uninsurable?

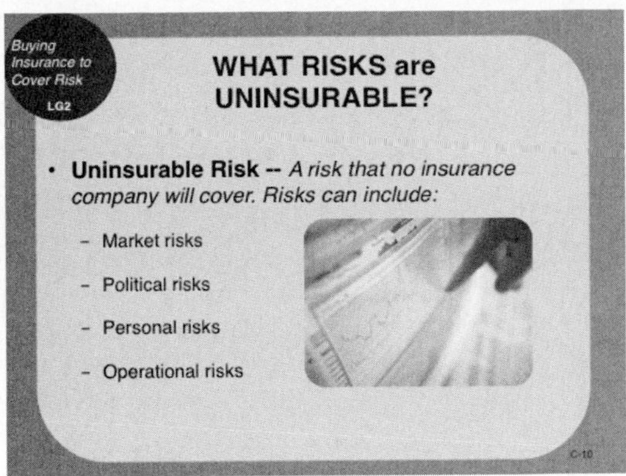

PPT C-11
What Risks Are Insurable?

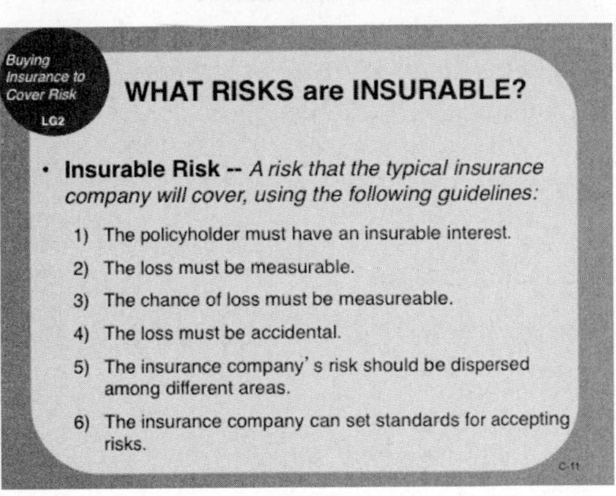

PPT C-12
Progress Assessment

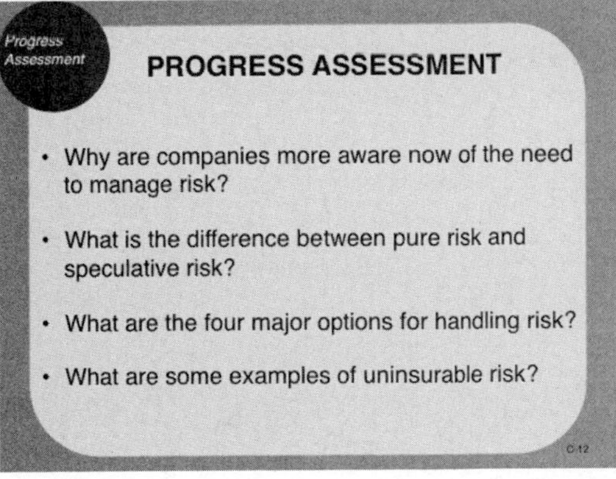

1. Hurricanes, terrorist threats, identity theft, and an unstable economy have all contributed to additional risk and the need for greater risk management.
2. Pure risk is the threat of loss with no chance for profit, such as the threat from a fire. If your house burns to the ground you lose money, but if it does not you gain nothing. Speculative risk can result in either profit or loss. An entrepreneur's chance to make a profit is considered speculative risk.
3. The four major options for handling risk are (1) reduce the risk, (2) avoid the risk, (3) self-insure against the risk, and (4) buy insurance against the risk.
4. Examples of uninsurable risk include market risk, political risk, personal risk, and some risk of operation.

PPT C-13
Insurance Policies

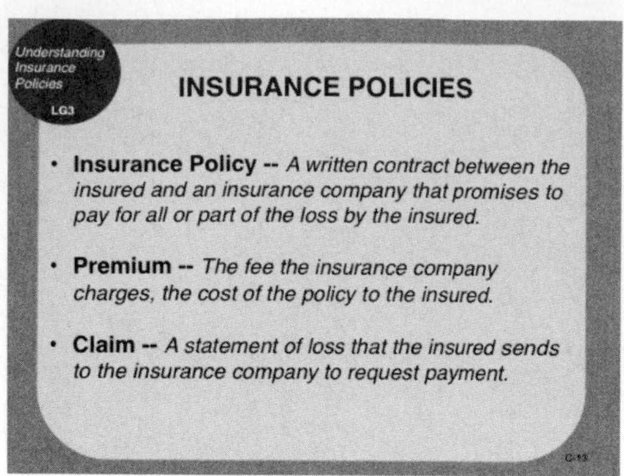

PPT C-14
Basics of Insurance Policies

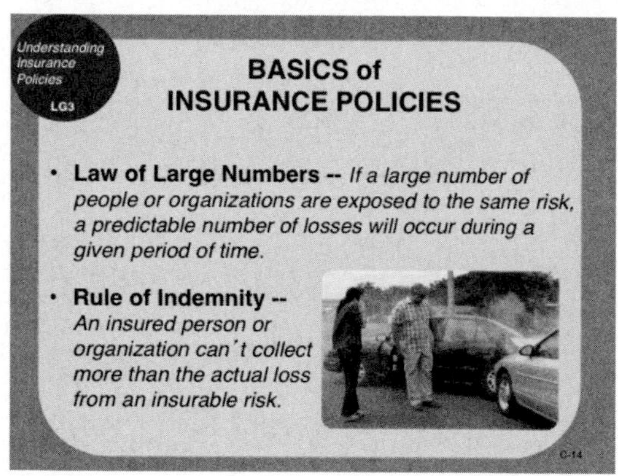

One of five U.S. adults, about 45 million people, say it's acceptable to defraud insurance companies under certain circumstances. Four of five adults think insurance fraud is unethical. (*Source: Four Faces of Insurance Fraud*, Coalition Against Insurance Fraud, 2008.)

PPT C-15
Types of Insurance Companies

PPT C-16
Stock and Mutual Insurance Companies

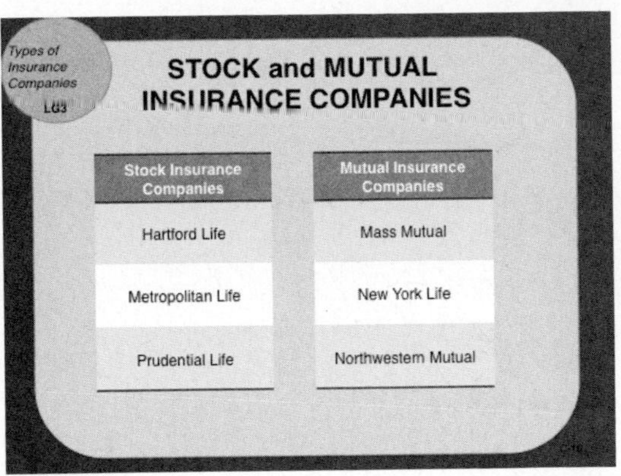

1. This slide profiles some of stock insurance companies and mutual insurance companies.
2. If time permits, have students examine some of the differences among the stock and mutual insurance companies listed on this slide.

PPT C-17
Progress Assessment

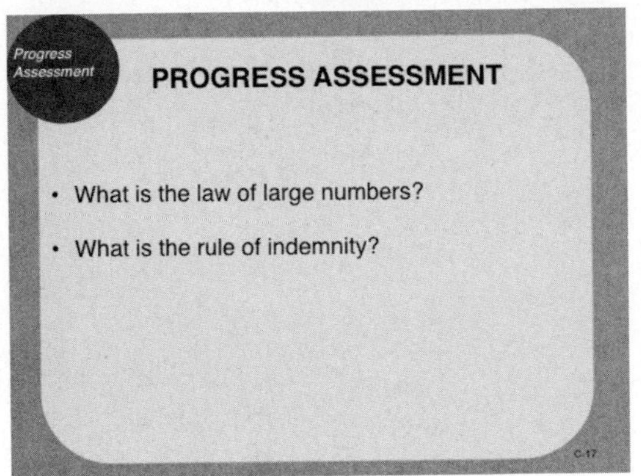

1. The law of large numbers means that if a large number of people or organizations are exposed to the same risk, a predictable number of losses will occur during a period of time.
2. The rule of indemnity says an insured person or organization cannot collect more than the actual loss from an insurable act.

PPT C-18
Heath Insurance Changes

PPT C-19
Employer Health Insurance Options

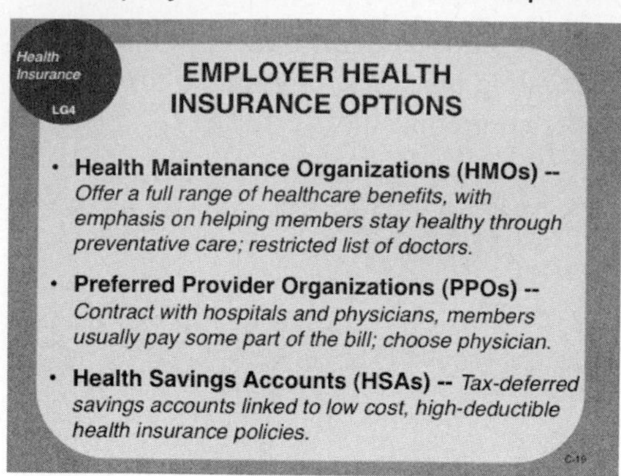

PPT C-20
Other Types of Insurance

Employers in all 50 states are required to provide workers' compensation insurance.

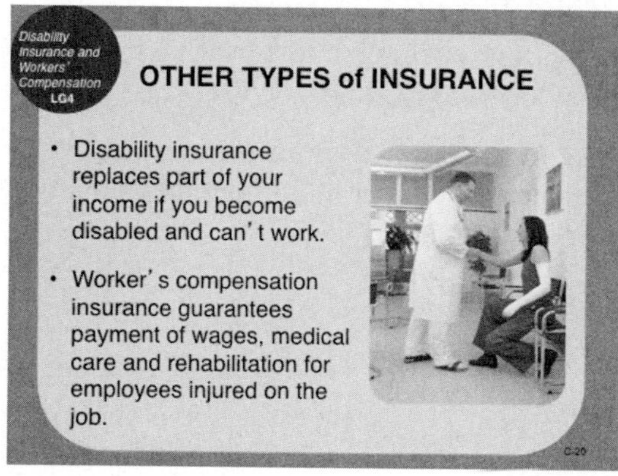

PPT C-21
Getting the Most out of Life Insurance

The cost of life insurance increases if you smoke or are overweight, so addressing these issues will reduce your premiums.

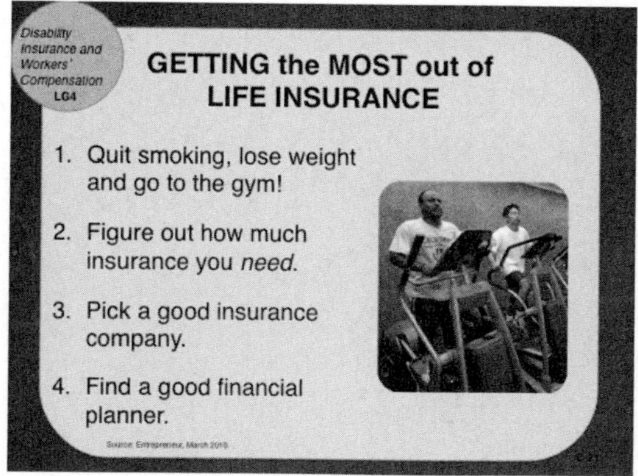

PPT C-22
Liability Insurance

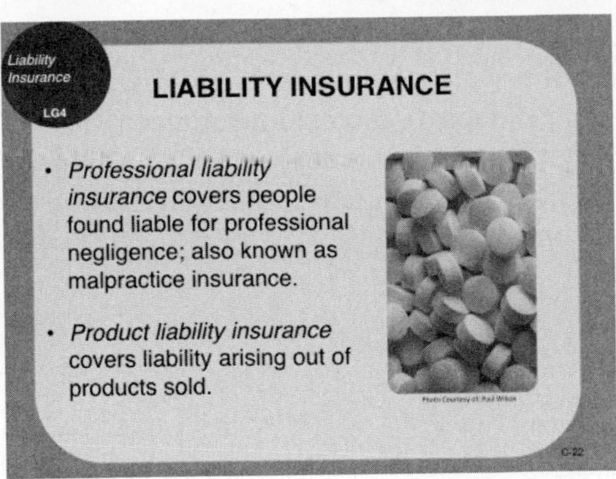

PPT C-23
Home-Based Businesses

PPT C-24
Home Matters

PPT C-25
Progress Assessment

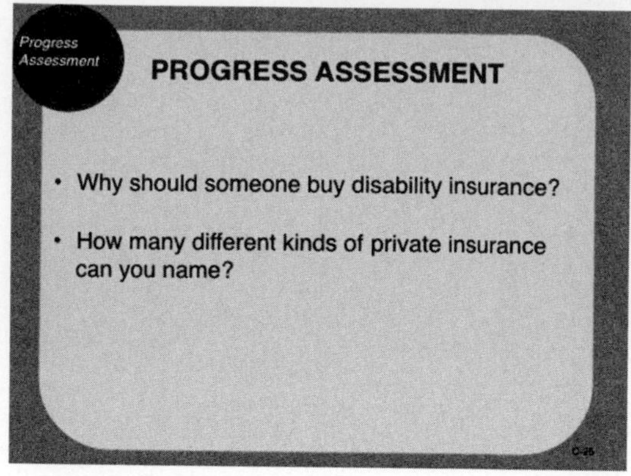

1. Disability insurance is important, because a young person is more likely to become disabled than to die.
2. The kinds of private insurance include life insurance (whole and term), medical insurance (PPO and HMO), property insurance, renter's insurance, professional liability insurance, disability, and workers' compensation.

lecture links

"Insurance covers everything except what happens."
Miller's Law of Insurance

"If the lion didn't bite the tamer every once in a while, it wouldn't be exciting."
Darrell Waltrip

"The probability of anything happening is in inverse proportion to its desirability."
Guperson's Law

lecture link C-1

THE FOUR FACETS OF RISK

While many companies are doing a better job of cataloging their risks, many industry insiders think an entirely new approach may be needed. Most businesses approach risk within a "silo structure," where different risks are handled by different departments. As the business grows, everyone has a good understanding of the risks in their part of the business but not in other parts of the firm. If businesses coordinated all the parts, risk could be managed more efficiently.

This is why risk experts recommend a more integrated system: enterprise-level risk management (ERM). ERM is a way to get the big picture—how risks interact and affect the enterprise as a whole—then use this knowledge to minimize risk and maximize return.

Not all risks are equal, or equally probable. A successful risk management strategy requires companies to understand the different types of risk they face, and create a strategy for transferring or controlling each of them.

The risk of an earthquake damaging or destroying a factory is a *hazard risk.* The best course of action is to *transfer* the risk by insurance. The risk that the price of oil will increase is a *financial risk.* The company can *hedge* against this risk by purchasing options in the commodity market, creating a ceiling on the price of oil. An example of an *operational risk* would be a computer virus putting IT systems out of action. The best course of action would be to *control* the risk by investing in antivirus software.

For many companies, risk management stops with these three facets—hazard risk, financial risk, and operational risk. But business must also consider a fourth facet of risk—*strategic risk.* This is the most dangerous type of threat businesses face. Strategic risk isn't as easy to define or protect against as an earthquake or the fluctuating price of oil. Strategic risk is an external bad thing that can happen to your business model, like the collapse of your brand's reputation or the risk of a new technology overtaking your own. Strategic risk is not only the most dangerous type of risk, but also the most prevalent, accounting for 60 to 70% of a business's risk.

However, once strategic risk is identified, several tools can be used to handle it. If the risk affects a particular industry, companies may be able to collaborate and cooperate. When the aircraft industry faced declining profits in the 1970s, several companies combined to form the joint venture Airbus. There is also a risk when two technologies are competing for acceptance. The best approach could be double-betting, or investing in both. In the 1980s, Microsoft embraced both Windows and OS/2 until one system prevailed. In both these cases, the companies not only managed their risk, they also grew their businesses.

There are also numerous examples of companies that didn't identify and deal with strategic risk. By staying too long with analog phones, instead of double-betting on both analog and digital models, Motorola opened the way for Nokia to dominate the digital side. The music industry also failed to anticipate the significance of the Internet distribution model and handed a lucrative opportunity to Apple's iTunes stores.

Companies have become successful at cataloging and managing traditional risks, like earthquakes, tornados, currency fluctuations, and failing IT systems. However, most are still ignoring 60 to 70% of their risks. With an enterprise-wide risk management program, they can to put the same efforts into cataloging and managing the most important one: strategic risks.[i]

lecture link C-2

RISK PERCEPTION: ANALYTICAL VERSUS INTUITIVE

Washington Post writer Joel Achenbach recalls the man he encountered on the morning of September 11, 2001. In the hours after terrorists flew a plane into the Pentagon, Achenbach joined the hasty evacuation near the Federal Reserve. He came across a man sitting calmly on a park bench reading a newspaper. The man had no interest in the evacuation or even listening to the news bulletins. He told Achenbach that he figured the danger was over and went back to his stock listings.

The man's reaction illustrates the two components of perceived risk—logic and emotion—two very dissimilar elements. The man could have reasoned through the situation carefully and determined it was safe to go back to the newspaper. That would be the logical and analytical approach to risk. But he could also be using his gut instinct to know that the danger was over.

The intuitive and emotional system is based on images burned into our brains during past experiences, and it often trumps the analytical one. Gut instinct warns us when something in the familiar environment doesn't seem right. Over the course of human evolution, that instinct has kept the human species alive. However, the intuitive instinct may not warn us of dangers from unfamiliar sources, such as airplanes descending from the sky to bring down skyscrapers.

Feelings can also cause us to make illogical decisions. A 1993 experiment offered people a chance to win a dollar by drawing a red jellybean from one of two bowls. One bowl had 200 beans, 7 of them red. The other had 10 beans, only 1 red. Many people preferred the bowl with the 7 red beans, even though they knew the odds were worse. However, they said they *felt* as if they had a better chance.

Another experiment highlights the emotional, intuitive element in decision making. Clinicians at a mental hospital were more likely to release a patient from a hospital if told he had a 20% chance of becoming violent than if told 20 out of 100 such patients would become violent. The visual image of the second scenario was more frightening, although the two risks were actually equivalent.

A risk taker analyzes both the emotional and analytical systems to make good decisions. Says psychologist Paul Slovic of the University of Oregon, "You need your feelings to put a cross-check on your analysis, and you need analysis to keep your feelings in check."[ii]

lecture link C-3

THE ECONOMIC IMPACT OF A CATASTROPHE

The chief concern after the devastating earthquake and tsunami that rocked Japan in March 2011 was preserving lives. With a death toll in the tens of thousands and a leaking nuclear reactor, Japan still had many tragedies to overcome before the nation could turn its eyes to the future. Like many of the earthquake's grisly consequences, the long-term economic outlook for Japan is uncertain. But as a potential $235 billion rebuilding price tag looms overhead, the fiscal future of Japan is worth examining at least to find out if this disaster could push Japan into a debt crisis.

First of all, Japan has the consolation of its wealth. Traditionally, the richer the country, the less one event can significantly affect its GDP. Although the quake likely destroyed many businesses and infrastructure, Japan has ample resources to draw upon for rebuilding. But Japan's robust GDP doesn't tell the whole story. For all intents and purposes, Japan is already mired in a credit crisis. Public debt accounts for an astronomical 228% of GDP, compared to 144% for Greece and 77% for the United States. Government officials rarely mention the problem publicly, and the low interest rates that keep businesses borrowing only make the problem worse.

Given those circumstances, any fiscal hit taken from the earthquake would be just another drop in a very deep bucket. So far the government allotted $12 billion for recovery in the 2011 budget and will likely increase that amount over the coming years. And unlike the debt crisis, business leaders are at least addressing the aftermath of the earthquake head on. A Japanese business lobby recently gave the government its blessing to scrap plans for a corporate tax cut to ensure that recovery efforts have as much funding as possible.[iii]

lecture link C-4

RECONSIDERING FLOOD INSURANCE

After Hurricane Katrina devastated the Gulf Coast in 2005, shocked residents and businesspeople called their insurance companies. Many found out—too late to do anything about it—that their losses weren't covered by insurance.

Nature can be cruel, and disasters occur with alarming frequency. Floods are more confined and predictable than other disasters, but their scale is sometimes so huge that private insurers have been scared away. That's why Congress created the National Flood Insurance Program (NFIP) four decades ago.

Since then, the federal government has made flood insurance available to property owners, filling a gap left by private carriers, which generally decline to write the coverage. The program has grown controversial over the years. Critics have argued that it encourages Americans to build on beaches, flood plains, and other sites that shouldn't be built on—and wouldn't be if the government wasn't willing to compensate owners when such homes and vacation spots are washed away.

The insurance can be immensely valuable. Policies under the NFIP will pay up to $250,000 for residential buildings, plus another $100,000 for contents that are lost. It will also pay up to $500,000 for nonresidential buildings and $500,000 for their contents.

The premiums average around $400 a year for $100,000 of coverage—higher in very flood-prone areas. That's very reasonable, considering the risks. Many mortgage lenders require it, at least for property located within a flood-prone area. Fannie Mae, for example, requires coverage of 80% of the replacement cost of the home, or the program limit of $250,000, whichever is less.

The federal flood insurance program has about 4.6 million policies in place, covering more than $743 billion in assets. Annual premium collections run about $2 billion. Still, the program is not as popular as you might expect. On the Mississippi Gulf Coast devastated by Katrina, just one in four homes were covered. The national average is 10 to 20%. It is much higher in New Orleans, where it covers about half the homes.

The hurricanes of 2005 created staggering losses and focused attention and concern on the federal flood program. From 1978 through 2005, the program paid $31.6 billion to 1.5 million policyholders nationwide. Louisiana's share, thanks to Hurricanes Katrina and Rita, was $14.9 billion. Next came Florida, at $3.3 billion; Texas, at $2.8 billion; and Mississippi, at $2.7 billion. Pennsylvania and New Jersey's losses were far less, though each topped $600 million.

Previously, the premiums collected have kept the program self-sustaining. But according to Robert Hunter, former head of the federal flood insurance program, the 2005 hurricane season will throw the program into deficit. According to Hunter, Hurricane Katrina is the first disaster in which flood claims exceed those for wind, which are typically paid by private insurers or state-run risk pools.

Hunter also sees an interesting question developing among claims adjusters—Who pays for what damage? The federal program uses private insurers and their adjusters to evaluate claims, and "company X may say, 'I can't tell if this is flood or wind, so it looks like flood because they pay it and we don't,'" Hunter said.[iv]

endnotes

---

[i] *Source*: "Risky Business," *Fortune*, April 4, 2005.

[ii] *Source*: Joel Achenbach, "Time to Hit the Panic Button?" *National Geographic,* September 2003.

[iii] *Sources:* Annie Lowrey, "Economic Devastation?" *Slate*, March 11, 2011; Eric Talmadge and Mari Yamaguchi, "Japan Death Toll Rises to 18,000, Rebuilding May Cost $235 Billion," Associated Press, March 20, 2011; Junko Fujita and James Topham, "Japan Business Lobby Gives OK to Scrap Corporate Tax Cut," *Reuters*, March 28, 2011.

[iv] *Sources:* Albert B. Crenshaw, "Under-Bought' Flood Insurance Proves Its Value," *The Washington Post,* September 4, 2005; Jeff Gelles, "Buying National Flood Insurance," *The Philadelphia Inquirer,* July 3, 2006; Becky Yerak, "Plaintiffs Lose on Katrina: Policy Excludes Water Damage, Judge Rules," *Chicago Tribune*, August 16, 2006.

Managing Personal Finances

bonus chapter **D**

critical thinking exercises

what's new in this edition

additions to the 10th edition:

- Getting to Know Nathan Myhrvold and Other Millionaires
- Name That Company: CardRatings.com and CreditCards.com
- Discussion of Credit Card Act of 2009 added to subsection Learning to Manage Credit
- Video case

revisions to the 10th edition:

- Text was revised to eliminate redundancy and tighten discussions.
- Statistical data and examples throughout the chapter were updated to reflect current information.

deletions from the 9th edition:

- Getting to Know Many Millionaires: How to Be a Millionaire
- Name That Company: eHealthInsurance.com

brief chapter outline and learning goals

bonus chapter D

Managing Personal Finances

Getting To Know NATHAN MYHRVOLD AND OTHER MILLIONAIRES

learning goal 1

Outline the six steps for controlling your assets.

I. THE NEED FOR PERSONAL FINANCIAL PLANNING

A. **Financial Planning Begins with Making Money**

B. **Six Steps to Controlling Your Assets**

learning goal 2

Explain ways to build a financial base, including investing in real estate, saving money, and managing credit.

II. BUILDING YOUR FINANCIAL BASE

A. **Real Estate: Historically, a Relatively Secure Investment**

B. **Tax Deduction and Homeownership**

C. **Where to Put Your Savings**

D. **Learning to Manage Credit**

learning goal 3

Explain how buying the appropriate insurance can protect your financial base.

III. PROTECTING YOUR FINANCIAL BASE: BUYING INSURANCE

A. **Health Insurance**

B. **Homeowner's or Renter's Insurance**

C. **Other Insurance**

learning goal 4

Outline a strategy for retiring with enough money to last a lifetime.

IV. PLANNING YOUR RETIREMENT

A. Social Security

B. Individual Retirement Accounts (IRAs)

C. Simple IRAs

D. 401(k) Plans

E. Keogh Plans

F. Financial Planners

G. Estate Planning

V. SUMMARY

lecture outline

Getting to Know NATHAN MYHRVOLD and OTHER MILLIONAIRES.

Myhrvold earned his money as chief technology officer at Microsoft. Extremely brilliant and with expensive tastes, you might expect him to be the model millionaire. However, the majority of millionaires are entrepreneurs who own one or more small businesses. Self-employed people are about five times more likely to be millionaires as people who earn a pay-check working for others.

One way to save money is to use your credit card wisely. There are organizations that can help you compare credit cards to get the most out of them. What is the name of one of those organizations?

(Students should read the chapter before guessing the companies' names: Credit-Cards.com *or* CardRatings.com)

learning goal 1

Outline the six steps for controlling your assets.

I. THE NEED FOR PERSONAL FINANCIAL PLANNING

A. The secret to success in a capitalist country is to have **CAPITAL**.

1. You have to earn the money, then save, spend, and invest it wisely.

2. However, students are poorly educated about financial matters.

B. **FINANCIAL PLANNING BEGINS WITH MAKING MONEY.**

1. **HAVING A GOOD EDUCATION** is one of the best assets in finding a well-paying job.

2. A typical full-time worker with a **FOUR-YEAR**

lecture notes

PPT D-1
Chapter Title

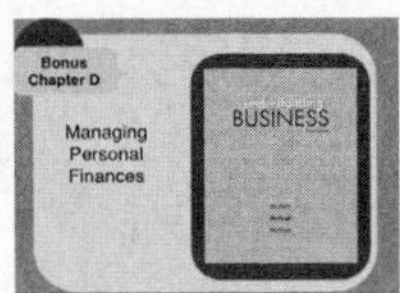

PPT D-2
Learning Goals

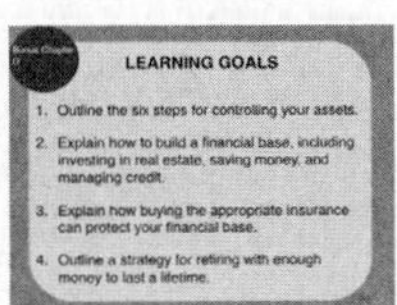

(See complete PowerPoint slide notes on page D.40.)

PPT D-3
Nathan Myhrvold

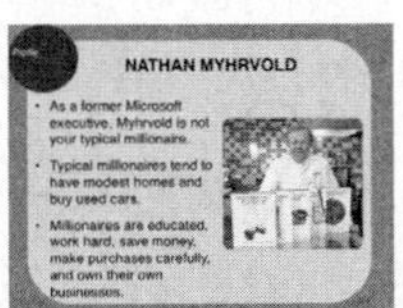

(See complete PowerPoint slide notes on page D.40.)

PPT D-4
Name That Company

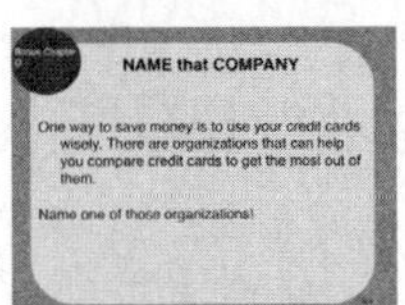

(See complete PowerPoint slide notes on page D.41.)

PPT D-5
Financial Planning Begins with Making Money

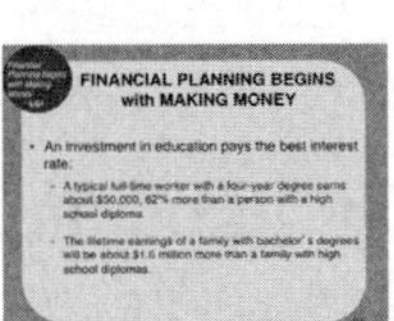

(See complete PowerPoint slide notes on page D.41.)

COLLEGE DEGREE earns about $50,000—**62% MORE** than one with only a high school diploma.

3. The government helps by giving various tax breaks for you to go to college.

C. **SIX STEPS TO CONTROLLING YOUR ASSETS**

1. The key to saving is to spend less than you make.
    a. In order to be financially secure, you have to save.
    b. Less than 10% of the U.S. population has accumulated enough money by retirement age to live comfortably.
    c. Also 36% of U.S. households don't have a retirement account.
2. **STEP 1**: Take an **INVENTORY** of your financial assets.
    a. First, develop a **BALANCE SHEET** for yourself.
        i. A balance sheet starts with the formula:
        Assets = Liabilities + Owners' Equity
        ii. **ASSETS** include anything you own, and should be evaluated based on their **CURRENT VALUE**, not purchase price.
        iii. Subtract your **LIABILITIES** to determine your **NET WORTH.**
    b. An **INCOME STATEMENT** starts with **REVENUE**, and then subtracts **COSTS** and expenses to calculate **NET INCOME**.
3. **STEP 2**: Keep track of all your **EXPENSES.**
    a. If you often run out of cash, write down every

PPT D-6
Six Steps to Control Your Finances

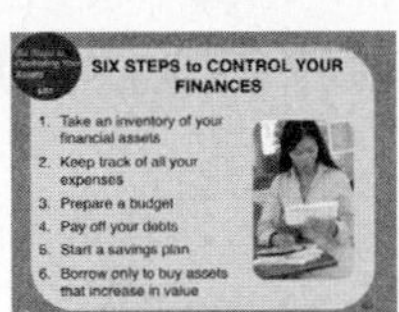

(See complete PowerPoint slide notes on page D.41.)

critical thinking exercise D-1

PREPARING A PERSONAL BALANCE SHEET

This exercise asks students to calculate the assets, liabilities, and owners' equity for a couple. (See complete exercise on page D.60 of this manual.)

penny you spend each day.

b. The only way to trace where the money goes is to keep track of every cent you spend by keeping a **JOURNAL**.

c. Develop **CATEGORIES** for expenditures, based on what is important to you.

d. Cutting back on luxuries can add up over time.

4. **STEP 3**: Prepare a **BUDGET.**

   a. Your personal budget (revenue and expenses) is your financial plan—you will have to make **CHOICES** on how to allocate your resources.

   b. What you spend now reduces what you can save later.

   c. Running a household is similar to running a small business—it takes careful record keeping, budgeting, control, and the need to borrow funds.

5. **STEP 4:** Pay off your **DEBTS.**

   a. Use any extra money to pay off your debts.

   b. Start with the debts that carry the highest interest rates.

6. **STEP 5**: Start a **SAVINGS PLAN.**

   a. Each month save some for large purchases in a separate account.

   b. The best way to save money is to **PAY YOURSELF FIRST**—take money out of your paycheck for savings, and then plan what to do with the rest.

critical thinking exercise D-2
DEVELOPING A SPENDING PLAN

This exercise asks students to develop a monthly budget and judge the impact of an increase in monthly rent. (See complete exercise on page D.62 of this manual.)

PPT D-7
Managing Your Household Budget

(See complete PowerPoint slide notes on page D.42.)

PPT D-8
Possible Cost-Saving Choices

TEXT FIGURE D.1
Possible Cost-Saving Choices
(Text page D-4)

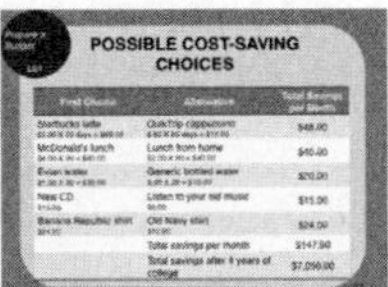

(See complete PowerPoint slide notes on page D.42.)

PPT D-9
How Money Grows

TEXT FIGURE D.2
How Money Grows
(Text page D-5)

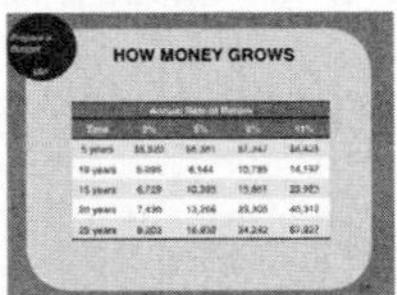

(See complete PowerPoint slide notes on page D.42.)

7. **STEP 6:** Borrow money only to **BUY ASSETS** that have the potential to increase in value.
    a. Don't borrow for ordinary expenses.
    b. Ideally, you should **SAVE SIX MONTHS OF EARNINGS** for contingency purposes in highly liquid accounts.
    c. You should borrow only for very unexpected expenses.
    d. Instead, you can try to produce more income.

learning goal 2

Explain ways to build a financial base, including investing in real estate, saving money, and managing credit.

II. BUILDING YOUR FINANCIAL BASE

A. Accumulating capital takes discipline and careful planning.

1. Savings can help you become an **ENTREPRENEUR**, one of the fastest ways to wealth.
2. A capital-generating strategy may require a **FRUGAL LIFESTYLE.**
3. Married couples need to discuss financial goals.
4. Ideally, the couple should live on one income and save the other.
5. The first investment might be a **LOW-PRICED HOME**.
6. Through the years, homeownership has been a wise investment.

B. **REAL ESTATE: HISTORICALLY, A RELATIVELY SECURE INVESTMENT**

1. The real estate bust that began in 2008 is a

PPT D-10
Easy-ish Budget Cuts

(See complete PowerPoint slide notes on page D.43.)

PPT D-11
Billionaire's Tab

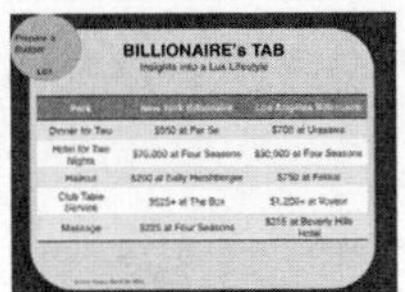

(See complete PowerPoint slide notes on page D.43.)

lecture link D-1
MILLIONAIRE WOMEN NEXT DOOR

Thomas J. Stanley and William D. Danko, the authors of the 1996 book *The Millionaire Next Door*, undertook a three-year study of wealthy women with some interesting findings. (See the complete lecture link on page D.52 in this manual.)

PPT D-12
Building Your Financial Base

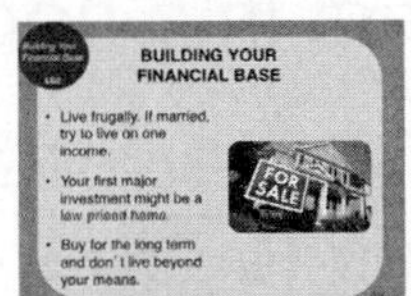

(See complete PowerPoint slide notes on page D.43.)

PPT D-13
Five Rules of Frugality

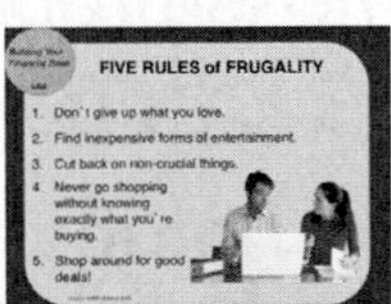

(See complete PowerPoint slide notes on page D.44.)

relatively rare occurrence.

2. **HOME OWNERSHIP**
    a. The one investment that you can live in is a home.
    b. The mortgage payments are also relatively fixed.
    c. Paying for a home is a good way of forcing yourself to save.
    d. Some people have used the strategy to **BUY DUPLEX HOMES.**
    e. By living in one and renting the other, a couple can live very cheaply while their investment in a home appreciates.
    f. The ownership versus rental analysis can be applied to other large purchases.

C. **TAX DEDUCTIONS AND HOMEOWNERSHIP**
    1. Buying a home is probably the largest and **MOST IMPORTANT INVESTMENT** you'll make.
    2. **INTEREST** on home mortgage payments is **TAX-DEDUCTIBLE**, as are real estate taxes.
    3. Almost all of the mortgage payments in the first few years go toward interest, so the early payments are tax-deductible.
    4. The key to getting the optimum return on a home is **LOCATION, LOCATION, LOCATION.**
    5. Buying a small house in a great location is usually better than buying a large house in a not-so-great setting.

PPT D-14
Financial Benefits of Buying a Home

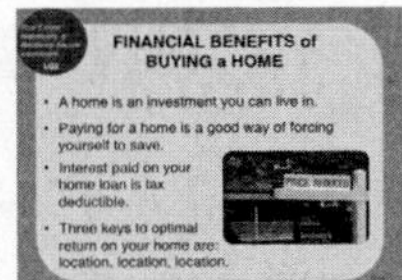

(See complete PowerPoint slide notes on page D.44.)

PPT D-15
How Much House Can You Afford?

TEXT FIGURE D.3
How Much House Can You Afford?
(Text page D-7)

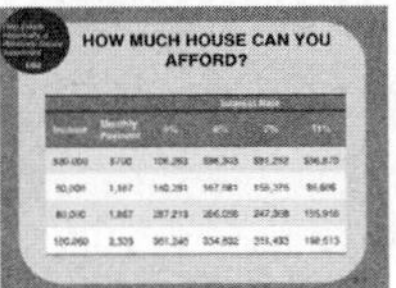

(See complete PowerPoint slide notes on page D.44.)

lecture link D-2
THE RENT-VERSUS-BUY DECISION

Although buying is generally better than renting, there are situations in which it is better to rent. (See the complete lecture link on page D.53 in this manual.)

critical thinking exercise D-4
CHOOSING THE RIGHT MORTGAGE LOAN

How much would the monthly payment be to purchase an $85,000 house? It depends on the interest rate, type of loan, and down payment. (See complete exercise on page D.66 of this manual.)

D. **WHERE TO PUT YOUR SAVINGS**

1. One of the **WORST PLACES** to keep your long-term investments is in a bank or savings and loan, even online banks.
2. However, it is important to have about **SIX MONTHS OF SAVINGS** in the bank for emergencies.
3. One of the **BEST PLACES** to invest over time has been the **STOCK MARKET.**
4. The stock market will rise and fall, but over time it has been a good investment.
5. Times of financial crisis may be the time to invest.
   a. The greater the **RISK**, the greater the **RETURN**.
   b. Low stock prices may be an opportunity to invest in the stock market.
   c. The average investor buys when the market is high and sells when prices are low.
   d. ***CONTRARIAN APPROACH*** is buying stock when everyone else is selling or vice versa.
6. Bonds have traditionally lagged behind stock as a long-term investment.

E. **LEARNING TO MANAGE CREDIT**

1. Even if they are rarely used, having credit cards is important.
   a. Some merchants require credit cards as a form of **IDENTIFICATION**.

PPT D-16
Saving and Managing Credit

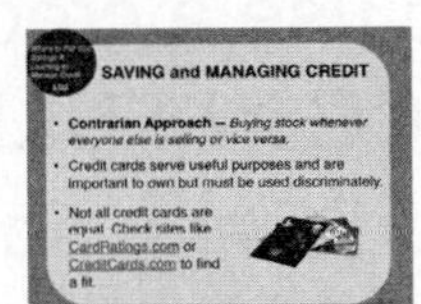

(See complete PowerPoint slide notes on page D.45.)

   b. Credit cards help **KEEP TRACK OF PURCHASES.**
   c. It is easier to write one check at the end of the month than to carry cash.
   d. Credit cards are **SAFER** than cash—you can cancel a stolen credit card.

2. Credit is expensive.
   a. **50% of college students** have four or more cards and only **17%** regularly pay off their balance.
   b. The financial charges on **CREDIT CARDS** are 12 to 26% annually.
   c. If you do use a credit card, **PAY THE BALANCE IN FULL** each month during the period when no interest is charged.

3. Choose a card that pays you cash back or gives you purchase credits or frequent flier miles.
   a. The value of these givebacks can be from 1 to 5%.
   b. Some cards charge an annual fee whereas others do not.

4. The **DANGERS OF CREDIT CARDS** are:
   a. It is easy to buy goods and services you normally would not buy.
   b. You can pile up more than you can repay.
   c. If you have trouble sticking to a budget, it may be better **NOT TO HAVE A CREDIT CARD AT ALL.**

lecture link D-3
KNOW YOUR CREDIT SCORE

Your credit score determines the interest rate you are charged for credit. This lecture link gives some practical tips for improving our score. (See the complete lecture link on page D.54 in this manual.)

PPT D-17
Credit Cards and Debt

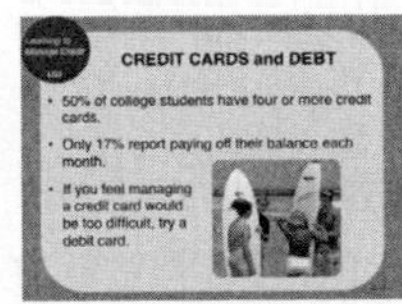

(See complete PowerPoint slide notes on page D.45.)

PPT D-18
Credit Card Act of 2009

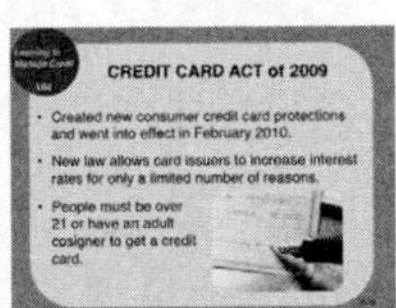

(See complete PowerPoint slide notes on page D.45.)

lecture link D-4
AMERICA'S GROWING CREDIT CARD AVERSION

As new credit card regulations come into effect, more and more Americans are still turning away from plastic, (See the complete lecture link on page D.55 of this manual.)

PPT D-19
America's Credit Card Debt

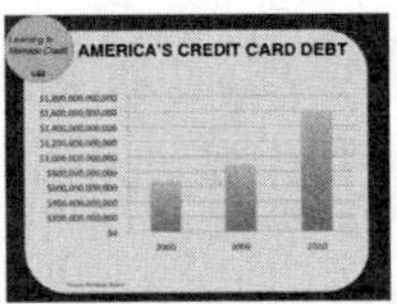

(See complete PowerPoint slide notes on page D.46.)

PPT D-20
Clean Credit

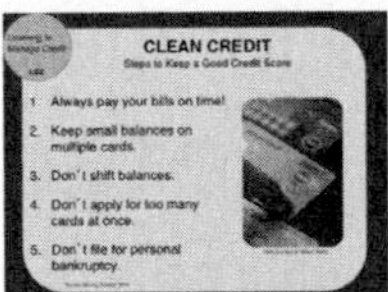

(See complete PowerPoint slide notes on page D.46.)

   d. Credit cards can be convenient, but they can also be a **FINANCIAL DISASTER** if you have little financial restraint.
5. For some people it may be better to have a debit card.
6. **DEBIT CARDS** are like credit cards, but they won't let you spend more than a certain amount.
7. **THE CREDIT CARD ACT OF 2009** went into effect in 2010 and protects consumers.
   a. Card issuers can raise rates only for a limited number of reasons.
   b. You must be 21 or have an adult cosign to get a credit card.

learning goal 3

Explain how buying the appropriate insurance can protect your financial base.

III. PROTECTING YOUR FINANCIAL BASE: BUYING INSURANCE

A. BUYING LIFE INSURANCE

1. The death of one spouse can mean a sudden drop in income for the survivor.
2. To **PROVIDE PROTECTION** from the loss of a spouse or business partner, you should buy life insurance.
3. ***TERM INSURANCE*** is pure insurance protection for a given number of years.
   a. Term insurance costs less the younger you buy it.

PPT D-21
What's Your Score?

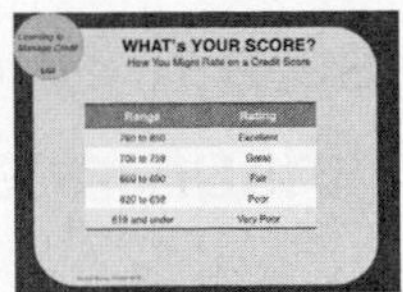

(See complete PowerPoint slide notes on page D.46.)

critical thinking exercise D-3

FINDING THE BEST CAR LOAN

This exercise asks students to use online financial sites to find the latest interest rates for car loans and calculate the monthly payment. (See complete exercise on page D.64 of this manual.)

lecture link D-5

DISCREDIT REPORT

Maybe you've never seen your credit report, but dozens of strangers have. (See complete lecture link on page D.55 of this manual.)

progress assessment

(Text page D-9)

PROGRESS ASSESSMENT

- What are the six steps you can take to control your finances?
- What steps should a person follow to build capital?
- Why is real estate a good investment?

PPT D-22
Progress Assessment

(See complete PowerPoint slide notes on page D.47.)

PPT D-23
Insuring Your Life

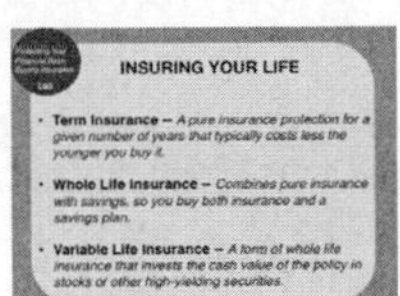

(See complete PowerPoint slide notes on page D.47.)

TEXT FIGURE D.4
Why Buy Term Insurance?
(Text page D-10)

This text figure shows the reasons for purchasing term insurance.

b. You can use a financial formula to figure out how much insurance you need at different points in your life.

c. **MULTIYEAR LEVEL-PREMIUM INSURANCE** guarantees that you'll pay the same premium for the life of the policy.

4. ***WHOLE LIFE INSURANCE*** combines pure insurance and savings.

   a. It places part of the premium in savings and the other part toward pure insurance.

   b. This type may be right for people who have trouble saving.

   c. A **UNIVERSAL LIFE POLICY** lets you choose how to divide the premium between insurance and investment.

5. ***VARIABLE LIFE INSURANCE*** is whole life insurance that invests the cash value of the policy in stocks or higher-yielding securities; it is vulnerable to stock market dips.

6. An ***ANNUITY*** is a contract to make regular payments to a person for life or for a fixed period.

   a. With an annuity you are guaranteed to have an income until you die.

   b. **FIXED ANNUITIES** are investments that pay the policyholder a specified interest rate.

   c. **VARIABLE ANNUITIES** provide investment choices identical to mutual funds; they are becoming more popular.

PPT D-24
Purchasing Annuities

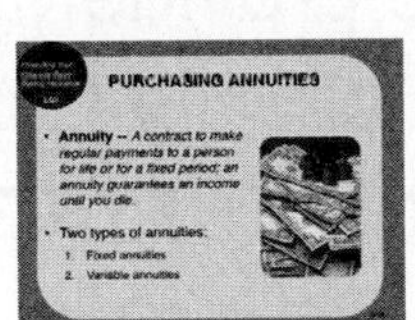

(See complete PowerPoint slide notes on page D.47)

lecture link D-6
SOCIAL SECURITY AND YOUR RETIREMENT

Back in the 1980s there were five active workers paying Social Security taxes for each retiree. Today it's 3.2 workers and dropping. (See the complete lecture link on page D.58 of this manual.)

d. Variable annuities are riskier; be careful choosing the insurer.

7. Before buying any insurance, it is wise to consult an independent financial adviser.

B. **HEALTH INSURANCE**

1. Individuals need to consider protecting themselves from losses due to health problems.

   a. Many have health insurance coverage through their employer.

   b. If not, you can buy insurance from a health insurance provider, a health maintenance organization (HMO), or a preferred provider organization (PPO).

   c. Health insurance coverage on a national level may change in the next few years.

2. You should also have **DISABILITY INSURANCE** because the chances of becoming disabled at an early age are higher than your chances of dying from an accident.

3. ***DISABILITY INSURANCE*** is insurance that pays part of the cost of a long-term sickness or an accident.

C. **HOMEOWNER'S OR RENTER'S INSURANCE**

1. **APARTMENT INSURANCE** or **HOMEOWNER'S INSURANCE** covers loss of your possessions.

2. It is best to get guaranteed **REPLACEMENT INSURANCE**, which means the insurance company will give you whatever it costs to buy things new.

PPT D-25
Other Insurance Protection

(See complete PowerPoint slide notes on page D.48.)

PPT D-26
Who Pays for Health Care?

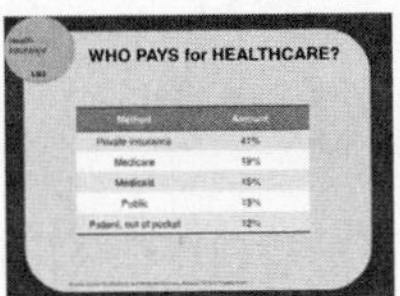

(See complete PowerPoint slide notes on page D.48.)

PPT D-27
Where Health Care Money Goes

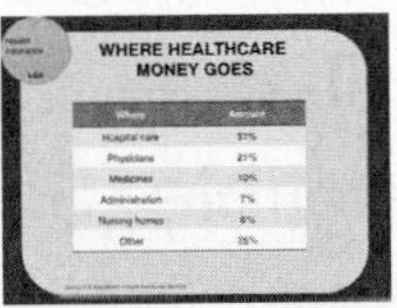

(See complete PowerPoint slide notes on page D.48.)

PPT D-28
What to Know about Health
Savings Accounts

(See complete PowerPoint slide notes on page D.49.)

3. Another option is to buy insurance that covers only the **DEPRECIATED COST** of the items.
4. You need to buy a **RIDER** to your insurance policy to cover expensive items such as jewelry or silver.

D. **OTHER INSURANCE**

1. Most states require that drivers have automobile insurance.
2. Be sure to insure against losses from uninsured motorists.
3. A large deductible ($500 or so) will keep the premiums lower.
4. An ***UMBRELLA POLICY*** is a broadly based insurance policy that saves you money because you buy all your insurance from one company.

learning goal 4

Outline a strategy for retiring with enough money to last a lifetime.

IV. PLANNING YOUR RETIREMENT

A. Successful financial planning requires long-range planning, including retirement.

B. **SOCIAL SECURITY**

1. ***SOCIAL SECURITY*** is the term used to describe the Old-Age, Survivors, and Disability Insurance program established by the Social Security Act of 1935.
2. By the time students retire, there will be huge changes in the Social Security system.
3. The number of people **RETIRING AND LIVING LONGER** is increasing while the number of workers paying into the fund is declining.

PPT D-29
Social Security

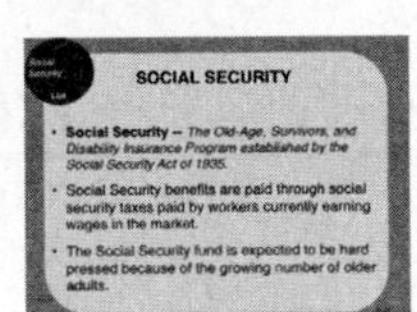

(See complete PowerPoint slide notes on page D.49.)

4. As a result, expect cuts in benefits, later retirement age, or higher Social Security taxes.
5. Don't count on Social Security to provide you with all your funds for retirement—**SAVE FUNDS NOW.**

C. **INDIVIDUAL RETIREMENT ACCOUNTS (IRAs)**

1. An ***INDIVIDUAL RETIREMENT ACCOUNT (IRA)*** is a tax-deferred investment plan that enables you (and your spouse, if you are married) to save part of your income for retirement.
   a. A **TRADITIONAL IRA** allows people who qualify to deduct from their reported income the money they put into an account.
   b. ***TAX-DEFERRED CONTRIBUTIONS*** are retirement account deposits for which you pay no current taxes, but the earnings gained are taxed as regular income when they are withdrawn at retirement.
   c. A traditional IRA is a good deal for an investor because the **INVESTED MONEY IS NOT TAXED.**
2. The earlier you start saving the better, because your money has the chance to double and double again.
   a. Saving $5,000 in an IRA at 10% interest will yield $1.5 million in 35 years.
   b. The actual rate of return depends on the type of investments you choose and can vary widely over time.

PPT D-30
Individual Retirement Accounts

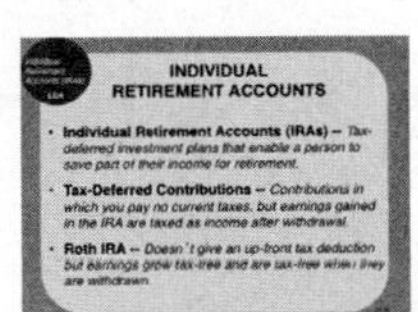

(See complete PowerPoint slide notes on page D.49.)

3. The earlier you start, the faster you will accumulate retirement funds.
4. A ***ROTH IRA*** is an IRA where you don't get up-front deductions on your taxes as you would with a traditional IRA, but the earnings grow tax-free and are also tax-free when they are withdrawn.
    a. Traditional IRAs offer tax savings **WHEN THEY ARE DEPOSITED.**
    b. Roth IRAs offer tax savings **WHEN THEY ARE WITHDRAWN.**
5. Both types of IRAs have advantages and disadvantages.
    a. In general, a Roth IRA is best for younger workers.
6. You cannot take the money out of an IRA until you are **59½ YEARS OLD** without paying a 10% penalty and paying taxes on the income.
    a. You cannot tap the fund for impulse purchases.
    b. However, you can now take out some funds for an **EDUCATION** or a **FIRST HOUSE.**
7. A wide range of investment choices are available.
    a. Banks, savings and loan, credit unions, and insurance companies all have IRA savings plans.
    b. If you can accept more risk, put your IRA funds into stocks, bonds, mutual funds, or precious metals.

lecture notes

c. Mutual funds have multiple options and allow you to switch from fund to fund.

8. Opening an IRA account may be one of the wisest investments you make.

D. **SIMPLE IRAs**

1. Companies with 100 or fewer employees can provide their workers with a **SIMPLE IRA.**

2. Employees can contribute a large part of their income annually, and the company matches the contribution.

E. **401(k) PLANS**

1. A ***401(K) PLAN*** is a saving plan that allows you to deposit pretax dollars and whose earnings compound tax free until withdrawal, when the money is taxed at ordinary income tax rates.

   a. 401(k) plans now account for half of America's private pension savings.

   b. Only 70% of eligible employees make any contribution—a huge mistake.

2. 401(k) plans have three **BENEFITS:**

   a. The money you put in **REDUCES YOUR PRESENT TAXABLE INCOME.**

   b. **TAX IS DEFERRED** on the earnings.

   c. Employers often **MATCH** part of your deposit.

3. About 61% of employers match your contribution—often 50 cents on a dollar.

4. You can usually select **HOW THE MONEY IS INVESTED** (stocks, bonds, and real estate).

PPT D-31
401(k) Plans

(See complete PowerPoint slide notes on page D.50.)

PPT D-32
Benefits of 401(k) Plans

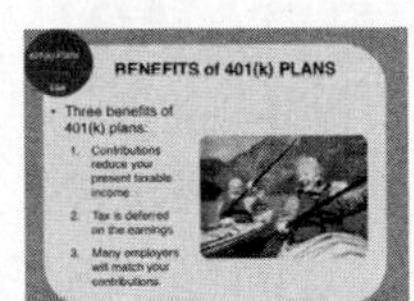

(See complete PowerPoint slide notes on page D.50.)

   a. Don't invest all your money in the company where you work.
   b. As with any investment, it is best to **DIVERSIFY** your 401(k) funds.
5. There is a simple 401(k) plan for those firms with 100 or fewer employees.

F. **KEOGH PLANS**

1. **KEOGH PLANS** are retirement plans for small-business people who do not have the benefit of a corporate retirement system.
2. The maximum amount you can invest in Keogh plans, $40,000 per year, is higher than for an IRA.
3. Like IRAs, Keogh funds are **NOT TAXED UNTIL WITHDRAWN**, nor are the returns the funds earn.
4. As with IRAs, there is a 10% penalty for early withdrawal.

G. **FINANCIAL PLANNERS** are people who assist in developing a comprehensive program that covers investments, taxes, insurance, and other financial matters.

1. Many people claim to be financial planners; find one who is a **CERTIFIED FINANCIAL PLANNER (CFP).**
2. **ONE-STOP FINANCIAL CENTERS**, or financial supermarkets, provide a variety of financial services in one place.
3. Most financial planners begin with **LIFE**

PPT D-33
Keogh Plans

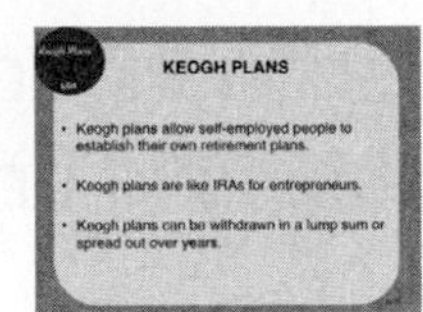

(See complete PowerPoint slide notes on page D.50.)

lecture link D-7

THE TROUBLE WITH SUING YOUR BROKER

The recent market crash left investors feeling misled by their most trusted financial advisors. Many want to seek legal action, but that might not be a possibility. (See the complete lecture link on page D.59 in this manual.)

INSURANCE, usually term insurance, and add health insurance plans.

4. Financial planning covers all aspects of investing, all the way to retirement and death.

H. **ESTATE PLANNING**

1. The first step is to **SELECT A GUARDIAN** for your minor children, someone with a genuine concern for your children.
   a. You should leave sufficient resources to raise your children, often through life insurance.
   b. Choose a contingent guardian in case the first choice is unable to perform the functions.
2. The second step is to **PREPARE A WILL.**
   a. A ***WILL*** is a document that names the guardian for your children, states how you want your assets distributed, and names the executor for your estate.
   b. The ***EXECUTOR*** is a person who assembles and values your estate, files income and other taxes, and distributes assets.
3. A third step is **TO PREPARE A DURABLE POWER OF ATTORNEY.**
   a. This document gives an individual you name the power to take over your finances if you become incapacitated.
   b. **A DURABLE POWER OF ATTORNEY FOR HEALTH CARE** delegates power to make health decisions for you.

PPT D-34
Planning for Those Who Will Inherit

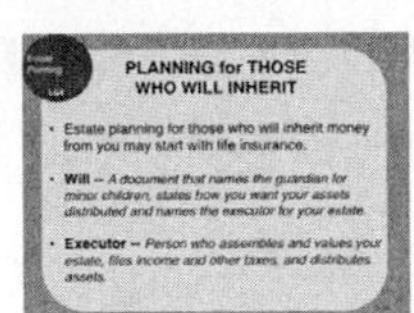

(See complete PowerPoint slide notes on page D.51.)

4. A financial planner can help you do the planning needed to preserve and protect your investments and your children and spouse.

V. SUMMARY

progress assessment
(Text page D-16)

PPT D-35
Progress Assessment

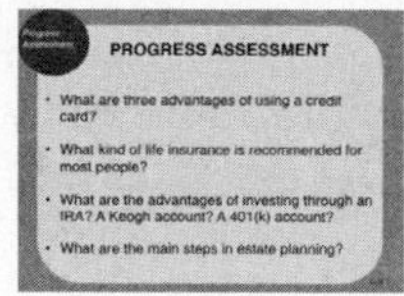

(See complete PowerPoint slide notes on page D.51.)

PowerPoint slide notes

PPT D-1
Chapter Title

PPT D-2
Learning Goals

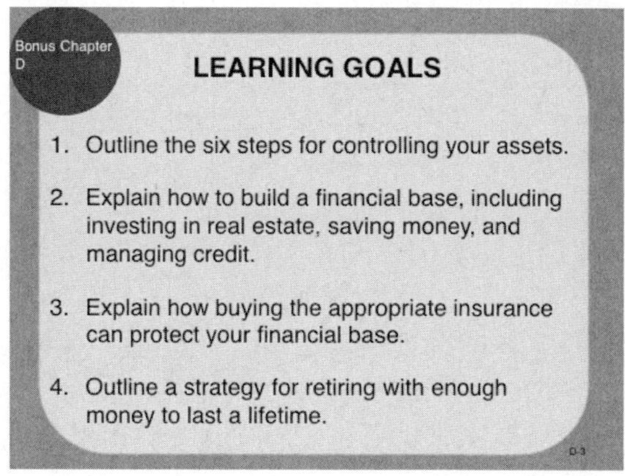

PPT D-3
Nathan Myhrvold

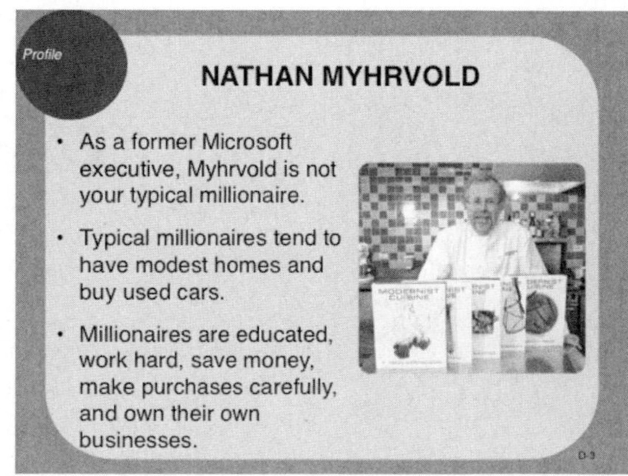

PPT D-4
Name That Company

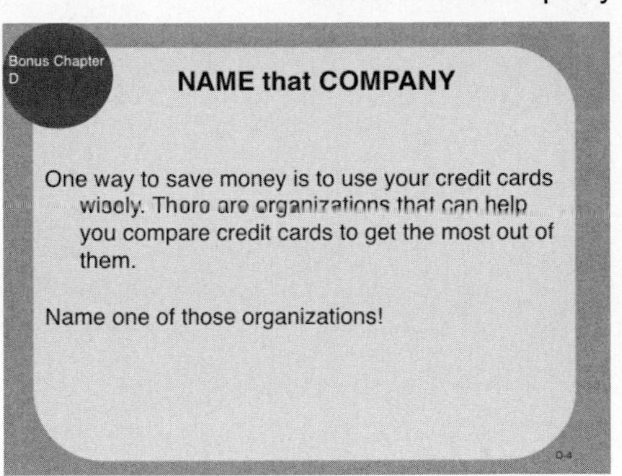

Companies: CardRatings.com or CreditCards.com

PPT D-5
Financial Planning Begins with Making Money

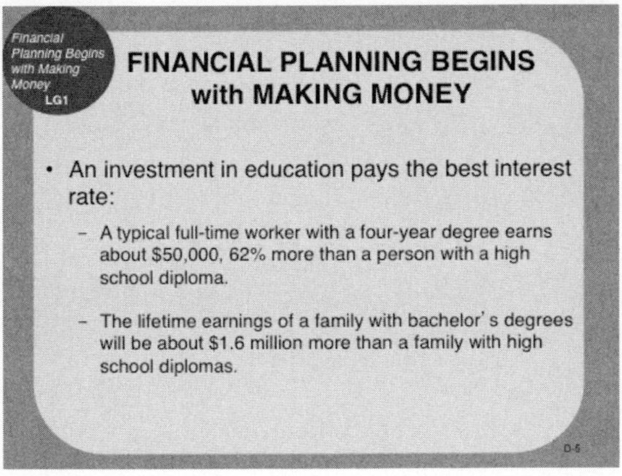

Investing in yourself through education is your best long-term investment.

PPT D-6
Six Steps to Control Your Finances

PPT D-7
Managing Your Household Budget

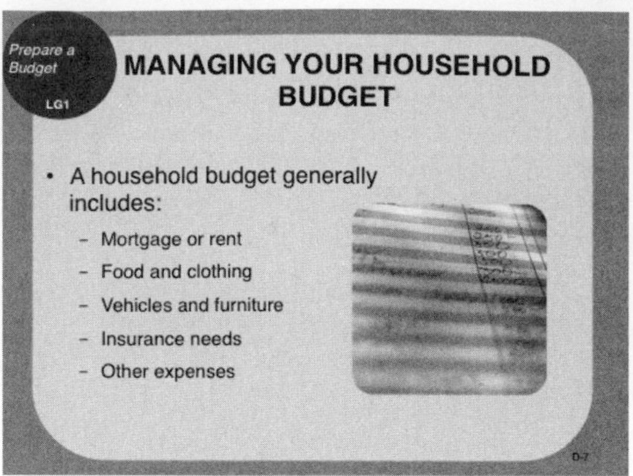

PPT D-8
Possible Cost-Saving Choices

Living frugally is not about doing without but rather making wise choices.

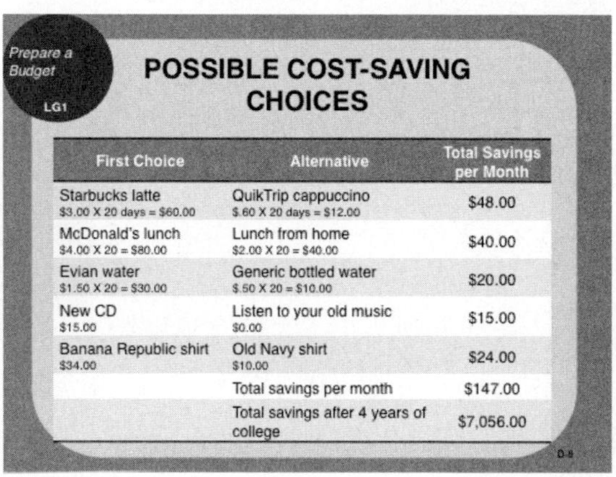

First Choice	Alternative	Total Savings per Month
Starbucks latte $3.00 X 20 days = $60.00	QuikTrip cappuccino $.60 X 20 days = $12.00	$48.00
McDonald's lunch $4.00 X 20 = $80.00	Lunch from home $2.00 X 20 = $40.00	$40.00
Evian water $1.50 X 20 = $30.00	Generic bottled water $.50 X 20 = $10.00	$20.00
New CD $15.00	Listen to your old music $0.00	$15.00
Banana Republic shirt $34.00	Old Navy shirt $10.00	$24.00
	Total savings per month	$147.00
	Total savings after 4 years of college	$7,056.00

PPT D-9
How Money Grows

The time value of money and compound interest are the saver's best friend.

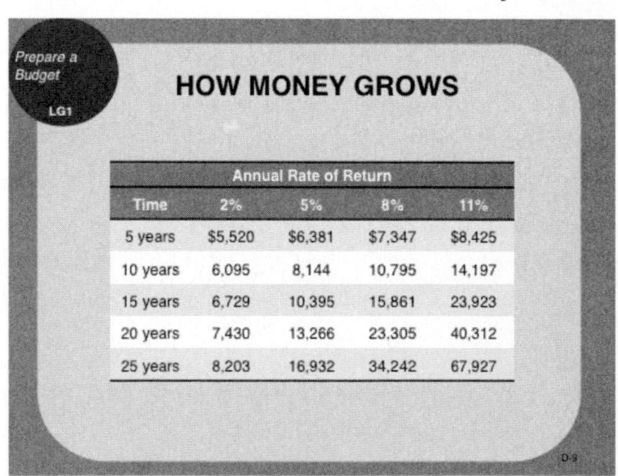

	Annual Rate of Return			
Time	2%	5%	8%	11%
5 years	$5,520	$6,381	$7,347	$8,425
10 years	6,095	8,144	10,795	14,197
15 years	6,729	10,395	15,861	23,923
20 years	7,430	13,266	23,305	40,312
25 years	8,203	16,932	34,242	67,927

PPT D-10
Easy-ish Budget Cuts

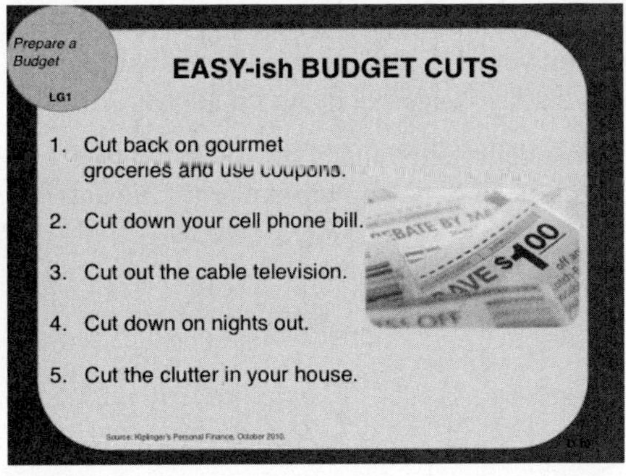

1. This slide shows the student how to trim the fat off their monthly budget.
2. Cutting cable! Shock! Horror! Many shows are available through free sites like Hulu.com; a lot of people are going cable-less.
3. Encourage students to visit free budgeting sites (like Mint.com) so they can track their spending. This might surprise them.

PPT D-11
Billionaire's Tab

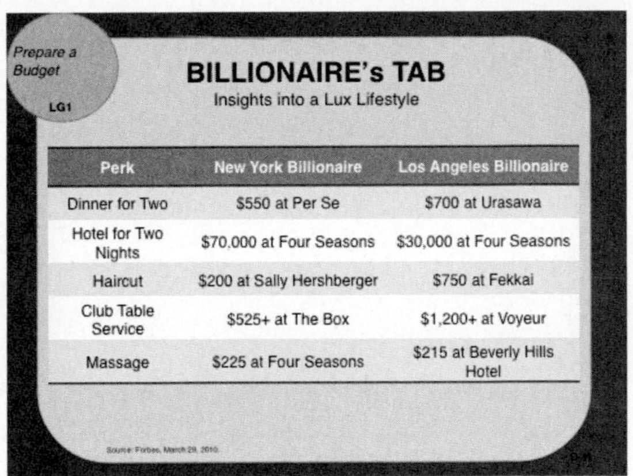

1. And you thought Fekkai's shampoo was expensive! This slide shows students what two billionaires in two American cities pay for services.
2. Ask the students, What do these services give the person above what others can afford? Is it really worth it to pay this much?

PPT D-12
Building Your Financial Base

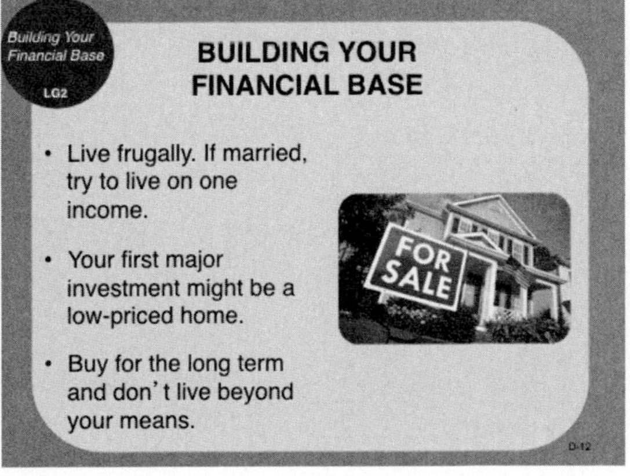

PPT D-13
Five Rules of Frugality

1. This slide shows five steps to saving money.
2. These are easy steps. Many think you have to give up all fun if you want to live frugally. This slide shows that you just need to spend time thinking before you buy instead of being impulsive.
3. Ask the students, How many of you attend free concerts instead of paying top-dollar for big acts?

PPT D-14
Financial Benefits of Buying a Home

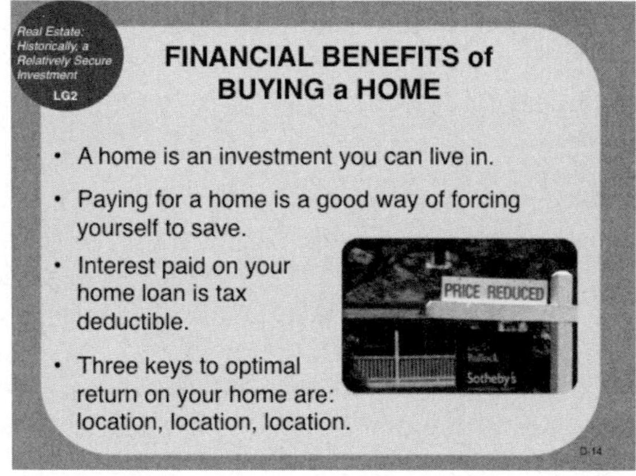

Although the housing crisis has dampened home prices, historically real estate has been a sound investment.

PPT D-15
How Much House Can You Afford?

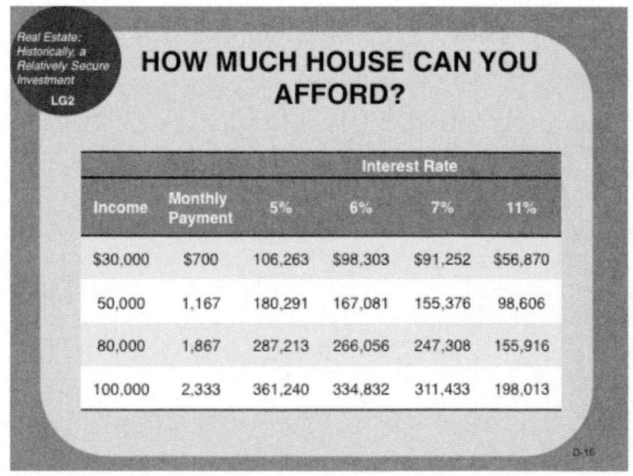

		Interest Rate			
Income	Monthly Payment	5%	6%	7%	11%
$30,000	$700	106,263	$98,303	$91,252	$56,870
50,000	1,167	180,291	167,081	155,376	98,606
80,000	1,867	287,213	266,056	247,308	155,916
100,000	2,333	361,240	334,832	311,433	198,013

PPT D-16
Saving and Managing Credit

Where to Put Your Savings & Learning to Manage Credit
LG2

SAVING and MANAGING CREDIT

- **Contrarian Approach** -- *Buying stock whenever everyone else is selling or vice versa.*
- Credit cards serve useful purposes and are important to own but must be used discriminately.
- Not all credit cards are equal. Check sites like CardRatings.com or CreditCards.com to find a fit.

D-16

Warren Buffet is considered a contrarian investor.

PPT D-17
Credit Cards and Debt

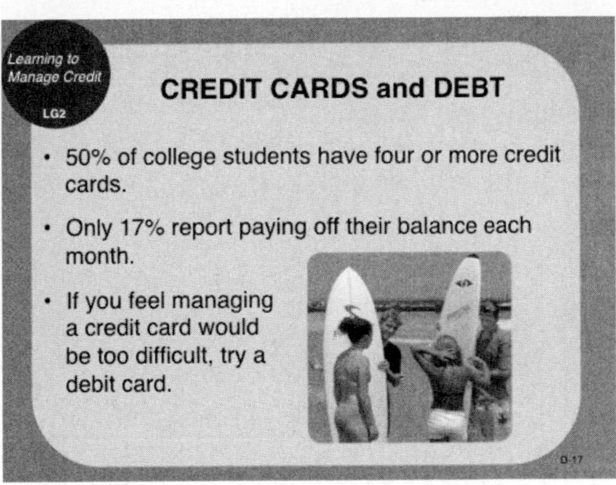

PPT D-18
Credit Card Act of 2009

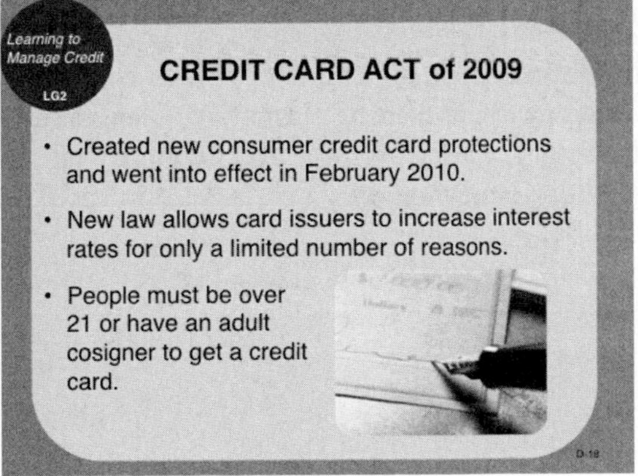

PPT D-19
America's Credit Card Debt

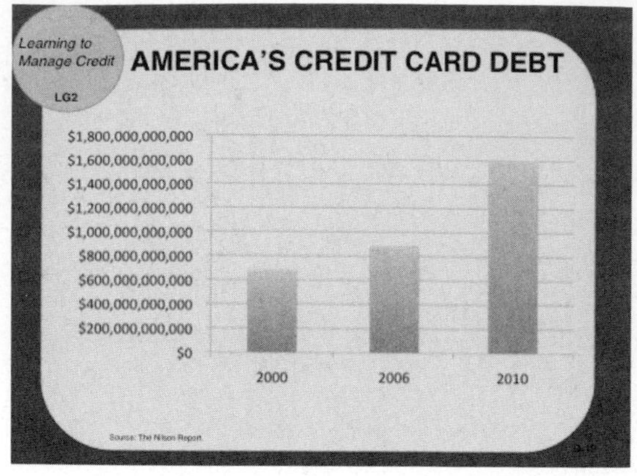

1. This slide illustrates the incredible jump in U.S. consumers' credit card debt since 2000.
2. Today many employers are using credit checks as a method of screening potential employees.
3. One way to protect your credit score is to use credit cards wisely.

PPT D-20
Clean Credit

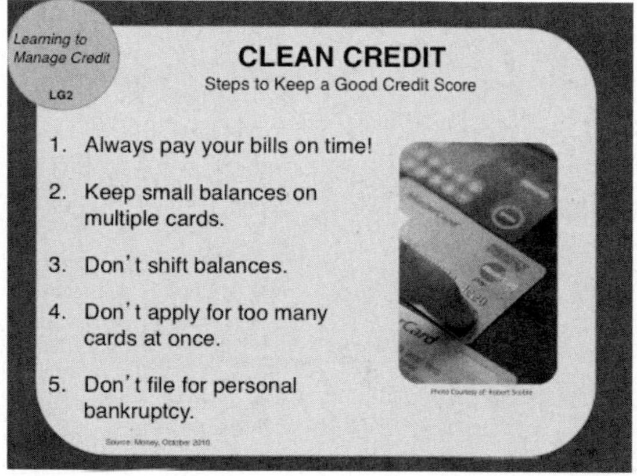

1. This slide shows the students how to ensure that they have a good credit score.
2. Students don't often understand the drawbacks of just paying the minimum amount due. Focus on paying bills in full and on time.

PPT D-21
What's Your Score?

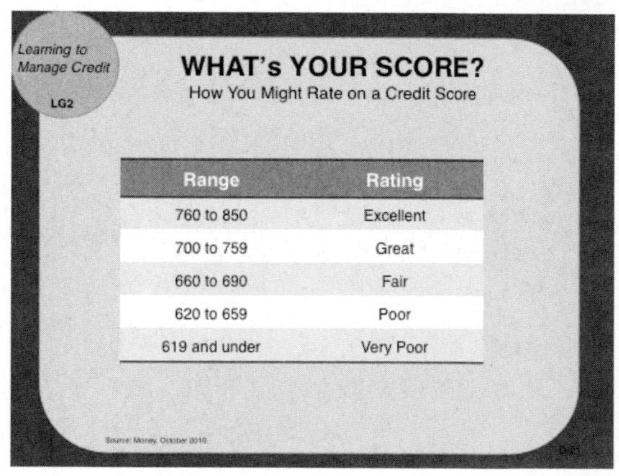

1. This slide shows the students what is a good credit score.
2. Scores range from 300 to 850.
3. Ratings also depend on a number of factors including credit payment history, current debt, length of credit history, credit type mix, and frequency of application for new credit.

PPT D-22
Progress Assessment

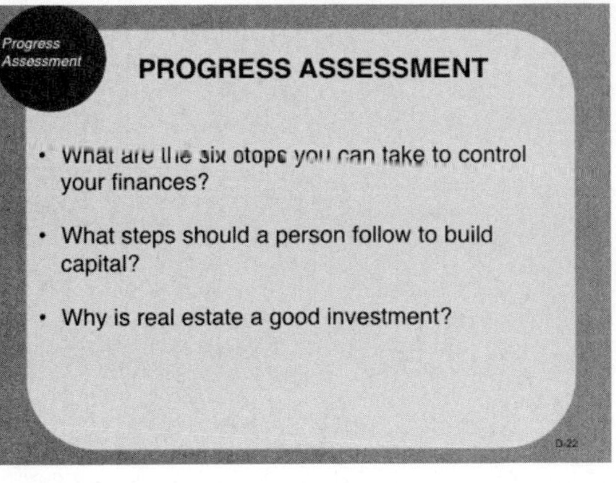

1. The six steps you can take to control your finances are (1) take an inventory of your financial assets, (2) keep track of all your expenses, (3) prepare a budget, (4) pay off your debts, (5) start a savings plan, and (6) borrow only to buy assets that increase in value or generate income.
2. The steps a person should follow to build capital are find a job, create a budget, and live frugally. Warren Buffet became one of the world's richest people but still lives in the house he purchased in the 1950s! Invest the money you save to generate more capital.
3. Historically real estate has been a sound investment. It is the only investment you can live in. Also, the payments are fixed with the exception of taxes and utilities. As your income increases, the house payments get easier to make, while rent tends to increase overtime.

PPT D-23
Insuring Your Life

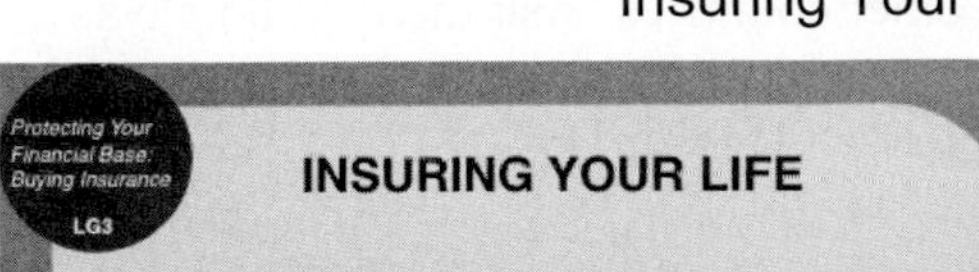

Nearly one-third of U.S. households are without life insurance coverage. Due to the cost difference, many recommend the purchase of term insurance rather than whole life.

PPT D-24
Purchasing Annuities

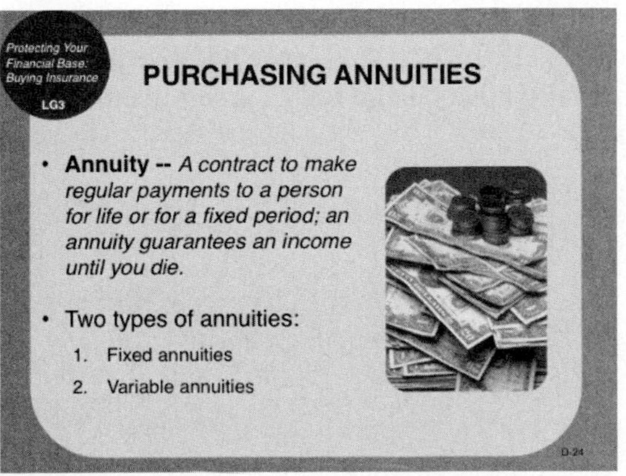

1. Fixed annuities are investments that pay the policyholder a specified interest rate.
2. Variable annuities provide investment choice identical to mutual funds.

PPT D-25
Other Insurance Protection

Health & Other Insurance
LG3

OTHER INSURANCE PROTECTION

- **Disability Insurance --** *Insurance that pays part of the cost of a long-term sickness or an accident.*
- Homeowner' s or renter' s insurance covers the cost of things you own if they are destroyed.
- **Umbrella Policy --** *Combining all your insurance (life, health, homeowner' s, auto) from one company is less costly.*

D-25

Disability insurance is an important coverage, since the likelihood of a young individual sustaining a disability is higher than the likelihood of dying.

PPT D-26
Who Pays for Health Care?

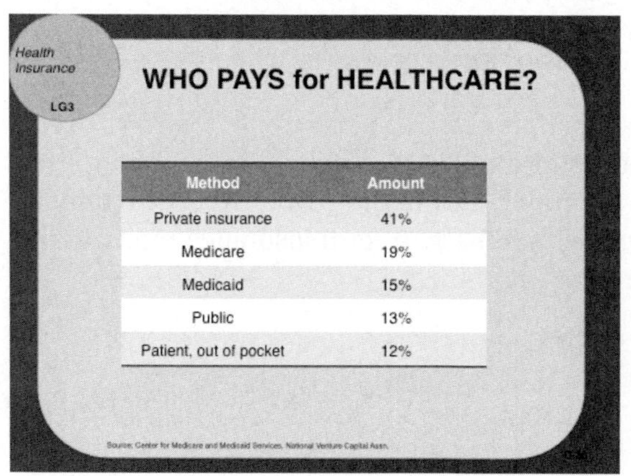

Method	Amount
Private insurance	41%
Medicare	19%
Medicaid	15%
Public	13%
Patient, out of pocket	12%

1. This slide shows who pays for health care.
2. Health care debates have been going on for many years. Ask the students, Who should pay for health care?
3. Give students time to research and compare health care expenses in the United States to those in other countries. Ask them, Who pays for health care in other countries?

PPT D-27
Where Health Care Money Goes

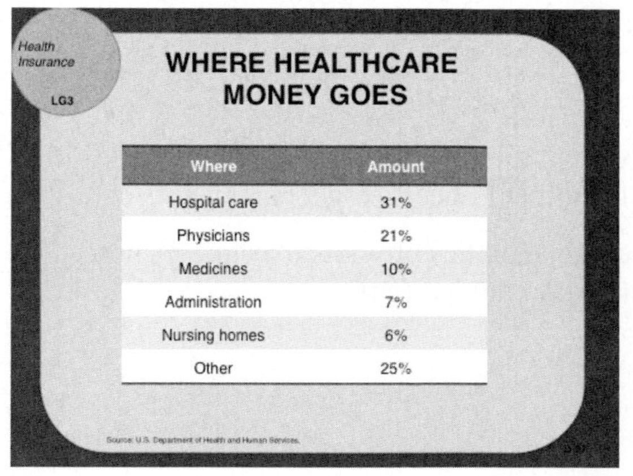

Where	Amount
Hospital care	31%
Physicians	21%
Medicines	10%
Administration	7%
Nursing homes	6%
Other	25%

1. This slide illustrates the percentage of money that goes to different aspects of health care.
2. Before showing the slide you could give the students these categories in a random order and ask them to rank which ones they think are the highest percentage based on money spent for health care.
3. Note to students that hospital care is the highest percentage, which makes sense because people are usually hospitalized only for serious medical issues.

PPT D-28
What to Know about Health Savings Accounts

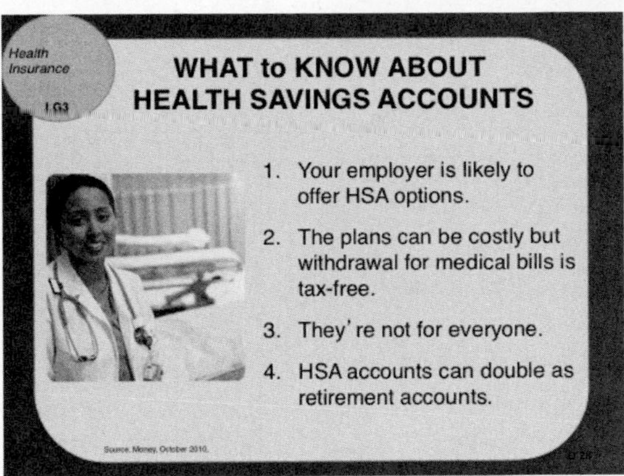

1. Health savings accounts (HSAs) are not for everyone. Some people choose to save money by choosing a high-deductible plan.
2. Those plans might work for young, healthy people. Consulting a financial planner should be the first step.
3. If you have cash to pay medical bills, keep your money in the HSA. At 65, you can withdraw the money penalty-free and use it for anything.

PPT D-29
Social Security

Social Security
LG4

SOCIAL SECURITY

- **Social Security --** *The Old-Age, Survivors, and Disability Insurance Program established by the Social Security Act of 1935.*
- Social Security benefits are paid through social security taxes paid by workers currently earning wages in the market.
- The Social Security fund is expected to be hard pressed because of the growing number of older adults.

D-29

It is important that students understand they cannot rely on Social Security alone as their sole retirement option.

PPT D-30
Individual Retirement Accounts

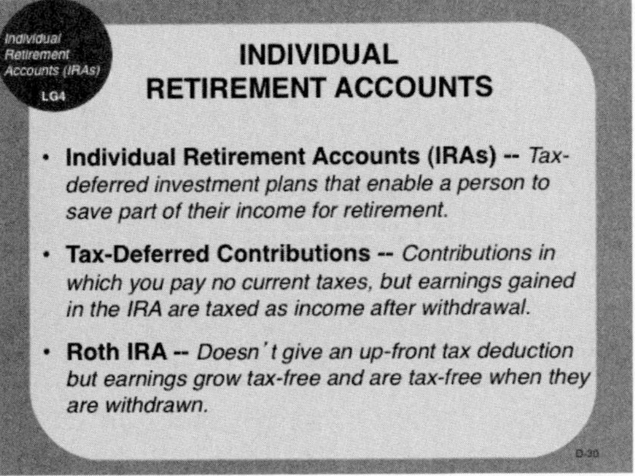

PPT D-31
401(k) Plans

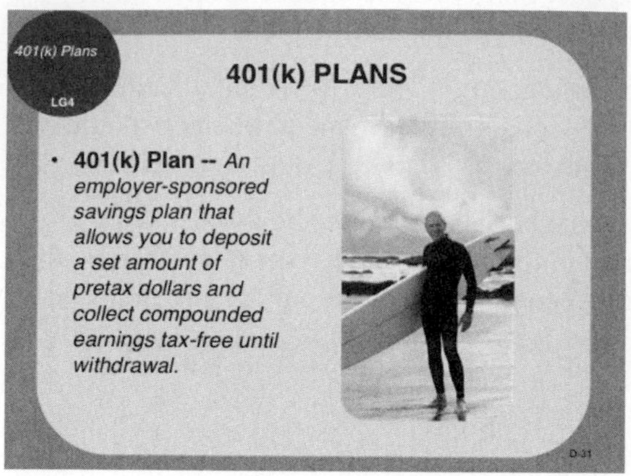

PPT D-32
Benefits of 401(k) Plans

If an employer matches your contribution, it is like free money. About 61% of companies will match your contribution, sometimes 50 cents on a dollar.

401(k) Plans
LG4

BENEFITS of 401(k) PLANS

- Three benefits of 401(k) plans:
  1. Contributions reduce your present taxable income
  2. Tax is deferred on the earnings
  3. Many employers will match your contributions.

D-32

PPT D-33
Keogh Plans

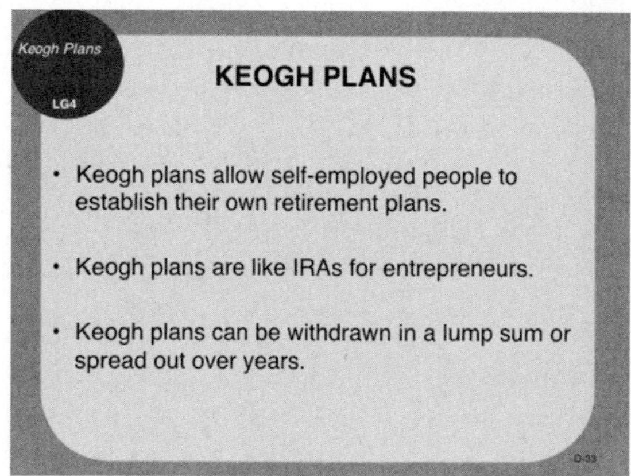

PPT D-34
Planning for Those Who Will Inherit

PLANNING for THOSE WHO WILL INHERIT

- Estate planning for those who will inherit money from you may start with life insurance.
- **Will --** *A document that names the guardian for minor children, states how you want your assets distributed and names the executor for your estate.*
- **Executor --** *Person who assembles and values your estate, files income and other taxes, and distributes assets.*

D-34

PPT D-35
Progress Assessment

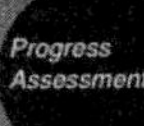

PROGRESS ASSESSMENT

- What are three advantages of using a credit card?
- What kind of life insurance is recommended for most people?
- What are the advantages of investing through an IRA? A Keogh account? A 401(k) account?
- What are the main steps in estate planning?

D-35

1. Three advantages of using a credit card are (1) you may have to have a credit card to buy certain goods or rent a car, (2) credit cards allow you to easily track your expenses, and (3) they are more convenient than carrying cash or writing checks.
2. Term insurance is often recommended for most people, since it is cheaper than whole life.
3. The primary advantage of an IRA and Keogh is that the money invested is not taxed until it is withdrawn. A Keogh plan is like an IRA for the self-employed. While the current IRA contribution limit is $5,000, it increases each year in line with inflation. An additional $1,000 can be added if you are over the age of 50.
4. The main steps in estate planning are (1) choose a guardian for your children, (2) prepare a will, and (3) assign an executor for your estate. It is also important to sign a durable power of attorney to enable someone else to handle your finances in the event you are not able to do so.

lecture links

"Avoiding the phrase 'I don't have time . . .' will soon help you to realize that you do have the time needed for just about anything you choose to accomplish in life."
Bo Bennett

"Why is there always so much month left at the end of the money?"
Anonymous

"The tax-payer—that's someone who works for the federal government but doesn't have to take a civil service exam."
Ronald Reagan

lecture link D-1

MILLIONAIRE WOMEN NEXT DOOR

Thomas J. Stanley and William D. Danko's 1996 book *The Millionaire Next Door* examined today's millionaires, who turned out to be small-business owners that drove old cars, shopped in warehouses, and pinched pennies. But years later Stanley realized that he was getting a lot of mail from wealthy women who complained that this portrait of the millionaire didn't fit them at all. Stanley noted that 92% of the people in the original study were men, who would have different experiences and outlooks than women do. Stanley then started a new project—a three-year study of wealthy women, *Millionaire Women Next Door*, published in 2003.

The typical millionaire woman is 49 years old, a wife, and a mother. Her workweek averages about 49 hours doing work she enjoys. Her income—$414,000—represents 71% of her household's income. She is college-educated and owns her own home. It is important for her to give to significant causes.

"Most millionaire women zeroed in on a skill or hobby that interests them, then stuck with it until they reaped financial rewards," says Stanley. Research bears this out—people who enjoy what they are doing are worth 50% more than the average person their age.

Stanley found several common characteristics. Women millionaires:

1. **SET GOALS, NOT LIMITS.** Most women millionaires have specific daily, weekly, monthly, and annual goals; and they believe that all their goals are possible. They also have several possible endgames planned—as opposed to men who tend to be more single-minded.
2. **SWEAT THE SMALL STUFF.** These wealthy women keep a detailed record of household expenses. Most are responsible for family financial planning and budgeting.
3. **SELL THEMSELVES.** Although running an antiques store or clothes boutique may seem attractive, the study found that these are among the hardest ways to make a living. Women do much better if they promote themselves as the product.
4. **DON'T LOOK BACK.** Four out of five millionaire women say they never look back. Instead, they use experience to look forward. They believe it is up to them to turn their situations around.

5. **THINK LONG QUALITY**. Rather than going on regular payday spending sprees, women millionaires stash a percentage of their wages in a bank account. Typically, they save 12% of their income in a 401(k) or an IRA.

Stanley's findings are echoed by findings in a 2005 British study. That study found that there were more 16- to 44-year-old women worth seven figures than men. The BBC program *Filthy Rich and Female* claims that the number of millionaire women is on the rise, and that within 20 years, 60% of the world's wealth will be controlled by women.[i]

lecture link D-2

THE RENT-VERSUS-BUY DECISION

The argument has always been "obviously" buying a home is a much better economic decision than renting. But, depending on how you figure it and how long you stay in a house, that may not be true. The real estate industry's logic always has been, "Buy now, make monthly payments, and write them off your taxes. Then, in a couple of years, the house will have appreciated, you sell it, and you get back all the money you put into it, plus a profit. It's like living free."

As powerful and persuasive an argument as that was in the 1970s and 1980s, it bears reexamining in the current era of mortgage points, escalating maintenance costs, and the fairly rapid rate with which the average American seems to change homes every seven years. And you don't need a calculator to know that those who bought homes at the peak of the housing market in 1989 have seen their property values depreciate 10, 20, and even 30%.

Nevertheless, if you crunch the numbers, buying remains a better deal than renting. But it is neither "obviously" nor "of course" the right decision. It takes a little more thought.

If you plan to stay in one place long enough to recover the fees of buying, say five to seven years, you are going to be a lot better off in the long run buying. Rent and real estate conditions vary dramatically city to city and even neighborhood to neighborhood, so a banker, accountant, or broker who knows the local market can help you compare the merits of renting versus buying.

Some factors to consider include:

BUYING: Consider down payment, closing costs, mortgage payment, insurance, property taxes, maintenance, inflation, appreciation, real estate commission when you sell, and the tax break for deducting monthly interest.

RENTING: Consider monthly rent and insurance, plus the profit you can earn on the money you would have used for maintenance and a down payment if you had bought a house instead, minus the income tax you pay on the profit.

What can't be factored in are "lifestyle choices." And really, that's what it comes down to. There's always going to be a trade-off. You can always decide to rent a less expensive house, and that would affect the way the numbers come out for you. Maybe you can rent a place for $500 instead of $750. But is that going to be the kind of place you want to live in?

The same is true of buying a house. How much house do you really need, and can you get by with less house to save a little more money?

The issue isn't whether it's better to rent or buy; the issue is really an individual one based on lifestyle.

lecture link D-3

KNOW YOUR CREDIT SCORE

Lenders have long used credit scores and reports to determine whether or not to lend you money and how much interest to charge. But other stakeholders are also interested in your credit report—auto insurers, employers, landlords, even utility companies.

A company called Fair Isaac developed the present credit scoring system in 1989 to give lenders a shortcut for judging applicants' credit worthiness. Based on the data they collect about you from banks, credit card companies, and public records, the three major credit bureaus calculate a so-called FICO score. Fair Isaac says its formula involves 22 pieces of data and that the final figure, from 300 to 850, is based on mathematical models that forecast behavior. (See Lecture Link D-5 for details about your credit report.)

The credit score can be compared to the letter grade system familiar from childhood. It reduces the complexity of credit information and provides a quick way to separate the good credit performers from the bad. The median U.S. credit score is about 720. More than a quarter of consumers fall into the 750 to 788 score range.

You're being judged on five major areas:

1. **PAST PAYMENT HISTORY.** Your payment punctuality weighs heavily (about 35%) on your credit score. The more recent your tardiness, the more points you sacrifice.
2. **AMOUNTS OWED.** All of the account balances are added up and compared with your credit limits. As you near your credit limits, your credit score will go down. This part of your credit makes up about 30% of your credit score.
3. **LENGTH OF CREDIT HISTORY.** Fifteen percent of your credit score is determined by how long you've been using credit. The longer your credit history, the better your score. But don't open up a lot of new accounts at once to establish a credit history. That will lower the "average account age" on your score.
4. **AMOUNT OF NEW CREDIT.** Each time you apply for new credit, an inquiry shows up on your report. Red flags start waving when you take on more credit, or even just apply for new credit, in a short period of time.
5. **TYPES OF CREDIT.** These include credit cards, retail accounts, and installment loans (like car loans and mortgages). Your use, or overuse, of these has a 10% impact on your overall score. If you have had no credit, lenders will consider you a higher risk than someone who has managed credit cards responsibility.

Your credit report influences lenders and can affect your finances in significant ways. A consumer with a credit score of 730 applying for a $150,000 30-year mortgage, for example, may be charged a 5.5% interest rate. For those with a score of 620 to 684, the rate rises to about 7.4%. The 5.5% interest rate equals a monthly mortgage payment of $856. The 7.4% loan translates to $1,034 per month. (These interest rates are used as examples. The actual percent interest charged will be based on current economic conditions.)

Your credit score is not part of the free credit reports guaranteed by the Fair and Accurate Credit Transactions Act of 2003. However, for a small fee, you can purchase this information from one or all of the credit bureaus.

After reviewing your credit report, there are several steps you can take to improve your credit score.

1. **SIGN UP FOR AUTOMATIC BILL PAYMENT.** If you accidentally miss a bill payment, your credit score can drop as much as 100 points.

2. **WATCH THE TIMING OF YOUR SPENDING.** If you plan to apply for a loan in the next few months, cut down on your spending and try to reduce your debt. The lower the balance, the better your credit rating.
3. **LIMIT CREDIT CARD APPLICATIONS**. Each time you apply for credit, a lender's inquiry to view your report is noted, which can reduce your score.
4. **THINK TWICE BEFORE CANCELLING CARDS.** The more companies you owe money to, the worse your credit score will be. But closing accounts may not improve your score. This is because you gain points if you only use a small percentage of the total credit available on your cards. Eliminating accounts can reduce that ratio.
5. **MAKE SURE CREDIT LIMITS ARE POSTED.** When creditors don't report your available credit, the credit scoring system may assume that those cards are maxed out no matter how much you've borrowed. Ask lenders to report your credit limit if it is not included on any accounts.

lecture link D-4

AMERICA'S GROWING CREDIT CARD AVERSION

On February 22, 2010, the provisions of Congress's Credit CARD Act of 2009 came into effect.

The law's central reform prohibits card companies from suddenly increasing rates on fixed rate cards. Also, companies are no longer allowed to institute over-the-limit fees without first consulting the cardholders. If the customers don't agree to pay the fines, they are simply barred from spending anymore on their card, thus halting a vicious cycle that drove many people deep into debt.

But while the new regulations are intended to make credit cards more transparent and trustworthy, card companies used the months before the new law took effect to find ways to circumvent it. Issuers raised rates, added new fees, and cut back on rewards while they still had the freedom to do so. For disgruntled consumers, this was just another example of the ways that card companies tried to take advantage of their customers. As a result, studies have shown that more and more people plan to reduce their credit card usage in the future. In fact, a Federal Reserve study shows that outstanding credit card debt has been unprecedentedly decreasing in recent months.

According to financial experts, consumers are experiencing an "emotional realignment" with their cards. What was once a convenient purchasing tool has transformed for some into an uncontrollable debt accumulator. For cardholders already burdened with debt, their natural inclination is to avoid the same behaviors that led to their problems. Others avoid the danger of credit cards by switching to debit instead. At the end of 2008, for instance, Visa announced that the purchase volume of debit cards outweighed that of credit cards for the first time. Still, economists fear Americans may become too afraid of using credit. Jumping from such an excessive credit boom to almost no card activity at all could cause a slower economic recovery in the long run.[ii]

lecture link D-5

DISCREDIT REPORT

Maybe you've never seen your credit report, but dozens of strangers have. Among those who've looked to see how much debt you have and whether you pay your bills on time are banks and mortgage companies, credit card companies, retailers, insurance companies, maybe even a landlord or prospective employer. You should add your name to that list.

Consumer advocates strongly recommend you review your credit report at least once a year if you use a credit card or make installment payments. The incidence of identity theft is exploding. Credit reporting agencies that compile the reports have been under fire from federal and state regulators who've heard nightmarish stories about reports riddled with errors and consumers struggling to get them corrected.

Our nation's credit reporting system includes a handful of major national reporting agencies as well as hundreds of smaller bureaus that operate in only a single state or county. Millions of bits of information are fed daily into their computers and into individual consumer credit files.

According to a survey by the Public Interest Research Group, one in four credit reports has errors serious enough to disqualify consumers from buying a home, opening a bank account, or getting a job. Of the 197 credit reports surveyed from people in 30 states, 79% had some error. Fifty-four percent of the reports included personal identifying information that was misspelled, outdated, belonged to someone else, or otherwise incorrect. Thirty percent contained credit accounts that consumers had closed but that remained listed as open. A common error is confusion over names—somebody else's credit woes get scrambled with your file.

Your credit report contains information about where you work and live and how you pay your bills. It also may show whether you've been sued or arrested or have filed for bankruptcy. Companies called consumer reporting agencies (CRAs), or credit bureaus, compile and sell your credit report to businesses. Because businesses use this information to evaluate your application for credit, insurance, employment, and other purposes allowed by the Fair Credit Reporting Act (FRCRA), it is important that the information in your report be complete and accurate.

You should review your credit reports once a year, or several months before applying for a loan. Check for errors, negative data, or any suspicious activity that may signal identity theft. The government has made it easier to review your credit rating. Under the Fair and Accurate Credit Transactions Act of 2003, all consumers are entitled to free annual credit reports from the three major credit bureaus. If you find any errors, there are appeal procedures available to clear up credit report mistakes. (You can access your free credit reports through www.annualcreditreport.com, a website sponsored by the three credit reporting agencies.)

WHAT'S IN YOUR CREDIT REPORT?

Your credit report will include the following basic information:

IDENTIFYING INFORMATION. Your name, address, phone number, and Social Security number appears on your credit report. The report may also include a list of your current and previous employers, even your previous home addresses.

YOUR CREDIT HISTORY. Your credit history includes a breakdown of your debt, including:

- Late payments
- Outstanding debt
- Total amount of credit currently available to you

ANY PUBLIC RECORDS. This section includes any filings of personal bankruptcy or court judgments against you. These items remain on your credit report for 7 years, except bankruptcies, which remain on your credit report for 10 years.

INQUIRIES INTO YOUR CREDIT. Whenever you or someone else checks your credit report, it shows up in your file as an "inquiry." There are two types of inquiries: hard and soft. Hard inquiries come mainly from lenders from whom you are seeking a loan. Lenders look at your report to see what kind of credit risk you pose. A "soft" inquiry will show up when you request a copy of your credit report or when your existing creditors routinely review your credit. These do not count against you.

In reviewing your information, ask yourself these questions:

1. Is the identifying information correct, including middle initials and Social Security numbers?
2. Are the accounts accurate? Check the account numbers, credit limits, and payment records.
3. Is the information current? By law, negative information can remain in your file for 7 years; bankruptcies, for 10 years.
4. Are old, closed accounts included? If they're listed as current accounts, a creditor might assume you have access to too much credit.

When negative information in your report is accurate, only the passage of time can ensure its removal. Accurate negative information can generally stay on your report for 7 years. There are certain exceptions:

- Information about criminal convictions may be reported without any time limitation.
- Bankruptcy information may be reported for 10 years.
- Credit information reported in response to an application for a job with a salary of more than $75,000 has no time limit.
- Credit information reported because of an application for more than $150,000 worth of credit or life insurance has no time limit.
- Information about a lawsuit or an unpaid judgment against you can be reported for 7 years or until the statue of limitations runs out, whichever is longer.
- Criminal convictions can be reported without any time limit.

DISPUTING A CREDIT REPORT ERROR

If you wish to dispute an item on your credit report that you feel is wrong, you can do so for free. When you contact the credit reporting company, it will investigate the dispute and issue you a revised credit report for free.

1. **START A RECORD.** Every step of the way, be sure to keep good records of all your conversations and copies of each letter you send. Send all letters via certified mail and be sure to include copies of any documentation that supports your claim. Also, be sure to tell the credit bureau exactly what you want it to do.
2. **INFORM THE CREDIT REPORTING AGENCY** and tell the agency what information you believe is inaccurate. The Federal Consumer Information Center provides a sample dispute letter (www.pueblo.gsa.gov). Within 30 days, the credit reporting agency will reinvestigate the items in question. It will forward all relevant data you provide about the dispute to the "information provider" (lender, creditor, etc.). The creditor is then required by law to investigate your complaint and report its findings. If the disputed information turns out to be inaccurate, the creditor must notify all nationwide credit reporting agencies, so they all can correct the information in your file.
3. **INFORM THE BUSINESS THAT** sent the erroneous information of your dispute. Let the creditor know in writing that you are disputing an item it put on your report. Include copies of the communication you have had with the credit bureaus.
4. **GET POSITIVE INFORMATION PUT INTO YOUR FILE**. If you have accounts with creditors that don't appear in your credit file, you can ask the credit agencies to add this information to future reports.

If your dispute results in a change to your credit report, the credit bureau will give you the written results and a free copy of your report.

But if you are unsuccessful in removing information from your credit file and reach an impasse, you always have the legal right to attach a letter of explanation to your credit file. Make sure all three credit bureaus receive the letter, as well as the business that provided the negative report. The business is obligated to include your letter in any future input to the credit bureaus.

REPAIRING YOUR CREDIT

If you find that you have less than stellar credit, there are two key ingredients to improving your creditworthiness: time and responsible use of credit. Nothing else will improve your credit image in the eyes of the lending world. When someone tells you they can wipe your credit record clean, they are lying. Worse, they could be telling the truth but using an illegal method to "clean" your record—creating fraudulent identities, producing false documents, or making false claims.

To heal your past credit abuses, you simply have to pay your bills on time and demonstrate responsible credit management consistently over time. Nothing else will work.[iii]

lecture link D-6

SOCIAL SECURITY AND YOUR RETIREMENT

The headlines have recently been filled with speculation about the future of Social Security. Social Security is not a pension fund with money put aside to pay future benefits. The taxes of current workers are used to pay the Social Security and Medicare benefits of current retirees.

That was workable back in 1980 when there were five active workers for each retiree. It is barely workable today with 3.2 workers per retiree. It won't work at all when baby boomer retirements reach their peak early in the 21st century.

By then, there could be fewer than two workers per retiree. By the year 2030, the Social Security system, including Medicare, would be paying out $1.8 trillion more each year than it takes in, if it had the money to pay.

No matter which scenario occurs, retirees will have to rely more on their own savings, and they can't depend on Social Security and Medicare to see them through. There are steps anyone can take now to secure their future.

SAVE MORE THAN YOU EVER THOUGHT POSSIBLE

Social Security benefits may have to be cut by up to 25%. Also, typical Americans in their 50s are staring at retirement with only $12,000 in net financial assets. To make up for those factors, Americans must quintuple their rate of savings and invest for an average return of 10% a year.

Can the average household really hope to quintuple its savings rate? Maybe not right away, but you can move in that direction:

RETHINK YOUR SAVINGS. Do a thorough retirement diagnosis of when you will expect to retire, what your expected sources of retirement income are, and how much you will actually need when you retire.

FORCE YOURSELF TO ACKNOWLEDGE HOW BIG A RETIREMENT GAP YOU WILL FACE—with a Social Security benefit that is significantly smaller than promised. Confronting that retirement gap can produce a dramatic change in expectations. Most people who do that calculation soon start trading some of the dollars they are spending today for the dollars they will need later.

Examples include eating out less often, taking one vacation each year instead of two and making that vacation much less costly than ever before, and buying fewer things—paying off credit cards instead of letting balances and interest charges pile up. Saving more and spending less can take you a long way toward closing your retirement gap.

INVEST MORE AGGRESSIVELY

There may be more stock market investors than ever, but few of them invest aggressively enough. Saving more won't close the retirement gap if you don't earn sufficient returns on your money.

STRATEGY. Unless you are within a few years of retiring, saving for your retirement is a long-term goal. When you're dealing with the long term, you can invest most of your money in higher return, higher risk investments such as stocks.

FAVOR MUTUAL FUNDS. Most people don't have the time or expertise to pick individual stocks. The prudent investment strategy is to pick a number of mutual funds.

DIVERSIFY. Don't put all your money in one type of fund. Diversify among different types of stock funds and between stock and bond funds.

Also, don't put all your money in one country. Diversify between funds that invest only in the United States and funds that invest in foreign markets. About 15% of your portfolio can be invested abroad—if you're in your 40s or early 50s; less if you're older. Maybe you won't earn a 10% return on your money every year, but history suggests it is reasonable and prudent to expect to earn that return on average over time.

Finally, you can prepare for a postretirement career. The way retirement works today, you wake up on a given day and go from working many hours a week to not working at all. Despite much longer and healthier lives, only 16% of men now work past age 65. In the new model of retirement, most people will want to work beyond age 65 and most will be physically able to do so.

lecture link D-7

THE TROUBLE WITH SUING YOUR BROKER

The recent stock market crash left many investors feeling spurned or mislead by those financial minds they trusted most, namely their stockbrokers. In fact, complaints against brokers have risen 81% since 2008. Despite the passage of time, investors are still rankled by the nosedive their portfolios have taken since October 2008, with many even pursuing legal action against the brokers who gave them such bad advice.

Sadly, those unlucky people may just be setting themselves up for yet another disappointment. In the world of securities arbitration, claims of more than $100,000 are heard before a three-person panel sponsored by the Financial Industry Regulatory Authority (FINRA), not a court. Present on every panel is one representative of the brokerage industry, essentially leaving each decision against one broker in the hands of a fellow broker. The practice has been decried as biased and unfair, but FINRA doesn't see it that way, citing its streamlined arbitration process as consumer-friendly because it costs less than a long, drawn-out lawsuit. FINRA also claims that over half of the customers who file complaints receive a settlement.

But FINRA's assertions don't tell the whole story. Investors who emerge victorious from the arbitration process usually receive only 50% of their claim, and awards received go down as the size of the brokerage gets bigger. Customers who challenge the top three brokerages usually only receive 21% of their claim. Some brokers even boast about their arbitration record, such as Morgan Keegan, which proudly states on its website that of 113 cases levied against the firm, 95 were dropped or dismissed. While complaints from customers and consumer groups continue, intervention from the highest authority in America might not be too far away. President Obama has already proposed that arbitration reform could be included in a new wave of financial regulation.[iv]

critical thinking exercises

Name: ______________________

Date: ______________________

critical thinking exercise D-1

PREPARING A PERSONAL BALANCE SHEET

Angela and Chris North are recent college graduates. They own a three-year-old car valued at $5,400, have $700 in a savings account, and $200 in their checking account. They owe $2,200 on their car loan. The Norths also have personal items valued at $1,800, plus a CD collection worth $300. They owe $4,800 on student loans and $150 on credit cards. Chris owns General Motors common stock worth $660, and Angela owns a $1,000 personal computer.

1. Prepare a simple balance sheet for the Norths.

2. The Norths decide to buy a $5,000 motorcycle, using $500 from their savings account as the down payment and borrowing the rest from the bank. Modify their balance sheet to reflect these changes. Has their net worth changed?

notes on critical thinking exercise D-1

1. *Prepare a simple balance sheet for the Norths.*

ASSETS	
Car	$ 5,400
Savings Account	700
Checking Account	200
Personal Items	1,800
CD Collection	300
General Motors Stock	660
Personal Computer	1,000
TOTAL ASSETS	**$10,060**
LIABILITIES	
Car Loan	$2,200
Student Loan	4,800
Credit Cards	150
TOTAL LIABILITIES	**$7,150**
NET WORTH	
10,060 – 7,150 =	**$2,910**

2. *The Norths decide to buy a $5,000 motorcycle, using $500 from their savings account as the down payment and borrowing the rest from the bank. Modify their balance sheet to reflect these changes. Has their net worth changed?*

ASSETS	
Car	$ 5,400
Motorcycle	5,000
Savings Account ($700 – $500)	200
Checking Account	200
Personal Items	1,800
CD Collection	300
General Motors Stock	660
Personal Computer	1,000
TOTAL ASSETS	**$14,560**
LIABILITIES	
Car Loan	$ 2,200
Motor Cycle Loan	4,500
Student Loan	5,800
Credit Cards	150
TOTAL LIABILITIES	**$11,650**
NET WORTH	
14,560 – 11,650 =	**$2,910**

The net worth has not changed. Assets have been increased, but so have liabilities.

Name: ____________________

Date: ____________________

critical thinking exercise D-2

DEVELOPING A SPENDING PLAN

Pam Washburn earns $19,080 a year as a file clerk. She also earns $100 a month selling home-made cakes. Her monthly rent is $420, monthly groceries run $200, and monthly utility bills are about $275. Auto and renter's insurance runs about $600 a year. Health insurance costs $110 a month. Her car payment is $315 per month. Annual medical expenses are $900, and she spends $150 a month on entertainment and recreation. Miscellaneous personal expenses run $30 a month.

1. Develop a monthly budget (income – expenses) for Pam and determine her surplus or deficit.

2. Her landlord has told Pam that the rent will be raised $50 per month beginning next month. Can Pam afford the same apartment?

3. What advice would you give Pam about her finances?

notes on critical thinking exercise D-2

1. *Develop a monthly budget (income – expenses) for Pam and determine her surplus or deficit.*

INCOME	
Salary (19,080 ÷ 12)	$1,590
Sales Income	100
TOTAL INCOME	**$1,690**
EXPENSES	
Rent	$ 420
Groceries	200
Utilities	275
Auto/Renter's Insurance (600 ÷ 12)	50
Health Insurance	110
Car Payment	315
Medical Expenses (900 ÷ 12)	75
Entertainment	150
Miscellaneous	30
TOTAL EXPENSES	**$1,625**
SURPLUS	**$65**

2. *Her landlord has told Pam that the rent will be raised $50 per month beginning next month. Can Pam afford the same apartment?*

INCOME	
Salary (19,080 ÷12)	$1,590
Sales Income	100
TOTAL INCOME	**$1,690**
EXPENSES	
Rent	$ 470
Groceries	200
Utilities	275
Auto/Renter's Insurance (600 ÷ 12)	50
Health Insurance	110
Car Payment	315
Medical Expenses (900 ÷ 12)	75
Entertainment	150
Miscellaneous	30
TOTAL EXPENSES	**$1,675**
SURPLUS	**$15**

Name: ______________________

Date: ______________________

critical thinking exercise D-3

FINDING THE BEST CAR LOAN

Finding information about automobile loans is easier than ever by using the Internet. Use one of the online loan calculators (example: www.bankrate.com)[v] to calculate the following information. Use local rate function to find your zip code. (Sometimes the Web address for a location changes. You might need to search to find the exact location mentioned.)

1. In your zip code, find the following information for a **30-month car loan.**

   a. What is the highest interest rate quoted?

   b. What is the lowest interest rate quoted?

   c. Using the lowest rate quoted, calculate the monthly payment for a $20,000 car loan.

   d. What is the total amount you will repay (monthly payments · 30 months)?

2. In your zip code, find the following information for a **48-month car loan.**

   a. What is the highest interest rate quoted?

   b. What is the lowest interest rate quoted?

   c. Using the lowest rate quoted, calculate the monthly payment for a $20,000 car loan.

   d. What is the total amount you will repay (monthly payments · 48 months)?

critical thinking exercise D-3 (continued)

3. In your zip code, find the following information for a **72-month car loan.**

   a. What is the highest interest rate quoted?

   b. What is the lowest interest rate quoted?

   c. Using the lowest rate quoted, calculate the monthly payment for a $20,000 car loan.

   d. What is the total amount you will repay (monthly payments · 72 months)?

4. Next, explore the cost of car loans in other areas of the country. Choose one of the zip codes below and find information for a 36-month car loan using the lowest interest rate quoted.

   New York 10013

   Chicago 60601

   Los Angeles 90230

   New Orleans 70130

   a. What is the interest rate for a 36-month loan?

   b. What is the monthly payment for a $20,000 36-month loan?

   c. Is this less, more, or the same as the rates quoted for your zip code? What do you think are the reasons for the differences, if any?

Name: ______________________

Date: ______________________

critical thinking exercise D-4
CHOOSING THE RIGHT MORTGAGE LOAN

What would be the monthly mortgage payment for your dream house? It is easier than ever to find this information by using one of the mortgage calculators available online. Try the website for your local bank, or use one of the national news or finance sites such as www.money.cnn.com, www.bankrate.com, or www.bankofamerica.com.[vi] (Search for "Mortgage Calculator." Sometimes the Web address for a location changes. You might need to search to find the exact location mentioned.)

You have found a great little house in an older section of town. Because it needs lots of renovation, the offering price is $85,000. You have saved $5,000 to use as a down payment.

1. What would be the monthly mortgage payment for a **30-year fixed-rate loan** if the interest rate is:

   a. 5.5%

   b. 7.0%

   c. 9.5%

2. What would be the monthly mortgage payment for a **15-year fixed-rate loan** if the interest rate is:

   a. 5.5%

   b. 7.0%

   c. 9.5%

critical thinking exercise D-4 (continued)

3. If you can afford a monthly payment of only $400 or less, what is the most expensive house you could buy (assuming 30-year fixed-rate loan) at:

   a. 5.5%

   b. 7.0%

   c. 9.5%

4. If your parents offer to lend you another $5,000 for the down payment ($10,000 total) for your $85,000 dream house, what would be the monthly mortgage payment on a 30-year fixed-rate loan if the interest rate is:

   a. 5.5%

   b. 7.0%

   c. 9.5%

5. Use the “local rate” function and enter your zip code. In your area, what is the current rate for an $85,000

   a. 30-year fixed-rate loan?

   b. 15-year fixed-rate loan?

6. Adjustable rate mortgages (ARMs) offer a low initial rate and then recalculate (“reset”) at intervals to reflect the current market interest rates. Use the “local rate” function on the website and enter your zip code. This time choose one of the ARM offers. ARM quotes give “caps,” or the maximum percentage points that can be added to your loan.

   a. What is the initial interest rate (annual percentage rate, or APR) for an $85,000 ARM mortgage in your zip code?

   b. What is the estimated monthly payment?

   c. What is the maximum amount percent interest that can be added to this loan when it resets?

endnotes

[i] *Sources*: Dana Hudepohl, "Could You Ever Be a Millionaire? More and More Women Are Ending Up with Fat Bank Accounts," *Cosmopolitan*, December 1, 2004; Alexa Baracaia, "Money, Money, Money, It's a Rich Woman's World," *The Evening Standard,* January 20, 2006.

[ii] *Source:* Rob Silverblatt, "A New Era Begins for Credit Cards," *U.S. News and World Report*, March 2010.

[iii] Sources: "One in Four Credit Reports Contain Serious Mistakes," *The Daily Leader,* June 20, 2004; Dayana Yochim, "Anatomy of a Credit Report," The Motley Fool, www.fool.com; www.annualcreditreport.com.

[iv] *Source:* Janet Paskin, "A Different Form of Justice," *SmartMoney*, August 2009.

[v] The Internet is a dynamic, changing information source. Web links noted in this manual were checked at the time of publication, but content may change over time. Please review the website before recommending it to your students.

[vi] The Internet is a dynamic, changing information source. Web links noted in this manual were checked at the time of publication, but content may change over time. Please review the website before recommending it to your students.